American Leader in War and Peace

*"Battle is the payoff. It's the objective that counts, not the incidents."*
—General John J. Pershing

Quoted in Richard Ernest Dupuy, *Men of West Point: The First 150 Years of the United States Military Academy* (New York: Sloane, 1951), p. 143.

# American Leader in War and Peace

*The Life and Times of WWI Soldier, Army Chief of Staff, and Citadel President General Charles P. Summerall*

W. Gary Nichols

WHITE MANE BOOKS
SHIPPENSBURG, PENNSYLVANIA

Copyright © 2011 by W. Gary Nichols

ALL RIGHTS RESERVED—No part of this book may be reproduced in any form without permission in writing from the publisher, except by a reviewer who wishes to quote brief passages in connection with a review.

Maps were prepared by Larry Hoffman.

The acid-free paper used in this book meets the guidelines for permanence and durability of the Committee on Production Guidelines for Book Longevity of the Council on Library Resources.

For a complete list of available publications
please write
White Mane Books
Division of White Mane Publishing Company, Inc.
P.O. Box 708
Shippensburg, PA 17257-0708 USA

Library of Congress Cataloging-in-Publication Data

Nichols, W. Gary (William Gary)
　American leader in war and peace : the life and times of WWI soldier, Army Chief of Staff, and Citadel President General Charles P. Summerall / W. Gary Nichols.
　　p. cm.
　Includes bibliographical references and index.
　ISBN 978-1-57249-399-5 (pbk. : alk. paper)
　1. Summerall, Charles Pelot, 1867-1955. 2. Generals--United States—Biography. 3. United States. Army--Officers--Biography. 4. United States. Army--History--20th century. 5. United States--History, Military--20th century. I. Title.
　E745.S86N53 2011
　355.0092--dc23
　[B]

2011018427

PRINTED IN THE UNITED STATES OF AMERICA

# Contents

| | |
|---|---:|
| List of Maps | vi |
| List of Illustrations | vii |
| Acknowledgments | ix |
| Introduction: The Warrior Citizen | xi |
| Chapter One: Growing Up | 1 |
| Chapter Two: West Point | 12 |
| Chapter Three: In the Army Now | 29 |
| Chapter Four: The Philippines | 63 |
| Chapter Five: China and the Boxer Rebellion | 94 |
| Chapter Six: Home and Hearth | 127 |
| Chapter Seven: Coastal Defense, the Militia Bureau, and West Point | 139 |
| Chapter Eight: Training an American Artillery Force and the Coming of the Great War | 152 |
| Chapter Nine: Over There with the Artillery | 176 |
| Chapter Ten: Cantigny and Soissons: The Price of Victory in the Turning of the Tide of Battle in the Spring of 1918 | 199 |
| Chapter Eleven: The St. Mihiel Salient | 229 |
| Chapter Twelve: The Meuse-Argonne, "Racing" to Sedan, and Peace | 245 |
| Chapter Thirteen: Mission to Fiume and Homecoming | 303 |
| Chapter Fourteen: The Home Front and Hawaii | 310 |
| Chapter Fifteen: Home to Stay and in Command: The VIII and II Corps Areas and Chief of Staff | 326 |
| Chapter Sixteen: The Citadel | 349 |
| Summerall Chronology | 377 |
| Notes | 379 |
| Bibliography | 431 |
| Index | 441 |

# Maps

| | |
|---|---|
| The Philippines | 65 |
| Early U.S. Operations in the Southern Tagalog Region | 73 |
| The Invasion, First Phase, Philippines | 81 |
| The Invasion, Second Phase, Philippines | 88 |
| Batangas Province, c. 1890 | 89 |
| Chihli Province, Northeast China | 97 |
| Peking | 100 |
| The Allied Advance on Peking | 111 |
| The Western Front, May 1918 | 200 |
| Cantigny-Montdidier Sector, May 1918 | 203 |
| French-American Attack South of Soissons, 18–22 July 1918 | 213 |
| First Army Plan of Attack, 12 September 1918 | 237 |
| German Defensive Organization in the Meuse-Argonne Region | 248 |
| First Army Plan of Attack, 26 September 1918 | 250 |
| First Army Plan of Attack, 4 October 1918 | 256 |
| Meuse-Argonne Campaign, 28 September–11 November 1918 | 266 |
| Ground Gained Near Barricourt Heights, 1–2 November 1918 | 275 |
| Operations of 1st, 42nd, and 77th Divisions Near Sedan, 6–7 November 1918 | 282 |
| Crossing the Meuse River by 2nd and 89th Divisions, 9–11 November 1918 | 294 |
| Oahu | 319 |

# Illustrations

| | |
|---|---|
| Cadet Charles Pelot Summerall | 12 |
| Charles Pelot Summerall in the army | 29 |
| Summerall in the Philippines | 75 |
| Lieutenant Robert L. Bullard | 77 |
| Firing on the Forbidden City | 114 |
| Captain Henry J. Reilly | 115 |
| Above the Crowd | 126 |
| Lieutenant General Robert L. Bullard | 187 |
| German Defensive Position | 195 |
| German Artillery | 212 |
| Major General J. L. Hines | 214 |
| Major General G. Harbord | 215 |
| Plains South of Berzy | 221 |
| German Infantry at Soissons | 223 |
| Montsec | 230 |
| General John J. Pershing and Major General Charles P. Summerall | 235 |
| Major General J. T. Dickman | 238 |
| Lieutenant General H. Liggett | 239 |
| General Ferdinand Foch and General John J. Pershing | 246 |
| Lieutenant Colonel George S. Patton, Jr. | 252 |
| Sergeant Alvin C. York | 258 |
| Brigadier General Douglas MacArthur | 262 |
| Major General John A. Lejeune | 274 |
| Major General Hansen E. Ely | 276 |
| Brigadier General Hugh A. Drum | 280 |
| Banquet Table with President Wilson | 300 |
| First Division Reunion at Monument | 328 |
| Bullard and Summerall | 331 |
| Summerall Becomes Chief of Staff | 338 |
| Major General Summerall and Mrs. Summerall visiting White House | 341 |
| Summerall with Charles, Jr., and Twins | 347 |
| Bliss Burial | 348 |

| | |
|---|---|
| The Citadel Campus, 1930 | 353 |
| Summerall at His Desk | 357 |
| Marshall and Summerall Review Corps of Cadets | 363 |
| Summerall at Home | 367 |
| Summerall with the Thurmonds | 369 |
| Citadel Campus with Buildings Added During Summerall's Presidency | 371 |
| Summerall Guards | 372 |
| Summerall Chapel | 374 |

# Acknowledgments

My interest in the life of General Charles P. Summerall began over 25 years ago, when, as director of The Citadel Self-Study, I realized just how important his leadership of the college was to its survival during the Great Depression. My colleagues in the history department, as well as Citadel alumni, encouraged me to look more closely into Summerall's 22 years as Citadel president. That endeavor was the beginning of a deeper study into his long life of 88 years, and a military career that spanned almost 40 years of American history.

Along the way, I have received the encouragement and generous assistance, especially from my colleagues in the history department at The Citadel, of many other Citadel faculty and staff, and from fellow historians, archivists, and librarians from across the country. Timothy Nenninger provided valuable guidance and insight into the archives of the AEF in the National Archives and Records Administration, and Mitchel Yokelson helped me track the wartime events and personalities recorded in this national treasure. The staffs of the Hoover Institution, the First Division Museum, and the Military History Institute introduced me to valuable collections where I found unique information on General Summerall's military career. John Votaw and Mac Coffman generously shared with me their insights into the personality and leadership of General Summerall.

The librarians of The Citadel's Daniel Library, including Debbe Causey, Kathleen Turner and Betsey Carter, cheerfully helped me locate hard-to-find books and information, and Ruby Murray and her colleagues renewed my shelves of overdue books time and time again. Jane Yates, the head of The Citadel Archives and Museum, responded with alacrity and good cheer to my many request for information, boxes of Summerall and Citadel records, as well as appropriate photographs and illustrations.

This book would not have been possible without the generous financial backing from The Citadel Development Foundation (now The Citadel Foundation). I am especially grateful for the financial commitment of Ben Hagood, Leonard Fulghum, Charles Cole, Guy Hecker, Cantey Higdon, Carroll LeTellier, Frank Mood, and Andrew Warlick. They are among the most loyal of Citadel alumni and have responded to every request to serve their alma mater throughout their private lives and professional careers.

Arthur M. Wilcox, the retired editor of the *Charleston News and Courier* (now the *Post and Courier*), an admirer of General Summerall and The Citadel, provided me with the records of the cadet "mutiny" of 1943. Huett Paul told me about Summerall's activities in the Charleston community. Edward Reynolds shared with me the poignant correspondence between his mother, Mrs. Maude Reynolds, who served as the secretary of The Association of Citadel Men (now The Citadel Alumni Association) and General Summerall during his brief retirement and final illness. Jake Burrows, Henry Rittenberg, Lewis Cauthen, Carol LeTellier, Walt Clark and R. L. Cockfield are among The Citadel alumni who shared with me their memories of cadet life under the watchful eyes of General Summerall. Russell Thompson and John Mettler, both retired after many years as Citadel faculty members, added their perspectives on life at the college during Summerall's last years on campus. Dr. Charles P. Summerall, III, the general's grandson, provided helpful insights into his grandfather's life at The Citadel, and graciously shared General Summerall's memoir with me.

During my teaching career at The Citadel, cadets and graduate students alike responded with interest and enthusiasm to my frequent forays into the life and times of Summerall. Robert Soukop, Citadel Class of 1953, assembled recollections of his classmates and shared their memories of cadet life with my seminar class at The Citadel on the life of General Summerall.

My former colleague and long-time friend, Larry H. Addington, Emeritus Professor of History of The Citadel, read every single word of the manuscript. He offered sound advice, constructive criticism, and provided expert guidance through the difficult passages of American military history. My friend Judy Hines and Citadel colleague Kyle Sinisi read the chapters on Summerall's early life and made many helpful suggestions. My thanks to Katherine Richardson Jones of the School of Education at The Citadel for her proofreading of the manuscript and for preparing the long lists of proper names and subjects. Thanks also to Larry Hoffman, who expertly drew the maps, and Philip Logan, who donated his time and expertise to locating photographs from the National Archives and Records Administration. Leonard Shurtleff generously included my presentations on Summerall in seminars sponsored by the United States Branch of the Western Front Association. My thanks go to the many members of the Association for their interest and support.

I very much appreciate the patient indulgence of Harold Collier of White Mane Publishing Company of my several requests to extend the date for the submission of the manuscript. Marianne Zinn, copyeditor and proofreader *par excellence*, with whom I had the pleasure of working throughout the editing process, made many valuable suggestions that greatly improved the readability of the manuscript. I much appreciate the editorial assistance of Angela Guyer of White Mane Publishing and the expertise of Dr. Diane R. Gordon who prepared the index. Vicki Stouffer was also helpful and understanding.

Most importantly, I am indebted to my wife, Liese, and to my sons Chris and Tony. Liese stoically endured my long stretches of isolation in libraries, archives, and before the computer, and always with unfailing love and understanding. The love and devotion of my sons have been sources of strength, inspiration, and solace. Chris's wife, Jeannemarie, and children Ella, James, and Margaret; and Tony's wife, Rosemary, and children Sam, Jane, and Will have brought even more love, joy, and laughter to our lives. And it is to these dear members of my family, and to Helen Gary Nichols, my mother, that I dedicate this book. Any errors or oversights that remain are solely my own.

# Introduction

## *The Warrior Citizen*

Charles Pelot Summerall was a remarkable warrior and citizen. General George C. Marshall, chief of staff, U.S. Army, in World War II, and subsequently secretary of state and secretary of defense, said that Summerall "was really the iron man. He was the nearest approach to the [Stonewall] Jackson type that I saw in the war [World War I]. He was a wonder to watch when the fighting was on as a leader. His influence on the men was tremendous. And my admiration for him was very, very great."[1] Like Thomas J. Jackson, Summerall experienced an impoverished childhood, was graduated from West Point, and stood fearless in command of soldiers in battle. As Jackson molded the lives of cadets at the Virginia Military Institute, in Lexington, so did Summerall shape and influence the lives of cadets at The Citadel, the Military College of South Carolina in Charleston. Both men have been memorialized by proud and grateful alumni. Jackson and Summerall both ruled their own lives with strict discipline, demanded strict obedience and absolute adherence to their orders and to the moral standards that governed their own actions. Any deviation from their orders or failure to conform to their standards of personal conduct would invoke their wrath. Historian Leonard J. Fullenkamp has written that Jackson "inspired confidence in the soldiers he led, though he drove them hard and used them hard in battle."[2] Like Jackson, Summerall inspired great confidence in the soldiers he led, drove them equally as hard, and used them relentlessly in battle. Some of his officers in wartime, as well as those who served him in his important peacetime commands, grew to resent his hard-driving style of command. But many others, like General Marshall, admired his devotion to duty, his enormous capacity for work, his seemingly inexhaustible energy, and his patriotic service to the nation. For 65 years, he wore the military uniforms of the Army of the United States of America.

Summerall was born dirt-poor in north central Florida and grew up amidst the poverty and violence of the post–Civil War South. Nevertheless, he won a competitive appointment to the United States Military Academy at West Point, where he achieved the top cadet rank of First Captain. His military career thrust him into the social life of *fin-de-siècle* San Francisco and the violence of the California railroad strikes, then into the Philippine Insurrection and onto the mainland of China, where his artillery breached the gates of the massive walls of Peking and helped crush the anti-foreign rebellion of the Boxers. In 1904, he returned to California, where he married Laura Mordecai, daughter of Colonel Alfred Mordecai, one of the army's few Jewish officers. Successive tours of duty took him to desolate posts in the Pacific Northwest, to dangerous settlements on the frontiers of Alaska, and to more stable and secure assignments with the National Guard, at West Point, and within the confines of the War Department in Washington, D.C.

In the Great War of 1914–1918, he emerged as one of the more indomitable battlefield commanders in U.S. history, leading the First Division and V Corps of the American Expeditionary Forces in some of the bloodiest and most decisive battles of the war. After the war, he remained a prominent military figure and rose to become the army's senior general officer of the line and its chief of staff in 1926, retiring in 1930 after 42 years of service. However, unlike many of his colleagues, Summerall chose not to retire to less demanding duties and more tranquil pursuits. Rather, at age 64, vigorous and in robust health, he accepted an offer to become president of The Citadel, and fought to save the small military college in Charleston, South Carolina, from the clutches of the Depression, and establish it as a viable educational institution. In 1953, at age 86, having accomplished his tasks after serving 22 years as president, he rejected overtures from the governing board that he retire, and resigned as president. He died two years later at Walter Reed Army Medical Center in Washington, D.C., and was buried at Arlington National Cemetery.

Summerall was a man of intense seriousness, loyal to friends and family, resolute in his devotion to the causes he believed in, and inexhaustible as he fought for their success. Whether in war or in peacetime, he drove hard both himself and those whom he commanded. He demanded obedience and loyalty from those who served under him. To those who were steadfast in their support and loyalty, he was just as loyal and supportive. For those who wavered or strayed, his wrath was severe, and those who incurred it were not forgiven or forgotten. His morals were shaped by deep religious beliefs, ingrained by impoverished but proud and dutiful parents, nurtured by the devotion of a clergyman-educator, and confirmed by the ideals and demands of West Point. He held himself rigidly to the moral standards and convictions of his upbringing; he believed that through his enormous energy and capacity for work, and the force of his powerful personality, he could lead men and institutions in the direction his moral compass pointed. To his friends and admirers, he seemed the model of what a soldier and a leader should be, and many were almost worshipful in their devotion to him. His critics and opponents, on the other hand, saw him as a rigid authoritarian, inflexible and doctrinaire in his approach to warfare, a martinet in his enforcement of rules and regulations, intolerant and thin-skinned, prone to hold grudges, self-righteous to a fault, and insensitive toward and excessively tough on subordinates. Rather than criticize or challenge his ideas or decisions, many of those who disagreed with him kept their own counsel, confided their criticisms to their friends, and avoided the general as much as possible. But when he retired as army chief of staff and closed his long military career, he had served with the support and approval of two presidents, and left his post at the War Department confident that no one could have accomplished more as chief of staff. He stepped down 22 years later as president of The Citadel, feeling that his resignation had been forced by the governing board, even though he was, as he put it, "as young as I ever was." He checked out of his office, turned over the keys to the college adjutant, and drove alone to his retirement home in Aiken, some 100 miles from Charleston. He remained there, wishing for the companionship of those who had served him loyally at The Citadel, until his final illness took him to Walter Reed Army Medical Center, where he died on 14 May 1955.

That Summerall could arouse such strong and decisive feelings among those, on the one hand, who were his devoted and loving followers, and those, on the other hand, who resented him, indicates the strength and decisiveness of his personality. This is a biography of that man and a study of the impact that this strong and imposing figure had on the men and institutions with which he so vigorously involved himself.

# Chapter One

## *Growing Up*

Summerall was born on 4 March 1867, in the pine barrens of north central Florida on the banks of the Suwannee River at the settlement of Blount's Ferry in Columbia County, about 30 miles north of the county seat of Lake City. His grandfather William Summerall had been one of the original land purchasers in Columbia County in 1853.¹ When he was in his late 40s, William, with his wife, Hetty, and their three sons and three daughters, moved there from Wayne County in southeastern Georgia. After settling in Columbia County, William began farming, acquired slaves and opened a store on his property.² He and his family prospered in the years before the Civil War and managed their interests well enough during the war that he could afford to buy an additional 159 acres in Columbia County in 1866 for $1,000.³

With the end of the war and the onset of Reconstruction, the prosperity that the Summeralls had enjoyed apparently ended. In 1869, William sold for $900 the land he had purchased for $1,000 in 1866.⁴ At home, affairs were also unsettling; within a year he moved his family twice, and one year after the sale of his land he divorced his wife, who moved in with the family of their eldest son, Elbanan Bryant.

William proceeded to remarry and went on to have several more children.⁵ After his father sold his land, Bryant Summerall and his family moved into an old, one-room log cabin in the settlement of Providence, in the southeastern corner of Columbia County. Along with his mother, Bryant Summerall's family included his wife, Margaret Cornelia Pelot Summerall, daughter Meta Margaret Ann, age seven, and sons William Bryant, age five, and Charles Pelot, age three. William, the grandfather, disappeared from their lives. Bryant Summerall and his family were on their own.

In his memoirs, Charles Summerall recalled that his father had been born in 1827 on grandfather William's farm in south Georgia. Bryant Summerall lived at home to help work the land and moved with the family in 1853, when they resettled on the land his father had purchased at Blount's Ferry in Columbia County. In 1862, according to his son's memoir, Bryant Summerall entered the Confederate States Army and served in one of the Florida regiments that, in early 1864, opposed the campaign of Union General Truman A. Seymour in north central Florida. Summerall stated that his father was mustered out because of sickness, but did not specify the date.⁶

Charles Summerall's account of his father's Civil War service seems in error, for Elbanan Bryant Summerall is not listed on the rolls of any of the Confederate regiments from Florida. The only Summeralls recorded on these rosters are Henry Summerall, who is listed on the roll of the 10th Florida Infantry; David Summerall, who is listed on a roll of "Miscellaneous" soldiers; and John W. Summerall, who was mustered into the 8th Florida Infantry on 14 May 1862, and deserted on 23 July

1862, thus having served just over two months.[7] However, on the rolls of the 26th Georgia Regiment in Company A, known as the Brunswick Rifles, of the Lawton-Gordon-Evans Brigade, the name Elbannon Summerall is listed. This Elbannon is undoubtedly Elbanan Summerall, for the spelling is obviously very close. But the 26th Georgia fought in Virginia and Pennsylvania and never was engaged in any campaigns or battles in Florida, where Summerall said his father had served.[8] Summerall was well into his eighties when he transcribed his memoirs, and could have confused his father's service with that of one of the other Summeralls, although there is no evidence that he knew or was aware of the service of any of the rest of them.

In his memoir, Summerall showed no enthusiasm or passion for either the Confederate or Union side in the Civil War. The only strong feeling he expressed about the war is his conviction that the conflict had denied Bryant Summerall the opportunity to pursue the career he had chosen. As Summerall put it, his father had a "passionate desire to study medicine," but the war thwarted his ambition. Attesting to his father's dedication and suggesting how successful his career as a doctor could have been, Summerall stated that his father spent as much time as he could reading medical books, and became so effective in treating his family's frequent illnesses that they rarely had to call a doctor. Frustrated by the war in his aspiration to become a doctor, Bryant Summerall was forced to seek other means to support his family. He tried setting up shop as a wheelwright; he worked with a physician to develop a patent medicine to treat eye diseases; and he repeatedly tried his hand at merchandising. In all these endeavors, he failed.[9] By stating that his father had put the call to duty before personal desires, and by placing his father in one of the major campaigns of the Civil War in his native state, Summerall may have been seeking subconsciously to honor Bryant Summerall by showing that his own distinguished military career had its roots in his father's service. Summerall's strong and driving personality, his powerful will to prevail and triumph, may well have been engendered by his determination to compensate through his own success for the setbacks and misfortunes of his father.

In his account of his formative years, it is evident that it was his mother, rather than his father, who had the greater influence on the development of her younger son Charles, and it was the history of her family that was of far greater interest to him. Margaret Cornelia Pelot Summerall was from Greenwood, South Carolina, one of the five children (three daughters and two sons) of Charles Moore Pelot and Margaret Ford Pelot. Charles Moore Pelot, for whom his grandson was named, was descended from French Huguenots who had left France for Switzerland following the Revocation of the Edict of Nantes in 1685. From there had journeyed to South Carolina where they settled along the upper reaches of the Savannah River. He and his wife were second cousins, both having been direct descendants of two colonial governors of South Carolina who were father and son. Margaret Ford Pelot's father was Major General Malachi Ford, who had fought in the Revolutionary War and later served as commander of the Second Division of the South Carolina Militia stationed at Walterboro, South Carolina.[10] Most impressive for her son Charles, however, was the record of her brother Thomas Postell Pelot, who had been graduated from the U.S. Naval Academy in 1853 at the age of 17. When the Civil War began, he resigned from the U.S. Navy and was commissioned a lieutenant in the Confederate States Navy.[11]

At the age of 25, Thomas Pelot took command of the iron tug *Lady Davis*, one of the small fleet guarding Fort Sumter, and on 21 June 1861, captured the much larger USS *A. B. Thompson* and took her into Beaufort, South Carolina.[12] He was promoted to the rank of first lieutenant, placed in command of the floating battery *Georgia* and assigned to the Confederate Savannah Squadron, commanded by Flag Officer William W. Hunter.[13] In late May 1864, Hunter placed Pelot in charge of an expedition to surprise and capture an enemy vessel reportedly anchored at the mouth of the Little Ogeechee River south of Savannah. Pelot organized a raiding party of 12 officers and 115 men selected from crews manning the *Georgia*, the ironclad *Savannah*, and the gunboat *Sampson*.[14] Led by Pelot and his second in command, Lieutenant (junior grade) Joseph Price, they set forth on the night of 1 June, in seven rowboats with muffled oars, but their quarry slipped away before they could locate it. Pelot then dispatched scouts who at last found the Union gunboat *Water Witch* anchored in Occabaw Sound, about three miles from where they had been searching.[15]

On the night of 2 June, they set out on their mission to capture the *Water Witch*. Winding through the twisting and confusing channels of the sound, in deep darkness and soaked by a drizzling rain, they had great difficulty finding the vessel. Finally, they spotted her at anchor. As they approached, around 0200 hours on 3 June, they were sighted, and under heavy, plunging fire, fought their way on board. Lieutenant Pelot was the first on deck, and in the brief but fierce fight that followed, he was shot through the heart and died instantly.[16] Five other Confederates were killed and eleven wounded, but Pelot's raiders succeeded in capturing the *Water Witch* intact and she was later commissioned in the C.S. Navy.[17] Of the 80-man crew on the Union ship, 2 were killed, 12 were wounded, and 66 were taken prisoner.[18] After-action reports filed by both Union and Confederate officers praised Lieutenant Pelot as "a brave and gallant officer," "a most gallant and accomplished officer," one of the navy's "most accomplished officers," and one "whose conduct was beyond all praise."[19] In his memoirs, Summerall hailed his uncle's action as "a daring and gallant deed," and noted that it had been accounted in the official records of the Union and Confederate navies.[20]

Summerall clearly admired Thomas Pelot's bravery and found more inspiration in the history of his mother's family than he had discovered in the family history of his father. He recorded carefully his mother's lineage, devoting almost five pages of his memoir to an account of her ancestral heritage, and identifying a number of the prominent forebears on both her paternal and maternal sides. This coverage contrasts with the description of the ancestry of his father, which he covered rather matter-of-factly in less than half a page, and for which he had only hearsay evidence and no documentation. Yet, with respect to his father, Summerall remained a devoted and supportive son.

In 1862, the year, according to his son's memoir, that Bryant Summerall entered the Confederate army, he and Margaret Cornelia Pelot were married in her hometown of Greenwood, South Carolina. She had taught school in several places around the state, and at the Columbia Female Seminary, located in the state capital, before moving to Quincy, Florida, about twenty miles west of Tallahassee. It is quite likely that it was in Quincy that she met her future husband.[21] After their marriage the young couple remained on father William Summerall's farm at Blount's Ferry, where all their children were born: Meta Margaret Ann in 1863, William Bryant in 1865, and Charles Pelot in 1867. In 1870, after Grandfather William had sold his land and divorced his wife, Bryant Summerall moved with his family to Providence, where he opened his wheelwright shop. Here, living at the edge of town in the crowded confines of their one-room home, they began their struggle to survive in the midst of the poverty, turmoil, and violence of Reconstruction in Columbia County.

Plantations that once were prosperous had been abandoned and were overgrown with weeds; coastal cities from Jacksonville on the Atlantic coast across to Cedar Key on the Gulf coast had been heavily damaged; railroads had been wrecked and left in disrepair; and although the interior had been saved from invasion by Confederate victories at Olustee and Natural Bridge, inland towns like Lake City struggled to restore order and prosperity.[22] Added to the depredations caused by the war were the effects of what Summerall referred to in his memoir as the "Tragic Era."[23]

The Reconstruction Acts passed by Congress in 1867, made it possible for adult black males to gain political office and influence in Florida and in all Southern states. However, the top positions in state and local governments were filled by white Republicans known as "carpetbaggers," men, who with all their belongings stuffed into carpetbags, had come south in 1865 and 1866. Many came for missionary-like reasons; others wanted to grab whatever political spoils they could get their hands on.[24] Native white Republicans were called "scalawags," and, like carpetbaggers, were made up both of men who sought to help Southerners move on to better lives, and those who merely wanted to exploit recovery any way they could.[25] In Florida, as in other states throughout the Deep South, native whites led by conservative Democrats regarded all carpetbaggers and scalawags as "merest trash that could be collected in a civilized community, of no personal credit or social responsibility."[26] They sought ways to get rid of them and their black political allies. Most often the means these white conservatives used were violent.

In Reconstruction Florida, many acts of violence had little to do with politics and race, and many racial problems had nothing to do with politics.[27] There would have been plenty of lawlessness and violence even without the political and racial difficulties brought on by the war and Reconstruction.[28] The state was still a frontier region where people acted angrily and without thinking to defend themselves against wrongs, whether real or imagined. Communities were isolated and separated by miles of unsettled land, transportation was difficult and communication limited, and law enforcement officials were scarce.[29] It was not unusual for men to pack guns and knives; Federal military officials feared that pistols and bowie knives were becoming the law of the land.[30] However, the most widespread and serious problem for law enforcement officials were acts of violence committed by the native whites against blacks and white Republicans to suppress political activity.[31]

Most of the violence in the state was limited to two areas. One was west Florida and the other was north central Florida, including Columbia, Alachua, Hamilton, Lafayette, Madison, and Suwannee Counties. Across these counties, secret regulator groups and the Ku Klux Klan unleashed a white terror against blacks and white Republicans. They struck often at night, hiding under masks, hoods, and long robes.[32] Columbia County was the most turbulent and violent area.

Between 1868 and 1871, 16 Republicans, most of them black, were murdered in Columbia County and many black and white Republicans were beaten.[33] In 1867, the Klan burned down the courthouse in Lake City; it was rebuilt the next year, but they burned it down again in 1874.[34] Late in 1868, when guns were being sent by rail from Jacksonville to Tallahassee to arm a state militia force, Klansmen boarded the train at Lake City, threw off the weapons and destroyed them.[35] In 1870, a band of armed, masked men seized the sheriff of Columbia County outside of Lake City, and forwarded a letter of resignation.[36] Leaving his office in Lake City on a hot July evening in 1875, Dr. Elisha G. Johnson, state senator and Republican Party boss in Columbia County, turned his head when he heard his name called out, and was greeted by a shotgun blast to the face. He died on the spot and his killers were never found.[37]

Senator Johnson's assassination was the last politically related murder in Columbia County during Reconstruction. However, the Klan and its supporters continued to terrorize black Republicans to the point where their leadership and morale were seriously weakened.[38] At the same time, as many scalawags and carpetbaggers drifted away from the Radical Republicans, Conservative Democrats mobilized the white vote and elected a Democrat as governor in 1876. The next year the so-called Compromise of 1877 led to the withdrawal of Federal troops from Louisiana and South Carolina and to the end of Reconstruction throughout the Southern states under the new Republican president, Rutherford B. Hayes.[39] It had been, indeed, a "tragic era" for Columbia County and north central Florida, and a time of grinding poverty for the family of Bryant Summerall.

He was 43 years old when he moved in 1870 with his family from his father's land to Providence. Impoverished by the consequences of the war and Reconstruction, their poverty was deepened by the depression that followed the Panic of 1873 and his customers could only pay with meager harvests of produce from their ravaged lands. To help out, Charles and his older brother William worked barefoot in the fields, since the family could not afford to buy them shoes. They planted potato vines and chopped cotton in the spring and summer and picked cotton in the late summer and early fall. Their mother tutored her children at home between school terms, made clothes for the entire family, and wove palmetto branches into hats to protect them from the sun. Since they could not afford kerosene lanterns or matches, she made tallow candles and covered the fireplace coals at night so that they could be used again the next morning. Young Charles was the baby of the family, and until he was six or seven, his mother let his blond hair grow down to his shoulders and curled it every day. Not surprisingly, the boys at school teased him and called him Sally, much to his annoyance. The only time for play was during the school terms, and they had but a few toys. Their food consisted mostly of potatoes, corn bread and hominy; hardly ever could they afford to have meat, and there were times when they had little or no food in the house.[40]

Margaret, small and slight, and suffering from "terrible headaches," taught in the school at Providence and in the surrounding schools, but, as her son recorded, "The pay was small and the term was [only] three months." When she was teaching away from home, she boarded with local families, and would walk as far as three miles to where she was teaching. According to her younger son, she was "always cheerful and never complained" and was able to carry so much of the weight and responsibility of the family only because of her "indomitable spirit and brave fortitude." Somehow she managed to find the time to teach her children to sing, and young Charles seemed to be the most proficient. While still a small boy, he was asked to lead the singing at religious services held at the Masonic Lodge and at the Baptist Church on nearby Olustee Creek. One of the happy memories of his childhood was of his family's walking together to church on Sunday mornings. On the Sundays they were not in church, Margaret would teach them lessons from the Bible.[41] These peaceful and pleasant memories were overshadowed by the violence that swept across Columbia County, and by Bryant Summerall's continuing struggle to provide for his family.

Bryant's shop continued to suffer from the widespread poverty of the area, but because of his standing in the community, as his younger son asserted, he was appointed justice of the peace and postmaster. This was enough, apparently, to provoke the hostility of some of the lawless gangs of regulators and Klansmen in the county. They tried twice to kill him, and he began carrying a shotgun loaded with buckshot. By the year 1879, Bryant Summerall had decided that it was unsafe for him and his family to remain in the county. He quit his jobs, closed his shop, sold their small cabin, and moved to the community of Live Oak in neighboring Hamilton County, where Margaret had found a teaching job. Bryant could not find work, and in vain collaborated with a local doctor to develop a medicine to treat sore eye.[42]

Charles Summerall came to believe that the setbacks and misfortunes his father suffered in Columbia County were the result of the lawlessness and violence that prevailed there during Reconstruction. He was proud that his father had remained an upright and honorable man, one of the "small number of good citizens," as he put it, amidst the lawless and murderous "gangs" of the county.[43] Confronted by threats of violence and the real prospect of death, Bryant Summerall had demonstrated courage, character, and fortitude. It was an example his son would follow in even the most ominous and dangerous of times.

In this immediate time of misfortune, the family did receive one bit of good news. Visiting a friend, Margaret learned about a school established in Charleston, South Carolina, by an Episcopal priest, the Reverend A. Toomer Porter, for the education of boys and girls from white Southern families impoverished by the war. She had written him to ask that he accept William; Porter agreed, and enrolled William without charge. Somehow his parents found the money to pay for his transportation and to buy him a school uniform, a new suit of clothes, and, quite likely, a pair of shoes. William, a bright young boy of 14, went on to do well, and was retained on the staff following graduation two years later.[44] As shall be seen, Porter and his school, Holy Communion Institute, soon would exert an especially important influence on William's younger brother.

In 1880, Bryant Summerall left Live Oak and headed south to the newly emerging frontier region of the state around Lake Eustis and Lake Apopka. Meta Margaret accompanied him, while Margaret remained with Charles in Live Oak where she still was teaching and where they boarded with a family on a small farm. Bryant found a little house beside the railroad track just outside the town of Umatilla, located about five miles from the shores of Lake Eustis. Soon he was joined by the rest of his family and opened a small store in the neighboring town of Glendale, while Margaret and their daughter found teaching jobs in Umatilla. Soon, Meta Margaret had saved enough from her earnings to enroll in the Columbia Female Seminary where her mother had studied years earlier.[45] It seemed that Bryant Summerall and his family finally were recovering, as was their home state, from the hard blows of war and Reconstruction. However, just two years after they had settled in Umatilla, a tropical storm struck the community, causing a great deal of damage and destroying the Summeralls' house.[46] Quite likely, the store was either wrecked by the storm or had failed, for the family left Umatilla soon after, and moved a short distance to the town of Eustis.

In this new town on the southern shore of the eponymous lake, and apparently at the suggestion and, perhaps, with the support of a Mr. A. S. Pendry,[47] Bryant opened a general merchandising store near the post office, advertising dry goods and groceries for sale.[48] Once again, his merchandising venture failed, and he moved his family into a small log cabin in Astatula, on Little Lake Harris, some 15 miles south of Eustis, most likely because it was there that his wife had found another teaching position.[49]

Astatula, Native American for "sparkling waters" or "rainbow waters," was on the edge of the Florida frontier. It had been settled in 1872, and was home to a small but lively number of families. Among the chief social events were bear and alligator hunts, made necessary because bears frequently snatched pigs from underneath cabins, and alligators killed cattle grazing by the lake; with their powerful tails, they swatted hogs from their wallows and ate them. Alligators were prized for their teeth, which the locals sold by the pound. Wild turkeys were plentiful, and had to be killed to keep them from eating up crops and gardens. At night, families were frightened by the howling of packs of red wolves; during the late night and early morning, they were startled by the screaming sounds of the Florida panther.[50] None of this probably alarmed Bryant Summerall, who had faced even more serious hazards to his health, and neither was he intimidated by his previous reversals in business, for in Astatula he opened a store once more. It was the third such place of business that had been started there.[51] Again, Bryant failed as a merchant and had to close down his store.[52]

The failure of Bryant Summerall's small store in Astatula ended his attempts to establish himself as a merchant and businessman. Now almost 60 years old, he turned to painting houses and working in the surrounding citrus groves, helped during the summers by Charles, while Margaret continued teaching in the public schools in Lake County. Daughter Meta Margaret had married, but her husband became ill and lost his business, forcing them to depend upon her parents for support. Fortunately, by this time, young Charles had been accepted by Reverend Porter, and already had joined brother William at the Holy Communion Institute in Charleston.[53]

Anthony Toomer Porter was a rice planter and slave owner when he decided in 1852 to sell his plantation and slaves and begin preparing for the Episcopal priesthood. Even before his ordination, he agreed to serve as rector of the small congregation of the Church of the Holy Communion, which met in an upstairs storeroom in a building on the grounds of the United States Arsenal in Charleston. By the time he was ordained in 1854, the congregation had doubled in size and they had raised enough money to build their own church.[54] While managing to find enough time to maintain his parish at Holy Communion during the Civil War, he served as a chaplain with the local Washington Light Infantry Volunteers and had accompanied them to war.[55] After the war and appalled by the devastation that he had seen and worried about the lack of money to build new schools, Porter journeyed north to seek funds to provide for the education of the next generation. He returned with enough money to start a school for black children and to begin the planning for one for white children as well.[56]

Early in December 1867, he opened a day school for boys and girls in the church building and a "Home" where boys from rural areas could live as boarding students. The first day-school class enrolled 425 boys and 125 girls; the first boy arrived at the Home in March 1867, and by the beginning of the fall term 33 had been enrolled. Expenses were high, however, since very few parents could afford even the 50 cents a month tuition. Porter resumed his travels to raise money. Again, northeastern congregations responded generously and paid for a journey to England, where Porter raised even more money.[57]

By the year 1879, thirteen years after its founding, the Holy Communion Church Institute had outgrown its facilities and had become a school for boys. Nearby were the buildings and grounds of the Arsenal, and Reverend Porter had gathered, quite likely from conversations with army officers who worshipped at his church, that it soon would be abandoned. Contacting military friends in New York and Washington, he learned that, indeed, the facility was scheduled to be closed. In April 1879, he arranged a meeting with General William Tecumseh Sherman, commanding general of the army, who remembered gratefully Porter's care for one of his officers who had been wounded in Sherman's assault on Columbia in January 1865. After their meeting, the general wrote to the secretary of war recommending the transfer of the Arsenal property and buildings to Porter, and on 19 December 1879, a joint resolution of Congress approved the transfer.[58]

Even before the formal possession of the facility, Porter had begun renovations to the main three-story building of the Arsenal, located on eight acres of land between Ashley and Rutledge Avenues in downtown Charleston. Soon, a kitchen and pantry were built, the storeroom converted into a dining room and study hall, and the second and third floors made into dormitory space. Old cannons and shot and shell were removed from the foundry, which was remodeled into the schoolhouse. By the middle of February, students and teachers had moved into the main building; and by the end of the year the old school building was closed and the new schoolhouse opened for classes. At the urging of General Sherman, Porter and his wife moved into quarters in the old arsenal building to be close to the students, and put up their home for rent.[59]

Formal possession of the old arsenal took place on 8 January 1880. It was preceded by a grand and colorful procession in which teachers and students from the Holy Communion Institute, local military, civic and religious leaders, state educational officials, and ordinary citizens marched around the block and through the main gate to the music of St. Patrick's Helicon Band of bass tubas. The bishop presided over the ceremonies, which were concluded when a United States flag, donated for the occasion by General Sherman, was raised to the top of the flagstaff. Porter and his staff were now well established to continue and expand their work to provide "our boys the best education in our power, and...to bring them up as loyal citizens of the government under the flag of which they live." "Ours," he said, "is not a political or partisan school, but an educational institution governed by the laws of religion and morality."[60] Throughout his own life, this was a mission and calling that would have special meaning and exert a strong influence upon the thoughts and actions of Charles Summerall.

In 1882, Charles joined brother William on the teaching staff at the Institute. That same year, Reverend Porter received the first of many subsequent gifts of $1,000 and more from a wealthy New York City widow, whom he and his wife had met at their hotel while vacationing in Palatka, Florida.[61] Perhaps it was this bequest from which Porter drew the funds to provide for the education of sons from upright, but poor Florida families like the Summeralls. The year 1882 was also when Bryant Summerall once more tried his hand at merchandising by opening a store in Eustis, down the road from their little cabin in Umatilla. Once again his business faltered, but nevertheless he and Margaret scraped together the money to buy a new suit, shoes, and a school uniform, and to put Charles on the train to Astor, about 30 miles north of Umatilla. At Astor he boarded a small steamer that took him to Palatka for the journey up the St. John's River to Jacksonville and on to Charleston on a ship of the Clyde Line and which provided him a free pass.[62]

Charles arrived in a city of about 3,300 acres containing some 50,000 people utilizing about 7,000 privies.[63] Economically, Charleston was experiencing its best year since before the Civil War. The fertilizer industry was thriving, construction was booming, and shrimp and crab boats were netting large and profitable catches. Charleston remained the state's largest city and its major port and rail center, handling about 10 percent of the nation's cotton crop. Schools and colleges were reviving; The Citadel, shut down since the war, reopened on Marion Square in 1882 with 185 uniformed cadets; the College of Charleston flourished on its impressive campus just below the major cross-town route of Calhoun Street; the High School of Charleston and the Charleston Female Academy, both public schools, charged tuition and maintained high standards for college-bound sons and daughters of prominent prosperous families; Memminger Normal School trained female teachers for city schools, and there were a number of private, church-related schools for both blacks and whites.[64] As indicated by the impressive and festive ceremonies marking the occupation of the new home of the Holy Communion Church Institute, it had assumed a prominent position among the city's educational institutions.

For young Charles Summerall, who was 15 years old when he arrived on campus, it was a very special place. As he exclaimed in his memoir, at the Institute "a new world opened to me. Whatever I have done in life is due to this beginning."[65] When he arrived, there were about 150 boarders and an equal number of day students ranging in age from 9 to over 20.[66] On campus, they dressed in civilian clothes; when they left the campus, they wore their school uniforms. Prior to his attendance at the Institute, Summerall had received only about three years of public school education, in addition to that provided at home by his mother.[67] However, this seems to have been adequate, for at Porter's school he asserted that he stood "well" in his class and "generally took a leading part." During his first year he was baptized and confirmed in Holy Communion Church. He was active in school literary societies, served as a dormitory monitor, and sang in the Holy Communion Church choir, where he also was a monitor.[68]

Having grown up in a household where personal discipline was essential in the conservation of meager resources, and where proper behavior and fidelity to the rule of law set one apart from the thieving and murderous gangs that roamed the countryside, Summerall found duty as a monitor both natural and satisfying. In his memoir, he remembered with pride that as a monitor, he "was responsible for order and compliance with the rules."[69] He did not hesitate to use his authority.

At one particularly solemn chapel service, Summerall noticed one member of the choir misbehaving and passed the word to him to stop it. The boy responded with a "very vile" remark that many in the choir overheard. After the service, back in the vestry room, Summerall confronted the unruly youth and demanded an apology. The youngster sneered back at him, whereupon Summerall knocked him to the floor right in front of the Reverend Porter. Furious at what he had just seen, Porter ordered Summerall to leave the school. However, when young Charles explained what had brought on the blow, Porter expressed his understanding and relented. Summerall was much relieved, but not at all pleased that the unruly choirboy had escaped punishment. In reflection, some 70 years after, he wrote that the whole incident taught him to control his temper. As shall be seen, it was a lesson, unfortunately, not well learned. Moreover, he seems never to have forgotten the young man's challenge to his authority. What he should have done, he later noted, since the boy was his own size and age, was to "have called him out and fought him." To the sober and disciplined mind of Summerall, regardless of time and circumstances, defiance of rules and regulations in the face of those entrusted with enforcing them should not be tolerated, forgotten, or go without punishment. He did manage to set aside some time for extracurricular activities, learning to dance and going out with girls, so long as there was no expense involved, for as he said, "I had no money."[70] Fortunately, Charleston was a city where a young man from the Institute could feel comfortable and enjoy his leisure time without money.

White Point Gardens, at the tip of the peninsula city, invited strollers, who could turn northward to promenade on High Battery along the harbor. The military atmosphere that had long prevailed in the city still endured, and a number of military organizations held shooting contests, tournaments and dances, and turned out in their uniforms to parade and celebrate national and local holidays. Ever more popular were ceremonies honoring the Confederate dead, highlighted by solemn commemorations, stirring speeches, and the music of military bands. With the revival of The Citadel, cadets once again became a familiar sight around Marion Square, and, along with the uniformed youngsters of the Institute, led boys throughout the city to "think a deal more of dressing up their bodies in...gaudy uniforms than in drilling their minds."[71] Altogether, it was an atmosphere not unlike that which would pervade the city when Summerall returned almost 50 years later to assume the presidency of The Citadel.

In June 1885, Charles graduated from Holy Communion Institute and returned to Astatula to work side-by-side with his father, as he had during summer vacations, cultivating citrus groves in Lake County and painting houses in the surrounding towns of Eustis, Mt. Dora, and Apopka City.[72] At home, Charles helped his mother with the cooking and did most of the family's washing in the waters of Little Lake Harris. Margaret's deaf sister, Susan Pelot, came to live with them and remained until her death. To communicate with her, the family learned sign language. An additional responsibility was the support they provided for Meta Margaret and her husband, who had lost his wheelwright shop and his health. As their family grew to include three children, they became increasingly dependent upon her parents and younger brother. Meanwhile, William continued to teach at the Institute, but according to his brother's record, provided no support for his kinfolk. He had, however, paid a bill for Charles at school for $210, which, as his younger brother stated pointedly, he repaid many times over.[73]

In the winter of 1886, as Summerall approached his 19th birthday, he was employed to teach in the Astatula school for the winter term of three months at the salary of $30 per month, which must have been a welcome addition to the meager household income.[74] The "little red school house" there probably had changed very little from when he had attended as a young boy of 12 years. It measured 16 x 20 feet, and stood close by the Baptist church. The children sat on benches made of split and hewed logs lined up in rows crosswise on either side of the room. Summerall would walk up and down the center aisle teaching the daily lessons as his students wrote their exercises on slate boards.[75] After the winter term was over, he returned to house painting alongside his father. As the winter term of 1897 approached, Charles, aged 19, was offered and accepted the job of teaching at the school in Leesburg, 20 miles northwest of Astatula.

Leesburg, a relatively new town, having been founded in 1887, was known as a "quiet, contented, easy-going, rather old-fashioned sort of a place....It has a good school and church, and an orderly society, which includes only one lawyer, who does not make a very large income...."[76] The school in this almost lawyer-less and placid little community was one of 72 that had been established across Lake County during the previous 10 years, and was equipped with a small table and chair for the teacher, benches for the students, a water bucket with a gourd dipper close by, and an outhouse.[77]

To his class of first graders, Summerall taught a carefully prescribed course of study beginning with reading, numbers, writing, spelling, and general physical, moral, and ethical instruction. Second graders continued with more demanding work in numbers, writing and spelling, and lessons through which "the teacher should try to teach the hearts of the pupils, and lead the expanding minds up to a love of nature and nature's God." Grades three and four received instruction in language, multiplication and fractions, writing and spelling, plus lessons in singing, where Summerall was quite probably an especially effective teacher. In grades five and six, geography was added to more advanced work in each of the other subjects. In grades seven and eight, U.S. history, physiology, bookkeeping, civil government, and elocution completed the course of study, after which the youngsters moved on to high school.[78]

For his work in simultaneously shepherding eight grades of boys and girls through their public school education in Leesburg, Summerall was paid $60 per month, but out of this salary he had to pay $25 per month for rent on the school building. Nevertheless, each month he netted $5 more than he had earned teaching at Astatula. Since he had to live in Leesburg, and pay room and board at the hotel where he lived, however, his take-home pay could not have been that impressive. Yet, for the frugal Summerall family in Astatula, whose burdens and obligations during the past few years had increased rather than diminished, any additional support was important. In his memoirs, he noted once again that his brother continued to teach at the Holy Communion Institute, but, as he stated pithily, "did not help the family."[79]

In the summer of 1887, Summerall again worked painting houses with his father, who had passed his 60th birthday on 5 July. During the fall term in Leesburg, in addition to his teaching duties, he began preparing for an examination that the county school board administered to teachers seeking a salary increase. A high score entitled one to a raise of $10 a month, and teachers "who had taught an unusually large number of students and 'managed them well'" received an added amount.[80] Summerall took the examination over the Christmas holidays and stated that his pay was then increased to $85 a month, an increase of $25. Thus, he scored high enough to receive the $10 raise, and in addition gained recognition as one of the teachers who had earned the special stipend, which in his case amounted to an additional $10 per month.[81] His overall performance seems to have been so effective that the school board appointed him principal of the one-room school.[82] With extra money coming in, he and his father bought a lot near the Baptist church in Astatula and enough lumber to start building a house. According to one of their neighbors, when they finished building, it stood two stories high, and "was a very nice house...finished inside with plastered walls."[83]

Reassured by the knowledge that his family now was more secure, and encouraged by his own professional accomplishments and the recognition of his ability as a leader, Summerall seems to have lifted his sights to goals that lay far beyond the confines of rural Florida. While he was preparing for the teacher examination during the Christmas season of 1887, he read a notice in the *Leesburg Commercial* that an examination for an appointment to the United States Military Academy at West Point by Congressman Charles Daugherty would take place the next day at the public school in Jacksonville. Excitedly, and with no time to waste, Summerall boarded the night train to Jacksonville, arriving at the examination site just in time. Assembling under the supervision of the school principal, more than a dozen young men took the examination, including the tired, bleary-eyed 20 year-old from Leesburg. A few days later the results were announced: Charles Pelot Summerall was the winner.[84]

Congressman Daugherty, however, did not nominate Summerall. Obviously concerned, Summerall and his mother wrote letters to the congressman, but received no reply. Instead, Summerall learned that Daugherty had selected a committee of prominent citizens to help him make the decision about whom to appoint. The committee consisted of Mr. Sherman Conant, a prominent Florida railroad builder, Mr. C. H. Jones, editor of the Jacksonville paper, *The Florida Times Union*, and the superintendent of the Jacksonville schools. Summerall regarded this move as an attempt by Daugherty to set up a "straw board" made up of his friends who would rubber-stamp his intention to appoint the son of a political ally. At any rate, toward the end of May, as the date for prospective plebes to report on 14 June approached, Summerall met Conant at the hotel in Leesburg and told him what he thought Daugherty was up to. Furious at Daugherty's attempt to manipulate him, Conant exclaimed, as Summerall quoted, "'That man cannot treat me that way.'"[85] Conant returned to Jacksonville, and apparently got busy setting straight the record of who was entitled to the appointment. A few days later Summerall received orders from the War Department to report to West Point on 14 June 1888.[86]

In his memoirs, Summerall did not explain why he sought an appointment to the Military Academy. However, in his second year at Holy Communion in Charleston he did describe a sudden burst of enthusiasm for a military education. In that year, 1884, the Democratic candidate Grover Cleveland was elected president, and, in Summerall's account, people in the South "took heart, and thought that a new day had dawned from the night of the Civil War." Swept up in the "great rejoicing in the South over a Democratic victory," and quite likely inspired and emboldened by the heroic gallantry of his uncle Thomas Postell Pelot, who had been graduated from the Naval Academy, young Charles audaciously wrote the newly elected president asking for an appointment to Annapolis. Laconically, he concluded his account of this episode of youthful exuberance with the remark that "no attention was [ever] paid to my request."[87]

Quite probably, Summerall's desire to secure appointment to West Point was like the wish of others in the Academy classes of the 1870s, 1880s, and 1890s who sought, according to historian Allan R. Millett, "not so much the positive selection of a military career as a flight from farming, rural teaching, or low-economic/low-status urban occupations."[88] From his account of his years of working in the fields and citrus groves of central Florida and painting houses in the summer, coupled with an apparently boring stint as a school teacher and principal, Summerall fits the first two of Millett's three reasons for "fleeing" to West Point. Millett also points out that "family size and limited income often put a university education out of reach. The young men who went to the Military Academy had little personal commitment to a military career."[89] Undoubtedly, Summerall's sense of obligation to help provide for the welfare of his parents and his sister's family and their collective and continuous financial struggles made improbable his chances of affording a university or college education. Even if he revealed no "personal commitment to a military career," for Summerall there was inspiration in the noble example of Lieutenant Pelot, and precedence in the service of his Revolutionary War ancestors. In his unpublished typescript of Summerall's life, Professor A. D. G. Wiles accounts that Summerall's sister Meta Margaret, writing in the *Eustis Lake Region* newspaper in February 1929, stated that "It was my mother's desire that Charlie go to West Point."[90] Summerall never mentioned in his memoir that his mother wished for him to make this journey. Perhaps the last word on this question should rest with Summerall's remark to Wiles that he went to West Point "Simply because I got the opportunity."[91]

# Chapter Two

## *West Point*

In early June 1888, at the age of 21, with not much more than $20 in his pocket and clutching a pass that the editor of the Eustis, Florida, newspaper had procured for him on a steamboat bound for New York City from Jacksonville, Charles Pelot Summerall embarked on the journey to the Military Academy at West Point. His sense of anticipation and his determination to succeed were intense, for the Academy offered him "the promise of a career, instead of hopelessness." Arriving in New York, he made his way to the docks on the west side of the city to book passage on the venerable, side paddle wheeler *Mary Powell*, "Queen of the Hudson," for the trip of some 50 miles up the Hudson River to West Point. When the ticket agent asked if he wanted a return ticket, Summerall answered "no," for, as he later wrote, "opportunity had opened up for me and I could not fail."[1]

The slow, riverine voyage took Summerall beneath the spectacular western palisades of the Hudson, and upstream between forested slopes that formed its verdant banks and shaded the small towns along the way. On the evening of 10 June, the elegant riverboat docked at the landing beneath the southern side of the high, triangular promontory that jutted out sharply from the western bank of the Hudson. On these heights spread a broad plateau known as the Plain, rimmed on the southern edge by the gray stone buildings of the United States Military Academy. Here began what in his later years Summerall regarded as "the process [that] would completely change my mental development by changing all that I had been to what it was intended that I should become."[2]

The beginning of this process was even less auspicious for Summerall than it was for the typical newcomer at West Point. Since he had arrived on the day before his orders specified, he had to spend the night in the West Point Hotel across the Plain on the northern rim, but he could not afford the price of a room, and had to sleep on the floor in the tower of the old structure. The next morning, stiff and apprehensive, he was escorted by army personnel back across the Plain to the southern edge where the library, the

*Cadet Charles Pelot Summerall*
Courtesy The Citadel Archives & Museum, Charleston, South Carolina

12

academic building, the mess hall, the chapel, the cadet barracks, and the administration building were clustered. In the administrative building, he was taken to the adjutant who examined his orders and letter of appointment. Then he signed in, writing his first name in large, heavy strokes. This was a bold and confident beginning, but his first name had taken up so much space on the horizontal line that he had to progressively diminish the size of the letters of his middle and last name, and squeeze in the last ones to fit his full name on the page.[3] Unconsciously, Summerall had created a metaphor for the system, through which, as shall be seen, the upperclassmen of the Corps of Cadets endeavored to suppress any boldness or cockiness in the new arrivals, and eliminate any sense of self-importance as they were molded into the absolute obedience of the Long, Gray Line.[4]

The next stop was at the office of the quartermaster, to pay the deposit of $65 required of all candidates for admission. When Summerall could only produce less than $20, which was all the money he had left, the quartermaster accepted it angrily, and only permitted Summerall to leave when he promised to pay the remainder later. Along with about 136 other candidates, he then was marched over to the hospital, just south of the mess hall, where they all were stripped of their clothes and examined from head to toe. Having passed this initial scrutiny, he was led to the barracks, and assigned a room he shared with two other aspirants, one from Vermont, and one from the Ozark Mountains.[5] Since most of the upperclassmen were now in summer camp, there was plenty of room in the barracks for all the candidates, who now fell under the supervision and command of cadets from the First (senior) Class and from the Third (yearling) Class. Immediately ahead lay a series of rigorous preliminary examinations that would determine who would stay.[6]

Each day, for one week, the new candidates assembled in the mess hall to take written tests in English, mathematics, writing, and American history. After the last test had been completed, the candidates were marched over to a grove of trees just in front of the library, where they formed a line facing the faculty of the Academy. The professors were dressed in their own distinctive uniforms, which consisted of a swallowtail coat and a waistcoat with brass buttons. They were seated in a row of desks with their tall, silk hats on the ground beside them. To Summerall, in their "superb appearance" they "seemed like supermen."[7] Each candidate was summoned before the faculty, and first required to read aloud a passage from a book, and then answer questions about his previous schooling. This "reading exam" and subsequent questioning gave the professors an opportunity for one final appraisal to determine whether a candidate had "the makings of an officer and a gentleman." If he could not pass this final muster, he could be rejected, even if he had passed his written examinations. On the other hand, a fine performance on the reading examination and demonstration of successful prior schooling could compensate for low test marks and convince the faculty that the candidate could make it at the Academy.[8] Summerall's reading most likely was with a strong and confident voice, as befitted his leadership in the choir at the Reverend Porter's school and his experience as a schoolteacher and principal. His account of his schooling must have been interesting; he was credited with "2 years, 6 months of 'common' public school, none of public high school; 6 months of private, 'common' school; 2 years 3 months of 'normal school or academy;' none of university or college; 11 months of teaching; 2 years of private study."[9]

The next morning, the candidates lined up in the barracks to hear the adjutant read the names of those who had failed. The young men who heard their names called out stepped from the ranks, returned to their rooms, packed their luggage and left. On 16 June 1888, the remaining 90 or so who had survived, took the oath of allegiance to the United States, and each was officially admitted as a "conditional cadet of the United States Military Academy"; unofficially they now were called "plebes."[10] Summerall had reached a major milestone on his journey toward "changing all that I had been to what it was intended that I should become," and, even at an advanced age, remembered how "devoutly thankful [I was] that I had passed, for I could not think of failure. It [passing the examinations] meant hope and life."[11]

When the new plebe class assembled in the chapel to hear the first sermon of the year, Summerall had the opportunity to give thanks for his good fortune. He recalled that the chaplain's text for his sermon was from Isaiah 51:1: " 'Look to the rock whence ye were hewn and to the hole of the pit whence ye were digged.'"[12] He believed that the rock was Jehovah, and the depths of the pit from which he was "digged" was the realm of evil from which the devil had assailed him and his family for so long.[13] A meaning even more powerful came from the text for the second sermon, First Samuel 18:14, that "'David was wise in all his ways, and the Lord was with David.'" Believing that God was with him as He had been with David, and feeling "overawed by the magnitude of the place," Summerall was convinced that he had come to the right place to chart a course for his life. With reverence and gratitude, he "hoped and prayed" that he might be wise in his search for the right path along this course.[14]

An important part of this early stage of his journey through the Military Academy toward a "career instead of hopelessness" was the system of hazing. It started as soon the new candidates arrived at the Academy in June, and lasted until the beginning of classes in the fall. As soon as they had assembled on the Plain, they were "greeted by the Third and First Classes, who immediately began a barrage of name-calling and 'bracing' at attention."[15] They were addressed as "beasts" and their quarters were known as "Beast Barracks." At any hour they were subject to "clothing formations," in which they were allowed two and a half minutes to race from the basement up to their rooms on the fourth floor, change into their full dress uniforms, and rush back to the basement, all for the yearlings' amusement.[16] This, however, was only a prelude to the more extensive and detailed hazing that soon would follow "Beast Barracks."

After examinations and "Beast Barracks," the newly anointed plebes were formed into four-man squads, assigned to companies, and moved into a tent camp consisting of three-man tents set up on the northern side of the Plain, and known as Plebe Barracks. Here, along with their familiar tormentors from the Third and First Classes, they lived for the rest of the summer. Summerall's tentmates were the brash and mischievous Leonard Morton Prince from Illinois, and also 21 years old, and John McAuley Palmer, a bright and congenial 18-year-old also from Illinois, who quickly came to admire his serious and determined tentmate from Florida. They were assigned to A Company, drew their uniforms, known as "plebe skins," and prepared to begin their "military education," as young Palmer put it.[17]

Their mornings consisted of drills in the manual of arms, infantry and basic artillery drills, and lessons in guard duty, all followed at regular intervals by inspections. Summerall had no difficulty with the manual of arms and the infantry drill, and he accumulated only a few demerits, or "skins" during Plebe Barracks. In July, he received "skins" for "rust in bayonet at s.m.i. [Saturday morning inspection]"; being "late at supper formation"; and for "loaning [his] dress hat in violation of rules." In August, he was assessed additional "skins" for being "slow fixing bayonet at formation for retreat parade"; again, for having "rust in barrel of piece at retreat parade"; for leaving his "overcoat unbuttoned at guard meeting"; for wearing his "shoulder belt too long at s.m.i"; and, finally, for reporting "late for s.m.i."[18] The only difficulty he seems to have encountered was in the artillery drill, which he found "very complicated,"[19] and during which on one occasion he received a "skin" for "giving the command 'fire' without authority."[20] As shall be seen below, it was quite likely during this particular drill that Summerall suffered his most memorable encounter as a plebe with a First Classman.

For both the First and Third Classmen, Plebe Barracks "was a welcome relief from their academic work, a gala round of dances, socializing, and games." Their favorite camp entertainment was hazing, which, over the three decades prior to Summerall's arrival, "had reached a fine flower of sadistic ingenuity."[21] Cadets and graduates justified hazing as the means to suppress the cockiness of the plebes, many of whom had, indeed, been the best athletes and smartest students, and had received the prized appointment to West Point. It also was the way in which the upperclassmen drove all sense of importance from the plebes and taught them unquestioning and instant obedience.[22] It was this latter lesson, perhaps, that Academy graduates had in mind when they insisted that the "experience [of hazing] was essential to their success as combat officers...."[23]

As the beneficiaries of this "experience," plebes could be required to perform for upper classmen menial tasks that included "'folding bedding; cleaning spurs, sabers, guns, breastplates, and shoes; sweeping the company streets; and, on hop nights, arranging clothing, putting on clean collars and cuffs, and making out the upperclassman's hop cards.'"[24] Along with the almost unceasing requirement to brace, whether they were told to or not, plebes could be forced to chew rope ends and rags; eat soap and quinine; drink Tabasco sauce; pick up each ant from a hill; permit hot, greasy wax from a candle to be dropped on their feet; recite any printed matter or sing any song an upperclassman wanted to hear; hold Indian clubs or a rifle at arm's length; "swim to Newburgh," which meant balancing on the stomach on a pole or lying face down on a box and pretend to swim; and, if an upperclassman spotted an idle plebe, he could order him to drop and do push-ups and any other of a series of exhausting calisthenics.[25]

Even for the solidly built and vigorous Summerall, a young man who had known hard times and hard labor, "The rough treatment and harsh manner of the cadets over us was a great shock, but all were undergoing the same experience and we tried to comply with our surroundings."[26] Like Robert L. Bullard, class of 1885, his future commander in the Philippines and comrade in arms in the Great War, and who would also become a mentor and close friend, Summerall had not been an arrogant or rebellious youth. Thus, the hazing quite likely was for him, as it probably had been for Bullard, "an anxious, irritating, but not traumatic experience."[27] If anything, it strengthened Summerall's resolve to remain. As he later put it, "Horrible as was the treatment, I wanted to stay and be a part of it [West Point] with all my being." With this kind of determination, he could take "whatever came in a philosophical way, " and was pleased that he and his tentmates had, in this way, accepted "our ordeal and licked our wounds with stoicism."[28]

Stoic, if not dogged, persistence helped Summerall master the West Point "method" of teaching swimming. All plebes were required to pass the swimming test by swimming for 10 minutes in the Hudson. They were marched about a mile north to the rifle range, and rowed out to a floating platform. Those who could swim plunged into the water and passed easily enough. For the non-swimmers like Summerall, a rope was tied around their middle, and they were ordered to jump in and start swimming. Time after time, over the course of several weeks, Summerall jumped in, flailed his arms and splashed about without success, and had to be pulled back to the float. Finally, after carefully watching a cadet "make the strokes," he jumped in and began "moving my hands and legs as he did." However, rather than ordering him out of the water after 10 minutes, the upperclassmen in charge of the exercise ordered him to keep swimming until they told him to stop. They told him to come out 63 minutes later. During the rest of his days at West Point he never went swimming again.[29] While in Plebe Barracks, however, he remained one of the focal points of the upperclassmen's interest.

During the last week of August, cadets marked the end of Plebe Barracks by staging the evening's festivities they called "color line entertainment." Probably to commemorate the entertainment that took place around the campfires of Civil War bivouacs, they gathered around an area of the camp where the colors were stored, and where their rifles were stacked. They amused themselves and their guests and visitors by singing, telling stories, and performing skits.[30] The fact that Summerall could sing had not escaped their attention. On several of these late summer evenings, he was ordered to step out and sing for the gathering the "Marseillaise" in French, "Die Wacht am Rhein" in German, or any other song which the Third or Fourth Classmen desired to hear.[31] John Palmer, who called Summerall by his middle name of Pelot, remembered his "earnest young" tentmate's singing as having been "greatly admired and frequently encored," and recalled that "He sang the words...as solemnly and earnestly as everything else he has ever done in the course of his earnest life."[32] For his part, Summerall was relieved that he could perform well enough to satisfy his superiors, took notice that on several occasions young ladies had been present, and was grateful for having learned to sing well at Dr. Porter's school.[33]

It is uncertain just how the upperclassmen discovered Summerall's singing prowess. However, unlike most cadets who learned quickly that "anonymity and passivity were the escape routes from hazing,"[34] it seems evident that Summerall was a determined and confident plebe, and was not reluctant to reveal his talent, rather than attempt to conceal it or ease himself into the background. In his memoirs, Summerall mentions, in fact, only one episode as a plebe that caused him to lose his customary stoic, earnest and confident demeanor. It also was an incident whose outcome revealed in him the development of less worthy characteristics.

It happened in Plebe Barracks, during the first artillery drill in which Summerall participated. He was part of the sponge and rammer staff, whose job consisted of a number of coordinated steps and movements to sponge out the gun barrel of their muzzle-loader after firing, and then ram home the charge and projectile. Summerall recalled that the First Class private, who was in charge of the gun crew, was so displeased with his work in the team that "He abused me and vilified me at the top of his voice, calling me all that was vile and denouncing me for every offense. He reported me for a long list of offenses which I could not have committed." Summerall was appalled when he saw the report published at parade, and "felt keenly the injustice [of the reports] and humiliation." The next morning, he went to Major Hamilton S. Hawkins, Commandant of Cadets, and "told him of my utter ignorance and my [true] efforts. He promptly removed the reports." As noted above, however, Summerall had received during the period of Plebe Barracks a "skin" in an artillery drill for "giving the command to 'fire' without the authority." He concluded his account of this episode with the assertion that the cadet private "was later placed in light prison for insubordination, and had become a worthless officer, retiring without rendering a worthwhile service. In after years, I, as captain of a light battery had a collision with him when he tried to interfere with my watering the horses in maneuver."[35]

As is evident from his response to the negative reports, when he was convinced he was right, Summerall possessed as a young man the courage to challenge the words and actions of someone in higher authority. It would not be the last time he would take such a strong stand. The record also indicates the possibility that the cadet had properly reported Summerall, who had then received the prescribed demerit for his "offense," rather than having the "reports" removed by the commandant. Of course, the "skin" could have been the result of his action or actions in a different artillery drill. Since he wrote the account of this incident some 60 years after it had occurred, his memory on this point could have failed him. What seems clear, however, is his hostility toward this cadet and his continued animosity, even across a span of more than 60 years, after both had become army officers. In recalling this incident, rather than checking his memory more carefully, or admitting that he could have slipped up as a plebe in an artillery drill and received a "skin," he asserted the absolute correctness of his actions, and assailed the untrustworthiness of his accuser. It was not the last time he would look back on an action or decision that had been criticized and refuse to admit the possibility that his critics were right, or that he had made a mistake. It was also not the last time that he would accuse his critics and accusers of being unworthy, hostile, and villainous characters. As enviable as was Summerall's personal and moral courage, it was unfortunate that over the course of his long life he developed a self-righteous, almost hyper-moralistic sense of pride, that led him to settle all accounts, and condemn as enemies those who criticized him, or with whom he clashed in personal and professional disputes.

On 28 August, Plebe Barracks ended. The three classes of cadets struck camp, and moved into two-man rooms in the barracks, where they were joined by the junior, or Second Class, which had just returned from summer furlough. Summerall's tentmates, Palmer and Prince, were assigned as roommates. He regretted losing them as roommates, but was pleasantly surprised when Donald W. Kellogg, a yearling who had been turned back, or forced to repeat the plebe year academic course, asked Summerall to room with him. He gladly accepted Kellogg's invitation, for he regarded his new roommate as "a man of unusual force and character [who] had many friends in the yearling class." Kellogg's past experience as a plebe and his knowledge of life in the barracks were especially helpful to Summerall in protecting him from "harassment by the upperclassmen, although hazing was supposed to stop in barracks."[36]

Quite probably hazing did continue, although officially hazing of plebes ceased with the end of Plebe Barracks. Cadet Regulations, the Academy's formal code of behavior, remained in force throughout the year, and applied to all four classes. The faculty and the officers of the tactical department, known as "tacs," enforced the regulations, which were designed "to govern every conceivable phase of cadet life; the arrangement and cleanliness of rooms; movement about the Academy grounds; relations with all Academy personnel; rigid time schedules for all meals, classes and formations; the performance of military duties; dress; the upkeep of uniforms and equipment; travel away from the Academy; and general deportment."[37] The tacs awarded "skins" for minor infractions; for many other violations, they could assign extra hours of guard duty or various kinds of restrictions. Once a month each cadet received a report on the number of "skins" he had accumulated, but in Summerall's day, as a reward for continued improvement, one-third of the "skins" could be removed at the end of the month. In addition, if a cadet had received in a month less than eight "skins," the difference between this number and eight was subtracted from the total number he had accumulated in a semi-annual period.[38] However, if a cadet had amassed more than 125 demerits from June through December, and more than 90 for the rest of the academic year, he could be dismissed.[39]

Summerall, earnest and ever dutiful, with Kellogg helping him "in keeping our room in superior condition," nevertheless accumulated "skins" throughout the year for infractions that included: speaking to the officer of the day at "carry arms"; not posting his class schedule; using an eraser in a mathematics class without permission; "not walking the proper post for times when visiting is allowed in barracks"; not properly arranging his clothes press at s.m.i. [Saturday morning inspection]; having his shoulder belt too long at s.m.i.; and for "causing confusion in the company by breaking through the sets of fours while attempting to regain his place in ranks returning from parade."[40] For this last transgression, ranked as a class four offense, he received the highest number of "skins" he was ever to receive as a cadet; namely four, out of a possible total of 10 that cadets received for offenses designated as first class. At the end of his plebe year, when the various subtractions were calculated, he was assessed only two "skins" and ranked number three in discipline in a class of 89.[41]

As an upperclassman, Summerall continued to accumulate "skins," but the infractions were few and minor: as a yearling, not properly sweeping the tent floor in summer camp and not extinguishing the light in the hall; as a Second Classman, reporting late for choir practice and being late for reveille and, actually for over-zealousness, in "appearing in an area equipped for guard mounting before first call for same"; as a First Classman, "failing to bring tables of ballistics to section room as directed," and "passing between officer of the day and sections." After having ranked third in discipline as a plebe, he slipped to seventh in his yearling year, but rose to second in his Second Class year, and, at the end of his First Class year, was graduated first in discipline.[42]

Since he was never cited for any uniform violations after his plebe year, he was a spit-and-polish cadet as well. Clearly, Summerall, like Bullard before him, "took the regulations seriously."[43] He admired "the dashing bearing of the cadet officers, the superiority of all [sic] cadets." For a young man who had lived his life without amenities in the harsh discomforts and uncertainties of rural poverty in the South, his sparsely furnished room, his bed with wire springs, the food which others scorned, were all "comforts of living...as I had never known or imagine...." As he stated in his memoir, he "respected, admired and revered the place and was proud and thankful to be part of it." This sense of gratitude and reverence, which he had felt as he listened to those first sermons in the chapel, returned to him on the Plain in the midst of the very first winter in which he had "experienced real cold and saw snow for the first time."[44]

In the face of a cold and cutting north wind on an afternoon late in January 1889, the Corps of Cadets stood in formation before the chapel, for the funeral service of a distinguished soldier, Brigadier General Ranald Slidell Mackenzie, first honor graduate of the class of 1862, who had been wounded at the battles of Manassas, Petersburg, and Cedar Creek during the Civil War, and had been a skillful and successful Indian fighter in the Oklahoma territory.[45] After the service, as the heavy, gray, twilight of winter gathered over the Plain, the funeral procession moved deliberately toward the cemetery, led by the caisson carrying the flag-draped coffin, with a caparisoned horse following at a slow walk, and the corps with shoulder arms reversed, marching at the slow pace of the funeral march played by the cadet band. As minute guns pounded a final salute, Summerall was reminded of the Biblical verse from the burial of Moses and realized now that he had been "captivated" by the military life, and "wanted with all my heart to become a part of it. The parades and guard mounting, the [entire] program from reveille to taps ennobled the life of the soldier." For Summerall, this was the life, and this was the course for which he had "hoped and prayed," and to which he would remain dedicated with all of his considerable strength and determination for the next 42 years.[46]

During the course of his plebe year, Summerall emerged as one of the leaders of the rising yearling class. When they met to organize, he was elected class vice-president. Not surprisingly, they also selected him to lead the singing of the class song.[47] Cadets like Summerall, whose delinquency list was short, who had done well in drill, had carried out their military duties responsibly, and who had demonstrated leadership ability and intelligence received rank. Captains and lieutenants were chosen from the rising First Class, sergeants from the rising Second Class, and corporals from the rising Third Class. Cadet rank was prized by those cadets who were ambitious militarily, and to win and hold rank, "a cadet had to be an ardent supporter of the Academy's ways."[48] When the list of rank holders, known as the "makes," was announced, Summerall was selected as the fourth ranking corporal in the Corps, and a member of the color guard. At that point in his life, he felt that "Nothing could have filled me with more pride."[49] When the two corporals ahead of him were reduced, he moved up to become the second in rank. At the end of his yearling year, even though the number of "skins" he received increased, he was named senior first sergeant, which was the cadet in charge of all other first sergeants and their various details of cadets in each company. He remembered this day as "one of the proudest moments of my life."[50] When the "makes" were published after graduation exercises in June 1891, Summerall's name stood at the top as First Captain, and thus in command of the entire Corps of Cadets for the year 1891–1892.[51] Some 60 years later, he looked back on that day as "the proudest moment of my life," and saw it as the confirmation of God's blessing.[52]

With the end of Plebe Barracks the cadets returned on 1 September to their barracks across the Plain to begin the academic program. Throughout the year, the daily schedule the cadets followed never changed. From Monday through Friday, reveille, or First Call, sounded at 0545 hours, with beds to be made and the room put in "superior condition"; then came Assembly and Roll Call, followed by breakfast at 0630 hours; Guard Mount was at 0700; from 0745 to 1215 hours; class periods of one hour to one hour and twenty minutes in length were held, with one period set aside for study hall; dinner was at 1230 hours, followed by more class periods from 1300 to 1500 hours; after the last class their time was filled by drills, riding, and physical training until supper at 1800; after supper they returned to their rooms to study until lights out and taps at 2000 hours. Saturdays began as usual, but after dinner they prepared for inspection, after which they were free for the remainder of the day, except for those who had to serve confinements or march off the "skins" they had accumulated. Each Sunday morning they were marched to the chapel for the mandatory Anglican service. On Sunday afternoons, they either slept, enjoyed whatever privileges they had managed to win, or received visitors.[53]

The academic program at West Point was based on the system developed by Sylvanus Thayer, the fifth superintendent of the Academy from 1817 to 1833, and known as the "Father of the Military Academy." The foundation and pillars for Thayer's program of study were courses in French and mathematics. French was important because many of the most advanced texts were written in French, and mathematics was basic to the understanding and practice of engineering. In his first year a cadet studied algebra, geometry, trigonometry, measuration, and French and English grammar. In his second year he continued in the same subjects, but with more emphasis on mathematics, French, drawing, and topographic sketching. The Third Class cadet studied natural philosophy (physics), chemistry, mineralogy, geology, and more drawing. In their First Class year the major course each cadet took was engineering, with an emphasis on civil engineering, as well as a capstone course in ordnance and gunnery, along with courses in military and civil law, a brief survey of world history, and a short course in Spanish. To teach these courses, Thayer attracted an outstanding faculty of soldier-scholars, who were among the country's best teachers in the fields of physics, engineering, and mathematics. Most were Academy graduates, and the textbooks they wrote in these disciplines were used in colleges and universities throughout the country. Many graduates went on to careers in the army, but others gained recognition as outstanding faculty members of other engineering schools, and builders of canals, railroads, and public buildings all across the United States.[54] Thayer also created the honor code, under which a cadet's word was always accepted. This bound him to always tell the truth, but neither Thayer nor his successors defined specific violations, or established a means to enforce the code. Nevertheless, cadets respected the code, and were vigilant in their support of it.[55]

As America entered the Gilded Age and approached the end of the century, knowledge "exploded" in all fields, and colleges and universities changed and intensified curricula and courses to incorporate and promote the latest technological and intellectual developments. At West Point, however, the success of the Academy's graduates in the Civil War further validated Thayer's program and policies. Until 1900, almost all the superintendents and professors were Civil War veterans, and they resisted any alterations in the system.[56] They believed their mission was to preserve the pre-Civil War curriculum, and to direct their classes through the prescribed texts, many of which had been written by their predecessors. The professors established the curriculum and had absolute control over it. Their power was institutionalized in the Academic Board, which, according to historian Stephen E. Ambrose, "was most responsible for the Academy's ignoring technological and intellectual ferment and remaining a changeless institution in a changing age."[57] As a result, Thayer's program had become as inflexible and unchanging as the cadets' daily schedule; by the late 19th century, as Robert L. Bullard's biographer and historian Allan Millett has written, "the Military Academy's curriculum had become a relic of what had been the nation's finest technological education program."[58]

The rigidity of the curriculum was matched by the firm and unchanging method of instruction, regardless of the course or subject matter. Each of the four classes was divided into sections made of eight to ten cadets in each course. Cadets were assigned to sections according to their academic standing; academic leaders were assigned to the first section of each course. Cadets were moved between sections on the basis of their academic performance, and demotion to a lower section could be a major blow to one's pride. They marched to classes, and stood at attention behind their desks or benches until the section marcher reported to the instructor. Then they took seats and class began. Each cadet was called before the instructor and required to respond to questions based on the assignment that was handed to him by the instructor. He was graded on how well his answers corresponded to the prescribed solutions in the text. When he had finished his "recitation," and answered any questions the instructor might pose, he returned to his seat, usually with great relief, to be followed by the next cadet in line. Young Frank Parker from South Carolina, class of 1894, was practically worn out, and somewhat vexed by the end of his recitations. "The method of recitation is very trying," he wrote. "When you get thro' [sic] with your subject on the board, you face about and stand at attention. You frequently have to stand in this one position for an hour and a half. As you are only allowed to put figures on the board, never a word [sic]. I have lost some of my mark by writing just a word or two. And again, if you move your body the least bit you suffer. I have lost one or two marks for moving a step backward in order to point out something."[59] When a bugle call sounded the end of the class period, the instructor dismissed the class and they marched off to the next one. As Millett has stated, "Except for occasional lectures and experiments and practical work in drawing, this was West Point teaching, day in and day out."[60] Examinations were held in January and June, and the results determined the cadets' academic standing in his class. If a cadet failed a single subject he was dismissed from the Academy.[61] In their later years, some cadets were not reluctant to criticize this regimen and the professors before whom they had stood with trembling hand at the blackboard.

Colonel T. Bentley Mott, class of 1885, wrote in his memoirs that "The work of an instructor was reduced almost to the sole function of listening to recitations, marking the students transferring them to higher or lower sections, passing on their examination papers." For Mott, an instructor was not a teacher but rather "a machine for grading cadets upon their knowledge of prescribed texts." He said that "As a rule, they know little beyond what they learned as cadets." Major General George Van Horn Moseley, class of 1899, complained that in his surveying class he was not taught to use surveying instruments, and, in fact, seldom was allowed to see any. He was especially critical of his French teachers, and stated that the language was "taught by men who could not speak it and it was in those days that the French instructor would invariably depart on a few days leave when the arrival of a prominent Frenchman to inspect the Academy was announced."[62]

In his memoir, Summerall commented critically on the teaching at West Point from his own experience as a teacher, and from the perspective of the "excellent teaching" he had received at Dr. Porter's school. To him, it seemed that the texts had little to do with what cadets were expected to learn, and the instructors were more interested in finding out what they did not know, rather than what they had learned. As he said, "We hesitated from asking questions because of the belief that the instructor would mark us low for what we did not know." He was sympathetic to the plight of his plebe roommate Donald Kellogg, who failed the mathematics examination at the end of the year and was dismissed from the Academy. It was not that he failed mathematics because of his own shortcomings, but rather, said Summerall, because "he could not learn the mathematics as taught." In another backhanded swipe at the pedagogy of his instructors, he stated that "The officers who taught us commanded great respect, and, no doubt, forced us to learn for ourselves instead of depending on them." Thus, he "devoted practically all my time to study." At times, the preparation of an especially difficult lesson, he said, "forced me to sit under the table [in his room] with blankets over it and study by a candle after taps." He thought he had been fortunate, on these faintly lit occasions, to have escaped detection by the "tac" making his nightly inspection tour.[63]

During their course of study at the Academy, cadets received a yearly stipend of $500, regardless of the resources of their families. From this amount they bought their books and personal items, and each month four dollars was deducted and deposited into a special fund to purchase uniforms on graduation. At the end of the year they received the balance remaining in their accounts.[64] Most of Summerall's classmates came from families of moderate means; none were listed as affluent, and none were in the lowest category of indigent. The occupation of Summerall's father officially was stated as a merchant of moderate means living in town;[65] unofficially, Bryant Summerall's means were much less than moderate, and although Astatula, Florida, might be considered a town, it was more like the country hamlet. Cadet Summerall had to watch carefully his expenditures, for, as he stated in his memoir, "I never received a cent from anyone while I was at West Point and never bought a class ring. I did not even have my photograph taken as First Captain."[66]

Summerall not only had proved to be a serious and thrifty young cadet, but also that he was a serious and hard-working student, but his memory once again seems to have failed him when he ranked his academic performance quite a bit higher than the record shows. In his memoir, he recalled that as a plebe, "I was in the first or second sections in English and French and in the third section in mathematics." According to records in the USMA Archives, among the 89 members in his plebe class, he ranked 24th in mathematics, 7th in English, and 19th in French. This was a respectable performance, but not quite as good as he had remembered. He was correct in noting that at the end of the year he stood 11th in his class.[67] Although in his memoir he mentions none of his rankings in specific courses during his remaining years at the Academy, the record indicates that in his third class year, which he considered as "by far the most difficult, especially in mathematics,"[68] he ranked 17th in mathematics, 11th in English, and 33rd in drawing. He noted correctly that he ranked 13th overall in a class that had diminished to 68 members.[69] Actually, his second class year appeared to be his toughest. He acknowledged that his added responsibilities as senior first sergeant limited the amount of time he had in the mornings to prepare for classes. Apparently, he felt that the professor of natural and experimental philosophy and head of the Academic Board, Peter Smith Michie, "Old Pete" to the cadets, was biased against first sergeants. He said that "The professor of philosophy [Michie] had a theory that first sergeants could not study properly and perform their duties and he acted accordingly."[70] At any rate, in his second class year he ranked 31st in natural and experimental philosophy, 25th in chemistry, physics, mineralogy and geology, and 36th in drawing. His class standing had declined from 13th to 23rd.[71]

Once he had gotten past "Old Pete," his performance and standing improved, and so did his enjoyment of academic work. He especially looked forward to classes in engineering and higher mathematics, and could even joke about an incident that happened in an engineering class. When he was asked by the instructor during recitation at the blackboard when he would come to an important detail in a problem, Summerall replied, "We'll come to that presently, Lieutenant." The instructor replied sharply that "'We'll come to it right now, Mr. Summerall.'" He noted that "the section was much amused at my expense."[72] His record at the end of his first class year as First Captain reflects Summerall's more positive recollections of his academic work in his final year as a cadet. In civil and military engineering he ranked 32nd, in law he ranked 30th, 28th in history, 25th in ordnance and gunnery, 9th in Spanish, and 4th in practical military instruction. His final ranking among the 62 members of the class of 1892 was 20th, which was one step below his friend John Palmer, who, as Second Captain, stood one rank lower than Summerall in the military chain of command.[73]

After the class of 1889 had been graduated in June, Summerall and his fellow yearlings moved into Plebe Camp, where, as a corporal in C Company and member of the color guard, he was kept busy drilling and instructing the new plebe class. He attended a few dances, and undoubtedly sang a few songs, but "devoted practically all of my time to my military duties in camp." His new tent mate and later roommate was George H. McMaster from South Carolina, "a superior character and we were very good friends." He was two years younger than Summerall, and later took part in the Punitive Expedition to Mexico in 1916, and commanded a regiment in the AEF in World War I.[74]

At the end of their yearling year, Summerall and his classmates were granted the traditional furlough for rising Second Classmen of two and a half months of freedom, until they had to report back at the Academy on 28 August. Before disbanding, they elected Summerall chairman of a committee to make arrangements for a class dinner and evening at the theater in New York City, and entrusted him with contributions from their individual account balances. In addition to his rank and position as vice chairman of the class, Summerall had become known as "Honest John," so it was logical that they would call on him to collect the money, and hold on to it until the bills came in for their night on the town. They went to see a play, and had dinner at the Murray Hill Hotel. Summerall remembered the evening as "a great success." The class prophet, with tongue-in-cheek humor that the serious and earnest young man from the backwoods of Florida might not have grasped, predicted for him, as Summerall recorded, a career as a socialite. The reason for this prediction, so said the prophet, was because to date Summerall "had refrained from social activities."[75]

The next day, with the money to pay the bills in his pocket, Summerall bought a ticket in steerage for the long journey home to Astatula, via Charleston and Jacksonville. As the steamer plowed into the rough waters of the open sea, the purser "must have guessed my status and my need," as Summerall said, and offered him a first-class stateroom. When they reached Charleston, the steamer tied up at the docks along the Cooper River on the east side of the city, and Summerall dashed ashore to see Dr. Porter at his school across town on Ashley Avenue. After a short visit with his former teacher, he returned to the dock, well before the time he understood the ship would sail. As he approached, he looked on helplessly as the ship steamed away from the dock, and turned south toward Jacksonville. Realizing that he had given all of his money, including the money for the class bills to the kindly purser for safekeeping, Summerall gathered his wits, and explained his "predicament" to a ticket agent for Clyde Line. This good Samaritan loaned the desperate young cadet enough money to stay overnight at a hotel, and to pay for a train ticket to Jacksonville the next morning. After arriving in the familiar port city, Summerall found the steamer, picked up his funds from the porter, and gave him the money to repay the "loan" to the ticket agent in Charleston. Then he boarded a river boat for the trip up the St. John's River to Astor, and from there caught a train to Astatula.[76]

Summerall had not been home for two full years, and apparently he had not seen anyone in his family during this period. Unfortunately, there exists no record of any letters between him and his parents or siblings during his years at West Point. He remained as steadfastly devoted to and supportive of his parents as ever, and worked alongside his father in the groves picking oranges "for small wages," and helping him at home to make improvements on their house. He suffered a puncture wound in his knee from an orange tree thorn, but was able to hobble around the house, and help his mother with the cooking, washing, and housework. He spent his spare time memorizing in alphabetical order the class roll of his company. As senior first sergeant in A Company, where he had begun as a plebe, he wanted to be ready for the competition among the other first sergeants at the first roll call, to see which one could recite his company roll the fastest.[77]

In late August 1889, Summerall returned for his third year at West Point, via the same route that he had taken more than two years earlier, with his pockets about as empty as before, but without having suffered any mishaps like those in his most recent journey home. After putting on his uniform, and taking his place at the first formation, he had no difficulty in calling the roll and detecting those who were absent, although he failed to mention in his memoir whether he had performed this duty faster than any other first sergeant in the corps. His new roommate was George C. Barnhardt from North Carolina, who served as company clerk, and became a "congenial friend."[78] Barnhardt was graduated 17th in the class, and commanded a regiment and a brigade in the AEF during World War I.[79]

As first sergeant, Summerall had to contend with several First Classmen who had managed transfers into the company, and apparently thought they could do as they pleased. They soon ran afoul of their strict spit-and-polish first sergeant, who would have none of their "gold-bricking," and reported them for being improperly dressed at reveille, and for many other offenses as well. He expected they might refute his reports and that, to defend his honor, he would be forced to fight one of them. However, they apparently realized, as Summerall said, that "I was acting from a sense of duty and soon conducted themselves properly."[80] During this year of increasing responsibilities, Summerall noted seriously that "I attended a few hops but I felt that I had little time for anything but my military duties and my studies." Not surprisingly, when the new "makes" were published after Exercises in June 1891, Summerall was appointed First Captain, the highest cadet rank, that carried with it the responsibility for the overall performance of the Corps of Cadets.[81] Other returning classmates like John Palmer were elated when what Palmer referred to as the "monotony" of cadet life was "broken by a revolutionary event": a football game, the first ever played by a West Point team, and against the team from the Naval Academy.[82]

American universities in the eastern states had started playing football in the 1870s. It caught on with students, alumni, and administrators, and by the turn of the century almost every college in the country fielded a team to fight it out on the gridiron. For a number of years Navy had been playing the game, but at West Point the sport remained virtually unknown, and only two cadets, Leonard Prince, Summerall's old tentmate, and Dennis Mahan Michie had ever played the game.[83] Michie was the son of Professor Michie, "Old Pete," who was the dean of the Academic Board, and dominated it as the Board itself dominated West Point. The elder Michie and his colleagues on the Board could be counted upon to resist any innovation, but Dennis was Michie's favorite son, and he assured his classmates that "Old Pete is against it now, but I will bring him around."[84] "Old Pete" and the Academic Board did indeed approve the match, and Dennis Michie was selected to coach the team. However, they could practice only on Saturday afternoons when rainy weather forced the cancellation of parade; the only way they could schedule any extra training was to get up a half hour before reveille, and jog around the parade ground.[85]

The day of the big game arrived on Saturday, 29 November 1890. A gridiron had been laid out on the southeastern corner of the Plain, and along the sidelines stood the cadets and the officers and their families, plus a group of young naval officers who had come up for the game from a ship anchored in the harbor of New York City. Soon the Navy team trotted out on the field, and to the astonishment of the crowd went through a series of organized calisthenics. This was their seventh game of the season, and they wore their dirty white uniforms to prove their toughness.[86]

Behind their powerful flying wedge formation, Navy dominated the action from the beginning. They had developed a system of play calling based on nautical commands like "Clear decks for action," "Helm's a lee," "Reef top sails," "Man the spanker sails." The cadets countered with hastily improvised military commands like "In battery heave," "As-skirmishers," "Forward guide center," "Left wheel," "Right forward, fours right." Michie's raw recruits managed to make several first downs, but failed to score. They could not stop the midshipmen, who scored three touchdowns in the first half, two in the second half, and made two of four conversions. A touchdown counted four points and a conversion after a touchdown counted two points, so Navy won the game by the score of 24 to 0.[87]

Undaunted in defeat, the cadets pressed for a return match the next year and received overwhelming support not only from the Academy, but also from army posts throughout the country. Contributions to buy uniforms poured in from every regiment, and a coach was hired to prepare the team to play a schedule of six games on the Plain during the 1891–1892 year, before the only game that really counted: the showdown with Navy. Michie, Prince, and their cohorts composed class yells, and fight songs were written to cheer on the team.[88] For Summerall, this new wave of excitement was more disturbing than thrilling.

He believed that class yells were a kind of unrestrained enthusiasm that weakened the cadet chain of command by introducing an unfavorable "change in discipline and in the relations between cadets and [cadet] officers." When the Academy hosted teams from other colleges and their supporters, he felt that they set a bad example as "Their presence in the mess hall, their college yells at meals and the non-military atmosphere introduced by them were in strange contrast to the ancient customs of the academy."[89] Nevertheless, the Army team won four of the six games during the season of 1891–1892, and hopes were running high that the loss to Navy would be avenged.

The day before the decisive battle, the band led the entire Corps of Cadets down the hill to the train station to give the team a rousing send-off. As John Palmer said, "We were not permitted to break ranks, but while waiting for the train, we were allowed to stand 'at ease.' This gave us a chance to sing our football songs, and to give the new Corps yell eighteen times, once for each player and an extra one for Captain Michie. If some old graduate had been a passenger on that train as it stopped at the West Point station, he would surely have died of apoplexy." Palmer might have been contemplating a similar but less lethal reaction from the First Captain himself! "After the train left," continued Palmer, and, he might have added, predictably, "'Battalion atten-shun' from Pelot Summerall, the senior captain, reconditioned us as soldiers and we marched up the hill again."[90]

Before the game started, cadets gathered in the barracks, where they anxiously awaited news from one of the substitutes on the team who had been delegated to send a telegram after each score. Tension and excitement mounted, as they learned that both teams had scored, and Michie had kicked a field goal to put Army in the lead at the half by the score of 10 to 6. In the second half Navy scored and went ahead, but then the substitute got so excited that he could not manage to send any more telegrams. At dusk an apprehensive Corps marched to the mess hall for supper and learned about a report in a New York paper that Navy had won the game. All through the meal nothing more was heard. The suspense was too much for the cadet quartermaster James Jervey of Virginia to stand, so he jumped up from his seat before supper was over, and dashed over to the telegraph office. In the meantime, the Corps had finished supper and marched back to barracks and lined up for dismissal to quarters. Just before they broke ranks, however, "Jim came running through the sally port waving a telegram. Pelot examined it and then announced with his customary solemnity: 'Final score, Army 32, Navy 16, dismiss your companies.'" Unrestrained and exuberant, the cadets rushed through the sally port and followed the band to an area on the north side of the Plain, where they had been authorized to light a bonfire if Army won. Said Palmer, "We danced around it like Indians and drowned out the music of the band with our songs and cheers. There was never such a night at West Point since its garrison of ragged Continentals got news of another victory down on the Chesapeake—Cornwallis's surrender at Yorktown." Looking back on this momentous day, Palmer saw it as a step forward for West Point, when he said that "Our football songs and cheers sounded the knell of the old monastic days and brought the academy into a broader contact with the modern world."[91]

As difficult as it may be to imagine the "solemn" Summerall dancing around the bonfire "like an Indian," he also wrote with excitement about the win, although, in contrast to Palmer's optimism, expressed concern and some bitterness about its consequences. "When our team returned from defeating the Navy," he said, "it was met at the train by the Corps and borne on their shoulders with such yells and pandemonium as the hills of the Hudson had never seen. We realized and [with] different emotions that, whether we liked it or not, a new era had been ushered in. Many old ideas died and many new ones were born. The effect on some of the athletes was marked. One of my closest friends during the first two years became an undisciplined bully. I could have nothing to do with him and I spoke to him only officially for nearly two years."[92]

The "bully" appears to have been Leonard Prince, his former tent mate, and one of the leaders of the football team, who had also written some of the class yells. Prince had been a candidate for president of the yearling class, while Summerall had been chosen as class chairman, with the job of presiding over the election for class president. Two factions emerged, one supporting Prince, and the other working for Henry Whitney. They carried on a vigorous and intense campaign, which Prince fully "expected to win," said Summerall. But Prince lost, and rather than accepting his defeat gracefully he and his "faction," Summerall wrote, "became very resentful and never fully accepted Whitney."[93] Since Summerall had presided over the election and also had been elected class vice president unanimously, and without opposition, he seems to have assumed that Prince resented him as part of the Whitney "faction." In Summerall's mind, a further reason for Prince's resentment toward him could have been his cool and critical response as First Captain to football at West Point, and his concern about its effect on the traditions of the Academy, while Prince had become one of the game's most enthusiastic supporters. If Prince were the "bully" in the memoirs, as appears highly probable, Summerall's reaction represents another example of his own perpetual animosity toward anyone who had opposed him, or who had challenged his own strongly held ideas and opinions.

In his riding classes Summerall found some diversion from his duties and responsibilities, and respite from antagonists like Leonard Prince. Classes were held in the riding hall, beginning in the Second Class year, and continuing through the First Class year, with instruction in hippology, the mounted drill, riding bareback, and dismounting and mounting at a trot and gallop. Summerall found all this "especially enjoyable," although he did have difficulty with the "acrobatic work" of dismounting and mounting, while the horse was trotted or galloped. With a strong and rather stocky build on his frame of 5 feet 9 inches, he was not agile enough to perform well in gymnastics, but boxed fairly well, enjoyed fencing, and wielded the broad sword with considerable skill.[94] The regimen, rigors, and physical challenges of cadet life seem, indeed, to have strengthened his solid physique and bolstered his good health, long since robust as a result of good genes, caring parents, abstinence from alcohol and tobacco, a moderate diet, and hard, physical labor. Altogether, it must have been evident that he was a young man well equipped to carry the weight that rested upon the shoulders of the First Captain.

Summerall bore his burdens proudly and discharged his responsibilities without hesitation. When he felt it necessary to report classmates for infractions, he promptly took action. After one such episode, he once again expected to be challenged to a fight by those whom he had reported. Fortunately, they apologized, backed down, and accepted their punishment. When he wrote of his duties and responsibilities, he could sound moralistic and self-serving: "I was not happy in my office [as First Captain]," he said, "but the responsibility developed character and moral courage and I believe that the experience laid the foundation for my future career."[95]

Yet, it would be unfair and cynical to imply that his assessment of his service as the highest ranking cadet meant any less to Summerall than the opportunity to prove himself worthy of the faith and confidence which he believed that his family, benefactors, friends, and superiors had vested in him. All of his responsibilities and duties carried the great weight of obligation, morality, and honor, supported by his conviction that God and his faith were directing him on the right course. It is understandable, therefore, that he would express his thoughts and feelings about these matters in highly moralistic terms. At the same time, instead of letting fade from his memory those who in their youthful years had opposed or criticized him, he retained the resentments he felt, and for too long held grudges against them all. It is regrettable that Summerall, a man with such a strong and commanding personality, and with such high standards for his own actions, could not see the justice and redeeming virtue of forgiveness and forgetfulness. Retaining resentment and harboring grudges only added heft to the burdens that he had assumed.

Nevertheless, he enjoyed some fun times during his First Class year. He escorted the daughter of a "wealthy family in New York" to several hops, and, along with two classmates, was invited over Christmas to the family's home in the city. It was, said Summerall, "my first experience with wealth. They took us to the theatre and gave us elaborate diners [sic] and lunches." The earnest, young, First Captain seems to have especially endeared himself to the grandmother of the family, who invited Summerall and more of his friends to spend a week after graduation at the family estate in Tuxedo Park, located not far from West Point.[96]

After their examinations in January, the class of 1892 began to "count the days till June," and consider their military assignments after graduation. Tailors came to take their orders for the uniforms they would wear as newly commissioned second lieutenants. Graduating seniors could request assignment to a specific branch of the army, but the general rule was that class standing determined the branch, with the top tier of graduates selected for engineers and artillery because of their mathematical skills; for the others, the only choices were cavalry and infantry. The class of 1892 was typical, with the top two graduates becoming engineers. Of the remaining 17 who ranked ahead of Summerall, 14 became artillery officers.[97] This placed Summerall in a dilemma, for, in his memoir, he said that he preferred artillery, but had learned that there were few vacancies, and realized that most of those ranked ahead of him had chosen this branch. There follows a certain confusion in his memoir about which branch he actually first requested. Initially, he said that he decided to make the 1st Infantry Regiment his first choice, and which was stationed near San Francisco. A few paragraphs later, he said that he had decided to request assignment to the cavalry "in my first application but later requested the 1st, 16th and 15th Infantry [Regiments] because the 1st was in San Francisco where I wanted to go." He chose the cavalry and then infantry, he said, because promotion in those branches was more rapid than in the artillery.[98] But on 11 July 1892, one month to the day after his graduation, he wrote from his home in Astatula a letter to the adjutant general of the army that reveals he had reached a more decisive preference than his memoirs indicate. In his memoir, however, he makes no reference to this letter. He wrote, "I have the honor to request that the following choices for regiments be substituted for those which I have previously submitted. My reasons for desiring the change are that these will be more advantageous to me and I shall like them better. First: Any Artillery. Second: The 7th Cavalry. Third: The 8th Cavalry. Fourth: Any Cavalry."[99]

Somewhat perplexed and vexed with what was a third request for assignment from Summerall, the adjutant general's office noted in a memorandum for the record dated 15 July 1892, that "Cadet Summerall is down on the graduating list as preferring Infantry, several regiments being named in order of preference. Subsequently he wrote a letter making changes in his first preference, but still naming infantry regiments. He now, a month after graduation, asks for artillery or cavalry. The assignments have been ordered, and presumably the nominations have been sent to the Senate. Cadet Summerall was given his second choice out of several infantry regiments. The assignments made cannot be changed without a great deal of trouble, and obviously there must be some limit to these changes." The major on duty added that "The Major Genl Comd'y [Adjutant General] says it is now too late to consider this request, as the assignments have been ordered and nominations made."[100]

Summerall's letter shows that in spite of the less promising chances for promotion in the artillery and cavalry, he genuinely preferred these branches, mainly because they would be "more advantageous to me," and "I shall like them better." He was not called "Honest John" for lack of candor. Also it is clear that his second choice for infantry assignment was the 1st Regiment, not the 16th, as he said in his memoir, since he "was given his second choice out of several infantry regiments," which was, indeed, the 1st. At any rate, upon reflection at home in Astatula, he reaffirmed his preference for the arm in which he would receive his baptism in battle, and in which he made his first mark as a courageous warrior.

As the parades, riding exhibitions, and gunnery drills of June Week took place, the class of 1892 made plans for their farewell dinner at the Murray Hill Hotel. When "the great moment of graduation" arrived on 11 June, the class of 1892 began their graduation leave, and as Summerall said, "We lost no time in changing to our civilian clothes and leaving. Our joy far exceeded our regrets."[101] Following their dinner in the city, he took several of his classmates and Second Class friends up to the Tuxedo Park estate of his "wealthy friends," whom, incidentally, he never named. There in the company of "as many young ladies" as there were cadets, they luxuriated in a week of "lavish entertainment." When it was time to leave, the grandmother who, said Summerall, "was the real head of the family" and "had come to look upon me as a sort of grandson," presented him with a ticket for the trip to Jacksonville by train, which was "at much greater expense" than the long, slow journey by steamboat would have cost; it was one of the "many kindnesses" which Summerall said he owed his elderly and unnamed benefactor.[102]

The opulent surroundings for his departure, and the comfort and security of his journey south toward home, were in great contrast to the bleak conditions in which he had departed four years ago, with such earnest and anxious hopes of deliverance. The deliverance he sought was even more complete than he imagined, for, as he had said, the four years at West Point had the effect of "changing all that I had been to what it was intended that I should become." Already a religious young man with high moral standards, dutiful and serious beyond his years, he embraced this process of change with impassioned determination, and with all of his strength and force of personality. He refused to be intimidated by the taunts and terrors of upperclass hazing, was meticulous in his attention to his duties and responsibilities, and held the respect and trust of his peers while remaining deferential toward the officers of the Academy, and rigorously enforcing the rules and regulations for which he was responsible. He was a natural for leadership and command at West Point. When he looked back at these years on the Plain, it is not difficult to understand why he thought the process of change he had gone through "was for the better."

The change that Summerall wrote about occurred during the period toward the end of the century that historian Thomas Fleming and others have called the "years of iron."[103] Unquestionably, the rigid and uncompromising regulations and demands of these years at West Point, as has been discussed earlier, helped to build strong, self-reliant men like Summerall, who learned to master the basic essentials of their profession, and how to exercise command. Ingrained in this period also was a kind of "harsh moralism" that was a part of the spiritual atmosphere of the Victorian era, and was embodied at West Point by authoritarian professors like Peter Smith Michie. What distinguished "Old Pete" as a teacher was his severity, and his deeply religious conviction that his course in natural and experimental philosophy proved the existence of God; if any cadet could not accept this truth he would be found deficient and expelled from the Academy.[104] He was described as a man who had "'developed a disposition originally positive and uncompromising into one of masterfulness that brooked no opposition or contradiction.'"[105] Summerall's deeply held religious belief that the God of creation had chosen his path, and his wrathful, almost Biblical-like judgments toward those who opposed or contradicted him, reflected the impression Michie had made upon him. Indeed, among the most important reasons for Summerall's intense determination to succeed at West Point might well have been his resolution to prove that not all first sergeants were like those who Michie believed, and as Summerall said, "could not study properly." By refuting the only negative reference to his work and performance at the Academy that he remembered and recorded, he revealed the full impact, both direct and indirect, of the man who, more than any other person on the Plain, had forged his character in the crucible of West Point during the "years of iron."

# Chapter Three

## *In the Army Now*

The United States Army Summerall had joined actually was about the same size as the division of some 28,000 officers and men that he would command in the Great War of 1914–1918. In the 1870s a frugal Congress, supported by a peace-minded people weary of war, had authorized a strength of 28,000, including some 2,100 officers commanded by three major generals and six brigadier generals.[1] It was organized into a corps of engineers and three major branches: infantry, consisting of 25 regiments; artillery, consisting of 5 regiments; and cavalry, made up of 10 regiments. In a series of wars with the Plains Indians, it had secured and advanced the western frontier and succeeded in defeating them by 1890. However, a survey of the armies of the world published in 1897 by the German General Staff described the armies of Spain, Portugal, Switzerland, and Montenegro, but omitted altogether the United States Army, which, apparently, it did not consider important enough even to mention.[2] Summerall's classmate John Palmer, newly commissioned as a second lieutenant in the infantry at Fort Sheridan, Illinois, read "with indignation" in the *Encyclopedia Britannica* that the American army was actually not really an army at all. The *Britannica* described it, according to Palmer, as "nothing more than a constabulary for the Indian frontier." Palmer reluctantly agreed with this assessment. He was also troubled that there was little if any cooperation among the various arms and that each had its own separate line of promotion, which remained in all branches notoriously slow. It was not uncommon, for example, for captains to wait more than two decades for their promotions to major. Consequently, by 1893 the average age for captains was 50, only four years younger than the average age for generals.[3] Resignations, however, were rare. For 17 of the 24 years between 1874 and 1897, it was annually less than one percent.[4]

Historian Edward M. Coffman asserts a number of reasons for officers remaining in the post-Civil War army. Whether the younger officers realized it, promotion in their army was much faster than in the antebellum army; undoubtedly as well, the authority of command and the lure of adventure continued to appeal to the officer corps; also, throughout the army there was a strong sense of pride and accomplishment among the men in blue after their triumphal victory in the Civil War; and for many, the

*Charles Pelot Summerall in the army*
Courtesy The Citadel Archives & Museum,
Charleston, South Carolina

29

financial security of an officer's pay (as young Summerall and his family would happily discover), was a welcome relief in the hard times of postwar deflation and recovery.[5] Additionally, as Palmer noted, the army offered "abundant leisure" and was a "wonderful place for a young officer who wanted to read and study."[6] Then too, a series of reforms and innovations initiated in the aftermath of the Civil War made for a more challenging and rewarding career for the army's young professional officer corps.[7]

The two men most responsible for these progressive changes were General William Tecumseh Sherman and Emory Upton. Sherman became one of the most innovative and brilliant commanders on either side during the war and succeeded Ulysses S. Grant as commanding general of the army, serving from 1869 to 1883. On the eve of the war he was serving as superintendent of the Louisiana Military Seminary; as commanding general the former educator was concerned that army officers, although well-trained by technical schools in their particular branch of service, were not educated at the higher levels of theory and command.[8] He decided to establish a system of postgraduate schools where officers would acquire the specialized knowledge of their branch before moving up to the apex of the system where they would study strategy and the principles and practice of higher command. Sherman hoped also to create a higher standard of professionalism for army officers, similar to systems of higher criteria being established in the 1880s and 1890s for lawyers, doctors, accountants, and other middle class professionals. In 1881, after reviving the artillery school and organizing an engineering school, he founded a School of Application for Infantry and Cavalry at Fort Leavenworth, Kansas. During the first decade, instruction at the Leavenworth school emphasized small unit tactics. In the late 1880s and the 1890s, two officer-instructors, Arthur L. Wagner and Eben Swift, emphasized at Leavenworth the study of abstract and theoretical issues of war and stressed the importance of staff work at higher levels of command.[9] By the time of Sherman's death in 1891, Leavenworth was evolving into the school that he had envisioned: the center of strategic planning and analysis for the emerging professional army.[10]

The second of these officer-reformers was Emory Upton, a protégé of Sherman, who had risen during the war to the rank of brigadier general at the age of 24, and attained the rank of lieutenant colonel in the postwar army. Seriously wounded in the war himself, Upton was appalled by the heavy losses suffered by both sides and blamed these excessive casualties on the lack of skillful leadership.[11] In 1867, he published *Infantry Tactics*, a revision of the infantry manual, in which he urged that infantry tactics be adapted to the more lethal rifled and breechloading weapons by abandoning frontal assaults in favor of less dense formations and more flexible groups of skirmishers. Quickly the War Department adopted Upton's revision. In 1870, he was appointed commandant of cadets and instructor in tactics at West Point, where he broadened his review and revisions of the army's tactical manuals to include those for the cavalry and artillery. As commandant, Upton developed a closer relationship with Sherman, and in 1876 the commanding general named him to a three-man commission to observe the armies of Asia and Europe. Upton already had pinpointed what he considered two main weaknesses in American military policy: the exercise of too much civilian control and the failure to develop and sustain a large professional army.[12]

After his return from his journey abroad, he published in 1878 *The Armies of Asia and Europe*. In this work he praised the German Empire's establishment of an all-military general staff that conducted the planning, preparation, and training for war while remaining largely independent of civilian control in peacetime as well as in war. He also expressed admiration for the German army's large professional cadre that served as the nucleus of an expandable force in wartime. In the last 54 pages of the book, Upton made specific recommendations based upon the essential elements of the German system. His recommendations were reviewed in hearings before the Senate Military Affairs Committee and incorporated into a lengthy legislative bill. Opposition from the administration, and heavy lobbying against the bill from military officers who feared they might lose their positions, killed its passage.[13]

Distressed but undeterred, Upton began work on a second book-length manuscript, *The Military Policy of the United States*. He turned to the history of American wars and his own personal experience to emphasize that men and materiel had been wasted at the beginning of almost every war the nation had fought because its armies had been poorly trained, poorly led, and weakened by excessive civilian control. Only the country's great wealth of resources and manpower and the courage of its soldiers had enabled it to prevail. Returning to the German model, he argued for the adoption of the German general staff system and a larger professional army, so organized that by civilian volunteers it could be increased rapidly in time of war to at least 100,000 soldiers. Ultimately, however, Upton remained pessimistic that any of his proposals would be adopted, and for reasons that remain unclear, he committed suicide in March 1881.[14]

For many, Upton's proposals conflicted with American traditions and current conditions. His praise of the professional soldier represented too much of a departure from American traditions of the "minuteman" and the National Guard concept of trained civilians. His belief that the military organization of the German Empire would serve well the interests of the United States ignored the political and cultural differences between this newly established empire and the American republic; and his notion that the United States needed an expandable standing army was unacceptable to a people who perceived no serious threat to their safety and security. Nevertheless, his ideas appealed to army officers, who perhaps felt unappreciated and neglected by the public. His recommendations might well have inspired General Sherman, two months after Upton's death, to order the establishment of a School of Application for Infantry and Cavalry at Fort Leavenworth.[15]

With reform in the army's educational system well under way, progressive-minded officers worked to change the military's executive command organization. At the top the army really had two masters: the commanding general and the secretary of war. As stated in army regulations, the commanding general was the senior officer and commanded "The military establishment...which pertains to discipline and military control." The secretary of war conducted "The fiscal affairs of the Army...through the several staff departments."[16] It seemed clear enough that the commanding general would command the "line" regiments that were stationed in the various territorial departments of the army, and the secretary of war would control the administration of the army through the staff offices (or bureaus as they came to be called). Since the bureaus through which the army was administered and supplied were excluded from the authority of the commanding general, his command and control of the regiments in the field, which obviously depended upon supplies and other support from the bureaus, was restricted. In addition, civilian secretaries of war came and departed, and usually showed little interest in strategic or administrative matters. Thus, the bureau chiefs, who themselves were senior officers permanently detailed to their positions, commanded their departments as if they were independent entities. When commanding generals sought to extend their authority over the bureaus, they encountered resolute opposition from the bureau chiefs. The chiefs made clear that they were responsible only to the secretary and that, in any case, officers of the line like the commanding general and his subordinates knew little about staff work. The entire situation generated bureaucratic infighting and led to lack of understanding and incessant feuding between staff officers on the one hand and line officers on the other. In addition, the army was unable to provide the secretary with unified advice and recommendations. Most seriously, the War Department failed in peacetime to develop plans to prepare the army for war and to establish clear lines of authority to decide what should be done in the time of war. In the 1870s, Upton and Sherman had blamed the entrenched bureau system for the War Department's shortcomings; in the late 1920s the bureau system and especially the chiefs who ran it would be no less a burden for Charles P. Summerall when he was the army chief of staff.[17]

If Second Lieutenant Summerall knew of the writings of Upton and the concerns of the reformers in the officer corps, he remained undisturbed on the long, leisurely train ride from New York City south toward home. Instead, in a more immediate and practical sense, he continued to weigh his choices and possibilities for duty in his new profession, and to consider what his "new life" would mean for him and his "impoverished family." When he arrived in Astatula he shared with them the good news that his salary as a second lieutenant would be $116.67 per month. As he said, "This to us was great riches. We had never dreamed of anything like it, and it meant what we had never known— security." Although as a yet unassigned young graduate he "knew nothing of what my living expenses in the army would be," it was enough to be used for "for the benefit of [us] all." Summerall unselfishly "determined that the greater part of my salary would be sent to my parents."

While Summerall had been at West Point, the chief support of his parents had been the income they had received from a boarder from Illinois, but who unfortunately had contracted malaria and died not long after Summerall arrived home. In addition to the money that he had remaining from his account at the Academy, he and his father finished building the house they had begun some six years before with money he had saved while teaching and serving as principal at the school in Leesburg. For the rest of his uneventful summer graduation leave, Summerall worked in the citrus groves alongside his father, now in his 65th year, and, as usual, helped his mother with the housework.[18]

Not long after he had requested in his letter of 11 July that his assignment be changed from infantry to artillery, Summerall received both his commission and orders to report on 30 September to Company "C" of the First Infantry regiment in San Francisco. With no apparent disappointment or hesitation (after all, he had hoped to be stationed in San Francisco) he wrote to the company captain to express formally his pleasure in this assignment and his hope that he "could be of some service." Responding from the Cosmos Club in San Francisco, where, as Summerall recalled, it was said he spent quite a bit of time, the captain gave Summerall two pieces of advice that he said would lead the young lieutenant to the top of his profession. The first was never to play cards for money; the second was to read military history. As Summerall said, "I did follow his advice and I did rise to the top of my profession." With lofty detachment he added that "There may or may not have been some connection." As for the captain, Summerall discovered "that he was noted for not following his own advice...and was one of the best card players in the city."[19]

Before leaving for San Francisco, he received news from his wealthy admirer back in Tuxedo Park that she and her granddaughter, whom Summerall had escorted to several cadet hops, would be staying at the Palace Hotel in San Francisco at the end of September. He did not record the reason for their trip, or if her letter was in response to his having written about his assignment. It is tantalizing, however, to wonder whether their presence in the city could have been arranged by the grandmother after she had learned where young Charles was headed, or whether grandmother and granddaughter just happened to be staying in San Francisco when he reported for duty. Since the grandmother looked on Summerall as a grandson, as he had recalled, she might well have been trying to arrange a match between her granddaughter and the young man she had befriended. In his memoir he gave no indication that such a plan could have been afoot; he did state, however, that he left Astatula "in time to spend a few days with them," but did not suggest that the relationship with the granddaughter was anything more than friendship.[20] Even if the relationship had been more than friendly, it would soon be swept aside by the intense and deep attraction he came to feel for another young lady who would grace the "new life" in which Summerall soon found himself happily immersed.

Thanks to a discount on tickets that the railroads offered to army officers, Summerall paid only $40 for the coast-to-coast, day-coach fare to San Francisco. He ate at meal stations along the way and found riding and sleeping in the coach cars "very uncomfortable," but for the frugal-minded Summerall, "It did not occur to me to ride in a Pullman and spend the extra money."[21]

In order to see something of the army along the way, he stopped for a day in Atlanta, Georgia, to observe the 4th Artillery Regiment at Fort McPherson; a day at Omaha, Nebraska, to observe the 2nd Infantry Regiment at Fort Omaha; and a day at Salt Lake City, Utah, to see the 16th Infantry Regiment at Fort Douglas. Probably quite pleased that a newly minted second lieutenant from West Point voluntarily would take time to visit their posts on the way to his first assignment in the army, his fellow officers treated him with "great courtesy and invited [him] to lunch in each place." At Fort Omaha, he was especially grateful to the post adjutant, Lieutenant William M. Wright and his wife, who "gave me my first glimpse of an army home and of army hospitality." He was also impressed by their seeming prosperity when they "drove me to the station in their phaeton drawn by two horses." Their meeting on the plains of Nebraska was the beginning of a close personal and professional bond that developed between Summerall and Wright. Mutual respect and admiration would underscore their collaboration as field commanders when they fought together some 25 years later against the formidable forces of nature and the enemy in the last great offensive of the American Expeditionary Forces in the First World War. In his memoir, Summerall praised Wright with his highest accolade when he said, "No one could have been more loyal to me."[22]

When he arrived in San Francisco in mid-September, tired and sore from the cross-country train trip and quite likely not looking his Sunday best, Summerall took a carriage to the Palace Hotel and entered the hotel's spacious marble-floored inner hall. Just a few years before Summerall, Rudyard Kipling also had stepped onto the same floor and observed a group of 40 or 50 men dressed in frock coats and top hats clustered together and making liberal use of the many spittoons that were "of infinite capacity and generous gape."[23] Summerall quite likely scanned a similar scene as he searched for his "friends." Looking up, he saw them waving down at him from an upper balcony. After a happy reunion, he was checked into his own room as their guest, and settled in to enjoy this "new world [whose] glamour quite overwhelmed me."[24]

Gazing with amazement from the inner court of the Palace, he beheld one of the city's most opulent hotels. Built in 1874 at a cost of $600,000, it covered an entire block on the south side of Market Street, between New Montgomery Street and Third Street, which would place it today southeast of Union Square and about five blocks northwest of the Museum of Modern Art. When it was built it was the largest hotel in the country, standing six stories high, accommodating 1,200 guests, and surrounded by a city of some 150,000 inhabitants.[25] The growth of this city by the bay had been as spectacular as the rise of the Palace Hotel.

In 1848, less than 30 years before the building of the Palace Hotel, San Francisco had been a settlement of tents and shacks with a population of 850. Then in 1849, the Gold Rush swelled the population to 5,000, with 800 ships riding empty at anchor in a cove of the bay, deserted by their gold-hungry crews. The panic of 1857 burst the golden bubble of wealth, but the discovery of the Comstock silver lode in the neighboring state of Nevada in 1857 ignited another boom, and by 1890 San Francisco's population had grown to 300,000, eighth largest in the country. "The city," as the inhabitants preferred to call it, had become a thriving urban center thousands of miles beyond the frontier. It was filled with hotels, restaurants, parks, churches, synagogues, schools, libraries, academies, and a number of private clubs like the Cosmos, where Summerall's company commander apparently spent quite a bit of his time and money.[26] Cable cars rumbled up and down the center of steeply inclined streets, and sidewalks served as promenades for Sunday strolls and became "hives of commerce and money-making" during the week.²⁷ Kipling found it all rather incomprehensible, remarking that "San Francisco is a mad city—inhabited for the most part by perfectly insane people whose women are of remarkable beauty."²⁸ For Lieutenant Summerall, however, it was a magical place where he would come to know strong, capable, and sensible men who would shape and inspire his career and where, along the shore of its magnificent bay, he would meet a woman of grace and charm who would remain in his heart for the rest of their lives.

One of the first men Summerall met who impressed him was Captain Thomas H. Barry, who called on Summerall just after he finished breakfast on his first morning in the city. Barry was assigned to the 1st Infantry Regiment with headquarters on Angel Island, north of the city, just off the Tiburon peninsula. It had been renamed Camp Reynolds and fortified by the Federal government in 1863 to protect the city during the war; afterwards it served as a depot for troops fighting in campaigns against the Apache, Sioux, and other Indian tribes. Recently, three gun batteries had been constructed on the southwest side of the island to strengthen the harbor defenses, and Barry invited young Summerall out to the island to meet the officers of the regiment and check out the new batteries. It was a pleasant outing, and Summerall felt honored that Barry had taken time to call on him and invite him to meet the officers of his command.²⁹ When Summerall returned in 1905 to West Point as a captain and instructor in tactics, Barry, by then a major general, was superintendent of the Academy, and according to Summerall, "one of the ablest officers in the Army," and who had over the years, "proved to be a loyal and helpful friend."³⁰

Returning to the city from Angel Island, he received orders to report to "C" Company of the First Infantry, stationed at Benicia Barracks, an army post close to the Arsenal, established in 1849 at Benicia, about thirty miles east of San Francisco. Before leaving for his new post, however, his friends from New York treated him to a visit down the coast to Monterey, where they spent a few days of sightseeing. It was a town prospering from the whaling industry, which supplied clean-burning whale oil for lighting and whale bone for women's corsets, and where buildings were being constructed with sturdy, fired brick. Summerall marveled at the luxury surrounding him, and wondered "how anyone could be so rich and generous" as his New York hosts. For him, the lavish expenditure of such wealth was the "antithesis of anything that I had known."³¹ Indeed, he had never possessed such wealth, and, for that matter, never would. However, as a youth and young man, the financial support he provided for his family entailed for Summerall a far greater personal sacrifice than that of his friend from Tuxedo Park, and revealed a generosity of spirit more intense and expansive than was common amid the opulence and self-indulgence of this Gilded Age of American history.

After returning from their visit to Monterey, Summerall and his "friends" said their good-byes and they left on the long journey back to New York, while he reported for duty as ordered at Benicia Barracks on 30 September. He was met by his company commander, a lieutenant, who picked him up in an ambulance, then the only means of passenger transportation available in the army. On the way to his quarters, Summerall listened as the lieutenant berated army life at Benicia as "hard and lonely" and tried to discourage him "in every way" from making the army his career. Brimming with enthusiasm, however, Summerall asserted that he found the life "filling and fascinating."³² Based upon his introduction to the bay area and his life over the last few months of 1892, this seems an appropriate description.

At Benicia, his duties consisted of a daily drill period of one hour, with an occasional assignment as officer of the day. He read books on military history, although in his memoir he mentioned no specific works, other than to say that they were books on the infantry and the art of war. He prepared an occasional paper to present to fellow officers at a Lyceum-style colloquia, and also utilized his experience as a teacher and principal. In 1889, the War Department began requiring soldiers who needed an education to attend post schools. Qualified teachers were hard to find, so it was logical that Summerall was placed in charge of the post school for enlisted men, gaining from the experience, he said, a better understanding of the men themselves and of their needs and capabilities. He and his fellow officers had time to hunt ducks and geese in early morning hours, and to sit around at night playing cards (but not for money). There was a lot of drinking, but Summerall remained a teetotaler, turning down offers at dinner parties of wine and champagne as well.[33] On one occasion, however, he slipped up.

After attending a military mass in the Roman Catholic church of the Franciscan monastery nearby in the town of Benicia on Columbus Day 1892, he and a small group of fellow officers sat down to lunch in the refectory with several of the priests. They all drank a lot of wine, and Summerall, sensing his legs go numb, was afraid he would not be able to stand up from the table without falling down. Feeling "panicky" and suffering "great stress of mortification," he managed to rise from his chair, clear his head, and make his way back to the post. From that point onward, he said, he "made it a rule not to drink any kind of alcohol or use tobacco in any form."[34]

Summerall worked out an arrangement with a fellow officer to "form a mess with a Japanese cook," and managed to get by on an expenditure of less than $80.00 a month. This enabled him to send home "more money than the family had ever seen." Occasionally the abstemious young lieutenant was invited over to sing with the young daughters of the commanding officer, no doubt calling upon the repertoire he had built up while singing in Dr. Porter's school choir and serenading fellow cadets and their dates at West Point. The lure of San Francisco remained strong; train fare to the city was cheap, and Summerall had brought along his dress suit and cutaway that he had purchased before leaving West Point. So, when he and other "eligible" officers began to receive invitations to debutante parties, teas, dinner parties, theaters, and concerts, they were eager and ready to go.[35]

At one of these affairs, a crowded afternoon tea at a wealthy home in the city, he spotted across the room a young man "talking earnestly" to a young woman and recognized him as having been "one of the boys with me at Dr. Porter's" in Charleston. He quickly walked over to him, asked him if his name were not Brooks Jones and said, "I am Charlie Summerall."[36] Jones greeted him warmly, quickly introducing him to the young lady and several of his friends. Afterwards, Jones took him along to meet his bachelor uncle, Winfield S. Jones, with whom he lived. The elder Jones was vice-president and general manager of the Security and Savings Bank, located downtown on Montgomery Street not far from the Palace Hotel, and was descended from one of the fine families of Virginia. One of his brothers had served as executive officer on the Union ironclad *Merrimac* during the war, and another had become adjutant general of the army. Winfield Jones "lived well" on Hyde Street, and opened up his home to his nephew's friend, insisting that Summerall stay with them on his visits to the city. In his memoir, Summerall remembered him as "the social arbiter of San Francisco" and "the best friend I ever had." As a friend and frequent guest of Winfield Jones and his nephew, the way for Summerall was opened to "another social world" where he met "the nicest people in the city who invited me to their homes and entertainments."[37]

For Rudyard Kipling, this "social world" was "a rush and a whirl. Recklessness is in the air. I can't explain where it comes from," he said, "but there it is. The roaring winds off the Pacific make you drunk to begin with. The aggressive luxury on all sides helps out the intoxication, and you spin for ever...as long as money lasts."[38] It was, apparently, in plentiful supply for Brooks Jones, who "arranged partners," as Summerall put it, for this energetic young pair. They attended concerts and productions of the San Francisco Opera, as well as musical performances that were held at the Joneses' home and dances at the Mare Island Naval Shipyard Yard, across the bay at Vallejo.[39] As they swept around the city and the bay, they may even have encountered other young men who, as Kipling observed, "gamble, yacht, race, enjoy prize-fights and cock-fights—the one openly, the other in secret—they break themselves over horse flesh and—other things; and they are instant in quarrel."[40] Adding to his "entertainments," Summerall's "friend" from New York paid for his membership in the Cotillion Club and sent him several gifts: a valuable watch, sets of the writings of William Makepeace Thackeray and other authors, and an expensive reclining chair.[41] He must have kept his "friend" well informed about his activities in San Francisco, but no correspondence between them has survived. Rather strangely, Summerall never recorded in his memoir either her name or her granddaughter's name, and after describing in his memoir how he met the young woman who eventually became his wife, he made only one brief reference to his "friends" from New York. Perhaps indeed, matching her granddaughter with Summerall had been the goal of his friend and patron from Tuxedo Park all along; if so, when it somehow became clear that she had failed, the friendship, patronage, and hope she had sustained apparently disappeared. For his part, Summerall seems to have been undisturbed by their withdrawal from his life.

Back at Benicia, tensions among his fellow officers concerned him, and once again he became ambivalent about his choice of branches. Summerall was troubled by what he saw as prejudice by infantry and cavalry officers against the artillery branch, which had been his first choice of assignment. He resented their referring to artillery officers as "coffee coolers" because they were stationed in the harbors of coastal cities, but also thought it unfair that artillery officers referred to their branch as the "scientific arm" of the army and "looked down on the infantry and cavalry." However, toward the end of 1892, after meeting Colonel William Montrose Graham, commanding officer of the 5th Artillery Regiment, and several of his officers stationed at the Presidio of San Francisco, Summerall's inclination toward the artillery returned.[42] Colonel Graham himself was another of the strong and decisive personalities of San Francisco who exerted a powerful influence on Summerall's life and career.

Graham was a nephew of Union General George S. Meade, and was graduated from West Point in 1855. During the war he had commanded an artillery battery at the Battle of Antietam, and successively won the brevets of major, lieutenant colonel, colonel, and brigadier general.[43] Now in his 37th year of active duty, he preferred to be addressed by the latter rank,[44] and enclosed it in parentheses after signing reports and orders as "colonel." According to a contemporary article in the *Sacramento Bee*, Graham "has a national reputation of being one of the strictest of military disciplinarians. Those who do not like him say he is a martinet."[45] Summerall, however, praised Graham as "uncompromising in high standards of duty, discipline and training," and credited him with commanding "the most efficient regiment in the army." He was "improperly called a martinet," said Summerall, but only by officers who had lingered in the army so long that "they were utterly unfit to serve...and would not retire voluntarily. These [were the kind of] men who found service under General Graham very unhappy and disliked him accordingly. Capable and industrious officers had no trouble with him."[46]

In Colonel Graham, Summerall had found, early in his career, another man and model for his own standards of duty, discipline, and training. When he wrote that Graham's enforcement of these "high standards" had made his command probably the most efficient in the army, he was unreservedly asserting why he considered his own commands successful, particularly that of the First Division in the Great War. In his view, the maintenance of high standards was not the work of a martinet, as he himself came to be called, but rather the way an officer assured the efficiency of his command. In addition, officers who were unhappy under such a command and disliked the commanding officer (as would be the case for those who chafed under the authority of Summerall, particularly the long serving army bureau chiefs), were "utterly unfit to serve" and "would not retire voluntarily."[47] Those officers who were capable and industrious (and, he might have added, remained loyal) "had no trouble."

So impressed was Summerall with Colonel Graham that he called at his office at the Presidio in mid-January 1893, and told him that he wanted to be transferred to his artillery regiment. Graham must also have been impressed with Summerall, for he received him cordially and told him that when his application was referred to him he would ask a friend in the War Department to approve it and assign him to a vacancy that existed in the regiment.[48]

Summerall returned to Benicia, and on 24 January wrote the adjutant general in Washington applying for a transfer from the 1st Infantry to the 5th Artillery, "to fill the vacancy of 2nd Lieutenant now existing in that regiment."[49] His action came as a "great shock to his fellow officers" at Benicia.[50] They knew, as did Summerall, that promotion in the artillery was very slow, partly because in each artillery battery there were three lieutenants, while in cavalry and infantry companies there were only two. The results of this slow advancement were particularly apparent in Graham's 5th Regiment, where there were nine lieutenants, each with twenty-four years service.[51] When the post adjutant heard about Summerall's application, he came to see him in "great distress" and cried, "My God, man, if you have the instinct of a soldier, don't transfer to the artillery." Others said that he was committing "professional suicide."[52] Nevertheless, his company commander endorsed and forwarded his application to the post adjutant, stating that "Lieut. Summerall is a studious and painstaking officer of exemplary habits, well qualified for the more scientific arm of the service to which he desires to transfer."[53] Here was one infantry officer, at least, who was not "prejudiced" against the artillery. The post commander added the second endorsement.

However, when his application reached the desk of Colonel William H. Shafter, commanding the 1st Infantry Regiment from his headquarters at Angel Island, it met with a different reception. Shafter, the hard-headed and portly officer who would later command the 5th Corps and lead it into Cuba during the Spanish-American War, forwarded the application. But he stated that "In consideration of the best interests of my Regiment I will not approve this application for the transfer from it of Lieut. Summerall. I have no personal knowledge of this officer, but his reputation in the Regiment and at his post is such that I do not care to lose him."[54] This would not be the last time a dedicated and seasoned veteran officer of the army would value his service highly and see in Summerall a man he would not "care to lose." In spite of Shafter's disapproval, however, the transfer was approved, quite likely because of Colonel Graham's support and that of his friend in the War Department, and Summerall reported to his new assignment at the Presidio of San Francisco in February 1893.

The Presidio was situated atop the long, level crest and along the sloping sides of the southern promontory of the Golden Gate. It had served as the guardian of the entrance to the San Francisco Bay since the Spanish established an outpost there in 1776 (in Spanish "presidio" means military outpost). Mexico took control in 1820, and fortified the site with a garrison and adobe buildings. In 1846, American forces landed in San Francisco and occupied the Presidio, finding most of the adobe structures in ruins. A rebuilding program began the next year, including the construction on the shoreline directly below the Presidio of a four-tiered brick and casement fort named Fort Point. It was finished as the Civil War began, and helped to secure the harbor and to shield work on fortifications around the southern and northern sides of the harbor that went on during the war.[55] By 1890, permanent brick construction had replaced all the old frontier structures of the Presidio and the post had been expanded to include a garrison of six artillery batteries, a cavalry troop, and two companies of infantry. It accommodated 30 officers and 562 enlisted men, as well as a canteen that had turned out to be an effective alternative to drinking binges in the city. In 1889, it was designated as a site for one of the army's first boards to examine officers for promotion.[56]

When Summerall reported to his new assignment, Colonel Graham appointed him to Battery K, commanded by First Lieutenant Henry J. Reilly. Standing just short of six feet tall and weighing about

145 pounds, Reilly appeared as thin as a rail and quite frail, with a thin mustache, close-cropped beard, and thinning grey hair parted in the middle above a high forehead. His steel-blue eyes looked down through prince-nez glasses perched on the bridge of his nose. He looked more professorial than soldierly. For all his academic appearance, however, Reilly was an army veteran of almost 30 years service, dating from the Civil War and including the last 25 years as a first lieutenant.[57]

Quite likely frustrated at the slow rate of promotion, particularly in the artillery, and contemplating retirement, Reilly had earlier taken a leave of absence to work for the Pullman Palace Car Company. After one unhappy year with Pullman, he came back with his family to the army. According to Summerall, Reilly had said that "no amount of money would induce him to change the Army for a civil[ian] career," even though, in Summerall's view, there seemed "little prospect of his promotion." In Reilly, Summerall saw a "remarkable personality," a man who was "able, enthusiastic and dominant," who commanded "by far the best battery on the post," and who "was entirely wrapped up in his profession." To be linked with such a man so early in his career was for Summerall "evidence of the destiny which shaped my career."[58] After their service together in the Philippines and before the walls of the Imperial City at Peking, China, during the uprising of the Boxers, one would be hard pressed to refute Summerall's judgment.

When Summerall joined Battery K, he found that the officers and men of the Presidio had been working for several years on extensive improvements to the installations and fortifications on both sides of the Golden Gate. The improved accuracy and range of rifled cannons during the 1860s had rendered obsolete large brick or stone forts like Fort Point, with their multiple tiers of gun batteries built on promontories or choke points to important harbor entrances like the Golden Gate. In the 1870s, technical developments such as improved casting techniques led to the manufacture of stronger guns in longer calibers; rifling became more precise and breechloading more practical and reliable; recoil systems were improved and of higher quality, and variable-burning powders were more widely available. Theoretically, artillery could be made safer to operate and more deadly at ranges of 10 to 12 miles. At the same time, the growing interest in sea power synthesized these advances in artillery with the development of the modern battleship. In order to be effective, coastal fortifications had to be outfitted with the new and improved guns, and with gun installations made of reinforced concrete and dug into the earth.[59]

To develop a plan for the restoration and modification of the nation's coastal defenses in light of the advances over the last 10 to 15 years, Congress created in 1885 a board headed by Secretary of War William C. Endicott. In 1886, the Endicott Board issued its report calling for new fortifications for the 26 principal harbors in the country and at three locations on the Great Lakes at what was then an enormous cost of $127 million. It recommended the construction of wide parapets of earthworks and steel-plated masonry to protect large numbers of breechloading rifles mounted on concrete platforms, rifled mortars mounted on floating batteries, searchlights, machine gun emplacements, and underwater mines. It ranked San Francisco as the most important port on the Pacific coast, and second only to New York in the importance of its harbor defense. In 1888, Congress passed an appropriation to begin the project, although funding was at much lower levels than recommended in the Endicott Board's report; two years later a New York Board of Engineers convened to develop a plan to modernize the seacoast defenses of San Francisco.[60]

In 1891, civilian construction crews and soldiers from the Presidio's batteries began the first phase of the project at a site to the south of the Golden Gate on the western side of the Presidio. This stage of the project provided for the destruction of the old West Battery above and to the west of Fort Point. The new site was called Battery Marcus Miller, and was constructed to contain three 10-inch breechloading rifles on disappearing carriages. (In 1912, it would be constituted into a separate coast artillery post and named Fort Winfield Scott.[61]) Summerall joined Battery K when its officers and men were at work on the Battery Marcus Miller project. In his memoir he states that he "dismounted some large guns from the top parapet of Fort Winfield Scott."[62] As noted above, the area that was named Fort Winfield Scott was not called that until 1912. In 1893, West Battery was still the prominent installation in this area, and when Summerall described his work at "Fort Winfield Scott," he probably was describing one of the final phases in the dismantling of West Battery. He seems also to have remembered incorrectly his work on fortifications at Lime Point, north of the Golden Gate. Construction began there in 1893, and Summerall stated that he "mounted a battery of 15-inch smooth bore guns at Lime Point across the Golden Gate from Winfield Scott [sic]."[63] The work at what was then called the Lime Point Military Reservation involved the mounting of three 12-inch breechloading rifles, rather than 15-inch smooth bores.[64] Since the modernization of all the installations around San Francisco involved the replacement of smooth bore guns by rifled ones, he and his men would not have been mounting obsolete smooth-bore guns.

While working at Lime Point, Summerall answered a phone call asking about fog conditions. After he hung up, the major in charge walked over and asked what the call was about. When Summerall replied, the officer asserted that, "If anyone else wants to know, you report to me and I will tell you the condition of the fog." For Summerall the major's response illustrated the attitude of the older men toward the younger officers.[65] Clearly it was one of jealous guardianship of whatever degree of authority they had managed to acquire in decade after decade of army duty and callous condescension toward junior officers like Summerall, who threatened their sense of self importance.

With the noncommissioned officers of the battery, Summerall's relations were far more pleasant and constructive. From them, he learned about cordage, or the use of ropes, mechanical principles and methods involved in the handling of the big guns, as well as first aid and much else of a fundamental, practical nature. He considered these men skilled and able soldiers. When someone asked Reilly why he always had such able noncommissioned officers serving under him, he somewhat haughtily answered, "I made them."[66] Rather, they helped to make him a knowledgeable officer.

In addition to his duties with Battery K, Summerall was detailed to serve on regimental court-martial boards and as recorder for various other boards, writing down the proceedings in his bold and clear script. He also wrote an occasional paper that he presented to officers assembled in their Lyceum colloquia, and continued his reading of the classics of military history, although, as was his practice in writing his memoir, he failed to specify the titles or authors he had read. Meanwhile, the first anniversary of his graduation from West Point rolled around and Summerall received his first pay increase, or "fogy" as it was called, that all graduates received five years after having entered the cadet corps. His pay now totaled $133.36 per month, an increase of $16.69, or over 12.5 percent of his beginning salary. In order to save money, he and several other young officers set up their own mess, calling it the "Scrub Mess," a step that enabled Summerall to keep his expenses for food, room and laundry to $30.00 per month.[67] As before, the money he saved enabled him without hesitation to come to the aid of his family, as once more they faced additional burdens and mouths to feed.

Summerall learned that Florida sister Meta Margaret Gardner's husband again had failed in business. Together with his wife and three children, he had moved in with Summerall's parents. They, in turn, had found a larger house in Eustis, and moved there with their daughter, son-in-law, and the three grandchildren. In addition, brother William had informed him that he had been granted entrance into Tulane University in New Orleans, Louisiana, to study medicine, and had left his teaching post at Dr. Porter's school in Charleston. William now had a wife and child, but had not managed to obtain enough money to pay his medical school fees and support his family at the same time. Brother Charles stepped in to help pay William's fees and to provide support for his older brother and his family. As ever, Summerall remained dutiful in his financial support of his family now having grown to 10 members, including six adults and four children. Yet, he never expressed any feelings of resentment about his own sacrifices for the sake of his family or any frustration or impatience over their lack of success. On the contrary, he expressed his gratitude that "Providence ruled over us and made me an instrumentality for their need."[68]

No longer able to afford the fees or keep up his wardrobe for the "cotillions" in the city, Summerall was forced to leave the social life of the bay area to the enjoyment of his fellow officers and to those well-heeled and well-connected men such as his friend Brooks Jones. Young Jones and his uncle Winfield apparently were concerned that Summerall's social life and "entertainments" were drying up. They decided that the elder Jones should use his connections in the War Department to inject some excitement into their young friend's life. In July 1893, E. F. Land and James G. Maguire, two Congressmen from San Francicso, wrote the secretary of war requesting that Summerall, whom they referred to as "a young officer of much merit," be assigned "to a term of service" at the Columbian Exposition in Chicago. For their convenience, they were provided with stationery imprinted with a letterhead that read "Security Savings Bank, 222 Montgomery Street, San Francisco." After a month had passed with no response, Winfield Jones himself asked an old friend, General J. C. Breckinridge, to intercede. Breckinridge wrote Lieutenant Colonel H. W. Lawton in the inspector general's office, and Lawton sent a letter to Adjutant General General R. Williams, requesting him to "approve and recommend" General Breckinridge's request, which Lawton extracted from Breckinridge's letter to him. It read as follows: "'My old friend, Winfield Jones, a brother of our late chief, writes urgently to me to get Lieut. Summerall of the 5th Artillery ordered to Chicago, praising him in stronger terms than he usually permits himself, and wishing him to get the advantages of the World's Fair....Will you please see if it can be done? It seems with the army competition going on there, the Columbian Guard, and various other details, it might be possible. I enclose the letter of two California congressmen, so that it can be used if necessary and filed, if the matter proves impossible for us.'"[69] In spite of the influence and urgent appeal of Winfield Jones, the support of two Congressmen who wrote unabashedly on the stationery of Jones's bank, and the endorsement of the inspector general's office, Lieutenant Summerall never received the orders that Jones had hoped for. That Jones would undertake such an effort indicates just how highly he esteemed his young friend and how strong was his concern about Summerall's well-being. Whether Summerall knew of Jones's actions or perhaps had forgotten this episode is uncertain, for he does not mention it in his memoir, even though it is recorded in his AGO file. Certainly, however, Jones's good intention supports Summerall's assertion that he "became the best friend I ever had."[70] What seems clear, at any rate, is that the year 1893 ended and the year 1894 began with more burdens and less excitement for Summerall than he had anticipated. With the approach of spring, new and more challenging assignments, as well as a rather unpleasant occurrence, made his life on the coast quite a bit more interesting after all.

Early in the year 1894, Colonel Graham appointed Summerall Post Exchange Officer. Since the principal business of the Exchange was the sale of beer, Summerall felt remorse that he was promoting the "drunkenness of the men." He was consoled by his success in making money for the company funds, which came from the profits of the Exchange.[71] For his part, Colonel Graham at least could be certain that he had appointed a Post Exchange Officer who would not drink up the profits. The busiest time came on payday, and for years Corporal Charles H. Drewes, the Exchange steward, had deposited the receipts of that day in a local bank.

After the close of business on a cold winter payday, with the receipts in hand, Drewes set out for the bank where he deposited checks in the amount of $100.00, but not the cash receipts. When he failed to return to post, he was reported AWOL, but soon the San Francisco police found him drunk in a "disreputable" house in the city with $772.50 in his pockets. Nevertheless, a shortage of $181.94 was discovered in the account books of the Exchange. A Board of Survey was convened on post to determine whether Lieutenant Summerall was justified in allowing Drewes to deposit the funds. He testified that Drewes had been entrusted with the job because he was familiar with the duties involved and had been recommended highly by several officers. The Board decided that, in view of Drewes's long service and heretofore clean record, he not be punished, but be required to pay back the missing amount of $181.94. It relieved Summerall of all accountability for Drewes's actions.[72] The lesson a somewhat shaken Summerall gained from the experience was never to trust money to an unbonded person.[73]

As far as Colonel Graham was concerned, however, the incident with Corporal Drewes was not worth mentioning in his "Efficiency Report in Case of C. P. Summerall, 2nd Lt. 5th Artillery," dated March 1st, 1894. This report is an example of the army's improved system for the evaluation of its officers,[74] and Graham gave Summerall high marks in every category. For "Professional zeal," "Attention to duty," and "Conduct and habits," Graham rated him as "excellent," the highest degree of proficiency.[75] Under "Scientific attainments" he rated him as "very good," the next highest degree. After "Prominent talents," Graham wrote, "an energetic and zealous officer." As to "Peculiar fitness, etc.," he stated that Summerall was "an excellent officer in all respects." With regard to "Special duties and how performed," Graham rated him as "an excellent exchange officer, well performed [in his duties]." In longer written comments, Graham noted that Summerall was "a zealous and able officer in all respects—very conscientious in the discharge of duty." Asked to respond to "Whether any important special duty has devolved upon him, and how he has performed the same," Graham reaffirmed his confidence in Summerall when he wrote, "yes [,] a very difficult duty—that of Post Exchange officer [in] which he has reaffirmed [his] conscientiousness." He also commented that Summerall "would be an efficient instructor in a college," and concluded his report with the remark that Summerall was "an excellent officer."[76]

With a blank social calendar and the Drewes episode behind him and with Colonel Graham solidly in his favor, Summerall could look forward to a more interesting year ahead. It began well, with his being detailed to Light Battery "D," a unit consisting of horse-drawn 3.2-inch cannons that were in great contrast with the large caliber guns of the coastal defense batteries he had been wrestling with. It was an assignment he was pleased to receive, since it raised his pay $10.00 per month and gave him the opportunity to work with horses, which he "loved."[77]

Lethal blasts of light artillery firing into charging lines of infantry and the rapid deployment of these guns by galloping teams of horses and riders churning up clouds of dust along the roads and across the fields and hillsides of North and South or plowing through muddy ruts and trails were distant memories for the army of the 1890s. Largely because of much tighter military budgets imposed after the war, the field guns of the horse artillery had been packed away and rarely had been deployed in the wars against the Plains Indians. In the five postwar artillery regiments, such as the 5th Regiment at the Presidio, there were 10 heavy units and only two of the light, or field artillery, armed with 3.2-inch guns. On war footing, however, a light battery was an impressive unit. It consisted of two or three platoons, with two sections in each platoon. A section was made up of one 3.2-inch gun with a caisson, or ammunition chest, and a limber connecting caisson and gun. It was drawn by six horses. The rest of the battery consisted of a field forge and wagons used for carrying supplies and equipment. Five officers, one captain and four lieutenants, commanding 175 enlisted men manned the battery, with a complement of 144 horses.[78] In just a few years, a battery much like this would be the fighting unit in which Summerall first would encounter hostile fire in battle and achieve his first success as a combat leader, and under Captain Henry J. Reilly, the man he admired, perhaps, above all others. He spent the next two summers in the Monterey area on frequent maneuvers for target practice with Light Battery "D," while at the same time mapping several hundred miles of roads and becoming familiar with land that he would later arrange to have the Federal government purchase for use as an artillery training center for the National Guard.[79]

Although work with Battery "D" was rewarding and constructive, Summerall, along with his fellow officers, continued to worry about the slow rate of promotion in the artillery branch. They calculated that he would not be promoted to the rank of major until shortly before he reached the retirement age of 64, 37 years in the future. Dismayed at this prospect, Summerall decided to seek a transfer to yet another branch of the army, this time to the Ordnance Department, where, as he believed, "promotion to 1st Lieutenant would take place at once and in twelve years I would be a captain." He learned that selections would be made following competitive examinations that were scheduled to take place in New York City that summer.[80] On 28 May 1894, he wrote the adjutant general requesting that he be "ordered to attend the next examination of applicants for transfer to The Ordnance Department." Captain Reilly added the 1st Endorsement, forwarding it to Colonel Graham with the comments "approved and recommended." Colonel Graham forwarded it to the Headquarters of the Department of California. He wrote as follows: "Approved and recommended to the favorable consideration of the proper authorities, as Lieutenant Summerall is, in my opinion deserving of this consideration by reason of his excellent character as an efficient, intelligent and conscientious officer in the discharge of his duty." On 1 June, the commanding general of the Department of California added the 3rd Endorsement and forwarded the request to Washington.[81] Summerall soon received orders to report for the examination and boarded a day coach in the city for the long train ride back across the country, but along a route more northern than the previous route he had taken from Jacksonville to San Francisco. Riding round-trip in a day coach enabled him to save most of the mileage reimbursement, based apparently on sleeping car accommodations, to send to his family.[82]

After his arrival in New York City, Summerall reported on 13 June to the Army Building for a physical examination. Standing 5 feet, 7¾ inches in height and weighing 153½ pounds, with a chest measurement of 33 inches at expiration and 35½ inches at inspiration, he appeared in perfect health: trim, solid and compact at age 27. His vision was perfect, 20/20 in both eyes, with only a slight astigmatism that easily could be "corrected by glass."[83] Three days later on 16 June, he took the competitive examination. The results surprised him. "While it did not appear to be very difficult," he stated in his memoir, "I was unsuccessful." He also pointed out that "I made two more efforts, but other competitors were selected." Of these latter "efforts," only the first in 1898 is documented in his AGO file. Late in life Summerall could conclude that even though all of these attempts failed, "destiny veiled my fate, for I would have been submerged in my career as an Ordnance officer."[84] At the time, however, as his family became increasingly dependent upon his devoted and conscientious support, he must have been concerned that no matter how well he performed, the slow rate of promotion in the artillery would limit severely his ability to help them.

Passing through Cheyenne, Wyoming, on the train ride back to the Presidio a few days after his brief and disappointing stay in New York, he read that the American Railway Union intended to go out on strike. Arriving in San Francisco, he learned that his train had been the last westbound one to reach the city and that striking railroad workers had forced rail traffic to cease on all lines west of the Mississippi. What had occurred and was surging westward behind Summerall's train as it steamed toward the coast was the great western railroad strike of 1894. Quickly the entire military manpower of the bay area was immersed in a major civil crisis and Summerall soon found himself right in the middle of it.

After the Civil War ended and in the year of Summerall's birth, the army was assigned major civil responsibility under the Military Reconstruction Act of March 1867, enacted through the leadership of the Radical Republicans in Congress. It forced Southern state governments to abandon the repressive codes against black citizens they had passed after the war and to rewrite their state constitutions to conform to the U.S. Constitution, particularly with respect to providing the identical right of universal male suffrage. Except for the state of Tennessee, which had ratified the Fourteenth Amendment, the other 10 states were divided into five military districts, each commanded by a general who had broad authority to maintain order and to protect individual and property rights. Less than a month later Congress passed the Second Reconstruction Act, directing the military district commanders to register to vote all adult males who swore they were qualified.[85] Thus the army in effect became a political policing force, not a role it welcomed, but, according to Allan Millett, one that it "undertook as a means of self-preservation" when no other mission could be found.[86] As has been noted, white Southerners like those in Summerall's native Florida retaliated against Reconstruction in the form of terrorist attacks on blacks and white Republicans. Led by the Ku Klux Klan and other gangs, the violence included assaults against local officials such as that against Bryant Summerall, justice of the peace and postmaster in the village of Providence, Florida, as mentioned above. The army tried its best to protect state and local officials, but its effectiveness was handicapped by insufficient manpower and by uncertainty about the scope of its legal authority.[87]

In 1871, Congress struck back by outlawing activities of the Ku Klux Klan and authorizing the president to suspend habeas corpus and undertake mass prosecutions, thus halting the violent outrages of the Klan. With the Klan on the run, and with Western expansion, Indian wars, economic growth, and trade issues gaining more attention, the North began to lose interest in what was happening in the South. At the same time, Conservative Democrats mounted campaigns that succeeded in voting out of office by 1876 all except three of the Radical Republican state governments.[88]

Reconstruction had ended, but no one, either in the North or in the South, seemed pleased with the army's role. Radicals claimed that it had not done enough to support the Congressional Reconstruction program; Conservatives asserted that it had done too much.[89] The latter group, composed of Democratic Congressmen, was particularly upset that soldiers had been called on in 1876 to supervise the presidential elections in a number of Southern states. One was so enraged that he introduced a bill to abolish West Point; another spoke of abolishing the War Department; while yet another wanted to eliminate the entire Regular Army.[90] Even more controversial than its involvement in Reconstruction and even more demanding of its resources and manpower was the army's role in major labor disputes in the latter part of the century.

The first of these was the Great Railroad Strike of 1877. The Panic of 1873 and the depression that followed deepened the poverty into which so many industrial workers and small farmers had fallen (like Bryant Summerall's neighbors in Providence). With revenues declining, the major rail lines in the East slashed wages. In June 1877, they imposed an additional 10 percent cut, provoking walkouts and demonstrations that spread in July from the East Coast to Chicago and on to San Francisco. As the wave of strikes rolled westward it became more violent, leaving in its wake more than 100 people dead and destroying property valued in the millions of dollars. Local law enforcement agencies were unable to repress the violence or restore order, and when governors called out the militia, also referred to as the National Guard, units often proved unpredictable. In Pittsburgh on 19 July, guardsmen joined the striking workers; in Philadelphia, however, National Guardsmen fired bullets into a crowd of strikers, killing 26 of them.[91] Not until President Rutherford B. Hayes ordered about 2,000 army regulars into the troubled areas did the violence and destruction end. They proved far more effective in restoring order than the National Guard, and they managed to avoid killing anyone.

However, the army was no more enthusiastic about strike duty and suppression than it had been about Reconstruction. As seen above, army "progressives," rather than expending energy and resources on domestic police actions, strove to create a more professional and modern fighting force to wage war.[92] That drive, however, would be deflected by the more violent strike that was rolling westward, one that had to be confronted by the military manpower of the entire bay area.

This new labor crisis had emerged, as had the previous upheaval, when the country slipped into another depression that followed the Panic of 1893. Problems began south of Chicago in the town of Pullman, where workers of the Pullman Palace Car Company were required to live and forced to buy goods in company stores and to pay rents and utility costs that were higher than in nearby towns. In response to the depression, owner George Pullman laid off 3,000 of his 5,800 employees and cut wages 25 to 40 percent; rents and other costs, however, remained unchanged. Then Pullman fired three members of a grievance committee, and on 11 May 1894, the strike began.[93]

A month later, the leader of the American Railway Union, the charismatic and dynamic Eugene V. Debs, called for arbitration. When Pullman refused, the union declared on 26 June a boycott of Pullman cars, and union workers stopped handling Pullman cars and the trains they were coupled to. The railroads responded by bringing in strike breakers from Canada and other places, telling them to couple mail cars to Pullman coaches. This action enabled the federal government to intervene and use the army to protect the mails.[94] According to historian Jerry M. Cooper, U.S. Attorney General Richard Olney intended to use the army from the outset of the strike, since he interpreted it as an insurrection engineered by the American Railway Union against the authority of the federal government.[95] As President Grover Cleveland asserted, "If it takes every dollar in the Treasury and every soldier in the United States to deliver a postal card in Chicago, that postal card should be delivered."[96] Another reason Olney might have wanted to use the army was the unreliability, as in 1877, of the National Guard, many of whose members sympathized with the workers. This was so, especially in the West, where the railroads had long had been unpopular among workers and the general public as well.[97]

By the time Summerall arrived back in San Francisco at the end of June 1894, the train service had also had ceased to Los Angeles, a city of some 68,000 people. On 28 June, Olney cabled George Denis, the federal attorney in Los Angeles, to make certain that trains carrying United States mails were not interfered with, but Denis ran into difficulty complying with his instructions. On 1 July, President Cleveland ordered the secretary of war to ensure the safe passage of the mails in southern California.[98] On the same day General John M. Schofield, commanding general, ordered Brigadier General Thomas H. Ruger, commanding the Department of California, to send the First Infantry Division to Los Angeles to make certain the mails got through.[99] On 2 July, Colonel Shafter and his regiment of about 300 men and officers left Angel Island by rail for Los Angeles. When they arrived on the morning of 4 July, the city was quiet and remained calm throughout Independence Day; by the next day local trains were making the run to Santa Barbara without any opposition.[100] In the northern part of the state, these July days did not pass so quietly.

From 1 July to 3 July, strikers in Oakland and Sacramento blocked attempts by the federal marshal and his deputies to get the trains running. On 4 July, the National Guard was called in but refused to clear out the striking workers from the rail yards in both cities. The guard's collapse surprised and concerned General Ruger, for he had counted on the guard to replace the men of the 1st Regiment he had ordered to Los Angeles under Colonel Shafter's command. However, the secretary of war secured 500 sailors and marines from the naval shipyard at Mare Island, about 30 miles from San Francisco on the northeastern side of the bay, and assigned them to Ruger. On 7 July General Schofield ordered Ruger to assist the commander of the Department of the Platte in Cheyenne, Wyoming (where Summerall had first learned of the strike), in opening the lines of the Union Pacific and Central Pacific eastward from San Francisco. To units of infantry, artillery, and cavalry, Ruger added the Marines and sailors from Mare Island, placed this force numbering 540 under the command of Colonel Graham and ordered him to Sacramento, where strikers had been the most determined and belligerent.[101] Graham decided to move his command by boat up the Sacramento River and promptly appointed Summerall quartermaster and commissary officer, detaching him from Reilly's Battery "K" and giving him the job of obtaining river transportation and supplies for departure on the following day.[102] "That night," wrote Summerall, "I secured ferry boats [sic], loaded supplies for troops and had the troops at The Presidio embark with horses for the cavalry, stop[ped] at Mare Island for the Marines and at Benicia for the infantry and reach[ed] Sacramento early the following morning."[103]

When Graham and his men arrived on Wednesday, the 11th, the rail yards were "filled with stalled trains, spoiling food and stranded, disgruntled passengers."[104] With Colonel Graham in the lead astride a black horse, and followed by soldiers and marines with bayonets fixed and cavalry with sabers drawn, they took possession of the yards and cleared out the strikers without incident. Next, they set up Gatling guns and pickets to secure the yards and established contact with local National Guard units.[105] Later that morning, Graham decided to dispatch immediately a passenger-mail train to San Francisco, protected by a combined force of 25 of his men and guardsmen from his command, with 65-year-old veteran engineer Samuel C. Clark and a fireman comprising the train crew.[106] A "railwalker" was dispatched and reported back at 1100 hours that the rails west of the city were secure and safe.[107]

Between 1200 and 1230 hours, a train consisting of an engine and coal tender, four mail cars, one baggage car, two day coaches, three Pullman sleepers and a dining car pulled away from the depot and eased through the rail yards, picking up steam as it rolled through the outskirts of the city and past the "howls, jeers, and insulting epithets of the strikers."[108] Soldiers and guardsmen, commanded by Lieutenant Skerrett of Battery "L," 5th Artillery, were posted atop the coal tender and throughout the train. Two miles outside of town, it slowed down to pass over the first of two trestles spanning the shallow water and reeds spreading out from the eastern levee of the American River. A few minutes later, as it crossed the second trestle, the engine and coal tender suddenly veered from the rails, crashed down on the crossties, and plunged from the trestle, twisting over to land with a burst of steam upside down in the shallow water and pulling two cars into the water behind them. One car was left hanging over the trestle and another had derailed. A "colored man" running into the depot brought the first news of the wreck; shouting that the engineer and fireman were dead and three soldiers had been shot and killed by strikers. Two doctors and a troop of cavalry immediately raced to the scene.

Upon their arrival, they found "Old Sam Clark" and the fireman crushed to death under the engine. Four enlisted men had been killed in the wreck, but not by bullets fired by strikers. One body was found in the water under the trestle and the other three under the engine.[109] When the cavalrymen on the scene examined the track they found that spikes and fishplates holding the rails to crossties on the trestle had been removed. This caused the rails to spread apart under the weight of the engine, which crashed onto the crossties and flipped over into the water. Captain O'Connell of the 1st Infantry contingent asserted that three strikers were captured "in the immediate vicinity of the wreck, secreted in the bush,...armed with revolvers and dynamite charges."[110] Although it is unlikely that anyone possibly connected to the wreck would be hanging around afterward "in the immediate vicinity," O'Connell's account of strikers "secreted in the bush...armed with revolvers and dynamite" made clear his belief as to who was responsible for the deaths of his fellow soldiers.

That afternoon Harry A. Knox, chairman of the Mediation Committee of the ARU in Sacramento, issued a statement asserting that the union "had not the remotest connection with the ditching of the train," adding that "We condemn this act as outrageous and barbarous, and entirely contrary to the spirit of the American Railway Union, which is engaged in a honorable struggle in the interest of labor, and is opposed to violence or the sacrifice of human life."[111] Knox's statement, however, failed to sway the opinion of the editors of the local morning paper, the *Sacramento Bee*.

In a scathing editorial on the 12th, the paper held the ARU accountable for the tragedy. It accused the union of promoting

> Anarchy—Anarchy, the devil's own viper and spawn from hell; anarchy nursed in Erebus and spewed out of Pandemonium; Anarchy that breathes arson and preaches murder; Anarchy that hates man, degrades woman, defies law and denies God. It is the serpent's tooth to humanity, the bastard snake of Ignorance and Vice to Deity, Man...it brutalizes into the essence of a cur and the quintessence of [a] hyena. Whelped in darkness, it turns mankind from the contemplation of that starry ocean in whose luminous bosom God eternal doth reign, and laughs as he sucks his inspiration from the seething depths of hell.

Defiantly, the editors demanded that Knox back up his words with deeds, "purge your organization of the stain which has been placed upon it," and use "the avenues of information denied to the officers of the law." They acknowledged that the vast majority of the railroad workers were "law-abiding and law-loving men," who had been "stirred to the depths by this damnable deed of devils, and would be well pleased if you [Knox] would send back to hell the spawn of hell guilty of this crime."[112] On the following day events along the riverfront revealed that no matter how respected and responsible were the majority of workers, relations between the strikers on the one hand and the army and the union's opponents on the other hand had grown increasingly hostile.

A squad of soldiers from Battery "L," led by Captain Roberts and Lieutenant Skerrett, were riding guard on a switch engine as it steamed slowly down Front Street by the river when a group of men began moving toward them across the barrier of the "deadline." Ordered to disperse, the men instead moved closer to the engine as one waved his hat as if to signal others to join them. Roberts ordered his men to fix bayonets and advance against the crowd, whereupon shots were fired at the engineer and rocks were thrown at the soldiers. Roberts then gave the order to fire, and two men fell wounded in the volley and later died at the City Receiving Hospital. The marines stationed at the depot heard the shots and rushed to the scene with fixed bayonets, prodding back the crowd and pricking a few in the rear. Then, the cavalry came, charging down streets and swooping around corners to scatter the crowd and clear the riverfront. Shortly before noon, the U.S. marshal appeared and ordered those remaining to disperse and go home, and was jeered by the crowd. Marines then stepped forward with bayonets still fixed to reinforce his words, pricking a few more in the crowd and causing them to disperse and walk away.[113] With the end of the bloody and deadly confrontation by the riverside, the violence that had hit the capital city during the June days of 1894 never reoccurred. As the *Bee* put it, the strike and all that went with it were as "dead as a mackerel on Monday."[114] In other areas of the state, the military succeeded in restoring rail transportation, even though scattered acts of sabotage continued until early September. Colonel Graham and his men remained on duty in Sacramento for another six weeks, patrolling the rail yards and escorting trains out of the city. Many, including Summerall, came down with malaria. When not on sick call, he was kept busy securing supplies of food and clothing and settling accounts with the railroad, "which charged us exorbitantly for everything we touched, including water and travel of train guards."[115] Meanwhile, the criminal investigation of the train wreck continued.

By mid-September, some 70 men had been arrested. The most prominent was none other than Harry Knox, who was charged with conspiring to delay the mail and violating the interstate commerce law. Knox posted bail, stoutly maintained his innocence and emphasized his commitment to the preservation of law and order by accepting the nomination of the Populist Party for sheriff of neighboring Yolo County, where the train had been wrecked. Perhaps to dramatize his candidacy, he acted in one of the lead roles in what the *Bee* referred to as a "lurid melodrama" called "The Great Strike" that was based on the recent labor disputes.[116] In spite of his notoriety, however, Knox was defeated in the election in November,[117] but, in December, he quite likely enjoyed the greater consolation of having the charges dropped against him and several other union members.[118] Another of the accused, however, was not so fortunate.

Salter D. Worden, a native of Syracuse, New York, who had lived in Sacramento for about 20 years and had worked as a messenger for Wells Fargo, was charged with the murder of train engineer Clark. The trial began on Monday, 23 October 1894, in Woodland, county seat of Yolo County. A young man walking ("tramping," as he put it) west from town along the trestle before the wreck occurred testified that Worden and some other men had stopped him and ordered him to turn around and go back. On Friday, 26 October, the prosecution presented as evidence against Worden a diagram written in his hand of the trestle, track, and general surroundings. On Monday, 29 October, one of the strikers testified that the night before the wreck Worden said to a crowd of workers, "'Boys, if we can't win this strike by fair means, we must win by foul; we will get claw-bars and each man will pull a spike, then no man can tell on the other. If there is a man in this crowd who is not an A.R.U. man, I will kill the s———n of a b———h.'" On Friday, 9 November 1894, the case went to the jury, which deliberated for less than an hour and found Worden guilty of murder in the first degree. Eight days later he was sentenced to be hanged on Tuesday, 12 February 1895. From the accounts of the trial in the *Bee*, which in any case had taken a strong anti-union position, Worden's defense seemed weak and passive, his lawyer at one point claiming that the rails across the trestle had been "bent by the sun." His lawyers also failed to shake the testimony of either the two witnesses who had implicated him, even though neither of the witnesses actually had seen Worden commit the crime.[119] Interestingly enough, Summerall seems not to have kept up with the Worden trial, noting only (and incorrectly) in his memoir that "The criminals who wrecked the train and killed the soldiers were never punished." On 3 September, he and the rest of Colonel Graham's command had returned to the Presidio, where Summerall's attention was focused on more immediate and pressing professional concerns.

What remained fixed in Summerall's memory was the ineffectiveness of the National Guard, which he found "entirely useless."[120] Perhaps this recollection provided the impetus, some 15 years later when he was serving as assistant to the chief of the Militia Bureau in charge of the field artillery for the National Guard. Summerall worked enthusiastically and successfully to improve the Guard's training and expertise in the use of field guns. He also retained a strong prejudice against labor unions and their leaders, especially Eugene V. Debs. But 30 years later, after Samuel Gompers, the long-serving head of the American Federation of Labor, led the union's strong support of the AEF in World War I, Summerall recognized him as an outstanding leader. When Gompers died in 1924, Summerall noted that "the army showed its sympathy for labor and its admiration of his patriotic services by according him a military funeral, which is the highest honor which can be bestowed to any man."[121]

Shortly after their return to the Presidio, Colonel Graham appointed Summerall regimental and post adjutant. While Summerall noted that the appointment was "legal," he realized that it was highly unusual, for army tradition held that only an older first lieutenant could occupy this important position. Older officers, he said, advised him to decline the appointment, warning him that if he accepted, he "might be ostracized by the regiment." In Summerall's view, however, to decline would be to disobey an order. Apparently, when a copy of the order reached the War Department, the "traditionalists" must have prevailed. Graham received a personal letter advising him to revoke the order, which he did. How long Summerall served in this position is difficult to determine; in his memoir he gives no dates and it is not listed on his service record. However, in the efficiency report Colonel Graham prepared on 30 June 1895, he credits Summerall with service as regimental and post adjutant and makes clear how highly he rated and valued the young second lieutenant's performance over the past year.

As in his report of 1 March 1894, Graham rated Summerall "excellent" in all categories. He noted that Summerall had performed "with battery engaged in suppressing the efforts of insurgents to obstruct and interfere with interstate commerce[,] maintaining law and order [and] the injunction of the U.S. Court's and President's Proclamation during the insurrection at Sacramento and along the line of the Southern Pacific Railway from July 11th to Sept 3rd, 1894." Under "duties other than those of routine," Graham wrote "those of Regimental and Post Adjutant at Presidio and those of an Adjutant General and Quartermaster and Commissary with troops engaged in suppressing strike in 1894, at Sacramento Cal., and in each and all displaying marked zeal and ability." He added that his "opinion [was] based upon my personal observation of the manner in which this officer has performed duty under my command as an adjutant, a quartermaster and commissary under conditions observed requiring the exhibition of the best qualities of a staff officer in each department named and in all of which he displayed marked aptitude of ability and a most conscientious loyalty to the obligations of duty." He concluded his report by remarking that Summerall was "a most efficient, zealous and conscientious officer in the discharge of his duty in all situations."[122]

From Graham's high praise of his prized second lieutenant, one could conclude, as the older officers had likely decided, that Summerall had been awarded a position that belonged to one of them mainly because he had become the colonel's "fair-haired boy." Summerall wrote that their attitude "seemed to me to be wrong," and he was quite right. However, he could have been more understanding and less critical of long-serving and deserving junior officers who had to wait a very long time, as he well knew, for any advancement or promotion. At any rate, he felt that the situation had been "composed," and seemed in this instance at least, to have held no lingering grudge or animosity toward his older fellow officers.

For the next two years, Summerall remained at The Presidio. In addition to making sure that the Commissary deposits arrived safely at the bank and taking care that the operation turned a profit, he performed routine duties on post as the engineering officer of Light Battery "D," and rode with the battery on practice marches and on maneuvers to conduct target practices.[123] The year 1895 seems to have been especially uneventful, since Summerall accounted in his memoir nothing from that year, not even a visit to the city to visit his close friends Brooks and Winfield Jones. In his personnel file he is listed on detached service and leave of absence from March to May 1895.[124] But in his memoir, Summerall mentioned that he took a leave of three months in 1896, beginning in December, and spent this time with his family in Eustis. Understandably, looking back over a span of over 50 years, he confused the years, although a check of his service record could have established the correct year of this, his first active duty leave. In any case, he remembered his stay in Eustis as a happy time, the last time, he said, that all the family was together. They were living very well, thanks to Summerall's support, and his brother William had just been graduated from Tulane University Medical School. Bothered by what Summerall called "a malignant ulcer in the palm of my right hand," he asked William to treat it, which he did "with much skill." With financial backing from his younger brother, William planned to establish his practice in Atlanta, but for reasons that Summerall never explained, "This did not happen."[125]

A more telling reason why Summerall's leave with his family must have been in 1895, rather than in the next year, was the death of his father, at age 69, in August 1896. The month of December and the Christmas season of 1896, just a few months after Bryant Summerall's death, could not have been a time of cheer, and he surely would not have recorded that "all the family were together." He learned of his father's death in a letter from his mother that he opened after returning from a practice march and target practice with his battery. It was the first death in his immediate family and, as he wrote, "it affected me deeply." The journey home for the funeral being too far and too expensive, Summerall was not able to return to Eustis, where Bryant Summerall was buried in a lot purchased in the city cemetery by his younger son.[126]

That Summerall loved and admired his hard-luck father is plain to see. He was pleased that his father was proud of him and remembered him as "always kind, loving and helpful." He deeply respected his father's bravery as he stood as justice of the peace in Providence against the violent gangs of Union county; he admired his knowledge of farming, medicine, and law, and his many skills: the design, construction, and painting of houses, cabinet making, blacksmithing, and the making and repair of carriages. To his son, Bryant Summerall was a man of "the highest integrity who wrote and spoke well," whose reasoning was sound and who "understood the mercantile business." Yet he failed to achieve success in any of his undertakings, particularly in the "mercantile business." Summerall could "never explain" his father's lack of success, "unless," he said, "it was due to complete unselfishness."[127] The unselfishness of the father, especially toward his family, was an indelible mark that Bryant Summerall left imprinted upon the character of his son. As stated above in Chapter 1, another deep paternal imprint, although of an indirect nature, was Summerall's "determination to compensate through his own success for the setbacks and misfortunes of the good and gifted man who was his father."[128] He also praised his father's love for his wife Margaret, asserting that both were "wholly devoted to each other,"[129] as they were to their entire family. This strong and vivid memory of his parents' mutual love and devotion and the knowledge that he himself had done much to comfort and sustain them and his family must have eased the heavy burden of his father's death. His parents' happy and devoted marriage would serve as a model for his own marriage that he came to see as "the most momentous part of my life," and one that "destiny" would decree and develop.[130]

If "destiny" indeed were at work, the beginnings were to be found in the home of Lieutenant John David Miley and his wife Sara Mordecai Miley. She was the oldest of the five children of Colonel Alfred Mordecai, Jr., and his wife, Sally Maynadier Mordecai (pronounced MOR-de-kee), and had married John Miley in 1892, five years after Miley's graduation in 1887 from West Point. Colonel Mordecai was the son of Major Alfred Mordecai, Sr., who was born in 1804 to prominent Jewish parents in Warrenton, North Carolina, and where he and his 12 siblings received their early schooling at home. Mordecai senior was graduated from the Military Academy in 1823 at the top of his class, and became one of the army's most distinguished and respected Jewish officers. While serving on the Ordnance Board, he helped create the first complete artillery system for the army and led the development in 1841 of the *Ordnance Manual*, the first set of ordnance regulations the army published. When faced with the difficult choice between service to his native South or loyalty to his country, Mordecai chose neither, and instead resigned his commission. He went on to have a successful career as an engineer and author and died in Philadelphia in 1887 at the age of 83. His son Alfred junior had been graduated ninth in his class from West Point in 1861 (his classmate George Armstrong Custer finished 34th and last), and had handled the logistics at Fort Sumter. He later fought at the first Battle of Bull Run in July 1861. He had followed in his father's footsteps as an ordnance officer, and in 1896 was serving as commander of the Springfield, Massachusetts, Arsenal.[131]

Colonel Mordecai's daughter Sara and her husband John were the parents of two young children, John David, Jr., aged three and a half, and Sally Maynadier, named for her maternal grandmother, aged one and a half.[132] They lived in an apartment housed in officers' quarters running south to north along the western side of the parade ground directly across from the enlisted men's barracks. It was not uncommon in the evenings for young bachelor officers like Summerall, nostalgic for the warmth of family life, to stroll along the walkway in front of "officers' row" and drop in for visits with their colleagues and their families. For Summerall and his friends, one of their favorite stops was at the Miley home. He considered John David as the "most superior officer on post." He found his wife Sara "brilliant and entertaining," and enjoyed entertaining their children.[133]

One evening in August, not long after Summerall had received the news of his father's death, and was quite likely looking for cheerful familial comfort to assuage his sorrow, he and some friends stopped by to visit the Mileys. There he learned that Sara's younger sister Laura, who at age 24 was five years younger than Summerall, would soon arrive from her home in Springfield, Massachusetts, for a visit. The morning after her arrival, while she and her niece and nephew were watching the guard mounting, Summerall saw the young woman, and realized who she was. He remembered that those who knew Laura Mordecai "spoke of her admiringly," and walked over to introduce himself. At that point, "destiny" seems to have taken over. "I was deeply impressed," he wrote, "by her sweetness, loveliness, and daintiness. I thought how small she was....After a brief conversation, I went on but the incident clung to me. I called on her at once, and met her occasionally."[134] The adverb "occasionally" seems out of place when used in the same breath as "at once," but because he was in mourning after his father's recent death, Summerall did not attempt to invite Laura Mordecai to any social events like the post hops at the officers' club, where, as he wistfully recorded, the other officers "said she danced beautifully."

One evening on his way home after working late on a court-martial board, he "happened" to walk past the Miley apartment and saw Sara's sister sitting on the stone steps. He asked her to walk along with him. His Victorian manners and modesty still evident in his 80s, he wrote almost apologetically that "Without intending to do so," (no formal invitation having been issued and no chaperon on hand to accompany them), "we walked along the beach to Fort Winfield Scott [sic]. The time and the distance seemed short to me, and I have no doubt that she enjoyed being with me."[135] They also met Sundays in the post chapel where Laura played the organ for worship services, doubtless under the admiring gaze of the strong-voiced singer who probably knew every hymn by heart.

In October, not long after his stroll with Laura along the beach beneath the promontory of the Golden Gate (the first time they were alone together), Summerall's regiment received orders to report to Fort Hamilton in New York harbor.[136] Laura extended her visit to help her sister, who was now expecting the birth of her third child in December,[137] so she and Summerall said their good-byes. He left, "feeling that she had entered my life for always, though nothing was said or done to indicate it." For the time being, it was consoling for him to know that when she returned to her home in Springfield she would not be far from his new assignment at Fort Hamilton.[138]

The journey in early October 1896 of the officers and men of the 5th Artillery Regiment across the continent from San Francisco harbor to the harbor of New York City lasted seven days. They left behind their horses and equipment, since they were to take over the animals and materiel of the 1st Artillery Regiment they were replacing at Fort Hamilton.[139] Situated on the northern side of the Narrows, the appropriately named waterway joined harbor and the sea. Fort Hamilton had long served as a seacoast fortification to protect the spacious and spectacular harbor and the surrounding city. It was quite probably named for Alexander Hamilton, who served there during the Revolutionary War as an artillery officer before becoming General Washington's aide-de-camp. Captain Robert E. Lee was assigned in 1841 as fort engineer, upgrading the batteries on both sides of the Narrows, and Lieutenant Thomas J. Jackson served as an artillery officer there after returning in 1848 from the Mexican War.[140]

Summerall began corresponding with Laura "at once." Living frugally on post, he heated only one room of his quarters during the winter months, and had his meals next door at a nominal cost with Lieutenant George Gatley and his wife and their three-year- old daughter, Ann Harding.[141] Gatley succeeded Summerall in command of the Field Artillery Brigade of the 42d Division in the Great War, and in later years his daughter Ann remembered fondly Summerall's playfully carrying her around on his shoulders,[142] entertaining her as he had the Miley children in their home at The Presidio. He seldom left the post, but when Laura returned home to Springfield early in 1897, he visited a classmate stationed at the Arsenal and called on her there. She, in turn, would stay with friends in Brooklyn, where they were able to see each other more frequently and at less expense for Summerall. He soon came to realize "that she meant more to me than anyone else had ever done [sic]." Although they must have talked about their future together, Summerall wrote that "my financial responsibilities precluded any thought of marriage." Probably hoping to deter a visit from his "good friends" from Tuxedo Park that might complicate his relationship with Laura and disrupt any future thoughts of marriage, he "made no attempt to revive my acquaintance in New York...."[143]

With the exception of visits with Laura Mordecai, the 18 months from October 1896 to April 1898 that Summerall spent at Fort Hamilton were filled with routine duties. As quartermaster for Battery "D," he was responsible for securing supplies and camp grounds for target practices that took place in the valleys of the Berkshire hills in eastern Massachusetts during the summer months of 1897. Some of the encampments were near Quaker and Shaker communities that eyed the soldiers rather warily, but remained friendly and tolerant of the unaccustomed proximity of fighting men to their pacific settlements. In other areas like Great Barrington, neighboring families invited officers to dinner; on one occasion the proprietor of a local inn treated Summerall and his battery of 125 officers and men to breakfast on the house.[144] The winter of 1897–1898 changed uneventfully into the spring of 1898, although Summerall noted that the New York newspapers, particularly the Hearst papers, "were beginning to stir up feeling for a war with Spain over Cuba." Even so, he said, "We could not take it seriously."[145] Soon, however, he would have to take it quite seriously. Indeed, tension with Spain increased and Americans began to press for a resolution to the fast-moving Spanish-American crisis over Cuba. It had become an issue that grew out of the revived spirit of expansion that surged forth in the United States in the 1890s.

Though dormant since the 1850s, expansionism had never really died out. It was revived in the 1870s after the purchase of Alaska from Russia in 1867, the acquisition of a naval base, and the right of extraterritoriality for Americans in Samoa in 1878, and the establishment of American control on 4 July 1894 of the Republic of Hawaii. With the closing of the frontier in 1890, a development that historian Frederick Jackson Turner referred to as the end of the "first period of American history," many Americans feared that the consistently expanding domestic market might now come to an end.[146] To ensure continued economic growth they believed the United States should follow the European example of the new economic imperialism. Traditional doctrines of imperialism had been based essentially upon the conquest of land and settlement by the conqueror's people to exploit the resources of the conquered. The "new imperialism" did not depart from this model, but was more clearly economic and emphasized the investment of capital to control local governments, markets, raw materials, and labor. Leaders like Senators Albert J. Beveridge of Indiana and Henry Cabot Lodge of Massachusetts, as well as the youthful Theodore Roosevelt, joined the traditional with the new brand of imperialism by advocating overseas possessions while promoting capital investment abroad to increase markets for American manufacturers.[147] They also added their belief that government under the American flag would provide freedom for all people. As Beveridge rhetorically asked in a campaign speech entitled "The March of the Flag," "Shall the American people continue their march toward the commercial supremacy of the world? Shall free institutions broaden their blessed reign as the children of liberty wax in strength, until the empire of our principles is established over the hearts of all mankind?"[148] It was the doctrine of Manifest Destiny now proclaimed beyond the vanished frontier at home to the waiting world beyond.

The writings of Captain Alfred Thayer Mahan, president of the Naval War College at Newport, Rhode Island, added forcefully to the case for expansionism. In his book, *The Influence of Sea Power Upon History, 1660–1783*, and in an article entitled "The United States Looking Outward," both published in 1890, Mahan asserted that sea power assured national greatness, prosperity, and security. Linking sea power directly with economic growth, Mahan called for a strong merchant marine, colonies, and a large navy, primarily made up of battleships, with supply bases. He envisioned American control of the Caribbean and expansion through an isthmian canal into the vast realm of the Pacific, and found among politicians and businessmen as much support for his theories and proposals as among generals and admirals.[149]

In 1888, two years before the publication of Mahan's seminal works, the keel had been laid for one of a new generation of ships designed to make the United States Navy the equal at least to the navy of the German Empire. Launched in 1890, the year in which Mahan's works appeared, this vessel, the battleship USS *Maine*, was longer than a football field, had a beam of almost 60 feet amidships, displaced over 6,680 tons, and carried a crew of 31 officers and 342 enlisted men. She was the first modern American battleship, the first in a new line of steel-hulled, steam-powered warships, and the first one built in an American shipyard of materials and components manufactured in the United States. She was also the first ship designed to use electricity and was equipped with a generator and electric lights, one of the newest technologies of the 1890s.[150]

In September 1895, the year the *Maine* was commissioned, a guerrilla army under Maximo Gomez rebelled against Spanish authorities on the Caribbean island of Cuba to free the island from Spanish rule. In retaliation, the Spanish sent to Cuba an army under General Valeriano Weyler to implement a "reconcentration" policy that forced much of the rural population into settlements and towns, while his army laid waste the countryside to deprive the guerrillas of men and supplies. As a result, guerrilla strength waned, but the economy of the island was wrecked, the sugar cane harvest almost ceased, and thousands of Cubans died of hunger and disease in Weyler's *reconcentrados*.[151]

American businessmen, initially critical of the guerrillas, became increasingly concerned about the security of their investments under Spanish rule in Cuba, and American public opinion, with much encouragement from a Cuban junta in New York and the New York press, turned steadily against "Butcher Weyler" and the Spanish. Moreover, the expansionist and imperialist followers of Senators Beveridge and Lodge, Theodore Roosevelt, and Captain Mahan strongly supported American intervention to free the Cubans from the brutality of Spanish rule, end the oppressive presence of Spain's decrepit empire in the New World, and launch the United States on its predestined path to world power status. Indeed, during the presidential campaign of 1896, all three major political parties (Republican, Democratic, and Populist) advocated independence for Cuba, using armed force if necessary. The Republicans even inserted a plank in their platform calling for the incoming president to use his office to restore peace in Cuba and to insure its independence.[152]

In the summer of 1897, however, a new and more liberal government under the elderly prime minister Praxades Sagasta came to power in Spain, hoping to retain the colony that for many years had furnished the mother country with much of its wealth. The Sagasta government recalled General Weyler and replaced him with Segismundo Moret, a capable and English-speaking Anglophile who announced a policy of home rule and scheduled elections for a Cuban parliament for April 1898. The plan satisfied no one. The guerrillas demanded independence, and executed a Spanish colonel who had come to talk to them about autonomy. Traditionalists in Cuba remained loyal to the *madre patria*, and opposed any home rule scheme. In support of the Spanish army, these loyalists inspired riots in the streets of Havana in January 1898, which led the American consul-general Fitzhugh Lee, a nephew of Robert E. Lee, to request that Washington send a warship to Havana to protect American lives and property.[153]

In the U.S. capital, President William McKinley, newly elected on the Republican ticket in 1896, was reluctant to implement the aggressive measures called for in his party's platform. But he accepted Lee's assessment of the risks to Americans and their property, and on 24 January 1898 ordered the *Maine*, which was sailing with the North Atlantic Squadron toward their winter base in the Dry Tortugas at the tip of the Florida Keys, to steam for Havana. The next day she eased into the harbor past the lighthouse at Morro Castle, and dropped anchor without incident. In Madrid, the government of Prime Minister Sagasta reluctantly accepted the presence of the American warship as a friendly visit and responded by sending the cruiser *Vizcaya* on a friendly visit to New York.[154] Sailing through the Narrows, the Spanish vessel anchored just off Fort Hamilton and fired a salute to proclaim her greetings to the city. From the fort the *Vizcaya*'s salute was returned on orders of the officer of the day, Lieutenant Charles P. Summerall,[155] who had just returned from special duty at the headquarters of the army's Department of the East on Governor's Island, just off the tip of Manhattan at the southern end of the East River.[156] As the sound of their salute reverberated across the harbor, Summerall and his men wondered whether the Spanish warship would be safe as she lay at anchor, surrounded by a city where the "yellow journalism" of William Randolph Hearst's *New York Journal* and Joseph Pulitzer's *New York World* had stirred up intense support for a war with Spain.[157] Their apprehensiveness did not inhibit preparations for a dance scheduled for Tuesday evening, 15 February, the day after St. Valentine's Day. In any event, the *Vizcaya* soon departed safely without incident.

Summerall was a member of the "hop committee" that had invited the officers and ladies of the Brooklyn Navy Yard to join with their fellow officers and their ladies at Fort Hamilton for a long and festive evening of dancing above the fluorescent winter waters of the city's spacious harbor. As the dancing hour approached at Fort Hamilton, news that the USS *Maine* had been blown up in Havana Harbor reached the mainland and "electrified the country," reported Summerall; a minor shock jolted the hop committee, which had to decide whether to cancel the dance. Since they had received no further details or information, and since their guests from the Navy Yard had begun to arrive, they decided to go ahead. Had they known that the ship had been sunk and lives had been lost, Summerall noted, they "of course would have cancelled the dance."[158]

What the officers and ladies of Fort Hamilton and the Brooklyn Navy Yard as well as the rest of the country soon discovered was that an explosion had blown up the *Maine* and that two officers and 266 enlisted men of the crew of 354 had died, and many more had been injured as she sank to the bottom of Havana Harbor. To Hearst's *World*, the cause of the disaster was clear. On 17 February the paper's headline proclaimed that, "THE WARSHIP MAINE SPLIT IN TWO BY AN ENEMY'S SECRET INFERNAL MACHINE."[159] A day later, Pulitzer's *World* urged the president to call on Congress to declare war against Spain.

Among the public, war fever climbed, heated by the yellow press and statements from younger members of the administration, like the young Assistant Secretary of the Navy Theodore Roosevelt who claimed that the sinking was "an act of dirty treachery on the part of the Spaniards."[160] With shouts of "Remember the Maine!" Americans brushed aside the comments of the acting Secretary of State John D. Long that the Spanish were not responsible for the explosion, as well as the report of a naval court of inquiry that there was not enough hard evidence to fix the blame. Public opinion held Spain accountable and demanded intervention in Cuba.[161]

With the country experiencing another depression, President McKinley had entered office in 1897 hoping to raise tariffs to protect and stimulate domestic industrial production and to ensure a "full dinner pail" for American workers.[162] A veteran of the Civil War, he had enlisted as a private in 1861, and served as a commissary sergeant at the Battle of Antietam in 1862.[163] He had had enough of war, confiding to an aide that "I have been through one war. I have seen the dead piled up, and I do not want to see another."[164] With the public crying for revenge, he realized he had to act and in March persuaded Congress to appropriate $50 million for defense and called upon Spain to grant Cuba independence.

In early April, the Sagasta government responded by announcing a unilateral cease-fire with the rebels and proposing an autonomous government for Cuba. It rejected independence, having decided that the loss of Cuba and the wealth it produced might well lead to revolution at home.[165] On 11 April, McKinley asked Congress for the authority to stop the conflict in Cuba and to protect American property and trade; 11 days later on 23 April, he announced a blockade of Cuba's northern coast and the port of Santiago. On 24 April, Spain declared war on the United States. On 25 April, Congress declared war on Spain, retroactive to 21 April 1898. It was an action that technically enabled the United States to declare war first.[166]

Since the passage of the $50 million appropriation in early March, the army and navy had been planning jointly for conflict with Spain. The navy would lead the way by imposing a blockade of Cuba, establishing command of the Caribbean Sea, and attacking the Spanish Squadron at Manila in the Philippine Islands. Meanwhile, the army would strengthen the country's coastal fortifications against possible enemy attacks, while undertaking the major task of mobilizing a large expeditionary force to invade Cuba as well as the island of Puerto Rico. Summerall soon saw firsthand the extent of these preparations.

As events and passions propelled the country toward war with Spain, Summerall left behind the festive yet frenzied surroundings of Fort Hamilton for duty far to the southwest where he was reunited with his mentor and model, William Montrose Graham. Recently promoted to the rank of brigadier general, Graham had been named commander of the Department of the Gulf at Fort Sam Houston, not far from the Alamo in San Antonio, Texas.[167] As his aide-de-camp General Graham had requested Lieutenant Summerall, who joined Graham early in April and moved on with the command when they were transferred to Atlanta, Georgia.[168] In Atlanta, Summerall lived with his brother William and his wife and two young children. William had set up his medical practice with $500 his brother had borrowed from Winfield Jones, of San Francisco fame.[169]

From department headquarters in Atlanta, Summerall traveled with Graham on several inspection trips along the southern coast. On 13 April, he was ordered to accompany Graham to inspect defenses under construction at Tybee Island, close to Savannah, Georgia, and on Sullivan's Island, just to the northeast of the harbor of Charleston, South Carolina. On 18 April, he received orders to accompany Graham on a trip to Key West, Florida, to inspect coastal defenses and barracks built to house American soldiers preparing for the invasion of Cuba.[170] After completing their work at Key West, they proceeded north to Atlanta via Jacksonville.

Arriving in the Florida port on 21 April, Summerall received a telegram informing him that his mother had died the night before. He immediately left for her home in Eustis, and got there in time for her funeral. She had requested that the words "She hath done what she could" be inscribed on her grave stone. Summerall saw to that and buried his mother next to her sister Susan and his father in the family plot in Greenwood Cemetery in Eustis. Reflecting on his mother's role in his life and in the life of his siblings, Summerall recorded in his memoir the depth of his love for her and the admiration he felt throughout his life for the strength of her intellect and character and for her devotion to family.

For his own dedication to the welfare of his parents and siblings and to his family to come, she was the perfect example. With affection and reverence he wrote that "it would be impossible to express what my mother had meant to me and the sorrow that her death brought. Whatever I have done worthwhile in my life has been due to her and her influence. Her loving, tender care in childhood; her understanding and encouragement in maturity; her inspiration of all that I ever did; her ambition and hope for us; her selfless sacrifice that we might live in the darkest days of poverty; her ambition for us to succeed; her intervention whenever we found difficulties; her strength as a refuge in our troubles; her fine intellect; her noble character and brave spirit made our lives and our success.... She taught me all that I knew before [my] going to Dr. Porter's, and I found myself thoroughly grounded. Her appeal to Dr. Porter to take my brother and myself was the turning point in our lives. She was never despondent and never complained. In the most abject poverty, she wrote the most beautiful verses. To have been blessed with such a mother and such a wife as mine [who was, of course, to be Laura Mordecai], is more than anyone could deserve."[171]

Rarely can one discover a more tender and grateful remembrance of a mother, and by joining his mother and his wife in this moving recollection, Summerall revealed at the same time the full measure of his love and devotion to Laura as well. The question of what to do about his mother's house was settled when, in consideration of his ongoing support for each of their families, his brother and sister agreed to give their younger brother quitclaim deeds to the house.[172] Returning to Atlanta, Summerall busied himself with routine duties, until on 17 May Graham was ordered to assume command of the Second Army Corps at Falls Church, Virginia, and Summerall again was detailed as Graham's aide-de-camp.[173]

Soon, they began the work of preparing volunteers for war with the forces of the Spanish Empire in Cuba. In Cuba, American soldiers would face some 150,000 regulars augmented by 50,000 Spanish volunteers and Cuban loyalists. On Puerto Rico the Spanish had in place over 8,000 regulars. Some 20,000 Spanish troops had been detailed for service in the Philippines, and 150,000 were under arms in Spain. Although large in number, disease, inadequate training, and poor leadership undermined the effectiveness of Spain's colonial army; moreover, if American sea power could seal off the Caribbean, as seemed likely, the army in Spain would be useless. In comparison, the U.S. Army of 28,000 regulars was indeed smaller than the enemy it would face, and had no experience in fighting a major war beyond the frontiers of the nation. It was a well-trained, well-led and disciplined army, and could call upon far greater resources of manpower than could the army of Spain. Added to the pool of American manpower were some 100,000 National Guardsmen, whose effectiveness was limited, however, by deficiencies of training, experience and leadership, as their action in recent labor crises had revealed.[174]

The president and Congress acted swiftly to expand the Regular Army, and tap the manpower resources of the nation to build a force large enough to overwhelm and perhaps intimidate the Spanish. In response to strong support in the States for the National Guard, legislation was passed on 22 April that limited the expansion of the Regular Army to about 65,000 and authorized the president to create as large a volunteer army as he considered necessary. These volunteers would serve for two years or for the duration of the conflict, whichever was shorter. On 23 April, McKinley called for 125,000 volunteers.[175] The next day he approved an attack on Manila by Commodore George Dewey's Asiatic Squadron by cable to Hong Kong, where Dewey was waiting. On 1 May, Dewey entered Manila Bay, and with expert efficiency, his squadron carried out his orders to destroy Admiral Patricio Montojo's squadron, which he found conveniently resting at anchor. The Spanish still held the city, however, and Dewey made clear to Washington that American soldiers were needed to take the city and hold the island.

Under the direction of the Secretary of War Russell A. Alger and Nelson A. Miles, the ambitious and contentious commanding general of the army, the National Guard and Regular Army units began to assemble in early May. Secretary Alger ordered the Regular Army concentrated at Tampa and Camp Thomas at Chickamauga Park, Tennessee; the volunteer units joined the regulars in these encampments or assembled in other camps in the Southern states, where they could be more quickly moved to ports for embarkation to Cuba. San Francisco was designated as the assembly point for units bound for Manila.[176]

As the army assembled, the War Department completed its command structure, organizing the volunteer and regular infantry units into eight army corps, each commanded by a major general.[177] For the concentration of one of these corps, designated the Second Corps, the department had selected a 1400-acre tract of land known as Woodburn Manor, located about 12 miles west of Washington, near Falls Church, Virginia. The land belonged to Charles Campbell and his wife, Emma, who gladly agreed to lease their property to the government for $300 a month. They were especially pleased that the lease allowed them to retain control of strips of land bordering the roads leading to the property. Along these roads they intended to open a few businesses and lease space to independent vendors.[178]

On 17 May, General Graham, newly promoted to the rank of major general, was ordered to assume command of Second Corps and arrived in Washington from Atlanta on 19 May with his staff, which included, of course, his aide-de-camp, Lieutenant Summerall.[179] After five days of work at the War Department, they boarded a train of the Southern Railway Company's Bluemont Branch steam railroad, and after a short ride stepped off at the Dunn Loring hamlet depot. This station was to serve as the gateway to the camp of the Second Corps and was just over a mile from the Woodburn Manor property. That same day, 23 May, the site officially was named Camp Alger, in honor of the secretary of war.[180]

Graham and his staff arrived at Camp Alger to find that some 6,500 volunteers from Pennsylvania and Ohio already had passed through the depot at Dunn Loring and had moved into tents supplied and set up on the dry, dusty land by a special detachment from the 1st Regiment, District of Columbia Volunteer Infantry. During the next two months, volunteer soldiers from 16 states north and south of the Mason-Dixon Line joined the men from Pennsylvania and Ohio, swelling the population of Camp Alger's tent city to some 23,600.[181] They reported to Camp Alger brimming with patriotic fervor for the war with Spain, and "promised to 'Remember the Maine,'" wrote Aaron Ward Hartley, of Company L, 7th Regiment, Ohio Volunteer Infantry, in a letter to the local newspapers in Meigs County, Ohio in June 1898.[182]

Like the thousands of their comrades pouring into other volunteer camps, those at Camp Alger arrived ill prepared to fight a war. State officials had failed to supply them with uniforms, tents or mess kits, and their training in basic drill and musketry skills had been neglected. Moreover, they arrived to find the camps poorly prepared to receive them. The demand for supplies for the large number of volunteers overwhelmed the War Department bureaus accustomed to meeting the needs of the small peacetime army. In addition, since the bureaus issued supplies only when requisitioned by commanding officers in the field, necessary supplies were not on hand at Alger and other camps when volunteers streamed in before their commanding officer had arrived. When supplies were requisitioned, the flood of paperwork led to long delays in Washington and confusion and logjams when supplies poured into small rail depots like Dunn Loring. Adding to the chaos was the misunderstanding between General Miles and the corps commanders regarding the role of the corps and the purpose of the volunteer camps. For Miles the corps were administrative organizations created to prepare soldiers for service in separate field commands. The corps commanders believed, however, that they were training soldiers to serve under their command in the field. They were largely unconcerned about the necessity to supply their camps for extended occupation. This misunderstanding and resulting confusion were never resolved during the war.[183]

At Camp Alger, no one was more disturbed about the lack of supplies and facilities than Lieutenant Colonel Alfred C. Girard, chief surgeon of the Second Corps. A medical officer in the Regular Army since 1889, Girard had studied European hospital systems and had an excellent reputation as a surgeon and administrator. He was deeply concerned that many National Guard units had arrived at camp without medicines, hospital tents, cots or ambulances, in spite of being notified by the War Department through their state governors that they must bring their own medical supplies until Washington could meet their needs. As Girard discovered, however, a few units had reported with some medical supplies, and with General Graham's approval he impounded their supplies while centralizing their use in hospitals equipped with 200 beds for each of the two divisions of the corps. Immediately, Girard encountered opposition from a number of regimental colonels and surgeons who refused to give up their supplies and from hospital stewards who protested that the new organization would reduce their pay and status. As adequate supplies began to arrive, and with the surgeon general of the army, Dr. George M. Sternberg, threatening to recommend the court-martial of any officer who continued to block Girard's plan, resistance largely disappeared.[184]

By mid-June, Girard's divisional hospitals were functioning, but were understaffed. Competent nurses were hard to find, for colonels were reluctant to allow their better soldiers to become nurses and saw in the hospital corps a way to get rid of undesirable men. Female nurses were not allowed in the camp until the last month of its existence, when only four, two of which were nuns, were permitted to work in Second Corps hospitals. Adequate staffs were assembled only after Girard hired contract surgeons and male medical personnel, which were recruited from as far away as Ohio. Additional help came from the National Relief Commission, which provided washing machines for cleaning the clothes of sick soldiers, religious literature, medical supplies, and all the ice Second Corps hospitals needed. With his plan in place and help arriving from far and near, Girard believed that his command could take care of the health of the Second Corps until they could be equipped for service in the field against Spain.[185] Morale also had improved. Corporal Hartley reported that "The men enjoy the practice marches and sham battles," and was proud that "a number of 'tenderfeet' dropped out" of a particularly long march to the Potomac and back.[186] Neither Girard, Graham, nor the other corps commanders, as noted above, had envisioned a lengthy occupation. None of them, including the men of the Second Corps, were prepared for the severity of the conditions and demands that resulted.

With several hundred soldiers arriving daily and with no units leaving, men found themselves living in crowded conditions, and increasingly more vulnerable to the spread of germs. Lack of space caused latrines to be placed too close to kitchens and tents, and contents were often left uncovered, attracting swarms of flies and giving off a nauseating stench in the summer heat. Surrounding woods were fouled by men who preferred to relieve themselves behind trees and in the bushes. Local springs, streams, and wells became polluted, and when rainfall amounts for May, June, and July dropped to lower than average levels, an acute water shortage developed. As temperatures rose to higher than normal levels and the air became hot and filled with dust, thirsty soldiers began drinking the water they found trickling in polluted streams and shimmering thinly at the bottom of wells. Water was too scarce for bathing, and men soon lost the battle to check the spread of body lice. The result of these natural and man-made conditions was a soaring sickness rate, from 578 men, or 2.7 percent of the Second Corps on 10 June, to 879 men or 3.8 percent on 20 June, just 10 days later. Camp Alger's hospitals rapidly were filling up. General Graham responded to the water crisis by bringing in water in sterilized barrels from wells far from camp and ordering the drilling of deeper wells on the Woodburn

Manor property. By the end of June, the new wells were providing a safe and dependable source of water.[187] This was good news and might well have led to improvement in the overall health of Camp Alger's soldiers had it come in time. Instead, typhoid fever condemned many soldiers to illness and death.

Typhoid fever was introduced in late May when at least 11 soldiers reported to camp already infected with the disease. At first, typhoid spread slowly and almost without being detected. Few understood the nature of the disease, and army surgeons had difficulty distinguishing the early symptoms of typhoid from those of malaria. By the time General Graham arrived, he found several men dying of it, and by early July the disease was sweeping through the camp, its progress accelerated by the cramped living conditions, polluted water, and germ-infested surroundings. By the end of July, 331 soldiers, or 3.5 percent of the corps, lay prostrate with the fever, judged by one of the Regular Army medical officers as "a most virulent type" that caused extremely high temperatures, intense thirst, and frequent periods of delirium. Never, he added, had he "seen worse cases of typhoid." During July, the rapid increase in the number of patients and the severity of the disease overwhelmed the capacity of the camp's hospitals and the ability of the facilities to provide care for the suffering soldiers. Many were transported to the general hospital at Fort Myer, some 15 miles to the east, but it quickly became overcrowded and had to be closed to additional patients. General Graham and the War Department then turned to more drastic measures to deal with the health crises at the camp.[188]

On 8 July, Graham obtained about 200 acres of land belonging to the Crittenden family close to Dunn Loring and ordered the First Division to move to the new campground. Rather than leaving the fever behind, they carried it with them, and the number of sick continued to increase. Secretary Alger then ordered the entire Second Corps to relocate to an area known as Thoroughfare Gap, near Manassas, Virginia, about 50 miles to the west. The Second Division left on 2 August, and spent an entire week meandering through Fairfax and Prince William counties before reaching their destination. Their march produced more sickness, and turned into a public relations fiasco. The fever continued to rage and claimed so many victims that a special field hospital had to be set up at Bristoe, some 12 miles from Thoroughfare Gap. Local inhabitants accused the men of stealing food, robbing and desecrating the grave of a Confederate officer, and assaulting a young girl.[189] The farmers were angry enough, according to Corporal Aaron Hartley, to "actually refuse to allow the soldiers a drink of water at their wells."[190] When the division finally reached the encampment at Thoroughfare Gap, the fever proved even more virulent. For the month of August, the number of men in the Second Division infected with typhoid rose to 389, an increase of over 300 percent over July.[191]

As the division wound its way toward Thoroughfare Gap, the Third Virginia Regiment of Major General Butler's First Division remained at Camp Alger. There an incident occurred that further complicated relations, not only between the division and their neighbors, but also between the Second Corps on the one hand and state officials and Virginia Congressmen on the other hand.

The trouble began on the evening of 8 August, when a white nurse who had once served with the Third Virginia was beaten up by a black teamster in a fight that occurred near a hospital, and close to where the regiment was encamped. When they heard the news of the fight, a group of about 65 soldiers and civilians who were mostly Virginians chased after the black teamster shouting, "Lynch him! Hang him!" He managed to elude his pursuers, who suddenly found themselves facing General Butler and his staff, who had ridden up to quell the disturbance. Butler immediately ordered the arrest of three men, confined the regiment to camp, and dispatched a Connecticut regiment to guard the Virginians. Incensed over what they considered unjust punishment of the Third Virginia, local newspapers, along with the attorney general of Virginia, condemned Butler's action. Pressured by two Virginia Congressmen, the War Department ordered General Graham to conduct a court of inquiry.[192] Graham, who also had received an appeal from the colonel of the Third Virginia for a court of inquiry, appointed Summerall as court reporter with the responsibility of presenting and recording the evidence. When the court convened, Summerall noted the presence of a number of prominent men who had come to support the Third Virginia and its commander. They included the two U.S. Senators from the state, the vigilant attorney general, Congressmen (probably those who had put pressure on the War Department), and "a very able attorney from Washington who conducted the defense." Awed by the challenge of presenting and recording the evidence, Summerall hired additional court stenographers and gratefully accepted the offer of General J. P. S. Gobin, the adjutant general of the Pennsylvania militia, to assist him as recorder. According to Summerall, many witnesses were called by the regiment and by General Butler, and the evidence and testimony "filled several volumes." In his own testimony, Butler "often became so violent in his attack upon the regiment," reported Summerall, "that I would ask the court to recess to let him become quiet."[193] In its finding the court exonerated the Third Virginia, but the decision was not published until September, after the Second Corps had left Camp Alger. By this time, among local citizens and national politicians the reputation and standing of the army and in particular of the Second Corps again had been tarnished and diminished.[194]

Responding quite likely to criticism from angry Virginians, and certainly to the admonition of commanding General Miles that the "fever-ridden camps of the United States be abandoned," Secretary Alger decided to relocate the Second Corps once again. He ordered the First Division to leave the Crittenden farm and move by train to Camp George G. Meade, named after the victor of Gettysburg, located near Middletown, in southeastern Pennsylvania. Next, he ordered the Second Division to leave Thoroughfare Gap and travel by rail to join the First Division at Camp Meade, where General Graham and his staff, who had remained at Camp Alger, would join the reunited command. The transfer from Virginia was completed by the end of August, and, much to the delight of the local population, Camp Alger was no more.[195]

The men arrived at Camp Meade depressed and demoralized. The United States and Spain signed a peace protocol on 12 August, ending all hostilities. Newspapers reported that a majority of Second Corps personnel wanted nothing more to do with the army, and wished only to go home. They were sick and tired of drills, false rumors of impending action, and marches to nowhere. As Hartley said, instead of getting ready "for a sojourn in Cuba, the Philippines or Hawaii," they had spent their days "tramping the same old drill ground," and "staging another practice march." For Aaron Hartley's brother Charles, the inactivity of the army became "tiresome in the extreme." He wrote that "To lie in one's tent and look out over the parched parade ground and see nothing but a soldier in blue moving listlessly along positively makes the eye tired." For him and his fellow soldiers, nothing broke the monotony of camp life. It was, he continued, "the same old grind, day in and day out." This grinding monotony hardened the attitude of the men toward those suffering and dying from the ravages of typhoid. As Charles Hartley wrote, "when a man gets sick enough he lies down and dies, he is buried and that is the end of the matter, so far as the impression made on the minds of the soldiers."[196]

At Camp Meade, soldiers from other camps joined the men of the Second Corps, swelling the population to over 40,000. The newer arrivals were just as downcast, bored, and disgusted as their longer-serving comrades, and, unfortunately, brought with them fresh typhoid germs from their previous encampments. By the time most of the men of the Second Corps finally left at the end of September, the sickness rate had risen from below 4 percent in Virginia to 11 percent at Camp Meade. Water and provisions were scarce, but, as Hartley stated, "we are getting used to such treatment and don't much care as we are going home in a few weeks like a lot of stampeded cattle. The Devil himself can not stop us when we get started for home. And may the good Lord keep another war from braking [sic] out while I live. I don't like anything that smells of war."[197] Finally, following the approval of the Peace of Paris by the Senate on 6 February 1899, the last soldiers left Camp Meade and headed for their homes. On 30 March 1899, it was closed, thus ending the hard times and many disappointments of the men of the Second Corps.

Among the most disappointed was undoubtedly General Graham. Instead of leading soldiers into battle and on to victory, as he had done in the Civil War, he had been ordered to train thousands of raw and ill-disciplined recruits, who were forced to march to escape disease rather than to confront and defeat his country's enemy. Later, testifying before the Dodge Commission, which had been set up by President McKinley to investigate the army's administration during the war, he described his struggle against typhoid and confessed that he "failed to do what I ought to have done."[198] For Summerall, who wrote that Graham himself had contracted the disease in November 1898, his mentor's work was heroic. "The task of organizing, training and caring for thousands of helpless and sick boys, most of whom were under age, was overwhelming," said Summerall. He insisted, "That some order and sanitation with reasonable food and shelter were obtained was due in the greatest measure to the indomitable spirit, high standards and broad experience of General Graham." Aware of the difficulties and hazards they faced, Summerall reflected that "His [Graham's] staff labored incessantly. Three of them had typhoid and one died. It is remarkable that any of us escaped."[199]

The only bright spots for Summerall in the dismal and disappointing summer of 1898 were the letters he received from "Miss Mordecai," with whom he had corresponded "intensely," and the chances to call on her in Washington when she came to the capital to visit relatives and to see Charles. In his memoir, he recorded that "There could be no thought about our future, for I was not in a financial position to marry." Yet they must have thought about and discussed the present situation and their future together, for in the next sentence he stated that "She accepted the conditions bravely."[200] He did not explain what these "conditions" were at that time. One circumstance they must have discussed, and one that certainly quickened their conversation, rested on the outcome of his third attempt to secure an appointment in the ordnance branch of the army.

Sometime in early July, he asked General Graham once more to endorse his request for the appointment. From Camp Alger on 9 July, Graham wrote Adjutant General H. C. Corbin, praising his aide-de-camp's abilities and performance on several levels and recommending Summerall's "appointment to one of the vacancies in the Corps of Volunteer Ordnance officers just created."[201] Taking advantage of his proximity to the capital, Summerall rushed from Camp Alger to Washington to deliver personally the letter to the Adjutant General's Office. That accomplished, he called on Florida Congressman S. M. Sparkman, and presented him with a letter requesting him to "use your influence with the Adjutant General of the Army" to secure Summerall's appointment as an "ordnance officer of volunteers with the rank of major."[202] Sparkman hurriedly wrote Adjutant General Corbin, endorsing Summerall's request and included the letter Summerall wrote to him.[203] Then Summerall must have rushed to the office of Florida Senator S. M. Mallory asking for his help, for also on 9 July Mallory wrote Corbin strongly supporting Summerall's request.[204] Why, for the third time, did Summerall seek appointment to the ordnance branch and work feverishly to secure it, even if this meant transferring from the Regular Army to a corps of volunteers, the kind of soldiers he had regarded with such scorn during the railroad strike in California? Certainly one reason for him to seek the more rapid promotion and increased pay that prevailed in the ordnance branch was the continuing dependency on his support of the families of his sister and brother.

An additional and more pressing reason involved his relationship with Laura Mordecai. In spite of his assertion to the contrary, in their intense correspondence and during their visits together in Washington, they must have discussed marriage and the possibility of his appointment in the ordnance branch. Appointment in that branch to a higher rank, coupled with the support from his future father-in-law, who remained an influential ordnance officer, could lead to the rapid promotion that would hasten the day of their marriage. His frantic campaign to win the appointment is indicative of just how eager and strong was their desire for marriage, and how desperately he worked to make it possible. Despite pressing hard with every advantage he could muster, the transfer never came through.

It seems clear that this failure was the disappointing blow that caused Summerall to record plaintively that "There could be no thought about our future, for I was not in a financial position to marry." This present condition and the realization he would remain in that position for a long time would seem to be the most immediate and decisive of the "conditions" that she accepted "bravely." That he omitted from his memoir a mention of this brief but intensive pursuit appears strange. Not long after it occurred he rejoined Reilly's Battery "K" and set sail for the Philippines and then to China, where the excitement of fierce fighting and fortuitous fame awaited. Perhaps, as he gathered his thoughts to record these adventures in the Far East, the memory of this intense pursuit had been swept aside. Perhaps also, he might have found it too remorseful and poignant to reveal the final, failed opportunity for them to be married before a continent and an ocean separated them for years to come. Then too, as he grew older and became hardened against any admission of failure, he could have decided to omit altogether an episode that represented a stunning and painful personal setback. As an old and aging widower, still in mourning after the death some seven years before of the woman who became his beloved wife of 46 years, he could take some consolation from the fact that the long years of their separation were among the most exciting and influential of this career, and had ended at long last with the great happiness of his marriage to Laura.

For the rest of the desultory and disappointing summer and fall of 1898, Summerall remained with General Graham at Camp Meade while the Second Corps gradually disbanded. Following his testimony before the Dodge Commission, General Graham retired from the army on 11 November 1898, and Summerall was relieved as his aide-de-camp and reassigned to the Department of the Gulf in Atlanta as aide-de-camp to Brigadier General A. C. M. Pennington. For the next five months his primary duty was to assist General Pennington on trips to inspect the condition of army facilities like rifle ranges, barracks, warehouses, and other government buildings used by the army.[205]

Toward the end of the month of March 1899, Summerall traveled to Fort Monroe, Virginia, where he was examined for promotion to first lieutenant. This examination went well, much better than the previous ones he had taken for assignment to the ordnance branch. He won the promotion, effective 2 March, and his pay was increased to $166.67 per month, a sum that "greatly helped me meet my financial obligations, including my sister's family." He noted that during his second stay in Atlanta, he visited often with friends he had made while serving there under General Graham, but failed to mention any contact with his brother, even though William lived with his family in Atlanta and presumably continued to practice medicine there.[206] Perhaps William no longer needed his younger brother's assistance, or perhaps the lingering dependency of the older brother upon the financial support of the younger had strained their relationship and had created a distance between them. At any rate, with his promotion in hand, Summerall turned to face the question of his next assignment in the army.

General Pennington's retirement was imminent, and thus Summerall soon would no longer be detailed as his aide-de-camp. Perhaps he hoped to remain in Atlanta and also to capitalize on his service as a court recorder and as a member of a courts-martial. When the post of acting judge advocate for the Department of the Gulf became open, Pennington requested Adjutant General Corbin to designate Summerall to the position, and added a rather expansive tribute to Summerall, stating that he had "received his promotion as first lieutenant...for increasing the efficiency of the army of the United States."[207] Summerall also requested support for the assignment from his prominent friend in San Francisco, Winfield S. Jones. From his desk at the Security Savings Bank, Jones wrote the adjutant general recalling an earlier visit to Corbin's office when he had requested assistance in having

Summerall promoted. In his letter Jones reminded Corbin of his remark on that occasion that he "would be pleased to aid him when the time came to act." In the excessively humble and solicitous manner of address of that time, Jones stated that he regretted "being among the number taking up yr [sic] valuable time, but Lt. Summerall is an especial friend & a most deserving young officer & being much interested in his welfare I take the liberty of asking for him the detail as acting Judge Advocate." He closed by cautiously reminding Corbin that "My father, the late Genl [sic] Roger Jones, once filled the Office you now occupy & I naturally feel an interest in the Adjutant Genl's [sic] Department & have perhaps less reluctance to seek a favor at the hands of its Chief Officer than of some other branch of the service [like the Ordnance Branch, perhaps]."[208] Before the adjutant general could act on these official and unofficial requests on behalf of this "most deserving young officer," events far across the Pacific caused others to take steps that would lead the young lieutenant on a course that neither he, General Pennington, nor Winfield Jones had envisioned.

The course that Summerall had followed during his first four years of service in the army had led him back and forth across the country from coast to coast, and had fixed in his mind models and experiences that would influence the long course of his life and career. He was pleased and excited with his initial duty assignment along the shore of the magnificent expanse of San Francisco Bay. There at The Presidio, he soon found models for his own conduct as an army officer. First stood William Montrose Graham, mentor and example of a proud and uncompromising disciplinarian, faithful supporter and ally of those who gave him loyal service, and inexhaustible in his performance of his duties. Summerall remained fiercely loyal to Graham, strongly endorsing his actions against the railroad strikers in California, and vigorously defending his command of the Second Corps during the long, hot summer of 1898. Second was Henry J. Reilly, who quickly attracted Summerall's attention at The Presidio, and became one of his ideals in the art of commanding arms and men. Both men were sober, serious-minded professionals, and Summerall revered them throughout his life.

Equally important was the value his superiors placed on Lieutenant Summerall's service and abilities. General Graham gave him demanding assignments and responsibilities, and rated his performance as excellent. Colonel Shafter, who had never met Summerall, noted that he had heard of his ability, and rejected his request for transfer because he did not want to lose him. When Graham moved up to command Second Corps, he kept Summerall at his side as aide-de-camp. He seems to have been as devoted to Summerall and his welfare as the young lieutenant was to him. He was ever willing to recommend Summerall (although he, like Shafter, certainly did not want to lose him), for the transfers he hoped would speed up his promotion. While Summerall was winning the praise and loyalty of his superior officers, he found comradeship and support in the broader world as well.

In San Francisco, he was welcomed into an influential circle of society and won the friendship of Winfield S. Jones, one of the city's most prominent bankers. With his "friend" and her daughter from Tuxedo Park, and especially in the company of Jones and his nephew, Summerall enjoyed the glitter and splendor of the booming times around the bay and moved easily within the higher circles of San Francisco society. He valued the friendship and support of Winfield Jones and through him understood how men of wealth and prominence could use their positions to advance his career. However, as he learned more about the splendors and powers of wealth and prominence, Summerall remained faithful to the example set by his parents and always placed his family's welfare above any consideration of his own pleasure and comfort. When his final and frenetic attempt to secure the transfer to ordnance failed, he realized that his marriage to Laura Mordecai had to wait. It was a painful decision, but he bore it with his customary fortitude, and she patiently accepted it with quiet understanding, with neither of them knowing what lay ahead. It is to these years, which would test further their fortitude and forbearance, that we now turn.

# Chapter Four

## *The Philippines*

While Summerall and his fellow officers and men of the Second Corps were fighting battles against boredom and disease in their festering encampments at home, his former commanders and comrades at the Presidio were experiencing their baptism of fire against the army of Spain in Cuba. On 20 June 1898, Major General William R. Shafter, with First Lieutenant John Miley, Laura Mordecai's brother-in-law at his side as aide-de-camp, led ashore some 17,000 men in a landing area just to the west of Guantanamo Bay and some 15 miles southeast of the port of Santiago de Cuba.[1] Shafter's force had been assembled in Tampa, Florida, and designated the Fifth Army Corps. It was made up mostly of Regular Army regiments, and included the 1st U.S. Volunteer Cavalry, the "Rough Riders," recruited and commanded by Lieutenant Colonel Theodore Roosevelt. They were ordered to help destroy the remaining vessels in the Spanish squadron of Admiral Pascual Cervera y Topete that had been trapped in Santiago Bay by ships of Admiral William Sampson's North Atlantic Squadron.

Shafter formed his corps into three divisions that advanced northwestward toward Santiago de Cuba and attacked Spanish positions along the San Juan Heights above the city. One division commanded by Major General Henry Lawton encountered surprisingly tough resistance from 500 Spanish defenders manning fortifications at El Caney before capturing the position on 1 July. General Joseph Wheeler's division attacked along the northeastern extension of the Heights, concentrating their assault upon a rise known as Kettle Hill.[2] Under orders from Lieutenant Miley, who had been sent forward by General Shafter to coordinate operations in the area, they charged up the Heights toward Kettle Hill. Spurred on by the exploits of Roosevelt and his "Rough Riders," the Americans seized the position on 1 July.[3] On 3 July, Cervera's six ships tried to steam through Sampson's blockade; five were sunk and the other, the *Cristobal Colon*, managed to escape from the harbor, only to be driven ashore by its commander when the pursuing American ships and guns found its range. Shafter laid siege to Santiago de Cuba, and on 17 July, the city's commander, General Jose Toral, capitulated. On 25 July, the commanding general of the army, General Nelson Miles, landed with an expeditionary force on the south shore of the island of Puerto Rico, captured the city of San Juan, and by 28 July, had taken possession of the entire island. A few weeks later, Spain agreed to a protocol signed on 12 August that ended hostilities and marked the end of the rule of Spain over lands that Christopher Columbus had claimed for Their Catholic Majesties Ferdinand and Isabella over 400 years before.[4]

Summerall's other colleagues and commanders from his days at the Presidio arrived in Cuba too late to join the fight for the San Juan Heights, or assist in the siege of Santiago de Cuba. Sailing from Tampa on 3 July, Captain Henry J. Reilly's Light Battery F, 5th Artillery, arrived at the landing area a week after the fall of the Cuban city, and was ordered to march inland to reinforce the American position at El Caney.⁵ They were bivouacked amidst the rich tropical growth in the hills overlooking the city with other batteries that were formed into a light battery battalion of U.S. Volunteers. There they remained in their hot and heavy khaki uniforms until late August, under the oppressive tropical heat and drenching rain of the summer sky. During the day, after they had fought off scorpions that crawled into their boots at night, they spent most of their time tending to their horses debilitated by hoof ailments caused by standing in the heat, rain, and sodden soil. Toward the end of August, about 70 men of the battery, led by second lieutenants Warren Newcomb and Manus McCloskey, retraced their march and embarked for home on board the auxiliary cruiser *Resolute*. Captain Reilly remained in Cuba for a few extra days, assembling the balance of the battery personnel, the guns, horses, and supplies before embarking on the transport *Specialist*. In early September, the detachments of the battery arrived at Montauk Point, Long Island, New York. In order to prevent the spread of yellow fever, which many returning soldiers had contracted in Cuba, they were assembled and then held there at Camp Wikoff, named for an officer who had been killed in the fight for San Juan Heights. On 19 September, the detachments of the battery were moved along the tracks of the Long Island Railroad to Fort Hamilton, where they were reunited under their captain. There, they remained for the rest of the year and into the spring of 1899, occasionally breaking their routines of garrison duty by participating in military displays of horsemanship in Madison Square Garden.⁶ Meanwhile, Charles Summerall, the battery's former second lieutenant, newly promoted in March to the rank of first lieutenant, languished in Atlanta.

Although, as noted above, Summerall was encouraged by his recent promotion, he was disappointed by his failure to secure the post of acting judge advocate of the Department of the Gulf, and, as a result, saddened by the necessity to postpone indefinitely any plans for marriage to Laura Mordecai. But, across the Pacific, far from the frustrations and disappointments of Summerall's life in Atlanta, and even farther from the rarely interrupted boredom of life at Fort Hamilton, the battle for the Philippine Island possessions of the old empire of Spain was well under way. Soon, this struggle would unite Summerall and his old battery in the first of two Asian adventures that would thrill and exhaust many of his comrades, end in disappointment and tragedy for some of those who were closest to him, and fill the new first lieutenant with renewed optimism for his professional success and with it, fresh hope for his personal happiness.

The Philippine archipelago of over 7,000 islands covers an area of 180,000 square miles, with a land area of just over 115,000 square miles, or slightly larger than Arizona. At the end of the 19th century it contained a population of 7,600,000, with about half of the population living on the island of Luzon, the largest and most important island, with about 35 percent of the land, and the site of the capital city of Manila. Five separate tribes, all speaking different languages, inhabited the island, and among them relations were often strained and violent. Along the coast of Luzon were large swamps, clusters of mangroves, and stands of nipa palm that stretched between magnificent bays and harbors. Inland were thickly forested mountains, jungles, sprawling upland lakes, rolling prairies of tall grasses, and numerous swiftly flowing rivers and streams. The tropical climate, the monsoon rains that pour down from June to October, and the persistent heat and heavy humidity, made life difficult for those unaccustomed to such conditions. During the rainy season, tropical diseases like malaria, dengue fever, and dysentery could be debilitating and life-threatening. Roads connected the important towns, but they were poorly maintained and almost impassable during the monsoon season. Travel along the coast and on lakes and rivers on boats and barges called *cascos* often was the most secure and safe transportation.⁷

The capital city of Manila is located about 4,300 miles west/southwest of Honolulu and 700 miles south/southeast of Hong Kong, and rests at the edge of the water on the eastern shore of the eponymous

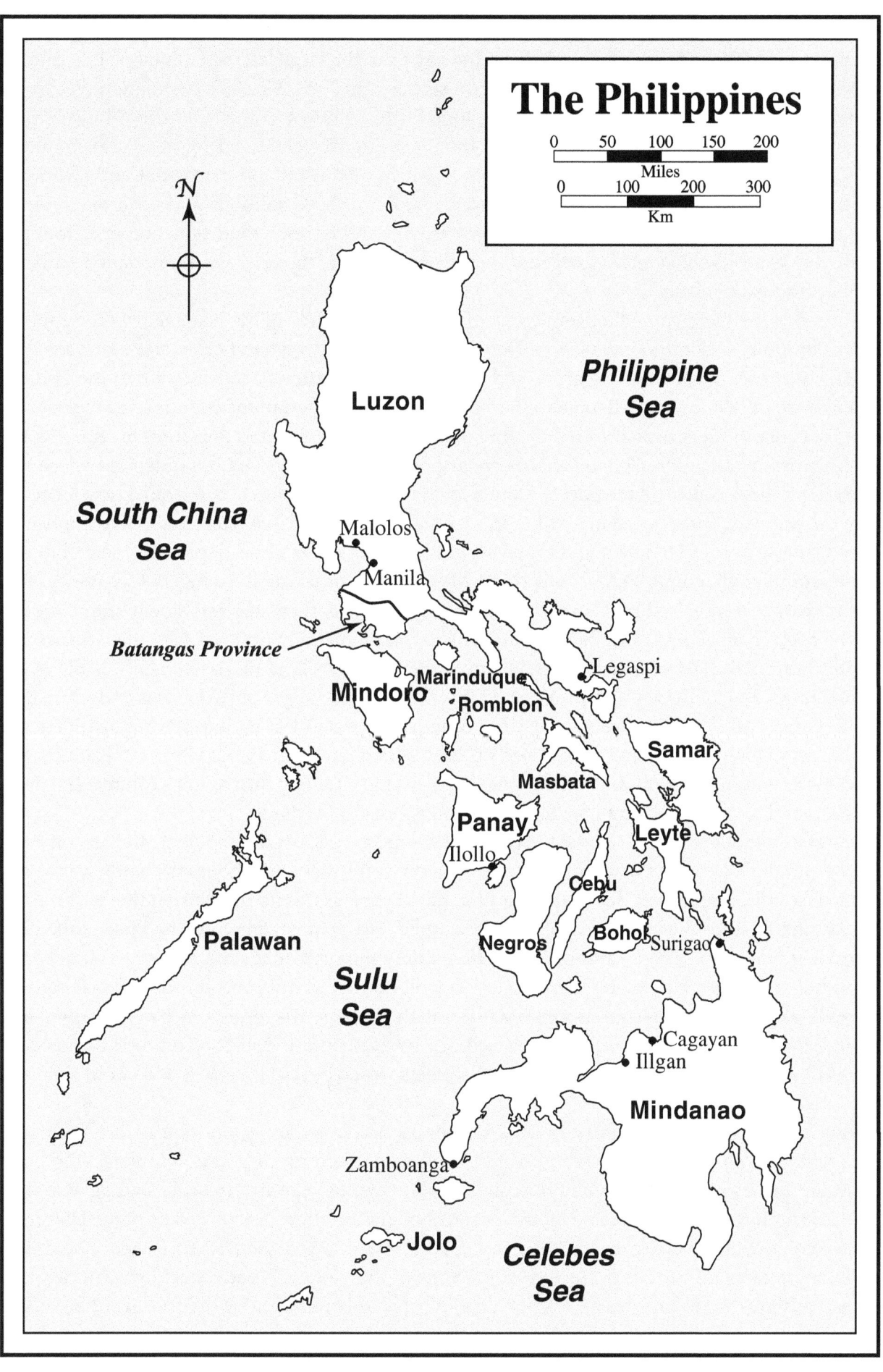

bay. The Pasig River flowed through the city into the bay from the large lake of Laguna de Bay, about eight miles to the east, and divided the city into two sections. In 1898, Manila's population was over 300,000, and its center was dominated by a large stone fortress known as the "Old City," built in the 18th century along the bay on the south bank of the river. Suburbs clustered for about seven miles north and south of the fortress and extended only about two miles inland across flat and swampy land. To defend Manila, the Spanish had stationed fewer than 13,000 soldiers, and positioned more than 100 guns around the city, but these weapons were old and in poor condition, and only four of them were modern breechloaders.[8] As events soon were to prove, the city was vulnerable to attack from the bay and from inland.

The United States had planned for some time to strike the first blow of the war against the Spanish fleet in the Philippines. Commodore George Dewey's Asiatic Squadron had been stationed in the Far East for this purpose. In contrast, the army had no plans for operations against Spain in the Philippines.[9] However, in 1896, a young lieutenant had proposed a campaign in the Islands as part of a war with Spain in order to apply pressure on the vulnerable colonial outpost, and thus force the Spanish to stop fighting and make peace. This is what Secretary of the Navy John D. Long intended when he proposed later to seize control of the port of Manila and thereby force Spain to come quickly to terms.[10]

When the war with Spain began in April 1898, Dewey's squadron of five cruisers and two gunboats was at the Chinese port of Hong Kong on the end of the Pacific cable. On 27 April, they left Chinese waters and around midnight on 30 April sailed into Manila Bay, dismissing the danger of sea mines laid across its narrow entrance. Led by Dewey in his flagship *Olympia*, they steamed slowly into the bay through the deep channel past Corregidor Island. About 0500 hours on Sunday, 1 May, they turned to starboard in front of the city of Manila as shells fired from the city's batteries passed harmlessly over their smokestacks. Two of Dewey's ships returned fire. However, Dewey's objective was to destroy the rather antiquated and decrepit Spanish squadron of two cruisers and five gunboats commanded by Admiral Patricio Montojo, anchored dead ahead off the fortified naval yard of Cavite. At 0540 hours, as *Olympia* came to within five thousand yards of the Spanish ships, Dewey turned to its commander and said in a clear and calm voice, "'You may fire when you are ready, Gridley.'"[11]

In the fight that followed, Dewey's ships proved far superior in speed, firepower, and armor, and their crews, although lacking in marksmanship, were more skillful. By 1230 hours the battle was over. The Spanish squadron had been decimated and the naval yard at Cavite had surrendered. Three of Admiral Montojo's ships were sunk and six were scuttled; 161 Spanish crewmen had been killed in action, and 210 wounded. Dewey's ships had suffered only minor damage; no Americans had been killed, and only nine men had been wounded. Dewey blockaded Manila and informed Washington that he could take the city if he were supplied with enough soldiers. His report reached the capital on 7 May, but American officials had already learned of Dewey's stunning victory from press reports. President William McKinley decided that American soldiers would be sent to seize Manila from Spanish rule.[12]

Fighting against Spanish authority in the Philippines had been going on long before Dewey's squadron sailed into Manila Bay. It started in the 1890s when a group of young Filipinos, who had been educated in Europe, organized a nationalist rebellion against Spanish misrule, and against the economic and political power exercised by the major Roman Catholic religious orders of the Dominicans, Augustinians, and Franciscans. In 1892, young nationalists organized a secret society called the Katipunan, a Malay word meaning "Society of the Sons of the People." It advocated violent revolution and secretly worked to prepare for a rebellion against Spanish rule and to achieve eventual independence. They appealed mostly to the Filipino masses, and their most important base of support was among the members of the Tagalog tribe in the province of Cavite, south of Manila.[13]

In August 1896, Spanish authorities discovered a Katipunan plot to massacre Spanish officials, to be followed by a general uprising. The leader of the conspiracy fled to the hills, but his followers immediately began attacks on the Spanish garrison in Cavite. Regional animosities and personal conflict among their leaders weakened the movement, and the rebels repeatedly failed to capitalize on their successes. But, in early November, and under the command of a young man of mixed Tagalog and Chinese blood named Emilio Aguinaldo y Famy, the rebels repulsed a Spanish attack and inflicted heavy casualties on their enemy.

Aguinaldo came from a prosperous family of landowners and had studied law in Manila. As a municipal captain in his community of Kawit, he had led the local militia against bandits. But, resisting Spanish rule and the refusal of the government to reward his service with higher office and authority, he joined the Katipunan. His victories over the Spanish troops elevated him to leadership of the insurgent movement. On 5 November 1896, he declared the Philippines independent, announced that he was now the president, and called for a popular uprising against Spain. For the next few months, Aguinaldo led sporadic guerilla attacks on Spanish detachments, but the Spanish besieged his guerilla bands in the mountains, where disease and hunger had decimated their ranks. Yet, the Spanish were also under strength and exhausted, and in December they proposed a truce that Aguinaldo promptly accepted. Subsequent negotiations produced an agreement that Spain would reform the government of the Islands and pay an indemnity of 800,000 Mexican pesos in three installments to the rebel treasury; in return, Aguinaldo and 27 of his key followers would be banished to Hong Kong. The truce between the Kapitunan and Spain did not last long. The rebels claimed that Spain, even though Madrid paid the indemnity, had done nothing to reform its rule of the Islands, and in March and April 1898, they renewed their attacks on the Spanish in Luzon.[14]

Meanwhile, in Hong Kong, a Kapitunan-American entente seemed to be emerging. Aguinaldo and his men saw renewed hope for their cause in the approaching war between Spain and the United States. As Dewey prepared for war with Spain and a possible assault on Manila, he saw in Aguinaldo and his men a means to rally Filipinos against the oppression of Spanish rule, and to hasten the end of the war in Cuba. Meetings were arranged in Hong Kong between Aguinaldo and the American consul general E. Spencer Pratt. During the discussions, the Kapitunan leader came to believe Pratt had promised that fighting on the side of the Americans against the common enemy would win the support of the United States for Philippine independence. Upon his return to the Philippines, Aguinaldo insisted that Dewey had confirmed Pratt's pledge, while Dewey insisted that no one had made such a promise. At any rate, Dewey lent his prestige and the services of an American steamer to transport Aguinaldo and his men to the Philippines, along with over 2,000 rifles that the U.S. consul had purchased in Hong Kong for the use of their fellow insurgents.[15]

Aguinaldo's party landed in Cavite on 19 May, rapidly raised an army of 15,000 men, and equipped them with rifles supplied by the Americans and captured from Spanish arsenals. Sweeping through southern Luzon, Aguinaldo's guerilla forces swiftly defeated Spanish detachments. On 23 May, he proclaimed himself dictator for the duration of the crisis, and, as the month ended, began making preparations for an assault on Manila.[16]

In the meantime, Commodore Dewey waited on the *Olympia* for the arrival of American soldiers. As noted above, Secretary of the Navy Long had planned to capture Manila to force Spain to come to terms quickly and thus shorten the war. Neither at this point nor in the early stages of the conflict in the Philippines did Washington show any interest in annexing the Islands.[17]

On 12 May, the day before Commodore Dewey's promotion to the rank of rear admiral, the Administration appointed Major General Wesley Merritt, a veteran of the Civil War and the second ranking officer in the army, to command the expedition to the Philippines. McKinley's orders for the expedition called for continuing the reduction of Spanish power in the area and for United States forces to establish order and security in the Islands. According to historians T. Harry Williams, Graham Cosmas, David Trask, and Brian Linn, the president had yet to decide upon a long-term policy for the Philippines. Yet, he had determined that Merritt should establish a military government that would sever ties between the Spanish and the Filipinos, protect the inhabitants and their property, guarantee individual rights, and promote trade and commerce. So that he could avoid any long-term commitments or entanglements, the president also decided not to recognize Aguinaldo's insurgents, as previously he had refused to recognize those in Cuba.[18]

After considerable discussion and debate between the War Department and Merritt over the size of the Philippine expedition, they agreed upon an initial force of some 10,000 to 12,000 men. Designated as the Eighth Corps and consisting of regular and volunteer components, they gathered in good order at San Francisco, and set out for the Philippines in three main groups. The first, consisting of 2,491 officers and men, and commanded by Brigadier General Thomas M. Anderson, left on 25 May; the second contingent of 3,500 under Brigadier Francis V. Greene, sailed on 15 June; the third group of 4,600 with Brigadier General Arthur MacArthur in command, and with General Merritt on board, steamed westward through the Golden Gate during the period 25–29 June.[19]

In the meantime, Aguinaldo's men had captured all of the scattered Spanish garrisons in the provinces around Manila, and had begun to besiege the city. On 12 June, Aguinaldo formally had proclaimed the independence of the Philippines with himself as head of a revolutionary committee, set up municipal and provincial administrations, organized various departments of government, and formed his first cabinet.[20]

On 30 June, General Anderson arrived with the vanguard of the American force, disembarked his men at the naval base at Cavite, and on 1 July met with Aguinaldo. The meeting did not go well. As instructed, Anderson would not recognize Aguinaldo's government or cooperate with him in besieging Manila. Although Aguinaldo initially had viewed the Americans as friends, he now considered their presence a danger to the successful conclusion of his military campaign and to the establishment of his government in Manila. Subsequently, Anderson reported that Aguinaldo was trying to stop supplies from reaching the Americans, and that the Filipino leader had tightened the siege of Manila, hoping to capture the city before any more Americans landed. When Merritt arrived late in July, he refused to meet or speak with the revolutionary leader, and immediately began planning an assault on Manila that would exclude all of Aguinaldo's forces.[21] This would be difficult, however, since the rebels surrounded the city and stood between the Americans and Spanish forces. Help came from an unexpected source.

Early in August, from inside the capital, the ruling Spanish official, Governor General Don Fermin Jáudenes y Alvarez, realized that with Dewey's squadron sealing the harbor and with Filipinos and Americans blocking off the city from reinforcements and supplies from its landside, any further resistance was hopeless. He let Dewey know that he preferred to surrender to the Americans and not to the Filipinos, for, as Graham Cosmas states, Jáudenes and his men feared retaliation by the insurgents for previous Spanish atrocities.[22] With Dewey and Merritt, Jáudenes arranged for a "mock battle," during which only Americans and no Filipinos would attack the outer defenses of the city, while Dewey in the *Olympia* would steam toward the city flying signal flags demanding surrender. Having resisted, and with his honor intact, Jáudenes then would surrender to the Americans. Merritt informed Aguinaldo on 12 August that his forces would not be allowed to enter Manila.

On 13 August, the "battle" began, and unfolded in a driving rainstorm according to plan, with all three of the American contingents attacking Spanish positions in the suburbs of the city. From muddy trenches and blockhouses, the Spanish fought hard, and both sides suffered casualties. With greater firepower and fire support from the navy, the Americans broke through Spanish resistance and into the heart of the city by late morning. In defiance of Merritt's instructions, insurgents attacked Spanish positions in the suburbs, and occupied them when the Spanish withdrew into the heart of the city. Around 1130 hours, sighting Dewey's signal flags, Jáudenes hoisted a white flag and Manila fell to the Americans. Aguinaldo's angry insurgents confronted the Americans and demanded to join in the occupation of the city. Negotiations calmed the situation, and a temporary settlement provided for the Americans to control the inner city and Aguinaldo's men to occupy the suburbs.

While both sides awaited further developments, news arrived on 16 August that the war between Spain and the United States had ended four days earlier. The protocol had been signed on 12 August and provided for an immediate cease-fire; the cession by Spain of Puerto Rico and Guam to the United States; and the relinquishing of Spanish sovereignty over Cuba, with the Americans and Cuban insurgents to decide the eventual political fate of the island. Spain agreed to the continuing American occupation of the city of Manila and its bay, pending a final settlement on the future of the Islands. That issue would be determined by a peace conference to begin on 1 October in Paris.[23]

For the rest of the year, while Spanish and American negotiators deliberated in Paris, a virtual state of siege existed between Aguinaldo's men and the Eighth Corps. The insurgents built new field fortifications in the suburbs, occasionally disrupted the water supply to the city, harassed American outposts, and even shot and killed an American sentry. Merritt's tight control of his men prevented further hostilities, but he was anxious to leave, and was pleased when his request for relief was granted late in August. He was reassigned to advise the peace delegation in Paris. He was succeeded by Major General Elwell S. Otis, a rather pedantic and moody officer, not well liked in the army, but a commander whose forces in the Islands were never to be defeated. When "Judged by conventional standards of military victory," according to historian Linn, Otis won the Philippine War.[24]

In Manila, Otis concentrated on strengthening his position. He used his soldiers, increasingly made up of State volunteers arriving in the city from the United States, to staff the departments of the military government, to police the streets and neighborhoods of the city, repair and rebuild roads and bridges, and improve the city's lighting and water systems. At times unruly and even hostile toward their Regular Army officers, the volunteers nevertheless performed well in their military/civilian tasks, and when the time came to fight in the field, they proved to be spirited and courageous soldiers.[25]

Aguinaldo, in the meantime, worked to consolidate his insurgents around Manila into a cohesive and conventional Regular Army. He called his force the Army of Liberation of the Philippines and organized it into battalions and divisions with units divided into line and light infantry, cavalry, or artillery. Essentially, it remained a loosely federated militia consisting of municipal volunteers under local leaders. As officers of this army, its leaders generally viewed their commands as personal and exempt from orders from the chain of command, particularly if family status and connections had placed them in the higher ranks. Through excessive demands and requisitions they exacted from villages and municipalities, they abused their authority and turned against them the very people they were supposed to protect. Aguinaldo wanted to fight a guerilla war, but they convinced him to fight a conventional one, even though they knew very little about how to fight such a war, and never trained their men in conventional warfare tactics such as maneuvering in formation or fighting in coherent units. According to historian Linn, Aguinaldo's officers were "the most glaring weakness in the Army of Liberation."[26] However, its infantry was made up of tough and durable men, who could move rapidly in rugged mountain terrain, nimbly cut their way through plains of cogon grass four to six feet high, and move through the dense tropical jungles of the Islands. They fought well when they were protected by field fortifications, but they lacked artillery, their rifles and ammunition were inferior, their marksmanship was poor, and when they managed to capture modern rifles like Mausers, they never learned to use them effectively.[27]

As the tense standoff continued in Manila, negotiators in Paris neared agreement on a peace treaty. In the United States the weight of public opinion, the commercial and territorial ambitions of those who wanted to establish an American empire, and feelings of national pride and altruism expressed by President McKinley, led to his decision to annex the Islands. After the Spanish protested that the United States had no claim by right of conquest, and had not even taken control of Manila, the American side offered the Spanish compensation of $20 million. They accepted the financial offer, and on 10 December, the Treaty of Paris was signed. It added Puerto Rico, Guam, and the Philippine Islands to the territory of the United States.[28]

As noted previously, the president had justified, in part, the acquisition of the Islands on altruistic principles, stating that Americans should "educate the Filipinos, and uplift and civilize and Christianize them, and by God's grace do the very best we could by them."[29] Accordingly, he ordered Otis to extend the military government "with all possible dispatch to the whole of the ceded territory." Through its conduct and authority the army was to "'win the confidence, respect, and affection of the inhabitants,'" and in this process, demonstrate "'that the mission of the United States is one of benevolent assimilation, substituting the mild sway of justice and right for arbitrary rule.'"[30] In Linn's view, McKinley's policy of "'benevolent assimilation'" was of "vital importance." It made clear the United States' claim to the entire island chain, ruling out the possibility for national or regional independence, and assigned to the army the dual task of establishing the authority and lawful rule of the United States and "protecting Filipino lives, property, and civil rights." In other words, the United States Army now had the job not only of achieving peace, but also of making sure that peace was secured and sustained.[31] This was the first time, but not the last time that American soldiers would be ordered to win the war and maintain the peace, as the mission of the army in post World War II Europe and Asia, as well as in the Balkans, Afghanistan, and Iraq in recent years has proven.

Aguinaldo also faced a difficult course of action as he prepared to resist American control. On 23 January, in the town of Malolos, about 20 miles north of Manila (see map, p. 65), he proclaimed the Philippine Republic and established a strongly centralized government. This action inspired and emboldened his forces around Manila, and strengthened the nationalist movement in Luzon. However, many landowners, professionals, and businessmen preferred a more federal system that shared power between the central government and the provinces. Some even advocated an accommodation with the United States rather than independence. In addition, thus far Aguinaldo had not been able to extend his authority beyond Luzon. With the United States determined to exert its authority over the entire archipelago, with Luzon as his only island base, with prominent interests divided in their support of independence, and with an army ill-suited to fight a conventional war against an army equipped and trained to fight this kind of war, Aguinaldo's mission to achieve independence appeared even more daunting than the difficult dual mission of the American army. As Linn observed, Aguinaldo's declaration of independence "was essentially a hollow gesture."[32] Nevertheless, as T. Harry Williams stated, Aguinaldo and his followers "had not entered on their revolution merely to exchange one foreign master for another."[33]

In Manila, as the talks between Otis and Aguinaldo stalled and then collapsed, tensions increased. Fights and scuffles between Filipino and American soldiers broke out in the city's streets and racial slurs were shouted back and forth. Soon, firing erupted between opposing outposts, and in the early morning hours of Sunday, 4 February, Filipinos and Americans began shooting at each other from positions all around the city. Full-scale war broke out as American commanders launched an all-out offensive against the enemy.[34] The second battle of Manila had begun.

Supported by fire from the heavy guns on Dewey's cruisers in the harbor, and by light artillery and machine gun fire from gunboats on the Pasig River, 13 regiments of the army attacked along a 16-mile front around the city. Infantry units outflanked and drove the Filipinos from their trenches and took over their outposts. They captured the city water works and seized the rail center at Caloocan, 12 miles north of Manila on the direct line from there to the Philippine Republic's capital at Malolos, and turned back to crush an uprising in the city behind their lines. In the process, they inflicted severe casualties and punishing defeats on their enemy. The Filipino insurgents fought hard and bravely, but their leaders failed to seize the initiative, and, as noted above, their units were not trained in either defensive or offensive maneuver, their arms and ammunition were inferior, and they were poor shots. On 23 February, after two weeks of fighting, Filipino resistance in and around Manila collapsed giving Otis and the Eighth Corps a complete and decisive victory.[35]

With Manila and its suburbs controlled by his forces, Otis prepared to carry the fight against Aguinaldo and the Army of Liberation into the interior of the Islands. He informed Washington that he would need more men if he were to retain his hold on the area of Manila and fulfill his mission of defeating the insurgents, as well as pacifying the people through the "benevolent assimilation" policy of the president.[36] On 2 March, Congress facilitated his task by passing an army bill that contained three important components: (1) an increase in the size of the Regular Army to 65,000 men, (2) provision to extend the enlistment of the State volunteers already on duty in the Islands whose service was required, and (3) creation of a separate volunteer force of 35,000 organized into 25 regiments.[37] Otis knew that he would have to wait until the fall of 1899 before these men were trained and sent to the Philippines for action, but he also realized that he would then have the manpower to complete his mission. In the meantime, he focused on the Luzon theatre. He developed a plan to attack first the three major provinces east of the city, where many insurgents had fled after the fall of Manila, and secondly Aguinaldo's capital and military base of Malolos.[38]

The eastern provinces of Cavite and Laguna bordered Laguna de Bay on the western side, and both provinces shared a common southern border with the province of Batangas. Since 1890, Filipino insurgents had utilized all three provinces as a base, first against the Spanish, and then against the Americans. Under the command of Aguinaldo's trusted aide, Lieutenant General Mariano Trías, these toughened fighters of the Army of Liberation had armed themselves with Remington and Mauser rifles, and a few artillery pieces captured from the Spanish. They were no better marksmen than their comrades, but they had dug trench works in thickets of cane and cogon grass, and from these positions had harassed the southern and eastern flanks of Otis's forces. Otis was determined to end this threat and isolate, if not defeat, Trías's forces to keep them from supporting Aguinaldo's army in the Malolos region.[39]

In early March, Otis appointed the tough and popular Civil War veteran, Brigadier General Lloyd Wheaton, to command an expedition to move against Trías. Wheaton formed a provisional brigade out of newly arrived regular and volunteer regiments of infantry, cavalry, and artillery, including the gunboat *Laguna de Bay*, equipped with cannon and .45 caliber Gatling guns. On 12 March, they attacked the main Filipino force entrenched to the southeast of Manila at Guadalupe Church, advancing along a broad front of two miles that swept in a long arch south of the enemy position. They blasted the enemy from their trenches with artillery fire, and drove them toward the Pasig River. As the Filipinos turned along the riverbank, the gunboat *Laguna de Bay* raked their flanks with heavy fire from its guns, and forced them to flee to villages and towns up the river. Over the next few days, Wheaton's brigade captured these settlements, overcoming strong resistance from Trías's forces entrenched in cane and cogon grass thickets. With Americans in control of the Pasig River all the way from Manila to the great lake of Laguna de Bay, and with his southern flank secure, Otis could turn his attention toward the campaign to capture Malolos. But the Army of Liberation still controlled towns beyond the Pasig River along the western shore of the lake, and villages and towns in the interior of the southern provinces of Cavite, Laguna, and Batangas. While Wheaton's campaign was successful, it was also highly destructive, as his brigade destroyed crops and farms, and burned towns that he asserted had supported the insurgents. It was a hallmark of war that would be left on the Islands throughout the duration of the Philippine War (see map, p. 73).[40]

On 25 March, Otis began the campaign to capture Malolos and destroy the main force of the Army of Liberation. In less than a week of heavy fighting through jungles, thickets, rain, mud, and heat, across rivers, and along muddy and slippery river embankments, the men of 8th Corps outmaneuvered Aguinaldo's men in their trenches and decimated their lines with concentrated fire. By 29 March, the Army of Liberation was in full retreat, but escaped destruction when their pursuers ran out of energy and supplies.[41] By setting fire to their capital as they fled through Malolos, the Filipinos signaled their failure to defend and secure their most important political and military base in the north.

While his northern forces rested and prepared for their next offensive in northern Luzon, Otis organized expeditions to the south to strengthen the American position on the Pasig River line and drive the Filipinos from towns along Laguna de Bay and northern Cavite. Under the command of Major General Henry W. Lawton, the tall, courageous, alcoholic, and impetuous veteran of the war in Cuba, this first expedition left San Pedro Makati, just south of Manila and the Pasig River line, with 1,500 men on 8 April. Their objective was Santa Cruz, an important supply and distribution center diagonally across Laguna de Bay on the southwestern shore of Manila Bay, some 60 miles south of San Pedro Makati. Moving across the lake in 17 *cascos*, they landed four miles from Santa Cruz on 9 April, and attacked a Filipino bulwark of trenches and breastworks in a driving rainstorm before nightfall forced them to break off the assault. The next day, supported by a cavalry squadron and advancing behind artillery fire from 3.2 inch guns dragged through the mud, Lawton's infantry routed the defenders from their trenches and cut them down with withering rifle and machine gun fire. On 10 April, they occupied Santa Cruz, but by the 16th their supplies were exhausted, and, since they had achieved their objective, Otis ordered them back to Manila. According to Brian Linn, Lawton's expedition had demonstrated "that the 8th Corps could go wherever it wished with relative impunity. As Filipino documents show, the expedition shocked the revolutionaries." In addition, Linn states that Aguinaldo was forced to commit manpower and resources to meet what he feared were more attacks in the south, thus reducing the number of men he could send north. Clearly, fighting in the south was far from over, but as American reinforcements began arriving in the late spring, Filipino forces in the region of Laguna de Bay had been forced on the defensive (see map, p. 73).[42]

Among the officers and men landing in Manila after the journey across the Pacific, were those of Reilly's Light Battery F. They had left Fort Hamilton on 3 April, aboard two trains bound for San Francisco, where they would board a merchant transport headed for Manila. After receiving his orders, Captain Reilly requested the assignment to the battery of First Lieutenant Louis R. Burgess to lead one platoon, and Second Lieutenant Manos McCloskey, who had served with Reilly in Cuba, to lead a second platoon. To lead the battery's third platoon, he requested the newly promoted First Lieutenant Charles P. Summerall, who had served with him so well at the Presidio.[43] On 31 March, Summerall had received orders relieving him as aide-de-camp to Brigadier General A. C. M. Pennington in Atlanta, and directing him to proceed "at once" to Fort Hamilton for duty with the light battery that had been ordered to "proceed to the Philippines."[44] Learning that Reilly's Battery already had left Fort Hamilton, Summerall arranged to join them en route at the rail center in Ogden, Utah, about 30

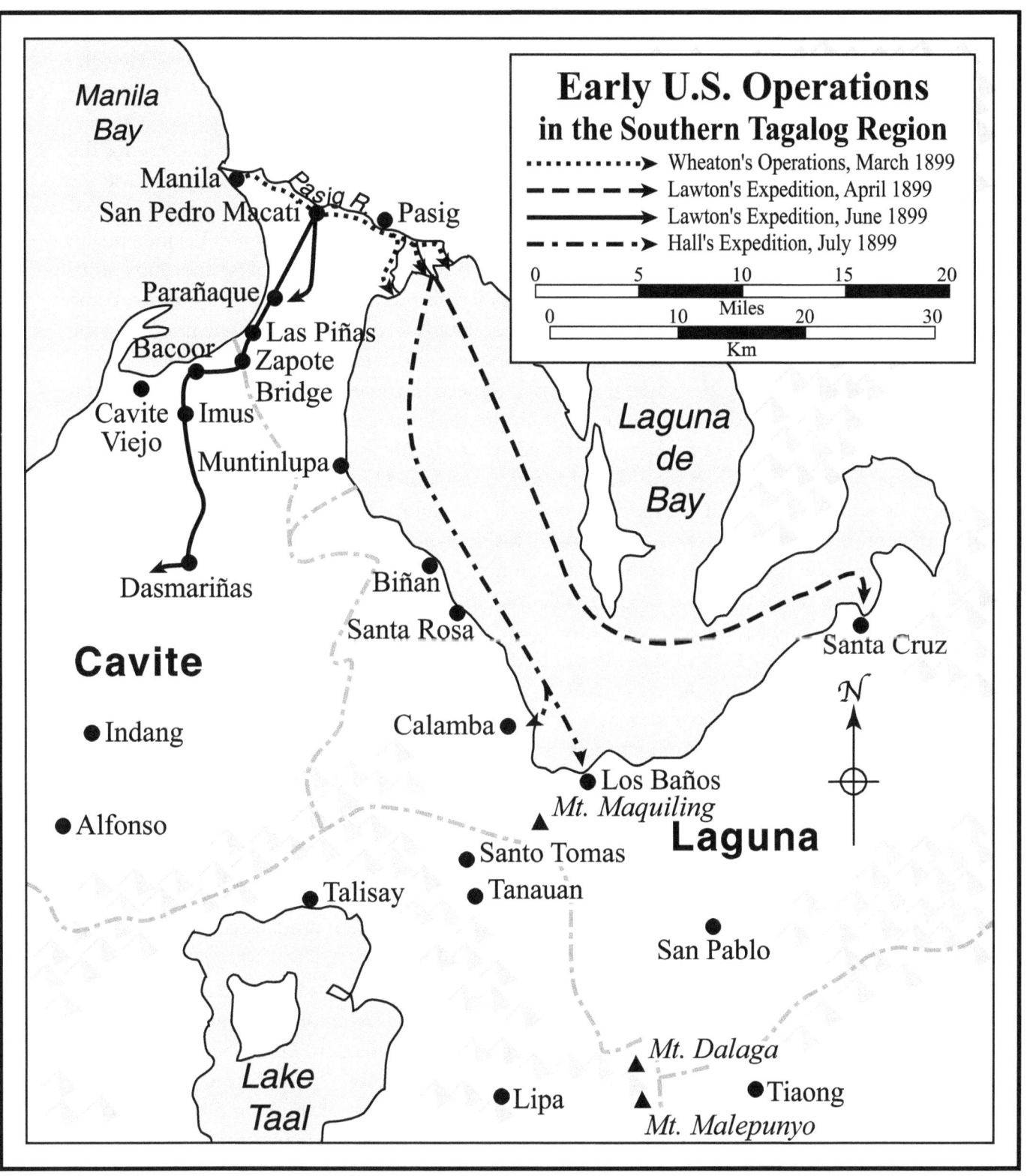

miles north of Salt Lake City. Among the personal possessions Summerall carried with him on the journey westward to Ogden were "the most beautiful letters" that Laura Mordecai had written to him and that he revered as "an inspiration to me in every way." For some reason that he never explained, he was "compelled with deep regret to destroy them" when he arrived in Ogden.[45] Perhaps they were too voluminous and bulky to be included in a soldier's campaign pack, although considering the proper limits that governed their relationship, it is unlikely that these letters were sufficiently incendiary to cause a spontaneous combustion and thus threaten his life, or the lives of the battery's men.

When Summerall met his unit in Ogden, Reilly placed him in charge of the train carrying the horses, mules, guns, caissons, and wagons. On 10 April, the two trains—the other carrying the battery's personnel—pulled into the rail yards at Oakland. Their contents of men, animals, weapons, ammunition, weapons, and equipment were moved by ferry to the Presidio, where Reilly and his men began preparations for the voyage to Manila. Ten days later, Reilly's Battery, along with personnel and equipment of the 4th Artillery and a battalion of marines, sailed through the Golden Gate on board the transport *Newport* and headed across the Pacific for Manila Bay. A few weeks later the steamer *Leelanaw* followed, carrying the guns, horses, mules, and equipment of this latest American contingent.[46]

The *Newport* was, like the other ships that carried American forces to the Philippines, an ocean packet that had been converted to a troopship, with comfortable quarters and excellent food for officers, but with terrible food and cramped and crowded spaces for the men. The constant pitching and rolling of these vessels on the high seas caused many to lose quickly what they had just eaten, and more, regardless of the quality of the food or how well the galleys had prepared it. Summerall, for example, never found his sea legs, and spent most of his time on board in a condition he described as "very sick."[47] After steaming with an erratically functioning engine for 10 days, the *Newport* arrived in Honolulu, Hawaii, where it took five days to make repairs and ready the ship to continue the voyage.[48] This extended stopover, however, gave the wobbly soldiers from the ship a chance to enjoy a taste of the Islands and the solid and stationary sensation of terra firma under their feet.

In early May, the *Newport* weighed anchor and set sail for Manila. In spite of the continued heaving of the ship and of his own stomach, Summerall sensed the "drama in the air," and felt strong enough to join in singing "songs of war and of farewell." All were "buoyant," he remembered, "but filled with sadness at going so far [away] from loved ones."[49] After a 20-day voyage from Honolulu, the *Newport* and its contingent of soldiers sailed past Corregidor Island into Manila Bay and straight into a gale howling through the darkness of the night of 22–23 May. Dropping anchor several miles from shore, they rode out the storm, and the next morning wearily climbed on board the ubiquitous *cascos*, and were towed to the docks by steam launches. They were relieved to leave behind them, at last, the *Newport*, which Summerall had deemed, not surprisingly, "entirely unsuitable for the voyage."

During the journey, the two artillery batteries had been organized into a battalion under the command of a Major Tiernan, and Summerall had been appointed the battalion adjutant. He accompanied Tiernan to report to General Otis and stopped to greet First Lieutenant Fred Sladen, Otis's aide, who had been graduated from West Point two years ahead of Summerall. "'Well, I suppose you are all glad to be here,'" responded Sladen. Summerall, ignoring the misery of the long days and nights aboard the *Newport*, replied that yes, they were. Sladen answered that "'We all want to go home.'"[50] Touched by the sadness and loneliness in Sladen's voice, Summerall realized, perhaps for the first time, just how alone a soldier can feel when duty and commitment take him far away from those back home whom he loves. The newly-arrived batteries were attached to the First Division, still commanded by General Lawton, and went into camp along the shore of the bay at Camp Otis, with little other than routine camp duties to occupy their time until their animals, guns, caissons, and wagons arrived. At

The Philippines

*Summerall,* **second from right,** *in the Philippines, 1899*

Courtesy The Citadel Archives & Museum, Charleston, South Carolina

length, on 18 June, the *Leelanaw* sailed into the bay carrying the means and instruments of war, and by 20 June, had unloaded all of its cargo.[51]

Lawton's division had just recently returned to Manila after defeating the Filipinos in one of the hardest fought battles of the war at a strategic bridge over the Zapote River, south of Manila. In the fight they had cleared the enemy from the northern area of Cavite province and extended their line to secure the Zapote bridge, but casualties had been numerous, and Lawton's remaining force was too depleted and exhausted to undertake any additional large-scale operations south of Manila. In addition, the summer monsoon season had begun, and in the face of unrelenting rain, the best policy was to maintain the security of the American garrisons along their lines south of the city.[52] The first of these lines that Lawton's campaigns had established ran southward along Manila Bay about 10 miles into Cavite province. The second line extended through the towns along the Pasig River to Laguna de Bay, then along the southwestern shore of the lake to Calamba, about 30 miles from Manila.[53] The three platoons of Reilly's Battery, each with two guns, were ordered to reinforce positions along the second line.[54]

On 21 June, the battery left Manila, with Summerall commanding the left platoon of five noncommissioned officers, one cook and eighteen privates, and Lieutenant Burgess in command of the right platoon consisting of five noncommissioned officers and twenty-five privates. Under the direction of Captain Reilly, Lieutenant McCloskey commanded the center platoon that included the battery headquarters and was the largest of the three units. With rain falling at the rate of one and a half inches a day, they made their way to their assigned positions along Guadalupe Ridge, overlooking the towns of San Pedro Macati and Pateros, and a few miles southeast of Manila. Reilly's and Burgess's platoons were stationed on one knoll of the ridge and Summerall's platoon occupied another knoll about three miles away. Within a few days, the rain-swollen river had flooded the town and the surrounding countryside, isolating Summerall's platoon from the rest of the battery. The continuous rain left their tents and uniforms soaking wet and their animals drenched and unable to forage for grass and grains. After a few days of this sodden suffering, the animals were sent back to Manila, but Summerall and his fellow sufferers remained, subsisting on hardtack, canned salmon (derisively known as "goldfish"), and fighting off attacks of dysentery and malaria. Each day a doctor walked the lines making his rounds, but, according to Summerall, "could do little for us."[55] Two months of this misery, plus daily drills in mud and rain did nothing to lift their sinking morale or fend off waves of depression. Finally, as it became clear that neither the insurgents nor the Americans were willing to stir up the other side in these conditions, the three platoons returned to Manila on 4 September in order to prepare for the next miserable monsoon mission.

The rains had also bogged down other units of Lawton's First Division as they struggled to advance their lines more deeply into Cavite. During the summer, Colonel Jacob Kline's 21st Infantry had occupied the lakeside town of Calamba, and Kline had deployed his soldiers in trenches around the town in a strictly defensive position. They managed just barely to hold their line against the ravages of disease and the repeated assaults and nightly sniping attacks from Brigadier General Miguel Malvar's militia from neighboring Batangas province.[56] According to Alan Millett, "The Twenty-First was an unhappy unit, its commander ill and happy to remain on the defensive…Fearing attacks from the encircling Filipinos, Kline compounded his regiment's malaise by keeping his men overlong in the trenches."[57]

On 7 September, Summerall's left platoon received orders to reinforce Kline's position at Calamba, just two days after Reilly's center platoon and Burgess's right platoon had marched out of Manila to join regiments of Brigadier General F. D. Grant's 1st Brigade in northern Cavite.[58] Summerall's men loaded onto *cascos* their horses and mules, two 3.2 inch guns, two 1.65 inch Hotchkiss revolving cannon, and two 3 inch mountain guns that were disassembled and carried on the backs of the mules.[59] Tugs towed the heavy barges up the river beneath a canopy of high trees and tangled vines. Overhead, giant-sized pythons curled around thick branches. As their *cascos* entered the lake and were pulled through the water toward Calamba, they saw along the shore, ferns growing as large as cherry trees, and birds flashing bright plumage as they suddenly took flight. Long-necked lizards, five feet tall, rocked from side to side through the dense undergrowth, and fruit bats with wingspans of four feet swept through the steamy air.[60]

After this short, smooth, and exotic trip, Summerall reported to Kline, while his men unloaded their animals, weapons, and equipment. He found his new commander, not surprisingly, in a foul mood, apparently, or so Summerall believed, because his artillery platoon had relieved an infantry platoon that had been with Kline for some time.[61] To Summerall, Kline's attitude represented another example, like the one he remembered from his days at the Presidio, of the infantry's long-standing "distrust" of the artillery and the "prejudice" of infantry officers against the artillery branch. He was convinced, however, that the officers and men of the infantry "liked an officer who gained its confidence."[62] In other words, Summerall reiterated the belief that through the exercise of his own will and personal action he could make right what he considered to be wrong. From this belief grew his conviction that the paths he chose, the missions he assigned, and the actions he undertook and directed were the only right ones. The self-confidence that flowed from this conviction enabled Summerall to forge himself into a courageous, strong, and resilient leader. In later years and with loftier rank, when his self-confidence turned into self-righteousness, he came to resent criticism, and turned against those who questioned or doubted his words or actions.

Summerall responded to what he considered the challenge of Kline's "prejudice" against and "distrust" of the artillery by deploying his guns around the town and clearing a path so that they

*Lieutenant Robert L. Bullard*
Courtesy Military History Institute

could be quickly moved from one position to another to repulse the attacks of the insurgents. He welcomed the advice of Lieutenant Colonel James Parker, a tall, gangling, and ambitious cavalry officer who was attached to the 21st Regiment and whom Summerall had grown to admire when they were both stationed at the Presidio, where Parker served as a captain of one of the cavalry troops. Summerall wrote that he was also "very fond of his lovely wife and their attractive children," and noted that many years later that "one of them would be an important part of my command."[63] Together, they planned an attack that drove a small enemy force from a hill that overlooked a segment of the American trench line. The next day, when Filipino artillery fired on the American lines from an abandoned sugar mill some 3,000 yards away, Parker called on Summerall and his platoon to destroy the position. Having already determined the exact range to all prominent points around the town, Summerall galloped up with his two 3.2 inch guns, and with quick and accurate fire destroyed the mill in bursts of shells, fire, and smoke. Through their glasses, Summerall and Parker saw the Filipino gunners abandon their guns and run for cover.[64] Summerall praised the skill and accuracy of his gunners, and noted with satisfaction that he had now gained the confidence of Colonel Kline and the entire regiment, as well as Parker's approval. He was shocked and saddened, however, when an officer asked him if he could borrow a bamboo ammunition cart to carry dead soldiers back to Calamba. He had found the experience of his first attack so exhilarating that he had failed to notice that Americans had been killed.[65] It was the first time he had ever seen men killed in action, and the sight of their bodies being lifted up onto the cart and taken away left upon the 31-year-old lieutenant a deep and unforgettable impression.

Over the next few months, Summerall's platoon and the 21st Regiment remained in Calamba in a virtual state of siege while both the center and right platoons of the battery were busy attacking and destroying insurgent entrenchments along the Imus River in northern Cavite.[66] With his own health failing, and with malaria and dysentery forcing almost a third of the men into the hospital, Kline was reluctant to strike out against the Filipinos,[67] even though in Parker's opinion, "the enemy could easily been punished and driven away."[68] Medical care was excellent, however, and when fresh meat, bread and vegetables began arriving daily from Manila, both the health and the morale of the regiment improved. As they recovered their strength, Summerall, Parker, and their men increasingly grew restless and became more active. They built houses of nipa palm and bamboo, grew beards, and according to Summerall, who sported a full, dark beard himself, "became hard and tough."[69] Those in Summerall's platoon were especially fortunate to have achieved that distinction, for they were about to find themselves commanded by a soldier who was just as hard and tough as anyone in the entire 8th Corps, or anyone in Aguinaldo's Army of Liberation.

On 7 December, Colonel Robert Lee Bullard stepped ashore in Manila in command of the 39th Infantry Regiment, U.S. Volunteers. A graduate of the West Point class of 1885, Bullard was born in the Civil War year of 1861, in Russell County in east Alabama, and, like Summerall, struggled with his family through the violent and hard times of the war and Reconstruction.[70] Also, like Summerall, as a young man he taught school, and won a competitive appointment to the military academy. For Bullard, as for Summerall, West Point represented much more than a college education. It symbolized, asserts Bullard's biographer Allan Millett, "an experience representing the very meaning of American life."[71] As an average cadet, finishing 27th in a class of 31 graduates, Bullard's choices for military assignment were limited to cavalry or infantry. He chose assignment to an infantry regiment, for essentially the same reason that Summerall would cite seven years later, albeit in the latter's case with much uncertainty, because he thought his chances for promotion would be greater than in the cavalry.[72] He went west, as had Summerall, but not to San Francisco, but to New Mexico, for duty with the 10th Infantry Regiment at Fort Union. While serving under First Lieutenant James Parker, Bullard got his taste of the Indian wars when he took part in the chase after Geronimo, the Chiricahua Apache warleader. They were close by when the Apache warrior surrendered in August 1886, and watched together as he and his band were loaded onto wagons that would bring them to the train to begin their long journey to Florida.[73]

Bullard spent the next few years serving garrison duty at posts in Kansas, Nevada, New Mexico, and Oklahoma, rising to the rank of first lieutenant, and marrying Rose Douglas Babson, a young widow from Tennessee. After moving back East, Bullard became a father and hoped for a return to his native Alabama, but was assigned as an instructor of military science at the remote North Georgia Agricultural College at Dahlonega in the foothills north of Atlanta.[74]

By 1898, bored and frustrated with his career as a line officer, Bullard, like many other middle-aged lieutenants, searched for ways to advance his rather stalemated career. He was deliberating just how he might arrange for a staff position at the War Department when war broke out with Spain. The 10th Infantry was ordered to Tampa for training, but Bullard, while excited about the possibility of going to war, hoped to secure a commission to command volunteers, and with it promotion to a higher rank. His chance came when Joseph F. Johnston, the governor of Alabama, ran out of able-bodied white youths to fill his state's quota. He responded to the requests of black men to serve and decided to create a battalion of black Alabama volunteers. He obtained the approval of the War Department and asked one of his state's native sons to take the command and begin the organization of the new unit. At the end of May, after lengthy discussions with Johnston and consultation with his friends, Bullard accepted the command with the rank of major. He was assured that the battalion would be immediately equipped for service in the field.[75]

During the first week of June, a camp for the 1st Battalion of Alabama Volunteers was set up outside of Mobile. Plenty of recruits arrived, and training began. Because the battalion was expected to remain for some time in the Mobile area, and because they were sensitive to the concerns of white Mobilians, Johnston and Bullard had agreed that all the officers would be white. This condition did not please the black leaders of the city, but Bullard encountered no difficulties between white officers and black enlisted men. He was especially pleased with the ability and effectiveness of his staff. In fact, in view of how well the training went and as the need for volunteers grew, Governor Johnston decided to add two more battalions and form the 3rd Alabama Volunteer Infantry Regiment. Bullard was promoted to colonel, and by the end of July, had led the successful transition of the battalion to a regiment. He had high hopes that soon they would be on their way either to Cuba for occupation duty, or to Puerto Rico, or to the Philippines.[76]

Yet, much to the disappointment of Bullard and his men, the War Department decided to disband the 3rd Alabama, and in late August, ordered them to Camp Shipp, just outside Anniston, Alabama. In spite of intense lobbying by Bullard, his officers, and many of his men, the regiment remained at

Shipp during the winter of 1898–1899, enduring harassment and race baiting from the townspeople, and even attacks from units assigned to the camp. On 24 November, fueled by an angry crowd encouraged by men from the 3rd Tennessee, a white unit, a riot broke out in town. By the time the rioters were brought under control, the 3rd Tennessee's provost guard had killed the 3rd Alabama's clerk and wounded three of its black soldiers. Bullard was angry and upset, but kept his men under tight control. No charges were ever filed in the incident, and tension in the camp remained high until the 3rd Tennessee was mustered out in January 1899. Bullard feared that the same fate soon would befall his regiment and tried to persuade the War Department to use it as part of a volunteer unit in the Philippines. But rather than receiving orders for the Philippines, he received orders in February 1899, to disband his regiment. The process was completed in March, and the 46 officers and 992 men of the 3rd Alabama went home, bringing Bullard's first regimental command to a quiet and disappointing conclusion. Nevertheless, Bullard believed their work and experiences represented solid achievements. He was especially proud of his black soldiers, recording in his diary, as Allan Millett notes, that their discipline was "'as good as any I ever hope to obtain from any troops.'" In addition, Bullard's leadership had won the praise of a number of generals, and he believed that he had learned valuable lessons in command and in the psychology of leadership.[77] His service with the 3rd Alabama had prepared him well for his second regimental command, and it was not long in coming.

While Bullard lamented the end of his first regimental command and his regression to the rank of captain, the War Department was busily engaged in raising the new volunteer regiments authorized by the army bill of 2 March. The brilliant and well-organized lawyer from New York, Elihu Root, had replaced the controversial and unpopular Russell Alger as Secretary of War, and Root proceeded deliberately in his selection of the officers for the new regiments. In choosing the commanding officers, he consulted with the president, with prominent men in government and in the private sector, and with military leaders in Washington and the Philippines. He carefully examined efficiency reports, and when he made his final choices, none of the colonels selected had served fewer than 14 years in the Regular Army. To command the 39th Infantry Regiment, U.S. Volunteers, he chose Robert L. Bullard, who received the news with great pleasure and surprise, and left Mobile by train for the regiment's assembly ground at Fort Cook, Nebraska, 10 miles south of Omaha. Bullard arrived on 24 August, and after two months of hard training, he and his officers were confident that they had molded their men into a first-rate and eager fighting unit.[78]

On 2 November, the 49 officers and 1,310 men of the 39th boarded a train headed for the docks at Portland, Oregon, where they marched on board the transports *Pennsylvania* and *Olympia*, and sailed for the Philippines. For over a month they steamed westward, pitching and rolling through the Pacific swells. They dropped anchor in Manila Bay on 7 December, and Bullard, lean, mustachioed, and impatient to fight, went ashore to report to 8th Corps headquarters. He was surprised that no one expected them, but the War Department had not sent the cable with the news of their assignment and departure. Nevertheless, Bullard was pleased to learn that their arrival had coincided with a plan Otis was developing to renew the offensive into southern Luzon to bring an end to the virtual siege of Calamba, smash the Army of Liberation in Cavite, and drive it out of all the southern provinces.[79]

Following the death on 19 December of General Lawton from a sniper's bullet in the chest, Otis promoted Major General John C. Bates to command the First Division. Cautious and competent, and willing to give his field commanders freedom to exercise their initiatives, Bates did not assume command until 4 January, the day Otis ordered the division to begin the campaign. Otis assigned to the division two brigades, one commanded by General Wheaton, and consisting of the 4th, 28th, 38th, and 45th volunteer infantry regiments. The second brigade was commanded by Brigadier General Theodore Schwann, Otis's German-born chief of staff, who saw in this campaign his best chance to earn a star in the Regular Army. Schwann's brigade was made up of the 30th and 46th volunteer regiments. Schwann's brigade also included an artillery detachment, engineers, signal corpsmen, cavalry troops and two companies of Macabebe Scouts, mercenaries from the town of Macabebe, located just north of the Rio Grande River in the northern province of Pampanga.[80]

With his two brigades, Otis planned to envelop the main elements of the army of General Trías, now the political and military commander of southern Luzon and a confidant of Aguinaldo. Schwann's brigade was to assemble at San Pedro Macati, just south of Manila, move southeastward through Muntinlupa to Biñan, and then turn west into the interior of Cavite, seizing the towns of Silang, Indang, and finally the coastal town of Naic, some 23 miles south of Manila. Wheaton would concentrate his brigade around the Zapote Bridge, about 10 miles south of Manila, in order to contain Trías while Schwann's brigade secured the line from Biñan to the coast. If the plan worked, it would trap Trías's army of 3,000 men between the two American brigades. After destroying Trías's army, the two brigades would combine to sweep southeastward to occupy the remaining southern provinces of Batangas, Laguna and Tayabas. Otis also assigned four other infantry regiments to the operation, but kept them separate from the two brigades. One of these regiments was the 39th, and Otis quickly sent Bullard to Calamba with the specific task of breaking the siege (see map, p. 81).[81]

Taking his headquarters staff and one of his three battalions, Bullard and his men left Manila by boat and arrived at Calamba in mid-December to relieve Kline and his ineffective 21st Infantry.[82] When he met Summerall, Bullard suddenly relieved him as commander of the revolving cannon and mountain guns and replaced Summerall's trained gunners with infantry. Shocked by his dismissal, Summerall again was quick to attribute Bullard's action to the prejudice of the infantry against the artillery, even though he never had met Bullard and knew nothing about him. He reported to Kline that if he and his men were replaced by a "strange" officer and untrained men, the regiment's entire position would be weakened and endangered, especially since they expected renewed attacks by the enemy at any moment. In one of his last and perhaps most constructive actions, Kline protested to Bullard, who revoked his order and restored Summerall to his command.[83] Once repaired, the relationship between the two Southerners and former schoolteachers soon flourished into one of mutual admiration and respect, as they fought together in the torrid Philippine campaign, and years later when they were reunited on the soil of eastern France in the Great War of 1914–1918.

Summerall came to revere Bullard in the same manner as he had come to regard Colonel Graham and Captain Reilly, praising him in his memoir as "one of the best friends and greatest influences in my life, in spite of a bad beginning [to our relationship]."[84] In the Philippines, Bullard soon came to value and respect Summerall as a courageous and skilled artillerist. When Bullard took command of the First Division of the AEF in 1917, he listed Summerall as one of two choices to command the division's 1st Artillery Brigade, and was delighted when Summerall was selected. As Summerall later wrote, "This gave me my start in the AEF."[85] When Bullard moved up to head the 2nd Corps in the last American offensive of the Great War, he recommended that Summerall take over the division. Summerall believed, quite correctly, that Bullard "did what he could to have me promoted and assigned to the command of the First Division."[86]

While serving as Army Chief of Staff in the late 1920s, Summerall found an opportunity to help his old friend, whose name and reputation gradually had faded away after the war. Bullard had been keenly disappointed and upset that Congress failed to restore him and First Army commander, Hunter Liggett, to their wartime rank of lieutenant general, while elevating General John J. Pershing to the special rank of General of the Armies and increasing his pension. Gathering the support of a number of Southern representatives, Summerall intervened, and persuaded Congress to restore Bullard and all other retired officers to their highest AEF rank. Because they already were drawing the highest

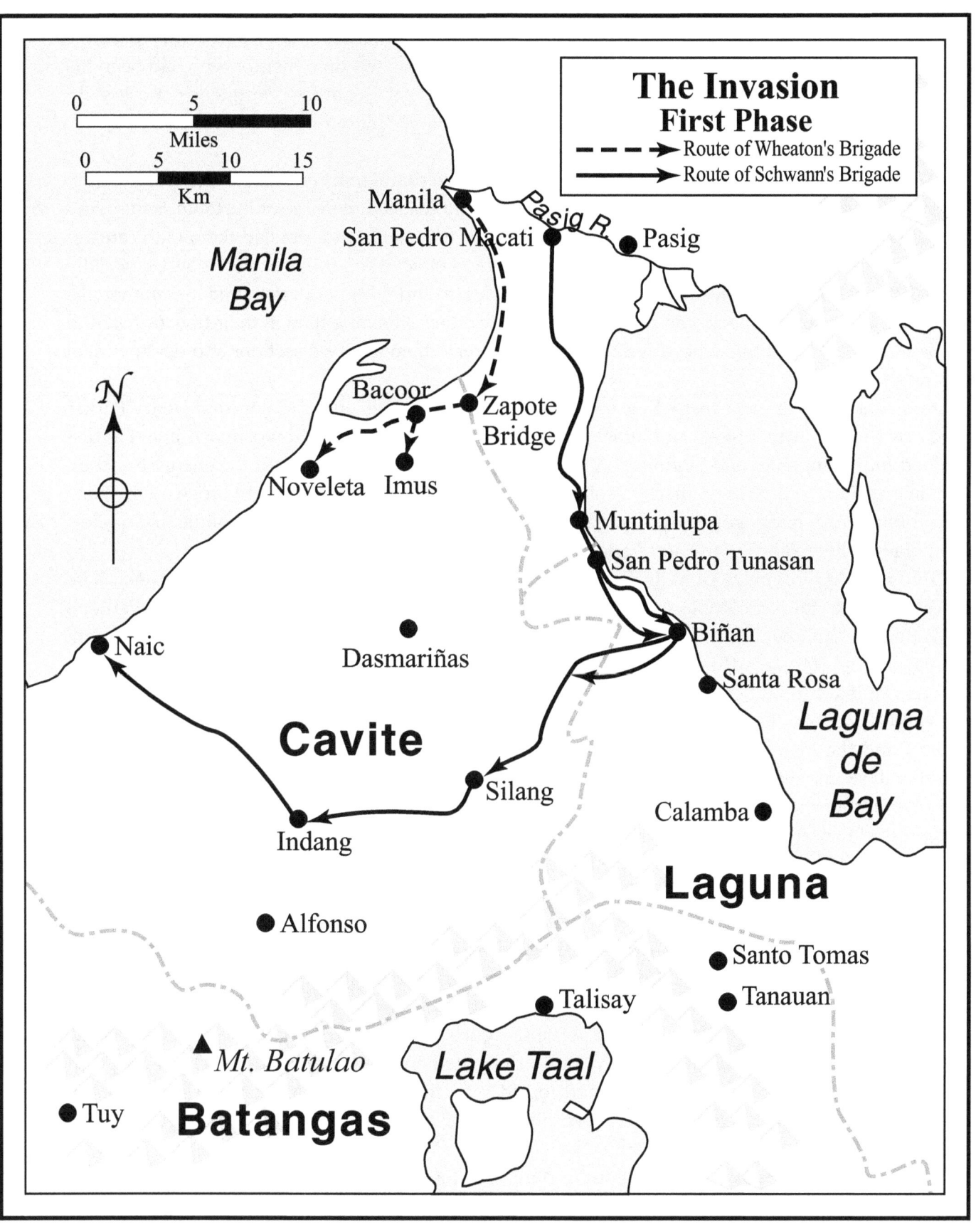

possible pensions, these amounts remained the same.[87] The two old soldiers and comrades lived well into their 80s, with Bullard dying at age 86 in 1947, six years before Summerall's death in 1953, at age 88. In his final years, as he looked back upon the memory of his wartime mentor who had been his close friend for over 50 years, Summerall noted gratefully that Bullard's "confidence and loyalty never wavered." He remembered also that he owed to Bullard "more than [to] anyone else my advancement in the AEF."[88]

As the "strong and robust" men of the 39th marched toward Calamba on a late December evening, the insurgents drove them back with a ferocious attack that reached the edge of the town. Summerall moved his guns quickly to intercept them at the point of the attack, and repelled them with canister and shrapnel, an action that Summerall said, "had a good effect upon the new troops and especially upon Colonel Bullard."[89] The next morning Bullard, Parker, and Summerall gathered in Summerall's nipa palm and bamboo shack, and developed a plan to attack Malvar's men in their trenches behind the San Cristobal River to the northwest of Calamba, break them into two sections and destroy them separately.[90]

In the darkness of New Year's Eve, Bullard sent two companies under Major John Henry Parker on *cascos* to land at first light, and attack behind the left flank of the Filipino trench line. He dispatched four companies and Summerall's platoon up the road directly toward the enemy trenches, with instructions to time their attack to coincide with Major Parker's. As daylight broke on the New Year, Summerall's guns opened fire, covering the Filipino trenches with shrapnel, while the infantry companies delivered heavy fire and Parker's men began their attack from the rear.[91]

Two months after the fight at the San Cristobal River, Bullard recommended that Summerall be brevetted major "for conspicuous gallantry in action," and described his actions as follows. As Parker's men attacked, Summerall saw that two of Parker's companies were pinned down by enemy fire from a range of about 600 yards. Running forward toward their position under "hot fire," Summerall brought up one Gatling gun and one mountain Hotchkiss gun, and positioned them about 25 yards to the right and 10 yards to the front of the right flank of the two companies. From there, closely watched by Bullard and the men of the two companies, he directed fire parallel to their front. The fire from Summerall's guns suppressed the rifle fire from the Filipinos, allowing Parker's companies to rise up and rush forward, driving the enemy before them. Again under "hot fire," Summerall and his gunners pressed forward, firing their guns as they advanced. They passed 200 yards beyond the flank of the retreating Filipinos and had to fall back to avoid firing into Parker's men who were moving past the enemy on the opposite flank.[92] Quite likely this is the scene Bullard had observed when, as Summerall rather gratuitously recorded, "Colonel Bullard rode up to me and exclaimed: 'I am surprised at you! I am surprised at you!' I was shocked with the feeling that I had displeased him and that he was going to censure me. I replied, perhaps somewhat resentfully, 'What have I done?' He replied: 'You and your men stood in the road fully exposed while my men had cover, lying down.' I said that we could not do otherwise and serve the guns, and that artillery was always exposed." Summerall went on to say that Bullard "was delighted in the performance of his guns, and complimented me profusely."[93] Battered and forced from their trenches, Malvar's men took flight, leaving bodies, debris, rifles, and cannon behind as they fled northward toward the town of Biñan, nine miles down the bay toward Calamba.[94]

The next day Bullard's men set out in pursuit of the Filipinos and encountered a contingent behind a strong position across a stream. Bullard went forward to the left with a flanking party, while Parker led the main attack straight toward the enemy. Later, Parker recommended that Summerall be brevetted captain for this action. He described how Summerall, riding on horseback in advance of Parker's skirmish line and under constant fire, pushed forward a 3.2 inch gun, along with the Gatling and Hotchkiss pieces. Calm and upright in the saddle as his platoon advanced, Summerall directed their fire until they were within 300 yards of the enemy, "at which point," noted Parker, "the enemy's fire ceased." Summerall then ordered his guns forward toward a stone bridge on the outskirts of Binan where some of the retreating Filipinos were entrenched. Parker continued that Summerall, after dismounting, "cooly [sic] walked up to within 30 yards of their stone barricade to reconnoiter. He then selected a position within forty yards from which his gatling [sic] could deliver nearly a reverse fire, helped personally to run it up by hand, and stood in the open to observe the effect [of his fire]." Parker concluded his recommendation by stating that "I have never seen his gallantry surpassed, nor the efficiency of his work equaled."[95] When the brief fight was over, fire from Summerall's gunners and Parker's infantry had cleared the Filipinos from around the bridge, and opened the way for Bullard's command to cross over and occupy Biñan on 2 January. In his endorsement of Parker's recommendation, Bullard reiterated his previous recommendation that Summerall receive "the highest brevet of Major for conspicuous gallantry in action on the two occasions named, one in this letter, [and] one in enclosed letter of Major Parker." He added that "The authorities cannot afford to pass over without recognition the conduct of this officer, whose skill and daring, in my opinion, saved the lives of my men on these two occasions."[96]

The next day, when Otis learned of Bullard's presence in Biñan, rather than congratulating Bullard for his initiative and success, he cabled his displeasure. Bullard was right to attack the insurgents and break the siege of Calamba, but he should not have pursued them, stated Otis. He was disturbed because Bullard's offensive had not been approved by his superiors, and because his men had moved into the area where Otis was about to send in Schwann's brigade. He ordered Bullard back to Calamba, and instructed him to stay there until he received orders to move. Mildly upbraided by Otis, Bullard and his command returned to Calamba during the night of 3 January, with Summerall's guns rolling along with the rear guard to protect against harassing fire.[97]

In spite of the mild censure that Bullard received, he and his men had performed well. The "strong and robust" fighters of the 39th and the skilled gunners of Summerall's platoon had killed 200 insurgents and had suffered only 14 wounded, seriously weakening Malvar's force in Cavite.[98] Had Otis looked more tolerantly and carefully at Bullard's seizure of Biñan, he would have noticed that Bullard's action had protected the flank of Schwann's march into Cavite. Bullard's offensive certainly had demonstrated his eager, aggressive, and independent spirit, one that might well have inspired Summerall's subsequent actions in their first combat operation together. In Bullard, Summerall had found fortuitously another strong personality who not only would become "one of my best and most helpful friends,"[99] but whom Summerall would regard as a role model for the rest of his life. On the road to Biñan, Summerall demonstrated great courage and bravery, advancing on foot and on horseback calmly and coolly under hostile fire, as he directed the aim of his gunners. It would not be the last time that he would defy the threat of enemy bullets to point his gunners toward their targets, although around Calamba he probably realized that his chances of being hit by rifle fire from enemies who were such bad shots were rather remote. Meanwhile, Bullard and his band of eager and able fighters waited impatiently in Calamba, while Schwann's brigade launched their invasion of Cavite.

On 4 January, Schwann's force of 2,500 infantry swept aside several hundred Filipinos in Biñan and quickly captured the town. They headed for the coast on 7 January, drove one of Trías's brigades from their fortifications in front of Indang, scattered them in all directions, and moved into the town. On 9 January, they set out for the coast, and after routing a contingent of 300 of Trías's soldiers, occupied their final objective of Naic. In a march of five days, Schwann had completed his task and awaited Wheaton's advance that would begin the final phase of the envelopment that would destroy Trías's army. However, Wheaton and Schwann soon discovered that there would be no major battle:

there were no longer any Filipino soldiers in Cavite to envelop and attack. Trías had gone into hiding, and his officers and men had either slipped through the American lines to join other Filipino units in neighboring provinces, or hidden their weapons and uniforms and returned as civilians to their homes and villages.[100]

As other units of the First Division won victories in Cavite, including the regiments supported by the other platoons of Reilly's Battery, Bullard and his command continued to cool their heels in Calamba. They soon returned to action, however, when Bates ordered Bullard to support Schwann's drive into Batangas by attacking General Malvar's headquarters at Santo Tomas on 9 January. Eager for a fight, Bullard assembled all three of his battalions, a total of 1,000 officers and men, along with Summerall's platoon and a battalion of the 37th Regiment, commanded by Lieutenant Colonel Benjamin F. Cheatham. He divided his force into three columns to attack the road barriers, trench lines, and fortified positions that Malvar's men had devised to defend Santo Tomas. Bullard led one column of two battalions to sweep the foothills east of the main road from Calamba to San Tomas, and deployed two companies under Captain William Taylor across the hills to the west of the road. Up the road, he dispatched the third column, commanded by Major George Langhorne, consisting of three companies, spearheaded by Summerall's artillery platoon (see map, p. 88).[101]

Blowing away roadblocks and shelling trenches cut across their path, Summerall's gunners had little difficulty clearing the way for Langhorne's advance until they reached an iron bridge over a deep gorge cut by a tributary of the San Juan River. Summerall wrote that on the opposite side of the ravine Malvar's men had fortified a crest with deep trenches with two tiers of loopholes on either side of the road that approached the bridge. However, the fortifications provided a clear target for Summerall's gunners, who pounded the trenches, reducing them to piles of debris and broken bodies. Langhorne's infantry then rushed across the bridge, picking off more of the militia, capturing a number of them, and forcing the rest to flee toward San Tomas. They left behind 4 cannon, 25 rifles, 24 dead, and 60 captives.[102]

Meanwhile, Bullard's and Taylor's columns met little resistance as they cut through the hills east and west of Santo Tomas, and entered the city shortly after Summerall and Langhorne had fought their way across the iron bridge. Malvar's militia fled westward toward Lake Taal, and the officers and men of Bullard's command filed into Santo Tomas, clearly the victors in their march from Calamba. At a cost of only one killed and two wounded, they had inflicted on Malvar's forces significant losses of men and materiel, and had driven them farther from their strong points and key bases in southern Luzon. Bullard returned to Calamba and reported the day's activities to Bates, who responded with praise for Bullard's successful campaign and for the seizure of Santo Tomas.[103]

Summerall's platoon had been increasingly effective against the rebels and played an important role in the success of Bullard's actions. He led their march along roads thickened with mud, up and down hills drenched and made slick with monsoon rain, through matted thickets of brush and stands of cogon grass, and rode forward boldly to direct the fire of his guns, standing confidently beside his gunners as they blew away the men and barriers thrown up against them. On 13 April, *The American*, a newspaper published in Manila, praised their action, noting that "Time and time again have Lt. Summerall's guns mightily assisted the infantry in their work, and on many occasions did the insurgents bitterly regret the existence of such an organization as Battery F of the 5th Artillery.... because of their excellent fighting qualities and the fact that the artillery could always be depended upon, the other troops here have more than an ordinary liking for Lt. Summerall and the boys of Battery F."[104] The news of Summerall's performance far away in the Philippine War quickly attracted the attention of the folks back home.

In April, an article in the *Florida Times-Union* in Jacksonville described a report on the recent actions of Summerall's platoon that appeared in the *Army-Navy Journal* issue of 7 April 1900, and added a brief account of Summerall's life. The article called attention to Summerall's winning a competitive appointment to West Point, pointing out that the paper's editor at that time, C. H. Jones, had been a member of the examining board. The next month the *Eustis Lake Region* reprinted for its readers the article from the *Times-Union* under the title of "Lieutenant Charles Summerall-This Former Eustis Boy's Brilliant Career in the Philippines." They added a statement of a certain Colonel Anderson about Summerall that "His judgment was ever sound; he was full of vigor and activity, and [as] cool and brave as any one I ever saw. He should receive some reward."[105]

Shortly after the article appeared in the Eustis paper, Summerall's sister Margaret, known in the family as Meta, wrote Secretary of War Elihu Root from Eustis and enclosed a copy of the *Times-Union* piece. In her letter to the secretary, she pointed out that "many prominent friends here and also in other states are watching his [Summerall's] career with deep interest and are anxious for <u>promotion</u> [bold underlining in her letter] for him. I can assure you," she confidently stated, "that you would always feel more than gratified with the result of any favor you might bestow on him." She recalled that Summerall had escorted President and Mrs. McKinley when they had visited Camp Alger, and assured Secretary Root that "They were very pleasant to him, and upon their departure kindly invited him to call upon them whenever he was in Washington." Whether Summerall knew of her letter is uncertain, for he does not mention it in his memoir. What does seem certain, however, is her pride in her brother's accomplishments and her conviction that he should be rewarded with a promotion. Perhaps also she was inspired to her own bold action by the bravery of her brother, and believed that she could help advance his career, and, at the same time, express her gratitude for the financial support he had provided for their parents' family, as well as for her and her husband.[106]

Back in Calamba, now that Bullard's actions had won the praise rather than the rebuke of his superior, he was ready for more, as was General Bates, who sent Schwann's brigade from Cavite into Batangas. He reinforced Bullard's regiment with the 38th Regiment commanded by Colonel George S. Anderson, the officer quoted in the *Eustis Lake Region*. A bearded, rather portly cavalry officer, who, like Bullard, was a veteran of the frontier Indian wars, Anderson had led his regiment in Schwann's campaign to smash General Trías's army in Cavite, and had been disappointed in their failure to trap and force Trías into a final battle. Impatient and determined to find and engage the rebels, he left central Cavite on 10 January, leading his regiment across 33 miles of mountainous terrain to link up with Bullard at Calamba on 14 January.[107]

In order to open and secure the way for Anderson's arrival, early that morning Bullard sent Summerall's platoon and Cheatham's battalion to clear a band of insurrectos from trenches they had dug across the road leading into Calamba from central Cavite.[108] Following a familiar pattern, at dawn, Summerall's guns opened fire on the trenches from the road while Cheatam's infantry picked off the rebels with enfiladed fire, forcing the survivors to scatter and take flight. Shortly afterwards, Summerall and Cheatam met Anderson and his regiment on the road approaching from the west. Summerall wrote that Anderson spoke to Cheatam, but ignored him. He stated pointedly that when Cheatam introduced Summerall as commanding the artillery, Anderson remarked, "in the most contemptuous way, without looking at me that 'Artillery ———,' using the filthiest word that he could utter." Noting that Anderson was a cavalry officer, Summerall again concluded that such foul-mouthed abuse indicated just how bitter was the "hatred" among the branches of the army. Anderson moved on to join Bullard in Calamba, followed the next day by Cheatam and Summerall, who was still smarting from Anderson's offensive outburst.[109]

With orders to attack any enemy concentration they discovered, Bullard and Anderson decided to march against Malvar's new headquarters at Lipa, some 10 miles to the south. Since Anderson was senior to Bullard, he assumed command of the advance, much to Bullard's annoyance, noted Summerall.[110] They left the next morning at 0600 hours, with Anderson's regiment taking the lead and Bullard's men following behind (see map, p. 88).[111]

They had not gone far when Anderson's adjutant rode back to Summerall and gave him direct orders from Anderson to report to him with his guns at once. Summerall, still seething from Anderson's "contemptuous" disregard of his presence and use of the "filthiest word" against the artillery, replied that he was under Bullard's orders, not Anderson's. Apparently overhearing Summerall's curt response, Bullard told him to comply with Anderson's order. Some distance ahead, Anderson waited on Summerall, not to ignore him or spit hatred at the artillery, but to welcome him, "in the most friendly and cordial manner." Apparently, Anderson had by then learned about the courage, skill and importance of Summerall and his platoon, stating as Summerall rode up with his guns, "I am glad to see you, Summerall. They [the insurgents] are right ahead of us." Quickly Summerall located an enemy trench "from which a good deal of fire was coming."[112] His gunners found the range, and with shell and shrapnel, again blasted the insurgents from their trench and cleared the way into Lipa, which the regiments entered that afternoon, having lost only one man killed and one severely wounded.[113] But the march had been a tough, uphill climb; horses had fallen in their harnesses, and the men were exhausted and suffering attacks of malaria and dysentery. Yet, when he "heard a young corporal say when the going was hard: 'Fellows, I would not change places with anybody in the world,'" he concluded they were all "fierce fighters with unbreakable morale."[114] These were the characteristics Summerall believed all soldiers, including him, should possess, regardless of circumstances and in all conditions.

When the Americans pulled into Lipa, they found it deserted, except for 130 Spanish prisoners, who greeted their liberators with jubilation. The Spaniards embellished their celebration with news that some of the insurgents had ridden off toward the town of Rosario with more Spanish prisoners and several American captives. The first part of their account turned out to be true, but not the second. But the entire story was credible enough for the irrepressible Bullard and the hard-charging Anderson, and they quickly assembled a mounted party of 12 and dashed off to rescue what they believed were the Spanish and American soldiers held captive by the insurgents. With guns blazing, they burst into Rosario that afternoon, chased off the few Filipino defenders, and scared off the townspeople and children, as well as donkeys, *caraboas* or water buffaloes, chickens, and birds. They soon located the Spanish prisoners, but after a thorough search of the town found no Americans. What they did find, however, was a cache of 20,000 Mexican pesos in silver coins that the fleeing insurgents had abandoned.[115]

Following behind Bullard and Anderson with his platoon, Summerall met up with them just as they were celebrating the discovery of the treasure, and rode back to Lipa with their party. What Summerall remembered about this episode, was not the excitement of the cavalry's riding in to rescue the prisoners and capture the treasure, or the euphoric celebration of Bullard, Anderson, and their party that continued on the way back to Lipa, but the serious remark of an officer who rode up to Summerall and said, "'I hear Colonel Anderson is praising you too.'" What really impressed him was the fact that Anderson had recognized his ability (as the *Eustis Lake Region* proudly would record), had seen the error of his "hatred" toward the artillery, and for the rest of his life would become "very friendly to me."[116] Late in life, as he thought of Anderson's initial "hostility," Summerall must have been pleased and comforted by the knowledge that early in his long career he possessed the strength and skill to win the praise and confidence of those who once had doubted his ability. Almost to the very end of his long life, he believed that he retained in undiminished measure that same power and ability to accomplish every mission he undertook.

While Bullard and Anderson rode back to Lipa excited and more than satisfied with the results of their ride to Rosario, General Schwann rode in the next day less than pleased with the entire episode. Schwann could have been a little jealous of Bullard's and Anderson's élan and success, but he was definitely disturbed because their dash to Rosario had left their rear and flanks unprotected, and had cost them time in their mission to trap Malvar's army. He promptly sent Bullard with one battalion of the 39th back to establish garrisons at Santo Tomas and Tanauan to keep open communications between Calamba and units to the south, effectively sidetracking him for the rest of the expedition, or so Bullard believed. He treated Anderson more leniently and kept him close at hand as Schwann planned an attack by his brigade on Batangas City, the capital of the province as well as the chief port on Batangas Bay, through which the insurgents received much of their arms and ammunition.[117]

Schwann divided his force into three columns and set out on 15 January for Batangas City. Summerall's platoon and a battalion of the 39th remained with Anderson, who commanded the column on the right that took the main road from Lipa. A second column, consisting of a battalion of the 38th Infantry under Major Charles Muir, headed farther eastward through Rosario, and across a mountain trail that led westward to the capital. Colonel Cornelius Gardener's 30th Infantry led the center column that moved east of Anderson's column through the town of Ibaan, then south toward Batangas City (see map, p. 88).[118]

Leading Gardener's column was the 1st Company of the Macabebe Scouts. The mercenaries were from the town of Macabebe, located just north of the Rio Grande River in the northern province of Pampanga. They were old enemies of the Tagalog people of southern provinces of Luzon, and fiercely opposed Aguinaldo and the Republic. In the fall of 1899, with General Lawton's support, First Lieutenant Matthew A. Batson had organized the Macabebe mercenaries into a battalion of five companies that eventually became a part of a Filipino auxiliary corps of over 15,000. They were tough and fierce fighters, skillful guides and scouts, but cruel interrogators of their captives.[119]

The 1st Company was commanded by Lieutenant Lee Hall, a former captain in the Texas Rangers and, at one time, an Indian agent. He was fair-haired, erect and thin, with a weather-beaten face, and with deep furrows and ridgelines across his neck. Hall had achieved fame and the rank of captain as a ranger, but while an Indian agent, he had been tried for misconduct and for mishandling agency accounts. Though he had been acquitted, the Department of the Interior dismissed him from its service.[120] At 49 years of age, and determined to redeem his reputation, Hall secured an appointment as a first lieutenant in the 33rd Volunteers, known as the "Texas Regiment." He arrived in the Philippines not long after Batson had organized the Macabebe Scouts, and when the commander of the 1st Company was killed, Hall was named to replace him. He joined Batson's battalion of Scouts as they spearheaded Brigadier General Samuel B. M. Young's fall campaign against Aguinaldo in the Rio Grande valley. Exhausted and stricken with malaria after a month of hard fighting in a tough campaign, Hall was hospitalized in Manila for the latter part of December. By January, he was well enough to leave the hospital and returned in time to command the 1st Company at the head of Colonel Gardener's column as they marched on Batangas City.[121]

Schwann had planned for all three columns to reach Batangas City at the same time, but Muir's column got there first, arriving by midmorning on the 16th, having encountered only weak resistance from rebels, who fired a few volleys from a ridge before fleeing into sprawling fields of sugar cane. Gardener's men, led by Hall and his company of Macabebe Scouts, began arriving about 30 minutes later, having killed a number of Filipinos, and captured about 70. Anderson's column reached the city by noon, without meeting any resistance along the way.[122]

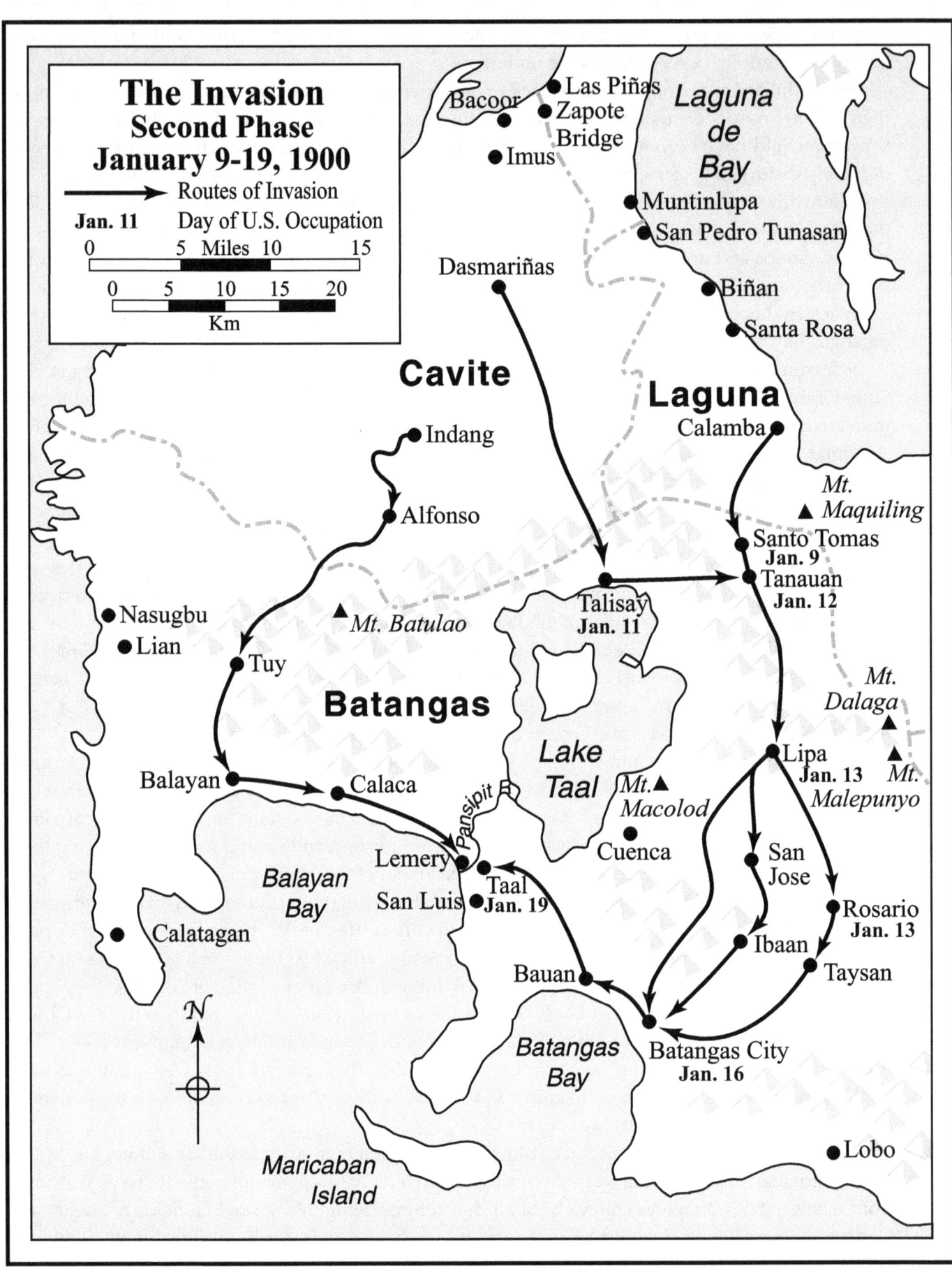

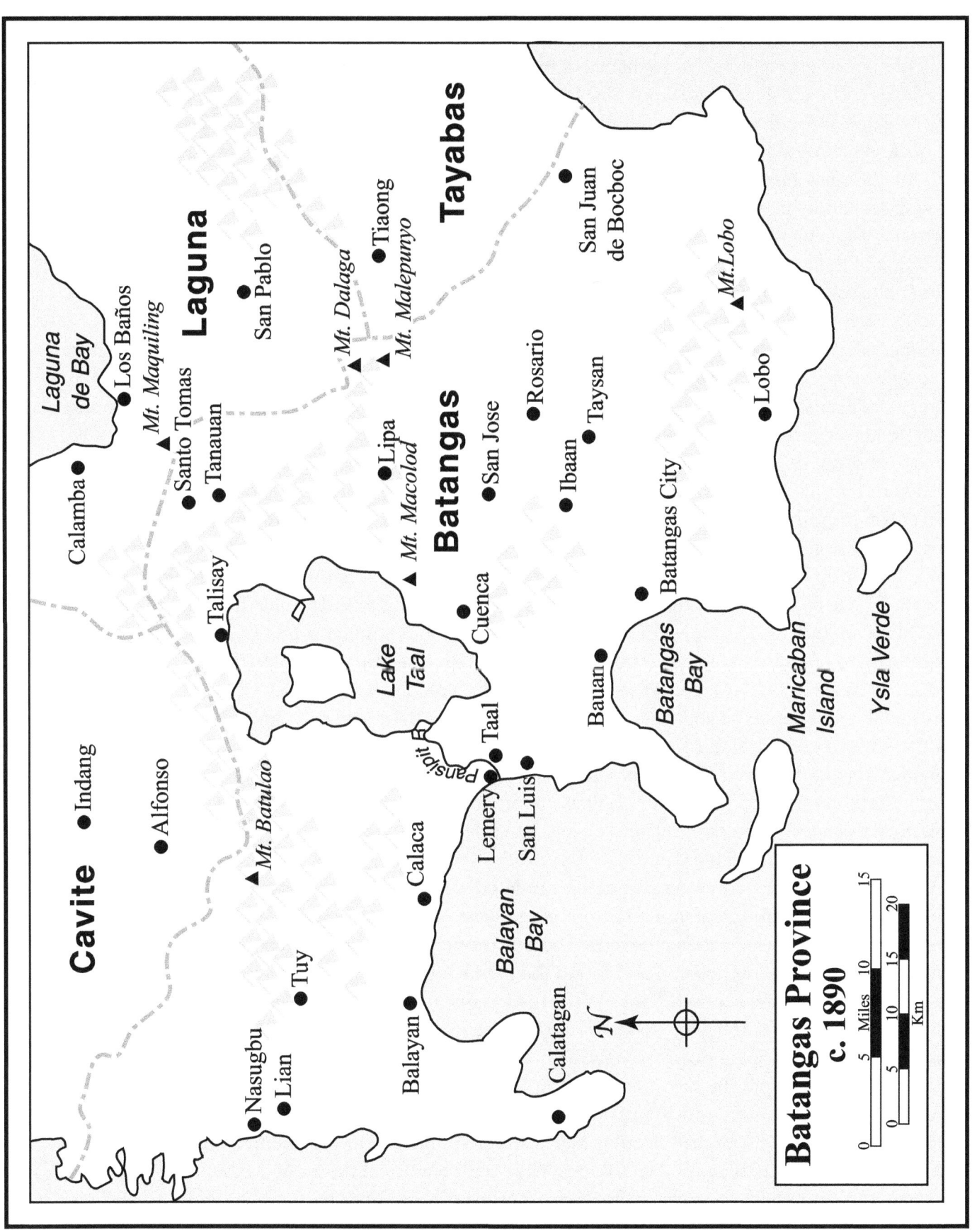

With the seizure of Batangas City, Schwann's soldiers had completed their occupation of the major towns and political centers of Batangas, which they would hold for the duration of the war. But many of his soldiers were sick and exhausted, their uniforms torn and tattered, socks and underwear were dirty, and their shoes were worn out. They were unwashed, and their faces were streaked with dirty sweat.[123] When Summerall rode into Batangas City, he wearily dismounted, and walked down to a dock of the bay where he found some food and some forage for the animals. Sitting down on the dock, he afforded himself the small luxury of opening a can of *pate de fois gras* that he had been carrying around in his saddlebag since receiving it in a Christmas package, probably mailed by Laura Mordecai. While he was enjoying this belated Christmas treat, quite likely lost in nostalgic thoughts of Laura and their time together, an officer walked up and asked if he could borrow a bar of soap to bathe in the river that flowed into the bay. Summerall obliged, but noted that he had to leave before the officer returned, and lamented that he never saw that bar of soap again.[124]

General Bates had decided to complete the conquest of southern Luzon and ordered Schwann into the provinces of Laguna and Tayabas to the east of Batangas. Schwann left Anderson's regiment in Batangas to garrison the eastern towns of the province and sent Muir to reinforce the towns to the west. He kept the battalion of the 39th with the rest of his brigade that still included Summerall's platoon, and on 19 January they left Batangas City and headed toward Laguna and Tayabas.[125] Summerall and his battalion commander rode ahead of the battalion's advance guard toward the town of San Jose and soon ran into a band of insurgents. Jumping down from their horses, they began firing their pistols and noticed that the advance guard was nowhere in sight. After chasing off the rebels, they rode back toward Batangas, discovered that the guard had taken the wrong road, and redirected them and the rest of the battalion along the road to San Jose. The next morning they broke camp at dawn and joined the rest of the brigade, pushing into Laguna province and advancing toward the town of Majayjay, about 30 miles northeast of San Jose (see map, p. 89).[126]

As the advance guard was composed of Summerall's platoon and the First Company of Macabebe Scouts, Hall and Summerall rode together. Summerall wrote that "We were ambushed several times and there was a good deal of firing, but the guns soon drove the insurrectos back. There were some casualties among the scouts." As Summerall and Hall rode and fought together, they became "very friendly," and he went on to describe Hall as "a remarkable type of man with proven courage. His blond face was weatherbeaten [sic], and deeply lined. His eyes were like blue steel and his hair and moustache were like blond wires."[127]

On 22 January, Schwann's expedition encountered a strong and impressive series of entrenchments blocking the passage across a narrow gorge west of Majayjay. Summerall's platoon was ordered forward with Hall's Macabebe Scouts to occupy the heights above the gorge. Hall and Summerall reconnoitered the Filipino position and found the flanks unprotected. Summerall placed his mountain guns to fire into the exposed flanks of the insurgents, while two companies lowered ropes and scaled down the sides of the gorge to attack the Filipino trenches. Facing Summerall's guns and with American soldiers dropping down around them, the defenders abandoned their strong position, and fled before firing a shot. The next day, Schwann's command continued their advance into Laguna province, with Summerall and his platoon marching with the advance guard, once again with Cheatam's battalion.[128] Now that his guns had won the confidence of the infantry, Summerall noted that they would do anything for the artillery. They built bamboo bridges and practically lifted the guns across deep ravines; later an entire company rigged ropes with hooks and toggles to pull his guns through boggy ground when the horses got stuck.[129]

Late in the evening on 24 January, Schwann's command reached the town of Santa Cruz (see map, p. 73) on the southeastern shore of Laguna de Bay, completing a course that had taken them through the provinces of Cavite, Batangas, Tayabas, and Laguna.[130] They settled down for the night before embarking the next day in *cascos* for Calamba. Summerall made a pallet in a nipa shack and was lying down to sleep when Lee Hall stopped by to say good-bye. Summerall asked him what he meant by that. According to Summerall, Hall replied that he was "going to Manila on that boat tonight and resign and go home. I have been thinking a lot these last few days. Every day, I have been going along these trails with the insurgents shooting and killing some of my men and some day it will be my turn. I am not going to let that day come. I will never go out there again." Summerall wrote that he "tried to remonstrate by saying that I must continue to go [on], and he could not leave me, but he was adamant." They shook hands and Hall left, as Summerall asserted, because he knew "by some intuition that the end of a life of danger and daring had come."[131]

In her biography entitled *Captain Lee Hall of Texas*, published in 1940, Dora Neill Raymond described a different reason for Hall's leaving the Philippines. She wrote that Hall fell ill in early February and was hospitalized in Manila until 19 March, when he returned to duty. For the next few months he was in and out of the hospital in Manila, and in June, was informed that he would serve no longer with the Macabebe Scouts. In September, when, for the fourth time, he was pronounced unfit for duty, he was honorably discharged and returned to Texas. There, he rejoined his wife, and sought without success to make a fortune in Mexican mining, oil drilling, and real estate. Broke and in poor health, Hall was hospitalized in San Antonio in March 1911, and died there before the end of the month at the age of 62.[132]

In his memoir, Summerall acknowledged a biography published "many years later" (after their service in the Philippines), in which the reason given for Hall's leaving the Philippines was his illness. Undoubtedly, Summerall had read Raymond's biography but had dismissed her well-documented account of Hall's illnesses and hospitalizations during his final months in the Philippines. Even though he actually had known Hall for just a few days, he loftily stated that "I am probably the only one to whom he [Hall] confided," thereby stubbornly insisting that Hall had left because of his premonition that an insurrecto's bullet soon would find him and not because he was ill. Summerall continued, stating that "He was an unforgettable character. I can understand the story that where he went, only one ranger was necessary to stop a riot. He was said to have killed a number of desperados."[133]

As he reflected on his admiration for Hall and the intense friendship that had developed between the 32-year-old first lieutenant and the 51-year-old ranger-warrior, it must have been inconceivable to him that such a man who had inspired and befriended him would not be truthful in confiding to him the real reason for leaving, in spite of Summerall's plea that Hall remain with him. Perhaps in Hall, a man who had "killed a number of desperados," Summerall had found a heroic figure that recalled his father and his courageous stand against the lawless gangs who had tried to kill him during the dark days of Reconstruction in Columbia County, Florida. Like Colonel Graham, Captain Riley, and Colonel Bullard, for Summerall, the old ranger was a strong father figure who had achieved the success that was denied to the talented and courageous Bryant Summerall.

The day after Summerall and Hall said their farewells, General Schwann's brigade loaded their guns, horses, supplies, and personnel onto the waiting *cascos* at Santa Cruz, and were towed to Calamba. They had completed roughly a circle in their campaign through the southern provinces of Cavite, Batangas, Tayabas, and Laguna. They had fought through rugged terrain and skillfully swept aside Filipino opposition, occupying the important towns and "setting the stage," according to Brian Linn, "for the imposition of political control over the populace."[134] Indeed, by the beginning of February 1900, Schwann's success had been matched by other commanders, and almost all of the key towns of the archipelago had fallen to the Americans.[135]

Meanwhile, the insurgents had learned painfully that with inferior weapons, insufficient ammunition of inferior quality, poor marksmanship, and without cavalry and naval power, they were no match for the Americans in conventional warfare. But as Linn and Glenn Anthony May point out, most enemy soldiers survived the invasion and continued to fight the U.S. soldiers. What made their resistance more effective thereafter, even though their efforts continued to be undermined by tribal and personal rivalries and organizational problems, was their shift to guerilla tactics.[136]

For two more years the war continued, marked by hit and run tactics staged by small guerilla bands led by local chieftains against American patrols and their use of terror to discourage native cooperation with the invaders. The Americans countered by using their superior fighting skills and firepower, and by developing means to maintain military operations in the jungles and mountains. They employed a reliable intelligence network to separate the guerillas from the general population, and did not hesitate to use harsh and punitive measures when "benevolent assimilation" failed. In March 1901, Brigadier General Frederick Funston captured Aguinaldo, causing many of the Filipino's followers to desert or surrender. By April 1902, the other important leaders had surrendered as well, and on 4 July, President Theodore Roosevelt pronounced the successful end of the war.[137]

About the time the Filipinos switched to guerilla tactics, Summerall and his platoon were detached from Schwann's brigade at Calamba, and ordered to return to Manila to rejoin Reilly's Battery for special artillery training. They boarded the familiar *cascos* on 8 February 1900 and docked the next day, where they were reunited with the other two platoons of Reilly's Battery. Reilly's other platoons had returned a few days earlier from northern Cavite, where they had made their way across rushing rivers, blasted insurgents from trenches dug into thick stands of bamboo along lush river banks, and received accolades much like the ones Summerall and his platoon had won. Their casualties also had been light, but Lieutenant Burgess had been wounded seriously in the leg fighting along the banks of the Imus River and had been sent back to San Francisco.[138]

While American commanders and their field units were developing and employing the tactics to defeat the guerilla tactics of the Filipinos, the three platoons of Reilly's Battery settled into the routines of garrison life at Camp Dewey just south of Manila. Early in March, they marched to Guadaloupe Heights above the capital to conduct experimental firing tests with shells containing a new high explosive charge called thorite. During April and May, they stayed busy test firing for the Ordnance Department a Hotchkiss gun and a Maxim-Nordenfeldt mountain gun, and conducting the usual marching drills and exercises with their horses. Occasionally, they took their horses down to the shore and let them swim in the waters of Manila Bay.[139]

One day, Colonel Bullard stopped by for a brief visit. While he and Reilly were discussing their recent campaign, Summerall overheard Bullard say that "He [Summerall] did not have to have a hammer to drive a nail."[140] Quite probably, Bullard was recalling Summerall's ability to overcome the challenges of nature, and to use to maximum effect the firepower of his small platoon against the insurrectos of Luzon. After leaving Camp Dewey, Bullard went on to lead his 39th Regiment on more victorious campaigns in southern Luzon, effectively implementing the policy of "benevolent assimilation," while forcing the surrender of many insurgent generals and their bands of fighters.

With the collapse of the insurrection in Luzon in March 1901, the 39th returned to Manila and sailed for home. Bullard followed them in September, but came back to the island of Mindanao, home of the insurgent Muslims known as Moros, in June 1902. There he took command of the 28th Infantry, led them in a series of victorious campaigns against the Moros, and concluded his service in the Philippines as governor of the Lake Lanao district of Mindanao. Tired and anxious to get home to his family and kin in Alabama, Bullard left Manila for San Francisco, on 15 July, and returned home to prepare for the challenges that lay ahead for him and the army, both domestically and abroad.[141]

After Bullard left in early February 1900 to rejoin his regiment in southern Luzon, Reilly's Battery resumed their routine at Camp Dewey, doubtless learning of new victories won by other units in the field, as they dutifully and routinely honed their skills. While wondering when they would return to action, they could not know that they had fought their last campaign in the Philippine War, nor what lay ahead were new dangers in a land even more exotic, amid circumstances just as complex and challenging as any they had confronted during their fight in the Philippines.

While Summerall and his battery mates worked through the hot and dry months of March and June into the rainy season of June and July, he could be pleased with his service during the war in the Philippines. Certainly, his colleagues and immediate superior officers had praised his work. He had impressed others as well. In January 1901, Colonel John I. Rodgers, then in command of the 5th Artillery Regiment, responding to a request from the headquarters of the regiment at Fort Hamilton, New York, for a list of officers having a "special aptitude for field artillery," named Summerall and seven other lieutenants, including Burgess, along with five captains.[142] Meeting in Manila on 25 May, an examination board headed by Colonel Tully McCrea of the Artillery Corps rated Summerall in eight subject areas: administration, drill regulations, exterior ballistics, fire discipline, hippology, military field engineer, military law, and minor tactics. In administration, drill regulations, ballistics, fire discipline, and military field engineering, he received a perfect score of 100. In hippology, military law, and minor tactics, his score was 90. Each score was multiplied by the relative weight of the subject matter, ranging from one to three. Out of a possible final total of 1,400 points, Summerall received 1,340, for an overall average of 95.71;[143] it was an impressive score by any standard.

Clearly, Summerall was pleased to have won the respect of the veteran officer James Parker and the friendship of Lee Hall, the rugged ranger from Texas. He also noted with satisfaction Colonel Anderson's swift reversal of his "prejudice" against the artillery, but he was most pleased and gratified to have won the praise and confidence, as well as the friendship and support, of Robert L. Bullard. The latter emerged from the Philippine War as one of the army's most energetic, aggressive and successful commanders, and not surprisingly, Bullard's energetic and aggressive style of command was a model that Summerall would follow when he succeeded his friend and mentor in command of the First Division, and when he served as V Corps commander in the last year of the Great War. Indeed, as the AEF fought toward victory in the final and climactic Battle of the Meuse-Argonne in 1918, Summerall might well have allowed the eager and aggressive spirit he had admired and acquired to overwhelm the necessity also for caution and careful deliberation before he ordered an attack. As will be seen, his actions during the concluding phases of the battle erupted into a controversy whose impact influenced his behavior and decisions for most of the remaining years of his life.

In the Philippine War, Summerall acquired characteristics in combat that came to distinguish him as a commander in the field, whether of small units or large ones: upright and courageous under fire, leveling heavy and concentrated fire against the enemy and his fortifications; and ordering an all-out, straight-ahead attack on his objectives. He seemed undaunted by opposition, whether from the rugged and diverse challenges of nature, or by the stubborn, if erratic, resistance of Filipino fighters. With a resilience toughened by the rigors of life during Reconstruction in central Florida and on the Plain at West Point, he emerged from the muddy roads, struggling villages, tangled jungles, and tall grasses of the Philippines, convinced that there was no obstacle that he could not overcome and sweep aside. He was well prepared for the next challenges he would face at the center of the vast, but crumbling, empire of the last of the Manchu rulers of China.

# Chapter Five

## *China and the Boxer Rebellion*

The Manchus had swept down from the north and seized Peking in 1644, and established the ruling family of China's last dynasty, called the Qing, which would rule China for more than 250 years. Two centuries of expansion incorporated Outer Mongolia and Tibet into their empire, but corruption and stagnation steadily weakened their rule. During the course of the 19th century European powers, including Great Britain, France, Germany, and Russia took advantage of these weaknesses to force trade concessions from the regime and to carve out their own spheres of influence. They stirred deep resentment among peasant masses, as their railroad tracks desecrated ancient burial sites, and their telegraph lines emitted low, moaning sounds in the wind, and dripped rusty red drops in the rain, suggesting that foreigners were torturing the spirits of the realm.[1]

In the wake of foreign expansion came increasing numbers of Christian missionaries. China moved ahead of Africa as the most important field for missionary activity. Through their devotion to their faith and good works, both Catholic and Protestant missionaries gained converts, built churches, and even cathedrals, increasing the reach and influence of the West throughout China. However, people from all classes across the country resented Christians for taking valuable land out of cultivation to build churches, schools and hospitals; for intervening in legal disputes that involved converts; and for the refusal of converts to practice ancestor worship and participate in traditional village ceremonies and rituals. Chinese converts to Christianity especially aroused intense animosity in the eyes of many of their countrymen. They believed these converts ceased being Chinese when they became Christians, and thus personified the grave danger that foreigners presented to the integrity and survival of China.[2]

In mid-century the combination of floods, droughts, famines, and the inability of the government to cope with these disasters, as well as with the corrosive inroads of foreigners, led to an uprising known as the Taiping Rebellion. It turned into a huge protest against Manchu rule, as thousands rose in the south and demanded a return to a legendary ancient state where the peasants owned and tilled the land, and practiced esoteric rituals in quasi-religious, secret societies dedicated to enforce a strict morality. Not until British and French forces came to the aid of the Imperial army, thus affirming Manchu political and military weakness, did the government succeed in crushing the revolt. When it ended 14 years after it began, more than 30 million people had been killed.[3]

Exploiting China's declining power, Europeans seized countries on the periphery of China that long had paid tribute to the emperor. In 1894 Japan, after having been jarred awake by the appearance in Tokyo Bay of Commodore Matthew Perry's U.S. squadron of four vessels in 1853–1854, and having gone through a thorough modernization, declared war on the enfeebled empire. The Japanese army drove the Chinese from their protectorate in Korea, marched into Manchuria, and was preparing to advance on Peking when the Qing administration dispatched an envoy to Japan to negotiate peace. The Treaty of Shimonoseki, signed in April 1895, in the port city on the southwestern tip of the island of Honshu, forced China to recognize Korean independence; acknowledge Japanese hegemony over the Korean peninsula; cede Taiwan and the Penghu Islands to Japan; pay an enormous indemnity; and agree to the establishment of Japanese industries in four treaty ports.[4]

Japan's unexpected victory reaffirmed China's political and military weakness, and led the great powers to expand their spheres of influence. The British added to their foothold in Hong Kong by securing a lease on the port and adjacent waters and territory of Wei-Hai-Wei in the northeast province of Shantung; the French gained control of the city and excellent harbor of Kwangchow, south of Hong Kong; the Germans took over Kiaochow Bay, to the south of Shantung Peninsula; and Russia secured the right to build a railroad across Manchuria to Vladivostok, and to establish control over Port Arthur and the Liaotung Peninsula that jutted out across from the Shantung Peninsula into the Gulf of Chihli.[5] The United States, with British support, urged the preservation of China's political and territorial integrity, not so much for altruistic reasons, but rather to prevent the great powers from using their spheres of influence to keep American businessmen from exploiting Chinese markets. In September 1899, Secretary of State John Hay outlined the Open Door Note, whereby all foreign countries would have equal duties and privileges in all areas of a sovereign China. Although Great Britain was the only country to accept Hay's policy, no country actually rejected it.[6]

If the Qing administration were to regain complete control of the empire and restore its integrity, either it could follow the example of Japan and open the country to Western ways and embark in earnest on a process of modernization; or it could reject Westernization altogether, rid the land of foreigners, and isolate China from the outside world. For 103 days, from 11 June to 21 September 1898, modernization appeared to be the course set by the government. The young emperor, Kuang Hsu, sought to establish a de facto constitutional monarchy and ordered a series of reforms that he hoped would revolutionize the legal and educational systems, remake the military, send students abroad for technological training, and transform agriculture, medicine and mining. Not surprisingly, his radical moves provoked a strong reaction among the conservative elite. They condemned the proposed reforms as too extreme and advocated a policy that would promote a more moderate and gradual approach to change. The Dowager Empress Tsu Hsi, the emperor's aunt, who twice had been regent and regarded the emperor's reforms as a threat to her status and influence, allied herself with the reactionaries. She engineered a *coup d'etat* against her nephew on 21 September 1898 and forced him into seclusion. The new edicts were rescinded, six of the reform leaders were executed, others were arrested, and some managed to flee abroad. The so-called Hundred Days' Reform ended with the return of reactionary and conservative elites to power in the capital of Peking.[7] Whether they could stir the people to revitalize the empire by ridding it of "foreign devils" and accept gradual change only within the confines of China's traditions remained an open question.

A young and talented American mining engineer named Herbert Hoover, working in northern China, believed that an anti-foreign atavistic movement among the people already had begun. In his memoirs, the 26-year-old Stanford graduate, and future U.S. president, wrote that "The constant encroachment by the European powers—Britain, Russia, Germany, France—on the independence and sovereignty of China had at last touched off hidden mines in the Chinese soul. There swept over North China one of those blind emotional movements not unusual among Asiatic masses."[8]

The movement that Hoover said gave him and his wife Lou "something to talk about for 'the rest of their born days,'"[9] came to their attention in the spring of 1900, when the Hoovers heard about a new secret society called the "Fists of Righteous Harmony" that foreigners called "Boxers." It had emerged in the difficult period of the mid-1890s among the peasants of Shantung province, where there existed a long tradition of the martial arts. They were organized into militia bands, tied red handkerchiefs around their heads and red ribbons on their arms and legs, and wound red sashes around the waist of their loose-fitting shirts. They practiced their rituals in Buddhist temples and before village audiences, where they twirled red banners, engaged in kowtowing and incense burning, as well as elaborate calisthenics that featured whirling and trusting of swords, spears, and long pikes, and thrusts with fists and feet. Some became "possessed," and claimed to be invulnerable to sword blows, spear jabs, bullets, and cannonballs. As it grew, this cult of invulnerability proved to be a powerful recruiting agent, particularly among the young, many of whom were no more than 12 or 13 years old. If one were wounded or killed in these ceremonial exercises, so these Boxers believed, it was because he had not conformed or remained faithful to the elaborate rituals of the movement.[10]

Like so many Chinese, the Boxers hated the "foreign devils" for their alien religion and desecration of the past and present and blamed them for all of China's ills, including recent floods and droughts that led to bad harvests and outbreaks of disease. Special hatred was reserved for those whom the Boxers called "secondary devils"; namely, Chinese converts to Christianity, whom, as mentioned earlier, many Chinese already had come to regard essentially as traitors.[11]

The uprising began on the last day of 1899, under the tolerant eye of the governor of Shantung, when the Boxers claimed their first victim, the British missionary, Reverend Sidney Brooks. He was attacked about a mile from his church and beaten to death by a band of about 30 armed men who chopped off his head, threw it into a roadside gully, and dumped his body in after it.[12] In response to messages from the British and other foreign legations in Peking urging that the government suppress the violence, the Tsungli Yamen, the Chinese foreign office, promised that Brooks' murderers would be found and arrested. On 11 January, the Court issued a decree that stunned foreign officials in the capital and filled them with apprehension for their safety. Rather than condemning the entire Boxer movement, the decree drew a sharp distinction between those Boxers who were "'peaceful and law-abiding'" practitioners of their skills in martial arts, and those who were causing "'disturbances.'" The foreigners' fears were soon confirmed, as bands of Boxers, interpreting the decree as a sign of the Court's approval, surged northward through Shantung, crossed the Yellow River into the province of Chihli, and advanced toward the fortified city of Tientsin, some 70 miles south of their ultimate goal, the great, walled, capital of Peking (see map, p. 97).[13]

Initially, the Boxers concentrated their fury against Christians and their converts, burning churches and butchering congregations. As their numbers and influence increased, however, they attacked all things foreign, including railroads and telegraph lines, as well as any foreign workers they could find. Many of those who escaped the rage of the Boxers fled to Peking, where they sought refuge in the compounds and churches of the foreign legations. Herbert Hoover felt the danger had grown so great that he withdrew the men of his geological expedition into Peking, even though they had "outlined a field of anthracite coal larger than all the other anthracite fields in the world put together."[14] By May 1900, bands of Boxers had infiltrated Tientsin, as well as Peking, and were roaming freely through the streets of the capital.

Fearing for their safety and the lives of their personnel and families, foreign ministers in Peking now demanded that the Court suppress and abolish the "Fists of Righteous Harmony," but the Empress Dowager paid no attention to their messages. Accordingly, the ministers agreed to summon guards stationed upon ships dispatched by the American, British, French, German, Russian, Japanese, Italian, and Austro-Hungarian governments, and anchored off the town of Taku as a show of support.[15] This small settlement of 700 inhabitants lay along the eastern bank at the mouth of the Han River, some 37 miles east of Tientsin, and was guarded by four mud-walled forts, two on each riverbank

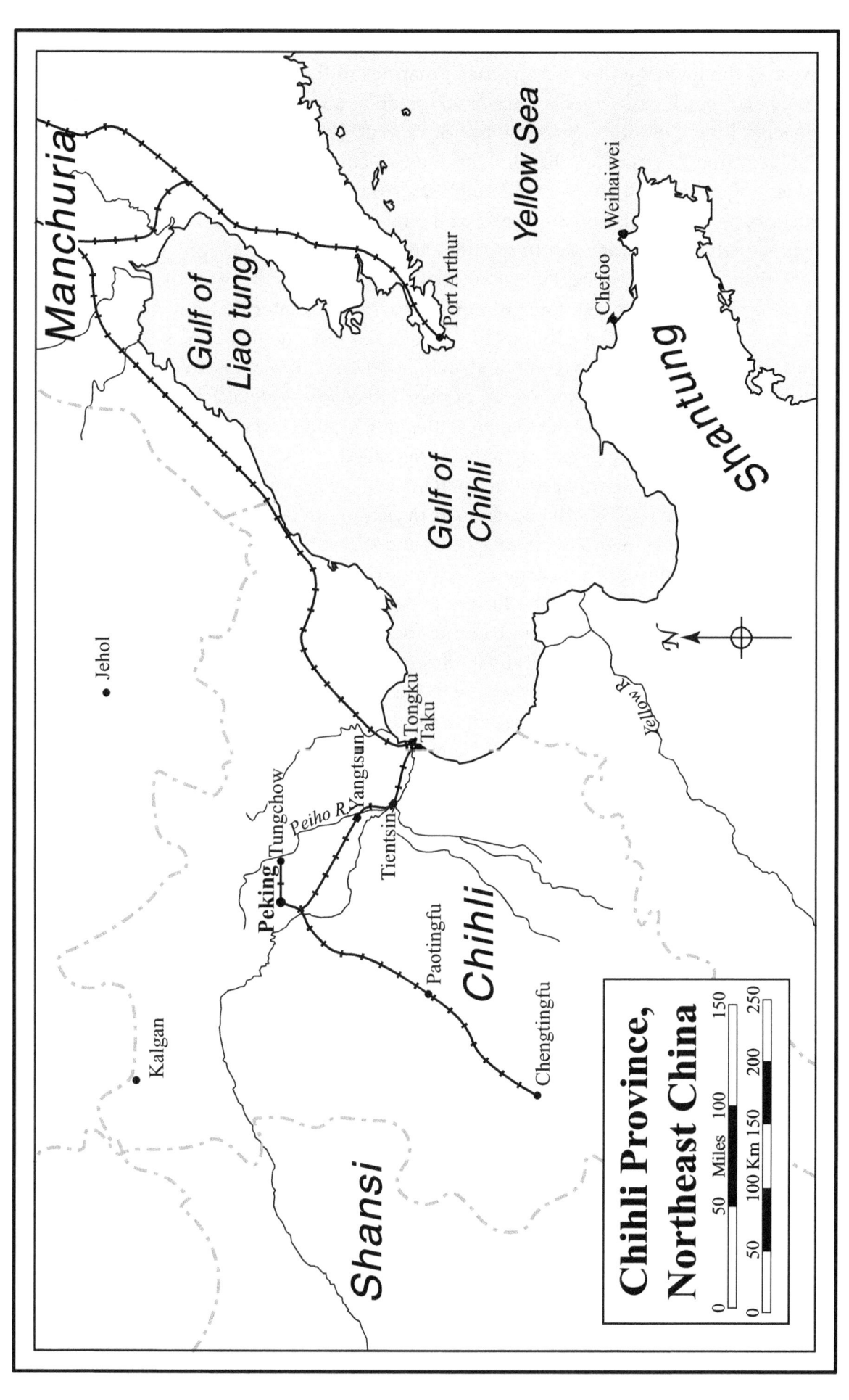

just west of the town. Led by 150 American marines of the 9th Infantry Regiment from the U.S.S. *Monocacy* and the U.S.S. *Newark*, a force of 400 legation guards from the other powers arrived in Peking in early June. Tensions increased when Boxers cut the rail line between Tientsin and Peking on 6 June and severed the telegraph line linking the two cities three days later.[16] According to historian Peter Fleming in his book *The Siege of Peking*, "the straw that broke the camel's back" was the Boxers' destruction, on 9 June, of the grandstand at the racetrack just outside Peking. This act forced some Englishmen who were riding out to the track to reverse course and spur their horses back to their legation, firing their pistols over their shoulders at the Boxers as they fled their screaming pursuers at a fast gallop.[17] At any rate, the foreign ministers assembled later that day at the British legation in Peking and agreed to ask the admirals to dispatch reinforcements at once. British Vice Admiral Sir Edward Seymour was named to command an international force of just over 2,000 troops. On 10 June, they left Tientsin on five trains made up of over 100 coaches. He left behind a force of about 1,100 soldiers and marines to defend the foreign settlement, located just outside the thick, high walls of the Chinese City, as the old, inner city of Tientsin was called.[18]

As the train bearing Seymour and his men made its way slowly toward Peking, the troops painstakingly repaired the rail lines the Boxers had ripped up. In order to do so, they had to fight off the Boxers' spirited attacks. Swinging their swords and thrusting with pikes, screaming "Kill! Kill!" and believing in their invincibility, the fanatical Chinese charged the coaches, only to be mowed down by rifle and machine-gun fire. Still, the Boxers pressed their attacks, and by 16 June, had cut off the expedition from its supply of food and ammunition at Tientsin.[19]

Responding to these attacks, the naval officers on board their ships off Taku ordered an attack on the Taku forts. They hoped to clear the way to Tientsin, secure the necessary supplies, and establish communication with Seymour's Expedition. On 16 June, they issued an ultimatum to the Chinese commander to surrender the forts. When he rejected their demand, naval vessels began bombarding the forts, and the next day infantry units attacked and captured them.[20]

News of the allied ultimatum of 16 June reached the Manchu court the next day as the Empress Dowager met with her council to consider what should be done about escalating attacks of the Boxers in Peking. She reacted angrily to the allied demands, issuing a decree calling for provincial governors to send soldiers to Peking, and ordering the Imperial army to attack Seymour's Expedition and the foreign settlement in Tientsin.[21]

Facing a combined force of Boxers and Imperial soldiers, and realizing that he could neither advance nor retreat by rail, Seymour ordered his men to abandon their train and retreat on foot to Tientsin. On 20 June, they began a grueling march down the Pei Ho River toward Tientsin, fighting off imperial cavalry attacks and artillery bombardments from the rail bed that ran parallel to the river. They carried their wounded and their dwindling supply of food and water. Spare ammunition was loaded on four junks that were towed through the muddy, shallow waters of the Pei Ho. Swirling dust storms kicked up by the dry wind from the northern deserts were a further hindrance. Two days later, they reached the safety of an old arsenal, six miles from Tientsin, where they met a relief column sent out from the city. On 24 June, they made it back to the foreign settlements of Tientsin in spite of heavy artillery and rifle fire from some 10,000 imperial troops and thousands of Boxer auxiliaries, many of them firing on them from within the strong walls of the old Chinese City. Seymour's Expedition had suffered casualties of 62 killed and 232 wounded; American losses were 4 killed and 28 wounded.[22] The expedition was finished as a fighting force, and the first Allied rescue attempt had failed completely. The fate of those under fire in the foreign settlement of Tientsin, and those who remained marooned and besieged in the Chinese capital, remained in great danger.

The ancient city of Peking, with a population in 1900 of about one million in a country of over 300 million inhabitants, lay just to the west of the Pei Ho River in the northern plain of China. It was less than 50 miles south of the Great Wall, some 20 miles northwest of Tientsin. Massive walls bounded the city on four sides, enclosing four distinct and delineated walled sections known as "cities." Behind the huge south wall lay the Chinese City, with its lakes and gardens of the Temple of Agriculture and Temple of Heaven. It was enclosed by four walls over 30 feet high and over 20 feet thick. Adjoining the Chinese City to the north was the Tartar City, enclosed by four massive walls over 40 feet high and 55 feet wide at the top, and more than 60 feet thick at the base. Another boundary of four more walls colored pink and as high, but less thick than the walls of the Tartar City, enclosed the Imperial City that contained palaces, temples, gardens, and public offices. Finally, four interior walls marked the boundary of the Forbidden City, where the emperor, known as the Son of Heaven, moved about in an inner sanctum of lofty gateways, courtyards, gardens, colorful pavilions and palaces. Six huge, iron-studded wooden gates, *men* in Chinese, sheathed in metal and crowned with pagodas that served as watchtowers, opened into sally ports (wide, arched openings) that led through the outer walls of the Chinese City. Three similar gates and sally ports were in each of the massive south and east walls of the Tartar City, while other fortified gates led into sally ports from the south through the walls of the Imperial City and into the Forbidden City.

The diplomatic missions, known then as foreign legations, were located inside the Tartar City in an enclave that covered an area about three-quarters of a square mile. Its boundary was the Tartar Wall to the south and the walls of the Imperial City to the north. The walled-in compounds of 11 nations contained just under 1,000 men, women, and children. Stores, shops, and trees lined Legation Street, which ran diagonally across the quarter outside the walled compounds, and over a foul-smelling canal that flowed through a sluice gate under the Tartar Wall and into a moat on the other side. The American Legation was located about 400 yards to the east of the Chien Men and right across the street from the Russian Legation. The British Legation was the most prominent and important of them all, occupying an area of almost three acres just behind the Russian Legation and across the street from the south wall of the Imperial City. The British compound adjoined Hanlin College, the center of Chinese scholarship, and home of the Hanlin Library that contained the oldest and richest collection of illuminated manuscripts in the world (see map, p. 100).[23]

As they listened apprehensively in their Legation Quarter for news of the Seymour Expedition, foreigners were kept busy arranging accommodations and food for the 400 guards that had arrived in their midst, and assisting the pastors and priests with the increasing number of missionaries and their converts that continued to converge on the Legation Quarter. Eventually, their numbers swelled to over 4,000.[24] Stories spread about the atrocities committed by Boxers throughout northern China, but no one at the Legations had yet seen one of these notorious characters. This suddenly changed on 13 June when Baron Clemens von Kettler, the German minister, noticed a Boxer in full regalia sitting on a cart in Legation Street sharpening a knife on his boot. The hot-tempered von Kettler attacked him with his walking stick, but he managed to escape. The German then administered a savage beating to another young Boxer in the cart, dragged him off, and imprisoned him in the German Legation. In retaliation, that same afternoon thousands of Boxers burst through the Ha Ta Men, just to the east of the Legation Quarter, burning shops and houses on Legation Street, and slashing their way through crowds of terrified men and women fleeing past the Legations. Brandishing torches, the Boxers set fire to several churches and cathedrals and stormed the walls of the Austro-Hungarian Legation, but bursts of machine-gun fire drove them away.[25]

On 15 June, American, Russian, British, and German marines went out on patrol to rescue survivors of the riot, and kill any Boxers they could find. When they returned, they reported that the streets

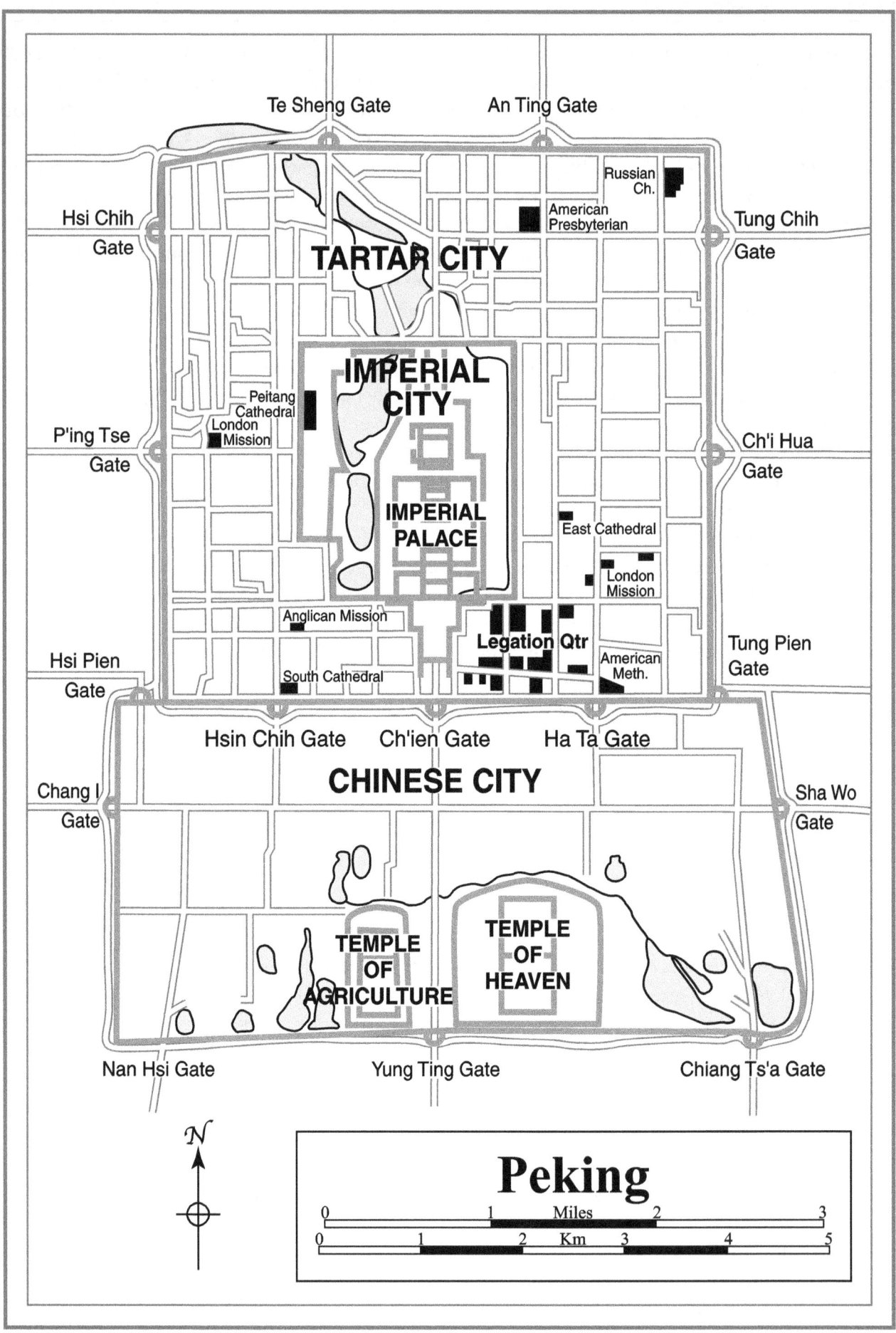

were littered with the mutilated corpses of men, women, and children, as well as the bodies of 100 Boxers. The next day, the hordes of Boxers returned, setting fire throughout the Chinese City to over 4,000 stores and shops that sold foreign goods. The fire engulfed the soaring 100-foot-high pagoda over the Chien Men, but the massive walls of the Tartar City shielded the Legation Quarter from the Chien Men fire.[26]

Convening in the wake of the deadly and fiery violence of the past few days, the imperial council, having already rejected the allied ultimatum to surrender the Taku forts, issued on 19 June, at 1600 hours, its own ultimatum. Its demands shocked the entire Legation Quarter. The Court considered the impending attack on the forts a declaration of war by all the Powers; hence, the foreign ministers were required to surrender their passports and depart Peking within 24 hours. They were to proceed under Chinese escort to Tientsin, and from there leave China. The stunned diplomats met and decided that current conditions were too dangerous for them to comply with the deadline and undertake the journey to Tientsin, but they did agree to leave. In hopes that the regime could stop the violence, or that a relief force could reach them soon, they requested more than 24 hours to make the necessary preparations.[27]

By mid-morning on 20 June, the Tsungli Yamen had not replied to the Legations' request, so Baron von Kettler decided to present himself to the Yamen and remain there until he received a response. Shortly before noon, he and his secretary left the German Legation in two canopied and colorful sedan chairs and turned east along Legation Street. As they approached Customs Street to turn toward the foreign office, an armed soldier walked up to the German minister's chair, leveled his rifle, and fired a bullet through a side window into von Kettler's head, killing him instantly. Though wounded with two shots in his thigh, the secretary escaped and dragged himself to the American Missionary Mission at the eastern end of Legation Street. There, he told of his minister's murder before passing out from loss of blood. The effect of von Kettler's death settled the issue for the Legations: no one would leave Legation Quarter, and they would defend themselves at any cost until relief arrived from the south.[28]

As the deadline of 1600 hours on 20 June approached, the foreign ministers decided to gather all legation personnel and families in the British Legation; thus shrinking the perimeter they might have to defend, including those under the looming, massive walls of the Tartar City. The various Legation personnel hurriedly collected food and ammunition, and soon a cosmopolitan crowd of over 473 men, women and children, along with just over 400 military personnel, had assembled in the Legation that normally accommodated about 60. Milling about in the gathering was an assortment of ponies, mules, a flock of sheep, and one cow. Prince Su, a wealthy courtier sympathetic to the plight of some 4,000 Chinese converts who were streaming into the Legation Quarter from throughout the city, agreed to provide sanctuary for them on the spacious grounds of his palace, directly across the canal from the British Legation.

At precisely 1600 hours, a low, bellowing horn sounded from beyond the Tartar Wall to the east, and gunshots rang out, killing a French soldier and wounding an Austrian.[29] The siege of Peking had begun.

Sir Claude MacDonald, the British Minister, was the "host" of those who had settled in his Legation, and the senior Allied minister serving in Peking. MacDonald was a military veteran of several African campaigns, and he logically assumed responsibility for directing the defense. He appointed a Fortification Staff that supervised the construction of trenches and barricades around the Legation compound and all other defensive measures. A detachment of guards was sent to protect Prince Su's compound, and another was dispatched to erect a barricade reinforced with sandbags. These were made from cut-off trousers and window curtains, and piled on a section of the Tartar Wall closest to the Legations and not yet occupied by the Boxers. They were determined to prevent the enemy from setting up artillery positions there that would enfilade the perimeter. Allied rifle and machine-gun ammunition was in short supply. The Legations' only artillery piece was an old Chinese iron cannon that was retrieved from a well. Once repaired, it was used on the barricades with surprisingly good effect, even though it belched black smoke with each round fired.

Other committees dealt with sanitation and supervised the collection of food. A hospital was set up on Legation grounds with a well-stocked supply of drugs. Large stocks of cereals and grain, especially rice, were accumulated and five sweet-water wells were tapped to provide plenty of water. Now that the racing season was finished (thanks to the Boxers' wrecking the track and burning the grandstand), ponies stabled nearby assured the Legations an ample supply of meat. Indeed, among the Legation personnel, optimism prevailed that the siege would be a short affair. But even if it dragged on, they thought themselves well prepared to withstand it until relief arrived from Tientsin.[30]

At nightfall on 20 June, the Imperial army and their Boxer auxiliaries began their full-scale assault on the Legation sector. They concentrated their attacks at night, firing shells from Krupp 9-pounder guns over the burned-out hulk of the Chien Men, launching flaming arrows and rockets, and catapulting hot bricks into buildings and barricades. Imperial and Boxer soldiers often followed these nightly barrages with charges against Allied barricades and suffered heavy losses when they ran into machine-gun and rifle fire. After one nighttime action, Allied soldiers collected the bodies of over 100 Chinese soldiers, hoisted them up to the barricade on the Tartar Wall, and tossed them over. But the siege had begun to take its toll on the Allies as well.[31]

Lack of sleep and constant strain exhausted both soldiers and civilians; bouts of dysentery broke out frequently, and the stench of human waste and bloated bodies lying in the streets in the summer heat added to the discomfort. Flies and the odor of blood pervaded the hospital, and over 100 defenders had been killed or wounded by the end of June. Supplies of food, ample enough to last through a brief encounter, were running alarmingly low, and the number of ponies dwindled swiftly as they were slaughtered for their meat. Infiltrators slipped into Hanlin College and set it on fire, destroying almost all of the ancient illuminated manuscripts, and almost succeeding in spreading the fire to the adjacent British Legation. The Allies still held the barricade atop the Tartar Wall and continued to repel attempts by the enemy to overwhelm and destroy this strategic position. As the siege continued into the even more debilitating heat of July, many began to wonder just how much longer they could hold out, and if relief from Tientsin would ever arrive.[32]

The spirits of the Legation personnel would have been even more depressed if they had known that Seymour's Expedition had failed, and their counterparts in Tientsin were under fierce assault. The 10,000 imperial soldiers and thousands of Boxers intensified the bombardment that greeted Seymour's Expedition as it staggered back into Tientsin. They concentrated artillery fire on the British and French legations and foreign settlements that lay southwest of the ancient walled city along the Pei Ho River, and fired rifles through loopholes in the thick mud walls of the ancient Chinese City at anyone within range.[33] Herbert Hoover and his wife Lou had just returned from a quick trip to Peking and carefully made their way to their house that "was on the edge of the [foreign] settlement and exposed to constant rifle and artillery fire." During the fighting that lasted just over a month, he estimated that some 60,000 shells were fired into the settlement.[34] With a force of just over 1,700 soldiers, Allies were not strong enough to mount an assault on the Chinese City. But events in Tientsin and Peking aroused the attention of their governments, and, fortunately for their compatriots that were under fire and besieged in both cities, relief was on the way.

On 27 June, the U.S. 9th Infantry Regiment, commanded by Colonel Emerson H. Liscum, along with a battalion of the 1st Marine Regiment, commanded by Colonel Robert L. Meade, embarked in

Manila Bay. On 6 July, they dropped anchor in the sweltering heat and shallow waters of the Bay of Chihli, just off the Taku Bar, some six to eight miles from shore.[35] They were ferried ashore and joined newly arrived forces from Russia and Japan, as well as contingents from Britain, France, Germany, Austria, and Italy. As these reinforcements neared the foreign settlements in Tientsin, the Chinese, surprisingly enough, stopped firing into the area. Amid this unexpected pause, the Hoovers heard sounds of the approaching soldiers, walked out of their house and climbed up on the roof of a warehouse. They soon caught sight of the marines and a group of Royal Welsh Fusiliers. Herbert Hoover recalled that he did not "remember of more satisfying musical performance than the bugles of the American Marines entering the settlement playing "'There'll Be a Hot Time in the Old Town Tonight.'"[36]

During the next few days, as the Allied contingent of some 6,000 men settled into their bivouacs, their commanding officers decided that they must seize the Chinese City in Tientsin before they could march on to Peking. They planned a direct assault against the City and to take it, essentially, by storm. Even though the Chinese outnumbered their forces, they reasoned that such an attack on all sides of the City would disperse the defenders so that Allied firepower could overwhelm them. The Japanese would lead the attack, advancing along a lengthy causeway that led up to the south gate. American and British units would support them on the left, and the French would advance in support on the right. The supporting attacks would cross a broad and difficult expanse of low-lying and swampy ground, broken up into ponds between six inches and eight feet deep, crisscrossed with ditches and low embankments, and interspersed with grave mounds. Coordination of the attacks would be difficult since the Allies had not appointed a supreme commander, and language barriers complicated communications across the attacking forces.[37]

At any rate, in the pre-dawn hours of 13 July, the Japanese, British, Americans, and French attacked the south gate of the City in three columns, while the Russians, with the support of the Germans and a few Austrians, circled around and attacked the north gate. Herbert Hoover was familiar with the terrain and accompanied the marines in their attack. As they advanced, they came under fire from the walls and sought cover behind grave mounds. "I was completely scared," he wrote, "especially when some of the Marines next to me were hit. I was unarmed and I could scarcely make my feet move forward. I asked the officer I was accompanying if I could have a rifle. He produced one from a wounded Marine, and at once I experienced a curious psychological change for I was no longer scared, although I never fired a shot. I can recommend that men carry weapons when they go into battle—it is a great comfort." As dawn emerged and the other forces came into sight, Hoover was dismissed and returned safely to his home and to his wife, who had decided to remain and help care for the sick.[38] To many of those who remained in the field such a safe return seemed doubtful.

Heavy fire from the walls pinned down the supporting forces in water holes and behind the grave mounds, and they suffered heavy losses while gaining little ground. The 9th Infantry was caught in a dangerously exposed position and lost Colonel Liscum, who fell mortally wounded in the stomach. He had attempted to pick up the flag that a bearer had dropped when shot in the knee. Swinging around to attack the north gate, Russians, Germans, and Austrians also came under fire that pinned them down for most of the day. Before dawn, the main attacking force of Japanese infantry charged up the causeway in the face of fierce fire from the south wall. Several hundred men were cut down, but with the Allies providing some cover from the flanks, the Japanese succeeded in establishing positions close to the wall. Early on 14 July, they blew open the south gate, and their *banzai* charge took them through the streets and into the heart of the Chinese City. They rushed past frightened inhabitants, but found no imperial soldiers, or Boxers; they had fled to the north and west just after the explosion that had destroyed the south gate. Soon the City filled with Allied soldiers, who released their frustration and anger in an excess of violence, looting, and pillaging. They stripped the City of anything of value and left it a smoldering ruin. Its streets were littered with dead bodies of all ages and sexes.[39] The sack and seizure of the Chinese City of Tientsin was complete, and Peking lay ahead.

In the Chinese capital, the fall of Tientsin stunned the Empress Dowager and forced her to yield to the more moderate faction at court that insisted the government's policy was leading to self-destruction. On 17 July, she declared a truce in the siege of the foreign legations. The besieged and hungry foreigners were joyous at the news, and encouraged when a group of Chinese soldiers appeared the next day atop the Tartar Wall carrying a flag of truce, offering fruits, vegetables, and chickens. That same day their spirits soared when a Japanese messenger reported that Tientsin had been captured and that a relief force of over 11,000 troops was preparing to march on Peking.[40] During the next two weeks, however, the besieged foreigners became more and more apprehensive. The Chinese soldiers failed to provide the food they had offered; supplies of rice and other foods stockpiled in the British Legation dwindled; and they had eaten most of the ponies and all of the stray dogs they could round up. Many small children had died and many more were sick; no one was certain just when the relief force would arrive.[41] A sudden and dramatic change in the Forbidden City soon justified their apprehension.

Emboldened by the arrival at court of her fiercely anti-foreign favorite and former governor of Shantung province, Li Peng-hing, the Empress Dowager drew more Boxers into her inner circle, and, in a sweeping ideological purge of the moderate faction at Court, executed five of their leaders. Then, on 4 August, suddenly and without warning, she shattered the truce by ordering a full-scale bombardment of the Legation compound and an assault on the barricades on the Tartar Wall.[42] The siege of Peking had resumed, and neither the besieged nor those poised to save them, could be certain of the outcome.

After the fall of Tientsin, the major powers had agreed that the German Field Marshal Count Alfred von Waldersee would command the international relief force, but Waldersee was not scheduled to leave Germany for China until 18 August.[43] In the meantime, soldiers were disembarking at Taku and piling into Tientsin, with nothing more to do than to mill about amid the rubble and ruin of the Chinese City. However, after General Alfred Gaselee, the British commander-in-chief, arrived in Tientsin on 27 July, he argued for quick action. With strong support from two American officers, Major General Adna Chaffee and Colonel A. S. Daggett, the allied council agreed on 5 August that an international relief force would march to the rescue of the foreign legations in Peking.[44]

General Chaffee, the stocky, jut-jawed successor to Major General Arthur MacArthur as commander of the U.S. Army in the Philippines, had reached Tientsin at the end of July in order to take charge of all American soldiers in China. In addition to the 12 companies of the 9th Infantry and the battalion of marines that had participated in the attack on the Chinese City, Chaffee's command of just over 3,700 men now included the 6th Cavalry, the 14th Infantry, commanded by Daggett, and Battery F of the 5th Artillery, under the command of Captain Henry J. Reilly. Apparently, Chaffee was just as eager as Gaselee to march on Peking, but Reilly's Battery had encountered problems in coming ashore at Taku, and the American general was unwilling to move until Reilly and his men were ready to go.[45]

Captain Reilly and his battery of 138 men and Lieutenants MacCloskey and Summerall, along with two companies of the 14th Infantry, had sailed from Manila on 15 July, on board the transport ship *Flintshire*.[46] Lieutenant Summerall had supervised the loading into the hold of the ship of the horses, guns, supplies, and some 10,000 rounds of ammunition of the battery, as well as the men, mules, and the wagon train of the two infantry companies. He recalled that it was far from a pleasant voyage. The ship was outfitted with storage areas, and with holding pens below deck for the transportation of livestock, not of soldiers; the only place to sleep was on deck; the only toilet facilities were reserved for the use of the officers; and the only way to take a bath was to be hosed down on deck with saltwater. The galley was only large enough to accommodate the small Annamese crew, so everyone ate on deck a twice-daily ration of "canned beef, tomatoes, and hard tack," and sipped carefully the daily serving of coffee, provided one could keep down the mixture of food and drink as the steamer pitched and rolled on the high seas. Not long after the *Flintshire* had sailed into the open sea on course to Nagasaki, Japan, to refuel before heading toward the Gulf of Chihli, the coal on board ignited from spontaneous combustion. Officers and men fought the fire with the saltwater hoses, formed bucket relays, and succeeded in putting it out before it spread to the ammunition.[47]

After 18 grueling days at sea, the *Flintshire* steamed slowly into the gulf on 1 August 1900, and dropped anchor off the Taku bar, more than 14 miles from the mouth of the Pei Ho River. Lieutenant MacCloskey marveled at the grand sight of a fleet of over 50 battleships, cruisers, torpedo boats, transports, and hospital ships "of every nation and of every description," as well as launches, tenders, junks, and lighters "without number." They set the area aglow at night with their shimmering lights. Summerall and McCloskey were placed in charge of transferring to a lighter and a barge the ammunition, guns, tents, and harnesses for shipment across the bar in the shallow waters of the gulf to the landing area at Tangku, just up river past the battered forts at Taku.[48] For Summerall, navigating that relatively short journey turned out to be even more hazardous and arduous than the long voyage from Manila.

On 2 August, with the *Flintshire* resting at anchor, a tugboat nudged a large 70-ton barge to the starboard side of the transport, where it was secured and loaded with the six guns and caissons of the battery. Then, a lighter eased up to the port side and was lashed into place to receive the animals that were hoisted by winches from their stalls in slings and lowered into the lighter's hold. Summerall closely supervised the ticklish hoisting process and remained on board the lighter as it pulled around the *Flintshire* for its crew to attach cables to the barge. That night, as the lighter towed the barge through the choppy waters of the gulf toward the mouth of the Pei Ho, a gale suddenly arose and caused the cables to break apart with a loud pop that sounded like a shot from one of the battery's guns. Summerall ordered the lighter's captain to steam ahead to Tongku, where he supervised the unloading of the animals before returning on the afternoon tide. In the meantime, the barge holding all the battery's guns drifted dangerously out to sea.

Fortunately, on board the floundering vessel was a young, tall, and toothless Korean sailor who had stowed away on the *Flintshire* in Manila, and whom Summerall had discovered after the ship had gotten under way. Rather than putting him ashore when they reached Nagasaki, Summerall enlisted him, feeling that his skills might be useful to a battery of soldiers who had no nautical ability whatsoever. As gale-force winds and rough seas battered the barge, a desperate search by the crew discovered two sails that they lashed to a mast and stepped it, while the Korean rigged a rudder and managed to bring the vessel under control. Throughout a sleepless night, he sailed the barge in circles to maintain his general position. Finally, around daybreak, the crew of a British customs boat, with a pilot on board, spotted them. The pilot came aboard the barge, took over the tiller in relief of the exhausted sailor-soldier from Korea, and eased the vessel across the dangerous Taku bar and into the Pei Ho, where Summerall met it as he returned from Tongku.[49]

On 3 August, the somewhat wobbly and weary complement of crew, soldiers, and animals disembarked at the port to find Captain Reilly waiting at dockside impatiently grooming his horse and eager to gather his command for the campaign that lay ahead. Aided by 200 Chinese coolies, the battery loaded their guns, wagons, horses, supplies, and ammunition onto narrow boxcars, and climbed aboard for the slow journey of some 20 miles to Tientsin. After their arrival early the next morning,

Reilly reported to General Chaffee (who undoubtedly was pleased that his artillery now was in place) and returned to his men with orders to march that afternoon toward Peking. They would join the men of the 9th and 14th Infantry, and the 1st Regiment of Marines to form the China Relief Expedition, the designation of the American contingent of the International Relief Force.[50]

This international army presented a fascinating and unique picture as it assembled in the shadow of the ruins of the Chinese City of Tientsin. Marine First Lieutenant Smedley D. Butler recalled the spectacle of "French Zouaves in red and blue, blond Germans in pointed helmets, Italian Bersaglieri with tossing plumes, Bengal cavalry on Arabian stallions, turbaned Sikhs, Japanese, Russians, and English."[51] With some of their number wearing regulation blue flannel shirts and others dressed to suit their own fancy, the American troops hardly presented an inspiring sight, but they were generously supplied with food, their camps were the cleanest and most sanitary, and they had plenty of light and heavy wagons to haul their abundant supplies and equipment. Altogether the relief force numbered between 18,000 and 20,000 men. It consisted of about 10,000 Japanese, 3,000 Russians, 3,000 British, 2,200 Americans, 800 French (most of whom were diminutive Tonkinese exhausted by the fighting in Indo-China), and around 200 Germans, Italians, and Austro-Hungarians, who were mostly sailors poorly prepared or trained for combat ashore. The relief force was well equipped with artillery but was weakened by the lack of adequate cavalry for reconnaissance and pursuit. Chaffee had counted on the 6th Cavalry Regiment to fill these needs, and it had landed safely at Tongku. But their horses were so sickened by the sea voyage that they were unfit for service, and the regiment was forced to remain behind. A few Cossacks and Bengal Lancers were useful, and the Japanese provided a cavalry regiment, but its horses were so weak that only 60 out of 400 animals managed to complete the march to Peking. No one could be sure, but rumors estimated that some 70,000 imperial soldiers and between 50,000 and 100,000 Boxers lay ahead along the route to the capital.[52]

With General Gaselee in charge, the expedition left Tientsin late in the afternoon on 4 August and headed toward Peking, marching along the twisting banks of the Pei Ho. The French, Russians, Germans, Austrians, and Italians began their advance on the east bank, but flood waters forced them to cross over to the west bank and march behind the Japanese, British, and Americans. Mules and ponies carried food and ammunition, but the heat drained the stamina of the animals, and deep ruts in the narrow roadways slowed and frustrated their pace. Several hundred coolies towed and poled through the shallow river waters a six-mile long fleet of junks and sampans loaded with reserves of supplies and ammunition. In view of the multinational and multilingual composition of his command, Gaselee kept his tactics relatively simple and straightforward. If opposition were anticipated, cavalry were sent out in reconnaissance. Then the leading elements of the column would hurriedly re-deploy as skirmishers, the horse artillery would rush forward and bombard the enemy positions, and the infantry would sweep forward in a frontal assault. Any mopping up that was necessary would be left to rear echelons, although the inadequacy of cavalry meant that Gaselee's forces would not be able to exploit fully a defeat of the Chinese.

The first battle began shortly after midnight on 5 August, when Japanese cavalry uncovered imperial soldiers, rumored to number about 20,000, entrenched at Pietsang, a few miles north of the old arsenal at Hsiku, where Seymour's Expedition had found safety as they retreated to Tientsin. Advancing in the early morning mist behind fire from two 12-pounder naval guns of the British artillery, Japanese infantry charged the Chinese positions, suffering numerous casualties before overwhelming the enemy and causing the survivors to flee before they were bayoneted or shot down. Reilly's Battery caught sight of a retreating column and fired several rounds at the Chinese fleeing eastward across the river toward the city of Yangtsun. Japanese losses were 60 killed and 240 wounded; the

British lost one killed and 25 wounded; six Russians were wounded, but none of the other allies suffered any casualties.[53]

General Gaselee ordered the British and Americans to lead the assault the next day on Yangtsun, strategically located where the railroad crossed the Pei Ho, some 10 miles north of Pietsang. An intricate system of trenches and earthworks protected the city that was held by a sizable force, well supplied with artillery. Reilly's Battery advanced abreast of a column of Sikhs and Bengal cavalry, with a British and Russian battery in support. As Reilly's men entered a field of six-feet-high millet and corn, they came under heavy fire. They could not see the enemy, but Summerall quickly unpacked a bamboo ladder he had used in the Philippines, climbed up high enough to see above the tall stalks of grain, and called out the firing data to his gunners below. Lieutenant MacCloskey stood up on a caisson to direct the fire of his platoon, while enemy fire ripped through the grain stalks and popped into the ground around the young officers. Quickly the shell and shrapnel of the two platoons began to explode on top of the Chinese and forced them to cease firing.[54]

Shortly after midday, under the searing heat of the sun and in the thick of the fight, a company of the 2nd Battalion of the 14th Infantry came under artillery fire as they entered the outskirts of the town. British naval lieutenant Roger Keyes, who rose to the rank of rear admiral in World War I, was nearby, and heard the Americans screaming that their own artillery was shelling them. Believing that Russian guns were at fault, Keyes galloped up an embankment and hoisted a white handkerchief on the tip of his sword as a signal to the Russians that they were firing on Allied soldiers. Meanwhile, the commander of the American company, fearing that the British were to blame, sent a lieutenant to tell their battery to cease firing. The officer collapsed of heat exhaustion before he could deliver the message, but a mounted orderly finally got through to the British. By the time the shelling stopped, 4 Americans had been killed and 11 lay wounded, most of them fatally.[55]

During an inquiry into the causes of what today would be termed an incident of "friendly fire," the British asserted that the Russians had asked for the range to the Chinese trenches. They relayed the range in yards, but did not warn or remind the Russians, who used the metric system, that the distance was measured in yards not meters. The Russians apparently failed to realize that the data had been calculated in yards. Consequently, their salvo fell short and exploded among the Americans. In his account of the incident, Colonel Daggett stated that the American advance had been so rapid that General Gaselee did not realize they were already in the area that his battery and that of the Russians were shelling.[56] Strangely enough, while every major work I have consulted dealing with this period mentions this case of "friendly fire," neither Summerall in his memoir, nor MacCloskey in *Reilly's Battery* (or in his father's diary excerpted in the book), mentions the incident. Quite likely, as O'Connor in his *Spirit Soldiers* and Fleming in his *Siege* conclude, the incident was an example of the difficulties of combined operations undertaken by a multinational and polyglot force.[57] Certainly, the history of warfare through our own day abounds with incidents of "friendly fire," some of them even more tragic.

Spearheaded by British and American attacks on Chinese entrenchments before Yangstun, the allies swept through the city gates at sunset, and seized the city on 6 August. After an uneasy rest the next day in the battered city, whose streets were laden with bloated corpses, they resumed their march toward Peking. The eager Japanese were in the lead, followed by the Russians, Americans, and British. (The ill-prepared and exhausted Germans, Italians, Austro-Hungarians, and French Tonkinese decided to return to Tientsin to rest and regroup.)[58] The route to Peking traversed a vast and nearly treeless plain, most of which was covered by dense fields of tall corn and millet, much like those encountered earlier on the march, and which had forced Summerall to climb his bamboo ladder to direct the fire of his gunners. An elevated road from six to 12 feet high wound crookedly through the fields and connected Yangtsun with the capital. Colonel Daggett explained that all Chinese roads were "very crooked," since "The object is to prevent the passage of evil spirits, for they always fly on straight lines according to Chinese lore. Part of the way, the armies marched on this road, for it raised the soldiers above the cornfields, where they found refreshing breezes and comparative freedom from dust. But to follow the crooked road too closely would increase the distance; so, like the evil spirits the Chinamen doubtless thought they were, they descended to the cornfields to cut off the angles. There were no bridges; none were needed. Not a stream of water was crossed on the route."[59]

The searing and terrific heat of the August sun compounded the rigors of the terrain. Smedley Butler claimed that "The temperature rose as thigh as 140 degrees [sic] in the sun. There was no shade, not a drop of rain, nor a breath of air. The cavalry and artillery kicked up clouds of dust, which beat back into our faces. The blistering heat burned our lungs. Nearly fifty per cent of our men fell behind during the day, overcome by the sun."[60] Daggett managed to find shade, but complained that "There was a fierceness in that China sun's rays which none had experienced in the tropics or [in] our Southern States during the Civil War."[61] For Summerall, who knew something about the rays of the sun in the Southern States and in the tropics, "The heat was terrific. Our canteens soon were empty and the men and horses suffered horribly for water. We camped on the Pei-Ho River, and in spite of the many bodies floating in it, we drank the water."[62] He later would pay dearly for these desperate drinks from the Pei Ho.

Along the painful and torturous trail to Peking, soldiers encountered a number of villages of mud houses that were mostly deserted except, as Daggett observed, for an occasional Chinese man or woman "found crouching in some hidden corner expecting to be killed every moment. And, to the disgrace of humanity, especially to soldiers of Christian nations, some of these innocent, unresisting people were shot down like beasts, *but not by Americans* [his italics]." He condemned the "considerable and needless destruction of property," implying that this was the work of the 12,000 Japanese and Russian soldiers who preceded the other allied troops.[63] Summerall more emphatically blamed the Japanese and Russians for the "Slaughter and destruction that marked their path. Along the road, heads were mounted on poles. Bodies [of Chinese] littered the roads and floated down the river. In the poor houses of the villages, women and children were slaughtered. Nothing living was left. It filled us with disgust and contempt, especially for the Russians, who were the lowest class of brutes. I saw women at one place running from them and drowning themselves in a canal."[64] Historian Peter Fleming concluded that "The Russians excelled at living off the country; 'they had nothing, yet lacked nothing,' as somebody put it."[65]

With the Japanese still in the vanguard, the allies cut their way through the fields of tall corn and millet and marched through clouds of dust along the crooked roadway leading toward the walled commercial city of Tungchow that rested on the west bank of the Pei Ho, only 14 miles from Peking. In the predawn hours of 12 August, the Japanese blew open the main gate of the city and charged through, with the other allies close behind. They expected fierce resistance, but found that the Chinese garrison had fled and left Tungchow deserted, except for the looters and pillagers who were joined in their ravaging of the city by the newly arrived contingents from abroad.[66] Smedley Butler observed that the city "must have been a rich town before it was struck by war. Now, corpses, with skulls smashed in, lay sprawled across the street. Brocades and fragments of porcelain spilled out of the broken fronts of shops. The gilded archways were shattered. Carved teakwood furniture was being split up by the Allied soldiers for firewood." He contended, however, that the destruction of lives and property was not the work of the allies, but the Boxers, who "had done most of the damage before we arrived."[67] In the evening of 12 August, the allied generals gathered amid the ruins of Tungchow to plan their assault on Peking. The French contingent of 400 had returned from Tientsin, so now there were five nations whose soldiers would march to the rescue of the besieged foreigners in the Legation Quarter.

Haste was critical, for the Chinese had launched one final attack on the Quarter, and the fighting was as fierce as ever. The allied plan called for the International Relief Force to start out together just before dawn on 14 August, and advance in four parallel columns astride the Imperial Canal that connected Tungchow with Peking. Each contingent headed for one of the four gates on the vast eastern wall of the city. The Russians advanced on the right flank along the northern bank of the canal and made for the Tung Chih Men, the northern-most gate. The Japanese used an old, paved road to the north of the canal and headed for the Chih Hua Men, just to the south of the Tung Chih Men. Across the canal, the Americans aimed for the Tung Pien Men, with the French sandwiched in between them and the Japanese. The British advanced to the left of the Americans on the extreme left flank to attack the Hsia Kuo Men. In order to coordinate their final attack on the city on the 15th, it was agreed that all contingents would halt on the 14th when they reached the line held by the advance guard of the Japanese, about three miles from the city walls (see map, p. 111).[68]

On the night of 13 August, in a torrential downpour of rain that soaked their tents and left the roads slippery and muddy, the allies bivouacked outside ruins of Tungchow.[69] Quite likely, Summerall and his fellow officers of Reilly's Battery tossed and turned worriedly in their pup tents dripping with rainwater, for, as he remarked, they did not know "anything of plans." During the night, they were awakened by the sounds of rifle and machine gun fire followed by artillery blasts coming from the general direction of Peking.[70] Since the allies had agreed to wait until the 14th to begin their joint advance on Peking, it seemed strange that such heavy fire should resound from that area. Daggett wondered if the Chinese had attacked the Legation and were massacring all the "foreign devils." As the firing grew fainter towards dawn, he feared that even though relief now was imminent, it might be too late. Thus, for Daggett and "many an anxious member of that relief expedition, there was no sleep that night."[71]

At daybreak on the 14th, the fears and uncertainties of the night became even more disturbing. A Japanese staff officer rode up to General Chaffee's tent and asked if he knew where the Russians were. Surprised by the question, Chaffee responded that they must be on his right, across the canal, preparing for the assault on Peking. The Japanese officer replied that there were no Russians across the canal. Chaffee quickly ascertained that during the night of the 13th, the Russians had left their camp at Tungchow and, "for reasons unknown to me," swerved to their left, cutting diagonally across the intended advance of the Americans. They had attacked the Tung Pien Men that had been designated as the American, not the Russian objective.[72] Although Chaffee could not understand why the Russians had attacked the wrong gate and prematurely, others assumed that the Russian General Linievitch deliberately had violated the plan for the final assault and had ordered a preemptive attack on the Tung Pien Men. They alleged that he had done this because it was the gate nearest to the Legations and offered the Russians the opportunity for being the first troops to breach the walls of Peking and thus rescue the Legations (see map, p. 111).

What actually happened is uncertain, but the historians Preston and Fleming both believe that the Russian attack was more likely the result of chance than of design. In order to secure the approaches to the gate, General Linievitch sent an advance guard with artillery under the command of his chief of staff, General Vassilievski. Moving under the shadow of the outer wall through a light rain in the darkness of the early morning hours, the Russians surprised the personnel in a guardhouse protecting the gate, and killed them. Hearing gunfire from the Legation quarter and fearing that the foreigners there were endangered, Vassilievski ordered his artillery to open fire on the ironclad outer gate. After about the twentieth shot, a hole was blasted in the gate, and Vassilievski led his men into the courtyard between the outer and inner gate. From atop the inner gate, the Chinese fired down point-blank on the Russians, inflicting heavy losses. But by sunrise, the Russians had killed or driven away the last defenders and controlled the Tung Pien Men, becoming the first of the allies to breach the great walls and enter Peking. For the remainder of the day, during which Vassilievsky was wounded seriously, they fought along the wall and in the streets behind it. It was not until early evening that they were able to advance toward the Legations and join the allied troops that had already arrived.[73]

While Chaffee and others were unclear about the reasons for the preemptive Russian attack on the Tung Pien Men, Summerall believed that it had been deliberate. He wrote that "They thought that they could reach the legations by our route, so during the night they disregarded the agreement and attacked our objective with the result that they lost heavily and failed [sic]." Clearly, Summerall erred in asserting that the Russians had failed in their attack on "our objective." He also was mistaken when he stated in his memoir that when his artillery platoon blasted through the huge, ironclad Chien Men a day after the Russians had fired through the Tung Pien, "Nothing of the kind had ever been done before."[74]

Perhaps his memory in his advanced years or his notes failed him. Perhaps, in his condemnation and misrepresentation of their actions in China, he transferred to the Tsarist-era Russians, the strong anti-Soviet beliefs that he held as he composed his memoirs in the era of the Cold War. He already had singled out the Russians as "the lowest class of brutes" for the atrocities they committed against the Chinese, even though the Russians were not the only ones among the allies who had violated and brutalized Chinese people. Perhaps, he came to resent, and eventually refused to recognize the fact, that it was the Russians, and not the Americans, who first had blasted their way into Peking. Although it seems unlikely, he may have never learned that the Russians had been the first to blow apart the massive, ironclad gates through which they became the first of the allies to enter Peking. There may well be at least still another explanation for his errors, and I will deal with this possibility further on.

Whatever the reasons for the premature Russian attack, it caused the allies to abandon their plans for a coordinated assault and to push forward independently on the morning of 14 August, toward the closest gate. To the right of the Russians, the Japanese mounted a fierce assault on the Chih Hua Men, bringing up their entire artillery of 54 small caliber guns, and firing more than 1,000 shells. Still unable to break it down, engineers blew it apart with high explosive charges.[75] General Chaffee ordered Colonel Daggett and the 14th Infantry forward on the left of the Russians toward the Tung Pien Men, as Lieutenant Burgess's right platoon of Reilly's Battery began firing at the great tower of the gate, and the left platoon under Summerall concentrated fire along the top of the wall of the Tartar City just behind the Tung Pien Men. The lead Company E of the 14th made it safely to shelter under the shadow of the wall of the "Chinese City," just to the south of the towering wall of the Tartar City and the Tung Pien Men, and pressed closely against the wall along with the Russians. Under covering fire from E Company, H Company dashed forth and joined the huddle of Americans and Russians. Daggett and his adjutant quickly arrived and concluded that it was too dangerous to charge across the remaining 200 yards toward the gate.[76]

The Tartar Wall that stretched out on either side of the Tung Pien Men was topped by a crenellated parapet that Daggett feared might hide any number of Chinese soldiers. He realized that the only way to deal with this danger was to climb to the top of the wall of the "Chinese City," and from this height, fire on any soldiers that might be behind the parapet. The 14th Regiment had no scaling ladder or ropes or tools for climbing, but one officer noted gaps and protrusions in the 30 feet-high wall left by bricks that had fallen out. He asked rhetorically whether it might be possible for someone to climb to the top of the wall by using the holes and projections as a ladder. Corporal Calvin Pearl Titus,

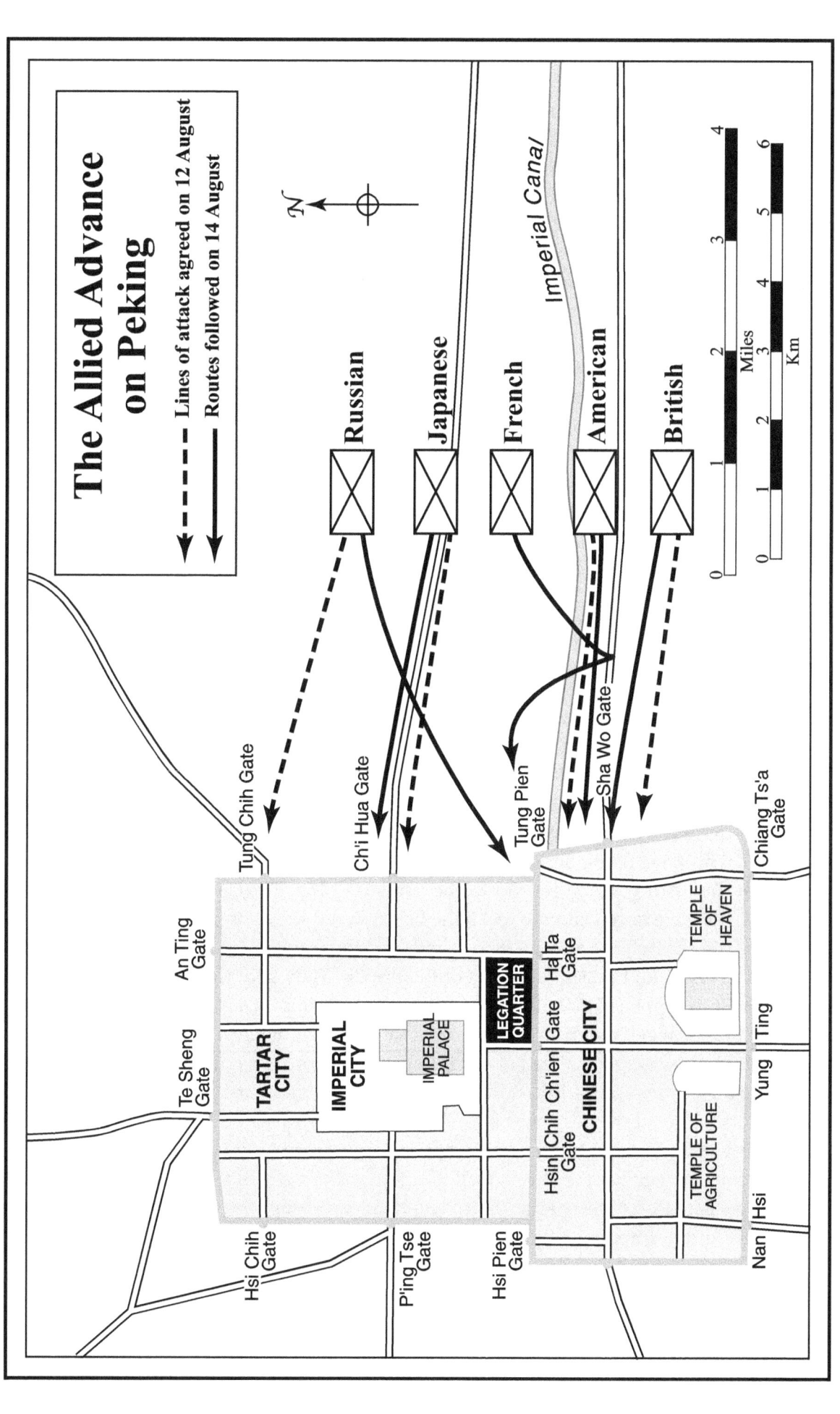

the 20-year-old regimental bugler, stepped forward and volunteered to try. Laying his bugle and rifle aside, he made his way up the wall, testing carefully each cavity and protrusion as he hoisted himself higher. When he reached an embrasure along the top of the wall, he stretched and peered through, not knowing whether he might find himself staring into the barrel of a Chinese rifle. Fortunately, he saw and heard nothing of the enemy, pulled himself through the opening, and called down to the others to climb up and join him. As the men of E and H companies clambered up the wall and took up positions along the top, Chinese soldiers manning the tower of the Tung Pien Men caught sight of them, and began firing with rifles and artillery. Daggett's men, supported by two platoons of marines led by Lieutenant Butler, returned fire, and with their number steadily increasing, forced the Chinese to abandon the gate. Butler led his men forward, but suddenly a bullet in the chest stopped him in his tracks, spun him around, and felled him. One of his men said that he had been shot through the heart, but Butler replied, "No, not the heart."[77] Actually, the bullet had hit a brass button on his uniform blouse and pounded it into his breastbone "with outrageous force. The shock was terrible," as he wrote his mother, "and for about half an hour I could hardly breathe."[78] After resting for some time, Butler rose to his feet and was leaning unsteadily against the Tung Pien when "Lieutenant Summerall, subsequently Chief of Staff of our army, was riding by with his artillery. When he saw me staggering and reeling along, he lifted me on his horse and escorted me in style to my company."[79] Butler kept the button and carried it in his pocket for years.[80] By noon the action was over. With the Chinese soldiers no longer manning the wall, the Americans brushed through the disorganized Russians, threw aside the debris that they had piled up around the gate and pressed forward into the Tartar City, hoping to be the first to reach the Legations.[81]

The attacks of the Russians, Japanese, and Americans forced the Chinese to concentrate forces against the main approaches to the Legation Quarter. This unexpected opposition slowed the American advance and allowed the British, moving up on the left of the Americans, to slip through a sluice gate. They moved in behind the Chinese defenders and burst into the British Legation, where they were greeted by a "sobbing cheer" and the grateful shouts of the many who had been under siege for almost two months.[82] The Americans of Daggett's 14th Infantry, along with Reilly's Battery, arrived a few hours later with flags flying and cheers ringing in their ears, only to realize, with much disappointment, that they had come in second to the British. Colonel Daggett, dismayed that his hard-fighting Americans were not the first to reach the beleaguered Legations, wrote that "As it was, they [the Americans] did the fighting and the British gathered the fruits." However, he bore no resentment and noted that "This is not in disparagement of the British. They kept their agreement [to attack the closest gate], and it so happened that the Chinese were not in their front as they advanced."[83] Summerall, less charitable than Daggett, begrudgingly wrote that "Unfortunately, the British, who were better informed, entered the water gate ahead of our infantry."[84] Regardless of how piqued Summerall was at the "unfortunate" success of the British, he soon became more than irritated, once again, by what he believed were additional transgressions of the Russians.

While British and American troops worked their way toward the Legations, Reilly's Battery had provided covering fire against the Tartar Wall and had moved steadily forward through the Chien Men, the massive gate to the west of the Tung Pien, that led through the south side of the Tartar Wall toward the gates of the Imperial City.[85] As the battery advanced toward the Legations, Summerall noted that "a Russian officer sent me a note asking me to cease firing until a Russian column could pass in front of my guns. I did so, but it soon abused my confidence [he did not explain how]."[86] Apparently, the battery remained close the Chien Men, for after several "alien contingents, including *these Russians* [italics mine]" entered the gate, Summerall stated that Reilly prepared to open fire on the first gate of the Imperial City, about a hundred yards inside the Chien Men. At that moment, wrote

Summerall, "a Russian colonel with his flag wrapped around his body, placed himself at the muzzle of the gun and told Reilly not to fire as the gate belonged to the Russians. Reilly would have fired," continued Summerall, "if the Russian General Linivitch [sic] had not asked him to wait until he could confer with the American General Chaffee. Reilly consented and Chaffee sent him orders not to fire." To Summerall, it appeared that the American and Russian generals had agreed to attack the next morning and "jointly capture the Imperial City."[87] Although Daggett reported the meeting between Chaffee and Linievitch, he said nothing about an agreement for a joint capture of the Imperial City. In his own words, "It was decided that the troops would be ready to move the next morning at 7 o'clock, and if the Russian troops were ready, they could pass the Americans." He added that "At the hour named there was no appearance of any movement in the Russian camp."[88] Since they were not ready, the Americans moved past them. In addition, Daggett wrote that when the regiment had broken camp that morning, they expected that they were "going into camp in another part of the city. It was rumored that possibly we might find some of the enemy on the ground to be occupied and have to brush them away. No other thought was in our mind."[89] Apparently, although Chaffee had decided to attack the Imperial City as late as the early morning of the 15th, he had not determined how to carry it out, much less agreed on an attack with Linievitch.

In none of the other accounts of the closing days of the Boxer Rebellion is there any indication or mention that Russians and Americans at this point would attack together in any direction, or toward a specific objective. Summerall went on to say that "the Russians encircled the Tartar City during the night and occupied and looted the Summer Palace twelve or fifteen miles to the west [the actual distance is 15 kilometers or approximately eight or nine miles] on the 15th while we were attacking alone."[90] But, if at 0700 hours of the 15th there had been "no appearance of any movement in the Russian camp," as Daggett has stated, and there exists no reason to doubt his statement, the Russians could not have "encircled the Tartar City during the night." In fact, it was not until after the allied victory parade through the Imperial Palace on 28 August that the looting of the capital spread to the Summer Palace, and which, indeed, the Russians ransacked and looted. Their plundering was hardly more widespread and thorough than that carried out by other allied soldiers, who had looted every place they had occupied, including the entire expanse of the Chinese capital. Once again, apparently, Summerall's lingering resentment of Russia and the Russians led him to make additional misstatements and to engage in partisan and excessive criticism of their behavior.

The American assault on the gates of the Imperial and Forbidden Cities, the last phase in their attack on the Chinese capital, began early on the morning of 15 August. Daggett's regiment, along with Reilly's Battery that had been withdrawn from the Chien Men, led the way and headed back toward the towering gate past the Russian camp. Beyond that, they had no firm idea of what lay ahead.[91] After they had marched a short distance, Chaffee rode up to Daggett and said that he wanted him to enter the Imperial City. As Chaffee wheeled his horse aside from the line of march, a member of his staff came up to Daggett and said that "The General directs that you enter the Imperial City. I will show you the way. There is the gate. My duty ceases, yours begins." Having no idea of the layout or what was inside the Imperial City, and having been issued no precise orders about how to conduct the operation, and possessing no equipment for scaling the walls or battering down the gates, Daggett felt it was all "a step in the dark."[92] What seems likely, as others have also suggested,[93] is that Chaffee's abrupt decision to enter the Imperial City resulted from his determination to win a measure of glory for the commanding general of an expedition that so far had produced little in the way of glory or distinction at any point, with the possible exception of the wall-scaling feat of Corporal Titus. Since the Americans had lost the race to reach the Legations, Chaffee could have resolved that they would be the first to arrive in the Imperial City, especially since, in historian Peter Fleming's view, Chaffee was a character "to whom inter-allied cooperation was a novel and distasteful concept."⁹⁴ If this were indeed a "race to glory," it was not the first one, and as will be seen later, it definitely was not the last of such "races" that involved American commanding generals fighting in a foreign land.

With Summerall's left platoon in the lead, the 14th Infantry, with the 9th Infantry following close behind, moved past the Russian camp and passed through the vast opening of the Chien Men around 0800 hours on the 15th. Summerall was ordered to park his guns and caissons about 200 yards in front of gates that barred passage through three archways that pierced the 45-foot high wall protecting the Imperial City.⁹⁵ Burgess's and MacCloskey's platoons used ramps along the Tartar Wall to wrestle their guns up to the top on either side of the Chien Men and were joined by Chaffee and Reilly.⁹⁶ Chinese soldiers quickly began firing at them from the walls of the Imperial City, but returned artillery fire from the two platoons blasted enemy soldiers from their positions and ripped large chunks of masonry from the walls. Chaffee and Reilly asked for guns to blow open the gates. Within a few minutes, Summerall galloped at the head of his platoon to the gate of the middle archway. As Daggett put it, "There was no doubt in our minds about the outcome of the request, nor the speed with which the guns would come."⁹⁷

The gate that loomed before Summerall and his gunners was about 15 feet high and 12 feet wide and blocked the entrance through the center archway. The gates were made of very heavy timber, eight to ten inches thick, fastened together with crossbeams of the same dimensions that were secured by heavy metal locks. Metal sheeting covered the outward facing surface of the gates, but they failed to close tightly, leaving a narrow gap. Summerall positioned one of his guns about 12 to 15 feet in front of the center gate, and as bullets kicked up dust at his feet, walked up to it, and, according to his memoir, "scratched with my thumb nail a cross [an "X"] on the metal covering of the gate opposite the bar [a cross beam] and ordered the gunner to fire at that spot. The gunner was Corporal Smith from the mountains of Tennessee and he had an accurate eye [shades of Alvin York!]." Since "nothing of the kind had ever been done before [*sic*]," Summerall feared that the shell would burst on impact, and that he and his gunners would be hit by shell fragments. As he sighted his guns, Corporal Smith reaffirmed the target, asking if he should fire "Right thar, sir?" at the cross mark. "Right there," replied

*Summerall's platoon firing on the Gate of the Forbidden City, Peking*

Courtesy The Citadel Archives & Museum, Charleston, South Carolina

Summerall.⁹⁸ Smith fired and the shell did its job, piercing a hole through the gate and the beam. But the beam remained in place, so Summerall walked up to the gate again, and "made two other scratches [*sic*] opposite the uncut parts of the bar, and, with two more shells [fired] through them, the bar was cut and the gate swung open."⁹⁹ As shells tore through the other two gates as well, a soldier came to Summerall with news that brought tragedy to the successful and dramatic scenario unfolding before the gates to the Imperial City.

Standing beside General Chaffee, near one of his guns atop the Tartar Wall, Captain Reilly, with field glass in hand, was watching Summerall's guns as they opened fire on the second gate. Suddenly, a Chinese rifle bullet ricocheted off the wall and struck him in the mouth, passed through his head, and knocked him senseless to the ground, killing him within a few minutes.¹⁰⁰ On hearing the report of

*Captain Henry J. Reilly*
Courtesy Colonel Robert R. McCormick Research Center

Reilly's death, Summerall told the messenger that it could not be true, and, believing it was a wild rumor like the one that he had been killed at Yangtsun, ordered him not to say anything to the other men. A few minutes later, one of General Chaffee's staff officers came to ask Summerall how his ammunition was holding out, and confirmed that Reilly, indeed, had been killed. For Summerall, "The shock was indescribable," but, at the same time, "I had much else to think of."¹⁰¹

Unaware of their captain's death, his gunners were rolling through the shattered gates into a long courtyard toward a second wall, some 700 yards ahead, that also shielded the Imperial City. Archways through the wall were barred by other heavily timbered gates sheathed in metal. Summerall's men quickly came under sniper fire from a crenelated parapet on the top of the wall, and from low brick buildings along the face of the wall. They loaded their guns with solid shot and shrapnel shells, shattered the parapet and, as Daggett put it, "made things lively for the Chinamen."¹⁰² Behind the fire of Summerall's platoon, riflemen from the 14th ran across the courtyard and scaled the wall with ladders that he had procured that morning from the Japanese. From its height, they poured down fire to protect the platoon, as Summerall brought his guns up to the gates. Striding forward he again chalked, rather than scratched, an "X" on the center gate; again Corporal Smith called out, "Right thar, Sir?"; again Summerall replied, "Right there"; and again shells began tearing through massive gates.¹⁰³

Meanwhile, from atop the Tartar Wall beside the Chien Men, French soldiers began firing small mountain guns at the gates Summerall had just wrecked and at the walls that rose in front of the advancing Americans. Chaffee immediately dispatched on officer to the French position, where he demanded to know "if the commander of these damned pop-guns knew what he was firing at." He warned that the shells might fall short on American soldiers, but the French commander ignored the warning, and his men kept firing. After about 30 minutes, a second American officer appeared with a direct order from Chaffee, stating that the firing cease. Only then did the French guns stop firing. Fortunately, no Americans were injured, although, for Chaffee, the incident undoubtedly confirmed his disdain for "inter-allied cooperation."¹⁰⁴

Ignoring the French fire, Summerall's gunners, along with the 14th and 9th Regiments, burst into yet another courtyard that led to a third wall pierced by archways barred with the familiar heavy, sheathed gates, but with wider gaps through which the Chinese were firing sporadically. As Daggett was more concerned that enemy soldiers might occupy the top of the wall and pour fire down on the masses of Americans assembled below than he was about scattered fire through the gates, Summerall's guns promptly demolished a parapet and killed the defenders behind. Soon men from both regiments clambered to the top and laid down covering fire for Summerall's guns to advance and blow open one more of a trio of archway gates.[105]

Led by E Company of the 14th, Summerall's platoon moved through the shattered gates and entered a courtyard about 500 yards long that led to another set of gates that blocked archways through a fourth wall. Shots rang out from Chinese soldiers atop the wall, and two riflemen fell, one mortally wounded. A fusillade of fire from E Company soon swept the Chinese from the wall, clearing the way for Summerall's men to advance to the gates. While his gunners prepared to fire another devastating blast, some of the men of E Company peered through the openings between the gates and beheld the elaborate courtyard of the Forbidden City, that sacred and legendary heart of the Manchu Court with its splendor of palaces, temples, and gardens. Daggett referred to it as the "holy of holies," and believed that he could grasp this fabulous prize within a few minutes. However, just as Summerall was about to open fire, General Chaffee's aide dashed up to Daggett and said, "The General directs that you suspend all further operations."[106]

Obedient, yet deeply disappointed and frustrated, Daggett wrote that "There was the Forbidden City, whose pavements, it is said, the foot of white man had never pressed. The enemy had been driven away. American soldiers had sacrificed life. Only an undefended gate barred the way. The means were at hand. The skill and nerve to use them were there. Five minutes' time only intervened between those victorious soldiers and the fruits of their sacrifices."[107] Summerall was equally frustrated, for he was ready to fire, and had to leave a shell in one of his guns. Not surprisingly, he maintained that behind Chaffee's order were the perfidious Russians, who had protested the American advance because they wanted to enter the Forbidden City along with, and not after, the Americans. For Summerall, their protest was another example of their treachery, just like their premature attack on 14 August, and their subsequent looting of the Summer Palace.[108] Actually, while Summerall's charge against the Russians of treachery was extreme and inaccurate, in this case it was not totally off the mark.

As the Americans advanced toward the Imperial City, allied commanders, sans Chaffee, of course, hastily called a conference at about 1600 hours, where the Russians, supported by the French, proposed that the allies adopt a conciliatory approach toward the Manchu Court; they argued that an invasion of the Forbidden City would make that policy impossible. After some discussion, the Russo-French proposal was approved, along with the corollary instruction that the entire area of the Imperial City also be evacuated.[109] Since allied soldiers would later loot the "holy of holies" under the eyes of their commanders, the approval of the joint Russian-French proposal, without American participation in the discussion, leads one to question intentions. Perhaps, the French resented Chaffee's earlier brusque orders that they cease firing with their "pop guns" at the enemy ahead, and wanted to seize an opportunity to rein in the American general; perhaps the Russians were anxious to halt Chaffee's attack before the Americans could sweep ahead to possess the prize of the Forbidden City, and leave them behind once again; perhaps the British resented American displeasure at their having beaten the Americans in the "race" to liberate the legations. Perhaps, however, the most accurate assessment of their action was posed by Daggett himself, when he asked whether it "Was the success of the Americans during those eight hours [between 0800 and 1600 hours] that caused the conference to reach that conclusion."[110]

Outraged and embittered, the Americans turned away from the Forbidden City and trudged back through the shattered remains of the massive gates to the American Legation, where they stopped to leave their wounded and arrange for the burial of their dead.[111] They continued through the Chien Men and set up camp outside the Tartar Wall in the southern part of the Chinese City. There they received the news of at least one joyful outcome of the long days of siege and conflict: the relief of the besieged Peitang Cathedral, the only Christian building in the Imperial City (see map, p. 100).

Throughout the siege of Peking, the cathedral had been under attack by Boxers and Chinese soldiers, who were especially enraged that many Chinese Christians had escaped their wrath by taking refuge in the Peitang, along with more than 3,000 foreigners. The besieged Christians managed to survive continuous and unrelenting attacks by the Chinese with the help of a company of French marines, defending the walls around the cathedral, and through persistent attacks on the besiegers by French artillery and infantry. Finally, on 16 August, a force of French, British, and Russian infantry captured a gate in the Imperial City wall close to the cathedral, surged onto the grounds of the cathedral, and rushed in to liberate its defenders from their almost totally destroyed refuge. Much to their surprise, however, they found that the cathedral already had been liberated by some 250 to 300 Japanese soldiers, who had simply slipped through ahead of them, and beat them to their goal. Nevertheless, they were elated by the welcome they received, although not cheered, perhaps, by the smug smiles on the faces of the Japanese. Altogether, during the siege of the Peitang, over 400 people, including 165 children, had died. Those who survived vowed to begin their work all over again.[112]

While the survivors of the siege of the Peitang Cathedral joyfully welcomed their liberators on the 16th, Summerall, and a burial detail of his men, solemnly returned from their encampment in the Chinese City to the American Legation, where they "prepared the body of our beloved Captain as well as possible."[113] Chaffee, Daggett, and soldiers and marines from both regiments, as well as Americans from the Legation, stood with them as they buried the body of their captain and those of their comrades with full military honors in the Legation compound. As Reilly's coffin was lowered into the grave, the American minister, Edwin Conger, stepped forward and noted that since there was a need for American flags, the one that shrouded Reilly's body should be removed. At once General Chaffee bellowed that "If it's the last American flag in China it will be buried with Reilly."[114] With that, Conger stepped back, and Reilly's flag-draped body gently was lowered into the ground, as his devoted men stood at reverential attention.

After the burials, Reilly's Battery returned to their bivouac area in the Chinese City on the grounds of the Temple of Agriculture, which stood in the center of the Chinese capital city. Nearly half of the local population had fled, and in the early morning hours of 15 August, the Empress Dowager, dressed in peasant clothes, and her court slipped out of the Forbidden City. They paused at the Summer Palace, then hurried from the city and headed southwest. Two months later, after completing a rather circuitous journey of some 1,000 miles, they returned quietly to the capital.

With the flight of the Manchu Court, the authority of the central government collapsed. Having made no plans for a military government, the allies failed to contain the indiscriminate and often brutal looting committed by all the nationalities. In an attempt to impose some degree of order, they divided the city into zones of occupation, headed by the various powers. This measure did nothing to halt what amounted to a race among the Americans, British, French, Japanese, and Russians to see which of them could amass the biggest haul of Chinese loot. In his memoir, Summerall attempted to put the best light possible on the looting by Americans. When Li Hung Chiang, the Chinese official who later led their delegation in the treaty negotiations, visited the battery, Summerall noted that he "embarrassed us by asking where we had gotten certain articles of Chinese furniture." Although Reilly had forbidden "the taking of anything," nevertheless, continued Summerall, "a certain amount of looting became general and our men and officers had a small share." However, he weakened his case when he concluded that "Some officers accumulated rich stores of treasure,"[115] and he himself, according to A. G. D. Wiles' typescript, took home five small Chinese dolls, two cushions, a marble top mahogany stool inlaid with mother of pearl, a small bronze Buddha, some rare mandarin coats, and a dragon design that he pulled from one of the gates of the Forbidden City. Except for the coats and dragon design, everything was lost when a train carrying the goods wrecked near Mount Shasta in northern California in 1901. Interestingly, Summerall referred to the lost items as "loot."[116] As Smedley Butler noted, "Some allowance should be made for the fact that during the excitement of a campaign you do things that you yourself would be the first to criticize in the tranquil security of home."[117]

Meanwhile, as allied looters continued their forays in the city, their diplomats and military leaders met on 18 August and decided that to impress their victory upon the Chinese, they would stage a victory parade through the Imperial City. They agreed that the parade would be led by the country with the largest number of soldiers, a distinction the Russians promptly claimed, even though the Japanese clearly outnumbered them. However, no one challenged the Russian assertion, and the parade was scheduled for 28 August 1900.[118] One officer or soldier from each company in every contingent was chosen to represent his country, and Summerall was selected as the representative of Reilly's Battery. The colorful parade formed at the Chien Men, and with flags flying and bands playing, they marched along the same route where Summerall had led his platoon some two weeks before. This time, however, they advanced through the gates of the Forbidden City and entered the Imperial Palace. Inside, they passed through three throne rooms, which Summerall said were filled with "richness and luxury," before exiting along lotus ponds that he said, "were the most beautiful." Later, he escorted visitors through the throne rooms and court apartments that were filled with "richness and luxury [that] was alien to the western mind. The gorgeous peacock throne room was magnificent." He pointedly added, that "No looting took place there and all was left as we found it."[119]

After the so-called "victory parade," Summerall and his men returned to their bivouac area and the routines of encampment, amid the ruins of a city where bodies lay piled up in the streets, and the smell of decaying flesh mingled with the stench of rotting garbage. En route to guard one of the gates to the Chinese City, Summerall's platoon had to drive across a marshy area filled with headless corpses, apparently the victims of a Chinese execution squad. Poison ivy vines, full of shiny, green, three-leaf clusters, dangled from walls, and crept along city streets and gutters, causing ferocious itching and reddish swelling to break out on those who came into contact with their leaves and tendrils. One of the unlucky ones was Summerall, who wrote that he had always been susceptible to poison ivy. This encounter caused his face to swell so severely that his eyes were almost closed shut, and his arms became so swollen that they had to be wrapped in bandages and placed in slings. His orderly had to feed him, and he could not remove his clothes for days.[120]

With the approach of winter, morale and conditions deteriorated. "Without Captain Reilly," Summerall wrote, "there was a deep depression. We realized that a great change had taken place though all tried to maintain his [sic] standard of efficiency. Men and horses were worn out and tired and reflected the hardships of the campaign." Cold winds brought snow from the Manchurian Mountains to the north, just when clothing and camp supplies began to run low. Camel caravans delivered powdered coal that was mixed with clay and formed into small balls that, in turn, were burned down to glowing coals to eliminate lethal carbon dioxide gas before bringing them into the tents. Summerall had learned that in other commands, men had been asphyxiated by carbon dioxide when they brought coals into their tents before the gas had burned off. Eventually, they all received small, coal-burning tent stoves.

Adding to their misery, a scourge of "the most malignant, deep-seeded boils" broke out among the Americans; over the next few months, Summerall counted on his body 15 that were clustered around his glands, and a "very painful one" in the palm of his hand. He believed, understandably, that the outbreak resulted from their having drunk from the fetid waters of the Pei Ho, contaminated by the decaying bodies that floated past their eyes as they marched through the parched countryside toward Peking. The regimental doctor was kept busy lancing more than 80 boils a day, before the "plague of boils" finally disappeared. On top of all that, an epidemic of glanders erupted among the horses and mules, forcing Summerall and his men to kill most of their animals, including Captain Reilly's horse, which was one of the first to be put down. In late October, Captain Thomas Ridgway, USMA, Class of 1883, arrived to take over the command of the battery. "All knew him well and liked him," according to Summerall, "and the battery functioned admirably under him."[121]

One of Ridgway's first orders dispatched Summerall to Tientsin to pick up clothes, food, and equipment for the battery. Still suffering from the pain of the boil in his hand, Summerall and a detachment from the battery went to the river port of Tungchow, some 14 miles from Peking, where he procured a river junk and crew of coolies.[122] These vessels were 30 to 40 feet long, with a cargo hold amidships, and a mast stepped forward of the hold. At the stern was a small cockpit where the Chinese pilot and six or seven coolies had their quarters. They set out for Tientsin, a journey of four or five days down the twisting course of the Pei Ho. With a long rope tied to the top of the mast, the Chinese crew towed the junk from a towpath along the shore; the pilot held the rudder and kept the junk away from the riverbanks. Occasionally, the coolies would pause to gather vegetables, which Summerall's orderly prepared when they tied up for the night at small settlements along the way. At Tientsin, Summerall procured the supplies and equipment he needed, and obtained 18 river junks with teams of coolies for the return trip.[123] Bending into their harnesses, they slowly towed the junks upstream; when the river widened into long, lake-like stretches, and a wind blew up from the south, they dropped their towlines, jumped on board, and hoisted large, square sails that caught the following wind.[124]

While Summerall's flotilla made its way upstream toward Tungchow, another fleet of 12 river junks was sailing downstream toward Tientsin. In charge was First Lieutenant John McAuley Palmer, Summerall's erstwhile roommate in their plebe year at West Point. Palmer commanded Company D of the 15th Infantry Regiment that had been in China at Tientsin since 19 August. Having missed the action and excitement of the 14th and 15th, his battalion had been serving as guards for the supply base there, and as military police for the entire Tientsin area. Palmer's junks, with his detail of soldiers and crew of coolies, were returning to Tientsin after delivering supplies to an army depot south of Tungchow. From there, he had expected to take a trip to Peking, but he was informed that General Chaffee was "mad as hell because his winter supplies are arriving so slowly. He knows you are here and has just issued orders for you to take your junks back to Tientsin just as soon as I can unload them." Many years later, still disappointed, even after years of distinguished service and promotion to brigadier general, Palmer wrote that "after I had traveled halfway around the world to within ten miles [sic] of Peking, that hardboiled old warrior Chaffee sent me back to Tientsin without a glimpse of the ancient city."[125]

As Palmer's fleet lay tied up for the night north of Tientsin, he greeted a junk moving upstream and manned by American artillery soldiers. He was delighted when they shouted back that Lieutenant Summerall, their commanding officer, was on a boat behind them. As Palmer told it, "I challenged every passing boat by crying out 'Summerall!' Finally somebody cried out from the darkness, 'Who is that?' to which I replied: 'Palmer of the class of '92.' Thereupon, Pelot moored his boat alongside mine, and we had a class reunion for 2 or 3 hours until he resumed his journey upstream."[126] Summerall recalled as well in his memoir the chance meeting with Palmer, and wrote that "we had a reunion in that tragic and desolate place."[127]

The two friends then went on their separate ways, Summerall bound for Tungchow, and Palmer headed for Tientsin, where he arrived toward the end of October. Still eager to visit Peking, he gained Chaffee's approval to accompany a Chinese general to the capital. Just as Palmer was preparing to leave in the general's houseboat, he was handed a copy of a telegram from the War Department to General Chaffee, informing him that his six-year-old son had died of diphtheria. A month later, he left China, never having seen Peking, and was reunited with his wife Maude in Petersburg, Illinois, south of Chicago. After a brief assignment at Fort Porter, in Buffalo, New York, he reported to West Point, where the birth of daughter Mary made the Palmers' sojourn there an especially happy time in their lives. He served as an instructor at the academy for five years before going on to become an outstanding staff officer, and a persuasive advocate for an army made up of citizen soldiers based upon universal military training and an organized reserve force.[128] For Summerall and Palmer, their next crossing would be on the other side of the world, in the midst of the Great War of 1914–1918.

A few days after saying farewell to his friend, Summerall landed with his fleet at Tungchow, where his men loaded their supplies onto wagons for the final leg of their journey back to the Chinese City and to their encampment, which his battery had named Camp Reilly. As winter of 1900–1901 closed in, they stayed busy pitching new tents, equipping kitchens, building shelters for the horses, and repairing guns and carriages. Among the few diversions to the routines of camp life were firing demonstrations of their guns by Russian, Japanese, British, and American artillery units in the Imperial Hunting Park. The French, however, did not fire, and kept all observers away from their new 75 mm quick-firing, recoilless cannon. Summerall noted that this weapon "was a major secret with them." In their off duty hours, Summerall and his men ventured into the different allied zones of occupation and bought silks from British soldiers, who had confiscated them from Imperial stores, and furs from Russians, who had taken them from the same source. All of these wares, according to Summerall, were purchased at a "high price." He wrote that before leaving Manila, he had been examined for promotion to captain, but had not received it, even though his pay had been increased. This extra money, combined with minimal costs for living, enabled him to continue to support his sister's family, to repay the money that Winfield Jones in San Francisco had loaned him, and to send Dr. Porter money for taking him in as a "charity boy."[129]

As Reilly's Battery settled into their new surroundings in the Chinese City of the capital, and learned more about the entrepreneurial and shooting prowess of the Russians, Japanese, and British, a large German contingent, known as the East Asiatic Corps, arrived in Peking in October under the command of Field Marshal Count von Waldersee, whom the allies had appointed in July as Supreme Commander of the international force.[130] Along his journey from Tientsin to Peking, Waldersee became convinced that the Boxers still posed a threat. By the time he had arrived in the capital, he had decided on a series of punitive expeditions to give his soldiers a taste of combat and crush any remaining pockets of resistance, as well as avenge the deaths of innocent foreigners like Baron von Kettler, the German consul who had been shot and killed by a Boxer assassin.[131]

During the winter of 1900–1901, Waldersee directed a series of brutal German raids that, according to most accounts, killed many more civilians than Boxers. The American government would not allow its soldiers to join the Germans, and General Chaffee condemned the raids for killing harmless women, children, and innocent coolies. The British took part, but one of their officers lamented that "'We fired about 2,000 rounds, mostly at inoffensive people I believe, and killed about fifteen of them.'"[132] Summerall did not comment on these raids, but did state his unfavorable opinion of the Germans in Peking, when he wrote that "The soldiers were subordinate but the officers were arrogant and patronizing. We respected their efficiency but did not like them and we had nothing to do with them." But, he carried too far his disdain for German officers when he incorrectly wrote that "Count von Waldersee wanted to assume command of all the contingents but the Americans and perhaps some others declined to recognize this."[133] Perhaps, his remembrance, late in life, of the Germans in China was shaped by his having fought against the Kaiser's army in the Great War, and then having seen, again, the results of German officers and soldiers goose-stepping across other lands, under the command of a new and more fearful commander: the Fuehrer.

Looking back, in his 80s, on the tribulations, trials, triumphs, and tragedies of the dangerous and demanding time in the Philippines, and in "The Land of the Dragon," as he titled the chapter on China in his memoir, Summerall wrote that "the most important thing in my life and that which was uppermost in my mind and heart [was] Miss Mordecai." He kept her photograph carefully sealed under the cover of his pocket watch. They had written constantly to each other, and "Every mail brought the most beautiful letters from her to inspire and hearten me." In his letters, he returned her love and devotion, and when his increase in pay came through, he felt free to propose their marriage, which they "determined" would take place whenever he returned to the States, "although we could see no prospect of such an event." Early in 1901,[134] she wrote that her father had been transferred to command the Benicia Arsenal, Summerall's first active duty assignment, and that she was going to Manila to visit friends. She included the schedule of the steamship *Sheridan* that would take her to and from Manila. Elated with the news, and thrilled that, although far away in California, she was now "much nearer to me," Summerall decided that it would be best for them to meet in Nagasaki, Japan, on her way back to California.[135] In view of his careful and chaste courtship of Laura Mordecai after their meeting at the Presidio, it is intriguing to imagine how they spent their days and nights together in Japan. In his memoir, he said nothing about having arranged accommodations for himself in Nagasaki, or elsewhere in Japan, much less anything about where Miss Mordecai would stay. Perhaps she remained onboard the *Sheridan*, although Summerall did not mention how long the ship remained in port. At any rate, one can picture his waving excitedly as he caught sight of her leaning over the ship's railing, his enraptured gaze following her down the gangplank, and their tender meeting as they gazed lovingly and devotedly into each other's eyes. Perhaps they walked together arm in arm, with porters scurrying to keep up, toward a more private place to share their joyful reunion, as the romance of spring filled the air in the "Land of the Lotus Blossom."

Before any of this could happen, he had to get General Chaffee's authorization for a leave, and, since "No one had ever thought of asking for a leave in Pekin [*sic*]," Summerall doubted that Chaffee would grant it. However, much to his delight, the crusty, old Indian fighter was "most kind in his attitude" and approved in late March 1901 Summerall's request for a leave of three weeks for him to travel to Nagasaki and return. He immediately wrote Laura and set about trying to secure passage to the Japanese port.[136] Thus began one of the most highly anticipated journeys of his life.

Summerall soon discovered that no American or commercial vessel was available. But after downing several bottles of bitter Japanese beer with a Japanese customs official (a most difficult "ordeal" for the teetotalling young lieutenant, but he could not risk giving "offense" by refusing), he secured passage on a Japanese ship that was anchored some 18 miles from Taku in the Gulf of Chihli. He hopped a train to Tientsin and from there made his way to Taku, where he boarded a small launch, appropriately named the *Captain Henry J. Reilly*, for the trip out to the ship. It was dark when the launch reached the Japanese vessel, and the waters of the gulf were so rough that it could not pull alongside the larger ship. The captain yelled down to Summerall that they would throw a rope ladder down over the side, and for him to grab hold and climb up to the deck when the waves tossed the launch close to the ship. As the *Reilly* pitched and rolled in the surging water ever closer to the ship, the ladder swung down erratically and slowly; Summerall reached out and grabbed hold of a rung, clambered up to the deck, and hoisted his bag up with a line. After he had enjoyed a meal of stew and rice with the crew, the ship sailed for the port of Shanhaikwan, now known as Linyu, on the Gulf of Liaotung, at the eastern end of the Great Wall. As they anchored early the next morning, Summerall looked up to see the Wall "climbing up the hills for a long distance." From Shanhaikwan they sailed to the Korean seaport city of Chemulpo, now known as Inchon, just west of Seoul, and from there to Shimoneseki, where Summerall left the ship, went to the train station, and bought a ticket for Nagasaki, about 150 miles to the south on the island of Kyushu.[137]

After arriving in this thriving seaport on one of the most beautiful harbors in the world, he went directly to the quartermaster in charge of the coaling and provisioning of all ships from Manila, and asked him when the *Sheridan* was expected to arrive. The answer he received shocked and dismayed him. The quartermaster said he had never heard of the *Sheridan*, knew nothing of any possible arrival date, and seemed to resent Summerall's persistent questions. According to the schedule Laura had sent him, her ship would arrive in two or three days, so he settled down to wait patiently. Three days passed, and still there was no sign of the *Sheridan*. He cabled Laura in Manila (at $3.85 per word he had to be brief), but in his haste and anxiety, he forgot to head the cable from Nagasaki. He waited for several more days, and sent more cables, but still received no response. The quartermaster remained as indifferent and unconcerned as ever. A side trip of a few hours to see a cherry blossom festival and an overnight trip to Unzen and its famous volcano, failed to lift the gloom that seized him. It must have pained him even more sharply that Laura was not along to share these unique sights and splendors of the Japanese spring. With his leave about to run out in early April, he booked the return passage to China on a small Japanese passenger ship, and "with a heavy heart and bitter disappointment," left Nagasaki and Japan for good.[138]

On the way back to Peking, Summerall's gloom was at least partially lifted by the performances of a theatrical troupe that he found "very decent." When they reached Tientsin, they found that the hotel there had no rooms for them, so Summerall took them to where some American missionaries were staying, and asked them to provide shelter for the women in the troupe. At first, the missionaries refused to take the actors under their roof, but upon Summerall's "insistance," they finally agreed to take them in. Irritated by the lack of hospitality and generosity of these missionaries, and perhaps reflecting on others he had encountered in China, he remarked that "We were not favorably impressed by the missionaries we saw." The next day, he took the train to Peking, and went directly to his tent where Lieutenant Burgess, his tent mate, greeted him with the comment that "Some fellow has been cabling you from Manila. The cables are on the table." He picked them up and saw immediately that they were Laura's replies to the cables he had sent her from Nagasaki. In his haste to find out why her arrival in Nagasaki was delayed, he had forgotten to head his cables from there, so that, when she received them, she assumed he had sent them from Peking. She replied then to his Peking address, and, in due time, he learned that she had arrived in Nagasaki on the same day that he had returned to Peking. Deeply disappointed and depressed that his oversight had dashed their reunion, however brief it might have been, Summerall repeated his melancholy assessment that "There was no prospect of my returning to the states," and added that, "the situation seemed hopeless."[139]

During the long, lonely, and rigorous winter at Camp Reilly, Summerall's gloomy outlook was not improved by tiresome and frustrating work as the recorder on administrative boards, and as judge advocate of general courts martial.[140] In one of the courts martial, Private Alfred H. Calvin of the 9th Regiment was charged with manslaughter in the death of a private in the French marines, who had died after Calvin had struck the Frenchman in the head with the butt of his rifle. The American pleaded not guilty to the charge and to its specifications.[141] A certain Dr. G. Machenau of the French army was summoned,[142] and he testified that the French soldier had suffered from "brain trouble," and would have died even if Calvin had not hit him with his rifle butt. The court believed him, ruled that Calvin's blow had been "coincidental," and acquitted him of all charges.[143] Summerall wrote that he did not believe the doctor and went on to lament the laborious amount of time it took him to record the minutes of all the trials in long hand. He testily complained that "it also fell to me to fire the salute of a hundred and one guns on the death of Queen Victoria."[144]

The coming of spring did nothing to lift Summerall's spirits and, if anything, deepened his sadness, for on Sunday 24 March 1901, just over two months after the death of the British monarch, and almost two weeks after Summerall's 34th birthday on 4 March, a funeral service was conducted for Captain Reilly and six enlisted men who had been buried in the grounds of the American Legation. It was followed by a procession headed by Captain Ridgway, Reilly's successor as battery commander, from the legation down Legation Street. Behind Ridgway marched the band, a cavalry troop, an infantry company, and then the caissons, with Lieutenants Summerall and MacCloskey riding abreast of Reilly's body and six soldiers marching abreast of the other six bodies. After them, came General Chaffee and his staff, and as the band played funeral marches, the procession turned slowly to the left and passed under the Chien Men, where Reilly had been killed, and into Camp Reilly, where the bodies were deposited in the quartermaster storehouse. In early April, as the battery fired a 21-gun salute, Reilly's remains were placed on a train to Tientsin and from there transported to Washington for burial in Arlington National Cemetery, where his grave was marked later by a monument paid for by contributions from the 5th Artillery Regiment.[145]

Meanwhile, across the Potomac in Washington, Congress for some time had been faced with a manpower shortage in the army, as the end of the enlistment of thousands of volunteers was fast approaching. Large numbers of soldiers were still needed in the troubled Philippines, and on 20 March 1901, four days before the funeral for Captain Reilly, legislators passed a law increasing the size of the army to 30 infantry regiments, 15 cavalry regiments and one corps of artillery, altogether 100,619 officers and men. The most significant change was in the artillery corps, which combined all of the various artillery units under a single commander, who was given the authority to make transfers as needed between the coast and the light artillery.[146] With this reorganization Light Battery F, known proudly for so long as Reilly's Battery, became the 10th Battery, Field Artillery, and its name, along with its beloved captain, passed into a realm reserved for those men and their units who have fought gallantly and served their country with pride and distinction.

As the sad and heavy days of April faded into the month of May, the 10th Battery at Camp Reilly at last received orders to leave China, not to sail for home, but rather to return to Manila and to their old camp at the Agricultural Grounds. It was a dejected Summerall who wrote that, once again, "There was no prospect of coming home and all were much depressed."[147] As they moved out toward Tientsin in what to them was hardly the "merry month of May," they left behind a city, and would soon depart a country still controlled by the "foreign devils." By the end of that month, a treaty that would establish peace and remove all allied forces from China finally began to take shape.

After she had fled the capital, the Empress Dowager had appointed Li Hung Chiang, Viceroy of Canton, as plenipotentiary to represent China in any dealings with the allies. They regarded him as China's leading statesman and respected him for his leadership of his fellow viceroys in the south against the Boxers, and for his support for severe punishment of pro-Boxer ministers in the Chinese government.[148] As mentioned above, when Li visited the battery after Reilly's death, Summerall encountered him and found in him "an impressive character." On Christmas Eve 1900, the allied ministers presented to Li what they called the Joint Note. It contained 11 demands, of which two were the most important: (1) the death penalty for government officials identified by the Manchu Court, and designated by the allies as having committed crimes in support of the Boxers; and (2) the payment of "An equitable indemnity to Governments, Societies, private individuals, as well as for Chinese who have suffered during the recent occurrences in their persons of property, in consequence of their being in the service of foreigners."[149] Pressured by Li, the Dowager Empress and her Council yielded to the demand for the death penalty, and at the end of February 1901, death sentences or suicides ended the lives of 119 minor officials and seven princes of the Manchu Court.[150]

The demand for an "equitable indemnity" was a much more difficult matter to resolve, for China hovered near financial collapse. The allied ministers wrangled throughout the spring and into the summer over how large an indemnity they could extract without causing the regime to go bankrupt. Through a complicated and rather arcane process that combined various allied demands and estimated occupation costs, they finally calculated the Chinese liability at $335,000,000. The American side insisted that this sum would bankrupt China and urged a decrease of more than a third. The other powers, however, demanded full payment of the liability, and on 26 May, an Imperial Edict announced a guarantee that the entire sum would be paid in full over a period of 39 years.[151]

Finally, on 7 September 1901, a peace treaty, known as the Boxer Protocol, was signed by representatives of 12 powers at the Spanish Legation, home of the most senior diplomat in Peking. It contained 12 articles and 19 annexes, and provided for the payment of the indemnity; that conveyed the Chinese Emperor's regret to the German Kaiser for the death of Baron von Ketteler, and provided for the erection of a suitable monument at the site of his assassination. The Legation Quarter was to be enlarged and placed under foreign control; the Taku forts be razed, along with any others that might impede communication between Peking and the sea; and 12 places between Peking and the coast were to be garrisoned by the powers to safeguard communications with the legations; membership in any anti-foreign society was to be punishable by death, and officials who failed to repress anti-foreign outbreaks would be dismissed and never reemployed; China was to prohibit the importation of arms and armaments, and the Tungsli Yamen be elevated to the status of a ministry of foreign affairs. Finally, the court ceremonial was to be modified as regards the reception of foreign representatives. On 17 September 1901, the last of the foreign troops left Peking, clearing the way for the return of the Dowager Empress and her court, all of which arrived by train in the capital on 7 January 1902, four months to the day after the signing of the Boxer Protocol.[152] Her entry on a British train underscored the weakness of the regime and the degree of humiliation the Protocol had imposed upon its empire.

For the remaining 10 years of their rule, the Manchu dynasty undertook a series of educational, economic, and military reforms, and drafted a constitution with provision for the election of a parliament. But, continuing civil and political strife weakened these efforts and led to the collapse of China's currency, the exhaustion of its reserves of specie, and to severe foreign restrictions on the country's credit. These crises undermined the system that regulated the redemption payments and caused the Americans and British to use their share to fund educational and public service programs in the country. The other powers soon followed the Anglo-American lead.[153] But neither their efforts, nor the reforms of the regime, could save it from revolutionary upheaval that broke out in 1911. One year later the last Manchu emperor died.

The outcome of the Boxer Rebellion dramatized to the world China's weakness before the might of the Western and Japanese powers. In itself, the rebellion demonstrated the intensity of native hostility toward foreign cultures and contempt for the avarice of their people, as well as the hatred for Chinese converts to Christianity. It illustrated the conflict between those who accepted the need to adapt the country's economic, political, and social institutions to Western standards, and those who opposed any measures that might change the complex institutions and traditions of the vast realm. The Boxer Rebellion that launched the 20th century in China was crushed, but the internal conflicts embedded in it not only lasted throughout that era of violence and upheaval, but continued into the century that followed.

In his memoir, Summerall's reflections on his service in the Land of the Dragon were rather sharply divided between pleasure and pain on the one hand, and criticism of other allied powers on the other hand. He encountered in China conditions and was assigned duties that, in several respects, were as tough and demanding as those he had faced in the Philippines. The summer heat and winter cold of northern China turned out to be about as severe as the torrid heat of central and southern Luzon, and the pain and discomfort of his "plague" of boils and poison ivy infection added to the misery of the climate, but still did not undermine his robust health. The misadventure of his eagerly anticipated reunion with Laura Mordecai and the death of Captain Reilly seem to have deepened his sense of loneliness and depression in a land so incredibly different from and far away from his homeland. After his own oversight dashed his hopes of meeting Laura, and after she had traveled halfway around the world to see him, he lamented more than once that a return to home and his fiancée was "hopeless." With Reilly's death, Summerall lost a mentor and role model whom he felt no one could replace, but the spectacular sights of the Forbidden City and the Great Wall were memories he cherished. Although he stretched toward incredulity the story of his marking crosses on the gates of the walls of Peking, his energetic command, and his decisiveness and bravery before the gates to the Forbidden City impressed his fellow officers and men, as well as his superiors. He was pleased when he received a citation from General Chaffee.

Summerall's criticisms of Russian actions seem, in retrospect, to have been excessive and a consequence of his strong anti-Communist beliefs later in life. His irritation that the Americans were prevented from being the first to breach the walls of Peking, had lost the "race" to reach the foreign legations ahead of the British, and had been held back from assaulting the final set of gates leading to the Forbidden City, was much like Daggett's and Chaffee's reactions to these developments. Together, their comments not only indicate their displeasure with fighting in a coalition, but also suggest some of the difficulties inherent in future American participation in coalition warfare of any sort. They foreshadowed the determination to be out front and "first" in any operation; the conviction that Americans fought best independently and under their own command; and the belief that American men and methods of war were superior to those of friend and foe alike. When the United States next was engaged in a wartime coalition across an ocean, these were the concepts that its leaders and commanders like Summerall carried into battle. But to the officers and men of the 10th Battery, Field Artillery, the excitement and challenges of recent battles, and the likelihood of future combat, seemed increasingly remote as they sailed away from China and back to Manila to the depressing prospect of camp life on the Agricultural Grounds of the Philippine capital.

*Famous illustrator Benjamin "Stookie" Allen's views of Summerall's bravery and leadership. This illustration was taken from his syndicated Series "Above the Crowd" that likely appeared in the* **Chicago Tribune** *in June 1919.*

Courtesy Colonel Robert R. McCormick Research Center

# Chapter Six

## *Home and Hearth*

Summerall and the 10th Battery, Field Artillery, left China forever in late May 1901, when the officers and men loaded their horses, guns, and equipment on board a ship much like the *Flintshire* and set sail for Manila. Once again on board a slow-moving steamer in the stifling heat of southeastern Asia, the men slept on deck and ate canned goods chased with occasional tins of coffee. The heat in the hold where the horses were kept became so oppressive for the animals that the men were forced to hoist them topside to let them cool down and breathe fresh air, while watching them carefully to keep them from slipping and falling onto the rocking deck. In early June, the vessel dropped anchor in Manila Harbor, where the familiar *cascos* returned the battery to their old camp in the Agricultural Grounds. For Summerall and his colleagues, it was not a happy return, for they had sailed from China believing that "There was no prospect of coming home," and feeling "much depressed." For the next 12 days, the routines of camp life failed to lift their spirits, but suddenly, and completely unexpectedly, they received an order to return to San Francisco. They were ordered to board the *Pak Ling*, a one-stack cargo vessel outfitted to transport horses, to serve as guards for several hundred prisoners, mainly American soldiers who had been held in Manila. Horses, guns, and all equipment of the battery were left behind and transferred to other batteries.[1]

Among the happiest of the soldiers when they learned they were going home must have been the battery's lieutenants. During their two years in the Far East, all of them had become engaged, but had not dared to set a date for their marriages, because, as Summerall wrote, "Captain Reilly had always said that he would not have a married lieutenant in his battery."[2] The death of their respected and beloved commander, and the likelihood of their promotions to captain, "changed the inhibition for us," wrote Summerall, in his most disciplined and restrained manner. His relationship with Laura Mordecai remained a very private matter that he shared with no one, regardless of the change in inhibition, or of his great disappointment in missing their rendezvous in Japan, or of the stack of cablegrams on his desk that MacCloskey pointed out to him when he returned from Nagasaki. As he said, "I had never mentioned Miss Mordecai to the others." Now, however, shedding his reserve, he rushed over to the cable office and sent Laura a message with the date of his arrival in San Francisco. In his excitement, he failed to notice that he had written the message on the top sheet of a pad of onionskin paper and that his words could be read on several of the thin, underlying sheets. When MacCloskey entered the office to use the same pad to write a similar message to his fiancée, Summerall probably gasped, but then blushed and smiled as he realized that his colleague would read his message, and that "his secret" would be revealed.[3]

In the early 21st century, when so many individuals demand attention, and seem to have a need to tell everyone about themselves and find out the most intimate details about others, it may seem strange that Summerall would remain such an intensely private person. Yet, as the son and sibling upon whom his family depended, and as a leader and model for his men and fellow officers in peace and at war, he believed that he could not show fear or any feelings or emotions that might suggest softness or weakness. That conviction had carried him through early manhood, as well as through the trials of West Point, from which he had emerged as one of the "men of iron." In the Victorian Age of his youth and developing maturity, leaders in public and as well in private life were expected to bear with stoic acceptance and fortitude the weight of command, and to project a picture of calm composure and confidence untouched by one's personal feelings. Those feelings were to be shared only with those in one's innermost circle, and, for First Lieutenant Summerall, that circle was drawn tightly around the person of Laura Mordecai.

In early June 1901, the *Pak Ling* hoisted anchor, and, with its mixed cargo of soldiers and prisoners, sailed out of Manila Harbor in the late afternoon as the sun set beyond the starboard side of the ship. Just after nightfall, as the ship moved slowly past Corregidor Island, Summerall turned to look back at the fading lights of Manila and wondered just how he had "endured so much hardship and privation" in the torrid and turbulent realm of the Far East. For 12 days, they sailed along the great circle route to San Francisco, through fog so thick that it shrouded the sun from view. Officers and men slept on the straw in the horse stalls below deck and took their meals topside. Some two years before, when he arrived in the Philippines, Summerall had joined his fellow officers in growing a beard and mustache. In a picture from that time, he is the thin, dark-bearded figure second from the right; hands folded behind him, with a bowler-shaped hat perched on his head just above two thick, black arches of hair looping across his forehead just below the hat rim. The carefully trimmed beard, a dingy, cotton khaki uniform blouse, and noticeably clean trousers complete the picture of a rather jaunty 34-year-old artillery officer. Now, with his ship approaching the California coast, and with his mind filled with thoughts of Laura, he shaved off beard and mustache, so that she would see him "as she remembered me."[4]

In the last full week of June the *Pak Ling* steamed through the Golden Gate and eased into a berth at the Port of San Francisco alongside other transports that had returned with decks crammed with soldiers celebrating their safe return from the dangers, toils, terrors and, for some, the thrills of war they had left behind in the Philippines and China. In fact, by the time his ship had arrived, Summerall noted that "returning soldiers were a common sight in San Francisco and no attention was paid to the landing of Reilly's Battery [he preferred the old name]." By the end of the week, the 10th Artillery had settled into their cantonment amid the familiar confines of the Presidio, and on Sunday, 30 June, Summerall boarded the train for the 30-mile trip to the Benicia Arsenal. He had begun there his active duty service, and he was now returning, almost nine years later, to begin a new chapter, so long and poignantly delayed, that would join his life with that of the woman who had become the love of his life, and the one person with whom he could share his deepest feelings.[5]

Summerall arrived at the quarters of Colonel Mordecai as the family, with the exception of daughter Laura, was seated around the dining room table enjoying their Sunday dinner. Laura Mordecai, quite likely too excited to sit calmly at the table, had gone out to the front porch to watch for her fiancé, and was standing on the top step when Summerall "alighted from the express wagon that took me from the station." The joy of their reunion must have been deep and exquisitely tender and touching, but Summerall, drawing the cloak of privacy around the loving pair, would only say after their meeting that "Much of the rest need not be told." That evening, Summerall told Laura's father that he "wanted to marry his daughter." As the blunt spoken and determined suitor saw the situation, Colonel Mordecai "had little option, though he had no objection."[6]

Apparently realizing its significance, Laura fixed 14 August, the anniversary of the fall of Peking, as the date for the wedding that would take place in Colonel Mordecai's spacious quarters at Benecia. During the next six weeks, she spent her time making arrangements for the wedding, visiting friends in San Francisco, and meeting with her fiancé at the Presidio. Winfield Jones gave a lavish dinner party for them, and Summerall informed his old friends and colleagues of his engagement and wedding date, including, "the young ladies I had known," who, as he laconically recalled with apparent relief, "scratched me off their lists." He heard from Lieutenant MacCloskey that his fiancée in Pittsburgh, without knowing the date for Summerall's wedding, had also chosen 14 August for their wedding date; Lieutenant Burgess's fiancée had fixed 15 July for their marriage, and Lieutenant Hall of the battery was to be married later that year. So, had Captain Reilly still been in command, his lieutenants, as Summerall, with a touch of restrained humor stated, would have "disqualified themselves for his battery."[7]

In early July, his idyllic interlude by the bay was interrupted when the battery was ordered to Fort Walla Walla, Washington. All of the lieutenants had gone on leave, so Summerall and Captain Ridgeway, along with several non-commissioned officers from the battery, were sent ahead by special train to organize the command before the full battery arrived. As the train traveled north through the night past the base of Mt. Shasta, it collided head-on with a southbound passenger train. The two locomotives crashed on their sides, but fortunately no one was killed, although several on the passenger train were injured. No one riding in Summerall's train was hurt, but one of the cars was telescoped, and the Chinese "loot" that he and Ridgeway were carrying with them was ruined, and "lay scattered everywhere." Repair crews cleared the wreckage and another locomotive soon arrived to pull the remaining cars on to Fort Walla Walla.[8]

The fort located at the confluence of the Walla Walla and Columbia Rivers in the southeastern part of the state, just north of the Oregon border, had been constructed in the early 19th century as a trading post for trappers plying the local rivers. It became a permanent military post in 1858 and had remained an important outpost in the suppression of subsequent uprisings from the Yakima, Spokane, Nez Pierce, and Modoc tribes. The town of Walla Walla had grown up around the fort as an outfitting point for the Idaho gold rush of the 1860s.[9] As the region stabilized and the town prospered, the fort's garrison had been steadily reduced, so that by 1901, it consisted of a cavalry troop, and, according to Summerall, "several hundred wild horses and a number of cowboys employed to break them." This would be his and Laura's first home, so he carefully selected a good set of quarters among the officers' row of modest clapboard houses, with sheltered front porches, along one side of the parade ground, directly across from the enlisted men's barracks. He bought a minimum amount of furniture and had the good fortune to hire as the cook for his new household Mrs. Margaret MacInturff, the wife of a non-commissioned officer serving in the Philippines. He called her by her given name, and she became, as Summerall wrote, "one of the greatest blessings in our lives"; she began her work by getting his quarters ready for the arrival of his new bride.[10]

With the day of wedding fast approaching, and with the command structure in place at Fort Walla Walla for the arrival of the battery, Summerall returned to the bay area for his marriage to Laura. Precisely at noon on 14 August 1901, on a bright, sunny Wednesday, they were married in the parlor of the Mordecai home at an improvised altar, draped with flowers. As described in a column in the *San Francisco Examiner* of 15 August, "The house was decorated with flowers and evergreens and the large porch at the east side of the house was draped with United States flags. In the reception hall [foyer] many Chinese curios were suspended on the walls as momentoes of the fall of Pekin [sic]." Four children scattered flowers as Laura's two bridesmaids, the sisters Helen and Miriam Clark, slowly preceded her. To the strains of the wedding march from Richard Wagner's opera *Lohengrin*, Laura was escorted by her father to the altar, where Summerall was waiting, along with his best man, the just-married Lieutenant Burgess, both officers attired in their full-dress uniforms.[11] As Summerall noted, "My promotion to captain took place on July 1st, but I had not received my commission. However, I wore my captain's bars on my full dress epaulets with my full dress uniform and sabre."[12] Laura's gown was "of white crepe de chine, trimmed with duchessse lace; the bridesmaids were attired in white organdie, and the bride's mother in grey [sic] brocade and black lace."[13] The Reverend D. O. Kelly, chaplain at the Presidio, performed the ceremony. Of his diminutive and delicate 29-year-old bride and their wedding, Summerall happily recalled that "No one was ever so lovely as the little bride and the whole setting was like a paradise." A reception and "breakfast" followed, "on the lawn in front of the house, and under the natural canopy of foliage."[14] Many of their guests and friends, including General Shafter, Winfield Jones, and Captain Miley's widow, came from San Francisco by train and harbor steamer, and, according to the *Examiner*, "Many and costly gifts were received."[15] Over 50 years later, Summerall could look back on this memorable and indelible day as "the culmination of life and the richest reward that any man could have."[16] Would that every husband could remember and hold his wedding day in such a vivid and cherished memory.

Naturally, Summerall wrote nothing about where they spent their honeymoon, not even going so far as to write that "Much of the rest need not be told." However, the article in the *Examiner* noted that "Captain and Mrs. Summerall, after a short stay in San Francisco, will go to Fort Lawton, Washington, [sic] to which post the Captain has been assigned."[17] Quite probably, they left San Francisco late in the afternoon on either the Saturday or Sunday after the wedding on Wednesday, took the train to Oakland, and from there caught the Portland train that would have arrived in Oregon's largest city about 12 hours later in the early morning hours. While waiting there for the train to Walla Walla, they noticed a train pulling out of the station, and when Summerall asked a porter where it was going, he answered Walla Walla. Quickly, he took Laura by one arm and told the porter to take her other arm. Carrying her between them, they dashed after the train, and tossed her up to the platform of a car, with Summerall leaping up after her. Their bags were thrown up after them, and they frantically were off to the high plains of Washington State, to Fort Walla Walla, and to their first home.[18]

The trip from Portland took more than the entire day, and Summerall wrote that "The day was terrifically hot. The car windows were opened for air and we choked with dust. We kept wet handkerchiefs to our faces. The train carried freight, animals [as well as], passengers and stopped at every station. We reached Walla Walla about eight o'clock [in the evening]."[19] His brief account of the journey from Benecia to Walla Walla corresponds to the timetable described above, which would have had them arriving at Walla Walla after a journey of some 800 grueling miles, with about the last 400 sounding something like the trek of Reilly's Battery along the Pei Ho from Tientsin to Peking. The exhausted newlyweds arrived either Sunday night on the 18th, or Monday night on the 19th (depending on whether they left on Saturday or Sunday), only to find Margaret ill, and "suffering great pain." As much as he wanted to be with Laura, and she certainly felt the same way, he understood why "my little wife spent most of the night nursing her." By the next morning, Margaret had recovered sufficiently to prepare their meals and assist Laura in setting up the household. In the meantime, Summerall's promotion to captain had arrived. It provided them with "the munificent salary of $180.00 per month." With his savings of almost $300, he suddenly felt rich, "even though I sent my sister $30.00 per month."[20]

Just one week after the Summeralls had settled into their new quarters, he received orders to report to Fort Lawton in Seattle, Washington, and take command of the 106th Company of the Coast Artillery. In spite of the need to pack up and move after such a short stay in Walla Walla, Summerall recorded no complaints, and neither, apparently, did Laura, who was probably well accustomed to the sudden and frequent moves of an army family. After another long train ride, this time a journey of some 250 miles across the Cascade Mountains and past Mt. Rainier, they arrived in Seattle in late August, and rode out to Fort Lawton, where they moved into a new set of captain's quarters. Neither their furniture nor Margaret had arrived, so, for a time, they sat around a packing box, eating the meals that Laura prepared. Summerall, of course, did not mention how or where they slept. After a few days the furniture arrived, soon followed by Margaret, whom the Summeralls "welcomed whole heartedly. She prepared the meals and kept the house clean."[21]

Fort Lawton originally occupied much of Seattle's Magnolia Bluff, which commanded the entrance to Puget Sound and to Elliott Bay, the city's waterfront. In 1896, the secretary of war had authorized the construction on the site of an artillery battery to defend Seattle and the south Sound from naval attack. Four years later, the army officially named Fort Lawton in honor of Major General Henry W. Lawton, who had fought in Cuba and had been killed by a sniper's bullet in the Philippines in 1899. (See above, Philippines, pp. 72, 75–76, 79.)[22] Summerall was stationed at the post for 10 months, but wrote very little about his duties and work there. His remembrances of that time were filled, essentially, with recollections of Laura in these first months of their marriage. He wrote that she was the only woman on the post (he forgot about Margaret), and, fearful of leaving her alone at night, took her along with him to inspect the guard. He described how much she enjoyed "working over the knots [used in cordage] with me and learn[ing] their names and how to tie them. She was keenly interested in all that I did to plant trees and to improve the post."[23] Certainly, Summerall was conscientious and attentive as ever to his duties and responsibilities,[24] but they had faded away, as he recalled what obviously was the glow of his first months of marriage and his enchanted fascination with "my little wife."

While they were stationed at Fort Lawton, the Summeralls learned that Laura was pregnant and would give birth to their child sometime toward the middle or latter part of June 1902. He did not mention just when they heard the exciting news, but surely it added immeasurably to the private bliss of their life together on the shaded heights of Magnolia Bluff. However, in April 1902, the eighth month of Laura's pregnancy, Summerall was ordered to duty in Skagway, Alaska, over 1,800 miles from her side. He left her in the capable hands of Margaret and a contract doctor at the post, but far away from the tender and loving care of her adoring husband. As he noted, "The situation was heartbreaking."[25]

In March 1867 (incidentally, the month and year of Summerall's birth), the United States had purchased Alaska from Russia for $7.2 million, relieving the Romanov dynasty of an unprofitable possession, and thus eliminating one more colonial power from the New World. The United States took over the Russian territory that had been delineated in 1825, in a treaty between Russia and Great Britain, upon which the Russian-American Treaty of 1867 was largely based. At that time, the entire area was unexplored and seemed worthless, and the boundary line between British Columbia and Alaska in the south had been described loosely in both treaties as running along the crest of the mountains, and not to extend inland more than 10 leagues (30 miles) from the coastline. The distance of 10 leagues from points along the coastline to the mountain crests was plain enough on maps of the region, but the coastline and mountain crests were ragged and undulating, and it was difficult to mark accurately the boundary on the ground in the remote wilderness of Northwest America. Nevertheless, both Canada and Britain accepted the boundary line as delineated on the map. However, the discovery of gold in 1896 in the Klondike River region of the Yukon Territory in Canada made every square foot of land a potential gold mine of enormous wealth, and that made the precise location of the border a critical issue. Of special importance were the inlet known as the Lynn Canal, along the southwestern coast of Alaska that opened the way to the gold fields, and to the town of Skagway, located at the head of the inlet. The United States took possession, claiming that the "sinuosities of the coast," as defined in the 1825 treaty, meant that the heads of all inlets, to include Skagway, belonged to the United States. However, Canada claimed that Skagway was more than 10 leagues from the ocean, and thus, was within Canadian territory. To back up this claim, in 1898, Canada stationed a customs officer and a detachment of North West Mounted Police in Skagway. The Canadian government also sent a 200-man army unit, known as the Yukon Field Force, to Fort Selkirk, some 300 miles northwest of Skagway. This unit could be dispatched to deal with troubles along the boundary, yet was not considered a threat to Skagway, even though tension between the United States and Canada remained high in the disputed area around the Lynn Canal and Skagway.

The town of Skagway rested on a flat stretch of land rimmed by rugged mountains at the head of the Lynn Canal, the inlet that was, actually, a deep fjord, 80 miles long and six miles wide, which led north from Juneau. Skagway was settled in the late 1880s by an old seafarer, Captain William "Billy" Moore, as a supply center to serve the route to the upper Yukon region of Canada, which Moore believed was rich in minerals waiting to be discovered. The precipitous and dangerous Chilkoot Trail was the only entry from the tidewater at Skagway into the upper Yukon valley, so Moore enlisted the help of a Canadian government survey party, headed by William Ogilvie, and opened a lower and safer trail, through what Ogilvie named the White Pass, to the river and downstream to the town of Whitehorse. In 1896, Moore's predictions came true when rich, gold-bearing gravel was discovered in the creeks that fed into the Klondike River, a 90-mile-long tributary of the Yukon, which flowed into it near the town of Dawson, 50 miles from the Alaska border and some 450 miles northeast of Skagway. News reached the U.S. in early 1897 and was followed by what became known as the Klondike Gold Rush of 1897–1899, sometimes called the "greatest stampede in history," when more than 30,000 persons, Argonauts, as some called them, made their way north via the Lynn Canal, Chilkoot and White Passes, and down the Yukon. Moore's settlement at Skagway was overrun. His claims were jumped by speculators like Frank Reid, a former county official in Oregon, who had been charged with killing a man, but was acquitted on the grounds of self-defense, even though the man he killed was unarmed. In 1897, Reid and his cohorts established the town of Skagway on Moore's land, divided it into lots, and sold them at steep prices. After a court battle that lasted four years, Moore was awarded 25 percent of the assessed value of his former property. As Skagway historian Howard Clifford said, "the town of Skagway was conceived in lawlessness and grew up in violence."[26]

To deal with this kind of lawlessness and disorder, and to contain the exuberance of men determined to find their fortunes in gold, two companies of the 14th Cavalry from Vancouver Barracks in the state of Washington were sent to Skagway, and two more were dispatched to the settlement of Dyea, at the head of the Lynn Canal, some 15 miles from Skagway. After the war with Spain broke out, most of these soldiers shipped out for Manila; those who remained faced the possibility that the boundary dispute between the United States and Canada could lead to a confrontation with the Canadian police and the Yukon Field Force. They also confronted the challenge of maintaining order amid the chaos of the Klondike Gold Rush.

By the summer of 1898, Skagway had become a boomtown of some 15,000 persons living in tents, shacks, and rooming houses, and reveling in 61 saloons and gambling dens. Adjoining many of the drinking and gambling establishments were "dance halls" that featured "queens" with names like Sitting Maude, the Montana Filly, Ethel the Moose, Sweet Marie, the Oregon Mare, Molly Fewclothes, The Virgin, and Diamond Lil Davenport. Business picked up when construction workers poured into town to begin work on the White Pass and Yukon Route Railroad from Skagway to Dawson. The previous summer the notorious con man and outlaw Jefferson "Soapy" Smith blew into Skagway, bought a saloon, and with his gang of fast and smooth talkers preyed on railroad workers and swindled and robbed gullible prospectors out of their money, valuables, and claims. In July 1898, a miner lost his poke of $2,700, and Smith was suspected of stealing it. A vigilante committee met, accused him of the theft, and proceeded with his trial, but refused to allow Smith to attend. Enraged, Smith tried to break into the meeting in a building on the Skagway wharf and was challenged by Frank Reid. Both men drew their pistols and began firing. Smith fell dead to the ground, and Reid died 12 days later. The vigilantes then went on a rampage through the town, looting stores and saloons, and chasing down suspected members of Smith's gang. In Juneau, the commissioner of Alaska was forced to call in reinforcements from the 14th Cavalry in Dyea to restore order. They arrived just in time to stop a hanging, ended the looting, and restored order, before returning to their post at Dyea.[27]

The 14th Cavalry was relieved in May 1899, after 15 months in Alaska, and was replaced by Company L of the 24th Infantry, one of four black units in the Regular Army. As part of the 5th Corps in the Spanish-American War, the 24th had fought with distinction in battles around Santiago, Cuba, as stated in an article about the regiment written by one of the officers in Company L and published in the *Skagway Daily Alaskan* on 1 January 1900. He noted also that the regiment had subsequently suffered losses of over 50 percent to the disease of yellow fever.[28] When they returned from Cuba, two new companies, L and M, were added to the regiment and the former, commanded by Captain Henry W. Hovey, was sent via the Presidio and Vancouver Barracks to Skagway (Dyea had seen its best days, and when the first few miles of the White Pass and Yukon Route opened in February 1899, Skagway completely superseded it). L Company settled into quarters on a dock that were in a "sad state of repair," and Captain Hovey began looking for other billets, when, as Skagway historian Clifford wrote, "a forest fire destroyed the facilities."[29] The author (who remained unnamed) of the article in the *Alaskan* wrote that they stayed on the dock "until burned out on the 28th of July last,"[30] which was a little over two months after they arrived in Skagway. The phrase "burned out" clearly indicates that a violent act of racial hostility had occurred, but the unnamed officer adds nothing more to his account. Skagway historian Clifford ignored this possibility and pointed out the hospitable response to the soldiers' misfortune. He stated that "Temporary headquarters were set up in a rented warehouse in Skagway and the troops were moved into property belonging to Captain Moore, who let them stay without charge. Later the troops moved into the Astoria Hotel, where the company was charged $175 a month."[31] At any rate, when railroad construction workers went out on strike and tried to destroy the roundhouse and shops of the White Pass and Yukon Route, it was clear that Skagway needed the soldiers of L Company. They routed the strikers, arrested the ringleaders, and broke up rowdy gatherings of workers across town. With conditions calmed and tempers cooled, the workers lined up and returned to their jobs.

The situation in the disputed boundary areas remained precarious. Stories circulated that a group of heavily armed Americans had demanded that the Canadian flag on the police station be taken down, or they would shoot it down, and that a few hotheads in Skagway were rumored to be plotting an uprising to seize the Klondike from Canada.[32] In December 1901, the commanding officer in Skagway reported to the War Department that the rumor of an insurrection had been generated in Canada to force a settlement of the boundary issue. The British ambassador reported to Secretary of War Elihu Root that only a few people had been stirring up these rumors and that reports of an insurrection were greatly exaggerated.[33] Nevertheless, according to historian and biographer of President Theodore Roosevelt, Lewis L. Gould, "an armed clash would produce a crisis that none of the three countries [the United States, Great Britain and Canada] wanted."[34]

The president had been watching the situation carefully, and in late March 1902, his secretary George B. Cortelyou wrote Secretary Root to send additional American soldiers "as quietly and unostentatiously as possible to southern Alaska *so as to be able promptly to prevent any possible disturbance along the disputed frontier line* [his italics]."[35] Roosevelt's unusually cautious instructions reflected his determination not to allow local disturbances to complicate settlement of the boundary dispute, about which he had firm convictions.³⁶ In July 1902, the president wrote Secretary of State John Hay that the Canadian claims were "'an outrage, pure and simple.'" Roosevelt was willing to have three American and three Anglo-Canadian commissioners meet to negotiate a settlement, but only with the understanding that the American representatives "'were not to yield any territory whatsoever, but were as a matter of course to insist on our entire claim.'"³⁷ Roosevelt knew that the Anglo-Canadian position was undermined by the fact that Canada and Britain had acquiesced in the American assumption of Russian rights, until the gold rush began in the Klondike. He also was confident that the Canadians knew that they had a weak case and that domestic political reasons lay behind their actions. Throughout 1902–03, he pushed the British and the Canadians hard and kept the American commissioners on a short leash to achieve his goals.³⁸

Meanwhile, perhaps in order to avoid the possibility of a clash between unruly racist settlers and the black soldiers of L Company that might escalate into the kind of "disturbance" that the president feared, the unit had been sent back to the States. In their place arrived soldiers that the president, in late March 1902, had instructed Secretary Root to send to southern Alaska; namely, the 106th Company of the Coast Artillery (C.A.) that was ordered to Skagway under the command of Captain Charles P. Summerall, who also had been ordered to send ahead to the town the 32nd Company, C.A.³⁹ Summerall very likely was the officer Secretary Root had selected to fit the president's desire, as expressed in the letter from Cortelyou to Root, "'to have some first-class young officer who can be absolutely trusted go along the border line and report on conditions, and especially as to whether there are any signs of Canadian aggression or any improper action by our own people.'"⁴⁰

Early in April 1902, Summerall received his orders and the next day he embarked the 32nd Company, followed by the 106th, which sailed from Seattle on 11 May. Laura was just one month away from the expected arrival in June of their baby, and Summerall was forced to leave her behind, with only "the good Margaret to care for her." This separation was further proof that the army was "cruel to families," and, for Summerall, it was "heartbreaking."⁴¹

When he arrived in Skagway, he was ordered to send the 32nd Company to the port of Valdez, some 500 miles north-northwest from Skagway, which he did at once. In his memoir, Summerall stated that with Root's decision to occupy "the disputed territory with two companies of Coast Artillery, one thousand miles apart [sic]," the secretary had stopped a "daring plan" of the "Northwest Police [sic]" who "were ready to seize Skagway and Valdez and take over southeastern Alaska by force." He also said that he expected to be attacked and had ordered a field gun sent to Skagway, and had prepared a defensive position.⁴²

As noted above, what mostly concerned the president and Secretary Root was not the threat of an attack by a Canadian armed force, for which there seems to have been no firm indication, but rather the possibility that rumors of uprisings and threats and actions by hotheaded miners and settlers on both sides of the border might escalate into a crisis that neither the United States, nor Canada and Britain wanted. TR and Root expected their soldiers in Alaska to monitor carefully conditions and developments on both sides of the border to prevent any disturbance that could undermine what the president saw as the strong American position in the boundary dispute.

In Skagway, Summerall waited desperately for word about Laura's condition in the last month of her pregnancy. A telegram finally brought the news of the birth of Charles, Jr., on 16 June, but the joy of that moment was depressed when he learned, after mother and child had landed in Skagway three weeks later, that both had been near death after the birth. Margaret had been caring for them, and came with them, but Summerall wrote that Laura was still sick, and that his infant son "was starving." Quickly he found an "excellent doctor," and under his care and that of the "leading saloon keeper's wife [!] and the doctor's wife," as well as a foster mother and Margaret, "the baby's life was saved, but both continued very ill."[43] He remained greatly concerned about their health, especially in view of sanitary conditions in the town, and the fact that, in 1898, more than a hundred people had died in Skagway in an epidemic of spinal meningitis. To meet this emergency, a hospital had been set up in a large log cabin, and the Episcopal church provided funds to keep it open, but raw sewage continued to flow down the muddy streets, and the town lacked "any hygienic measures whatever."[44]

Summerall found two rooms for them in the Pulliam House Hotel, but the weather remained cold, and they had difficulty sleeping, because it was impossible to shut out the light from the summer sun that shone continuously. A local man built for the enlisted men an "excellent house," and Summerall kept his men busy practicing on a pistol range he had built. They also served as sentinels along the streets of Skagway, watched carefully by their lieutenants, less they stray into the "large saloons, gambling houses and disreputable places" that "did an enormous business with the prospectors coming and the miners with gold going out."[45]

Summerall's first significant assignment came when he received a telegram ordering him to Haines Mission, located on the south side of a peninsula that juts into the Lynn Canal, some 15 miles down the fjord from Skagway at the mouth of the Chilkat River. The town had been founded in 1881 by Presbyterian missionaries and had been named for Frances Haines, the secretary for the church organization that helped found missionary sites throughout North America. It had been chosen as the location for Alaska's first permanent army post, and Summerall was to select the site for the construction of the post on 4,400 acres of land that the 57th Congress had deeded to the army early in 1902.[46] He hired a surveyor, procured a small launch, and set out with 20 soldiers through the rough waters of the Lynn Canal. He reported that when they landed, he "found a number of Northwest Police [sic]," who "forbade him to begin any construction, and said this was disputed territory." He replied that "this was American territory and if they interfered I would use force." Apparently, the Canadians had learned about Summerall's mission simply by reading the order that was sent "In the clear over Canadian telegraph lines as there was no American telegraph or cable line to Alaska." As the Mounties looked on, Summerall's men began surveying an area two miles wide and four miles long, just above the town and below a mountain peak that offered protection from the north wind. A noted claim jumper named "Shellgame" Jackson and several other locals showed up and protested that the army was taking their lands. Summerall directed them to take their complaints to Washington. As the day ended, the Mounties rode away, and Summerall and his men settled into their "dog tents" for the first of many bitterly cold nights at Haines Mission. Their days were filled with the work of laying out sites for the various buildings for the new fort, cutting through dense undergrowth and trees (that Summerall referred to as a "jungle") to reach a mountain lake from which they took water samples to test for potability, and planning the construction of a dock.[47]

After more than a week at Haines Mission, Summerall felt that he must get back to his loved ones. Even though a strong, northerly gale was blowing, his party, along with a few civilians, embarked on a Saturday night. As they moved into the deep waters of the Lynn Canal and turned north toward Skagway, the gale began to howl, and a heaving sea sent a surging wave crashing over the bow, shattering the windows around the engine house, and flooding the engine compartment. Remembering that many ships had wrecked in the stormy waters, and on the undulating, rocky shores of the fjord, Summerall feared that the boat would either capsize or founder, and ordered the captain to return to the Haines harbor. Afraid that a turn in those conditions would cause the boat to capsize, and with the engine kicking in and out, the captain protested, but made the turn and managed to bring the boat back safely, under steady power from the engine. Luckily, a large vessel arrived at Haines Mission later that same night; the next morning it took the exhausted and weary passengers safely back to Skagway, where, fortunately and happily, Summerall found the health of his wife and baby improved under the devoted care of their faithful Margaret.[48]

Laura, in fact, felt well enough a few days later to accompany her husband on a trip on the recently completed White Pass and Yukon Railroad, as the guests of the railroad superintendent.[49] The narrow gauge railroad running from Skagway to Whitehorse, Yukon, a distance of 110 miles, was begun in 1898 and completed after only 26 months of construction. Climbing 3,000 feet in 20 miles, with grades up to 3.9 percent, winding around cliff hanging turns of 16 degrees, it passed through two tunnels and across numerous trestles and bridges. When completed in 1901, its steel, cantilever bridge was the highest in the world.[50] The railroad superintendent invited the Summeralls to ride in his car up to Lake Bennett, some 40 miles from Skagway. On the return trip they rode in the locomotive, with Laura sitting bravely in the fireman's seat, and gazing into snowy ravines that plunged thousands of feet from the tracks to the narrow slits of the bottoms below.[51]

Sitting in his office one afternoon, not long after the exhilarating ride on the rails of the White Pass and Yukon line, Summerall heard a violent explosion and the clanging of an alarm bell. He rushed out and saw the front of the bank and post office demolished and debris blown into the street. From the rear of the building an official staggered out and said that a stranger, brandishing two sticks of dynamite in one hand and a revolver in the other hand, had walked up to the teller's window and had demanded that the teller hand over $20,000, or he would blow up the bank. At that point, a customer walked in with $350 to deposit, startling the dynamite-and-pistol-wielding hold-up man. Just then the teller shouted, "'Look out, he's got a gun,'" and bolted from his cage toward the rear door. The man fired his pistol, either at the teller or the would-be depositor, but instead of hitting either of them, he hit the sticks of dynamite that he was holding. They exploded in a violent eruption, blowing the teller out the back door, splintering glass into the customer's face, scattering across the floor bank notes, gold, and silver coins, $2,800 in gold dust, wrecking the bank, and blowing a large hole in the floor. Next to the hole lay the mangled body of the stranger, who was never identified and died a few hours later at the railroad hospital.[52] Summerall posted sentries at the entrance and around the bank vault; in an attempt to recover the gold dust, other soldiers hosed down the remains of the building, and collected four to six inches of muddy gold dust residue. They placed it in barrels and boxes, hauled it down to a creek where sluice boxes were built to pan the rich residue, and, according to Howard Clifford's account, recovered more gold than the bank had on hand at the time of the attempted robbery. The unlucky customer, temporarily blinded by the flying glass, recovered all of his money, and bravely deposited it, after repairs were made to the bank. The remains of the hold-up man were cremated, except for his skull, which one of Skagway's locals seized and placed in his museum until it closed in the early 1920s.[53] For Summerall, the entire incident was not unusual for a town where "Many desperate characters and outlaws had preyed upon the gold seekers and murder had become quite common."[54]

As Summerall neared the end of his tour of duty in Skagway, he was notified that a General Randall from Vancouver Barracks in Washington state would arrive to investigate the complaints that Summerall had seized squatters' claims to build the army post at Haines Mission. Randall reached Skagway in early September, accompanied by Colonel Wilds P. Richardson, who had been the tactical officer of "A" Company at West Point when Summerall was first captain. Summerall liked Richardson and stated that he "was devoted to the life" in Alaska. He took Randall and Richardson to Haines Mission, showed them around the site he had laid out for the post, and got the general's endorsement, who subsequently reported his approval to the War Department. Seizing the opportunity to return to the life to which he was devoted, Richardson asked Summerall if he "would be willing to have him relieve me so that he could build the new post at Haines Mission." Summerall, noting that his wife and baby again were very ill, and fearing that he would lose both of them if he stayed, "eagerly consented." Soon after his visitors from Washington left, Summerall and his 106th Company, C.A., were ordered to Fort Flagler, and a battalion of the 8th Infantry, newly returned to Seattle from the Philippines, was ordered to Skagway. When the infantry battalion arrived from Seattle in September, Summerall reserved their space on the ship for his family and artillery company, and they sailed on the 22nd, a date that he carefully recorded in his memoir as marking the end of his service in the Land of the Midnight Sun.[55]

It had been a bittersweet experience. The joy of his homecoming and reunion with Laura and their marriage, his promotion to captain, and the beginnings of their blissful life as newlyweds filled Summerall with great pleasure that he fondly remembered for the rest of his life. The hardships of army life in remote lands under harsh conditions of man and nature, like those he experienced in the Far East and in Alaska, never daunted him. But he seems to have resented the fact that his duties as a soldier actually had come to endanger the life of his wife and their infant son. He also appears to have resented the natural realm of Alaska, for he never noted its beauty and splendor, and never saw it as majestic or awe inspiring. Instead, the uniqueness of the Alaskan wild for Summerall was a menacing and constant threat to the safety of his family. The people in and around Skagway did not fare much better in his assessment. With the exception of a few kind souls, he regarded most of them as part of a dangerous and untrustworthy rabble. Maybe they were, but he failed to appreciate, or note, that among them were also men and women who had braved the journey into the wild Alaskan north, were toughing out an existence there, and who worked diligently to protect and preserve their homes and families.

Perhaps to give a greater meaning and significance to his dour Alaskan duty, Summerall, as noted above, once again exaggerated the nature and purpose of his mission. His assertion that his command was part of Secretary Root's militant and "daring plan" of dealing with the Alaskan boundary dispute, contrasts, practically to the point of misrepresentation, with the cautious and careful approach of Roosevelt and Root to the problem. As a result, his presence and actions assumed a far greater importance than is justified. Instead of elevating his role in the Alaska boundary dispute almost to the level of thwarting a potential invasion of the Mounties and war between the United States and Canada, he might well have reflected upon the actual duties that he and his men performed, and their extraordinary experiences as pioneers in the assertion of the American government's authority in the unique circumstances of the great Klondike Gold Rush on the wild Alaskan frontier. There was indeed, very little glory in his work, but as his description of the actual duties that he and his men performed clearly shows, he appears very much like the "first-class young officer" whom, as Cortelyou had mentioned in his letter to Root, the president desired to send to southern Alaska in the first place. In addition, he could have made clear that the site he laid out for the fort at Haines Mission was where Wilds Richardson would build the installation that became Fort William H. Seward, named in honor of the man who, as secretary of state, had negotiated the purchase of Alaska from the Russians in 1867.

Summerall's departure from Alaska was almost a microcosm of this stay there. On boarding the ship for the return passage to Washington, he noted that "The weather was cold with high winds and sleet. When we reached the ship at night, we found that the train had brought the riff raff from Dawson who had left there on the last steamer of the season up the Yukon." They were mostly women from the dance halls and had taken all the accommodations that Summerall had reserved for his men. The Summeralls had to sleep in the public saloon, certainly an unfamiliar and unwelcome place for baby Charles and his parents, but the men "enjoyed the trip, talking and dancing with the girls." But their captain and his wife despaired, for their baby again seemed to be starving, and the howling gale and heavy seas further lengthened, and made even more miserable, their journey away from the menacing confines of Alaska. On board were a mining and railroad engineer and his wife, who told the Summeralls that she had nursed their starving baby back to health with a certain brand of condensed milk. After four long days at sea, the ship finally reached Port Townsend, just across the Straits of San Juan de Fuca from Fort Flagler. Summerall got the milk as soon as they arrived at their new post and was much relieved and happy as the health of their son improved, even though, as he noted, "it was years before he became healthy."[56]

# Chapter Seven

## *Coastal Defense, the Militia Bureau, and West Point*

Safely ashore at Port Townsend, Summerall found a room for his wife and child, and gratefully welcomed back "their good, faithful Margaret." He then set out across the Straits to Fort Flagler, where he unpacked their furniture, and set up their quarters before returning to Port Townsend to bring his family and Margaret to their new home. It was not a happy homecoming for the Summeralls. The post was entirely isolated from the town of Port Townsend; their house was only sparsely heated by coal-burning stoves; a cistern provided their drinking water, and a pump supplied brackish water for the bathrooms. Laura "was ill all the time," and their beloved Margaret left them to join her husband, who had returned from the Philippines. Tragically, Margaret was soon stricken with "some disease," and died in a hospital in Seattle. The Summeralls deeply mourned the woman who had "loved our baby as her own," and whose "help to us made her the best friend we ever had." They advertised in the Seattle paper for a cook, and soon hired a "very good one," but their life at Fort Flagler remained "very rugged."[1]

Fortunately, Summerall's work with the 106th Company of Coast Artillery, and its performance, raised his spirits and his hopes that better days lay ahead. Actually, this was the first time that the company had been assigned to its specific duty of coast defense, and they went right to work training for their mission. Their armament consisted of a battery of two 10-inch guns on disappearing mounts, a battery of 5-inch, rapid-fire guns, a range finder mounted in a tower, and the necessary equipment to plot the location of specific targets. Colleagues from other coastal defense installations supplied Summerall with the details of firing and target practice, and, with satisfaction, he noted that "the men were soon proficient in gunnery, vessel tracking, range finding, plotting and the service of the guns," and "earned much about the computation of range tables, and the technique of firing at a moving target." He was pleased also that they had attained a high level of morale and had excelled in the post athletic competitions.[2]

Another of his duties took Captain Summerall out to San Juan Island in the Straits of San Juan de Fuca to report on the condition of the graves of American soldiers who had died while on duty on the island. Their presence on the island originated in a dispute between the U.S. and Great Britain that began in the 1830s over the boundary of the Oregon Country, a vast area that swept from the present-day boundary between the states of Oregon and California into the northern reaches of what is today the Canadian province of British Columbia. In June 1846, the Treaty of Washington established the boundary between Canada and the U.S. from the Rocky Mountains westward to the coast along the 49th parallel (the U.S. had argued for the northern boundary along the 54°40² parallel). The treaty also guaranteed both nations navigation through the Gulf Islands and drew the boundary through the channel that separated Vancouver Island from the mainland. This latter provision allowed the British to retain this large island, and the U.S. to possess the smaller, but important, island of San Juan. However, both sides belatedly discovered that not just one but two major channels existed: Haro Strait and Rosario Strait. If the boundary were drawn through Rosario Strait, San Juan Island would belong to Great Britain; if it ran through Haro Strait, the U.S. would own the island.[3]

Asserting British control of San Juan, the Hudson Bay Company built several facilities on the island during the 1840s and 1850s. American settlers also moved in, and the Washington territorial legislature formally stated its claim to the island. Unaware of growing tensions on the island and between the British-Canadians and the Americans, a pig, belonging to the Hudson Bay Company, "invaded" the vegetable garden of an American farmer and began to root up and devour his entire crop. In defense of his land, and to save what little remained of his vegetables, the farmer shot and killed the pig. The angry officials of the Hudson Bay Company sought to arrest the farmer, and American settlers responded by calling for military support from the mainland. In July 1859, a contingent of soldiers under the command of Captain George E. Pickett (who later led, and survived, his regiment's charge at the Battle of Gettysburg) was ordered to San Juan Island. The British responded by sending three warships into the island's harbor. When Pickett's force remained in place, the British sent two more warships. The dispute quickly became known as the Pig War, although no shots had been fired, and President James Buchanan sent General Winfield Scott to defuse the situation. He arranged for a joint occupation of the island, but the outbreak and long course of the American Civil War delayed a permanent solution. In 1872, an arbitration panel, set up under the auspices of Emperor William I of the recently established German Empire, established the boundary through Haro Strait, placing San Juan Island in the U.S.[4]

In his memoir, Summerall noted that the soldiers' graves were in good condition and dealt briefly with the boundary dispute that brought them to San Juan Island in the first place. For Summerall, British claims amounted to an "attempt of England to seize our territory," as he had come to believe the British had tried to do later in Alaska.[5] He reached this judgment, as he had concluded in the case of Alaska, without noting the confusion over the boundary line that made a settlement more difficult, and without considering whether the territorial demands of the American side were any more justified than those of the British. His myopic condemnation of British actions on the one hand, and blanket approval of American policy on the other hand, are similar to his assertion that the British had unfairly beaten the Americans in the "race" to free the besieged legations in Peking. That he held these judgments into his final years of life, without ever having examined more carefully both sides of the various issues that were involved, indicates how convincingly he believed that his own opinions and decisions always had been correct. In addition, these conclusions may well reflect an entrenched resentment against those European powers, like Great Britain, under whose leadership, rather than under its own commanders, the U.S. had been forced to wage war, from the ravaged plains and desiccated cities of China to the killing fields of the Western Front in France.

Not long after completing his report on the military graves on San Juan Island, Summerall was ordered south to Fort Stevens, one of three coastal defense installations on a narrow, triangular area that pointed northward from the southern bank into the wide mouth of the Columbia River, in what is today the state of Oregon. He was assigned as counsel at a general court martial of a young lieutenant who had been arrested for allowing a prisoner to escape from one of the magazines where he had been locked up for setting fire to a number of buildings on the post. He had escaped by unscrewing nuts from the bolts that held two iron gates in place across the entrance to the magazine. On one of his nightly inspections as officer of the day, the lieutenant saw that both the iron gates were unhinged and the prisoner had fled. The young officer was seized and subsequently charged with neglect of duty.[6]

Meanwhile, the post commander and a railroad official caught a train to Portland to enlist police detectives to search for the escapee. En route, a hot box flared up under their car, and when the train stopped to allow the brakeman to fix it, he found the escaped prisoner stretched out along one of the brake beams that connected the brake blocks to opposite wheels of the coach. He was returned to the magazine-jail, and the iron gates were secured by hammering the ends of the bolts over the nuts so that they could not be removed, a method known as "upsetting."

With the culprit securely bolted in, the court martial convened, and Summerall entered a plea of not guilty for his client. He claimed that the conditions that allowed the prisoner to escape; namely, the badly secured nuts, were the responsibility of the command, and not that of the lieutenant, "who had performed full duty in visiting the magazines," including the one from which the prisoner had escaped. "Of course, he was acquitted," wrote Summerall. Looking back, perhaps, on this proceeding, as well as the court martial of General Billy Mitchell, who, as shall be seen, succeeded in getting Summerall removed from his court martial, Summerall noted that he "had a great deal of court-martial duty both as judge-advocate and counsel for the defense, and I have tried to do my full duty in each case." As if to assert his impartiality, which Mitchell later would question, as well as to proclaim his respect for military law, Summerall concluded that "Military justice is one of the most serious responsibilities of an officer."[7]

Early in the summer of 1903, just a few months past his 36th birthday, Summerall received a telegram from the War Department asking if he would accept an assignment at West Point. Citing the still delicate health of his wife and son, and lacking the money to pay for their cross-country journey, Summerall declined the detail, noting in his memoir that he was more interested in his work at Fort Flagler, and "much attached to the men who had been so loyal to me under difficult conditions."[8] The department honored his request, but in early August, ordered him to Camp George H. Thomas, Chickamauga Military Park, in northwest Georgia, to assume command of the 3rd Battery, Field Artillery, and lead it on a long training march northward to Fort Myer, Virginia, just across the Potomac River from Washington, DC.

Summerall departed his post at Fort Flagler and the soldiers of the 106th with mixed emotions. He felt that he had forged a strong bond of mutual respect with his company during their service together in Alaska and along the northern Pacific coast, and he noted that "it was a sad leave-taking," when they turned out to the last man at the dock to say goodbye. But he was pleased, and much relieved, that his wife and son, still far from healthy, would be in the comforting and secure care of her parents and sister in Sandy Spring, Maryland, some 21 miles north of Washington DC, with whom they would stay while he was at Chickamauga, and while he was leading the battery's march from Georgia. With some of the $500 that he had saved from the bequest of his friend and benefactor Winfield Jones, Summerall bought tickets on the Great Northern Railroad for the long ride eastward, and arranged for the shipment of their furniture and other belongings by freighter from the west coast around Cape Horn to Philadelphia.

It was a rough and fatiguing trip for the family; the baby was frightened by the noises from passing trains and clanging signals, and slept fitfully; his food had to be heated over an alcohol lamp; and they all got car sick as the railcar lurched side to side, and smoke from the locomotive drifted through windows that were opened to relieve the passengers from the August heat. In Chicago, they changed to a train of the Baltimore and Ohio Railroad, and after the weeklong and exhausting ride, they arrived in Washington. Laura's father met them at the station, where they caught a trolley car out to the Mordecai home in Sandy Spring. The next day, Summerall left for Chickamauga.[9]

Along with other Civil War battlefield sites, Chickamauga Military Park had been created by an act of Congress in 1896 to serve as a training ground for the army and to help educate military students, like West Point cadets, about decisive battles in American history. As war with Spain approached, the site was named after George H. Thomas, the Union major general, whose stand against fierce Confederate attacks at Chickamauga nearly 35 years earlier had led to his being called the "Rock of Chickamauga." Like Camp Alger in northern Virginia, Camp Thomas served as a concentration point and training ground for soldiers preparing for war with Spain. Poor sanitation, polluted water, and overcrowded living spaces led to epidemics of typhoid fever and other virulent diseases as also happened at Alger. A total of 425 soldiers died at Camp Thomas, more than were killed in the entire course of the brief conflict with Spain. After the war, the camp was cleaned up and rehabilitated, and in 1902, the army established it as a campground for the instruction of Regular Army and National Guard troops. That same year, Congress authorized the purchased of 813 acres outside the camp to accommodate a regiment of cavalry and provide a safe area for artillery and small arms practice.[10] When Summerall arrived in late August, both the 7th Cavalry Regiment and the 3rd Battery were already encamped.

He found the battery in superb condition, well trained and disciplined by its previous commander, Captain Eli D. Hoyle, with three very capable lieutenants and outstanding non-commissioned officers. Morale was high, and the battery seemed to be on the best of terms with the cavalry. When Summerall took them out for their first target practice under their new commander, they turned out to be rather poor shots, but he was pleased at their determination to improve and felt that the exercise had enabled him "to become identified with the men and to accustom them to my methods in the field."[11]

With a "loyal and cooperative" battery assured, Summerall sat down with his lieutenants and began planning for the long march to Fort Myer. They laid out a line of march that would take them across the Tennessee River and northward along the eastern slope of the Appalachian Mountains into the Shenandoah Valley of Virginia, then to camping grounds at the Natural Bridge. From there they would continue northward toward campsites at Virginia Military Institute, and on the grounds of the Battle of New Market, where VMI cadets had fought a gallant action against the Union army in May 1864. From New Market, their route would take them to campsites at Staunton Military Academy and Harpers Ferry, West Virginia, before turning south across the Shenandoah River toward their final destination at Fort Myer, almost 700 miles away. Summerall ordered the quartermaster to ride ahead to mark the route along back roads and byways, secure the campsites, buy forage for the horses, and make the necessary arrangements to provide for each of the battery's overnight encampments.[12]

On 8 September, the officers and men of the 3rd Battery formed a long and imposing column and marched out of Camp Thomas. Summerall noted with pride that the 7th Cavalry lined both sides of the dirt road and saluted their departing comrades with rousing cheers, as the camp band struck up favorite songs like *Garry Owen*, which lightened the battery's steps and lifted their morale.[13] He also could look back on the start of this long march with much pleasure and satisfaction for several more significant reasons. First, and most importantly, he knew that when he reached their destination at Fort Myer, he would be reunited with his wife and son, and, at last, would be able to provide for them the kind of comfort, safety, and care that army life in the lands of the western frontier had made impossible. Secondly, he could judge the beginning of this march as the start of a new phase in his military career during which he would take full advantage of new opportunities to secure his place as one of the army's rising young officers, and continue to prevail over anyone who might doubt or question his abilities and actions.

As the battery marched northward, they soon settled into an efficient and productive routine. The quartermaster would meet Summerall late in the morning and lead the battery to their campsite. They would usually make camp by noon; Summerall himself would lay out the camps, "announcing" where the officers and men would pitch their tents, where the kitchens would be set up, where the latrines would be dug, and where they could find water. Picket lines would be stretched, horses unhitched and unharnessed, rubbed down, and given hay. After lunch had been served, the men would be divided into various details to water and groom the horses, and clean the carriages and harnesses. They would then be free to rest or visit the nearest town, but had to return to duty by 1600 hours to tend to the horses, and prepare for supper. Frequently, visitors from nearby towns and settlements would stop by the camps. On one occasion "a large number of girls from a boarding school [Hollins, perhaps?] swarmed into the camp and quite excited the men, but the young ladies were treated with the greatest courtesy." Tattoo would be sounded at 2100 hours, and taps at 2130, when an inspection would be conducted to make sure that all were in bed. Reveille would wake the men at 0400 hours, followed by breakfast, harnessing and hitching the horses, breaking camp, policing it "perfectly," and starting the march before 0530 hours.[14]

Summerall was especially impressed by the welcome they received as the battery arched through the Shenandoah Valley of Virginia. "We were the first Union troops in the Valley since the Civil War," he wrote, and he felt that "the people wanted to show us that as they had been valiant foes, so they could be hospitable friends." Delegations of leading citizens and local officials came out to the battery's campsites to welcome them on their arrival, and "offered any service to make our stay pleasant." On one occasion, Summerall was met by a former colonel in the Confederate army, who invited him to dinner at the colonel's home. They rode together for several miles through the countryside and entered the grounds though a large iron gate, riding slowly under a canopy formed by the branches of live oak trees that lined each side of a broad avenue leading up to "a beautiful old home," where "a negro [sic] took the horses and we were received by the most exquisite lady, the colonel's wife." After a "delicious supper" had been served, the colonel, "as eagerly as a boy," regaled Summerall with stories of his experiences in the war, and of his proud service on the staff of the famous Confederate cavalry commander Jeb Stuart. He accompanied Summerall back to camp, and, as they rode along, he asked his guest where he was from. When Summerall replied that he was from Florida, the colonel "said in his most disgusting and familiar way: 'O hell, I thought you were a damned Yankee, or I would not have been half as nice to you.'" Summerall explained that every man and officer in the battery came from the South, but the stubborn old colonel insisted that they "wore the Yankee uniform and looked and acted like Yankees." More amused than angry, Summerall brushed off the remark and said that they "parted [as] good friends, and no more 'sirs' were used."[15]

Summerall selected the next campsite at the Natural Bridge himself, "so that the men could see this marvel of nature." He was surprised that there was an admission charge, and disappointed that his men could not afford to pay it, as the officers could. As they walked along the gorge, however, he noticed that the men were close behind, and when they returned, the gatekeeper gave the officers back their money, saying that he "couldn't keep the men out, and therefore would not charge the officers."[16]

For Summerall, the most interesting experience of the long march was their reception at the Virginia Military Institute, and in Lexington, where they arrived at an attractive campsite some 20 miles north of their previous camp at Natural Bridge. General Scott Shipp, the superintendent of VMI who had commanded the Corps of Cadets at New Market, had dispatched several officers to meet the battery and escort them to their campsite, where they were welcomed by a prominent local judge and other leading citizens of the town. A busy round of social engagements followed. General Shipp gave a dinner for the officers at his quarters on campus, and the men were invited to supper in the mess hall with the cadets. Visitors, including "many ladies," thronged the camp, and the judge invited the officers to his home to sample his "famous mint juleps," which Summerall, of course, politely declined, much to the judge's surprise. The next day, the officers were conducted on a tour of VMI, pausing to pay their respects at the statue of General Thomas J. "Stonewall" Jackson, before walking next door to Washington and Lee University, where they stopped to honor the memory of General Robert E. Lee at his recumbent statue. Summerall was much impressed by the appearance of the cadets at VMI, and, at the same time, believed that his "hardy soldiers could not fail to arouse admiration and respect of all who saw them." As they broke camp and left at 0530 hours the following morning, one of the VMI professors brought Summerall a bag of Albemarle Pippins, the rare and prized apples of Virginia that were not available for local sale, since all were exported. Not having enjoyed the benefit of the professor's generosity, one of the battery's soldiers jumped over a fence around one of the valuable apple orchards and stole a bag full, but was found out when he returned to camp. Summerall, noting that such conduct would have given the battery a bad name, ordered the culprit to walk the rest of the way to Fort Myer: no riding on caissons and limbers for him, or hitching a short ride on one of the battery's horses, as others were allowed to do occasionally for rest and recuperation.[17]

They soon were immersed in more Civil War history, camping at New Market and touring the battlefield, and hearing much about Stonewall Jackson's famous Shenandoah Valley campaign when they stopped and camped near the town of Winchester. At Staunton, city officials and members of the faculty at Staunton Military Academy received Summerall and his officers "with much ceremony," and when the battery reached Harpers Ferry, West Virginia, a few days later, city officials conducted them to "a beautiful campsite on a precipitous bluff on the Potomac River." When Summerall noticed the traces of tent ditches on the site, he feared that recent encampments by other army units might have left it in an unsanitary condition. But the mayor assured him that no soldiers had camped there since the Civil War. These ditches, as well as the ditches, trenches, and earthworks they found at Civil War campsites in northern Virginia, were well marked, and, even after some 40 years, looked to Summerall as if they had been made only recently.[18]

On 20 October 1903, as the battery approached the gates of Fort Myer, they were welcomed by a battery that Major Hoyle had sent out to meet them, and escorted up the hill, where the handsome buildings, quarters, and carefully groomed grounds and stately trees of the fort overlooked Arlington National Cemetery, the Potomac, and the capital city that stretched beyond the river to the east. When they marched toward the crest, Summerall caught sight of "my precious wife and baby," as they stood waiting for him. Looking back on that moment, he wrote that "I could not describe my joy at seeing them." After settling his men into a set of new barracks, and the horses into new stables, which "seemed luxurious to the men who had lived in camp for years at Chickamauga and Cuba," Summerall joined his family at the house of one of the captains where they had been staying and waiting for his arrival. The next day they moved into their set of quarters, along with the furniture and household goods that had recently arrived in good condition after the long trip from the west coast around Cape Horn. They soon found "good servants" for their new home and a nurse for the baby, and, with Laura's relatives and friends close by, the trials and tribulations of their lives in Alaska and on the west coast were replaced by what the Summeralls viewed, understandably, as a life of luxury. Most important for Summerall was the health of Laura and Charles, Jr., which improved rapidly, and left them, as he wrote, "very happy in our home."[19]

Summerall's happy home life carried over into his work. He took great interest in the keen rivalry between the two artillery batteries at Fort Myer that Major Hoyle had formed into a battalion. He trained the men and horses each day in drill regulations and gunnery exercises and worked them hard in the riding hall to execute the indoor drills that were performed for the public each Friday. He made sure that the guns, caissons, harnesses, and horses were maintained in "show condition." For the many funerals that took place in Arlington National Cemetery, he made sure that one caisson was varnished and draped, and six "handsome horses with shining harnesses" were kept ready at all times. Both batteries were called on to fire salutes for visiting generals and admirals and to serve as escorts for the funerals that were held in Washington for high-ranking military officers and governmental officials. In January 1905, they marched in President Theodore Roosevelt's inauguration parade. Summerall wrote that his battery "aroused much admiration," as they marched down Pennsylvania Avenue, and he felt their appearance led to their being selected that spring to represent the Field Artillery at a horse show in Madison Square Garden.[20]

For the rest of the spring of 1905, Summerall stayed busy. He was ordered to the Rock Island Arsenal, located on the eponymous island in the Mississippi River, between Davenport, Iowa, and Moline, Illinois, to learn the characteristics of the army's new 3-inch cannon, which used smokeless powder, fired high-explosive and shrapnel shells, was outfitted with optical sights and equipped with a recoilless carriage. It was an excellent gun, and the recoilless carriage enabled the gunners to fire without having to reposition the piece before firing the next round. Shortly after he returned in early May, both batteries went on maneuvers to Mount Gretna, Pennsylvania, a little over 33 miles east of Harrisburg, and a march of almost 150 miles from Fort Myer. During their week in camp, he felt that his officers and men had gained proficiency in gunnery, marching (they certainly had had enough practice in that foot-weary aspect of soldiering), as well as in the complex and detailed process of determining firing data.

On the return march they camped for a week at York, Pennsylvania, not far from the bright lights and attractions of the York County Fair, where most of the battery's men headed on their first night in camp. Not long after they arrived at the fairgrounds, several of them got arrested and then thrown into jail. Summerall sent an officer to their trial the next morning, and he returned to report that the men had been arrested because the town government, in the hands of Republican Party members, was angry that their Democratic Congressman had ordered the battery into their Republican district, apparently without their approval. The men had been arrested, said the officer, not because they had violated some local ordinance, but merely because the town government had chosen this way to show their resentment against the congressman. When the town authorities showed up at Summerall's tent later that morning, he refused to talk to them, demanded the release of his men, and ordered the dignitaries out. He then commanded the bugler to sound "boots and saddles," the order for the men to get themselves and the horses ready to leave, and within an hour, the battery, with all of its men in line, had marched away.[21] This was the first time, but as shall be seen during the first year of his presidency at The Citadel, it would not be the last time that he would take an unshakable stand against political interference in a realm where he considered his authority preeminent.

The batteries returned to Fort Myer in time for Summerall to celebrate with Laura the third birthday of Charles, Jr., on 16 June 1905. Young Charles had developed a "love of horses" and delighted in leading them around the battery stables. The highlight of the birthday party came when Summerall hoisted his son onto the back of his horse and let him ride it around the paddock all by himself. This was the moment, according to his proud father, that Charles, Jr., began his "fine horsemanship." The Summeralls' "very happy period" of their lives at Fort Myer continued and included their attendance at receptions at the White House, for which Summerall had to buy a new full dress uniform, along with formal civilian attire that included a Prince Albert coat and a silk top hat that his son called a "coachman's hat." These expenditures, coupled with the support that Summerall continued to provide for his sister Meta's family, compelled him and Laura to forego any entertainment in their home, but there is no indication that their tight budget, to which they had long been accustomed, in any way diminished the happiness of their home life, or soured Summerall's pleasure as an army artillery officer.[22]

Suddenly and without warning, as the summer of 1905 drew to a close, Summerall received orders, not a request this time, to report to the military academy at West Point, for duty as senior instructor of artillery tactics and commander of the artillery detachment. He was excited about returning to his alma mater and found an "excellent house" at the south end of the post, not too far from the main gate, for his family, who had stayed behind with a neighbor. They arrived a week later, and, as he lifted Charles off the train, he saw that his son looked "very pitiful," with his arm in a sling, and learned from Laura that he had hurt it badly when he tumbled out of bed at the neighbor's house. As usual, since he, and not the army, had to pay for the move of his furniture and household essentials, he was forced to use the rest of Winfield Jones's bequest of $500 to pay for it all.[23] Nevertheless, he and his family were together and had already discovered that his work at West Point presented far more difficult and demanding challenges than their financial struggles.

At the military academy, Summerall was in charge of the instruction of the cadets in field and coast artillery. He was also the commander of the artillery detachment that was stationed there, for West Point was, as it is today, a military base and military reservation. The resources provided by the academy, both in terms of instructors and equipment, however, were far from satisfactory. He had no assistant and had to depend on officers in the various academic departments for classroom instruction in gunnery terms and theories, as well as for assistance in practical instruction with guns, horses, and instruments in the field. The only equipment at hand consisted of materiel and horses for a small mobile battery, mules and lightweight, portable guns for a mountain battery, one battery of field guns for standing gun drill, and several obsolete coast artillery guns at Trophy Point. Not only was all of this inadequate for effective training, but also all of it—guns, horses, mules, and harnesses—was in poor condition. The artillery detachment battery at the post numbered about 45 men, who had to care for the guns and horses, and had to maintain, to Summerall's disdain, the polo field. They were quartered in run-down barracks at the north end of the post, and the horses were stabled in a temporary building close to the polo field. Their food was skimpy, their daily ration only 25 cents, and Summerall said that they were "regarded and treated as laborers and desertions were frequent. The conditions were the reverse of the beautiful battery I had left at Fort Myer."[24]

One of his first actions was to order a Saturday morning inspection that found the men "badly clothed, unshaven and dirty." A week later he found them looking no better, so he "gave some extra fatigue to a few." It must have been a tough penalty, for five men deserted. He began to see gradual improvement and soon had the battery executing fast, mounted drills on the Plain, with cadets participating as drivers and cannoneers. He was also pleased with the instruction of his non-commissioned officers, who assisted Summerall with practical instruction that put into practice the theories that he and his colleagues taught in the classroom.[25] Only second year cadets, or third classmen, did not take any courses in artillery. Their plate was full with courses in mathematics (including solid geometry and calculus), modern languages (French and Spanish), drawing (topography, cartography, and surveying), drill regulations, and military engineering. First year cadets, or fourth classmen, took courses in mathematics (algebra and trigonometry), modern languages (English and French), and were instructed in artillery drill regulations and target practice, as well as in the use of the sword. In addition to steadily advancing courses in the sciences, philosophy, law, and military engineering, the upper two classes received intensive theoretical and practical instruction in all the elements of artillery. Third year, or second classmen, learned drill regulations for infantry, light artillery, and cavalry, and the use of seacoast artillery. Fourth year, or first classmen, were taught the use of ballistic tables and instruments, the determination of velocities and pressure, as well as how to use logarithmic tables.[26]

Nowhere in the curriculum, however, was there a course or any provision dealing with the major reforms that Secretary of War Elihu Root had developed and that Congress had enacted in 1903.

Neither was there any provision or forum for the discussion of these measures and the impact they would have on the future course and development of the army. It is also rather surprising that Summerall never discussed the "Root reforms" in his memoir, particularly since Root made serious efforts to curtail the influence and strength of the bureau chiefs with whom Summerall would struggle when he was army chief of staff. Perhaps, he remained too immersed in the memories of the dual responsibilities of teaching the theoretical and practical matters of soldiering to cadets, and of his work in reforming the post's artillery battery.

At any rate, in response to the criticism directed at the War Department for mismanagement of mobilization and supply of the army in the war with Spain, President McKinley had dismissed Secretary of War Alger in 1899, and appointed in his place the Wall Street lawyer Elihu Root. The new secretary studied the shortcomings of the war with Spain and took into account the recommendations of progressive-minded army officers. He also read carefully Emory Upton's writings and was particularly impressed by *The Military Policy of the United States*, in which Upton argued (as noted above, in Chapter IV, In the Army Now) for the creation of a general staff that would direct the planning and strategy for a larger professional army that could be expanded in time of war to a force of at least 100,000 men.[27] Root concluded that the mistakes of the last war resulted from faulty organization and planning.[28]

To provide for central army planning, investigation, and coordination of military activities, Root proposed, and Congress adopted in 1903, a General Staff, headed by a chief of staff, who replaced the commanding general of the army. The chief of staff also supervised the staff corps of 45 officers and served as the principal advisor to the secretary of war. The legislation also required that the chief of staff serve a term of no more than four years and provided that some of the staff corps would rotate between Washington and the army's geographic departments. The chiefs of the existing bureaus, along with their Congressional allies, worked to limit the effectiveness and authority of the general staff, but, at the very least, the army had, for the first time, in peacetime a means of planning for future conflicts.[29]

To provide the army with better educated and specialized officers, Secretary Root expanded the army's postgraduate schools, reorganized several of them, and established an entirely new one, the Army War College, to educate field-grade officers in the problems of high command. Working with Congressman Charles Dick, chairman of the House Militia Affairs Committee, and a National Guardsman who had served in Cuba in the war with Spain, Root introduced and Congress passed in 1903, the Militia Act, also known as the Dick Act, which brought the National Guard's training program, organization, and materiel up to federal standards. It also reorganized the militia into two groups: the Organized Militia (National Guard), under federal and state control, and the Reserve Militia, defined as all able-bodied men between the ages of 18 and 45, which were required to meet both federal and state obligations in emergencies. The Dick Act also provided for a one-time grant of two million dollars to modernize National Guard equipment, and for the federal government to pay for summer training camps, while the states had to meet federal standards in organizing equipping, and training their units. In 1908, the act was amended. The nine-month service limit was eliminated, and the president now had the right to decide the length of federal service and the authority to appoint all National Guard officers while they were in federal service. The amendment of 1908 also established the Division of Militia Affairs, or, as some called it, the National Guard Bureau.[30] In view of how much time and effort Summerall devoted to the training of National Guard units, and to his later assignment as assistant to the chief of the Militia Bureau, that will be considered below, it is again surprising, in this case, that he failed to consider major changes in the organization and training of this important source of military manpower, for which he had an important professional responsibility.

As a classroom teacher, and in the practical exercises he conducted with the United States Corps of Cadets, Summerall quickly came to enjoy teaching them, found them "responsive and attentive," and felt that his relations with them were "all that could be desired."[31] On Friday afternoons he would take a battery of first classmen out for a practice march and to work on solving plotting problems. They would make camp, look after the horses and guns, cook supper, build a campfire, and sit around it, while the cadets asked him questions, and they all "talked artillery." He also took first classmen down to Fort H. G. Wright on Fishers Island, off the eastern tip of Long Island, or Fort Hancock on Sandy Hook, off the northern coast of New Jersey, where they used the various guns and fire control equipment of the forts in target practice.[32]

One of the most "responsive and attentive" cadets was George S. Patton, Jr., class of 1909, who wrote his father that he "'went down to see Capt. Summerall to day and asked him about things in general. He said he would advise me as a choice between cavalry and infantry to take cavalry and he gave a lot good reasons. In fact he was very nice about it.'"[33] Patton talked again with Summerall, this time about "the business of being a soldier," and Summerall reiterated his opinion that cavalry was better than infantry because there was more to do, and if you were busy, then you were more likely to be happy. Promotion in peacetime would be slow in any case, but in time of war it would come, he continued, to anybody, "'just as long as he could win,'" and had proven that he was "'good in his profession.'"[34] This was hardly a gratuitous remark to a young and impressionable cadet. Rather, as shall be seen, when Summerall led his division and corps in some of the toughest fighting of the Great War, his desire to win became the most powerful driving force of a man who had long since proven that he was "good in his profession."

Patton's talks with Summerall led to a mutually supportive relationship. They exchanged letters of congratulation and admiration as both rose through the ranks; Patton was pleased to serve in Summerall's 5th Corps in World War I;[35] and, when Patton, in command of an army in north Africa in 1942, attacked what Summerall called a "most impregnable position," he wrote Summerall that "I knew my artillery. I tore them to pieces with my 155s [howitzers] and took the position without loss."[36]

Summerall also was proud to have taught a number of cadets who became generals in World War II, including Harold H. Arnold, Carl Spaatz, Jacob L. Devers, Alexander H. Patch, William Hood Simpson, Robert L. Eichelberger, and Simon Bolivar Buckner. Although John M. Palmer, his roommate at the military academy, said that Summerall was called "Honest John" as a cadet, Summerall wrote in his memoir that he gained that nickname while teaching at West Point, and "always regarded it as a compliment."[37]

Patton and his classmates were not the only ones who regarded Summerall as an officer who could counsel and inspire young men who aspired to become military officers. Just over two months after he arrived at West Point, Summerall received a letter from General Shipp, the superintendent of VMI, stating that the current commandant of cadets would leave his position there at the end of June 1906, and asking whether there would be "any hope of getting you as his successor." He emphasized his request by adding that "I should very much like to have you here."[38] Strangely enough, Summerall did not mention General Shipp's request in his memoir, but retained in his papers two letters from Shipp, as well as related documents from the War Department and the headquarters of the military academy. Apparently, he informed General A. L. Mills, superintendent of West Point, about the request from VMI. Mills, in turn, referred Shipp's request to the War Department, where the military secretary asked for Mills's recommendation. In his brief, the superintendent responded that "Captain Summerall is an exceptionally capable officer and is performing very valuable service at the Military Academy. I have conferred with him regarding his wishes in the matter and he prefers that it should be decided by the government. I will be sorry to have the Military Academy deprived of Captain Summerall's services, but am not inclined to offer objections thereto if the War Department finds it advisable to approve this application."³⁹ One month later Superintendent Mills continued his praise of Summerall and wrote that "I would esteem myself especially fortunate to have this able and excellent officer under my command at any time." He also stated that he considered Summerall "especially well fitted to command troops," and concluded his report by writing that Summerall "has performed all his duties throughout the year in the most satisfactory manner. He is an exceptionally excellent and capable officer of pleasing presence and courteous deportment."⁴⁰

Meanwhile, as the wheels of decision-making, at least in this case, turned ever so slowly at the War Department, General Shipp had become increasingly concerned. In May 1906, he wrote Summerall that "We are very anxious to have you as Commandant of Cadets. Unless your mind is definitely fixed, I should like to have an opportunity to talk over [the] subject with you. There is no time to lose. If you think an interview will be of any use, could you meet me at the Park Avenue Hotel [in New York City] any morning you might name."⁴¹ Apparently, Summerall did not answer him, but on 15 June 1906, Henry P. McCain, the military secretary in the War Department, wrote Shipp that the secretary of war had considered the detail of Summerall as military instructor at VMI, and had instructed McCain to advise General Shipp that "The detail of Captain Summerall cannot be approved, in view of the fact that his services are needed at West Point where he is the senior instructor in artillery tactics and his duties are very important. The Department appreciates the necessity for a suitable officer at the Virginia Military Institute, but as Captain Summerall is on important duty at West Point, *for which he was specially selected*, [italics mine] the interests of the services demand that he remain there."⁴² The secretary's letter ended the matter, and Summerall, of course, stayed at West Point. There, living in comfortable quarters, with his wife and son enjoying at last a measure of good health, and having had success as teacher, winning the admiration of cadets like George Patton, as well as having gained the support and esteem of the superintendents of West Point and the War Department, it is startling to read in his memoir, that the time he spent at West Point "was the most difficult and disagreeable part of my service."⁴³

The reason for this negative assessment of his tenure at the military academy might well be found, like his encounter with the cavalry officer in the Philippines, in his reaction to the outright "hostility," as he saw it, that other officers directed toward him and the artillery. At West Point, it was the commandant of cadets, Lieutenant Colonel Robert Howze, who was a cavalryman, and one of his assistants, who was an infantryman, who were "hostile to me and said derogatory things about the artillery to others." With his ire intensifying, he continued that "During a field exercise," this same commandant gave him "an impossible assignment and then criticized me severely at the critique. He no doubt deliberately intended to humiliate me and make me ask to be relieved. I went so far as to prepare my request for relief and then resolved that I would fight it out with him." Summerall did not record what happened next, but went on to implicate Howze's wife in the web of hostility for her intent "to omit us [the Summeralls] from the invitation list" for a reception that the Howzes gave for Summerall's department. Howze and his wife did invite them, but only after "The wife of an officer in the department made her invite us."⁴⁴ Needless to say, had one been at this reception, it would have been possible to cut the tension with a knife.

But, Summerall was not finished with Howze. He wrote that in World War I, Howze "asked me to help him get a division, which I did, and after the war he asked me to help him to be promoted to major general, which I did. I also promoted in after years, his assistant who had been hostile to me. I am sure that they changed their opinion of me but they would have injured me at that time."⁴⁵ These were the words of a man, who, as has been seen before, retained late in his life vivid memories of the actions of those whom he believed had wronged him, or had intentions of doing so. Perhaps, Howze and his assistant were envious and jealous of Summerall's record and reputation. Perhaps, Mrs. Howze felt the same way, or just didn't like the Summeralls. But Summerall never seems to have made allowances for these human frailties that were exaggerated in an institution like the army (or in academia), where the scarcity of rewards and promotions intensified competition and fierce rivalries. He seems also to have been compelled to indict them with charges of "hostility," while never considering the possibility that he might have acted in a presumptuous or self-righteous manner that might provoke a retaliatory, or "hostile" response. It is regrettable that, in his last years, Summerall still held on to these "grudges," and used his memoir as a means of settling these old "scores" in his own mind, while asserting with each "settlement" that he was right, and they were wrong. And it is unfortunate that he allowed the incidents with Howze to darken in any way the memory of a very special and successful period in his life, when he enjoyed such rewarding and constructive relations with cadets, his battery, and when his wife and son were safely at his side.

For Charles, Jr., his years at West Point were healthy and happy ones, and for Laura also, in spite of the snub from the Howzes. Under the care of the excellent doctors at the military academy, and of a specialist at Newburgh, Charles' health greatly improved, and he and his mother always enjoyed the parades. With his father's help, he learned to ride a bicycle, and went out riding with him as much as possible. He enjoyed playing with the sisters of his parents' friends, the Henry McKays, who often came up from their home on Long Island to visit. When he and his parents visited the McKays, they all had fun on their trips to Coney Island. Laura took great pleasure in attending the officers' hops in Cullum Hall with her husband, and enjoyed short, afternoon rides in the light surrey that Summerall bought for them. On one of these outings, the horse suddenly bolted, ripping the reins from Summerall's hands, and plunged toward a wagon directly in front of their surrey. Quickly, Laura grabbed the reins, pulled them back, and guided the horse away from the wagon. Summerall generously acknowledged that her prompt response was an action that he himself should have taken at once.[46]

Another satisfying aspect for Summerall of his duty at West Point was his involvement in major construction projects that greatly improved the facilities, services, and the appearance of the campus. New and enlarged barracks and stables for the use of the field artillery were completed, and his men kept them "beautifully." He equipped the coast artillery section with the latest in plotting equipment, telescopes, and searchlights for night exercises. He secured a battery of 6-inch guns on disappearing carriages, a battery of 12-inch mortars, and increased the number of men and horses up to the level of an army light artillery battery. He felt his men had become "the equals of the best service batteries." They grew their own vegetables behind the stables in a garden (that undoubtedly was well fertilized); got their milk from a cow that Summerall bought for them, and eggs from chickens that ran around in the woods behind the stables; and had apples and cabbage delivered from local markets. "Bowling alleys, a pool room, a player piano, and a gramophone were provided for recreation." Not surprisingly, "desertions, drunkenness and absent without leave rarely occurred."[47]

As Henry P. McCain, the military secretary in the War Department had written, Summerall had been "specially selected" for duty at West Point. Most likely, he had been chosen for this duty not only to supervise the education and training of cadets to be disciplined officers and knowledgeable artillerists, but also to forge the miserable artillery battery on the post into a unit that could serve as a model of appearance and performance for the cadets, as well as for the tax-paying public. In both respects, his work at the military academy more than justified the expectations, not only of the War Department, but also of his superiors at the military academy, with the exception of the condescending commandant, Robert Howze.

As an indication of his success, and evidence of how important the War Department regarded his work at West Point, his tour of duty was extended beyond the normal term of three years to a second three-year tour. Superintendents like General Mills, who urged the War Department to keep Summerall

*Coastal Defense, the Militia Bureau, and West Point*  151

at West Point rather than post him to VMI, and Colonel Hugh L. Scott, who wrote in Summerall's efficiency report that "His battery is the best I have ever seen," clearly valued highly his work at the military academy.[48] And, as he prepared to leave West Point for his next assignment, General Thomas H. Barry, the superintendent who had also served in the Philippines and China, wrote Summerall that "it is a pleasure to record in this way the very satisfactory manner in which you have performed every service required of you." He noted how successful Summerall had been in instructing cadets and added that "Under my supervision you have served but a short time, but for a part of that time acted as Commandant of Cadets in addition to your other duties, and displayed those qualities of effective and efficient command and administration which prompt the opinion that you need only the opportunity to demonstrate your thorough efficiency for much higher command than has as yet come to you."[49] General Barry sent a copy of this letter to General George B. Davis, the adjutant general, and Davis wrote back, saying that "I know something of his [Summerall's] excellent character, high soldiership and great and unusual efficiency. The compliment was fully deserved and was most gracefully paid."[50]

As he left West Point, Summerall was pleased that he had established a genuine rapport with the cadets, and had earned their respect and trust. He was particularly proud of the work he had accomplished with the post's artillery battery, and wrote that, when he left, "It was in the highest state of efficiency and morale. The non-commissioned officers were the equals of officers in the practical instruction of cadets. The artillery, both field and coast, commanded the respect of the cadets and it was a popular choice [for their army branch after graduation]."[51] He was relieved that Laura and Charles, Jr., had remained healthy, and gratified that he had been able to enjoy special times with his wife and son within the comfortable and safe confines of the campus. He was fully satisfied that he had more than justified the confidence of his superiors, and believed that he had secured his standing as an officer who was ready and qualified for higher command.

He was surrounded by a loving and devoted family, by admiring and appreciative young men in the corps of cadets, by a proud and exemplary battery of soldiers, and basking in the glow of praise from his superiors, including the secretary of war. Indeed, a month before his next assignment, he received from the War Department the news of his promotion to major,[52] certainly a cause for satisfied reflection across the years of his career, including his most recent duty at West Point. He was in the prime of his health, and the summary of his physical condition, noted in the efficiency report cited above, confirmed a picture of an imposing young officer who was "erect, muscular, with a good and strong pulse rate condition."[53] He had shown that that he was more than equal to the rigors of the long march from Camp Thomas, and had impressed men of military stature through the length of the Shenandoah Valley with his expertise and authority as a military commander.[54]

As he wrote about his personal happiness, and described the strengths and accolades that enhanced an already impressive career, it is disappointing that Summerall, in his twilight years, would allow his sensitivity to criticism, however misplaced, to cast a shadow over his final years at West Point, where, as a young plebe, he had been "captivated" by the military life, and had "wanted with all my heart to become a part of it." Summerall had truly become an important part of the "military life," and his next duty further indicated that his superiors clearly understood and highly valued his importance as an expert artillerist, as well as an exceptional military leader.

# Chapter Eight

*Training an American Artillery Force and the Coming of the Great War*

As the Summeralls left his alma mater in April 1911, they found themselves in rather familiar circumstances. He had been assigned to command the 2nd Battalion, 3rd Field Artillery Regiment that was based at Fort Myer, but was currently on maneuvers in San Antonio, Texas. Naturally, his wife and son could not accompany him, so Summerall had to find a place for them to live. Charles, Jr. was ill again, this time slowly recovering from the measles. Fortunately, their friends, the Henry McKays, invited them to stay at their home in Brooklyn, and Summerall took a few days' leave to be with them. He and Laura soon located a boarding house that was close to Laura's sister and her family in Markham, Virginia, about 55 miles west of Fort Myer. He arranged for his wife and son to stay there until he returned from Texas and located permanent quarters at Fort Myer.[1]

Summerall headed for Texas to join his new battalion that was a part of what might well be called the first U.S. Army division of the 20th century. It originated, mainly, in the policies of two recent appointees at the top of the military hierarchy. The first was the new secretary of war, Henry L. Stimson, who was a former law partner of Elihu Root (whom President Roosevelt had appointed secretary of state, and was serving as Republican senator for New York), and a strong supporter of Root's reforms.[2] The second was General Leonard Wood, whom President William Howard Taft had appointed army chief of staff in 1910. Wood had ridden with the "Rough Riders" in Cuba and had remained as military governor, before serving as governor of the Moro province in the Philippines. Wood had entered the army as a contract surgeon, after being educated at Harvard College and Harvard Medical School, and despite his military record, was always regarded as an outsider by most career officers. As chief of staff, the ambitious Wood was determined to establish his authority firmly as head of the general staff, increase its authority over the bureau chiefs, and reorganize the field army.[3]

Working closely together, Stimson and Wood sought to improve training procedures and the speed and efficiency of mobilization. They also were impressed by the designs of the large European armies for permanent divisions and saw the need to abolish the small installations, which many called "hitching posts," and which had dotted the landscape of western America since the days of the constabulary army (such as Summerall's posts in Alaska and Washington) and the Indian wars. They developed a plan to create a larger garrison that would speed up mobilization and give officers the experience they needed to handle large bodies of men. This larger grouping also would permit testing and experimentation with new Signal Corps equipment, such as the telegraph and radios, as well as airplanes.[4]

The beginnings of the Mexican Revolution afforded a convenient pretext for mobilizing this force, as political opponents in Mexico raised armed bands to gain influence and fought among themselves to seize the office of president. The conflict spread to the U.S. border when outlaw bands conducted raids across the border into southwestern American states in areas where central authority was weak. To deal with these incursions, President Taft ordered some 13,000 troops to be assembled in San Antonio, Texas, beginning in March 1911.[5] They formed what became known as the "maneuver division," and it included the 2nd Battalion of the 3rd Artillery Regiment, the unit that Summerall had been assigned to command.

Summerall's battalion was known as the "rotten battalion," and he believed, quite correctly, it appears, that he had been chosen to straighten it out, or "to change it," as he put it. I have not located the order that Summerall received; but, given his performance and standing, it is doubtful that his superiors would have selected any other officer for this job. At any rate, when he joined the battalion, he found that to call it "rotten" was a conservative assessment. A few of the officers were "excellent, but others," he concluded, "were worse than useless. The men were uninstructed, the materiel in deplorable condition and the horses much neglected." The efforts "to establish camp sanitation, care of animals and equipment and a course of instruction" were met with "indifference or resistance by the poor officers." He noted that "After my soldiers, batteries and cadets at West Point, the contrast was distressing. The target practice was a farce because so many officers could not conduct fire."[6]

The general officers who showed up were not any better. He was "shocked" by their "ignorance" of artillery, although it is difficult to believe that they did not understand direct fire, the traditional use of the guns to fire on targets in the line of sight of the crews. But, he was especially "shocked" that these generals knew nothing about indirect fire, the more advanced and technical use of artillery fire on targets that were out of a gun crew's line of sight. Their fire was directed by forward observers using telephone, telephone cables, or wireless communication. To hit these targets, gun crews, or cannoneers, as Summerall liked to call them, fired shells in a high arc out to long distances and/or over terrain that blocked their view of the target. "A brigadier general," wrote an astounded Summerall, "criticized me placing the guns where the cannoneers could not see the target." If these ignorant observations were not distressful enough, Summerall developed a "severe ulceration of a front tooth and my face was badly swollen and painful." Fortunately, the generals soon left, and so did the pain, thanks to "A remarkable dental surgeon at the post hospital who bored through the gum [without some kind of anesthesia!?] drained the root [anesthesia?] and saved the tooth."[7] For someone who could "drive a nail without a hammer," as Bullard had said of Summerall in the Philippines, gum-boring and root-draining, without, apparently, the use of anesthesia, were tolerable procedures.

Soon recovered from the pain and treatment of his ulcerated tooth, and minus the distractions of clueless generals, Summerall went back to work, training his battalion hard, and noting their improvement in marking and locating map positions and targets. Nevertheless, he had not been pleased with their preparedness, and the army had reached a similar conclusion with respect to the level of preparedness of the entire maneuver division. Summerall clearly had more work ahead of him to bring his battalion up to his standards, and the army faced the task of improving its entire organizational structure to support its divisional plan, especially if the country had to fight a strong and determined enemy.[8]

After three months of training in the dust, rain, and mud of Texas, Summerall and his battalion returned to Fort Myer, with the men and horses settling into some of the best buildings on the post, while Summerall took a short leave and headed to Markham to join his wife and son for a few days. He returned to unpack their belongings and move their furniture into "a nice set of quarters" that went along with his rank of major, and bought a pony for Charles, much to the surprise and delight of his son. With his family comfortably settled into their field-grade quarters, Summerall turned to a fresh challenge; namely, to continue his work to improve the "rotten battalion," at a post that was commanded by "the most worthless and contemptible officer I have ever known." In Summerall's opinion, this officer's idea was "to have the troops do as little as possible and let officers run wild." He also issued orders that prohibited any duty after 1200 hours.

Citing orders from the department commander that the troops should be trained as much as necessary to make them efficient, Summerall ignored the post commander's intentions as well as his orders, and forged ahead. He believed that all "impulses," or movements for change, flowed from the top down, and would succeed only if the officers set the proper example. To make sure his officers met his standards, he established a "school" and conducted it himself each morning, after which he led them in battery and battalion drills; in the afternoons he took them out on terrain exercises. In spite of this demanding workload, several of them "spent the nights drinking in Washington, and were unfit for duty in the morning." Those he termed "delinquent" were held accountable for their offenses. Charges were preferred against one lieutenant, and Summerall "relieved" him from the officers' class; a second, caught cheating on a tactics problem, was tried and dismissed from the service. This latter officer was a stubborn case, and after Summerall had talked with him "about his dissipation and neglect," he defiantly asserted that "I would rather die than live the way you want me to live."[9]

In response to Summerall's strict requirements, high expectations, and severe penalties, "The post commander ["the most worthless and contemptible officer I have known"] objected and an inspector investigated complaints that I was overworking the officers."[10] Colonel Charles G. Treat, the commander of the 3rd Field Artillery Regiment, received the report that expressed "dissatisfaction" at the strenuous work that Summerall had demanded. In his remarks, Treat wrote that the unfavorable comment [about Summerall] should be leveled on "those expressing dissatisfaction at strenuous work and trying service than on the Battalion Commander." Leaving no doubt as to where he stood, Treat added that "The thorough supervision of his work and conscientious attention to duty by the Battalion Commander and the requirement of similar action on the part of his subordinates is a valuable asset to the command. *In my opinion, the efficiency of the Field Artillery would be greatly increased had we an increased number of Battalion Commanders* [my italics]."[11] These comments confirm not only Treat's respect for Summerall's record and expertise, but also his confidence in Summerall's judgment, as well as his belief that it was officers like Summerall who were needed to lead the field artillery of the American army. In addition, Summerall got results. With lazy, incompetent, and undisciplined officers thrust aside, Summerall achieved the "improvement in discipline, instruction, gunnery, care of horses and equipment and morale" that had been expected of him, and that he had demanded. His battalion staged practice marches, and remained in overnight camps while conducting night exercises in establishing firing positions and orienting their guns.[12] Indicative of his solid stature and proficiency as an artillery officer was his selection to attend the School of Fire for Field Artillery at Fort Sill, Oklahoma.[13]

Following the three-month course during the winter of 1911–1912, he returned to Fort Myer, where he received orders from the newly established Militia Bureau of the War Department to locate a site and establish a camp east of the Mississippi for training the field artillery of the National Guard. Both the Militia Bureau and the General Staff were concerned that from one-half to three-fourths of the Regular Army and National Guard artillery units were located in the northeastern states and as far south as Virginia, yet the closest artillery training camp east of the Mississippi River was in Sparta, Wisconsin, some 184 miles northwest of Milwaukee. The expense and time consumed in transporting artillery units to Sparta, coupled with the expectation that the money spent instructing training officers at Fort Sill (about $30,000 per year), could be justified only if they spent more time with their organizations, meant that a suitable artillery training camp had to be located on the East Coast.[14]

Summerall's search for a suitable location took him to the Cumberland Plateau of middle Tennessee, where he checked out sites around the town of Tullahoma, about halfway between Nashville and

Chattanooga. From Tullahoma he headed southeast into the Pisgah Mountains of North Carolina, and from there to familiar ground in the Shenandoah Valley of Virginia. After returning to Fort Myer in late March, he informed the Militia Bureau that he had found nothing suitable, and was then directed to proceed to Oakland, Maryland, in the mountains of western Maryland, some 200 miles west/northwest of Baltimore.[15] He arrived on 2 May, "and spent the next three days traveling over the country with a view to find a range for artillery practice of regular and militia batteries."[16] When he returned to Fort Myer, he submitted two reports to the adjutant general's office, describing in progressively greater detail the topography and resources of the area, and recommending in his final report the purchase of a 12,000-acre tract of land at three dollars an acre,[17] which was owned by a lumber company whose superintendent had agreed to the sale.[18] Major William J. Snow, Summerall's fellow battalion commander in the 3rd Field Artillery, and future chief of the field artillery, wrote a memorandum for the record, supporting Summerall's recommendation, as did Colonel E. J.[?] Greble, writing for the Field Artillery Committee of the General Staff, in his memorandum for the chief of staff, and Brigadier General R. K. Evans, Chief of the Division of Militia Affairs of the General Staff.[19] In his memorandum to the adjutant general, dated 14 May 1912, General Wood stated his full support, as well as that of the secretary of war, of Summerall's proposal.[20] But for some reason, in spite of all of these endorsements, the site was not selected, and the land was never purchased. Summerall was instructed to keep looking.

On 10 April 1912, he was ordered to report on a campsite in the vicinity of Tobyhanna, Pennsylvania, in the Pocono Mountains, about 122 miles north/northwest of Philadelphia.[21] The landscape around Tobyhanna consisted of broad, flat, swampy areas intermingled with low hills that stretched across a plateau some 2,300 feet above sea level. The region was sparsely inhabited, with few roads and no settlements, but with plenty of good quality water, either from underground sources, or from two nearby lakes. The lakes supported an ice industry in the winter, as ice was cut and stored in large barns and added to boxcars hauling fresh produce and meat to East Coast cities, or shipped to cities for use in kitchen iceboxes; some of the ice was even shipped to hospitals in Florida.[22] Apparently, none was left over for the soldiers who might be headed that way. Summerall visited the area in August and found it "covered with the most forbidding rock, gullies, extensive bogs, jungle and impenetrable forest of second growth hard wood trees."[23] A local coal company owned most of it, and Summerall obtained their permission to use it as a firing range, and, before returning to Fort Myer in August, leased a tract of land near the rail station from a local physician for $300 as a campsite.[24]

Before bringing his battalion to Tobyhanna, Summerall led them on a march of just over 300 miles, through the countryside of Maryland, Pennsylvania, New York, and into Connecticut, where they participated in the Connecticut Maneuver Campaign in Fairfield County, near the town of Monroe, some 50 miles south of Hartford. They arrived in early August, in "blistering hot weather," along with 20,000 Regular Army soldiers and National Guard units from the states of New York, New Jersey, Connecticut, Vermont, Maine, and Massachusetts. The purpose of the "campaign" has been described as "an exercise to train soldiers under conditions which exist in the actual field battle," and "to promote a positive feeling toward the military." Some said that it was also an attempt to entertain and impress several visiting European generals. To achieve these goals, the soldiers were divided into two teams: the Red Team, whose objective was to "capture" New York City, and the Blue Team, whose mission was to stop them within a period of eight days. Summerall's battalion "fought" for the Red team and engaged Blue team forces at the "Battle of Newton," which was declared a draw, thus ending the campaign, but, at the same time, preventing the Reds from "capturing" the prize of New York City.[25]

As far as promoting "a positive feeling toward the military," the campaign seems to have been a resounding success. Reporters from 11 newspapers, a newsreel team, and approximately 50,000 people from the surrounding towns turned out to watch the action. Many of the local townspeople had brought lemonade, other cold drinks, and fresh baked cookies to the campsites, and, as the soldiers marched toward the climactic showdown, admiring spectators pressed cookies into their hands and handed them cups filled with cold refreshments.[26]

Summerall and his men received high praise for their performance. Lieutenant Colonel Ernest Hinds, commander of the 5th Artillery Regiment, wrote that "I can not speak too highly of the energy, ability and efficiency of the officer of the regular battalion which formed a part of the Provisional Regiment [designation for the Connecticut Maneuver Campaign]. Major Summerall is an exceptionally able officer and his battalion one of the best I have ever seen in the service."[27] Brigadier General Fred A. Smith, commanding the Red Army, wrote Hinds that "the work of Major C. P. Summerall's Provisional Battalion of 3rd U.S. Field Artillery and Batteries 'A' and 'B', New Jersey N.G., was particularly fine."[28] With the townspeople of Fairfield County gathered at the train station in Monroe to cheer them on, and having said their farewells to their valiant opponents on the Blue team, Sumerall's battalion boarded their train for Tobyhanna, arriving at night, and then marching three miles from the train station to their campsite. The next day they began to locate future target sites and firing positions for the batteries, and work out the firing data to determine the conduct of fire. After a few days of planning and plotting, they returned to Fort Myer.[29]

Back in familiar surroundings, Summerall reviewed plans for the construction of the camp at Tobyhanna, and took time to prepare and deliver what was to be the first of a number of lectures on field artillery and military tactics at the War College. He continued to drill his battalion and to enjoy the more comfortable life for him and his family that his salary of $3,000 a year as a major provided.[30] On 4 March 1913, he and his men marched in the inauguration parade for the new president, Woodrow Wilson, and Summerall proudly recorded that "the superb appearance of the battalion swept every thing before it." General Wood seems to have agreed with Summerall's assessment and wrote him that he "was particularly impressed with the excellent appearance of the battalion of field artillery under your command at the recent Inaugural Parade. The appearance of both the personnel and materiel was such as to reflect the highest credit upon you and the officers of your command."[31] He bought a new closed carriage, used two battery horses to pull it, and detailed a battalion sergeant to drive him and Laura to official functions, such as receptions at the White House. They began to entertain in their quarters and served on the post hop committee; when it came their turn to prepare and serve champagne punch, they were amazed that the guests drank it as fast as they could make it.[32] Needless to say, the Summeralls were not accustomed to slaking the thirsts of champagne drinkers or any other group of alcohol aficionados.

Young Charles, now in his 10th year, and a proud tenderfoot Boy Scout, was thrilled when his father bought him a pony. "The child loved him dearly," wrote Summerall, and father and son enjoyed long rides along trails in the woods around Fort Myer in the afternoons after school. Before one of their afternoon rides, Summerall strapped a flat saddle on the pony instead of the standard, cavalry-issue saddle, known as the McClellan, which he had been using. As they were leaving the post, the pony, uneasy under the new saddle, suddenly bolted into the woods, pitching Charles, Jr. from the saddle, and dragging him along the ground with one foot caught in a stirrup. Summerall raced his horse up to them, grabbed the reins of the pony and pulled it to a stop. Charles was bruised and battered, but not seriously injured. The pony was not so fortunate. Summerall, practically exploding in anger and rage, "gave him a severe beating while the child cried and begged me not to punish the pony. I then mounted the pony and we returned to the post. I rode the pony [apparently Summerall had either forgotten the name or had blotted it out of his memory] back to the road and galloped him till he was worn out. He never gave any more trouble." The rest of the spring was considerably less risky for the Summeralls. Charles, Jr. continued his scouting activities, practicing his newly developed skills as a bugler; his father kept in top physical condition, leading his officers on a 90-mile ride in three days, while remaining in the saddle for six hours each day.[33] Laura, meanwhile, stayed busy with various social functions, and hosted a buffet supper in their quarters for a visiting general and his staff that had just completed their own 90-mile ride.[34]

As the springtime of 1913 yielded to the beginnings of summer across the greening grasses and wooded hills of Fort Myer with its stunning views of the capital city, Summerall prepared his battalion to return to the rugged terrain of Tobyhanna to complete the task of creating a major training camp for the National Guard batteries of the eastern United States. He placed special emphasis on qualifying gunners for firing duty and held exhibition drills in the riding hall to keep his horses and vehicles in top condition.[35]

Finally, the battalion left for Tobyhanna on 3 June and marched by way of Baltimore into Pennsylvania, arriving at their camp on 18 June. They immediately set to work, for they only had three days to prepare the camp before the arrival of the first National Guard units on 21 June. They drilled a well, built a water tank and a pumping station, and laid pipes to every part of the camp; they cleared the "jungle" from the campsite, and built roads and temporary buildings for kitchens, latrines, shower baths, and stables. Summerall was pleased with the work of his men. In an article he wrote about the camp that was published in the January–March 1914 issue of the *Field Artillery Journal*, he stated that "The men manifested a creditable zeal, and with a cheerful enthusiasm that spoke well for their morale, they adapted themselves to the situation and were soon ready for the real work of the camp."[36]

The "real work," of course, was the training of militia batteries by the officers and non-commissioned officers of Summerall's battalion, who were paired with the militia batteries and "took full charge of the instruction" of them. The first batteries arrived on June 21 and came from New Jersey and Rhode Island; batteries from Connecticut, Pennsylvania, New Jersey, and the District of Columbia arrived at the end of July. They came in by train on a Saturday, and departed on a Monday, 10 days later. On the first day, they pitched their tents and set up their messes, and on the second day their duties, camp routine, and the course of instruction were explained. From Monday, the third day, through Sunday, the ninth day, they received instruction that included the care of horses, harnesses, and carriages; service and firing methods for the guns; the use of telescopes, telemeters, and field glasses; reconnaissance, selection, and occupation of positions; preparation of firing data, smoke bomb practice, and target practice with service ammunition. Each evening in the large mess hall, Summerall and his officers conducted a critique of each battery's performance that day.[37] In addition, a special school that ran from 1 July to 15 July was arranged for artillery officers, and 53 reported from the eastern part of the country. Their training schedule was almost identical to that of the other militia, except that they received additional instruction in battery administration, subsistence and supply, and terrain exercises with battalion headquarters and special details. At the conclusion of the school, officers received a grade in each area of instruction; a measure that Summerall believed would form a basis for estimating their efficiency and placement in classes at future camps.[38]

When their long days of instruction and duty were over, officers and men took off for neighboring towns; Saturday afternoons were set aside for polo matches and baseball games.[39] The one special luxury that Summerall enjoyed was the pleasure of having "my little family" close by, and they found "comfortable boarding houses at Tobyhanna," along with the wives of the other officers in the battalion. In his memoir, however, Summerall mentions their presence only once in a brief sentence, an indication that there was very little extra time for any of them to spend with their loved ones.[40]

The first session of the summer camp at Tobyhanna drew to a close in September with a field day of sporting events that were attended by a large number of people from the neighboring communities.

Summerall enjoyed the day and was well satisfied with the work of his battalion and the results they had achieved. His officers and men "were anxious to do all that I required," and through their instruction and their own execution in the field, had become "the most efficient battalion in the army."[41] A total of 72 militia officers and 670 enlisted men attended the camp, and he found them "eager to learn and profited by all that was said. The officers and men were superior in intelligence and morale," and "the discipline of the soldiers was excellent," as was their health. Summerall saw the training of Regular Army batteries with those of the militia as having a "great educational advantage over the habitual isolation of batteries in their practical training." He predicted that "Each year should see increased facilities and improved methods of instruction." Indeed, arrangements already were under way for continued use of the camp, and he recommended the construction of new roads, clearing ground for moving targets, and additional instructors and inspectors. After all of the National Guard batteries had left for their home states, Summerall's battalion remained for their own target practice ("which was excellent") before breaking camp on 4 October, and reaching Fort Myer three weeks later on the 24th.[42]

Back in the familiar surroundings of the post above the Potomac, the Summerall family and his battalion spent an essentially uneventful winter and spring in 1913–1914. One encouraging development, however, was Congressional authorization for the War Department to purchase additional land around Tobyhanna for a permanent camp.[43] Also satisfying for Summerall was the copy he received of the report on the inspection of the camp by Major General Thomas H. Barry, formerly superintendent of West Point when Summerall had taught there, and now commanding the army's Eastern Department. Barry reported that he regretted that so few National Guard soldiers had taken advantage of the chance to attend the camp, because "The work done under Major Summerall at this school is the best opportunity ever given the Field Artillery of the National Guard to receive proper instruction." He urged that "Such troops should be compelled to attend, as it is only by attendance at such practical camps of instruction that we can hope to raise the Field Artillery of the National Guard to a proper plane of efficiency and at the same time give the War Department a proper line of National Guard officers of that arm of the service." In a final paragraph that really must have pleased Summerall, Barry stated that he was "very much gratified by the marked improvement in all respects of that [Summerall's] battalion, and I am satisfied that those pertaining to the National Guard who attended the school of instruction there [at Tobyhanna] received lasting benefit, credit for which is due to the professional zeal, ability and energy of Major Summerall, his officers and enlisted men."[44]

In early June 1914, with the solid prospect of additional funding for the future development of the camp, and with General Barry's support and confidence in his work and mission, Summerall led his battalion along the well-traveled route from Fort Myer to Tobyhanna. They arrived in time to prepare the camp for the second summer of instruction and training of National Guard field artillery. Regiments, battalions, and batteries came by train from Massachusetts, Rhode Island, Connecticut, New York, Pennsylvania, Ohio, Virginia, the District of Columbia, Louisiana, and for the first time, units from Georgia. They followed the schedule and assignments that Summerall and his battalion had developed for the first camp, and Summerall noted that "To urge them on I told them that the guns of the next war were being aimed at Tobyhanna. I also told them that if they could maneuver guns at Tobyhanna they could do so anywhere in the world." He added that "None of these troops were ever baffled by the difficulties in France in World War I."[45] During the summer of 1914, however, it is doubtful that anyone at Tobyhanna paid much attention to the crises that were simmering in the Balkans and soon would ignite smoldering coals of anxiety and resentment that would burst into a worldwide war. Summerall himself wrote that "We had no thought of war at first" and went on to suggest that many around him were assured of peace, when the Carnegie Foundation, as he ironically stated, "published a statement that it had abolished war and must find some other use for the [their] money."[46]

Indeed, in the late afternoons and evenings after the long workdays were over, and especially on the weekends, a festive atmosphere prevailed in the camp. Summerall and his officers delighted in again having their families close by in boarding houses, where they could be together in the evenings, or meet during visits to the camp. More visitors from neighboring towns and summer resorts came to "witness the firing," and some stayed to have lunch with the soldiers; among them was Miss Margaret Wilson, President Wilson's daughter. After evening mess, the camp veterinarian led group singings of favorite camp songs and even composed special "Tobyhanna songs that all learned and enjoyed."[47]

The only discordant note came from a group of Quakers from Philadelphia who were vacationing at one of the nearby lakes and protested the presence of soldiers in the area. A local attorney, who also was a Quaker, advised Summerall that if he could not placate the Quakers, he might not be able to use the firing range. Quickly, Summerall requested General Barry to assign the Fifteenth Cavalry Band from Fort Myer to the camp. Barry agreed, and soon the band's Sunday afternoon concerts began attracting hundreds of visitors, including Quakers, one of whom was the mayor of Philadelphia. He and his wife became friends with Summerall and invited him to Sunday dinner at their lakeside vacation home. As they sat together on the front porch one Sunday afternoon after dinner, a group of Quakers returning from church passed by and noticed Summerall with his hosts. "After that," he wrote, "I had no further opposition [from the vacationing Quakers]."[48]

As the time approached for the last battalions and batteries to return home from the second summer of the camp at Tobyhanna, disturbing signals from abroad interrupted their routines of military and social life. Summerall wrote that the Saturday night dance in the mess hall was well under way when the camp's radio operator rushed in, shouting that he had just heard that all British ships had been ordered to the nearest American ports, and that the ambassadors of "the European antagonists" had been recalled home. This is how, as Summerall recorded, they learned "That war was a reality."[49]

As the men of Tobyhanna packed for the march home, the guns of August 1914 continued to fire across the trenches and ripped through the opposing armies of the Triple Entente (Great Britain, France, and Russia) and the Triple Alliance (Germany, Austria-Hungary, and the Ottoman Empire), as each side fought for dominance over the other, and for supremacy in western and eastern Europe. Many of the officers in a New York regiment that was training at Tobyhanna were Wall Street brokers, and they left early to deal with the impact of the war on the stock exchange.[50] Amid this growing uncertainty and the severe onslaught of an early winter in October, with days of sleet, snow, and ice, a bright spot for Summerall was the splendid performance over the past two summers at Tobyhanna of his battalion. Exceeding General Barry's praise of his battalion, he believed now that "It was ready for action anywhere, anytime and under any conditions." No longer would anyone be able to refer to it as the "rotten battalion."[51] He was also pleased that General Wood, now commander of the Eastern Department, had commended his "most excellent work," and, after three visits to the camp, had concluded that "it should become a permanent feature of our relations with the militia, and that every effort should be made to bring to it the largest possible number of batteries." He praised the condition and care of the horses and equipment in Summerall's battalion and noted "that there was not a sore neck or back in the battalion, and that both horses and materiel were in excellent condition."[52]

On 14 October, Summerall's battalion broke camp and began their final march from Tobyhanna to Fort Myer. He and his men could look back on their work with a solid sense of pride in their work not only in preparing National Guard artillerymen to maneuver their guns "anywhere in the world," but also in preparing themselves to do the same. Without doubt or reservation, Summerall had reinforced his standing as a master of artillery weaponry, and his reputation as an efficient and hard-working officer with outstanding organizational ability. He had received high praise from his superiors, not only for the creation and efficient administration of the camp, but, most importantly, for his success in training the artillery battalions and batteries of the National Guard in the eastern U.S. to fight effectively with their comrades in the Regular Army. General Wood believed that because of "the splendid work you have done, which has been of far reaching effect upon the Field Artillery of the National Guard," Summerall's "method of instruction" should be applied throughout the country.[53] Summerall thought it was important to establish positive relations between the soldiers at Tobyhanna and surrounding communities and was pleased that he had succeeded in accomplishing that goal. General Wood felt the same way and was especially complimentary of Summerall's success in this respect. He wrote that "When the camp was established last year, the local sentiment was intensely hostile; at present, so far as I can judge, it is most friendly, and the atmosphere is one of cordial support. This change in conditions is the result of your efforts, good judgment, and tactful handling of the situation."[54] Quite clearly, Summerall's skillful handling of the public was an important consideration in his next assignment, which shortly will be considered.

Not everyone, however, was enamored of Summerall and his achievements. A. D. G. Wiles, in his unpublished manuscript of Summerall's life, recounts the comments of a "prominent Washingtonian," who had served some 40 years in the National Guard, and had attended the camp at Tobyhanna. Wiles interviewed him in Washington in 1958 and wrote that this individual, whom Wiles subsequently referred to only as the "interviewee," recalled that one day during the camp, as his battery was moving their guns across "a very rough, bumpy road, that gave the horses much trouble, Summerall ordered everyone to walk. When he had gone, a non-com decided that just the same he would ride." When he later caught sight of the man, so said the anonymous source, "Summerall cried in a great and infuriated voice: 'Get down off that wagon. Get that G—D— man off that wagon.' When the man had jumped down, Summerall said: 'Tear those chevrons off your sleeves. Now walk back to camp, and report to my tent, and stand in front of it till I return.'"

On another occasion, he said that Summerall, after gathering his officers in a circle, "called one who had done something wrong to the center of the circle and blasted him scathingly." Although the "interviewee" said that Summerall had reasons for his actions, nevertheless, "'He was just a martinet!'"[55] As Captain Reilly had said of his battery as they embarked on their journey to Asia in 1900, so would Summerall insist that, regardless of the time and circumstance, "There will be nothing to explain in my battery," or, for that matter, in any of his commands.

Indeed, his reform of undisciplined and ineffective artillery units, whether Regular Army or militia, into responsive and well-trained batteries and battalions, his energetic leadership in changing rugged landscapes into well-ordered artillery training camps, and his ability to assuage the concerns and win the support of a local officials and their constituencies, undoubtedly were major reasons why Summerall was called to Washington to serve as the assistant to the chief in charge of the field artillery of the Militia Bureau. He moved his family into a comfortable apartment at the Westmoreland, just off Connecticut Avenue beyond Rock Creek Park, where Laura's father and his second wife, whom he had married in 1892, after the death of Laura's mother, were living.[56]

Summerall reported for duty in his new assignment on 4 September 1914, the day that *The New York Times* reported that the German army had swept through Belgium, and was just 40 miles from Paris, where the citizens were calmly preparing for an approaching siege. The very next day, led by Generals Joseph J. C. Joffre, the commander in chief of the French army, and Joseph S. Gallieni, the military governor of Paris, with the British Expeditionary Forces providing valuable support, the French army and citizens of Paris recovered their spirit of *élan*, and began a counterattack. For the next five days, the opposing armies fought and maneuvered over a battlefield that stretched along the uneven ground south of the Marne River and east/northeast of the capital city. On the fifth day, the Germans disengaged, enabling the exhausted armies of Britain and France to claim a strategic victory. The Battle of the Marne had saved Paris and France from an early defeat and saw Joffre emerge a national hero and the savior of his country. After three weeks of war, each side had lost more than 500,000 men in killed, wounded, and captured.[57] And it was far from over.

Unable to break through the masses of men, weaponry, and field fortifications on either side, the opposing armies tried to outflank each other, maneuvering along a front that stretched some 470 miles from the Swiss border to the North Sea. When their attempts failed, the soldiers of these formidable alliances huddled in vermin-infested, muddy bottoms and along the walls of trenches that stabilized the front, and served as the only refuge on the battlefield. Attacking troops were mowed down by machine gun fire, ripped apart, suffocated, burned and vaporized by the exploding shells of artillery fire and mortar blasts. They were speared by double-edged bayonets and gouged by "trench" knives. They were channeled by barbed wire directly into the sights of rifles, machine guns, and quick-firing artillery pieces. The Great War, a brutal conflict that would claim more than two million of them as casualties after just three months of combat,[58] was only the beginning. This era of trench warfare would consume millions more. It would exhaust much of the blood and treasure of western civilization, while leaving millions more to grieve for the fallen.

In November 1914, seeking desperately to break the stalemate on the Western Front, the British mined the North Sea as part of a blockade of Germany that they hoped would choke their enemy's ability to sustain the wages of war. Germany retaliated by establishing a "war zone" around the British Isles, warning that merchant vessels would be attacked without advance notice. The rules of cruiser warfare provided that merchant ships suspected of carrying contraband must be warned before they were boarded and searched; if contraband were found, the crew's safety had to be assured. The Germans insisted, however, that the vulnerability of the submarine, which had to surface to issue a warning, invalidated this principle. In response, the British declared the war zone to be illegal, and stated that they would arm their merchant ships and attack submarines whenever they surface. The United States, still a neutral in the war, and profiting from its trade and loans to the Allied powers and also with Germany (until the British blockade prevented it), warned Germany that it would be held accountable for any loss of American lives and property. For its part, the German government, attempting to keep the U.S. neutral, wanted to print in newspapers a warning against Americans traveling on British ships. With the approval of Secretary of State William Jennings Bryan, the warning appeared in American newspapers on 1 May 1915.

On that day, the Cunard luxury liner *Lusitania*, one of the biggest and fastest ships afloat, set sail from New York bound for Liverpool, carrying almost 2,000 passengers, which included many Americans. Its cargo included over 50 tons of shrapnel shells, 74 barrels of crude oil, over 10 tons of rifle ammunition, and a large amount of guncotton, an explosive compound used in mines and as an ingredient in smokeless gun powder. Less than a week later, on 7 May 1915, as the liner slowly steamed into the approaches of the Irish Sea, the German submarine *U-20* fired without warning a torpedo that struck the *Lusitania*. The explosion blew out the bottom of the bow, and in less than 20 minutes it sank to the bottom. Almost 1,200 lives were lost, including those of 128 Americans. The American public was outraged by the attack, but President Wilson, determined that the U.S. remain neutral, and intent on avoiding a break with Germany, on 13 May said that the American people were "too proud to fight." He demanded reparations, a disavowal of U-boat warfare, and the acceptance of his interpretation of neutral rights. Germany deplored the loss of life, but asserted that the ship with its cargo of munitions and explosives was not an unarmed merchant vessel, and claimed that the submarine acted in self-defense. Wilson sent a much stronger note on 9 June, causing Secretary of State Bryan to resign in protest over the president's unequal treatment of the British and German blockades. In early 1916, Germany accepted liability and agreed to pay reparations. Wilson considered their acknowledgements inadequate, and the entire incident provoked an intense rise in anti-German sentiment throughout the country.[59]

Summerall did not comment on the *Lusitania* affair in his memoir but noted an awakening of "much interest" in the war, as letters from National Guard units piled up on his desk, many asking that new artillery batteries be organized. One appeal that he remembered came from the adjutant general of Connecticut, who requested that a battery be organized at Yale University.[60] It would include students, faculty, and staff, and an alumnus had volunteered to donate funds to build an armory and stables. Summerall responded positively by sending a major to New Haven to organize the battery and give them basic instruction to prepare them for training at Tobyhanna. This learned battery, commanded by Captain Robert M. Danford, with Dr. Edward B. Reed, Professor of English, serving as its sergeant major, trained at Tobyhanna during the summer of 1916, and was one of a number of National Guard batteries that subsequently served along the Mexican border in the pursuit of the revolutionary outlaw and Mexican popular hero, Francisco "Pancho" Villa.[61] An article that appeared in the January issue of the *Field Artillery Journal* praised Summerall "whose interest in the organization was always keen, and who never failed to encouragingly respond to every appeal for advice and assistance."[62]

In response to many other similar requests, and in continuing efforts to improve the caliber of militia artillery, Summerall was ordered to search for additional campsites and firing ranges in the southern and western parts of the country. For most of the remainder of the year 1914, and into the winter and spring of 1915, he was "on the road," looking for suitable sites again around Tullahoma, Tennessee, then south to Anniston, Alabama, some 60 miles east of Birmingham, and from there to Monterey, California. He found nothing on his second trip to Tullahoma, but in Anniston, he found a suitable tract of 16,000 acres that adjoined 2,000 acres of government land and arranged for its purchase. In Monterey he located 16,000 acres and negotiated an agreement to purchase it; and, on the return trip, he stopped at Tobyhanna and completed arrangements there to purchase an additional 28,000 acres. As with Tobyhanna, the Anniston and Monterey tracts subsequently were expanded and became permanent military posts. Funding for all three acquisitions was included in the War Department budget for the next fiscal year.[63]

The European powers continued to wage war incessantly and indecisively, while the *Lusitania* episode increased hostility toward Germany, and American soldiers were fighting in Mexico against government regulars and Villa.[64] Not surprisingly, private individuals as well as governmental officials were as interested in the war as were the National Guard units that Summerall had observed. Actually, since the outbreak of the world war, the Preparedness Movement, led by former President Theodore Roosevelt, former Secretary of War Henry Stimson, Wall Street financier J. P. Morgan, and Henry Cabot Lodge, the powerful Massachusetts senator, and supported by partisan organizations, had been working hard to prepare the country for war, and for intervention on the Allied side. The sinking of the *Lusitania* increased pressure on the president to call on Congress to increase military appropriations, but in his determination to remain neutral, he steadily refused to do so. For Summerall, the sinking of the *Lusitania* meant that war was inevitable, but he and Laura tried to avoid taking sides in heated discussions around town and at the Westmoreland about whether we should fight for or against the Allies. As he saw it, his duty "was to prepare for war and to respond to any order."[65]

Secretary of War Lindley M. Garrison, a blunt-spoken New Jersey lawyer and former judge, advocated the creation of a large, federal reserve force of 250,000 men, the so-called Continental Army Plan. It failed to gain Congressional support, since it was seen as diminishing the status of the

National Guard, and moving the country toward intervention in the world war. When President Wilson rejected Garrison's plan, the secretary abruptly resigned, and the president appointed Newton D. Baker, the intelligent, persuasive, and progressive former mayor of Cleveland, Ohio, to replace him. While a student at Johns Hopkins University, some 20 years earlier, Baker had studied under Wilson, and they became well acquainted while living in the same boarding house.[66]

Meanwhile, Lodge and Roosevelt continued to press hard for military preparedness and gained the support of General Leonard Wood, commander of the Eastern Department, and New York attorney Grenville Clark. Wood and Clark worked together to establish special camps, where well-educated and successful young men could be trained to become officers. With funds from the army and from private sources, the first and largest of these camps was located at Plattsburg, New York, and the entire project became known as the Plattsburg Movement. Young volunteers were offered officer training in the function of specific weapons and in basic infantry tactics, and spent a summer or six months (at their own expense), with the reward of a possible commission in the Regular Army, or "reserve corps," after successfully completing the course. In 1915, camps were held in four different locations and were attended by over 1,000 volunteers; in 1916, the number of camps had increased to 10, with an enrollment of over 10,000 volunteers. The camps were sponsored by business, labor, professional, and religious groups, many with strong Republican leanings, and although the War Department supported the camps with equipment and training personnel, volunteers still had to pay their own way. The program quickly drew criticism from Wilson's Democratic administration, and from the public as well, as a way for young men from elitist East Coast families to get commissions in the army, and as a vehicle to promote the preparedness views of Wood, Roosevelt, and their associates.[67] Historian James W. Pohl has concluded that the legacy of the Plattsburg Movement and the Military Training Corps Association (MTCA), which followed it in the next three decades, was that young men needed to be educated in time of peace to become proficient junior officers in time of war.[68]

More immediately, the Preparedness and Plattsburg Movements helped to prepare the United States to wage modern war by paving the way for passage of the National Defense Act that Congress enacted on 3 June 1916. By then, legislators realized that important segments of the public were willing to support preparedness in peacetime. In addition, earlier that year in March, a U-boat had torpedoed another vessel, the French steamer *Sussex*, with the loss of several American passengers. President Wilson threatened to break diplomatic relations with Germany, and this forced the German government to state that it would no longer attack merchant ships without warning. This so-called *Sussex* pledge prevented the diplomatic breach between the two powers and strengthened Wilson's policy of protecting American rights. Once again, German belligerence had taken American lives, and the president realized just how precarious American neutrality had become.[69] By signing the National Defense Act, he created the means through which the United States could build and organize a mass army.

The Act of 1916 restructured the army and provided for a major expansion of the land forces of the United States. Over a five-year period, the Regular Army would be expanded to a peacetime strength of 175,000 men; with the inclusion of volunteers in wartime, that number could increase to 286,000, to include 65 infantry regiments, 25 cavalry regiments, 21 field artillery regiments, 7 engineer regiments, 2 mounted engineer battalions, 263 coast artillery companies, 8 aero squadrons, and supporting units. The law also established tactical divisions and brigades, with three brigades to a division and three regiments to a brigade. In war, therefore, a tactical division would consist of around 17,400 officers and men, a brigade about 5,800, and a regiment around 1,900.

National Guard strength was increased from 100,000 to a maximum of 450,000 soldiers, but in order to receive federal subsidies, guard units had to drill a minimum of 48 times a year, and attend a two-week summer camp (like the one at Tobyhanna), under supervision of the Regular Army. Upon enlistment, guardsmen were required to take a dual oath, federal and state, and, when called into federal service in a national emergency, were required to serve abroad for as long as the president ordered. When they went to war, they would enter and serve as guard units, not as individuals. With the Plattsburg Movement as a model, the Act established an Officer Reserve Corps (ORC) and a Reserve Officer Training Corps (ROTC) at colleges and universities. Students enrolled in these programs could receive reserve commissions after completing the required curriculum and attending training camps. It also authorized the president to force any business to give priority to government orders in wartime, and to set limits on prices that the government was charged, as well as profits gained from governmental contracts. The Act also gave the president the authority to deal with issues involving economic mobilization, a provision that the president used to create the Council of National Defense.[70] The National Defense Act of 1916 had made possible the creation of an army far larger than any that the country had ever established in peacetime. Whether the public, the government, business, labor, and the army itself would be ready for, and equal to, the enormous demands of modern warfare, if the country no longer were shielded from its fury, was, however, another issue altogether.

With the expansion of the National Guard under the National Defense Act, the number of artillery batteries increased accordingly, and Summerall kept busy visiting as many of them as possible, recommending additional sites for training camps, and maintaining close contact with many of the officers with whom he had worked at Tobyhanna. He was appointed a member of a board to study the organization of the Field Artillery and prepared a plan for the organization of an artillery brigade for an infantry division. After examining combat operations in Europe, he recommended that each artillery brigade consist of two regiments of 3-inch guns, and one regiment of 105-mm (3.6 inch) howitzers. Additional brigades of large caliber guns and howitzers would be constituted as corps and army artillery with divisional brigades in corps and army reserve. Except for the substitution of the 155-mm howitzer for the 105-mm that he had recommended, Summerall's organization of an artillery brigade was adopted, and he extravagantly asserted that "It was the most efficient organization of the artillery in any army and did much to win our battles [in the world war]."[71] While this assertion may well account for "much" of the success of American divisions in World War I, the same could be said for the artillery brigades of the other great powers on both sides whose massive and lethal barrages dominated so many of the battles of that conflict.

In 1916, those battles increased in scope, intensity, and lethality, as both sides in the conflict desperately sought to break the deadlock on the Western Front, and exhaust the strength of their enemy's ability to wage war. In January, the Germans sent two Zeppelin airships in raids over the English countryside, killing four people, and causing considerable panic, out of all proportion to the death toll. Altogether, in 1916, 23 Zeppelin raids dropped 125 tons of ordnance that struck villages as well as urban centers, including London, and killed 293 people.[72]

In February, the Germans began their assault on the fortified, but lightly defended area of Verdun-sur-Meuse, unleashing an enormous bombardment, and attacking along an eight-mile front. Their goal, as General Erich von Falkenhayn, chief of staff, informed Emperor William II, was not to achieve a breakthrough but to "bleed white" the French army trying to stop it. Indeed, when General Joffre sent General Henri Philippe Pétain to assume command, Pétain declared, "They shall not pass." Attacks and counterattacks consumed vast quantities of men and materiel, and when the guns fell silent across that ravaged landscape in December, the French had suffered approximately 542,000 casualties, including 162,000 killed, and the Germans 434,000, including 100,000 killed. The outcome left the French army close to mutiny against the offensive tactics of their commanders, and staggered the German army, whose leaders had hoped for a two to one casualty ratio.[73] In late August, General Paul von Hindenburg replaced Falkenhayn as chief of the German general staff, and appointed as his deputy General Erich Ludendorff, who became the real power behind Hindenburg and the emperor. Together they headed what was named the Third Supreme Council and established essentially a military-industrial dictatorship of the German Empire.

As the Verdun campaign raged on the Western Front, Italy, allied with the Entente (Allies) since 1915, and Austria-Hungary, Germany's declining ally, fought a series of bloody battles along the Isonzo River, northwest of Trieste, and in the mountainous region of the Austrian Trentino. By September, the Dual Monarchy's casualties were over 184,000, while the Italians had suffered some 273,000 casualties. Austria-Hungary's army was left exhausted; the Italians, while stunned by massive losses in the Trentino, were encouraged when their forces, under General Luigi Cadorna, chief of staff, took the city of Gorizia, along the eastern bank of the Isonzo, some 15 miles inland from the northern Adriatic coast.[74]

Desperately seeking to weaken Austro-Hungarian attacks in the Trentino, the Italians had called on their new Russian allies for help. From the *stavka*, headquarters of the Russian general staff, Tsar Nicholas II ordered the Southwestern Army Group, commanded by General Alexei A. Brusilov, to attack along a 300-mile front. Brusilov's offensive began in June, and routed the forces of the Dual Monarchy, until the Russians ran out of supplies and were checked by German reinforcements rushed into the battle from Verdun in September.[75] The Empire of Austria-Hungary was saved by these reinforcements, and Russia, having suffered more than one million casualties, was plunged deeper into the crisis that would cost the tsar his throne just six months later.

With French resistance forcing Germany to pour men and materiel into the Verdun campaign, and with Russia and Italy pressing the Dual Monarchy on three fronts, Great Britain launched on 1 July a massive attack against strong German defenses north of the Somme River in the northern French region of Picardy. Under the command of Generals Henry S. Rawlinson and Edmund Allenby, the British made small gains but sustained over 60,000 killed and wounded on just the first day of the battle. It was the greatest one-day loss in the history of the British army. To the surprise of the Germans, the French supported the British by attacking south of the river, making greater gains than their ally, and forcing their enemy to shift reinforcements from Verdun. For four and one-half months, fighting continued along the Somme; the British suffered 420,000 casualties, the French 195,000, and the Germans some 650,000. Especially costly for the German army was the high percentage of losses among prewar officers and non-commissioned officers. Deprived of these experienced small-unit commanders, "That army would never be the same again."[76]

While initially concerned more with French rather than British military forces, the German High Command had become increasingly worried about the threat of British military and naval power. Their concern increased with the realization that, after the naval Battle of Jutland, the German Seas Fleet would not be able to seize control of the Atlantic from the Grand Fleet of Great Britain, and that meant that Britain would continue to receive materiel from the U.S.[77] Hindenburg and Ludendorff decided on a strategy of unrestricted submarine warfare as a desperate and deadly form of *guerre de course* that they hoped would force the British to capitulate by exhausting their resources. The Germans were quite aware that this policy could lead to war with the United States, with whom relations were increasingly hostile, but neither they nor any other observers believed that the American army would be a factor in Europe. Even if the U.S. declared war, the High Command estimated that it would take over a year for the Americans to have a fighting force on the ground in Europe. By that time, they expected that Allied shipping losses would have crippled the British economy, and forced an end to the war on terms laid down by the Triple Alliance. On 31 January 1917, Germany proclaimed unrestricted submarine warfare, and on 3 February, the U.S. severed diplomatic relations between the two countries.[78]

Three weeks later, British Foreign Secretary Arthur Balfour turned over to the American ambassador to Britain, Walter Hines Page, the text of a telegram from Berlin that British Naval Intelligence had intercepted and decoded. In this message, Alfred Zimmermann, the German foreign secretary, proposed to the German minister to Mexico a defensive alliance between the two countries in case of a war between Germany and the United States, with the proviso that Mexico re-conquer the lost territories of New Mexico, Texas, and Arizona. Mexico should also urge Japan to join the Triple Alliance. Ambassador Page, long an advocate of American intervention on the Allied side, received a copy of the telegram and sent it to the president, who kept it under wraps while he won the approval of a bill in the House of Representatives to arm merchant ships. But, when the bill went to the Senate, a group of senators filibustered it, and a frustrated president authorized the State Department to release the telegram to the press. It appeared on 1 March 1917, quickly became known as the Zimmermann Telegram, and touched off a furious anti-German reaction all across the country.[79] On 18 March, German submarines sunk three American ships with the loss of 15 lives, but Wilson still hesitated to plunge the country into war. After all, the slogan, "He Kept Us Out of War" had been decisive in his narrow electoral college victory less than six months earlier. Finally, on 2 April 1917, he convened the Congress, and that evening called for a declaration of war against Germany, hoping to make the world "safe for democracy," and shape the peace that would preserve that goal.[80] Four days later, on 6 April, Congress declared war on the German Empire. Hoping to divide Austria-Hungary from Germany, Wilson did not ask for a declaration of war against the Habsburg Empire, but when that split between the two Central Powers did not occur over the course of the next few months, he called for, and Congress responded with, a declaration of war against the Dual Monarchy on 7 December 1917.

With the latest bloodbaths of Verdun and the Somme having drained their manpower; with the French army in an actual state of mutiny after a disastrous spring offensive along the Chemin des Dames plateau in the Aisne River valley of northeastern France; and with many Russian army units drawn more deeply into the revolutionary turmoil in their own country, while other units voted for peace "with their feet," and headed home to their villages, British and French delegations rushed to Washington to plead for help.

Foreign Secretary Balfour led the British delegation that came to Washington in late April, and three days later the French arrived, led by the massive, and massively popular, Marshal Joffre. They wanted their new ally to supply ships, money, and, most importantly, men for the Allied cause. Since they doubted that the U.S. could raise, train, equip, and provide officers quickly enough and large enough to help defeat the German army, they urged that American soldiers be fed into Allied armies, either as individuals or in small units. The British called for 500,000 to be sent as soon as possible, and Joffre added that that number would be all the Allies would ever need. This was the best way, they argued, for American manpower to strengthen the armies of the Allies on the Western Front. When that proposal, which became known as amalgamation, was turned down, Joffre urged that one American division be sent to France to boost the sinking morale of the French.[81] President Wilson agreed and had already decided to recommend a draft as the best way to raise an army that clearly would have to be far larger than the force that the National Defense Act of 1916 had provided.

On 2 May, General Scott, army chief of staff, ordered Major General John J. Pershing, commander of the Southern Department at Fort Sam Houston, Texas, to select five regiments to form the division that would be sent to assure the French that the Americans were, indeed, coming. Pershing had only recently returned from Mexico, where, as the "very hard taskmaster" and leader of the Punitive Expedition against Villa, he had impressed Scott and Secretary Baker as a vigorous and confident commander, who had been loyal and obedient, in spite of his concern about the restrictions that his government had imposed on that operation. From the standing army, Pershing selected the 16th, 18th,

26th, and 28th Infantry Regiments, and the 6th Field Artillery; later, when he added the 5th and 7th Field Artillery Regiments and some additional auxiliary units, he formed the First Provisional Division. As the First Division, they would be led to victory by Bullard and Summerall, and under the watchful eye of Pershing, emerge as his favorite. With his plans for the First Division now in place, Pershing left for Washington, confident in his ability to command whatever force the government would entrust to him.[82] He looked the part.

Handsome, ramrod-straight, toughened by his years of iron at West Point and by his military campaigns, in robust health, impeccably uniformed, and possessing a penetrating gaze that bore into one from above tightly pressed lips and a bristling triangulated mustache, Pershing was eager for the command that lay before him. In several respects he was a carbon copy of Summerall, or vice versa. Both had been school teachers before winning competitive appointments to the military academy; both were older than their classmates; and both had risen through the cadet ranks to be first captain and president of their class; Pershing had entered in 1882 and graduated with the class of 1886. Following graduation, he served as a frontier cavalryman and taught military science at the University of Nebraska for four years, earning a law degree along the way. Like Summerall, he became frustrated with the slow promotion that prevailed in the army, and, at one point, considered leaving the army and practicing law. In 1897, he returned to West Point as a "tac," rather than as an instructor like Summerall. His serious demeanor and "excessive strictness" earned him the "silent treatment" on one occasion at mess, and the nickname "Black Jack" for his having commanded black troops on the frontier. It stayed with him. After this unhappy experience at his alma mater, Pershing, like Summerall, fought with much success in the Philippines and completed three tours there. In 1905, he married Helen Frances Warren, the daughter of the rich and influential Senator Francis Warren of Wyoming. The Pershings celebrated their honeymoon in Tokyo (not too far from where Summerall and Laura had planned a reunion), where he was posted as a military attaché. While in the Far East, he served as an observer in the Russo-Japanese War from 1905–1906 and was suddenly promoted from captain to brigadier general, leapfrogging over 862 senior officers. In 1909, he began a four-year term as governor of the Moro Province in Mindanao and succeeded in subduing the rebellious Moro tribesmen. Meanwhile, his happy marriage had produced three daughters and a son, and in 1914, the Pershings returned to America, where he took command of the 8th Brigade at the Presidio. In August 1915, while he was at El Paso guarding the border with his brigade, Pershing's wife and three daughters perished in a fire that broke out in their home at the Presidio; only his son Warren survived. His biographer, Donald Smythe, noted that after Pershing had been promoted to major general in 1916, he told a friend that "All the promotion in the world would make no difference now." After his expedition into Mexico had broken up Villa's band and killed a number of his men, Pershing returned to Texas to await the command that he "ardently desired."[83]

Pursuant to an order from General Scott, Pershing reported to him on 10 May. Scott confirmed the impression in his message of 2 May that Pershing would command a division that would be sent to France. His next meeting was with Secretary Baker, who impressed Pershing as a man who understood the task ahead, and would not hesitate to make definite decisions on the "momentous questions" that would arise. A few days later Baker again met with Pershing and informed him that he would command a much larger force, the AEF—the American Expeditionary Forces. Pershing noted in his memoir that he and the War Department were "decidedly against our becoming a recruiting agency for either the French or British," and emphasized also that "it was definitely understood between the Secretary of War and myself that we should proceed to organize our own units from top to bottom and build a distinctive army of our own as rapidly as possible."[84]

For Wilson, an independent and victorious American army would enable him to detach the United States from the entrenched animosities and hatreds that had arisen on both sides after the years of slaughter, and to shape the peace that would make the world "safe for democracy." For Pershing, "a distinctive army of our own" would enable him to train his soldiers to abandon the entrenched, exhaustive, and demoralizing warfare on the western front that was marked by "the regulation of space and time by higher commands down to the smallest details * * * fixed distances and intervals between units and individuals * * * little initiative." Instead, he would train his soldiers in what he termed "open warfare," marked by "irregularity of formations, comparatively little regulation of space and time by higher commanders, the greatest possible use of the infantry's fire power to enable it to get forward, variable distances and intervals between units and individuals * * * brief orders and the greatest possible use of individual initiative by all troops engaged in the action * * * The infantry commander must oppose machine guns by fire from his rifles, his automatics and his rifle grenades and must close with their crews under cover of this fire and of ground beyond the flanks."[85] Key to the success of open warfare was marksmanship with the rifle. Pershing viewed the rifle and bayonet as "the essential weapons of the infantry," and, although he believed that machine guns, grenades, Stokes mortars, and one-pounders "were all valuable weapons for specific purposes, they could not replace the combination of an efficient soldier and his rifle."[86] Aggressive in the attack, and skilled in his use of the rifle, Pershing believed that American soldiers would be invincible in battle. It was a belief that would be sorely tested in the war that lay ahead.

President Wilson and Congress decided that the wartime American army would be raised through national conscription, and those who were drafted would serve for the duration of the war. On 18 May 1917, the president signed into law the Selective Draft Act. The draft agency was called the Selective Service System, and Brigadier General Enoch H. Crowder, the army's chief legal officer, and his key aide, Major Hugh S. Johnson, set up a system of some 4,648 local draft boards made up of local citizens, who decided who would be inducted and who, because of certain specified reasons, could be deferred or exempted. With local officials making these crucial decisions, the Selective Service System became one of the government's most successful and widely accepted wartime programs. It registered 23.9 million Americans, drafted 2.8 million, and established 16, later 32, training camps and cantonments across the country. In addition, another two million Americans volunteered for service, mostly in the navy. When the U.S. again went to war in 1941 and during the Cold War, as well, the Selective Service model was used again, although, as historian John Whiteclay Chambers II, points out, it "broke down" during the unpopular and controversial war in Vietnam.[87]

As he prepared to lead this army into France, Pershing chose as his chief of staff Major James G. Harbord, an astute, energetic, fellow-cavalry man, who had enlisted in the army as a private in 1889, served two years in Cuba and twelve years in the Philippines before his current assignment at the Army War College in Washington. Pershing knew him well, respected his ability and frankness, and valued, "above all," his loyalty. Together they selected the rest of his General Staff, or, as it soon became known, Headquarters, American Expeditionary Forces. It included, among others that Pershing knew well, Summerall's classmate and friend, Major John McCauley Palmer; First Lieutenant George S. Patton, Jr., Pershing's aide in Mexico; Major John L. Hines, who had served on Pershing's staff in Mexico; Colonel Fox Conner, a West Pointer whom Pershing increasingly came to rely upon; and Captain Hugh Drum, who had been on Pershing's staff of the Southern Department. They promptly began planning for the future first division, and for the organization of the AEF in France, and finished their work the day before Pershing reported to the White House to meet with the president on 24 May.[88]

In their first and only meeting, before the president came to Paris after the armistice, Pershing was surprised that Wilson did not say anything about the war or the army's part in the Allied effort. At the same time however, he was gratified when the president told him that he had "every confidence that you will succeed," and that he would have the president's "full support." Wilson gave Pershing complete freedom in the conduct of operations, a decision that Secretary Baker fully supported, and one that Pershing determined was "unique in our history."[89]

The day before he left for France with his staff, Pershing received a letter from Baker reaffirming his supreme authority in France, and instructing him to cooperate with the Allies, while, at the same time, to keep in mind that "the forces of the United States are a separate and distinct component of the combined forces, the identity of which must be preserved." Of course, that was fine with Pershing, but he had a hard time understanding why Major General Tasker H. Bliss, Acting Chief of Staff,[90] gave him a letter that essentially made the same points about maintaining the identity of the American army. He never figured out the reason, but he had more pressing matters to worry about, and when he got to France, he locked both letters in a safe, and never looked at them again.[91] More than likely, this redundancy was an example of the confusion and disorganization in the War Department in the early stages of the war. In addition, similar conditions prevailed within the undermanned General Staff, as it confronted the enormous task of mobilization, which the power of the bureau chiefs over the army's supply and administrative bureaus made even more difficult.

Another indication of the general lack of organization in the War Department was Secretary Baker's appointment on 28 May, two days after Pershing and his staff had sailed for France, of an independent commission of 12 officers to travel to Britain and France to study the overall situation, determine how the American army should be supplied, equipped, and trained, and report their findings to the department. These were the same issues that Pershing and his staff had been working on. Once again, a redundancy of orders stemming from a lack of coordination had created an awkward situation for Pershing, this time with the added potential to weaken his authority and his own recommendations.[92] In addition, it led to a forceful encounter and outcome between the commander-in-chief and some of his staff on the one hand, and, on the other hand, an important member of the commission; namely, Colonel Charles P. Summerall.

The commission that Secretary Baker appointed was headed by Colonel Chauncey B. Baker, a classmate of Pershing. Summerall was informed by General Bliss that he would serve on the committee as head of the artillery section. Bliss gave him a letter addressed to "General John J. Pershing. For your eye[s] alone" and told him to be in Halifax, Nova Scotia, the next morning and hand the letter to Pershing. Naturally, Summerall assumed that the letter contained important and secret instructions, and Bliss enhanced the aura of secrecy by instructing Summerall not to tell anyone where he was going. As ordered, he left his office in the Militia Bureau without telling the chief, returned home to pick up his trunk that Laura had helped him pack, and together they left their apartment for Union Station. He had told her that he was going to inspect an artillery camp, but as they parted on the platform, he felt that she knew where he was going, but, characteristically, said nothing more in his memoir about their good-byes.[93]

Late in the afternoon on 28 May, Pershing and his party of 191 officers and men indeed had left New York on the British steamer *Baltic*, bound for Britain via Halifax, where they were to transfer to another vessel for the voyage across the Atlantic to Liverpool. For 48 hours they waited off Halifax for a thick fog to lift before finally deciding to raise anchor and set sail for Britain.[94] When Summerall arrived in Halifax the next morning after he had left Laura, he went directly to the American Consulate, and informed the consul that he needed to see General Pershing. The consul said that he knew nothing about Pershing or his whereabouts, and left to find out who Summerall was. When he returned, seeming to be "more friendly," he took Summerall to lunch, where they met Captain John G. Quekemeyer, one of Pershing's aides, who was also a member of the Baker Commission, and had been a cadet at West Point during Summerall's tour of duty there. Quekemeyer had been looking for Summerall, and after their friendly reunion, the consul introduced them to another British captain who commanded the steamer *Olympic*. It was loaded with Canadian troops and was waiting for the arrival of Arthur Balfour's party from Ottawa before sailing. The captain told the Americans that German submarines had been sighted off Halifax, and, as a result, the *Baltic*, with Pershing's party aboard, had bypassed the port and set a course for Liverpool.[95]

Shortly afterwards, Balfour's party arrived and boarded the *Olympic*. Summerall went on board and discovered that the other members of the Commission were with Balfour's group, including three American field artillery officers who would work under Summerall's authority. As he was getting acquainted with his colleagues, Summerall received a radio message from Bliss ordering him to return and sail from New York. Knowing that Pershing had already sailed, Summerall was perplexed by Bliss's order and showed it to the *Olympic*'s captain, who told Summerall that he would sail earlier from Halifax than from New York. Summerall radioed Bliss that he would leave from Halifax and boarded the *Olympic*, which set sail the next morning, without Summerall's having received any response from Bliss. On board, he sewed the letter for Pershing into a pocket in a vest that he slept in, and settled into the cabin that he shared with Quekemeyer. Destroyers escorted the ship for two days, and after they turned back to Halifax, the *Olympic* began a zig-zag course at a speed of almost 30 knots.[96]

After an uneventful voyage across the north Atlantic, and by rail from Liverpool, Summerall and his fellow commissioners reached London on 9 June, just 24 hours after Pershing had arrived. When they entered the lobby of the Hotel Savoy, the first person Summerall caught sight of was Pershing. Summerall barely knew him, having first met him as a fellow usher at a wedding, and then later at their home at Fort Meyer, when Pershing and his wife called on the Summeralls. After a proper greeting, Summerall told him about the letter. They went up to Pershing's room, where Summerall "ripped the letter from my vest pocket and handed it to him. He read it, waited a moment and made a grunt. I saw that the interview was finished and left." The contents of the letter remain unknown, but Summerall surmised that it dealt with Pershing's departure from New York on the *Baltic*, which "was made public so that he could transfer to the fast *Olympic* in Halifax and thus deceive the German submarines."[97] Actually, as Summerall apparently never discovered, Pershing's voyage, while it was supposed to be a secret, could hardly have escaped the attention of any interested party, whether friendly or hostile. As Donald Smythe noted, the military men with him in New York City "blundered about like bulls in a china shop," and "the signal battery at Governor's Island boomed out a farewell salute as Pershing departed."[98] At any rate, Summerall believed that Bliss's letter was a very important one. His view that Pershing responded rather curtly and indifferently to its contents might well be a reflection of the aged general's long-standing and smoldering resentment of Pershing, a feeling that developed only in the wake of the latter's harsh judgment of Summerall's actions in the so-called "race to Sedan," an episode in the closing days of World War I that will be considered at length below.

After his brief encounter with Pershing, Summerall and the other members of the mission met with Colonel William Lassiter, the American military attaché in London, who had prepared an overall schedule of visits to the principal training camps, including those for the field artillery that were of special interest to Summerall and his team.[99] They left London the next day, traveling to posts in the southern part of England, with Summerall taking copious notes on training methods, types of artillery, and how the guns were used. His observations confirmed his contention that the more powerful 105 mm gun should have replaced the French 75 mm, and he might well have been right. The French 75 was a proven, effective gun, popular with the British as well as the French, and since France would be supplying artillery for the AEF, it was unreasonable for Summerall to expect a conversion to the 105-mm gun.

When they finished their tour of British installations, Summerall's party returned to London for a series of receptions and dinners honoring the Baker Mission. Ambassador Page gave a reception at the American Embassy, where Summerall met Field Marshal Lord Frederick Sleigh Roberts, "Britain's First Soldier," the victor in the Afghan War of 1878–80, and in the South African War of 1899–1902. At the embassy and in the hotels where he stayed, Summerall was much impressed with the cheerful demeanor and the "handsome blue uniforms" of British officers and their "elaborately dressed women," and concluded their appearance was an important part of an effort to "give officers and men on leave a maximum of pleasure and to keep up morale." "Our simple and inexpensive uniforms," he noted, "compared unfavorably with the British." In another swipe at Pershing, Summerall wrote that Pershing "at once adopted the Sam Browne belt, and his staff were soon wearing London-made uniforms."[100]

Shortly after Ambassador Page's reception, Viscountess Astor, the American born wife of Lord Waldorf Astor, invited Summerall's group to a lavish dinner party that included "several American ladies who [like Lady Astor] had married into the British nobility," with whom Summerall talked "as though we were at a family reunion." He found Lady Astor to be "charming, natural and cordial." After dinner, the Americans gathered informally in a smaller room, and as Lady Astor's sister led them at the piano, and with voices quivering with emotion, they "sang American folk songs like Ol'Virginny, Old Kentucky Home, S'wanee River, Casey Jones, and others." Perhaps that evening prompted Summerall to send Laura one of the many letters he wrote her after his arrival in Liverpool. All were censored, but he told her about his experiences and various activities, and recorded as well in his memoir how his leaving had "caused her great anxiety, but her courage and resignation were sublime and heartened me."[101] She remained, as always, "my dear wife."

Before the Baker Mission left London for a first-hand look at the war on the British and French fronts, he and Pershing agreed that Baker's group and the Expeditionary Headquarters staff should meet before the mission returned to the U.S. Pershing and his staff had no direct authority over Baker and his mission, or, as Summerall rather defiantly put it, they "had no control over us,"[102] but since Pershing would command the AEF in the fighting to come, it was certainly appropriate for Baker to discuss his recommendations with him.

With the conclusion of their professional inspections and the festive, if nostalgic, receptions in wartime London, Summerall and his colleagues in the Baker Mission sailed across the choppy waters of the English Channel, bound for a first-hand look at the war on the western front. They landed on the Belgian coast and were taken to a sector in the British front just to the west of the city of Ypres, where the Germans had established a strategic salient dominated by the Messines Ridge, which measured six by eight miles. Determined to relieve German pressure on the French army to the south, the British Second Army under General Sir Herbert Plumer had unleashed on 21 May a massive artillery bombardment with 2,500 guns that rained down three and a half million shells on the German positions for 17 days. On 7 June, just days before the Americans arrived, Plumer's men had literally blown up the German lines on the ridge by setting off over a million pounds of high explosives in over five miles of tunnels they had dug under the Germans. As Summerall's party reached the front, the Second Army had begun to consolidate its gains. Massive artillery barrages pounded German trenches, Allied planes swooped over enemy lines, and 72 Mark IV battle tanks led the assault of nine Allied divisions.[103] At Plumer's headquarters, the British explained the workings of army headquarters, showed the Americans the plans they had developed, and took them to the terrain where they had carefully rehearsed the attack. Summerall and his artillery team were especially interested in the sound ranging system that the British employed to locate enemy batteries and the liaison system that linked artillery batteries with infantry units. They also were impressed, to Summerall's considerable satisfaction, with the British desire to replace the 155-mm howitzer with the less powerful, but more mobile, 105-mm gun. After filling his notebook with the details of the British operation, Summerall settled in for the night, worried about becoming infected with lice that he had heard were contaminating all their billets. He had taken along a particularly potent anti-louse powder, but it burned his skin, so he could not use it. Fortunately, the lice left him alone, and he left, lice-free, the next morning with the Baker Mission, bound for Paris.[104]

In the French capital, the Americans settled into their accommodations at the elegant Hotel Crillon, on the historic Place de la Concorde. From there French officers took them to the artillery training school at the Château de Vincennes, located on the periphery of the city in an expansive hunting park, which had been a frequent residence for Emperor Napoleon I and Empress Josephine. At Vincennes, the French maintained an arsenal of heavy guns and "fine horses," which impressed the visitors, and had constructed a miniature trench system and terrain where they demonstrated deployments as well as methods of attack and defense.

From Vincennes, French officers escorted the mission to the front in Champagne, where they witnessed barrage fire to protect units in advanced trenches, techniques of camouflaging artillery emplacements, and, in general, made sure that French soldiers realized that America was now "in the war." A high point for Summerall was their lunch with General Henri Gourand, the popular commander of the Fourth Army, and former leader of the French expeditionary force in the ill-fated Dardanelles campaign in 1915, where an exploding shell broke both of his legs and severed his right arm. Gourand's slender face, dark, penetrating eyes, and sharp, aqualine nose, with his mustache sweeping out beyond his cheeks, and a wide, thick goatee covering his throat, reminded Summerall of the "prevailing pictures of the Christ." He was seated on Gourand's right, and listened intently as his host described how, after every battle, he would invite a soldier from each company to dinner. He would then shake hands with each one, and address them in the most "friendly and complimentary terms." As perhaps only a French general could put it, Gourand insisted that '"The best liaison is at the dinner table.'" Although he wrote that "Everywhere the French served excellent wines," Summerall pointed out that he could not personally vouch for it, since he "did not drink. No doubt they considered me...one of what they came to call the '"sauvage Americaines.'"[105]

On 2 July, Summerall and his colleagues in the Baker Mission returned to Paris and found the city decorated with American flags and bunting, as Parisians prepared to celebrate the Fourth of July, in honor of their new allies. For the next few days, Baker and Pershing met to set the agenda for the conference they had agreed upon in London. They designated several committees, composed of officers from both groups, to exchange ideas and reports, and to arrive at common conclusions and recommendations. Baker agreed that Pershing should serve as chairman, a position that would permit Pershing, according to Donald Smythe, to stamp his imprint and authority on the report. To ensure this outcome, Pershing "stacked the deck, bringing to the conference eighteen of his own people, to outvote twelve of Baker's."[106]

On 8 July, the conference convened at the large mansion on the rue de Varenne, which belonged to the American financier and philanthropist Ogden Mills, who had made it available to Pershing. Pershing had settled there along with Colonel Harbord, his chief of staff, two additional other staff members, and personal aides.[107] The conference opened positively, with both groups in agreement on most issues. Summerall was asked to present the report on the visits to the artillery section to the British and French armies. He noted that the organization of an American artillery brigade was superior to that of the British and French, and recommended the adoption of the 105 mm howitzer. But he contended that American divisions were undergunned, and, in his memoir, stated that he had urged the adoption of the Allied estimate of one 75-mm gun for every 15 yards of front, one 155-mm howitzer for every 50 yards of front, and one 155-mm gun, or similar piece, for every 100 yards of front. He pointed out that these figures were based on British standards, and "the [British] experience at the battles of Vimy and Messines."[108]

When he had finished his presentation, Summerall wrote that he was "at once viciously attacked personally and officially by officers of the staff whom I hardly knew for trying to promote a lot of artillery generals, for advocating the light howitzer and for [advocating] such a quantity of artillery. I replied with equal force and resentment. I told them that the infantry would pay in losses for the lack of artillery. This is what happened."[109] Pershing's Operations Section, headed by Fox Conner, had compiled a table, based on Summerall's ratios, which showed that the number of guns per 10 yards of front that Summerall recommended was more than two and one-half times as large as the British and French. In a second table, Fox's section showed that total number of guns per division employed by the British at Messines was 118, less than half of the 256 that Summerall cited, although Summerall had stated that his recommendations were based on the Messines attack.[110] Quite certainly, it was Fox, as well as others in his section, who vigorously and loudly pointed out Summerall's errors, and stressed that their figures, unlike Summerall's, were based correctly on the British and French experience. Summerall, as he stated, replied "with equal force and resentment," for he had asserted that his figures also were based accurately on the examination of British and French actions. Clearly, the Operation Section's tables that are printed in the *United States Army in the World War, 1917–1919* (see endnote 108) show that their figures were correct, and that Summerall's were wrong. But Summerall made a strong and valid point when he insisted that American divisions were undergunned, for Pershing's headquarters had planned for a division of some 28,000 men that was almost twice the size of those of Britain and France, but its artillery of 72 guns was to be no stronger.

After the flames of mutual antagonism and disputation had diminished, Pershing asked Summerall "to step out on the porch and said: 'Summerall, I want you to get together with my staff.'" Rather gratuitously, Summerall responded that "General, no one wants your success more than I. Your staff are wrong and I am going to Washington and fight for what I know is best for our artillery."[111] According to Donald Smythe, Pershing remained calm after this exchange,[112] but Summerall remembered that Pershing "seemed to be furious and turned and went into the house without a word. I felt that I would not be allowed to return to France and that my part in the war was ended."[113]

In his still smoldering resentment of Pershing's later criticism of those whom he considered responsible for the Sedan incident, Summerall totally had blotted out in his memory, and in his memoir, the facts, as he had known that Pershing had lauded his abilities and his performance at the highest levels of command. As Smythe stated, Pershing was "a man who liked strong men, including those who stood up to him, [and, following the mission's return to Washington] cabled the War Department, asking that Summerall be sent back to the AEF, where he consistently promoted him from one key position to another."[114] Perhaps inadvertently confirming Pershing's respect for Summerall's stance, Harbord observed that Summerall had "carried his argument as nearly to the limit of courtesy as I have ever seen an officer go and not be rebuked."[115] In addition, Smythe quotes Pershing's praise of Summerall after the war as "'An exceptionally able man in all respects. Possesses soldierly qualities instinctively. Thorough in his knowledge of his profession. Most loyal and reliable. Very energetic and determined. Inspires the highest ideals of service in his subordinates, and makes them feel that nothing is impossible. Brilliant in handling a command, none better. Would have been as army commander if the war had lasted. The highest type of man and soldier worthy of every confidence and able to fill any position.'"[116]

At the conclusion of the conference, Pershing got what he wanted when the two staffs submitted a common set of recommendations, known as the General Organization Project (GOP), dated 10 July. It incorporated the Operation Section's report on artillery, including the adoption of the 155-mm howitzer instead of the lighter 105-mm that Summerall had recommended. Most importantly, the GOP established the organization of a field army of one million men, with plans to increase that number in the future to at least three million men; by the end of the war, that number had swelled to over four million, with some two million having served in France. It created, as noted above, a division of approximately 28,000 men, which was larger than the entire army when Summerall received his commission. It consisted of two infantry brigades, each with two regiments and a machine gun battalion, totaling about 8,500, and each commanded by a brigadier general. Each regiment was composed of three battalions and a machine-gun company with 12 guns, about 3,800 troops, and commanded by a colonel. The battalions were made up of four companies, about 1,000 officers and men, each under the command of a major. Companies of six officers and 250 men were commanded by a captain, and platoons, the basic unit, consisted of 58 men under a second or first lieutenant. The division artillery brigade consisted of 72 guns organized into two regiments of 75-mm batteries, each totaling 24 guns, one regiment, also of 24 guns, of French 155-mm howitzers, and a trench mortar battery. Attached to this brigade were communicators, range-finding teams, and a headquarters staff that planned fire support.[117] In addition, this so-called "square division" had one engineer regiment, one machine gun battalion, one signal battalion, and trains. Since U.S. armories were unable to manufacture enough of the army's standard rifle, the 1903 Springfield, many American soldiers were equipped with British Lee-Enfield rifle, and, as previously noted, practically every artillery piece used by the AEF was manufactured in France.

These large AEF divisions were over twice the size of British, French, and German divisions, but Pershing and his staff believed that these big divisions would be able to absorb more losses than smaller ones, and thus sustain combat operations longer and more effectively. They also recognized that the AEF lacked men trained in command and staff work, and that larger divisions, rather than more numerous smaller ones, would mean that fewer officers would be needed to staff division headquarters. These large divisions proved to be more difficult to transport, supply, and deploy than those of the Allies or Germans, and, when they were organized into encampments, command and control of these huge units, with fewer officers, was difficult. In addition, combining National Guard and Regular Army divisions into the new organizations as they were being called into service led to considerable confusion and delay. These were some of the many and increasingly difficult problems that the War Department had to deal with, for which the ever impatient and demanding Pershing had little appreciation or understanding.[118]

With their hard work and a tough session with Pershing's staff behind them, Colonel Baker and his colleagues gave a farewell dinner at the Hotel Crillon for their French liaison officers, and set sail the following morning for London and the voyage home. Before they left, Summerall picked up a box of sugar at the American commissary to give to Lady Astor in appreciation of her hospitality. He stopped by her house after arriving in the British capital, but a servant told him she was at a hospital visiting wounded soldiers. He left his card with the box of sugar, "knowing that she would give it [the sugar] to her wounded." From London, the Baker Mission returned to Liverpool, where they boarded the *New York* at night for the voyage home, sailing around the northern tip of Ireland to avoid submarines, before heading west across the north Atlantic.[119]

During the uneventful homeward journey, Summerall spent most of his time writing the report of the Artillery Section that he would submit "to Washington," as he vowed to do in his face-to-face confrontation with Pershing in Paris. The report ran to 12 typed pages, addressed to the adjutant general, postmarked "Steamship *New York*," and dated July 21, 1917. In it, he reaffirmed in detail the Artillery Section's report that the number of guns per division recommended by the Operations Section of Pershing's headquarters was insufficient, "in both types and quantity." He labeled as "incorrect" and "erroneous" their analyses of the British artillery strength at Messines and Vimy. In an appeal to the adjutant general to endorse and implement his report, he wrote that "our infantry will suffer great and unnecessary losses if it attempts to advance over any reasonable ground under any artillery fire that can be established by the plans of the Operations Section. The differences [between the Artillery Section and the Operations Section] are not those of opinion but of fact. The lives of many thousands of our infantry depend upon a decision with reference to this all-important subject."[120]

When Summerall reached Washington, "the reunion with my dear wife and child was the great event of my return." Almost as important, however, was his determination to have his report to the adjutant general implemented. He invited to lunch Major Benedict Crowell, the Cleveland industrialist, and friend of Secretary of War Baker, who had recently received his commission in the reserves. While Summerall was assigned to the Militia Bureau, he had worked with Crowell on a board to examine ammunition production, and he had come to like and respect Crowell, whom Baker would later appoint as Assistant Secretary of War and Director of Munitions. Summerall explained his report to Crowell, as well as the nature of his "experience" with Pershing's headquarters in Paris, and asked him to inform Secretary Baker about the situation, or, in other words, to persuade Baker to implement his recommendations instead of those of Pershing's Operations Section. The next evening Crowell invited Baker to have dinner on his yacht, where he did "discuss the matter with him [Baker]." The secretary responded, not by overruling the joint report signed by Pershing, his handpicked commander in chief, but by instructing Bliss to appoint Summerall to head a board to recommend types of artillery for the war, with the authority to appoint the other members. The next day Bliss informed Summerall of his appointment and of his authority to choose the members of the board. The latter recommended the 105 mm howitzer for divisional artillery, a measure that Summerall consistently had supported, but which was never adopted.[121]

Summerall never heard anything, however, about his report, or about his appeal for its adoption that Crowell had discussed with Secretary Baker. Neither did he mention either subject again in his memoir. He might well have pondered the fact that Secretary Baker and Army Chief of Staff Bliss apparently overlooked the consequences of an appeal over the head of his commander in chief, such as noting it for the record, or issuing a reprimand. He could also have pointed out that, by choosing him to chair an important committee on artillery weaponry, they had kept him involved in their efforts to build a victorious American army. And although he was right about the lack of artillery fire power and the need for more mobile artillery for American divisions in the war, he could have reflected on the other factors, as shall be noted below, that contributed to the great number of losses of men under his command in the AEF on the Western Front. But Summerall chose once again in his memoir to use a conflict with Pershing to express his bitterness over the commander in chief's criticism of his actions in the Sedan incident.

Upon his return to the Militia Bureau, and realizing that his report had not been accepted, Summerall must have spent considerable time speculating about his future in the army. At the same time, buoyed by the presence of his wife and son, he would have been encouraged in the knowledge that he, perhaps better than anyone else, could train and mold soldiers into first-rate performing units; that he could win public support for the army wherever he went, and that he had earned the respect of his men, many of his fellow officers as a master of his profession, an officer of extraordinary mental and physical toughness, and a principled man of fierce determination. Indeed, he did not have to wait long until he was given a mission to turn men into the soldiers whom he would lead into battles that would drive the German army from France, and assure the victory of America and its allies in the Great War beyond the sea.

# Chapter Nine

*Over There with the Artillery*

Not long after Summerall had returned from France, another crucial issue that bore directly upon the strength and composition of the AEF had to be resolved. At issue was the general staff's view that the National Guard was too inexperienced for combat service abroad. Instead, it planned to draft 500,000 men and send them to France as Regular Army soldiers, rather than call up the guard.[1] A brilliant and ambitious young major on the staff, Douglas MacArthur, disagreed, for he believed "that the Guard's strength could be increased by voluntary enlistments and its expanded units trained to combat effectiveness."[2] MacArthur had been an aide to President Theodore Roosevelt and was appointed to the general staff in 1913, where he worked with Assistant Secretary of the Navy Franklin D. Roosevelt on economic mobilization plans. After the passage of the National Defense Act of 1916, Secretary of War Newton D. Baker appointed him his military assistant, with special responsibility for the new Bureau of Information.[3] He became the link between the War Department and the newsmen who covered it and "was expected," as he modestly put it, "to explain our national military policy to the country and to shatter the prevailing delusion of a world living in security."[4]

After Secretary Baker read MacArthur's objections to the general staff's plan, he took him along when he called on the president to urge the full employment of the National Guard. Wilson agreed with Baker and thanked MacArthur for his "'frankness.'" Later, when Baker said that he wanted to field a division that would cover the entire country, MacArthur suggested that they take men from surplus units in the different states, "so that a division would stretch over the whole country like a rainbow." Baker agreed, and, while officially it was designated the Forty-second Division, it would be known as the Rainbow Division.[5] Pershing gave it his "hearty endorsement," and Summerall's boss at the Militia Bureau, Major General William A. Mann, was named its commander, and MacArthur its chief of staff.[6]

Not surprisingly, given his position at the Militia Bureau and his extensive experience and record of accomplishment as an organizer and trainer of National Guard artillery units, Summerall was promoted to brigadier general on 5 September 1917, and given the command of the 67th Field Artillery Brigade of the Rainbow Division the same day. Camp Mills on Long Island, New York, close to the town of Garden City, was selected as the training ground for the division, and guard units began arriving from all parts of the country. Since horses and the materiel of war were not available, and would have to be furnished by the French when the division arrived overseas, the men were kept busy by drilling, pulling guard duty, maintaining camp sanitation, and toughened by several 10-mile marches every week.[7]

The three artillery regiments that made up the brigade arrived from Indiana, Minnesota, and Illinois, with the latter under the command of Colonel Henry J. Reilly, the son of Summerall's beloved battery commander who had been killed as he observed Summerall's guns in action before the great gates of the walled city of Peking. Reilly was graduated from West Point in 1904, was a classmate of MacArthur, and, like his father, had served in the Philippines. He had returned to teach history at the military academy, where he also wrote a weekly military column for the *Chicago Tribune*. When the war broke out, the paper wanted to send him over as a military correspondent, but since he was an American officer, the British and French refused to grant him necessary permission. He then resigned his commission and joined a volunteer ambulance unit on the Western Front. When the U.S. entered the war, Reilly returned home and joined the First Illinois Field Artillery as a captain, served on the Mexican border in 1916 and 1917, and was promoted to colonel when his unit was called up to become a regiment in the Rainbow Division.[8]

When he left France, Reilly brought with him a complete set of pamphlets used by the French at their artillery school at Fontainebleau. French officers fresh from batteries at the front had written these pamphlets that emphasized methods of instruction on the very latest experiences on the front lines of battle. With Summerall's approval, Reilly supervised the draftsmen, men, and officers of his regiment at Camp Mills who knew French in translating the pamphlets, making copies of sketches and diagrams, and blueprinting them. They even employed a retired French artillery officer living in New York City to check the translation of all the technical terms.[9] By the time the division was ready to sail, every officer in the brigade had a complete set of translations of the most up-to-date information and instructional expertise from the French artillery school that was probably the best in the world.

Quite likely, it was the diligence and hard work of Reilly's regiment at the camp that Summerall was thinking of when he wrote that his "officers and men were superior in character and ability," and that "the highest morale and pride prevailed." He also noticed that "many young college men were in some of the batteries," although he did not mention if any of them were from the Yale batteries that had trained at Tobyhanna in the summer of 1916.[10] Apparently, however, not all of Summerall's men were as pleased with their commander. Historian James J. Cooke, in his book, *The History of the Rainbow Division in the Great War, 1917–1919,* states that Summerall was "noted for his sharp tongue and never liked by his National Guard gunners."[11] Their reaction recalls remarks of other officers and men of the Regular Army and guard who bristled under Summerall's hard and rigid discipline, such as the officer who said he would rather die than live by Summerall's standards, and the "prominent Washingtonian" who referred to Summerall as "just a martinet." Unquestionably, Summerall was a demanding taskmaster and drove his men hard. What is also without question was his success in fulfilling his responsibilities as a commander, whether the task was to toughen men for the physical and mental demands of war, turning undeveloped and rugged landscapes into artillery training camps where the gunners of the next war honed their craft, or transforming "rotten battalions" into proud and viable fighting units. What he required of his officers and men was obedience and conformity to his high standards of behavior and performance. Whether they liked him did not matter. What he really desired, and what he fully believed he had earned, was their respect for his leadership and their confidence in his expertise and ability.

Perhaps some of the guardsmen, like those who complained about Summerall, were among those young men who were away from home for the first time, and in their search for ways to break the boredom of camp life and to relieve the rigors of long marches, found the allure of bars and fleshpots in the neighboring towns impossible to resist. Summerall certainly would discipline them harshly, and Cooke pointed out that by mid-September it was necessary to ban the consumption of alcohol, and to put "off-limits" all bars in the towns of Hempstead and Jamaica. In addition, sectional and other antagonisms arose and led to a series of fights between the soldiers from Alabama and New

York that escalated into a nasty brawl, in which an Alabamian was killed. Although the damage was finally repaired, ill feeling between the two regiments persisted, even during their service in France.[12]

With these kinds of disturbances occurring, it would not be surprising if Summerall were pleased that he had settled Laura and Charles into a hotel in the peaceful and quiet town of Garden City, near Camp Mills, where he could see them every evening. They met Mary Pinckney MacArthur, ever vigilant and influential throughout most of her son's life, who was staying at the same hotel. Summerall noted that she "made particular efforts to be friendly with my wife." Also staying at the hotel to be near her son was the widow of Captain Reilly, and the Summeralls saw much of her during their brief stay in Garden City. A number of other families lived near the camp, including the Summeralls' old friends, the MacKays. They all were "most hospitable and entertained the officers and men in their beautiful homes."[13] One assumes that the rowdy or angry men of the division were kept at a safe distance, probably drilling or marching themselves into docile exhaustion.

At any rate, the Rainbow Division left behind the relatively safe shores of home and moved out of Camp Mills during the night of 18 October 1917, headed for Hoboken, New Jersey, New York City, and then to Montreal to board the ships that would carry them to France. Late that night Summerall's brigade arrived in Hoboken and filed on board an 18,000-ton freighter that had been confiscated in New York Harbor from its German owners, hurriedly reconditioned as a troop transport, and renamed the USS *President Lincoln*. On board were about 5,000 men of the brigade and some 1,500 crewmembers, all crammed into five decks that reached to the very bottom of the ship. Summerall, who does not mention saying his good-byes to his wife and son in his memoir, promptly met with the ship's captain and executive officer to make plans to evacuate the ship if it were torpedoed and disabled by torpedoes. Among the precautions taken, the men were instructed to wear their life vests at all times; the ship was equipped with only about a dozen life boats, so life rafts were constructed out of wooden crates filled with empty five-gallon cans; rope ladders were made to hang over the sides of the ship so that the men could climb down and hold on to the floating crates of cans; the men were ordered not to jump into the sea; sentinels were appointed to close off the ship's compartments after the men had left; and every day alarms would be sounded at different times to signal formation on deck prior to evacuation. The goal was to have every man on deck in formation and ready to abandon ship in less than five minutes.[14] At sea, the men rose at reveille at 0630 hours and spent the rest of the day drilling, washing down the decks and collecting trash. They paused for dinner (lunch) at 1200 hours, a band concert from 1430 to 1530, and supper at 1600 hours. Retreat was sounded one-half hour before sunset, and all white lights were extinguished before dark.[15]

Also on board was a battalion of black soldiers that Summerall described as "grave registration troops." He recalled that they "could not be trusted on [the top] deck and [were] formed between decks with orders to go on deck [only] when instructed."[16] He cited no specific reasons for that remark and expressed no reservations about their being formed between decks, spaces that must have been especially stifling and uncomfortable. Perhaps he retained the contention of Pershing, as well as that of other top commanders in the AEF, that black soldiers had been unreliable and would later claim that they had fought poorly in the war. Perhaps he had the engrained view of black soldiers that a segregated army perpetuated before and during the course of two world wars and their aftermath; or, perhaps his belief that black soldiers could not be trusted stemmed from his vivid memory of the violence and upheavals of his childhood and youth that swept across central Florida, and were fueled by racial conflicts.

The *Lincoln* steamed uneventfully across the Atlantic in a zigzag course for France, sailing with other troop ships and destroyers as part of a convoy, a system that the Allies had devised as the best protection from submarine attacks. While constantly on guard against this possibility, the most obvious and consistent problem for the brigade and its commander was seasickness. As Summerall put it, there was "vomiting everywhere," especially for Summerall, who heaved on his daily inspection tours to the extent that "all inside of me came up." Like most of us who have suffered from *mal de mer*, he felt "deathly sick." He recalled that on one such occasion, after interrupting an inspection tour with a sudden detour to the ship's rail, he turned around to find his staff of 15 standing smartly at attention behind him. He managed to say, "That will be all today, gentlemen," after which they saluted, and he staggered off to his bunk. His aide, Lieutenant Alban B. Butler, sketched a cartoon of the scene and included it in the day's mimeograph, "for the amusement of all."[17]

The day before they reached St. Nazaire, the old and beautiful city on the Bay of Biscay at the mouth of the Loire River, the engine on the *Lincoln* failed, because, Summerall believed, Germans had sabotaged it before the Americans had confiscated the ship. The *Lincoln* dropped out of the convoy and floated helplessly, an easy prey for German submarines. Fortunately, a repair crew fixed the engine, and to everyone's great relief, they reached St. Nazaire unharmed. They docked safely on 31 October, after a sickening voyage of 13 days.[18]

St. Nazaire was the most important of several ports on the western coast of France south of Brittany, where soldiers of the AEF would first land on French soil. Pershing and his staff decided that American divisions would appear in the line and train in trench warfare in a relatively quiet sector until they were ready to form an independent force. They selected the Lorraine sector between the Argonne Forest and the Vosges Mountains, an area about 50 miles wide, that lay some 400 miles to the east of St. Nazaire. In this area the AEF could find billeting, train in trench warfare, and prepare to strike a decisive blow against the Germans, but which they believed they might not be able to accomplish before 1919.[19]

In September, so that he could be closer to the sector, Pershing had moved his headquarters from Paris into a four-story barracks in the city of Chaumont, about 150 miles southeast of the capital, roughly 75 miles southwest of the Lorraine sector. Railroads from the ports to the sector ran south of the routes that supplied the Allies to the north, and thus were more available to supply the AEF with the men, weapons, and resources to fight the war. Jutting over 15 miles into the sector was the St. Mihiel salient, controlled by the Germans since early in the war, allowing them to concentrate fire on the rail line from Paris to the important industrial city of Nancy. It was a tempting target, and a successful American attack on the salient would eliminate this threat. It also would cut off from the German armies in the northwest their rail center at Metz, just north and east of the sector, deprive them of the coalfields of the Saar, and the iron ore deposits of the Longwy-Briey region, to the east of Lorraine. In addition, and perhaps just as importantly, a victorious American attack on the salient would be a huge morale boost for the home front.[20]

Summerall's brigade remained on board the *Lincoln* for three days, unloading the freight and cleaning up the ship. He granted them a day of shore leave, but before they were allowed to leave the ship, he ordered that they all take baths, put on clean underwear and socks, remove any spots from their uniforms, clean and shine their shoes, have their hair cut short and be neatly shaven, have all buttons sewed on, and all pockets buttoned.[21] He wanted to make sure they were in "presentable condition" that would reflect their professional expertise to the French.

Summerall recalled with disappointment how the French, who stood alongside the dock to witness the arrival of the brigade, unlike the crowds who lined the boulevards of Paris to cheer Pershing when he arrived, welcomed their new allies with a surprising lack of enthusiasm and an attitude that he considered downright unfriendly. He attributed this dour reception to their belief, as he saw it, that the coming of American soldiers only meant that the bloodletting and suffering of the war would continue, regardless of the outcome. He felt that "the French were completely defeated mentally and physically and they would have surrendered at any moment but for the arrival of the American Army."[22]

The recollection of Louis Collins, a Minnesotan with the 151st Regiment of the brigade, was just the opposite. He wrote that when his regiment paraded ashore on 3 November, under a brightly shining sun, "the streets were strewn with flowers, and lined with men, women, and children who greeted the Americans as their saviors. The children marched the whole way, under the men's feet most of the time." When the entire brigade left the ship, he noted that the "Americans really fraternized with the French."[23] Perhaps Summerall's gloomy assessment of the French was the result of his looking back on the egregious collapse, before the armies of the Third Reich in 1939, of the nation for which his men had suffered and sacrificed so much as they fought to free France from the burdens of war, as well as from the power and presence of the army of the German Empire.

As Summerall and his brigade prepared to begin the march that would bring them to the front lines of battle, they received some disturbing news. Pershing and GHQ had issued an order designating the division as a replacement division, that is, a division that would be essentially cannibalized to supply soldiers and equipment to a corps that GHQ was organizing. To Pershing and his staff this seemed reasonable. The divisions in France that would make up the corps were already short 20,000 men; if National Guard divisions were not used as replacement divisions, then the newly established divisions of the National Army (made up of draftees) would have to be, and they were not expected to arrive in France anytime soon; and since the brigades of the Rainbow Division had been transported to France in different ships, their dispersal would be faster and less disruptive. General Mann protested that the Rainbow had been a unifying force for the country, and its elimination would come as a great shock.[24] MacArthur appealed directly to Pershing's chief of staff, James Harbord, now a brigadier, and urged him to check out the division personally before disbanding it.[25] Harbord did, and submitted to Pershing a report stating the reasons for and against the replacement proposal. His most detailed reasons were against the proposal. He pointed out that although the relatively aged General Mann had since been replaced by Major General Charles T. Menoher, a classmate of Pershing, Mann remained, stated Harbord, "an active politician." He also stated that division had "perhaps more spirit than any other division" and "has figured more in the press [thanks to MacArthur] and has more friends to resent the matter." He closed his report to Pershing with perhaps his most persuasive argument, stating "that if you used it for replacement without notice to the War Department that you would be reversed; on the other hand if you ask the War Department that you will not be permitted to do it."[26] Harbord's report convinced Pershing to revoke his order, and he designated the Forty-first Division that arrived from the West in December, and the Thirty-second Division that arrived from Michigan and Wisconsin in February, as replacement divisions to sustain the ones already there.[27]

Curiously enough, Summerall did not mention in his memoir the concern among his officers about Pershing's replacement order. Henry J. Reilly, in his history of the division, *American All: The Rainbow at War*, states that, as their transports tied up to the docks at St. Nazaire, the division "faced one of its greatest crises!" The officers were not immediately aware of it, he wrote, but became suspicious when the artillery brigade was kept on board the *Lincoln*, even though Coetquidan (that once had been Napoleon's artillery base) and was one of two artillery training camps in France, was only 70 miles northeast of St. Nazaire, and just west of the city of Rennes in Brittany. They became even more worried when they were ordered not to Coetquidan, but to two nearby villages where there was no ground available for training and firing. Their worries were confirmed when Summerall called the three colonels of the brigade into his cabin and read them the telegram he had received from MacArthur with the news that GHQ planned to make the Forty-second a replacement division. They resolved to stop that from happening.[28]

Summerall, moving with "characteristic decision and energy," told Reilly and his fellow colonels that he would leave immediately for Coetquidan to find room for the brigade. He ordered them to get the brigade ready to unload the *Lincoln* and march the brigade to some temporary barracks outside of St. Nazaire. They left on 4 November, and when Summerall returned from Coetquidan, he chose a battalion from each of the three regiments and loaded them into boxcars with "40 hommes, 8 chevaux" (forty men or eight horses) stenciled on the sides, for the short ride to Camp Coetquidan to prepare the barracks for the entire brigade.[29] It is unlikely that Summerall's "preemptive strike" of occupying the barracks to prevent the division from becoming a replacement one had any impact on Pershing's final decision, but, as noted above, it certainly impressed Reilly and others with their commander's determination and decisiveness.

The barracks Summerall located were occupied by German prisoners of war. He persuaded the French commandant of Coetquidan to move them to a prison camp some distance away, even though the prison camp had not been completed.[30] The barracks were filthy, and Reilly wrote that none of the "horrors" of war left "such an indelible mark on the minds of those chosen for this cleaning up job as preparing these barracks for the occupancy of the brigade."[31] Summerall noted that they were infested with lice and vermin, and Reilly wrote that the lice were so thick that each morning the cleaning crews had to take off their uniforms, put on overalls over their underwear, and tie up their hair with handkerchiefs. To destroy the larvae, they dug up a foot or more of the dirt floors and disinfected the material before stamping it back into place. While talking with one of his colonels, Summerall noticed a fat louse crawling along his collar and wrote that the colonel probably saw some crawling on him.[32]

With the barracks deloused and cleared of rats, the brigade boarded boxcars for the ride to Coetquidan. Each car was provided with water bags from which the men could fill their canteens, candles and lanterns, and a small box of sand, along with one garbage can or two buckets "to be used in lieu of toilets in the cars, in case of necessity only." As far as practicable, the men were urged to "answer the calls of nature at places provided where the train stops."[33]

They arrived amid downpours of rain and the early approach of winter and soon faced another crisis that threatened the survival of the division. As Summerall put it, "a malignant form of measles broke out and most cases turned into fatal pneumonia. The young college boys especially became victims. There was no hospital and no nurses." He complained to corps headquarters, and a unit of nurses from Pittsburgh that had just arrived, were dispatched, after which the health of the camp improved.[34] Historian Cooke mentioned the outbreak of pneumonia and how worried the officers were about the overall health of the brigade, especially when two cases of infantile paralysis were diagnosed just before Christmas, leaving the men in intense fear of "this dreaded crippler."[35] Fortunately for the brigade and for the men of the AEF, no further cases appeared.

With the threat of disabling and debilitating diseases behind them, but having to cope with the cold, misting rain, snowfall, and the clinging mud of November, the brigade began its training under the watchful eyes of Summerall and his officers, and their French artillery instructors, who had arrived with shiny, new, 75-mm guns. Collins wrote that they were "enchanted" with the gun. He called it a "graceful war maiden, *Mlle. Soixante-quinze*," and said, "it was much lighter and easier to handle than the American three-inch piece."[36] Reilly and his fellow officers had studied carefully the French artillery pamphlets he had had translated, so they were able to move quickly to the use of firing tables without having to take much time with theory. Since their horses never showed up, they had to get by with smaller and weaker French and Spanish horses and an inefficient mixture of American and French harnesses.[37] The horse and harness situation slowly improved, and Summerall had tightened discipline. He insisted on crisp and snappy salutes, and on one occasion when a private saluted him in an "admirable manner," promoted him to corporal on the spot.[38] By February, historian Cooke stated, "the artillery men became so professional with their French 75-mm guns that they could fire an average of 32 shells per three-gun battery per minute."[39]

Once again, a National Guard artillery unit, this time an entire brigade, which began their training under the watchful eyes of Summerall and officers who respected and admired his leadership, would reach a level of performance that, as one of its division historian determined, marked them as exceptional professionals in the exercise of artillery firepower. They were fully prepared, as were the National Guard gunners who trained at Tobyhanna, to maneuver their guns "anywhere in the world."

As he had in other areas close to his commands, Summerall carefully cultivated the support and good will of the local people. He visited the French commander of the region at his headquarters in Rennes and presented him with a box of cigars that his host "greatly appreciated." In a gesture like that of General Gourand, the mayor of Rennes invited Summerall, and an officer and soldier from every rank, to a reception at city hall, after which Summerall addressed a large and appreciative crowd, as a university professor translated his remarks. He admired the prized medieval tapestries that depicted the major historical events in the history of Rennes, visited the largest printing press in the world for calendars, marveled at the most complete collection of butterflies in the world, and inspected the nearby training center for new draftees into the French army. When a local countess asked his permission for the nurses at the hospital in Rennes to sell lace and pastries at Camp Coetquidan, he "could not refuse." After she told him that she did not have enough money to buy sugar and flour, he gave her the money she needed. Soon she had amassed such a large amount of delicacies, clothes, laced articles, and "other things," that Summerall had to build a large storehouse for the items. When she asked that he hold a bazaar at the camp, he agreed. It turned out to be a grand affair, with pastries selling at high prices, and the men enjoying the food, and especially the company of the nurses and the women from the Red Cross, who came to help. The good will flowed, and the festive atmosphere broke the strain of camp life and boosted morale throughout the brigade.[40]

As the winter of 1917–1918 intensified during December into one of the coldest on record, the infantry regiments of the division were ordered to prepare to move to a training area at Rolampont, south of Chaumont, to begin intensive training in trench warfare. The artillery brigade would continue training at Coetquidan until February. It promised to be a long and unpleasant interlude. Temperatures were dropping toward zero degrees. The rains were turning into snow, making the roads even muddier and more slippery, and the transportation of supplies more difficult. Some of the men lacked heavy wool overcoats and other warm clothing, and their shoes offered little protection from the cold and mud.[41] Summerall wrote General Menoher that the feet of his men were constantly wet and that the recent cases of influenza and pneumonia had been aggravated by this condition, as well as by the fact that the shoes issued in the U.S. were "practically useless."[42]

On a brighter side, he received a letter from William Lilly, a family friend in New York City, with the cheerful news of a "delightful evening" that he had spent with Laura and Charles in Washington, where he "had found them both in good health, comfortably settled for the winter." He included a list of goods that he and his wife had packed into a "Christmas Box" that they would send along with their "hearty Christmas greetings and best wishes for a Happy New Year." Among the items they packed were tins of chicken and ginger; assorted nuts, cocoa, and potted tongue; an aluminum tea kettle and a fruitcake; eighteen cakes of vanilla chocolate, and two clusters of raisins; woolen and cashmere socks, undershirts, under drawers, rubber hip boots, a waterproof woolen-lined coat, and a pair of sheepskin slippers. Doubtless, the Lillys' hope that "these articles may add a bit to your comfort during the winter days and nights" was fulfilled.[43] If a brigadier general prized socks, underwear and rain gear, one can easily imagine how much the rank and file would have appreciated these essentials amid the bleak winter of 1917–1918.

Summerall also was cheered when the brigade received a shipment of 155-mm guns, and he recalled how much he looked forward to leading his officers and men into battle. He was surprised, therefore, when he received orders dated 16 December to relinquish command of the 67th Field Artillery Brigade and assume command of the 1st Artillery Brigade of the First Division. He replaced Brigadier Charles H. McKinstry, who, in turn, was ordered to command the 67th.[44] On 21 December, Summerall issued General Order No. 6 to the officers and men of his first brigade command, thanking them for their loyalty and devotion, and praising them for having "met the demands of their military service with a fortitude and a sense of obligation that bespeaks for the brigade a success in whatever operations the future may hold for it."[45] Late that afternoon, with the regiments of the brigade lining both sides of a soggy road to bid farewell to the commander who had led them to France, Summerall's car moved slowly between them. He was headed to Paris to catch a train that would take him to Lorraine and to the headquarters of the First Division. He looked back on that journey as the beginning of a new phase of his career that the "hand of destiny" had determined.[46]

The First Expeditionary Division was composed of the four infantry and one field artillery regiments that Pershing had cobbled together back in May to send to France as the first American soldiers to fight on French soil. They were all Regular Army, and although the lieutenants had been carefully selected from the various training camps, only half of the division's company commanders had any experience in combat. Its soldiers were "an undisciplined and nondescript lot," and "many were undersized and a number spoke English with difficulty."[47]

To command these hastily assembled men, the War Department had appointed as the division commander Major General William L. Sibert, an engineer who had been graduated from West Point in 1884. He had had been promoted to general for his distinguished service as commander of an engineer battalion in the Philippines and for his work in building the Panama Canal. Since Sibert had never commanded soldiers in combat, was little known to line officers, or to Pershing, his appointment was rather surprising. The two infantry brigade commanders, Brigadier General Omar Bundy, who had known Pershing at West Point, and Brigadier General Robert L. Bullard, Summerall's former commander and mentor in the Philippines, were seasoned and veteran leaders, as were their regimental commanders.[48] However, Sibert's staff officers did not seem likely to give him much help. As Mrs. George C. Marshall saw them walking in the rain in soaked, ill-fitting civilian clothes past her house in New York City, she remarked to her husband that they "were such a dreadful-looking lot of men that I cannot believe they will be able to do any good in France." Her husband, however, regarded them as men of "remarkable vision and broad judgment,"[49] and he was right.

Chief among them was Captain George C. Marshall himself, who was appointed assistant chief of staff, and then chief operations officer, the staff position designated G-3. Marshall had been graduated from Virginia Military Institute in 1901, had finished first in his class at the Army Staff College and School of the Line at Fort Leavenworth, Kansas, had served in a number of posts, both at home and in the Philippines, and had established a reputation as an exceptionally gifted planner and organizer. When he received his appointment to Sibert's staff, he was serving as aide-de-camp to Major General J. Franklin Bell, army chief of staff from 1906 to 1910, and commander of the recently organized Department of the East. Other staff members included Colonel Frank Coe, chief of staff, who rose to become chief of coast artillery in 1918; Colonel Campbell King, assistant adjutant, who would end the war as chief of staff, III Corps; Colonel James L. Collins, another veteran of the Philippine Insurrection, who had served as Pershing's aide-de-camp, was appointed secretary of the General Staff, and later commanded an artillery battalion in the Meuse-Argonne campaign, where he won a Silver Star for gallantry; and Major Leslie J. McNair, who served along with Marshall as assistant chief of staff, had been with Pershing in Mexico, had gained a reputation as an excellent trainer and artillerist, and went on to become the youngest brigadier general in the AEF.[50]

On 14 June, Marshall and his colleagues sailed from Hoboken in a convoy of 12 ships, arriving safely at St. Nazaire on 26 June 1917. Marshall noticed, as had Summerall, that the French who were gathered at dockside did not cheer the arrival of the Americans. There were only a few men in the crowd, most of the women were in mourning, and the entire scene seemed to Marshall more funereal than celebratory. A few days later, the Americans left these gloomy surroundings and marched out to their barracks, built by German prisoners of war, about three miles from town, and apparently free of lice and rats. Pershing arrived shortly after they had settled in and designated a battalion of the 16th Infantry Regiment to march in a Fourth of July parade in Paris. Marshall and his colleagues on the staff were depressed about the prospects of their raw recruits with their unmilitary appearance impressing the French, but the crowds in Paris, unlike the people at St. Nazaire, gave the Americans a tumultuous reception. He feared, however, that the Americans had not impressed those French military officials who were already skeptical of the Americans' military skills.[51]

On 5 July, the officers and men boarded the French "40 and 8" boxcars (as they became known) and headed toward the Lorraine sector and the Gondrecourt Training Area, about three hours by train from Paris, roughly half way between Pershing's headquarters at Chaumont and the town of Bar-le-Duc, just west of Nancy. They were billeted in the stables and barns belonging to the villagers of Gondrecourt and the surrounding hamlets, and ate in the streets out of their mess kits.[52] Trains carrying the components of the artillery brigade began moving east through Nantes and Dijon, headed for the village of Le Valdahon, just over 100 miles south of Gondrecourt, about 20 miles from the Doubs River port of Besancon. It was not until the last day of August that all of the artillery regiments—namely, the 5th, 6th and 7th—finally were in place.[53] By that time the First Expeditionary Division had been redesignated the First Division, and the three artillery regiments organized as the 1st Field Artillery Brigade. The artillery units were billeted in Le Valdahon and the neighboring villages. As was the case with their comrades at Gondrecourt, they did not find much to entertain them when they were not training, although wine and women presented two attractive temptations.

The men of the AEF, however, seemed strong enough to resist, or at least to limit, overindulgence in wine, and to exercise caution and restraint with respect to women. At home, men in uniform were not allowed to drink alcohol (a regulation that Summerall himself could have written), but Secretary Baker, following the admonition of "when in Rome do as the Romans do," relaxed that regulation, but, as historian Coffman observed, "one could hardly say that the AEF was debauched."[54] The venereal disease rate among American soldiers in France was low, thanks to Pershing's frequent orders, and lectures and pamphlets that reinforced his orders, as well as prompt treatment of infected men at the regimental level. In September of 1918, it was less than one case for every 1,000 soldiers.[55]

No sooner had the men of the First Division settled into their billets, than their rigorous training began. Under the watchful eyes of the elite French Forty-seventh Division, the Chasseurs Alpine (the "Blue Devils"), infantrymen learned how to construct frontline, support, and reserve trenches; and learned to handle their French-supplied weapons, the Chauchat automatic rifles, Hotchkiss machine gun, the 37-mm gun, the trench mortar, and hand and rifle grenades. According to the *History of the First Division*, "the entire day was devoted to work," with the men pausing only at midday for a sandwich and water from their canteens.[56] Practice with the bayonet emphasized the need to kill or disable the enemy, unless he surrendered. At Le Valdahon, a corps of French artillery instructors spent a week teaching the gun crews about their new weapons, the 75-mm guns and the 155-mm howitzers, and how best to use them. The first firing practices were held in early September, and for the next four and a half weeks, five mornings each week were devoted to target practice. During the final two weeks of the course, the American regimental and battalion commanders took over the supervision of the training, with the French officers acting only as observers.[57] When Summerall took over command of the brigade, a foundation was in place, as it was at Coetquidan, for the effective use of American artillery power in the battles that lay ahead.

Pershing was concerned that training at home had not incorporated his principles of open warfare, thanks to the inclination of the War Department General Staff "to accept the view of French specialists and to limit training to the narrow field of trench warfare."[58] To correct this "irregularity in training," as he called it, he established a system of schools in the AEF that would train units up to the division level and would include training for replacements, as well as corps schools for unit commanders and all noncommissioned officers. On inspection trips to Gondrecourt, he and his staff had been closely monitoring the training of the First Division. He had come to regard it as his favorite and determined that it must become the model in every respect, from appearance to performance, that future AEF divisions would follow.[59] Not surprisingly, he took men and officers from the division to provide some of the faculty and students for his schools. In late July, he assigned Bullard and Colonel James McAndrew, a regimental commander, to assist in setting up the system, with Bullard charged with establishing schools to train infantry officers.[60]

Pershing was never convinced, however, that General Sibert, an engineer, who, as noted above, had virtually no experience in commanding soldiers, was the right man to command a combat division, much less Pershing's favorite. In addition, Pershing concluded that Sibert lacked the vigor, military bearing, and spirit of aggressiveness that the commander-in-chief wanted to see in his division commanders. He especially noted the sharp contrast between the appearance of the French "Blue Devils" and his soldiers, and was not assured when Sibert fell ill during a review. He bristled when French Premier Georges Clemenceau visited Gondrecourt and criticized the readiness of the division.[61] Marshall noted that Pershing was not satisfied with Sibert's critique of the demonstration, and "he just gave everybody hell. He was very severe with General Sibert, very severe, in front of all the officers."[62] Marshall, who had chosen the ground for the demonstration and helped to organize it, tried to explain, but Pershing turned away, only to have Marshall put his hand on Pershing's arm and protest the lack of important instructional information from Chaumont. Pershing turned back to Marshall. He reminded him that "we have our troubles," to which Marshall replied that he knew that, but that "ours are immediate and every day and have to be solved before night." Their exchange continued, with Marshall becoming "mad all over." Afterwards, Marshall's friends came up to him and said that his career was finished, and that he would be fired right away.[63] Their reaction was similar to what Summerall's had been when he concluded, after his confrontation with Pershing and his staff in Paris, that his role in the war was over. But Marshall's outburst had much the same effect on Pershing as Summerall's protest had had, convincing the commander-in-chief of the strength of the man's courage, and earning his respect as well. On future visits to the First Division, Pershing often took Marshall aside to see how things were going, and Marshall came to admire Pershing for listening to whatever one had to say, as long as it was "straight and constructive criticism. He did not hold it against you for an instant. I never saw another commander that I could do that with."[64]

Sibert continued to be a marked man, and on 20 October, Pershing told Bullard that he might call on him "to take the command of this division at any moment."[65] The next day four battalions, one from each infantry regiment, entered the Sommerviller sector, a quiet area a few miles northeast of Nancy, and occupied trenches of the French position, supported by a machine gun company and three artillery battalions. With soldiers of Sibert's division preparing for their first action, Pershing was reluctant to replace their commander.[66]

Under French control of the sector, but with American officers commanding their infantry companies and artillery units, the division's battalions moved into frontline strong points connected by cordons of barbed wire. For a month, amid swirling snow flurries and chilling rain, they withstood German artillery fire, fired their own guns and machine guns in response, captured a German prisoner, and fought off German raids on their trenches in bloody, hand-to-hand fighting. In one such raid, soldiers of a Bavarian regiment captured eleven Americans, wounded several, and killed three, making the First Division the first American unit to suffer combat losses in the war. On 20 November, having lost one officer and 82 men in the Sommerviller sector, the troops were withdrawn from the line and returned to Gondrecourt, where the artillery brigade joined them, uniting the division for the first time.[67]

Meanwhile, the course of the war in November, on both the eastern and western fronts, made even more pressing the need for Pershing's divisions to be ready for battle. On 7 November, the Bolshevik Party had engineered a coup d'état in the Russian capital of Petrograd, toppling the unpopular and floundering government of Alexander Kerensky. They promptly began discussions with Germany that resulted in the signing of an armistice at Brest-Litovsk on 15 December, ending the fighting on the eastern front, and making it possible for Germany to shift its military power westward to press for victory before the Americans had a chance to stop them.

On the Italian front, a new and revitalized Austrian army, with the support of seven German divisions, and under the command of German General Otto von Below, crashed through an Italian army at the Battle of Caporetto in late October. The attack was spearheaded by German soldiers trained in techniques that became known as "Hutier tactics," developed by General Oskar von Hutier, and first employed in the successful attack on the Russian city of Riga in September 1917. Instead of long, preliminary bombardments before an infantry attack, the Germans positioned guns and infantry at the last possible moment to assure surprise. The guns began firing a short and heavy concentration of gas and smoke shells that masked the enemy's strong points. Close behind a rolling barrage and attacking aircraft, carefully picked small groups of infantry, to be known as storm troopers, bypassed the strong points. Armed with light machine guns, light trench mortars, flame throwers, satchel charges, and stick grenades, they overwhelmed weak areas behind the lines, rupturing communication and supply lines, leaving the strong points to be mopped up by following troops.[68] It was not until 12 November that the Italians, reinforced by 11 British and French divisions, were able to stop the Austro-German offensive and establish a defensive position that extended south of Trent in the Dolomites, down to the Piave River and along that line to the Gulf of Venice.[69]

As a result of the Italian disaster at Caporetto, the Allies created the Supreme War Council to establish a unified Allied command, and a means of coordinating grand strategy. It consisted of the British, French, and Italian prime ministers and had the full support of President Wilson, who appointed Army Chief of Staff General Tasker H. Bliss, as military representative. General Pershing felt that the Council represented the "realization that Allied success in the future would depend upon better coordination of effort,"[70] and during the coming months, he and Bliss would work well together.

For his part, General Sibert tightened his command, relieving the colonel of the 16th Infantry and replacing him with Colonel John L. Hines, a veteran commander in his late forties, who was on Pershing's staff at Chaumont. Yet, Pershing had come to believe even more strongly that Sibert was not the man to lead the division into full-scale combat. On 13 December, he sent a stinging letter with the subject "Pessimism" to Sibert and Major General Clarence Edwards, commander of the Twenty-sixth Division. He wrote that Americans who had visited training areas had "received a note of deep pessimism, including apprehension of undue hardships to be undergone." In addition, they had "come away with an impression that the war is already well along toward defeat for our arms." He stated that such an impression had originated mainly with general officers, and that no "officer worthy of command would give expression to thoughts of depression, much less communicate to untutored civilians false ideas of the morale of our troops." Pershing concluded by stating that if such an attitude had visible effects on an officer's command, it would "constitute grounds for his dismissal without application."[71]

On 14 December, Pershing relieved Sibert, and with the "moment" having arrived, appointed Major General Bullard to command the First Division. Sibert returned home to head the Chemical Warfare Service, where he served well. Marshall believed that Sibert had been relieved because Pershing's staff "didn't understand what they were doing at all. They had become very severe and they didn't know what they were being severe about. General Pershing was severe, so they modeled their attitude on him."[72]

*Lieutenant General Robert L. Bullard, AEF*
Courtesy National Archives

When Bullard arrived to take command of the division, Marhall and his fellow officers were still bitter over Sibert's dismissal, an attitude that caused Bullard to pass over Marshall as his chief of staff, and instead to appoint Colonel Campbell King, who was the division's adjutant general, and was "a much more moderate person and [one who] didn't get 'het up,'" as Marshall described himself at that point in his life.[73] Bullard retained Marshall as the division chief-of-operations, a decision, wrote Millett, that "he never had cause to regret."[74] Bullard also appointed as his two infantry brigade commanders George B. Duncan, from Kentucky, West Point class of 1886, and a veteran of the Philippine Insurrection; and Beaumont B. Buck, a Mississippian, and classmate of Bullard in the class of 1885, who also had served in the Philippines. Bullard retained Colonel Hines as commander of the 16th Infantry Regiment and was satisfied that Colonels Hanson Ely, commanding the 28th Infantry, and Hamilton A. Smith, commanding the 26th Infantry, were able and aggressive leaders. He relieved the stubborn Colonel Ulysses G. McAlexander as 18th Regiment commander, and replaced him with Colonel Frank Parker, class of 1894, a native South Carolinian, who was fluent in both French and Spanish and had studied at the École Superieure de Guerre. When the war broke out, Parker was serving as an observer with the French army and would prove to be a high-spirited, as well as an ambitious leader.[75]

Bullard quickly concluded that the artillery brigade commander, Charles H. McKinstry, an engineering officer, was not the man to lead the brigade into battle, and asked Pershing to replace him with either William Lassiter or Summerall. As Bullard wrote, "To my delight, I got Summerall." As noted above in Chapter IV, Bullard had praised Summerall's work and lauded his bravery in the Philippines, and wrote only in superlatives about his military and personal qualities. With Summerall's arrival, he noted that "the influence of a master artilleryman and commander was felt, and work increased, as did also for a while grumbling, but soon confidence and reliance succeeded the grumbling." He also wrote that Summerall seemed "incapable of thinking or doing a dishonorable, disloyal, or crooked thing." As a leader, Summerall was one "who was able to secure almost fanatical support and confidence from his inferiors. What he said should be done was done," wrote Bullard, and "Those who did it not from love or confidence did it from fear."[76]

On 23 December, Summerall, with Lieutenant Butler, his aide, reported to division headquarters at Gondrecourt, where Bullard welcomed him, and reviewed plans for brigade exercises and for a final division problem in open warfare. Summerall was then driven a few miles to brigade headquarters in an old stone mansion that was close enough to the front lines for all to hear the sounds of artillery fire. He spent the days before Christmas visiting each regiment and inspecting the batteries in their billets. He noted that the billets competed with each other to see which would have the most elaborately decorated tree, and was pleased that soldiers from every regiment in the division had bought all kinds of presents, decorations, candies, cakes, and chocolates to give to the children of the villages where they were billeted.[77]

The day after Christmas, he left his headquarters on an inspection tour of the three regiments that made up the brigade. He was shocked to discover that one major and four captains were absent without leave[78] and concerned to find that the officers of the brigade had not been vigilant in enforcing discipline, standards of appearance, maintenance of their arms and equipment, and proper care of horses and livery, as specified in requirements issued by First Division headquarters. In a sweeping memorandum sent to all of his officers on 30 December, he detailed their lack of attention to these matters. "Many men were not shaved," he wrote, "and a considerable number had long and shaggy hair. The clothing is generally dirty, and shows that no adequate effort has been made to clean it. Shoes in quarters are muddy and hard, and few show evidences of being oiled or greased. Harness and saddlery show that they are not habitually cleaned, bits are left with the saliva from the horse's [sic] mouths, collars have caked sweat on the bearing surfaces and mud between flanges, harness generally is dirty and trace chains and buckles are rusty. Wagons show the same neglect. Many revolvers and cartridge clips show rust." He stated that the men also showed little evidence of instruction in the use of the pistol, frequently pointed them at inspecting officers, and in one case, one was actually fired in the ranks.[79]

He rebuked the non-commissioned officers of the guard for their lack of "smartness of commands and movements." He found the prisoners "dirty and unkept" and mingling "freely in the same rooms" with the guards. He observed that salutes were totally inadequate. "While nearly all men salute, the hand is not moved smartly and often the men do not turn the head and look at the officer saluted. Many men fail to salute an officer in an automobile." He found the men in the kitchens and quarters were slow in coming to attention, and on the street he noted that "all the men in a group did not salute." He reminded the officers that they would be held accountable for the failure of their units to conform to the requirements laid down by the commander-in-chief and the division commander. He stated that "All officers must possess such firmness, zeal, industry and resourcefulness as will enable them to respond to whatever demands may be made upon their commands without occasioning adverse comment." Summerall continued his lengthy memorandum by noting, "with profound regret," that there had occurred "certain acts of indiscipline of officers of this command. Whatever disposition may be of such cases, the fact that it is possible for them to occur shows a lack of morale that is so disquieting as to require frank recognition and vigorous remedial action. Officers who are so wanting in professional pride and self respect as to commit any act that is incompatible with the high standards of deportment demanded of their positions, not only deprive the government of their usefulness, but they set an example that can not fail to be harmful to others." He admonished them for having attracted attention "by drinking conspicuously in cafes." It was essential, he continued, "that the spirit of temperance enjoined upon the army by the laws of our country shall be observed by all members of the command. Without fortitude and self-restraint and a single minded devotion to duty, on the part of every officer, this Brigade cannot fulfill its high mission." He concluded by exhorting the young officers "to avoid being influenced by false standards and to guard sacredly their professional reputations."[80] It was an exhortation that he himself had followed during his own life and one that faithfully echoed Captain Reilly's assertion that there would be nothing to explain in his battery. It also was a summons that had guided his command of his fighting batteries in the Far East, of the "rotten battalions" on the Texas frontier, of the companies of West Point cadets, and of guardsmen maneuvering across the rugged, eastern mountain chains of home.

Summerall quickly established a vigorous program of training for his brigade, drilling the batteries four times a day, at 0500 hours, 0800 hours, 1100 hours and 1800 hours. After the 6th Regiment had conducted an operation in an attack problem in early January, Summerall ripped apart their performance in a memorandum to the commanding officer. He pointed out the failure to recognize that the weakened condition of their horses would slow down the move of their guns to designated firing positions; he said that their communication system was not operative until after the attack had begun, and that there appeared to be no artillery communication forward. Most serious was a battalion's use of incorrect firing tables that would have placed their ordnance shells behind rather than in front of advancing infantry. He ordered the commanding officer to "investigate and report the responsibility for [this] failure" and personally questioned the battalion officers who said that the tables they had used were the correct ones for the exercise. He said this response had aroused "grave suspicion as to the mental attitude of these officers. Deception in any form," he continued, "is not only contrary to the fundamental doctrines of the military profession, but it is fatal to efficiency and injures most of all those who are weak enough to practice it." Expressing concern also about their lack of initiative, Summerall said that they should have informed him "that they had no table calculated for this problem."[81]

Two days later, on 7 January, Bullard, hobbled by painful neuritis in his left shoulder, called together his brigade and regimental commanders and told them that the division was going into the line to take over the Ansauville sector, currently occupied by the First Moroccan Division of the French 1st Army. It was an area of about four and one-half miles wide that extended east from the village of Seicheprey to the village of Bouconville, along the southern face of the St. Mihiel salient, about 15 miles northwest of Toul. Addressing his commanders in a "shaggy, wolfskin coat," Bullard informed them that the 1st Brigade would move first, followed in two or three weeks by the 2nd Brigade, along with the artillery brigade, and service units.[82] Their performance in this sector would determine if they were ready for a full combat mission. As part of the preparations that he found necessary, Bullard followed up his conference by engaging "in a hate-making campaign against the Germans. I am trying to imbue our soldiers," he said, "with a determined hatred of them, their method, their purposes and acts."[83]

For his part, Summerall continued to tighten discipline, and, in another lengthy memorandum, assigned liaison personnel to infantry battalion commanders, stressing the need for his men "to assist the infantry in securing quick and effective artillery support." They must show the infantry, he said, "the value of the artillery by constant helpfulness in the employment of the artillery." As soon as a call for a barrage was received, he ordered that "all guns concerned will be loaded and fired within thirty (30) seconds after receipt of the call." He instructed that in a normal barrage each gun would be "fired at the rate of six (6) to eight (8) shots during the first minute; then three (3) per minute for three (3) minutes, and two (2) shots per minute for two (2) minutes." Summerall's barrage would unleash a total of 936 rounds during a three-minute attack. If the enemy attacked, "then each gun would fire two shots per minute for as long as necessary." Should the infantry require the fire of a battery being shelled by the enemy, "the guns will be served, regardless of the enemy's projectiles." In paragraphs entitled "Aggressiveness," he admonished every officer and enlisted man "to feel the responsibility that rests upon him for the performance of a full measure of duty." Reviving once again the motto of Reilly's Battery, he said that each soldier "must so acquit himself of this responsibility upon every occasion that he will have nothing to explain afterwards." He told his men to remember that "the artillery is held responsible for giving all the protection in its power to the infantry, even though no call or signal may be made for such protection. Even the presence of our own prisoners in the hands of the enemy will not excuse our artillery for failing to fire at such an enemy." Summing up his view of the vital importance of artillery in the battles to come, Summerall underlined his assertion that "the rule of the artillery must be to fire as much as possible and not as little as possible."[84]

As British and French troops had moved through southern France and across northern Italy to reinforce the Italians after Caporetto, they had cut off the supply of forage from the south for the horses and mules of the First Division, leaving them emaciated, practically devoured by mange, and so hungry that they ate their leather harness straps, and chewed up the woodwork on their stalls.[85] Summerall kept his men busy scrounging for food for their animals and working to bring under control the scourge of mange. They managed some improvement, but recovery was slow. In the bitter cold of the Gondrecourt area, which became known as the Valley Forge of the war, officers and men also suffered as their feet became so swollen during the night that it was difficult for them to put on their shoes in the morning.[86] As various units struggled into position during the final division maneuvers in trench warfare tactics, the men stood around shivering in trenches knee deep in mud, snow, and ice water.[87] Adding to their woes, a blizzard raged during their final maneuver, and Summerall's brigade and its weakened horses had great difficulty moving the guns through deep snow and over ice. In spite of these conditions, Summerall stated that they were able to conduct simulated fire, and he finally "felt confident in our readiness," and pleased that his men had "responded wholeheartedly."[88]

On 15 January, the 1st Infantry Brigade, consisting of the 16th and 18th Regiments, along with five battalions of Summerall's artillery brigade, began their march in a driving rainstorm toward the Ansauville sector. The 2nd Infantry Brigade and the two remaining artillery battalions stayed behind in the Gondrecourt area to wait their turn in the trenches. As the two regiments plowed through muddy roads, the rain turned into snow and sleet. The men were loaded down with 60-pound packs on their backs and heavy overcoats that soon became soaked, and that seemed to weigh almost as much as their packs. Ice patches on the roads caused entire teams of horses to lose their footing, and their heavy loads dragged them down, tangled in their harnesses, and practically helpless. When they were unable to pull the wagons, guns, and carriages up steep hills, the gunners had to "put their shoulders to the wheel" to help them. Along the way, the men slept in billets, on cold, damp straw in haylofts, reaching the sector on schedule on 18 January; that very night they began to enter the muddy, water-logged trenches. Summerall's artillery battalions began arriving on 22 January, and by the 28th, had relieved all of the French batteries. Bullard, Summerall, and their staffs moved on to set up their respective headquarters about five miles south of the sector, at the village of Menil-la-Tour, just beyond a forest that separated it from the village of Ansauville.[89]

The brigades, plus their support units, including an engineering regiment, a machine gun battalion, a signal battalion, military police, an ambulance company, and two field hospitals, held a position that had been occupied since 1914. For some time it had remained a quiet area, where exhausted and depleted French and German divisions went for rest and recuperation. It lay in a valley facing eastward toward the expanse of the Woevre Plain, an area filled with villages, heavy forests, and ravines, all of which provided ample cover for German batteries and shelter for German troops. The terrain was low and marshy, the weather remained cold, with frequent, heavy rains, and even on sunny days the mud never dried out. Essentially, the country had turned into a quagmire. The front line trenches were knee deep in muddy water, and the engineers, as well as the infantry, constantly had to repair them, and if that failed, dig new ones. The men slept in cold, rat-infested dugouts that they had shoveled out of the mud. They suffered from body lice and had to wait for their food and ammunition to be delivered at night. Barbed wire entanglements stretched out from both sides for about half a mile into the area between the lines, known as no-man's land. Pock-marked by shell holes, gouged by water-filled trenches, it was dissected by a muddy and narrow creek named the Rupt de Mad. Beyond this stream, and well behind German lines stood the "picturesque hill" of Montsec, a barren butte that rose to a height of almost 400 feet, and whose slopes the Germans had fortified with machine guns and artillery observation posts. From their positions on Montsec, German soldiers could practically look down the throats of the Americans, and their artillery had had plenty of time to register for fire on any part of the terrain that lay before them. They also had a clear view of the highway linking the small towns of Rambucourt and Beaumont, and running along a ridge some four miles from Montsec and three miles from the village of Ansauville.[90]

During the first fifteen days in the Ansauville sector, while the French retained tactical control, Bullard's men worked to strengthen their positions in the low ground forward of the highway. Draped in his wolfskin coat, their commander "prowled" these positions, as his men settled into their training routine, strung miles of communication wires, and moved forward ammunition and supplies. He welcomed the visits and advice of General Marie Eugene Debeney, commander of the French First Army, and Debeney, in turn, invited Bullard to the weekly conferences of his commanders. Bullard met frequently to discuss tactical matters with General Duncan, the brigade commander, and Colonels Hines and Parker, Duncan's regimental commanders.[91]

Bullard also spoke often with Summerall and his regimental commanders, who were busily deploying their guns in French emplacements on the highway ridge, in positions where they could cover the enemy's rear areas, and any part of the division front. Summerall assigned artillery liaison officers to each of the infantry regiments, informing his officers that it was "the great mission of the artillery in coming instantly to the assistance of the infantry and of minimising [sic] in every possible way its losses and its exposure." Because the Germans on Montsec knew the location of all the brigade's battery positions, he instructed his regimental commanders to construct alternative emplacements under the cover of woods. If it were necessary to locate these emplacements in the open, they must be camouflaged. He stated that officers were "expected to have sufficient resourcefulness to overcome any shortage in camouflage, and this will not be accepted as a reason for delaying the construction [of alternative emplacements]." He impressed upon every artillery officer that it was his duty "to cultivate the most cordial relations with the infantry and to encourage, in every possible way, that spirit of co-operation which will stimulate the infantry to call without hesitation and with a full confidence in an effective and glad response under every condition of service that might arise."[92]

Under Summerall's careful observation, and in accordance with his instructions, his men established telephone lines of communication from his headquarters out to the regimental headquarters to all posts of command and to all battery positions. Summerall checked out each battery every day and frequently went with Hines or Parker to visit their regiments to make certain their front lines units were confident in the support they received from his artillery. His brigade had created code names taken from the names of American Indian chiefs for Summerall and his staff, assigning the name of "Sitting Bull" to their own chief. Quite likely, they picked it because they knew Summerall's reputation for remaining composed and resolute under fire, and ready to fight, no matter how fierce the fire of battle might rage around him. "Sitting Bull is on the way," was the message from one battery to the next, as Summerall inspected each emplacement.[93]

Although the Ansauville sector was supposed to remain quiet, the Germans began firing high explosive and gas shells as soon as the Americans had moved into the area. Enemy planes directed fire for their batteries and strafed the American lines. Casualties mounted among the men in the trenches and in the artillery, and those who had been sickened from the filth and cold of the trenches succumbed to their sicknesses, and, along with their comrades, began to fill in the cemetery that had been prepared for the war dead. During an inspection, Summerall's eyes became so inflamed from mustard gas he contacted that the doctor treating him ordered him to stay in bed with wet cloths applied to his eyes. Private William H. Steamer came to his bedside, and, as Summerall recalled, sent away the orderly who had been assigned to him. When Summerall asked Steamer who had sent him, "He said no one. I kept him," wrote Summerall of the faithful Steamer, "and he proved an invaluable help and friend during the war and for the rest of my life."[94] Three days passed before Summerall's eyes cleared enough for him to leave his billet.[95] Bullard's good relations with General Debeney paid off when the French commander, after much urging from the American, put the Ansauville sector under the control of the First Division on 5 February. Bullard was ready for aggressive action, and promptly published Instructions No. 1, ordering his men to "Be active all over no-man's-land; do not leave its control to the enemy." Front line commanders were ordered to "immediately locate and report all places where there is a favorable opportunity for strong ambuscades and for raids on the enemy's lines and advance posts."[96] Summerall made sure his gunners were ready by ordering daily exercises, in which each gun squad was drilled against the clock for sighting of targets, fusing projectiles, and loading and firing their gun. Each gunner was drilled independently against the clock in his duties, in order to see who was the fastest and most precise in his work. In this way, be believed that "a competitive spirit will be developed among them for excellence."[97]

All of Summerall's well-drilled and finely tuned artillery was now moved into the sector to provide full support for infantry patrols looking for the enemy's presence or any sign of enemy activity in no-man's-land. During the month of February, Summerall's guns fired more than 1,000 shells a day. The Germans responded by firing more than 800 shells a day, precipitating an artillery duel that dominated the fighting for the next two months as each side tried to knock out the other's gun emplacements. Quite probably, both sides used gas in one out of every 10 shells.[98] On an inspection trip in mid-February, Pershing and his staff found the infantry-artillery coordination excellent,[99] and Summerall wrote that "morale was high and pride grew with efficiency and confidence."[100]

Gas, however, had long been a problem in the sector, and before the Americans had moved in, the French had warned of the danger. In the early morning hours of 26 February, the Germans launched a gas attack on a wooded area just beyond the village of Seicheprey, about four miles from Montsec, and about one mile north of the Rambucourt-Beaumont highway. The attack hit the 3rd Battalion of the 18th Infantry, killing eight and incapacitating 77 others who had inhaled the vapors of phosgene gas. On 26, 27, and 28 February, the Germans shelled Summerall's batteries along the highway with mustard gas, concentrating their fire on the position on a battalion of the 6th Regiment.[101] The bombardment so overwhelmed the battalion that Summerall had to evacuate the men to a field hospital, "where they lay with their faces and burned bodies covered with bandages."[102]

As the shelling continued, Major Robert R. McCormick, commanding two batteries of the 5th Artillery Regiment, feared a German attack and requested permission from brigade headquarters to fire on enemy positions. McCormick, who owned the *Chicago Tribune*, and ran it with his cousin Joseph M. Patterson, was a National Guardsman, had entered the artillery training school at Valdahon, and had been assigned to the 5th Artillery, "because," as he frankly stated later, "I had to be attached to something."[103] When an inexperienced reserve officer on duty at brigade headquarters refused his request, McCormick angrily ordered his gunners to open fire, precipitating an artillery duel that lasted four hours. After the shelling subsided, Summerall ordered McCormick to report to brigade headquarters, and he arrived at lunchtime, expecting the worst. Instead, Summerall rose from the table, greeted McCormick with a handshake and surprisingly declared that "Thank God there is one man in this outfit who knows when to disobey an order."[104] As McCormick's biographer, Richard Norton Smith notes, "Summerall was not always so forgiving," and later gave McCormick a brutal dressing-down for leaving his Post of Command to check on a report that his shells were falling on attacking American soldiers. Smith notes that in his war diary, McCormick slighted Summerall's ability as an artilleryman and leader, but in his later years, he developed a deep admiration for his former commander, as did Summerall for McCormick.[105] It was a mutual admiration society that would prove especially beneficial to the fortunes of a struggling military college in South Carolina, and for the retired general who became its president in 1931.

The German attack in late February convinced Bullard that the enemy was preparing a major raid against that part of the sector. He withdrew the 18th Infantry into counterattack positions behind the trenches, and in the early daylight hours of 1 March, "a tornado" of high explosive shells and mustard gas burst across the sub-sector, followed by a German raiding party of 220 assault troops, equipped with light machine guns and flamethrowers. German shells deluged Summerall's gunners and wiped out their telephone lines; but his men regrouped and opened fire, as they had been taught and ordered. The battalion's machine gunners kept firing as well, and a fierce counterattack by the infantry stopped the assault, forcing the Germans to pull back across the churned and bloody ground of no-man's-land. They left behind 17 dead and four prisoners; the Americans suffered 54 casualties.[106]

The next day the French issued a general order congratulating the division and "in particular the 3rd battalion of the 18th Infantry, as well as the American artillery whose precise and opportune action contributed to the success."[107] On the following day, French Premier Georges Clemenceau arrived at Bullard's headquarters to express his admiration of the regiment's conduct. Bullard liked the short, stocky, and vigorous 77-year-old with the thick gray mustache, whose fierce and aggressive leadership had earned him the nickname "The Tiger." He reminded Bullard of Andrew Jackson, whom Clemenceau greatly admired, and, in a gesture the seventh president, but not Summerall, likely would have approved, Bullard offered a drink of American whiskey to the French premier, who "swallowed his without grimace."[108]

After Clemenceau and his party of French officers had left, Bullard's top commanders sat down with Colonel Marshall's staff to plan retaliatory trench raids for the First Division. They scheduled two raids for the night of 3–4 March. March 4 coincidentally was Summerall's 51st birthday. They carefully rehearsed every feature, leaving Summerall with the impression that their plans were perfect.[109] As the first raiding party prepared to move out at 0100 hours, his brigade, reinforced with French guns, unleashed a box barrage with the fire of 250 guns.[110] They fired a second box barrage, but then received reports that neither raid had taken place. "We were puzzled," wrote Summerall, who noted that when GHQ asked Bullard who was responsible for the failures, he replied that he himself took full responsibility. "The effect was electric," wrote Summerall, for "almost every officer and man in the division knew that he would never be a scape goat [sic] if he did his duty. From that moment, there was complete mutual confidence in all grades and a determination that no one should ever fail. I believe that what became known as the 'Spirit of the First Division' was born then and grew to perfection."[111] In his *History of the First Division*, he wrote that he later found out that the raids had been aborted because the long, so-called Bangalore torpedo tubes that were to be used to blast holes through the enemy's wire were too long to be maneuvered through the tight turns in the communication trenches. Colonel Marshall added that the engineers, in their haste to deploy the tubes, tried to find a more direct route and got lost in the dark.[112] In his memoir, Summerall stated that no one was to blame for the failure of the raids. But, as he looked back across the years through the perspective, once again, of his clash with Pershing's staff in Paris, and his resentment of Pershing's criticism of his role in the Sedan incident, he wrote that had it not been for the courage of Bullard and his loyalty to his soldiers, "G.H.Q. would have crucified some innocent officer for not thinking about the length of the tubes."[113]

Bullard and Marshall, as well as Pershing, were disappointed by the failure, but there is no indication that Pershing contemplated any sort of punishment for Bullard or any other officer of the division. Moreover, the French were pleased with the aggressiveness of the division, and no one thought of abandoning the plan.[114]

On 9 March, the 2nd Infantry Brigade replaced the 1st, with the raiding parties remaining in the sector, and Bullard rescheduled the raids for 11 March. This time the gaps in the German wire would be cut in advance by the artillery, followed by machine gun and artillery fire to prevent the Germans from repairing the gaps. The barrage worked to perfection, but the Germans did not cooperate. They had fallen back to their third trench line, about 300 meters from no-man's-land, and had avoided the barrage. Having encountered no Germans, the raiding parties returned safely, shielded by the counterbattery fire of Summerall's gunners that had suppressed any German artillery fire. That same day, Bullard wrote Summerall, expressing his appreciation of his artillery's efficiency and effectiveness in enabling the raiding parties to carry out their missions, and for inflicting heavy losses on the enemy.[115]

The Germans, however, were not finished with the First Division and its artillery brigade. They shelled and gassed the fresh infantry in the front lines, but most of the gas and high explosive shells burst on the positions and the billets of supporting units of the artillery. From Montsec, German gunners spotted and shelled every position the 6th Regiment occupied, killed nine men in the 5th Regiment, 14 in a machine gun battalion, and caught in deadly fire the relief and supply detachments. On 19 March, raiding parties from the 2nd Brigade's 26th and 28th Regiments retaliated. Skillfully they cut through German wire, crept up silently on enemy outposts, and bayoneted, clubbed, shot at close range, and grabbed prisoners to bring back and interrogate. Preceded by a heavy box barrage, the German infantry staged a major raid a few nights later, only to find themselves overwhelmed by a barrage that killed most of the raiders before they had cleared their own lines.[116]

Behind their lines, the Americans continued to endure daily and nightly gas and high explosive shelling; to struggle against the cold, mud, disease, and lice; to repair and rebuild dugouts and shelters; to cope with damaged and faulty communications; and to care for weak and mangy horses. For Summerall, the fight against the German army in these conditions marked an important stage in the growth of the division, forging bonds between individuals, arms, and services that would endure among those who succeeded the men of Ansauville, almost all of whom would be dead by the end of the war.[117]

As the Valley Forge winter slowly gave way to the unsettled month of March, the Allies feared that the German army, infused with divisions freed from the Eastern Front after the armistice and peace with Russia, would mount a great offensive to win the war on the Western Front. Their worst fears were realized on 21 March, when General Ludendorff, using the same Hutier tactics he had employed at Riga and Caporetto, unleashed 63 divisions transferred from Russia against the junction of the British and French armies between Cambrai and St. Quentin, some 75 miles east of the strategic railroad center of Amiens on the Somme River, and 125 northeast of Paris. It was the beginning of *Kaiserschlacht*, the "emperor battle" to end the war. Exploiting the lack of a unified command on the Allied side, the attack itself, code named *St. Michael*, created a wedge 40 miles deep and 40 miles wide

*German defensive position*

Courtesy National Archives

that divided British and French forces. By 24 March, the Germans were just 30 miles from Amiens; if it fell, the way to the Channel ports would be open.[118]

With a strategic disaster looming, the Supreme War Council met on 26 March at Doullens, about 18 miles northwest of Amiens, and appointed French General Ferdinand Foch coordinator of the Western Front. Two days later Pershing met with Foch and offered him "Infantry, artillery aviation, all that we have are yours."[119] It soon became clear, however, that the Doullens agreement did not give Foch the authority he needed to organize and launch offensive to reverse the German advance. On 3 April, the War Council met again, with Clemenceau and Lloyd George in attendance, as well as Bliss and Pershing, at the town hall in Beauvais, about midway between Amiens and Paris. They named Foch commander in chief of Allied forces, entrusting to him "the strategic direction of military operations." British, French, and American commanders-in-chief retained tactical control of their forces, and each had the right to appeal to his respective government, "if in his opinion, the safety of his Army is compromised by any order received from General Foch."[120] As the meeting broke up, Lloyd George asked Foch if he should bet on him or Ludendorff, and Foch answered, "You can bet on me, and you will win."[121] Although "Foch's influence was more personal and inspirational than organizational," as Donald Smythe points out, Pershing wrote that he was pleased that the question of supreme command was settled, and "with almost unlimited American reinforcements looming on the horizon, the chances of Allied success were much improved."[122]

The German offensive had occurred as Pershing continued working toward his goal of consolidating his forces into an American army in the Lorraine sector. In addition to the First Division, three other divisions had been training with the French in quiet sectors—the Second and Forty-second in Lorraine, and the Twenty-sixth ("Yankee" Division) in Chemin des Dames.[123] Already in January, he had organized I Corps, with headquarters at Neufchateau, about 50 miles northeast of Chaumont, and had named

Major General Hunter Liggett, the overweight and arthritic, yet robust and brilliant former president of the War College, as commander. When the Germans launched their offensive, Pershing was preparing to organize all four divisions under Liggett's I Corps and move the latter's headquarters to Toul, north of Neufchateau, and closer to the St. Mihiel salient.[124] As Pershing wrote of the German offensive, "the storm broke," and the occupation and organization of an entirely American sector had to be postponed indefinitely.[125] He ordered the Second Division to lengthen its sector and sent the Forty-second to relieve a French division at the front. At the request of Pétain and Foch, Pershing transferred the First Division from the Lorraine sector to a position in reserve at Gisors, just over 20 miles southwest of Beauvais, and ordered the Twenty-sixth to relieve the First in the Ansauville sector.[126]

As the First Division prepared for its relief, Bullard continued to struggle with neuritis in his shoulder and right arm, but it was not nearly so troubling as the matter that he called "the most irritating experience of my life,"[127] one that Summerall considered just as disturbing. The crisis developed after Bullard gave to Summerall and his staff the job of policing the sector, before turning it over to the Twenty-sixth Division.[128] When elements of that division began entering the First Division's lines on 1 April, Summerall renewed his acquaintance with his good friend, General Lassiter, who had succeeded him as commader of the 67th Brigade of the Forty-second Division at Camp Coetquidan, and was currently in command of the artillery brigade of the Twenty-sixth. Lassiter was apparently in charge of handling the details of the relief for his division, and, as Summerall wrote in his memoirs, "the relief was executed entirely to his [Lassiter's] satisfaction."[129] Others, however, were not as satisfied. Major General Clarence Edwards, the division commander, reported to I Corps headquarters that the First Division had done a poor job of policing the area, and added the far more serious charge that classified documents had been left behind. Liggett ordered Edwards's staff to investigate further, and they reported that unburned classified documents had been found in the Post of Command (PC) of an infantry battalion; they also found dead mules, sick horses and 15 prisoners who had been court-martialed and were awaiting disposition.

Acting on the division's report, Colonel Malin Craig, I Corps chief of staff, recommended to Harbord at GHQ that Summerall and other officers be court-martialed.[130] Harbord informed Bullard of Craig's report but told him that GHQ would clear up the matter. Later, after Pershing's investigators cleared the First Division of the charges, he told Bullard in so many words to forget about the matter and not to waste his time on it.[131] "This satisfied me," wrote Bullard, but he was furious, anyway. He continued to blame Edwards, who he said "was so fault-finding and made such bad reports of us to our common military superiors that for long afterwards we were kept explaining, fighting our own people behind while we fought the enemy in front."[132] For Summerall, the villain in the piece was not Edwards, but Craig, whom he described in his memoir as "having a sadist mind for injuring others," and who later would conspire to have Edwards relieved from command of the division on false charges that "blighted the career of an able officer." In his aged memory, long embittered by the controversy over Sedan, he believed that "We [the First Division] never felt safe from spying and false accusations, inspired by jealousy on the part of the men we were serving."[133]

With the completion of the relief, the First Division assembled in a large camp just southeast of Toul and rested for a few days before they boarded 200 box cars making up 40 troop trains for the 24-hour ride to Grisors, where the last of the elements arrived on 8 April. Bullard remained behind, hospitalized at Toul, in pain and with his right arm practically paralyzed from the effects of neuritis. After four days and nights of suffering, he "jumped the hospital," put on his wolfskin coat, and was driven to the division PC, where he joined his officers on 13 April to prepare for a division maneuver in "open warfare," or what the French called "warfare of movement."[134] It took place two days later under the observation of Pershing and the commander of the French Fifth Army commander, General Joseph Micheler.

Before the exercise began, Bullard and Summerall accompanied the French general on an inspection of the division. Both Bullard and Summerall were concerned about how Micheler would react to the thin and emaciated horses that had not yet recovered from the hard winter and the lack of forage in the Ansauville sector. Indeed, Micheler expressed his concern that the apparent weakness of the horses could delay the division's entry into battle. Deciding to bluff their way through, the American generals pointed out that these were the thin, raw-boned horses that were common in Texas, and were fully capable of doing their work on the field of battle. At that moment, either a mounted orderly or platoon commander rode by, and, as he tried to turn his horse to give a command, the "poor starved, worn-out horse"[135] collapsed and died on the spot. "Micheler looked at him sadly and rode away," wrote Summerall, and, as Bullard wrote, "the need for us at the front was too great for us to be detained back here."[136] As Marshall later wrote admiringly, "Even this did not faze General Summerall, who is one of the greatest living exponents of the principle that much more can be done than ever seems possible, if one has the will to do it."[137] Regardless of the effects of this "deadly moment," as Bullard called it, both Micheler and Pershing were pleased with the maneuver, and found the division "quite proficient."[138]

In the meantime, the great German spring offensive slowly weakened. British resistance stiffened, and French reinforcements stopped the German assault at Montdidier, just 12 miles from Amiens, forcing Ludendorff to halt the offensive on 5 April. Allied losses numbered about 240,000 and included over 160,000 British and over 77,000 French soldiers, with the loss of 70,000 prisoners and 1,100 guns. German casualties were about the same, and the carefully trained storm trooper divisions were hit especially hard. Initially, Ludendorff achieved tactical success, but as a result of Allied resistance, and because his army was unable to provide logistical support and sufficient firepower to sustain the drive, *St. Michael* was a strategic failure.[139]

Nevertheless, on 9 April, Ludendorff launched a second offensive, that like *St. Michael*, was intended to divide the British and French armies and seize the Channel ports. German storm troopers again struck in a Hutier-type attack, catching the British by surprise, and recapturing Messines Ridge.[140] On 11 April, British commander-in-chief General Douglas Haig issued his famous order and appeal to his armies that "There is no other course open to us but to fight it out! Every position must be held to the last man; there must be no retirement. With our backs to the wall, and believing in the justice of our cause, each one of us must fight on to the end."[141] Haig's order stiffened British resistance, and Foch sent in reserves for in-depth support. When he asked if the First Division was ready to go, Pershing, having just seen the maneuver on 15 April, said yes, they were ready.[142]

On 16 April, he assembled the division's officers, some 900 in all, in the courtyard of the chateau that served as Bullard's headquarters and spoke to them about what lay ahead. They were, of course, the leaders of his favorite division and formed, as he later wrote, a "rare group" that he believed had been "hardened by the strenuous work of the fall and by two months in the winter trenches," and who "fairly radiated the spirit of courage and gave promise that America's effort would prove her sons the equals of their forefathers."[143] In his speech, he urged them to "be an example in everything that personifies the true soldier, in dress, in military bearing, in general conduct, and especially an example on the battlefield. You are about to enter this great battle of the greatest war in history," he said, "and in that battle you will represent the mightiest nation engaged. Centuries of military tradition and of military and civil history are now looking toward this first contingent of the American Army as it enters this great battle. You have behind you your own national traditions that should make you the finest soldiers in Europe today." He told them that "You are taking with you the sincerest good wishes and the highest hopes of the President and all of our people at home. I assure you in their behalf and in my own of our strong belief in your success and of our confidence in your courage and in your loyalty, with a feeling of certainty in our hearts that you are going to make a record of which your country will be proud."[144]

In his *History of the First Division*, Summerall wrote of Pershing's appearance that "The scene and its significance were impressive and became one of the outstanding incidents in the life of the command." Of Pershing's speech, he continued that his words "sank into all hearts [as] he told them of their mission, of their responsibilities and of his confidence in them. His personality and his lofty sentiments were an inspiration, and he imparted the spirit of his own high resolves and resolute purposes." The day after Pershing's speech, the division left for the front. He had reason to believe, wrote an admiring Summerall in 1922, that "in his devoted band his hopes were [to be] abundantly fulfilled."[145] In his memoir, Summerall wrote of the event only that "General Pershing visited the division and talked to the officers. All felt the responsibility of taking over an active sector still reacting to the German attack."[146] This rather terse account contrasts with the words he wrote in 1922 and indicates, again, his refusal to praise the man who had come to support those who had been so critical of Summerall's actions in the Sedan incident. Yet, in the spring of 1918, Summerall was inspired by Pershing's vision and resolution. He was confident that his commander in chief would lead the AEF to victory, and that his "devoted band of followers" would help to achieve and secure that triumph.

# Chapter Ten

*Cantigny and Soissons:*
*The Price of Victory in the Turning of the Tide of Battle in the Spring of 1918*

On 17 April, the First Division began its march to the northeast toward Picardy, where it would join the French First Army, commanded by General Debeney, in their desperate defense against Ludendorff's second offensive in his great *Kaiserschlacht*. This time their line of march took them through countryside unscarred by the lashes of warfare, with flowers blooming and grasses greening under a bright spring sun. On 21 April, with the sounds of German artillery warning them of what lay ahead, they reached their billets in the rear of their new sector, named Cantigny for a small village that lay in ruins some three miles west of a major road junction at Montdidier, about 55 miles northeast of Paris. Cantigny had been seized by the lead elements of the German Eighteenth Army, under the command of General Oskar von Hutier, who had devised the innovative storm trooper tactics of *Kaiserschlacht*. The village lay in a small salient just over 300 yards deep and 500 yards wide and was the deepest penetration in the German March offensive (see map, p. 200).[1]

The mission of the First Division was to stop what appeared to be a drive northwest of Montdidier toward Amiens. To accommodate the division, two French divisions moved to the right and left of the sector, and all three divisions were assigned to the French VI Corps of the First Army.[2] By 26 April, the Americans had taken their places in the line in a wheat field lying in a shallow valley just west of Cantigny. There were no frontline or communication trenches and little barbed wire, so the infantry dug pits, or "foxholes," and were distributed in shell holes that they connected with shallow trenches. The frontline German trenches were so close to the American positions in the wheat field that it was almost impossible to tell where their lines were located. German artillery occupied higher ground in the woods around Cantigny and concentrated fire on the support positions of the division.[3] Summerall's batteries were among these positions, and his men worked to cover and camouflage their emplacements as much as possible. One German artillery burst killed all of the horses in one of his batteries, and German planes strafed the horses that had been taken to water in rear areas. German artillery fire disabled all of the guns in another of his batteries, wrecked some of their billets, and killed "many" men in the brigade. Summerall's men returned the German shelling, but it was difficult to tell just how effective it was.[4]

The long hours of sunlight made movement and trench work so difficult and dangerous during the day that food, ammunition, and water for frontline soldiers had to be moved to them during the night. Even then, German shelling continued. The division and artillery headquarters had been set up in a badly damaged house in the village of Mésnil-St.-Fermin, about three miles from the front. One night, a shell hit the corner of the house and destroyed a number of rooms, Summerall's included,

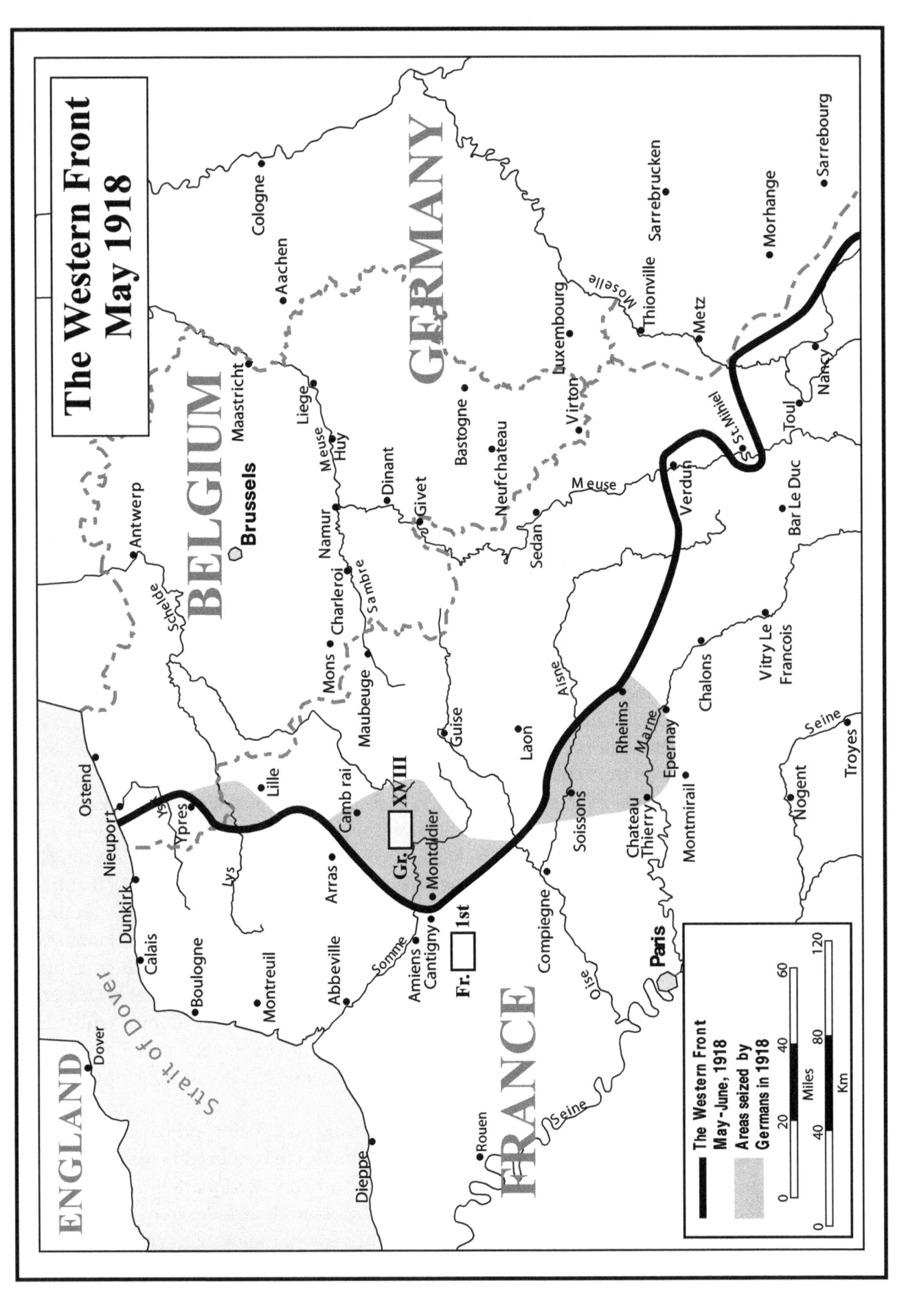

forcing everyone to work and sleep in the wine cellar. Gas attacks were routine, and one such attack eliminated almost an entire infantry battalion. "Our casualties in killed and wounded mounted rapidly," wrote Summerall. Among these losses were some of the division's most experienced and valuable officers.[5] Bullard also was concerned that American losses were excessive, running "from two to four times as great as those of the French." The reason for these losses, he concluded, was that his men, "either from ignorance or carelessness," were not taking cover. At the same time, he believed that his men could "sustain in fine spirits" their hardships and losses.[6]

Meanwhile, the Twenty-sixth Division, which had moved into the Ansauville sector in that controversial relief of the First Division, had taken their positions in the mud-filled trenches along an 11-mile front that was about twice as long as it was when the First had manned the sector. German artillery was still in place on the intimidating face of Montsec. A week after the men of the Twenty-sixth had arrived, and before they had really had become familiar with the sector, the Germans staged three raids before the Yankees managed to fight them off with artillery fire and in hand-to-hand fighting. Ten days later, on 20 April, preceded by a heavy artillery barrage, an enemy force of 2,800, led by storm troopers, raided the extreme right of the sector at Seicheprey, overrunning two companies and support platoons. Reinforcements forced the invaders to pull back at dawn the following day, but the Twenty-sixth's losses were 81 killed, 187 wounded, 214 gassed, and 187 missing or taken prisoner. The men had fought hard and well, but the 669 casualties were far more than the First Division had suffered in the German raid of November, and Pershing believed that the division's leadership, especially Edwards, was responsible. In addition, the German raid caused Lloyd George to raise questions about the leadership of American generals, and with American infantry and machine gun troops now arriving at the rate of 120,000 a month, the Allies began pressing harder for amalgamation.[7]

One week after the German raid at Seicheprey, and after a series of attacks and counterattacks, Ludendorff called off his second *Kaiserschlacht* offensive. Again, and for the same reasons as before, he had achieved a series of tactical successes, but had not won a strategic victory. His losses had been great, almost 100,000; his elite storm trooper divisions had been depleted, and their morale seriously weakened. British and French losses were about 110,000, but the Allies had prevented a breakthrough, and the Channel ports were safe.[8]

The French had expected the Germans to undertake a new offensive against their X Corps in the Cantigny sector in mid-May and were preparing a counterattack. When it became clear, however, that the enemy would not attack, plans for counterattack were dropped.[9] Instead, it was decided that the First Division would attack the Cantigny salient to eliminate the German artillery positions on the high ground and to strengthen the division's defensive position. With Lloyd George now strongly advocating amalgamation, the American command was anxious to prove their ability to plan and execute an offensive operation that would justify Pershing's argument for an independent American army. In addition, both Pershing and Bullard believed that it would also "demonstrate the skill and élan of the AEF."[10]

Bullard entrusted the responsibility for planning the operation to Marshall, who organized the infantry attack, and Summerall, who planned the artillery support. They selected the 28th Infantry Regiment, commanded by Colonel Ely, the hard-fighting, 51-year-old who had won the Silver Star in the Philippine Insurrection, to make the assault. It formed part of the 2nd Brigade, commanded by Brigadier General Beaumont B. Buck. They reinforced the regiment with divisional artillery, machine gun battalions, engineer and rifle companies, and added 368 French guns and trench mortars, 12 heavy tanks, flame-throwers, and air cover. This gave Summerall the massive artillery firepower and support he needed to isolate and destroy the German positions and batteries around Cantigny, and to establish fire superiority and suppress counterbattery fire. The entire regiment would participate in the attack, with its three battalions abreast, and three companies of each battalion up front, and one in reserve. A rolling barrage would lead the battalions forward, and smoke shells would cloud their advance. Both Summerall and Marshall realized that the division's counterbattery fire would be crucial to the success of the attack.[11]

Since the German lines were so close to the American positions, secrecy and surprise were critical to the success of the operation. Soldiers dug additional trenches, but thought they were reinforcing the front lines, and did not know they were digging jump off trenches for an attack. Supplies and ammunition were moved forward, and telephone lines were laid to battery positions, only at night. Aside from the 28th Infantry, only four officers, the colonel and his staff, knew that an attack was in prospect.[12]

As preparation and planning continued, Marshall and Bullard decided to withdraw the 28th Infantry from the front to rehearse the attack, and on 22 May, replaced it with the 18th Infantry. Rehearsals took place on a section of terrain about 12 miles in the rear of the sector and included simulated artillery fire, tanks, and flamethrower teams. The contours of Cantigny and the surrounding area were reproduced on a sand table measuring 20 by 30 feet, and the entire operation was rehearsed three times. Each time their practices improved, and on the night on 26 May, the 28th Infantry began to reenter the lines. The 18th Infantry withdrew but remained close in the rear to serve as reserve or support troops. A battalion of the 26th Infantry, led by Major Theodore Roosevelt, Jr., moved up to cooperate with the main attack.[13] On 27 May, Bullard issued the order that the attack on Cantigny would begin at 0645 hours on 28 May 1918.[14]

The Germans, with their lines so close to the American sector, had noted the increased activity in the First Division. Suddenly, they unleashed a heavy artillery barrage and surprised the 28th and 18th Regiments as they were moving into their positions. Close behind the barrage, the Germans struck both positions with two specially trained, commando-style raiding forces. The attackers were beaten back with heavy losses, and two prisoners were captured. Their interrogation suggested that the Germans knew nothing of the planned attack, so preparations for the attack on 28 May continued.[15]

A second surprise was not so reassuring. Early in the morning of 27 May, Summerall's guns began a general bombardment to destroy the enemy's trenches and gun emplacements, and to undermine the morale of the enemy. As the infantry prepared to follow the barrage, Bullard learned that two German armies had attacked poorly prepared Allied positions along the Chemin des Dames, a 15-mile-long ridge between Soissons and Reims. This was Ludendorff's third great spring offensive of his *Kaiserschlacht*. It ruptured Allied lines and moved rapidly toward the Marne River and the approaches to Paris. Late that evening, Bullard received the news that he had feared: the French corps and division artillery, as well as French planes, would be withdrawn after supporting the attack for one day, and would be sent to meet this new German threat.[16] "This was a heavy blow," wrote Marshall, for it left the division with only 72 guns, most of them the short range 75s, and deprived it of the counterbattery fire it needed to suppress the heavy German artillery that would pound the infantry as they moved toward their final objectives.[17] Nevertheless, after consulting with Summerall, Bullard decided that they would go ahead with the attack as scheduled.[18]

On 28 May, as the sun rose into a clear and glowing sky, over 560 guns of the 1st Artillery Brigade unleashed a "tremendous roar." Exploding gas and high explosive shells spewed pieces of Cantigny into the air with great clouds of smoke and dust, like the earthen debris from an erupting volcano.[19] The inferno lasted for two hours, and precisely on schedule at 0645 hours, "with rifles at high port and bayonets fixed,"[20] waves of infantry swept across no-man's-land, following close behind their artillery's rolling barrage, with the lumbering French tanks abreast or in advance. The attack completely surprised the Germans and caught them in the middle of a relief.[21] The artillery barrage had wiped out

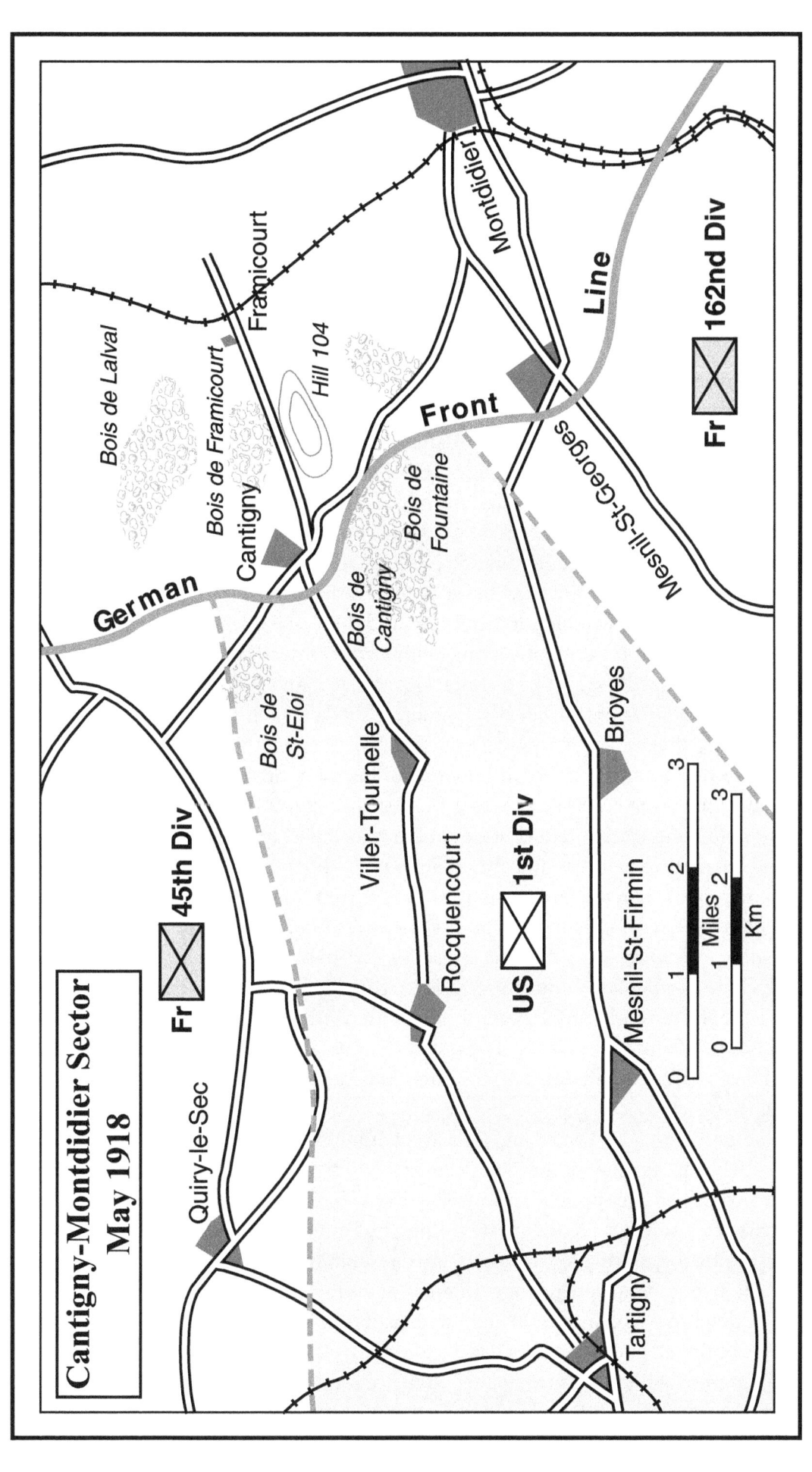

their soldiers in the forward outpost areas, and the appearance of tanks, "which our men had never seen before," wrote the German operations section, added to the surprise.[22] They fled into cellars and dugouts, where they were engulfed by the fires of flame-throwers, or were driven to the surface, captured or shot. Tanks and rifle fire silenced the machine-gun nests that had survived the bombardment, and the areas that were captured were engulfed by a box barrage, and swept with machine-gun fire.[23] Just before 0730, the operations section of the division reported that Americans were seen on the other side of Cantigny. At 0755 hours Bullard's staff reported that all objectives had been taken.[24] Cantigny was in American hands and the attackers had lost only about 50 men (see map, p. 203).

Summerall, Marshall, and their colleagues responded to the news with enthusiasm and delight, but, at mid-morning, their high spirits were dashed when they learned that the French artillery and aircraft were starting their withdrawal. By midnight, all of the heavy French guns were gone, and with them the divisions to suppress German artillery fire.[25] The "air was completely under Boche control"[26] as German aircraft flew spotting missions and strafed American lines with little resistance.[27] Almost immediately after the fall of Cantigny, the Germans began bombarding the newly captured positions and launched the first of what turned out to be some six or seven counterattacks. One of the heaviest of these assaults came about 1800 hours, and the first wave of Germans got to the other side of the defensive barrage before it hit them. The Americans held them off with rifle and machine-gun fire, and Summerall's artillery pounded the second and third waves.[28] For some reason, the German infantry had not been ready to attack at the outset, and there was a lack of coordination between their artillery and infantry. Reinforcements, along with flank protection from Roosevelt's battalion and withering fire from the artillery, broke the attacks, but German artillery continued to pour down fire on Ely's men.[29] Especially frightful were heavy mortar shells that left individual soldiers shellshocked, and in Ely's words, "half crazy, temporarily insane."[30] In his memoir of the battle, Captain Jeremiah M. Evarts, of the 18th Infantry, recorded how one of his men, during an earlier bombardment, wept and prayed out loud every time there was a bombardment. As the shells exploded, "he lay on his stomach in the mud and water on the bottom of the trench and wept and wept."[31] As Donald Smythe wrote, "There are many more such in battle than people like to believe."[32]

With his men badly shaken, and casualties in his front-line troops rapidly rising, Ely asked for relief, but Bullard had received reports that the enemy's infantry was not advancing and told Ely to hold the position.[33] Bullard was reluctant to use his last fresh regiment since there were indications that a major German offensive would soon begin in the sector.[34] As German artillery continued to punish the regiment throughout the second day, Bullard ordered soldiers from the 18th Infantry to strengthen Ely's left flank. The Germans resumed their assaults, and losses in Ely's regiment rose to almost one-third, with casualties among commissioned and non-commissioned officers running especially high.[35]

During the nights of 30–31 May, and 31 May–1 June, the 16th Infantry, commanded by Colonel Frank Bamford, began its relief of the 28th Infantry, with two battalions from Colonel Frank Parker's 18th Infantry positioned in support.[36] At sunrise on 30 May, German shells rained down on the Americans, and another assault surged toward their lines, but infantry fire and Summerall's guns broke the attack. German guns kept firing for the rest of the day, and their planes strafed and bombed across the Cantigny position, but there were no more infantry assaults.[37] On 31 May, the 16th Infantry completed its takeover of defense of the line and began to consolidate the American position. For the next four days, shelling continued and Bullard ordered a night attack that secured their flank. German artillery fire persisted, but the battle for Cantigny essentially was over.[38] The soldiers of the First Division had won their first major fight, and those of the German Empire would never again reclaim the sector named for the small, roadside village in Picardy.

The seizure of Cantigny had cost the division 45 officers killed, wounded or missing, and 1,022 men who had been killed, wounded, missing, or gassed.[39] The German soldiers whom they had defeated and driven from Cantigny were not from first class units, but they had fought hard, and Bullard thought their counterattacks would never end.[40] General Charles A. Vandenburg, who commanded the French X Corps, and whom Bullard especially admired, praised these "Sons of America" and informed them that he and his soldiers were happy to call them "The Men of Cantigny."[41] Marshall wrote that Cantigny "demonstrated conclusively the fighting qualities and fortitude of the American soldier."[42] Bullard acknowledged that "Cantigny, in itself, was a small fight," but nevertheless, was "one of the most important of the war in its import to our war-wearied and sorely tried Allies."[43] To his officers and men, he stated his appreciation for their gallantry and steadiness and noted that "The moral effects, to flow from this proof of reliability in battle of the American soldiers, far outweighs the direct military importance of the actions themselves."[44]

Pershing could not have been more pleased with the victory. He congratulated Bullard and concluded that the division's success marked a "distinct step forward in American participation [that is, an independent American army] in the war."[45] At dinner, he and his staff talked excitedly about how magnificent had been the conduct of American soldiers, and he cabled the War Department that his soldiers and staffs were equal to any others. In that same cable, he praised the artillery as excellent, and was strongly impressed with Summerall's work with Marshall in planning the attack, and with his command and control of the artillery brigade.[46] Lieutenant Butler recorded that an English visitor said that he had heard from many people, one of which was "a Prime Minister," that "Genl. Summeralls [sic] artillery "is as good as any in France."[47]

Pershing's pride in the division and his praise of Summerall and Marshall were certainly justified and proper. In his authoritative study of Cantigny, Allan Millett stated that the First Division, indeed, had proved its readiness, but he also concluded that the attack was hardly a test of Pershing's open warfare doctrine. The hard fighting also showed that attacking infantry could advance and deal with counterbattery fire, but only if they maintained close liaison with supporting artillery fire massed behind the line of departure.[48]

In his memoir, Summerall wrote that after Pershing had visited the division headquarters to express his great satisfaction for their victory, he took him aside and said, "Summerall, I am going to make you a Major General and I want you to learn to handle infantry as well as you handle artillery." Reflecting on Pershing's assertion, Summerall wrote that he responded, again from the perspective of his antagonism toward his former commander in chief, as follows: "General, all I know about artillery I learned from the study of infantry and how artillery should serve it." As Summerall recalled it, his reply apparently put Pershing in his place and left him virtually speechless, as they "returned to the house, and he said little more."[49] In spite of his apparently stunned silence, Pershing appreciated the fact that Summerall's masterful organization and use of artillery were crucial elements in their victory. Marshall relied upon Summerall's advice in planning the attack, and Bullard consulted him before every critical decision, most notably on the occasion when he resolved to attack on 27 May, and in spite of the fact that the French had decided to withdraw their heavy artillery. As in the Philippines, the fighting team of Bullard and Summerall in France was proving to be determined, aggressive, and victorious.

The First Division had won the Battle of Cantigny, but the Germans still held every other place in the salient, with its nose tilted to the south to include Montdidier, and its southern side stretching across the Oise River, some 25 miles from Montdidier. Ludendorff's offensive across the Chemin des Dames had carried the Germans into the Marne River valley south of the Oise River and had created a second and much larger salient, known as the Marne salient. Its nose was at Château-Thierry, with its bridges across the Marne pointed toward Paris, and its eastern boundary extended to Reims, about 30 miles east-northeast of Château-Thierry. Its western boundary extended just over 40 miles from Château-Thierry north-northwest to Noyon, just east of Montdidier. The base ran from Noyon to Reims, a distance of about 50 miles. These two salients, in Donald Smythe's description, were "like two huge breasts projecting into Allied lines," with a "cleavage" between them.[50]

To eliminate the "cleavage," French intelligence had predicted that a German offensive would strike somewhere in the Montdidier-Noyon area, and Bullard was concerned that it might strike his position, now more thinly manned with its front lines stretched out to cover the longer front. He was determined to hold his hard-won position and set up three lines of defense, echeloned in depth, with four battalions in the forward trenches, two in an intermediate location, and six battalions in the last and main line of defense.[51] In concert with Bullard's deployment, Summerall withdrew his batteries to defend the in-depth position.[52] The French X Corps had orders to hold the area, but these same orders allowed for a tactical withdrawal to a defensive position. To Bullard, the two aspects of the order left them in "irreconcilable conflict," and would not be understood by his men. His order was "to fight in the first line to the death, and if that line were lost, the second line troops were to counter attack."[53] Summerall issued orders that his guns would remain in action "until the last," and, if necessary, would become strong points for the infantry to make a stand.[54]

Life in the trenches remained hard. The men ate an average of only one meal a day; there was no water for bathing or for washing clothes; no issue of clothing was possible; so, soldiers wore the same filthy, lice-infested uniforms for days until they could return to rest areas to clean up and delouse.[55] Bullard set up headquarters for the division and artillery brigade at Breuteil, a few miles west of Cantigny, in the elegant Château de Tartigny that Marshall described as "something of a miniature Versailles," complete with broad, tree-lined avenues, and formal gardens.[56] It was safer than their former headquarters at Ménil-St. Firmin, but it soon became the focus of enemy aerial bombing raids. Summerall noted that one aggressive attack killed the division quartermaster and others in their billets.[57]

Aiming to wipe out the "cleavage" between the two salients, the Germans unleashed on 9 June, "an intense bombardment with shell and gas" that hit the entire First Division, and German planes began flying bombing missions over the rear areas. In keeping with X Corps instructions, the French division protecting the Americans' right flank fell back, exposing the 26th Infantry Regiment to heavy shelling that took severe casualties. When he learned of the French withdrawal, Bullard and Summerall went straight to General Vandenburg and told him that they could not understand how any "retirement" could be made, and that their division would fight to the last man. Just then, General Debeney, French First Army commander, came in and met with Vandenburg. He told the Americans that the X Corps order would stand but expressed great pleasure in Bullard's determination "to hold the line."[58] They held it, and by 13 June, the German offensive, while gaining some ground between Montdidier and Noyon, failed to reduce the expanse of most of the "cleavage." Their shelling and bombing steadily diminished, and Summerall's batteries responded in kind.[59]

A relative tranquility settled over the division, as spring turned Picardy into a landscape of fields covered with grass, stalks of grain, acres of red poppies, and other flowers of bright blues and yellows.[60] All four infantry regiments remained in line. The three battalions of each regiment were in columns, with one in the front line, one in support, and the third in reserve in the rear. Front line duty lasted 10 days, and Bullard ordered all of his battalion commanders to plan and carry out a raid during that period. Major Theodore Roosevelt's battalion conducted the most successful of these raids, cleverly planning it, executing it quickly, and capturing 35 prisoners, while suffering a small loss in men.[61]

As the First Division held fast to its hard-won position in Picardy, the German drive across the Chemin des Dames had reached the Marne River. It was now the turn of other American divisions to halt and contain this latest German offensive. The Third Division, commanded by Major General Joseph T. Dickman, the burly, thickly-mustached, former cavalry-man, had been in reserve in Picardy, preparing to relieve the First Division.[62] Instead, on 30 May, Dickman's division was ordered to Château-Thierry to shore up the French defenders, contain the Germans, and block their advance across the Marne. The division's motorized 7th Machine Gun Battalion traveled 100 miles in 24 hours and went into action on 31 May in support of a battalion of the French Tenth Colonial Division. For two days they repelled German attacks, blocked the enemy's attempts to cross the Marne, and forced them to shift their attacks to the west of Soissons. The remainder of the division then was brought up to stabilize and secure Château-Thierry and the south bank of the Marne.[63] The French praised their success in holding this line as "one of the most remarkable deeds of this war."[64]

With the Third Division on the way to Château-Thierry, Pershing ordered the Second Division onto trucks to head from its training area in Picardy to reinforce French forces northwest of Château-Thierry. They arrived on 1 June, in the area of Belleau Wood, a thickly forested, rocky, and rugged tract, traversed by ravines, and shaped like a "distorted hour glass."[65] It measured about 1,000 yards across at its widest northern section, and about 3,000 yards in length. The Germans had fortified it with mutually supporting machine-gun nests, shielded by massive boulders that made them almost impervious to artillery fire.[66] The division included the 4th Marine Brigade, commanded since early May by Brigadier General Harbord, Pershing's former chief of staff, who had taken over when the brigade's commander fell ill. Their mission, like that of the Third Division, was to "form a brick wall" and keep the Germans away from Paris.[67]

On 6 June, Harbord's men attacked Belleau Wood and for the next 20 days, fought a ferocious battle. They took the wood, but the victory cost them some 5,000 casualties, over 50 percent of the brigade. Again, Americans had stopped the Germans, wrung from their grasp a position they were determined to hold and had gained the gratitude and esteem of their French allies (who renamed the wood Bois de la Brigade de Marine).[68] The AEF staff considered Belleau Wood no more than a local engagement, and the land itself had little military value, as historian Donald Smythe has concluded. The Marines, however, thought it was worth the cost, and today, as Smythe noted, they still do.[69] At Belleau Wood, they triumphed over what seemed to be an impregnable German defense designed to crush the American attack, and to destroy their will to fight. Having failed to impose their will and power in this crucial battle, Belleau Wood would be what scholar George B. Clark called the "beginning of the end for the Germans."[70]

The two American divisions digging in to halt and reverse the German thrust toward the Marne and Paris did not reassure the French that the resurgent German army could be stopped. Parisians were streaming south from the city, the government was making plans to evacuate, and Pershing was prepared to abandon his headquarters at Chaumont.[71] Amid this crisis, Allied political and military leaders met at Versailles on 1 and 2 June, in the sixth session of the Supreme War Council, in order to press Pershing for more men.[72] There were already more than 650,000 American soldiers in France, but General Foch wanted increased numbers of infantry and machine gun units in June and July, a number amounting to 250,000 men each month. Pershing argued that the French railway network, already breaking down because of the lack of skilled operators and repairman, would have to be improved before it could handle the transportation of that many soldiers. He also stressed that the concessions he had already made to strengthen Allied armies with American units had made more difficult his program to build an independent American army. He also argued that it would be impossible to train in America as many troops as the Allies wanted before sending them to France.[73] Foch replied that they could be trained in France and made it clear that he was not impressed with any of Pershing's arguments. As Pershing wrote, Foch "became very excited, waving his hands and repeating,

'The battle, the battle, nothing else counts.'"[74] Pershing yielded and agreed to alter his shipping program to accommodate the transportation of 250,000 additional combat troops per month.

By the middle of June, another 650,000 U.S. troops had arrived in France. Pershing stopped by First Division headquarters to have lunch with Bullard and informed him that there soon would be two corps, each with two divisions, near Château-Thierry. On that occasion, Lieutenant Butler noted that Summerall for a long time had been advocating smaller corps but with the same numbers of corps artillery in order to increase the artillery support for attacking infantry.[75] By the end of July, the AEF had been expanded to more than a million men and organized into 24 combat divisions. This gave Pershing the grounds for creating the separate field army he so long had advocated. He already had created three more corps headquarters to manage the tactical use of these troops, as well as their training and administration.[76]

On 30 June, Pershing, much pleased with the efficiency of his three combat divisions, and especially elated with the success of the First Division, came to award the division the first Distinguished Service Cross, the new American decoration for valor.[77] As he said, much to the consolation and satisfaction of Bullard and his men: "To the 1st Division first."[78] He left the division in high spirits, and with their guns essentially inactive, Summerall and his brigade took the lead in boosting the morale of the division. Summerall's aide, Lieutenant Butler, ran off copies of a daily newspaper on his mimeograph machine and sent it out to the men in the trenches and battery positions every night.[79] It provided them with news of the war, and Butler contributed cartoons that depicted the conditions of the war with a touch of humor that "gave the men amusement and did a lot of good."[80]

The men of the artillery brigade gathered pieces of furniture and rugs from abandoned and ruined villages and placed them around their gun emplacements; they picked brightly colored flowers and placed them in empty shell casings set on rugs among the "scraps" of tables and chairs. They painted all the gun carriages and made sure that the latrines and stables were kept "in the most sanitary condition." They turned the horses out onto the fields of "luscious grass" that restored the weight their half-fed bodies had lost and groomed them carefully. They treated their animals for mange and lice, and whenever these afflictions disappeared from a battery, Summerall issued the unit a special commendation. As he remembered, "they wanted no greater reward."[81]

On the Fourth of July, the brigade staged a horse show for the division along one of the broad avenues, underneath the century-old trees of the Château Tartigny. At noon, the 155 mm guns of the 5th Artillery Regiment fired 48 shells toward the German lines in a salute to the Union. The batteries competed for prizes and paraded their fat, well-groomed horses and mules, gleaming harnesses, caissons, and wagons before judges that included English and French officers, and ladies from nearby Breteuil. The winners received money, a three-day leave in Paris, and transportation in army trucks.[82] It was a splendid show, a proper tribute to the outstanding performance in Picardy of the infantry and artillery brigades of the First Division.

Still, it had been a costly campaign, with 238 officers and 5,593 men listed as casualties.[83] Replacements were arriving daily to replenish the ranks, and as the division was enjoying the Independence Day celebration, Bullard learned that they would be relieved in the sector by two French divisions and would move to new billets in the Beauvais area, about 40 miles south of Amiens. There they would begin training for open warfare, which would take them up and out of the trenches, and to which the men, as Summerall wrote, "had long looked forward."[84] They did not have to wait very long.

In mid-June, with Allied infantrymen now outnumbering the Germans on the Western Front (thanks to the increasing number of American soldiers on the ground in France), Marshal Foch began drawing up plans for an Allied offensive that would "bring the war to a victorious conclusion."[85] He ordered General Henri Pétain, whose tactics had helped stem the recent German drives, to prepare a counter attack against the German forces in Marne salient. The main attack would strike the western edge of the salient south of Soissons, seize the heights of the Dommiers plateau, and cut through the highway leading to Château-Thierry, as well as the Paris-Soissons railroad, both of which were major supply routes to German forces to the south.[86] If these routes were severed or interdicted, the Germans would have to pull out of the salient, and if the attack were swift and forceful enough, it might be possible to entrap most of the enemy before they could withdraw.

Pétain assigned the attack to his Tenth Army, commanded by General Charles Mangin, who had been languishing in Paris after his part in the disastrous failure of the French offensive (directed by General Robert Nivelle) in April 1917. For his determination to press forward his attacks, in spite of massive casualties, the compactly-built and square-jawed Mangin had become known as the "Butcher."[87] With Mangin's Tenth Army conducting the main assault, the French Fifth Army would attack the eastern corner, while the French Sixth and Ninth armies would contain the Germans and attack from the vicinity of Château-Thierry.[88]

Within his Tenth Army, Mangin assigned the mission of seizing the Dommiers heights to the XX Corps, commanded by his offensive-minded, and hard-charging colleague, General Pierre E. Berdoulat.[89] Already in late May, General Pershing had suggested a counterattack against the flanks of the Marne salient and had offered American troops for the operation. He wanted his divisions to be given a corps area and asked that the Second, Third, Forty-Second, and Twenty-Sixth Divisions be concentrated near Château-Thierry. The French planned to use the First and Second Divisions as the assault divisions in the attack on Soissons, but agreed to form a corps under an American commander in Mangin's army and release a sector west of Château-Thierry to General Liggett's I Corps.[90]

On 8 July, AEF Headquarters informed General Bullard that he would command the III Corps, and direct the First and Second Divisions in the attack against Soissons.[91] In his memoir, Summerall wrote that Bullard sent him at once to AEF Headquarters to arrange for the assignment of artillery to III Corps.[92] Actually, according to the diary that his aide Lieutenant Butler kept, he accompanied Summerall to General Liggett's I Corps Headquarters on 12 July, where Summerall received and wrote out his acceptance of the order promoting him to major general.[93] Then, they drove to Chaumont, where, as Summerall wrote, he was offered the assignment as chief of artillery of the First Army that Pershing was organizing.[94] On 14 July, he and Butler returned to First Division headquarters, where Bullard was making plans to take command of III Corps, and where everyone, according to Butler, was "hoping Genl. Summerall will command the 1st Division."[95] Indeed, Summerall had made clear on his visit to AEF Headquarters that he preferred to be assigned to command the First Division, and Bullard, in the meantime, had urged Pershing to name Summerall as his successor.[96] Pershing had recently rated rated Summerall as his top commander, and his assignment to replace his friend and mentor Bullard as commander of the First Division was assured, and approved.[97] He assumed his new command on 14 July, as Bullard set off to command his new corps. Meanwhile, Pershing, disappointed with the performance of Omar Bundy in command of the Second Division, had replaced him with Harbord, who had commanded the Marine Brigade at Belleau Wood, and who now received his second star.[98]

On 15 July, the day after Summerall assumed command of the First Division, and on the day Harbord took over command of the Second Division, Ludendorff launched his fifth, and, what turned out to be, his last offensive, code-named *Strassenbau*. With a force of 49 divisions, the Germans attacked between Château-Thierry and Reims. The French had been warned of the attack by deserters, aerial reconnaissance, and prisoners; so, their heavy artillery forced the Germans to halt their attack east of Reims. Farther to the south, 14 German divisions crossed the Marne, but were stopped by the sturdy defense of General Dickman's Third Division. The division's 38th Infantry Regiment, under

Colonel Ulysses G. McAlexander, beat off the repeated attacks of two German divisions, and earned the nickname "Rock of the Marne." Two days later, after Allied aircraft and artillery destroyed the German bridges across the Marne, Ludendorff called off the offensive.[99]

As Ludendorff launched *Strassenbau*, General Mangin completed his plans for the main attack against the Marne salient at Soissons with elements of his Tenth Army, specifically the XX Corps, and its First and Second American divisions. They were augmented by the tough French First Moroccan Division that included the famous Foreign Legion. The French Fifth and Sixth armies on the west side of the salient would move forward to support the main attack. Mangin planned the attack to achieve complete surprise and, for that reason, did not inform the two American divisions of their mission or their ultimate destination. To tighten security, he ordered that the American divisions be held in reserve and marched to the line of attack only at the time of the assault. Unlike the usual procedure, there would be no long artillery preparation that would signal an imminent attack, only a rolling barrage scheduled to begin at the precise time of the attack, at 0435 hours, on 18 July. This meant that the infantry had to be in position on time, otherwise the rolling barrage would be useless.[100] Planning was hurried and confused, and Bullard, deciding that III Corps was not ready to function, allowed the First and Second Divisions to be under the command of the French XX Corps.[101] All that Summerall and Harbord could do was to wait until they were told where and when their divisions should deploy, and make certain they were ready to attack at H-hour.

Late in the afternoon on 12 July, the First Division left the Beauvais area loaded into French Model T-like truck convoys. They lurched along the narrow roads at night to conceal their movement and pulled off the roads into wooden areas and villages during the day. They were traveling toward the Compiègne Forest, also known as the Forêt de Retz, that stretched along the western face of the salient, south of Soissons. They reached the woods during the night of 15–16 July, but their horses and guns lagged behind and did not join the division until the following night. They found the First Moroccan Division already in place, but not the Second Division.

After a brief rest in Paris, Harbord arrived on 15 July at Beauvais to take command of the Second Division, only to find that the artillery had already left, although no one knew its exact destination or mission. The rest of his division was scattered all over the Château-Thierry area; and, because of their dispersal and delays in obtaining enough trucks, could not leave until late in the afternoon on 16 July. Harbord knew only that their destination would be in the French XX Corps area. Still, no one had told Harbord exactly where they were going. As he wrote in his diary, he "knew nothing except by rumor."[102]

At 1500 hours in the afternoon of 17 July, Summerall received the XX Corps order that would launch Mangin's carefully concealed and surprise attack. H-hour was set at 0435 hours on 18 July, but Mangin's order had mentioned nothing about the terrain, or about the enemy. Summerall and his staff spent the next several hours completing the operational orders for the First Division, without any knowledge of the ground they would fight over, or of the enemy that lay ahead.[103] They would attack across a two-mile front, with two brigades abreast, and all four regiments on line in battalion columns, with an assault battalion followed by a support battalion, and a reserve battalion in the rear.

General Buck's 2nd Brigade, consisting of the 28th and 26th Infantry Regiments, was assigned the northern sector of the division's zone; to their left was the French 153rd Division. Colonel Conrad S. Babcock had just assumed command of the 28th Regiment the day before the attack, succeeding Hanson Ely, who was promoted to brigadier general after his valiant role in the Battle of Cantigny, and given command of the Second Division's 3rd Brigade. Babcock, regarded by historians of the Soissons battle, Douglas Johnson and Rolfe Hillman, Jr., as a "very thorough, thoughtful, professional officer," was the former Inspector General of the First Division.[104] The 26th Regiment was commanded by Colonel

Hamilton A. Smith, who had been graduated from West Point the year after Summerall, and had fought in Cuba during the Spanish-American War and in the Philippines during the insurrection.[105]

The 1st Brigade, commanded by General Hines, was assigned the southern sector of the division's zone, consisting of the 18th Regiment, commanded by Colonel Frank Bamford, and the 16th Regiment under Colonel Frank Parker, both of whom had led their regiments in the victory at Cantigny. The First Moroccan division, with its Senegalese regiment and the Foreign Legion abreast, was on the right of the 1st Brigade.[106] The mission of Summerall's division was to press their attack across the Dommiers plateau toward the villages of Missy-aux-Bois and Chaudon, and then to keep moving forward.

Meanwhile, Harbord and his chief of staff, Colonel Preston Brown, had received a supply of maps and copies of the XX Corps attack order and worked into the night of 16–17 July, writing their operations order. A French major gave them a brief description of the ground over which they would fight, so they had a little more information than Summerall and his staff, but that was the only bit of intelligence they received prior to writing the division's attack order.[107] As elements of the Second Division began arriving in the Forêt de Retz, Harbord and Brown spent the entire day of 17 July, just 24 hours before the attack, locating the division's units, concentrating them, distributing orders, negotiating their way through roads and woods jammed with weary and bewildered soldiers, and trucks stuck in roadside ditches.[108]

Harbord's Second Division would attack across a front somewhat shorter than the two-mile front assigned to the First Division. Brigadier Wendell C. Neville, a highly respected Marine Corps officer, had succeeded Harbord as commander of the division's Marine Brigade, made up of two regiments, the 5th and 6th Marines. The 5th Marine Regiment, commanded by Lieutenant Colonel Logan Feland, would attack on the division's northern flank, to the right of the Moroccans, in the usual battalion alignment. The 6th Marine Regiment would be held in XX Corps reserve, so Feland's regiment would have to cover the front of an entire brigade.

The division's 3rd Brigade, under Ely's proven leadership, included the 9th Infantry Regiment, commanded by Colonel LaRoy Upton, and the 23rd Infantry Regiment, under Colonel Paul B. Malone. The 9th Regiment would attack along the flank of the 5th Marine, and the 23rd Infantry would advance along the right flank of the 9th Regiment.[109] The Second Division's mission was to push forward toward the village of Vierzy, and beyond. Their right flank was covered by the French 38th Division, and on their left was the First Moroccan. Thus, this elite and veteran French division was in the center of the attack, between the two American divisions, and was ordered to set the pace for their American allies (see map, p. 213).

During the night of 17 July, as darkness enveloped the Allied divisions and lowering clouds masked and dampened the rumbling noises of their preparation, some 67,000 men, 5,000 animals, and 3,000 trucks began moving toward their positions on the jump-off line that was just over five miles long. The few roads that existed were filled with artillery and trucks, and, with the addition of several battalions of heavy French tanks, the infantry was forced off the roads to trudge along in the roadside ditches.[110] As the infantry moved out in long columns, a thundering rainstorm, streaked by lightning flashes, deluged the men, soaking their uniforms and adding to the weight of their backpacks. Amid the blackness of the night, with their eyelids almost closed to keep out the driving sheets of rain as they slogged through water-logged ditches, each soldier had to place a hand on the shoulder of the man in front to maintain contact, and keep moving forward toward the jump-off line. Dazed, sleepless, and hungry, they stumbled and staggered through the night.[111] Forcing their way through the forest, the 5th Marines and the 9th Infantry of the Second Division would not reach their positions until five minutes before H-hour, and their machine-guns would not join the division until the next day.[112] Nevertheless, a huge American force was in position to attack, as scheduled, south of Soissons, on ground held by three German divisions of the Group of Armies under the command of the Crown Prince.

At 0435 hours on 18 July, the roar of artillery and flashes of fire announced the attack of the XX Corps, and Allied infantry surged forward behind the rolling barrage of more than 100 guns, at the rate of 100 meters to two minutes. Warned by deserters and captives from the French 153rd Division north of the First Division, the Germans fired a protective barrage that caused significant casualties in the 3rd Battalion (support) of the 28th Infantry, but the assault battalions of General Buck's regiments on the left, and of General Hines's on the right surged forward.[113]

Major Clarence Huebner, who had won his first Distinguished Service Cross at Cantigny, was in front of his 2nd Battalion of the 28th Infantry as they swept though enemy infantry in the fields of wheat, led by the machine-gun fire and roar of the heavy French tanks. The Germans were taken by surprise and were shocked by the effectiveness of the tanks.[114] Ahead, perpendicular to their line of attack, beyond the waist-high wheat of the Dommiers plateau, the Missy Ravine had sliced a crevice in the earth a mile long, and half a mile wide. Its banks sloped at a 60 degree angle and were covered with tangled vines, scrub trees, thick brush, and stinging nettles. A marshy swamp 600 yards wide covered the bottom, and a small, but deep, creek ran through the middle of it. The Germans had built wooden paths and bridges across the creek, and had set up machine-guns to fire along these routes. They also had placed about 30 artillery pieces along the bottom and had fortified the eastern bank with additional artillery, more machine-guns, and pillboxes. The stone house and buildings of the Saint Armand Farm stood at the eastern end of the ravine, and stone structures of the rather large village of Saconin-et-Breuil were located on the bottom of the ravine at the northern end. On the eastern lip of the ravine was the village

*German Artillery*

Courtesy National Archives

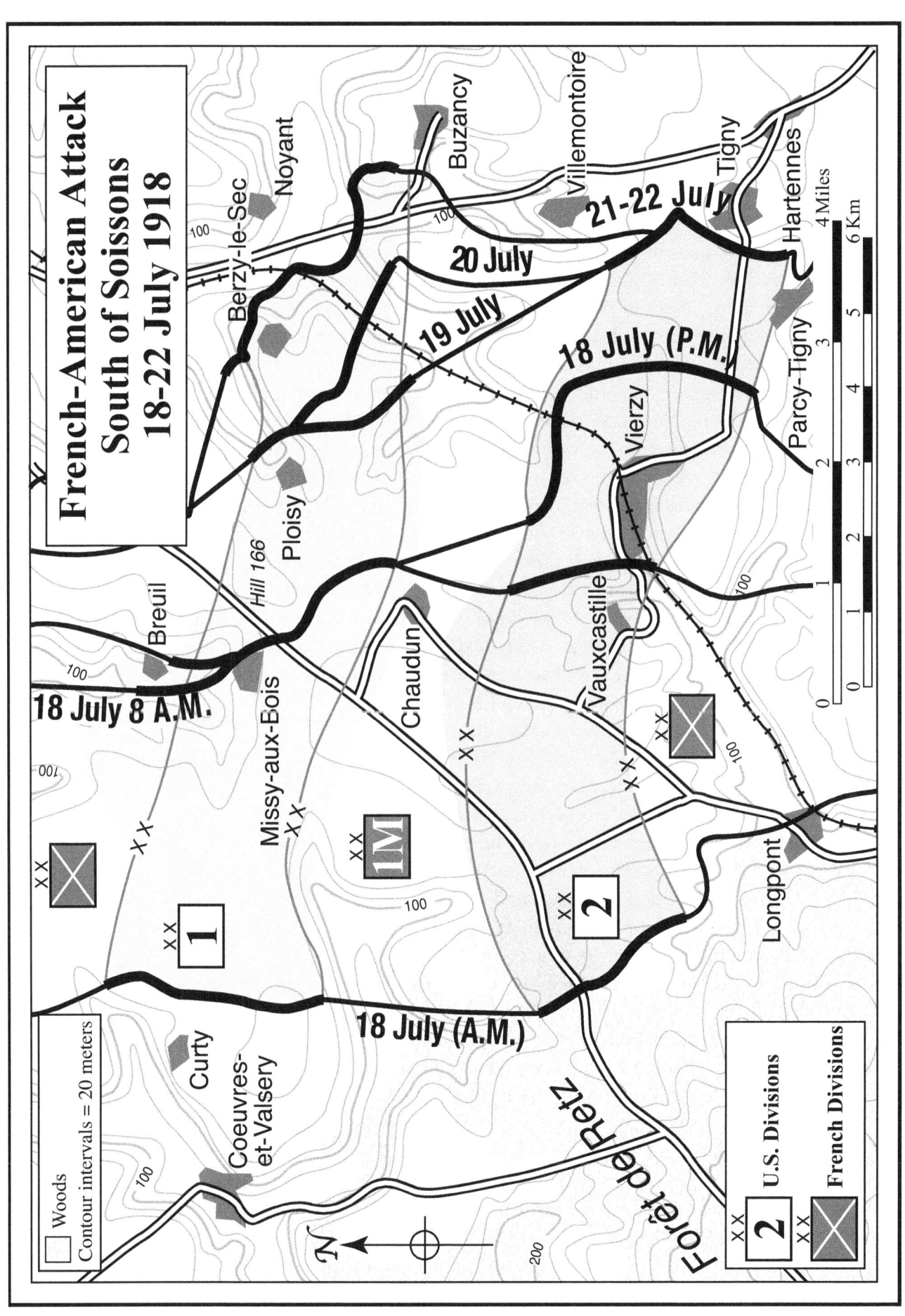

of Bareuil, and directly across on the western edge lay the village of Mont d'Arly. The Missy-aux-Bois village stood on the southeastern rim of the ravine. The Germans had fortified the farm and villages into strong defensive positions, with batteries of 155-mm and 77-mm guns.[115]

As Huebner's battalion neared the Missy Ravine, they were forced to shift part of their attack to the left to help the French 153rd Division, which had been stopped by fire from the Saint Amand Farm. By 0700 hours, his men had taken the strongly defended farm, but their swing northward had left them directly in front of the ravine. Attacking down the western slope, the assault battalion was ripped by enfiladed machine-gun fire from Saconin-et-Breuil and direct artillery fire from Breuil. Of the five French tanks that lumbered into the ravine, three were destroyed by artillery fire, and two sank into the swamp. Losses in Huebner's battalion surged to almost half of their fighting strength, and all of his company officers, except Huebner himself, had been killed or wounded.[116]

The 3rd Battalion, which had been in support and had suffered some 25 percent losses from the German protective barrage, moved forward to join the depleted assault battalion. With German machine-gun fire enfilading the wooden pathways across the bridges and through the swamp, the combined battalions waded through the swamp water and muck, somehow making it up the eastern bank of the ravine. In their rear, a large group of Germans that the Americans had overlooked in a cave around Mont d'Arly suddenly emerged and began firing. Two platoons of the 3rd Battalion returned fire and drove them back into the cave, where they held out until late that afternoon, when a battalion of some 500 soldiers, along with their colonel, surrendered. They brought with them a pile of trench mortars and machine-guns. Meanwhile, Colonel Smith's 26th Infantry Regiment had advanced without major losses, until it reached the Missy Ravine, where it encountered the same blistering, murderous fire, and suffered numerous losses, before taking the southern lip of the ravine by 0900 hours. By the end of the day, General Buck's two regiments were in line on the eastern rim of the bloody ravine, facing the heavily defended Soissons-Paris road, beyond which lay more fortified ravines, farms, and villages.[117]

*Major General J. L. Hines, AEF, at his old PC, Soissons, 7 August 1919*

Courtesy National Archives

To the south, General Hines's 1st Brigade, with French tanks in the vanguard, swept eastward, with no ravines in their way, leaving the First Moroccan behind, and crossing the Soissons-Paris road east of the village of Chaudon. Their advance had been costly and bloody, as direct hits destroyed two of the tanks, and artillery and machine-guns raked their lines. With the late-arriving First Moroccan and a hard-charging company from the 5th Marines joining the attack, the village of Chaudon was captured in hand-to-hand fighting. As the Moroccans withdrew and turned slightly to the north to link up with the 18th Infantry, German infantry retreated eastward, onto high ground and into the Chazelle Ravine, where the Americans could see them digging trenches and setting up machine-guns. By late in the afternoon on 18 July, the French 153rd Division, the First Division, and the First Moroccan Division held the line that extended east of Seconin-et-Breuil, across the eastern rim of the Missy Ravine, and past the villages of Missy-aux-Bois and Chaudun.[118] Casualties had been heavy, but Summerall had advanced the artillery

*Major General G. Harbord, SOS, AEF*
Courtesy National Archives

brigade to suppress enemy fire positions and to cover the division's next advance with a rolling barrage.[119]

The ground won by the First Division and its allies on this first day of the operation, forced the army of the crown prince to conclude that "the enemy was able to gain a great success." It also became clear to his army that it would now have "to dispense with the ideas of continuing its own offensive within a for[e]seeable time. Indirectly, but nevertheless surely, this means a great strategic success for Marshal Foch's counteroffensive, and looking at it from this viewpoint July 18 is a turning point in the history of the World War."[120]

While the divisions to the north of Harbord's Second Division were pressing their attack through the fields, ravines, farms, and villages of the Dommiers plateau, his men were rushing through the crowded Forêt de Retz to reach their jump off positions on schedule. The line consisted of General Ely's 3rd Brigade on the right, with the 9th Infantry Regiment on its right and the 23rd Infantry on its left. The 4th Brigade, with only the 5th Marine Regiment in line, was on the left of the 3rd Brigade, and to the right of the First Moroccan Division.[121] Without maps or landmarks to guide their advance, the Second Division attacked in the general direction of the Soissons-Château Thierry highway. On the left, the 5th Marines's jump off line was in the forest, and they had to fight their way through German machine-gun nests before they reached the wheat fields beyond.

The fighting was bitter and costly. Attacking fortified farms while maintaining contact with the Moroccans on their left, the marines veered to the southeast to support on their right the 9th Infantry's attack on yet another formidable ravine outside the village of Vierzy. As the sun bore down, units intermixed, men clustered in small groups and were separated, and the supply of water gave out. On the right of the division's sector, the 23rd Infantry, with the French 38th Division on its right, double-timed out of the forest behind the rolling barrage, clearing out Germans from farms and villages, before encountering stiff German resistance at the village of Vauxcastille. In bitter fighting that lasted all afternoon, Vauxcastille fell at 1800 hours, and Vierzy was taken about two hours later.[122] The Second Division had covered nearly six miles, creating a bulge beyond Vierzy and the line reached by the First Division on its left, and the French 38th on its right. Its flanks were exposed, and it had suffered heavy losses, particularly in officers, and several battalions ended the day commanded by lieutenants.[123] Harbord moved his division headquarters forward to the Beaurepaire Farm, just to the west of Vauxcastille. It also served as an advanced dressing station, where he observed "hundreds of wounded and dead men, infantry, marines, artillery, Moroccans, Germans and Americans all lying on the ground leveled in the common democracy of suffering and death."[124] Those who were left were exhausted, thirsty, and hungry.

Harbord could not sleep during the night and early morning hours of 19 July, and, with no wire communication with the rear, was concerned that his division had outrun its communications.[125] At XX Corps headquarters, the French also were concerned. They did not know just where his division was, so they sent an officer to find division headquarters. After searching for several hours, he finally located Harbord at 0200 hours and handed him an order from XX Corps to resume the attack at 0400 hours.[126] Harbord faced a real dilemma. With not enough time to inform XX Corps that his three brigades were in no condition to resume an offensive, he had to order the 6th Marine Regiment to make the attack, but it was in the support position, two miles from the front. He sent out the order at 0300 hours, but the regiment did not begin moving out until three and a half hours later. It did not arrive at the front until 0830 hours, beginning its attack, four and a half hours later than the order specified. The artillery barrage had begun at 0630 hours, which was the hour when the regiment had begun its march; so when its two battalions attacked, the barrage had long since passed. Their objective was the Soissons-Château Thierry road, and 28 French tanks led the attack across the open fields.[127]

With every German machine-gunner alert to the attack, and the French tanks attracting artillery fire as if they were magnets for the shells, the marines pressed ahead under a scorching sun into enemy fire that never seemed to let up. Within a few hours, more than half of the marines in the two assault battalions had become casualties, and the survivors sought cover in German foxholes that the enemy had abandoned.[128] They were swept by enfilading machine-gun fire, making it almost impossible to move from one position to another.[129] Finally, they managed to advance to the village of Tigny to within about 800 yards of the Soissons-Château Thierry road. By then, Harbord had concluded that they could go no farther, for, as he wrote in his *The American Army in France*, "It seemed evident to me that the force of my Division was spent and it had done its red-blooded best."[130] In his diary, he also wrote that "the attack had reached its limit beyond which it could not be supported by its artillery unless the artillery changed positions. This was not considered advisable under existing conditions."[131] He wrote General Berdoulat, XX Corps commander, requesting that his division be withdrawn, and, at 1700 hours, received word that the French 58th Colonial Division would relieve the Second Division.[132] That evening, the three officers, and some 200 marines that remained alive in the 6th Marines,[133] crawled out of their foxholes, withdrew from the front, rejoined the remnants of their division, and marched back to the Forêt de Retz.

In two days, the Second Division had advanced seven miles, captured almost 3,000 prisoners, 75 guns, and piles of machine-guns. They had suffered casualties of almost 5,000 killed and wounded. Their battalions had been reduced from 1,000 men to just a few hundred; companies had been diminished from a normal number of 250 to between 25 and 30 men. Later, when Pershing saw Harbord and his chief of staff Preston Brown at Second Division headquarters, he congratulated them on the splendid conduct of their division.[134]

In their analysis of Harbord's command, historians Johnson and Hillman point out that since no one had told the artillery that the time of the division's attack had been changed, the barrage that was fired two hours early on 19 July "was wasted." The Germans were given ample notice that an attack was coming and had time to prepare to resist it. In addition, they state that since artillery support was rarely a factor after the opening barrage, Harbord's statement that the attack of 19 July had to stop because it could not be supported by artillery was "badly off the mark."[135] They also state that Harbord should have maintained more effective communication with his senior headquarters in the rear, should have left his forward Post of Command on 19 July to go forward and get more information about the terrain, the status of his division, and the strength and nature of enemy defenses. Had he done so, he would have seen that the road to Vierzy "was certainly available" to assist the beleaguered 6th Marines. Yet, Harbord, standing with Preston Brown beside the road watching his men march back toward the

Forêt de Retz, noted their "independent attitude, the very swagger of their march," and their scattered conversations that "proclaimed them a victorious division." Harbord and Brown, like so many of their fellow officers, and, indeed, like Pershing and their commander in chief's French counterparts,[136] believed that victory countered above all other considerations on the field of battle, and victory is what they believed their division had achieved in two days of combat at Soissons. Nevertheless, the problems and challenges that faced Harbord and his division were no less than those that Summerall's First Division encountered as they fought to survive, and to win.

Unlike the trouble that XX Corps headquarters had in locating Harbord's headquarters during the night and early morning hours of 19 July, it knew where to find Summerall's headquarters. It was located in a large quarry cave, and Colonel Campbell King, his chief of staff, had organized it to function smoothly.[137] Still, Summerall, like Harbord, did not receive the attack order until the wee hours of the morning, sometime before 0300 hours, with the attack to begin at 0400 hours. Summerall's brigades had not advanced as far as Harbord's and were not as exhausted, but the 2nd Brigade had suffered severe losses fighting through the Missy Ravine, and the 1st Brigade, along with the First Moroccan, had managed to take Chaudon only after bloody, hand-to-hand fighting.

The division's mission required General Buck's 2nd Brigade to advance some two and a half miles, and General Hines's 1st Brigade about three miles to a map line that slanted from Berzy-le-Sec to Buzancy, exclusive of the two villages. To stop the attack, the Germans had moved in all their available reserves during the night and had concentrated machine-guns and artillery on the high ground in the northeast corner of the plateau at Vauxbuin, and in the 153rd French Division's sector.

To the right of the French, Buck's brigade faced the Ploisy Ravine, an obstacle that cut across the plateau, and was as well fortified and just as formidable as the Missy Ravine. Beyond Ploisy was the village of Berzy-le-Sec, the key to the entire operation. It was perched on the edge of a plateau, with Ploisy on the western side, and with the eastern side sloping steeply down to the Crise Ravine. The village overlooked the road and railroad that ran through the ravine and was assigned to the French division. Hines's brigade was to the south, with the Moroccans on their right. Ahead of them lay the Chazelle Ravine and then the Crise Ravine, presenting the same problems as Missy and Ploisy, as well as strongly reinforced machine-gun units.[138]

Buck's and Hines's brigades attacked on schedule, and the artillery covered their advance with a rolling barrage laid down by the 75-mm guns, while the howitzers fired concentrations at longer ranges on German support positions.[139] Because of an unfortunate failure of communication between division headquarters and the artillery brigade, and as a result of the failure of XX Corps to send the attack order with dispatch, the barrage fell in support of the "*assumed* jump-off line," which, as Johnson and Hillman state, the brigades had not yet reached.[140] General Buck went forward to confer with Colonel Smith and his adjutant, as shells burst ahead of them, and "machine gun bullets whistled through the branches of the trees." Smith told him that one of his battalion commanders, Major Theodore Roosevelt, Jr., had been wounded and had been sent to Missy-aux-Bois for treatment.[141]

More trouble lay ahead, as Babcock's 28th Regiment charged forward toward the strongly defended Soissons-Paris road in front of the Ploisy Ravine. The French division on their left again failed to advance, exposing Babcock's regiment to flanking fire from old French entrenchments the Germans had occupied, and strong points they had packed with heavy machine-guns. The regiment had to change course to deal with the German fire. Babcock reported the problem to the division and called for artillery support, but none was forthcoming to neutralize the enemy fire.[142] Johnson and Hillman concluded that this lack of response and support was "a command failure of major proportions."[143] Certainly, there should have been at least a response from Summerall's headquarters, but Johnson and Hillman point out that an officer indicated that the division did not have enough guns for an effective rolling barrage before the attack, so it is possible that it lacked enough artillery to neutralize this German fire from the flank. On the other hand, the two historians believe that Summerall, in command of the division for only a few days, was not prepared or willing to go beyond the boundary lines on the map that separated his division from the French sector.[144] In the not too distant future, he would make a controversial, albeit unrelated, decision that other boundary lines would not be observed.

As German machine-guns swept across the entire front of the division's attack, the 28th Regiment dug in and protected its flank, minus all of its tanks, which the Germans had either destroyed or disabled. With the 153rd French Division ready to attack at 1730 hours, Summerall ordered Babcock's regiment to attack simultaneously.[145] In his memoir, Summerall wrote that "At 4:25 the colonel of a regiment called me and said that he could not obey the order and would not attack. I told him as calmly as possible that he must not say anything to his battalion commanders whom I knew would attack. He showed himself unsuited to be a combat regimental commander. The battalion commanders led their troops to take their objectives."[146] Johnson and Hillman note that records indicate that the call came from Babcock, and that, indeed, battalion commanders had taken their objectives, but on the day before. One battalion of the regiment was held in reserve and was about to be released.[147] Clearly, Summerall believed that Babcock had been insubordinate, but felt, which he did not explain or clarify, that Babcock's "connections were such that it would be best not to relieve him." Nevertheless, "after the battle he was transferred out of the division." Summerall concluded by noting, sympathetically, that similar responses by regimental and brigade commanders were caused by "the terrible ordeal of battle."[148]

A week later, on 25 July, Babcock wrote Summerall to explain that his regiment could not have attacked because the position on the map where they were to form up was "exactly where the enemies [sic] machine guns were located." He stated that an artillery barrage had not silenced the enemy's fire, and noted that when he had informed Summerall that the French had not come up his left, Summerall responded that he would "fill in the gap." Babcock wrote that he had directed "the Major Commanding the battalion [Huebner] to advance when his left was covered." He closed by stating that "I do not understand in what way my telephone message has displeased you, or how I could have done otherwise…. If I have failed to carry out the fighting spirit you wish to have in the Division, I deeply regret it; but I am convinced that the Division Commander will do justice to us all, and will see that I have tried to do nothing but what I considered my duty as a regimental commander."[149]

Later, more deeply at odds with his commander, Babcock wrote a less deferential and more assertive account of this incident. He said:

> I directed Major Huebner to prepare to attack, but not to move forward until I directed him to do so. I sent a message to the brigade, stating that the 28th Infantry could not form up on the ground indicated as the area was fully occupied by the enemy, and that the French regiment had not taken it….I got the Division on the phone and explained, in detail the exact front line conditions of my regiment. General Summerall directed me to attack from the ground now held by the regiment, that troops would come up on my left. Later, he informed me that this message indicated to him that I was prone to see obstacles; that he did not want officers in his Division to make reports concerning obstacles in their sector. As a regimental commander, responsible for the lives of my officers and enlisted men, as well as the operations of the regiment, I thought it necessary, and still think it was my duty, to place all facts before my superiors. They, then, with all the information, just go forward. He [Summerall] liked to talk seriously in preposterously heroic phrases. Once I heard him say that he had visited many battalions that had not gained their objective; but as long as one man remained, there was no excuse.[150]

After his conversation with Summerall, the reserve battalion was released to Babcock, and it surged forward as soon as troops came up on its left.[151] As Summerall described it in the *History of the First Division*, "It passed through the rest of the regiment with a dash that defied all opposition. It swept over the most stubborn resistance at every step and clung to the heels of the barrage. Casualties were heavy and when the objective was reached only eight officers were left to command the front line."[152] Among the wounded were Major Theodore Roosevelt, 1st Battalion commander, and Major Huebner, the only officer in his battalion who had not been killed or wounded in the attack on the Missy Ravine the day before. Huebner had stumbled into Buck's headquarters with the front visor of his steel helmet split by a shell fragment and with his face and shirt streaked with blood. When he saw Buck he said, "Well General, they got me at last," but as Buck examined his wound, he said, "It doesn't amount to much."[153]

That night, long after dark, Babcock's 28th Regiment reached the eastern edge of the Ploisy Ravine and linked up with the Colonel Smith's 26th Regiment, which had just captured a German 77-mm battery and several hundred prisoners. Working through the night without any food, the men established a front line and dug foxholes to protect them from rifle and machine-gun fire from the fields, as well as from Berzy-le Sac, that lay just ahead.[154]

South of the bloody fight for Ploisy, the Germans had withdrawn their infantry along the front of the 16th and 18th Infantry Regiments of Hines's 1st Brigade and the Moroccan Division to their right, but had not pulled back their machine-guns and artillery. The Americans took heavy casualties, but steadily advanced toward Berzy-le-Sec. The Moroccans overcame German resistance by outflanking enemy positions around the Chazelle Ravine and fighting off counterattacks that lasted into the late evening of 19 July. Their fight seriously depleted German forces and weakened their resistance.[155]

In the early morning hours of 20 July, as an intermittent rain began falling on the Soissons battlefield, Summerall received an order from General Mangin to take Berzy-le-Sec. It lay in the zone of the 153rd French Division, but, as Butler recorded in his journal, "they cannot take it."[156] Thus, the First Division had the sole responsibility for the capture of Berzy-le-Sec, which, as noted above, was the key to the success of the entire operation. In their analysis of Summerall's command during what they refer to as "The Taking of Berzy-le-Sec,"[157] Johnson and Hillman focus on Buck's 2nd Brigade and raise serious questions, not only about Buck's conduct, but also about the decisions that Summerall made and the actions he took.

After he received Mangin's order, Summerall convened a conference at his headquarters to coordinate with the French on his left, assigned a reserve battalion from Colonel Frank Bamford's 18th Infantry to the 2nd Brigade, and moved forward five batteries and one battalion of artillery to support the attack. H hour was scheduled for 1400 hours. In the *History of the First Division*, Summerall wrote that it was preceded by an artillery barrage on Berzy-le-Sec at 1200 hours, which continued until H hour, and was followed by a rolling barrage as the attack began.[158] Johnson and Hillman refute Summerall's account of this artillery report and point out that "all of the infantry reports confirm the absence of any effective fire support," and add that these reports were "consistent on this point: there was no supporting barrage."[159]

The Moroccan Division and Hines's 1st Brigade began the attack in the morning, before the primary attack of Buck's 2nd Brigade at 1400 hours. After issuing the attack order, Buck wrote that he moved on to the front line of the Moroccan Division to visit with Colonels Frank Parker and Frank Bamford of Hines's 16th and 18th Infantry Regiments, respectively. He wanted to gather all the information they could provide and took a close look at the valley of the Crise River, which, as he wrote, "would be of very great value to me the next day."[160] Johnson and Hillman, who describe his movements as "riding off into the blue," point out that he mistook the Chazelle Ravine for the Ploisy Ravine in his own zone and was out of touch with his own troops. His behavior, they contend, was either cowardly, or a case of "considerable mental confusion." That afternoon, Buck continued to roam "all over the battle field," dodging bullets fired from German airplanes swooping across the lines, halting stragglers and calming a hysterical lieutenant, but without making contact with any of his regimental or battalion commanders or with Summerall's headquarters. Only when he returned to his post of command did he learn that "our attack on Berzy-le-Sec was a failure and that the men were digging in for the night." Johnson and Hillman conclude that these were "not actions of a leader in full control of his faculties; they are rather more suggestive of mental dysfunction from fear or exhaustion."[161]

Meanwhile, Babcock had received the order to attack at 1400 hours behind a rolling barrage but was worried that his regiment would suffer further heavy casualties attacking over a wide, flat plain swept by enemy machine-guns on three sides, unless they were given stronger artillery support. He discussed his concern over the telephone with General Buck, who, as Babcock stated, told him it was "your duty (or right) to report these matters, or words to that effect." Babcock wanted to get the division to understand the situation, and when Buck reported the conversation to Summerall, Babcock wrote that his division commander "noted it against me" and that "the attack arrangements were not altered."[162] Although Summerall did not mention this exchange in his memoir, one certainly can assume that Babcock's second objection to an attack order reaffirmed Summerall's judgment that Babcock was "unsuited to be a combat regimental commander." Johnson and Hillman state that Babcock's recommendation in this case was also correct, but that he simply could not prevail against Summerall and Buck.[163] He remained in command but quickly ran into another problem with his division commander.

With his plan for heavier artillery support rejected, Babcock devised another way to avoid the heavy losses of a frontal attack. He ordered one of his lieutenants to organize three or four small teams of two squads each, about 16 to 18 men each. They were to infiltrate through the trees along the border of the Ploisy Ravine and enter Berzy-le-Sec from the north. More teams would filter into the village until the force amounted to the size of a small battalion. The first teams reached the outskirts of Berzy, but heavy machine-gun fire stopped their advance. Babcock notified Buck what they had accomplished and reported that they could capture Berzy in a night attack. He then directed a company to reinforce the teams at 2400 hours, midnight. At 2300 hours, he was notified that an intense bombardment would fall on Berzy-le-Sec at 0445 hours on 21 July.

In a frantic state of mind, Babcock realized that "Either the brigade failed to notify the division, as to what the 28th Infantry intended doing that night, or the Division completely ignored the brigade. In either case, there I was with a few of my men near Berzy, another large group about to leave, and a heavy barrage designated to fall on them and the village in the early morning. Instead of saving some of the lives of my men, my plan, had it gone through, might have caused further heavy loss." Abandoning the night attack, he stopped the company from moving forward and sent a message to the infiltration teams to fall back.[164]

Johnson and Hillman regard the necessity to abandon Babcock's plan as "another tragic demonstration of inadequate communications and the regrettably standard failure of connection between infantry and artillery that had dogged the attacker for three years." They wonder whether Buck was again the problem, or whether it was Summerall's staff. At any rate, it was "A brilliant opportunity wasted."[165] Their questions and judgment are fair and reasonable, but Butler, in his journal, and Summerall, in his memoir, described decisions and developments that might well have been factors in the demise of Babcock's plan.

Butler noted that throughout the morning of 20 July, "There were conflicting reports as to whether our men were in Ploisy or Berzy,"[166] and Babcock's men also could have been an element in this

*Plains south of Berzy*

Courtesy National Archives

uncertainty. Once locations had been clearly established, Butler stated that "Our 75, 155 and Corps arty. finally began to fire on Berzy at 12:00 noon."[167] Summerall wrote that in order to make up for the shortage of artillery that resulted from the decision of Pershing's staff in Paris, he adopted for this attack a method of concentrating the barrage of all of his artillery to lead each successive echelon of attacking infantry.[168] The 26th Infantry led the attack on Berzy, and since all of the artillery was concentrated in the barrage that preceded the attack, Summerall could have concluded that none of his guns could be used for any other purpose.

The attack of the 2nd Brigade began as scheduled and the barrage that led the 26th Infantry landed properly, as Johnson and Hillman state.[169] As the attack progressed, an unnamed observer noted that the "artillery had been pounding Berzy-le-Sec and the heights above it," but it did not silence batteries of 105-mm and 150-mm howitzers. "Great gaps were left in the ranks as the shells crashed among them," and "our infantry was shrouded in smoke and dust…. Men struck by the enemy's fire either disappeared or ran aimlessly about and toppled over….The attack had met the resistance of a strong position occupied in great force by the enemy. It could not be taken at this time by our worn soldiers, and after this advance, they could go no further….Then appeared a sight which at first seemed inexplicable. Individual men and groups of twos and threes began to wander about all over the field. They were unit leaders, reorganizing their groups against counter-attack. Thus the afternoon passed and night fell."[170]

Late that afternoon, with losses mounting to nearly seven thousand, and with dead bodies lying everywhere, Summerall visited the front line to talk with his infantry regiments.[171] Pershing stopped by division headquarters, apparently to check on reports of the division's casualties that Summerall believed his old "enemies" at GHQ had criticized as excessive. When Pershing found that "I had gone to the front, nothing further was said."[172] The Germans spotted Summerall's presence, and, as Butler described it, "He was shot at with everything—shells, M.Gs., & rifles. He joked with the men….and they promised him that they would take Berzy-le-Sec. He encouraged them and told them that they would be relieved tomorrow night. Their tails were up. They asked for an Artillery barrage & when the General got back at 1.00 A.M. it was arranged for."[173]

Johnson and Hillman criticize Summerall for not requesting at this point the relief of his depleted division. They note that Harbord's request that his battered Second Division be relieved had been granted, and that, in late October, after his unit had fought to exhaustion, Hanson Ely had asked Bullard for relief, and his corps commander relieved it that night.[174] Yet, Summerall was encouraged by the fighting spirit of his men at the front and "knew that we were winning a great victory and deciding the fate of the war…. I felt that my life and that of everyone must be given to gain the final victory if necessary."[175] As he responded to a corps staff officer who asked if the division could mount an attack after such heavy losses, "Sir, when the 1st Division has only two men left they will be echeloned in depth and attacking toward Berlin." In that spirit, and upset that a battalion commander reported that he had been stopped, Summerall replied that "You may have paused for reorganization. If you ever send another message with the word stopped in it, you will be sent to the rear for reclassification."[176] Also, as he recalled the enmity of those at GHQ, he could well have believed that a call for relief at that point might well have given these "enemies" at GHQ another reason to undermine his authority. He did tell his men they would be relieved the next night, and he remained concerned about the impact on his commanders of the terrible ordeal of combat.

In his memoir, Summerall wrote that "One brigade had not reached its objective….On reaching the brigade command post, I found the brigade commander [Buck] much confused and worn. I told him to get some rest, that the attack would be resumed the next morning and that he would lead the attack."[177] The next morning, as his brigade again led the attack on Berzy, Buck was with them at the jump-off line. He moved forward with the first wave, and when he saw that the second wave had not started, he rushed back and personally rallied them, "… gathering up every man left, mostly machine gunners, directed them on the run to the brow of the slope, where they took posts. One of my men came running to me an[d] said if I would go to the brow of the hill I could see small parties of the enemy running down the slope toward the Crise [River]." Buck concluded that the fight was over. When a captured German captain told him that his men refused to support him when the Americans attacked, and after Buck hurriedly questioned other prisoners, he "hastened to the nearest telephone to report to the Division Commander that Berzy-le-Sec had been captured and was in our hands."[178]

Summerall's driving will, coupled with compassionate understanding, seems not only to have cleared and focused Buck's mind, but also to have inspired him to exceptional and heroic leadership. In the opinion of Johnson and Hillman, and that of a future major general, Summerall's next encounter with one of his commanders did not have such a fortunate outcome. As shall be noted below, their judgment, though understandable, is not conclusive.

After his visit with Buck, Summerall stopped by the command post of the 26th Infantry and wrote in his memoir that he "found the colonel [Hamilton Smith] exhausted. He was sullen and defiant. I asked him why his regiment had not attacked. He replied: 'The order was impossible and I did not try to obey it.' I could have relieved him but it was evident that he was over wrought and scarcely responsible. The strain had been too great for him. I told him that I had brought the lieutenant colonel [who] would be on duty while he rested. The colonel was killed the second day after this."[179] Summerall went on to the front lines, escorted by a captain, and described how they had to take cover in a shell hole when heavy artillery fire began. At the front, he "found the men in good spirits. I explained the situation and the necessity of taking the objective of Berzy-le-Sec….They said they would take it if I would give them our own artillery fire. I told them I would do so."[180]

In their account of Summerall's meeting with Colonel Smith, Johnson and Hillman did not mention Summerall's subsequent visit to the front, but include the description of the incident that retired Major General Joseph Patch wrote in his book, *A Soldier's War*, published in 1966.[181] They cite Patch's conclusion that "Summerall had treated Colonel Smith unjustly."[182] Patch wrote that "On a front line

*German infantry at Soissons*

Courtesy National Archives

tour he [Summerall] formed the opinion that Smith was too far to the rear and told him so, ordering him to go up and take personal command of his forward units. Smith got the idea that Summerall thought him lacking in courage. The result was that he went up and got himself killed. The men of the 26th never forgave Summerall for this. Smith was delicate, high-strung, and often sick, but so were Wolfe and Forbes in the French and Indian War. I was with Smith through all the trying days in the Ansauville sector and knew that he possessed all sorts of courage, and so did everyone else in the 26th."[183]

The two historians of Soissons quote the official history of the 26th Infantry, which describes Smith's last two days at the front, as working wonders among his men "by his courage and happy spirits."[184] In addition, a report contained in the historical file of the First Division in the National Archives, describing the operations of 18–22 July, states that "The regimental commander, Colonel Smith, was killed while personally supervising the readjustment of our lines."[185] These records confirm Smith's courage, high spirits, and popularity among his men. They also describe a man responsibly engaged in commanding his regiment, perhaps even more determined after his meeting with Summerall, and not someone bent on getting himself killed. Colonel Smith seems to have been an outstanding combat commander, and one of many officers under Summerall's command who found the courage and energy to lead men into battle, and died as he prepared them for the fight that lay ahead. And, Patch concluded, "It is the opinion of the men of the Division, that Summerall was the best Combat Commander of the war, probably one of the best of all time….Summerall, whether you like him or not, was a great soldier and a great American."[186]

As a revitalized (thanks to Summerall's bracing counsel) General Buck gathered himself and prepared to lead his 2nd Brigade in the attack on Berzy on 21 July. General Hines's 1st Brigade received their attack order at 0445 hours. The objective was the village of Buzancy, situated atop a high plateau, just about two miles to the southeast of Berzy, and fortified with elaborate machine-gun defenses. To reach the Buzancy plateau, Hines's regiments had to cross a succession of steep ridges covered with thick brush, and the muddy bottom of the Crise River, with its ravine and more thick vegetation. On their right was the French 87th Division, which had relieved the First Moroccan the night before.

In the afternoon before the attack, Summerall made his way to 18th Infantry's regimental command post. There he encountered another commander whose losses had left him distraught. Speaking "in a most resentful manner," as Summerall wrote in his memoir, Colonel Parker told Summerall: "'General, my regiment has lost 60 percent of its officers, nearly all of its old non-commissioned officers and most of its men and I don't think that is the way to treat a regiment.'" Summerall responded with compassion for Parker's feelings and understanding of the depressing weight of the losses his regiment had suffered. He wrote that "I could have relieved him for insubordination, but I replied calmly, telling him that the tide of battle had been changed by his troops and those of the division of which his were only a part and that the attack would be resumed with what he had. In repeating the incident later he stated that I replied: 'Colonel, I did not come here to have you criticize my order or to tell me of your losses. I know them as well as you do. I came to tell you that the Germans recrossed the Marne last night and are in full retreat and you will attack tomorrow morning at 4:30.' He added: 'from that day, I have never questioned your orders and I never will.' He was about the best combat officer I ever knew."[187] Indeed, as General Patch wrote in his brief account of Parker's career, "More than any other officer, Frank Parker represented the First Division…. No one appreciated his value as a combat leader more than General Summerall did…"[188]

Whether Summerall went on to the Bamford's command post is not known, but the next morning both regiments attacked on schedule behind a rolling barrage, while maintaining contact with Buck's brigade that was under enfilading fire from the plateau on the other side of Buzancy. They crossed the Crise Ravine and fought their way across the Soissons-Château Thierry road. To stay in touch with the 2nd Brigade, Bamford's regiment had to face north, causing him to complain that he had never had to fight without having an exposed northern flank.[189] Yet both regiments advanced in liaison through dense brush and enemy fire up the slope and onto the heights of Buzancy. Parker's men seized the fortified Château of Buzancy and captured more than 200 prisoners who had taken refuge in a deep cavern. That number was greater than the men that were left in the regiment's assault battalions. That night, as Hines's 1st Brigade established contact with Buck's 2nd Brigade at Berzy-le-Sec, the First Division consolidated its lines, pushed forward patrols, and organized the captured ground for defense. The division had won its objectives, severed the Soisson-Paris railroad and the Soissons-Château-Thierry highway, defeated four German divisions, and captured 3,400 prisoners and 75 guns.[190]

The exhausted survivors of the division's depleted regiments waited all during the night for the relief that the Tenth Army had promised. Summerall had been notified that the Fifteenth Scottish Regiment would be sent but was told that it would not arrive until sometime the next day. He sent his French aide to find out why they were not relieved as promised, but he returned with an explanation that it was just impossible for the regiment to arrive as scheduled.[191] Their advance parties finally began moving in during the morning of 22 July, as German planes strafed the American lines and Scottish infantry, and German artillery continued to harass their positions. The 26th Infantry, having lost all of its field officers, was led by Captain Barney Legge, who had been graduated from The Citadel in 1911, and had been in the army less than two years. They wiped out a nest of snipers at the Sucrerie, a sugar factory, and seized the building.[192] The taking of the Sucrerie further secured the Château-Thierry road to the south and east.

At midnight on 22–23 July, the command of the sector that now stretched from Berzy-le-Sec to the southeast beyond the heights of Buzancy passed to the Scottish division. At dawn, they attacked all along the front, but the barrage laid down by the First Division's artillery brigade was too far in advance, and the Scottish casualties were heavy. Later in the day, the artillery found the range, placed its fire accurately, and helped the Scots repel repeated German counterattacks.[193]

During the next two days, British artillery arrived to take over the firing missions of the 1st Artillery Brigade, ending the five-day battle waged by the First Division. During the nights of 23–24 July, and 24–25 July, the brigade marched back over the six and a half miles to join the rest of the division that had already reached the Forêt de Retz, where, long days ago, they had assembled to prepare for the Soissons attack.[194] "All were pitifully worn, hollow-cheeked, dazed and exhausted," wrote Summerall. "Practically every man fell sound asleep for they had had no rest and little food for over four days. The companies were pitifully reduced in numbers. All companies were mere skeletons of the well-filled ranks that entered the battle. Some companies were commanded by privates. One regiment [the 26th] was commanded by a very young captain [Legge]. Every battalion commander was a casualty."[195]

Soissons itself would not fall to the Allies until 2 August, but the French Tenth Corps now held the crucial routes to the south and east, and Mangin's Tenth Army was in position at the northwest shoulder of the salient, with the soaring, gray-stone spire of Soissons Cathedral right before their eyes. That shoulder would be the hinge for Dagoutte's Sixth Army to the south, which included the six American divisions that comprised Liggett's I Corps and Bullard's III Corps. The Sixth Army drove northeast across the Orcq River and reached the Vesle River on 6 August, officially ending the great Aisne-Marne Offensive, wiping out the Marne salient, and forcing the German Seventh Army into a disheartening reassessment of its position and prospects. On 8 August, the British Fourth Army smashed the Somme salient that the Germans had forged in their breakthrough of 21 March. They captured 400 guns and 27,000 prisoners, while suffering only 10,000 casualties. General Ludendorff called that day the "Black Day" of the German army and concluded that "The war must be ended."[196]

Prior to Ludendorff's bitter assessment of 8 August, the operations section of the German Seventh Army had reported on 24 July that a total of 18 German divisions had been rendered unfit for offensive action. It stated that "Under these circumstances this headquarters does not believe it to be expedient for us to fight the battle to a finish south of the VESLE. Considerable portions of the army and the services of supply are being used up, thereby more and more reducing the forces available for attacks from our side." The report concluded that "There is no doubt about it that the enemy will continue the battle. He has sufficient forces available for this purpose."[197] The 150,000 American soldiers who had fought through to the Vesle had proved that point, and, as Johnson and Hillman point out, "most did it without having the in-country training and field experience that had been acquired by the 1st and 2nd Divisions."[198]

The veterans of Soissons gathered in the woods outside the village of Couvres, welcomed back by the music of their regimental bands. After they had feasted on the hot food prepared in their company kitchens, Summerall stepped forth to address them. Butler wrote in his diary that "He apologized to them for not getting them relieved the night of the 21st as promised, he praised them for their work, talked with individuals, told them we had stayed in from one to 3 days longer than any other Division on this line & and gained more ground." In spite of their exhaustion, Butler noted that "The men's spirit is wonderful...The Foreign Legion sent us word that we were as good as they are [underlined by Butler]." That afternoon, Summerall and Butler visited the wounded in hospitals in Mortefontaine, west of Couvres, and some who had been cared for in a private home. They found the staff, nurses, and operating teams "overworked and very tired," after having cared for over 3,000 soldiers. At one stop, Summerall talked with hospital personnel who had come in the night before the wounded started to arrive, and before tents could be set up. He found flies everywhere, food being served from buckets, and a shortage of nurses. Butler wrote that "Any kind of women would have done to administer to the wants of the men & keep the flies off....The men's spirit was fine & most of them were very cheerful. They are being moved to Base Hospitals as quickly as possible."

Their tour ended the day at Dammartin-en-Goele, some 30 miles southwest of Couvres, where the division would follow and assemble, before being assigned to a new sector. When he and Summerall arrived, Butler wrote that "The General is very tired having slept hardly at all since the night of July 15th."[199] It was a feeling and condition shared by all who had survived those days and nights of combat that had followed. Together with those who had suffered the death and wounds of battle, they had fought to victory across the "killing fields," through the ravenous ravines and up the heights of the dangerous plateaus of the land south of Soissons. It had been a costly triumph.

No other American division sustained the number of casualties suffered by the First Division at Soissons. More than 7,300 men had been killed or wounded, as the division fought for four days over the ground that the Germans fought fiercely to retain. Together, the First and Second Divisions suffered more than 11,200 killed and wounded. They had captured over 6,400 prisoners, and the First Division alone had seized 90 guns.[200] Pershing wrote that the victory at Soissons had "snatched the initiative from the Germans almost in an instant. They made no more formidable attacks, but from that moment until the end of the war they were on the defensive. The magnificent conduct of our 1st and 2nd Division and the Moroccan Division marked the turning point of the tide. Pétain said it could not have been done without our divisions."[201] In a general order issued on 30 July, Mangin said of the Americans that "Your magnificent courage completely routed a surprised enemy and your indomitable tenacity checked the counter-attacks of his fresh division. You have shown yourselves worthy Sons of your Great Country and you were admired by your brothers in arms....I am proud to have commanded you during such days to have fought with you for the deliverance of the world."[202]

Summerall stated proudly that the First Division had "cut his [the enemy's] rail and road communications and was chiefly responsible for his recrossing the Marne July 20th and beginning the retreat that never ended till the Armistice. So powerfully did the division fight, that the Germans never captured a prisoner or crossed our lines to identify our dead." Yet, in his memoir, he again criticized GHQ for leaving the division without sufficient artillery. "With only its 72 guns to cover nearly three miles of front, the division, once again, lacked the artillery firepower it needed. Our heavy losses," he continued, "were directly due to our lack of sufficient artillery to neutralize the enemy, as I had warned the staff in Paris." Increasingly embittered as he looked back on what he regarded as their unjust criticism of his "warning" and his role in the "race to Sedan," he charged that "These men really knew nothing about fire power in battle or the meaning of artillery."[203]

Johnson and Hillman conclude that "There was plenty of heavy artillery available." They state that Summerall unaccountably missed the opportunity to suppress the flanking machine-gun fire from the Vauxbuin Position that ripped into Babcock's regiment on 19 July.[204] Yet, Summerall seems to have dismissed Babcock's concern about the danger his regiment faced because he believed that, at worst, Babcock lacked personal courage and, at best, was unwilling to follow orders. General Patch, in his account of the incident, stated that Summerall's subsequent relief of Babcock was *just* [his italics], although he did say that his relief [*sic*] of Smith was *unjust* [his italics].[205]

The two historians of Soissons believe also that Summerall was "handicapped by personal insecurities that haunted him and distorted his behavior throughout his life."[206] They fail to explain just what these insecurities were, but if they existed, they do not seem to have handicapped his rise through the United States Corps of Cadets to the rank of first captain; or to have undermined his courage and bravery in combat in the Philippines and in China; or to have stopped him from hopping on a Japanese ship in Chinese waters hoping to meet his fiancée in Nagasaki; or his leadership, and tireless and distinguished work at the Militia Bureau; or his frequently delicate, and successful dealings with the public; or the esteem in which he was held by cadets like George Patton, who saw him as a model. It seems also unlikely that someone "handicapped by personal insecurities" would have had the conviction and courage to stand up to Pershing at Paris; or would have possessed the self-confidence to request and assume the command of the division that had been led by his mentor, and had become the favorite of the commander in chief. In fact, their statement about his insecurities seems to conflict with their earlier assessment of Summerall, whose "acknowledged leadership ability and demonstrated fearlessness underlay gale-force self confidence and a sense of self-importance."[207] Again, without citing specific evidence or bases for their conclusion, Johnson and Hillman further state that Summerall's "ridiculous blathering and evident fear of any challenge to his authority made his performance as army chief of staff poor."[208] Comment on that judgment must await an examination of his term as army chief of staff, and that follows below in a subsequent chapter of this study. They apparently agree with historian Mac Coffman that by the second day of combat at Soissons, "Summerall had his command more in hand than did Harbord"[209] and add that Summerall "had a much better appreciation of affairs by the end of his journey than at the first...."[210] Soissons, indeed, had been a learning experience for Summerall, as it had been for every commander on that battlefield, and Johnson and Hillman fairly conclude that "Soissons...reflected an army in transition."[211] Summerall understood this, and ordered his headquarters to examine the operations of the division at Soissons, and report their recommendations. The first of two major reports dealt with the use of machine-guns in the battle.

The report, dated 5 August, identified a number of major mistakes and proposed measures to correct them. Infantry battalion commanders had given practically no orders on the use of machine-guns, and "What orders were given were simply to the effect that certain gun crews would accompany certain infantry companies. The objectives and the lines of march were not given the machine gun commanders; as a result, they followed the infantry blindly and almost without exception were lost from the units to which assigned." Apparently, in some instances, "the Battalion Commander, not knowing just what to do with his machine guns, let them follow with a view to utilizing them as the necessity arose." Also, there had been practically no communication between machine-gun and infantry commanders; machine-gun crews became lost and joined any infantry unit they contacted; infantry detailed at the last minute to carry ammunition "had no particular interest in getting this material up and apparently quit at the slightest provocation"; and "Such ammunition as was brought up was picked up from that dropped by gun crews which had been knocked out." Gun crews hardly ever located exactly enemy machine-guns and were forced to simply comb the ground where they were supposed to be.[212]

The report recommended that machine-gun companies be held intact well in the rear of infantry battalions, and that a reconnaissance team consisting of an officer, two non-commissioned officers, and four runners advance between the first and second waves of a battalion attack and locate enemy machine-gun targets and positions. The officer in charge of the team should then bring up the guns and give the crews the necessary firing data. The machine-gun company commander and the reconnaissance party must know the plans of the battalion commander with whom they are operating. Infantry battalion commanders must practice the dictation of orders and plans to the machine-gun commander and maintain close contact with him and with the reconnaissance party. Carrying parties must practice the organization and transport of the required load, as well as moving over different types of terrain a fast pace to keep up with the infantry. Interestingly enough, Colonel Babcock made quite the same points when he recommended in his report of 4 August "that machine gun companies do not follow their battalions into the action, but come up after the position is taken and hold it."[213]

First Division headquarters issued the second report on 11 August, and it covered a wider range of issues. It noted the problem that the division commander and other commanding officers encountered in locating the front line of the infantry, as well as other echelons during an advance. This often made it "impossible to utilize the artillery to facilitate the advance or to protect the infantry." The report recommended that panels be laid out to mark this line, so that an aerial observer could locate it accurately. Panels had been issued, but had not been displayed, and this "proved a great hindrance to the operations, and in some cases, exposed advanced positions to danger from friendly fire." Soldiers were instructed to carry pieces of white cloth and display them so that they could not be seen by enemy airplanes. Thus, it was important that soldiers be taught the "disinguishing marks of friendly and enemy aeroplanes."[214] Clearly, the doughboys had a lot to learn.

The most serious of the concerns addressed in the report of 11 August were division losses caused by "unnecessarily dense formations. In the advanced echelon especially, men must be taught not to crowd or to form in groups, and in the advanced line the interval between men should not be less than five paces."[215] To train their men not to follow their natural tendency to huddle together in the face of mortal danger would prove to be one of the most difficult challenges that Summerall and his commanding officers faced in the months ahead. Yet, their commander in chief believed that the victory at Soissons and the surging offensive toward the Vesle, clearly and finally justified the formation of an American field army that would "strike an offensive blow and turn the tide of the war."[216] Summerall's men would have a crucial part in that offensive. Their operations would test whether he could achieve the artillery firepower that he had long demanded, and whether his commanders and gunners could use that firepower to overwhelm the deadly resistance that had killed and wounded so many of the infantry that he had sent into battle.

# Chapter Eleven

## *The St. Mihiel Salient*

With the defeat on the Aisne-Marne battlefields of Ludendorff's fifth offensive, Supreme Commander Foch called together at his headquarters on 24 July the Allied commanders in chief—Sir Douglas Haig, General Henri Pétain, and General John J. Pershing—in order, as he wrote, to "bring all the Allied resources into play; as rapidly as possible, so as the prevent the enemy from recovering before we could effect his definite destruction."[1] He noted the large number of exhausted German divisions, the growing superiority of Allied air power and in the number of tanks, and took special note of the powerful reserve of American manpower that "pours 250,000 men every month upon the soil of France."[2] Pershing later recalled that nearly 300,000 American soldiers had been engaged in these operations, and had suffered more than 50,000 casualties.[3] Foch asserted the Allied armies had "arrived at the turning point of the road. They have recovered in full tide of battle the initiative of operations; their numbers permit and the principles of war compel them to keep this initiative."[4] He believed that the decisive year of the war would be in 1919, when "America will have reached the climax of her effort," but proposed for the remainder of 1918, a succession of blows by each of the Allied armies along the entire front.[5]

Foch's plan, outlined in his memorandum of 24 July, was based upon operations to clear the railroad lines and make it possible for the Allies to exploit the defeat of the Germans; namely to free the Paris–Avricourt railway line in the Marne region; to free the Paris–Amiens line by concerted action of the British and French armies; and, most significantly for Pershing, the freeing of the Paris–Avricourt railroad in the area around Commercy, about 190 miles southeast of Paris, "by reducing the St. Mihiel salient. This operation should be prepared without delay, and executed by the American Army as soon as it has the necessary means." In a footnote, Foch added that the American operation would bring the Allies within striking distance of the strategic Brey region, held by the Germans, and make possible operations "on a wide scale between the Meuse and the Moselle [Rivers], which might one day become necessary."[6]

Even before the meeting of 24 July, Foch and Pershing had agreed that the First American Army would be formed. The American commander in chief was delighted. After a year of planning and persistent advocacy, Pershing finally had his army. Now, with the agreement of 24 July, it had its own front, in Lorraine, where the First Division had occupied the Ansauville sector, before it moved to Picardy to prepare for the Battle of Cantigny. Pershing was also pleased that Foch had given to the First Army the mission to reduce the St. Mihiel salient, which was a project Pershing and his staff had supported as an American objective as early as June 1917, and had endorsed as a major American operation in 1918.[7] He and Foch also had agreed to form the Second American Army and assign to it a front in the Château-Thierry salient. After the conclusion of the Aisne-Marne counteroffensive and the elimination of that salient, they decided to concentrate on the formation of only one army. Foch wrote that he clearly recognized "the importance which American assistance was assuming on the French front," as well as "the ardent desire of American soldiers, so often expressed by General Pershing, to have the American Expeditionary Forces united as soon as possible under his orders, and given an autonomy similar to that of the other Allied Armies; they wished to see the Stars and Stripes waving over a battlefield at the earliest moment."[8]

As historian James H. Hallas noted, the St. Mihiel salient jutted out like a "200-square mile shark's fin" into Allied lines.[9] It lay between the Meuse and Moselle Rivers, with the wooden heights of the Meuse on the western side, along the east bank of that river. As described above in Chapter X, the broad plain of the Woevre River, dotted by forests, lakes and swamps, lay to the east toward the Moselle and the forested bluffs that rose high above both banks of the river. The Rupt de Mad was the only important stream in the salient. It flowed from the southeast into the soggy lowlands of the southern side, or "face" of the salient, and by the town of Thiaucourt, before emptying into the Moselle. Deep water and steep banks made the stream unfordable, and German machine gun emplacements on the embankments gave them excellent command of the approaches from the southern face.[10] The towering butte of Montsec, long since familiar to the veterans of the First Division, loomed over the Rupt de Mad from beyond the northern bank. The western apex of the salient included St. Mihiel, a town of some 10,000 inhabitants, about 150 miles east of Paris. The town of Haudiomont, about 13 miles northeast of St. Mihiel, and the Moselle River town of Pont-a-Mousson, about 25 miles to the southeast of Haudiomont, anchored the base. German attacks had carved out the salient in September 1914, and French attacks up to 1916 had failed to eliminate it. It split the railroad from Verdun to Toul and enabled German artillery to fire on the rail line from Paris to Nancy. The tip at St. Mihiel pointed straight toward the strategic Meuse-Argonne area and clearly indicated the danger to the flank of any Allied offensive that might be launched through that region and into Germany.[11]

For four years, the Germans had been fortifying the salient and had covered all approaches with three lines of barbed-wire entanglements, a network of trenches and machine guns, concrete bunkers and pillboxes, and artillery emplacements. It was held by nine German divisions and one Austro-Hungarian division. Pershing called it "practically a great field fortress."[12] After 1916, the French

*Montsec*

Courtesy National Archives

abandoned attempts to seize it, and the area became a quiet zone, where tired or untested units could rest or train for combat. In the meantime, the Germans had settled down comfortably and had planted vegetable gardens, made their dugouts cozy with comfortable furniture and curtains, married local women, and fathered a number of children. The German and Austro-Hungarian divisions that held the position were second- or third-class troops, their general morale was low, and they were eager for the war to end.[13] They had neglected to keep their defenses in good repair, and, as Pershing noted, their salient, like all others, had the characteristic weakness of vulnerability to converging attacks from both sides.[14]

On the day that Foch issued his memorandum, GHQ formally announced the organization of First Army, effective 10 August, with General Pershing commander.[15] Between 11 and 16 August, First Army headquarters was transferred to Neufchâteau, southwest of Nancy, where the staff began planning for the St. Mihiel operation.[16] Since Pershing now wore two hats—one as commanding general of the AEF, and the other as commanding general of the First Army—he had to divide his time between the two headquarters. This situation left Lieutenant Colonel Hugh Drum, whom Pershing appointed as First Army chief of staff, with considerable freedom and power. Drum was one of Pershing's most experienced staff officers and worked well with his old friend Colonel James W. McAndrew, who was the chief of staff at GHQ. Other key staff officers were Colonel Fox Conner, who was Pershing's most important battle planner at GHQ, and 37-year-old Lieutenant Colonel George Marshall, who came over to First Army from the First Division.[17] Drum directed Marshall to work with deputy chief of staff Lieutenant Colonel Walter Grant in planning the St. Mihiel attack. Marshall regarded Grant as "one of the most efficient people in the Army" and an officer who possessed "a highly developed sense of responsibility, who at the same time enjoyed the relaxation of a little frivolous badinage to lessen the strain."[18] The headquarters staff soon grew to number about five hundred, and was moved to Ligny-en-Barrois, closer to the salient, and about 50 miles west of Nancy. The supply and administrative services of First Army remained at Neufchâteau.[19]

On 23 July, French trucks conveyed the First Division to the Saizerais sector, some eight miles south of Pont-a-Mousson, not far from the west bank of the Moselle. They relieved the 2nd Moroccan Division and settled into an area that still bore the signs and scars of battle: successive rows of barbed wire entanglements, three lines of trenches, jagged and shattered tree trunks, as well as abandoned machine gun emplacements that had been echeloned in depth, and had changed hands several times during bloody fighting in 1914 and 1915.[20] Since then, it had been quiet; but, the Germans took notice of the division's presence and staged several raids that captured a few prisoners. An enemy artillery bombardment and raid took several lives; total casualties while they were in the sector amounted to 51 with one officer and 14 men killed or died of wounds.[21]

About 7,000 replacements, including a large number of officers arrived. As soon as they had been processed, the division began exercises in training and operations to implement the recommendations of the reports that division headquarters had issued on 5 and 11 August. They were told not to allow hostile strong points and machine guns to impede an attack. This enemy resistance would be reduced by the intense fire of machine guns, automatic rifles, Stokes mortars, and 37-mm guns and accompanying artillery. Covered by this fire, infantry, as recommended by the reports of 5 and 11 August, "must advance by rushes around the flanks, in small groups or individually, accompanied by automatic rifles."[22] Under the direction of Summerall and his veterans, the division trained in the elastic system of defense, in which battalions were rotated in three lines. They also worked to improve liaison to preserve unit cohesion and formations.[23]

More intensive training lay ahead, as the division, minus the First Artillery Brigade, moved westward during the night of 23–24 August, into the Vaucouleurs training area, where, one year before at Gondrecourt, they had begun their elementary instruction.[24] The artillery brigade remained in the Saizerais area to cover the arrival of Major General Henry Allen's Ninetieth Division. Both divisions received the order assigning them to the First Army, in the administrative area of IV Corps, on the south side of their objective, the St. Mihiel salient.[25] At Vaucouleurs, Summerall's division rehearsed the attack over similar terrain; drilled in the use of Bangalore torpedoes to blow paths through enemy wire entanglements estimated to be 25 rows deep; practiced the rapid construction of foot bridges across swampy areas and streams; and worked on the coordination of attacking infantry with machine gun companies and battalions.[26] Instructions, written under Summerall's direction, stated that

> All officers and men must be impressed with the necessity of enduring great fatigue, hunger, thirst and lack of sleep. These conditions do not prevent vigorous action and it must be borne in mind that they will pass away with the successful accomplishment of our mission....The subject of relief of the troops must not be considered or discussed by them. With skill and leadership the infantry must preserve its organization, cohesion and fighting power, and the division must be capable of continuing a successful offensive for several days. Success will always come from fortitude and skill, and from a resolute spirit in the troops and in subordinate commanders.[27]

As he had emphasized more than once, there must be nothing to explain, whether in a platoon, battery, or in any other of his commands.

The officers and men did have time to enjoy short vacations in leave areas. They received new uniforms and impressed French officers who visited frequently and praised the division's fighting ability. As the *History of the First Division* recorded, "the Division [had] not only regained its strength in numbers, but, if possible, it became more intense in pride and morale."[28] Occasionally excesses occurred, as when soldiers engaged in "unlawful fishing in ponds," by using grenades and other explosives to kill fish. Commanders were instructed to take strict disciplinary actions "in case of further violations."[29] Summerall frequently invited his officers to lunch, perhaps dining on fresh fish without his knowing how they were caught. He also "constantly visited commanders in the trenches," and noted in his memoir that "Morale was very high."[30]

Summerall hosted special lunches for Red Cross workers and met for the first time Clark Williams, a wealthy Wall Street financier and head of the Red Cross. He acquainted Williams with the plan of attack, for he expected many losses, and wanted to be sure that the Red Cross would be ready to care for the wounded. He wrote that Williams's "accomplishments were all that could have been desired," and that he became "my closest friend."[31] Their close relationship continued for the remainder of their lives. Years later, when Summerall took over as president of the struggling military college in South Carolina, Williams responded to his call for help by endowing five scholarships that continue to bear his name.

Meanwhile, the artillery brigade had moved into the Forêt de Reine, in the rear of the old Ansauville sector, and closer to the south side of the salient.[32] Another artillery brigade, an artillery regiment, and a battalion of howitzers were added to brigade, increasing its firepower to 120 75-mm guns, 40 155 mm howitzers, and 8 8-in. howitzers.[33] The First Division, with its training intensified, with its morale high, and with its artillery stronger than ever, was ready for the fight.

During the remainder of August and into September, as the First Division stepped up training, firepower, and boosted morale, GHQ and First Army headquarters finalized their plans for the St. Mihiel operation (Marshall noted that his working hours were from eight o'clock in the morning until two or three o'clock the next morning).[34] The attack would be the first operation controlled completely by AEF, and would include French divisions under the American umbrella of command. It would be a test of the competency of the First American Army, and of Pershing's consistent assertion that the American army knew how to beat the Germans and win the war.

Initially, Marshall and Grant were ordered to plan for six divisions to free the Paris–Nancy railroad that did not lie within German lines, but was threatened by enemy artillery in the salient. Then came the order to increase the number of divisions to 10, then to 14, and then to 16, in addition to six French divisions. The scope of the operation was increased to include the complete reduction of the salient by massive attacks from both sides, as well as against the nose of the salient at St. Mihiel, and the advance of the line of attack to the outskirts of Metz. If the offensive succeeded, Pershing wanted to continue it as far as possible.[35] Over 500,000 Americans and 110,000 Frenchmen, 2,971 guns, 200,000 tons of supplies, 50,000 tons of ammunition, including 3.3 million artillery shells, and 267 light tanks were massed for the attack that was expected to last five days. Engineer and communication equipment was necessary to the operation, as well as hospitals, and railroad and supply depots. The recently organized 1st Tank Brigade of 144 new Renault light tanks, commanded by Lieutenant Colonel George S. Patton, Jr., and organized into two battalions, was added to the operation. Patton had recruited his crews and had devised and supervised a training program for them. He would lead the only American tank brigade to see action during the war.[36]

Crucial to the success of the operation was the element of surprise, and, in order to conceal all preparations, most of the troops, supplies and materiel would have to be moved at night.[37] Finally, under the leadership of Colonel William Mitchell, the air combat veteran of the Battle of Château-Thierry, a coalition force of more than 1,400 American, British, French, and Italian airmen was assembled to support operations. It would be the largest concentration of air power in all of World War I.[38]

As First Army gathered resources for the attack, Pershing seemed to thrive on an increasingly heavy workload, and his spirits were high. First Army headquarters was up and running, General Foch had approved his general plan, and Field Marshal Haig had agreed to release three U.S divisions from the BEF to join the American army for the St. Mihiel attack.[39] Then, Pershing was stunned when Foch, who had been made marshal on 7 August, informed him on the morning of 30 August, that he and Haig had agreed on a plan that would require major changes in the St. Mihiel operation.[40] That afternoon the French marshal came to First Army headquarters with a proposal for an offensive that would produce "a far more important result than the mere disengaging of the Commercy railway line by the capture of the Saint-Mihiel pocket."[41] In view of the victories the Allies had won by the end of August, Foch proposed that all the Allied armies be brought together in a greater mission to attack the Meuse-Argonne region. It would combine the Franco-British attack already under way around Cambrai and St. Quentin, north of Soissons, with a Franco-American attack along both banks of the Meuse toward Mézières, the city north of Sedan between the Meuse and Aisne rivers. He was afraid that if the American army carried its St. Mihiel offensive too far, and in the wrong direction as well, it would not be in a position to support the projected mission that he called the Battle of Mézières. In order for Foch to direct the offensive against Mézières, from which he expected "very great results," he asked Pershing to reduce the force for the St. Mihiel operation to nine divisions, and limit the objective to clear the Paris–Avricourt railroad, an objective several miles short of the base of the salient. The remaining divisions would drive toward Mézières with the French.[42]

Pershing was not pleased. He stated that dividing American forces would destroy "the thing we have been trying so long to form—that is, an American Army." He also stated that limiting the objective in the St. Mihiel attack would make it more difficult to force the Germans out of the salient, and thus risk a disaster. Pershing repeated his long-standing objection to having American soldiers under French or British command, but he was mainly concerned with preserving his newly created American army.⁴³ After two and one-half hours of intense discussion, the meeting ended without an agreement.

The next day, Pershing wrote Foch, stating that he would not agree to any plan to disperse units of the American army, and reiterated his concerns about limiting the attack on the salient. He pointed out the difficulties of carrying out the St. Mihiel operation, and then immediately thereafter withdrawing divisions and transferring them to another region. But he concluded his letter by stating that if Foch decided

> to utilize American forces by attacking in the direction of Mézières, I accept that decision, even though it complicates my supply system and the care of my sick and wounded, but I do insist that the American Army must be employed as a whole, either east of the Argonne, or west of the Argonne, and not four or five divisions here and six or seven there.⁴⁴

Before he left Ligny-en-Barrois, Foch gave Pershing a summary and detailed explanation of the points he had raised. The next morning, Pershing consulted his staff, and that afternoon met with General Pétain, who understood the issues Pershing had raised.⁴⁵

On 2 September, Pershing, Pétain, and Foch met at the marshal's headquarters. After discussing French and American concerns, they agreed to press ahead with the St. Mihiel operation, and, just as importantly, to use Pershing's American army in the Battle of Mézières. They decided to limit the attack on the salient to the line, short of the base that Foch had originally proposed; the attack would use eight to 10 divisions, and begin on 10 September; the attack in the Battle of Mézières would be made between 20 and 25 September by from 12 to 14 divisions of the American army, in addition to those that would be refitted after the St. Mihiel operation; the American army would attack between the Meuse River and the Argonne, and would be supported on their left by the French Fourth Army. The entire Meuse-Argonne offensive would be commanded by General Pétain.⁴⁶

The agreement of 2 September preserved Pershing's American army. It would fight in two major offensives and have a crucial, if not decisive, impact on the course of the war. He had taken on an awesome task for it. After fighting a major battle, the army would have to disengage and move some 60 miles away to fight another great battle. All of this would have to be accomplished within a span of two weeks, with a First Army staff that had developed a plan based on the earlier mission to capture the entire salient. Now, not only would they have to revise this plan, but they also would have to prepare a plan within 14 days for the Meuse-Argonne operation. Was this really too large an undertaking? Historian Donald Smythe believed it was.⁴⁷ In addition, as shall be noted below, Smythe found much to criticize in the performance of First Army in the St. Mihiel operation. It seems that his critique would certainly apply to Summerall, who was an exceptionally important commander at St. Mihiel. It also seems that his question, with respect to the Meuse-Argonne operation, implied that Summerall could not manage his even greater responsibilities in that offensive. Whether Smythe's criticisms can be applied fairly to Summerall is an issue that will be addressed below as well.

Pershing informed Drum on 3 September of the new plans, and George Marshall and Walter Grant promptly were ordered to devote themselves "exclusively…to the revision of the orders, and the preparations concerned" for the St. Mihiel operation.⁴⁸ The plan that Pershing approved called for three coordinated attacks to reduce the salient (see map, p. 237).

General Liggett's I Corps and General Dickman's IV Corps would carry out the main attack against the southern face. The second attack would be against the western face and would be made by V Corps, commanded by Major General George H. Cameron.⁴⁹ (Like Dickman, a former cavalryman, Cameron had led the Fourth Division in the Aisne-Marne offensive when it established and held the first bridgehead across the Vesle River.)⁵⁰ The French II Corps would attack the "nose" of the salient

*General John J. Pershing and Major General Charles P. Summerall with officers*

Courtesy National Archives

and hold the Germans in their front as the two American attacks converged to trap the Germans and split it apart. General Liggett's corps consisted of the four divisions, the Eighty-second, the "All Americans," commanded by Major General William P. Burnham, who had entered West Point with the class of 1885 but had failed to be graduated and had then enlisted and worked his way up through the ranks; the Ninetieth, under General Allen; the Second, under its new commander, Major General Lejeune, USMC, who had commanded the division's Marine Brigade at Soissons; and the Fifth, commanded by Major General John E. McMahon, a veteran of the Philippine Insurrection. Colonel Paul Malone, who had commanded a regiment in the Second Division at Soissons, led the Fifth's 10th Brigade. Dickman's IV Corps included the Eighty-ninth Division, under General Wright, the Forty-second Division, commanded by General Menoher, Pershing's classmate, and the First Division, under the fearless and hard-driving Summerall.[51] Pershing depended upon the veteran First, Second, and Forty-second Divisions to delivery a "rapid and deep, powerful blow," and he had given them the most important strategic positions in the main attack opposite the most open terrain of the Woevre Plain.[52] On the west face of the salient, General Cameron's V Corps was made up of the veteran Twenty-sixth Division (of Ansauville sector-relief fame), under General Edwards. It also included a part of the Fourth Division under General Hines, the battle-tested and resourceful veteran of Soissons, and the French Fifteenth Colonial Division.[53]

In view of the necessity to coordinate and supply his huge army of over 500,000 soldiers, Pershing was concerned that two of his corps headquarters, IV and V, had never been involved in offensive operations. Their commanders, Dickman and Cameron, had been promoted in July, and had had less than a month to organize their headquarters and get ready for battle. In addition, four divisions (the Fifth, Eighty-second, Eighty-ninth, and Ninetieth) had never been engaged in offensive combat; and, in his newly-formed army, many soldiers had met their commanders and leaders for the first time. They were a part of a mixed command made up of French artillery, air service, tanks, and various other specialists.[54] He had great faith in his five proven strike divisions, the First, Second, Fourth, Twenty-sixth, and Forty-second, but he knew that using them to achieve victory in the St. Mihiel attack meant that they could not be transferred to the Meuse-Argonne in time to begin that attack. Thus, to lead that assault, he realized that he would have to use inexperienced divisions that had not even completed their training. Some of them would be without their own artillery and would have artillery brigades assigned to them with which they had never been in contact.[55] But, Pershing had decided to use his best divisions at St. Mihiel before Foch ordered the Meuse-Argonne operation, and it was now too late to make any changes.[56]

The St. Mihiel offensive was now set to begin on 12 September at 0500 hours. To conceal their attack, most of the soldiers in the huge American army would move all through the night of 11 September toward their jump-off positions. Just before his division moved out, Summerall conferred with his commanders as a cold and heavy rain poured through the jet-black night. They reviewed the division's intelligence report that the division intelligence officer, Captain Thomas R. Gowenlock had prepared, and Summerall pointed out the difficulties they would face.[57] He ordered the infantry to swim across the Rupt de Mad if the bridges (that were heavy and difficult to move through the mud) did not arrive. As Summerall remembered, George Patton, whose tank brigade had been ordered to support the First and Forty-second Divisions, was present, and said, with his usual gusto, that he would drive the tanks into the stream so that the infantry could cross over on them. Summerall cautioned that the men in the tanks might drown. Patton responded that, if so, he would be one of them.[58] Fortunately, Patton did not have to sacrifice himself, even though the rains had forced the creek over its banks and increased the depth to 20 feet.

As the Rupt de Mad swelled and overflowed, and the cold rain soaked the khaki uniforms that clung to their bodies, the men of the First American Army shivered in their waterlogged trenches and waited to attack. The artillery was parked almost wheel to wheel, and at 0100 hours on 12 September, almost 3,000 guns began firing. At 0500 hours the guns shifted to a rolling barrage, and the attack on the south face of the salient began, with the Americans plunging into no-man's land, through mud 18 inches deep, followed by the French supporting attack an hour later. The French attack against the nose of the salient, designed to hold the Germans, also began at 0600 hours, followed by the western attack at 0800, and another supporting French attack at 0900.[59] The German defenders were caught off guard and had just begun to withdraw some of their matériel, including heavy artillery. A deluge of artillery fire, intended primarily to damage the German wire, wiped out many machine gun nests. Smoke and mustard gas shells exploded in woods and along roads, making enemy communication and resistance much more difficult.[60]

As historian James Hallas points out, "the Big Red One had drawn the most difficult assignment in IV Corps." Their job was to advance through the mud and across the rising waters of the Rupt de Mad and protect their left flank dominated by Montsec.[61] But the feared butte remained strangely quiet, and the *History of the First Division* attributed this phenomenon to the artillery fire that had blinded its "baleful eyes."[62] As noted, preliminary artillery fire had been especially effective in eliminating machine guns, and, with assault battalions from each of the division's four regiments leading the way, by 0530 hours the infantry reached their first objective, the near bank of the Rupt de Mad. They paused while the artillery laid down a 20-minute barrage on the far bank. Five of Major Brett's tanks crept alongside (see note 53), firing at enemy pillboxes across the stream, while engineers laid down footbridges. Infantry threw down chicken wire matting and walked over the German wire that had not been cut by the engineers. The remaining 44 tanks crossed the stream to the left of the sector

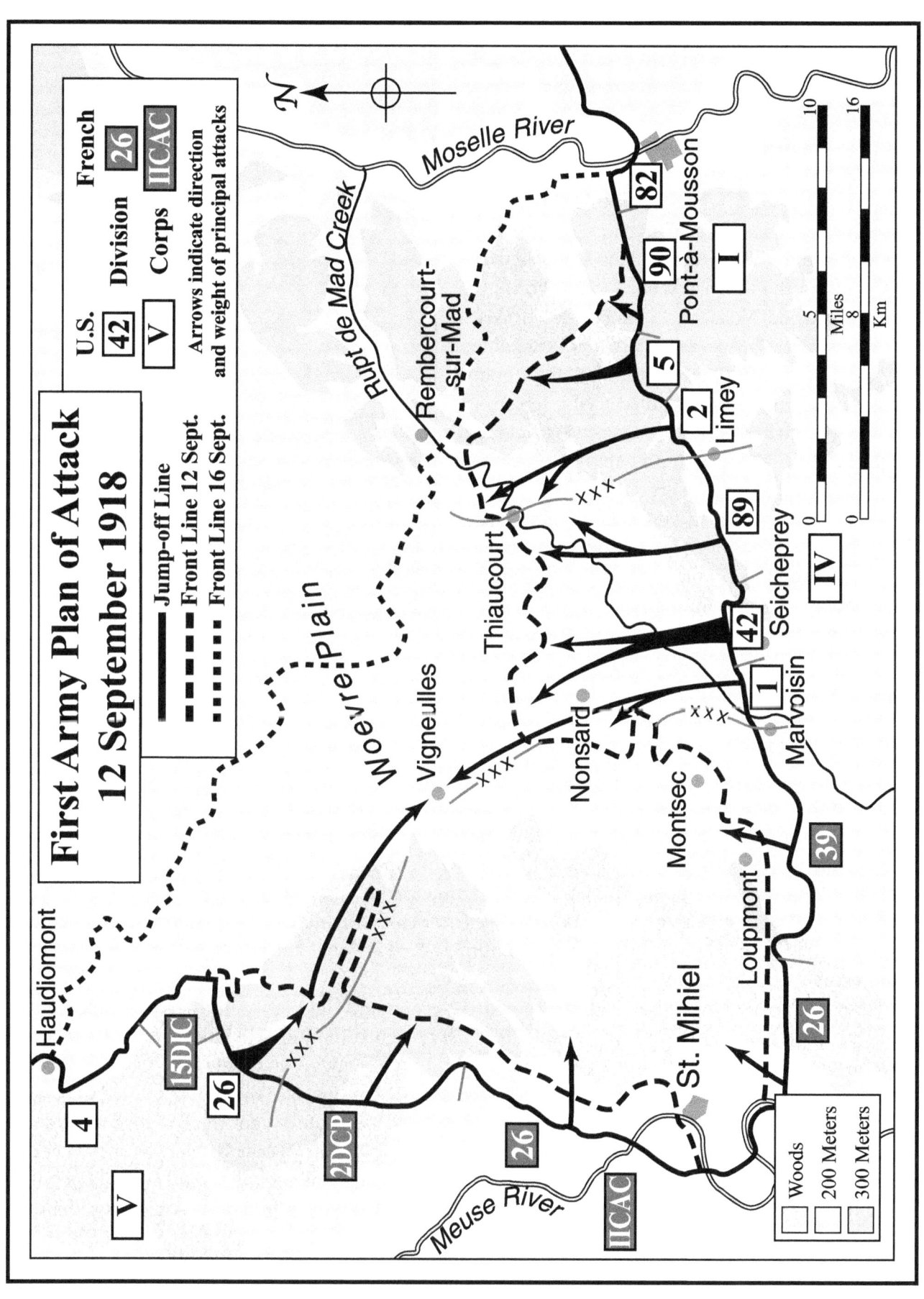

and moved up the far bank to link up with the advancing infantry. Some bogged down, but the 16th Infantry wiped out German machine gun nests in the rubble of a small town on the far bank.[63] On their left, the 18th Regiment cleared a dense forest and moved forward with the rest of the division toward the town of Nonsard, which was the objective at the end of the first day. The artillery barrage fell at 1100 hours, and the lines resumed their advance, stepping through the German wire. At 1230 hours the division reached Nonsard, having suffered losses that were "far less than expected" and "unbelievably small," and dug in to consolidate their gains. Some of the tanks were disabled trying to cross a creek with high banks.[64] Other tanks were delayed, but joined the division, as it prepared for a German counterattack that never materialized.

At IV Corps headquarters, General Dickman, the ex-cavalryman, sought to exploit what he considered the crumbling German resistance by sending three troops of cavalry through the First Division to reconnoiter toward Vigneulles and Heudicourt, northwest of Nonsard. Their mission was to cut the Vigneulles–Heudicourt railroad and be in position

*Major General J. T. Dickman*
Courtesy National Archives

to block an enemy retreat from the tip of the salient. They passed through the infantry lines at 0430 hours into the Nonsard Wood, about a mile and a half from Nonsard, where they encountered German soldiers, wagons, and guns on the move out of the salient. The Germans opened fire from machine guns that had remained hidden as the First Division had stormed through; their infantry charged toward the troopers, spooked the horses, and scared the inexperienced recruits into a mad dash back through the woods. A few veterans managed to retain control and led the fight through the woods, capturing ten prisoners and knocking out two machine guns.[65] They only lost one man killed and one captured, but, as Dickman noted in his book *The Great Crusade*, "they did not accomplish much that day, except the capture of a few prisoners."[66] Summerall's reaction to the failed cavalry mission will be noted below.

The other two divisions in IV Corps, the Forty-second and the Eighty-ninth, had jumped off on schedule to the right of the First Division. Before they reached the Rupt de Mad, the 3rd Battalion of Brigadier General Douglas MacArthur's 84th Brigade of the Forty-second met stiff German resistance in Sonnard Wood. Artillery fire had failed to dislodge the Germans, and they hit the doughboys with machine gun fire and mortar blasts. Major Compton's tanks (see note 53) got stuck in the mud, but the battalion continued to press the attack. They cut through the wire, leapt over barriers, and crouched in shell holes to gather their strength before rushing forward. They made it into woods and fought hand-to-hand with the Germans. By 0630 hours, they had taken Sonnard Wood and moved forward with the rest of the division, which had met with much less resistance.[67]

But MacArthur's brigade appeared to have stalled at the village of Essay, located on the near bank of the Rupt de Mad. Colonel Patton, who had been with Compton's tanks, joined MacArthur, who was personally leading his infantrymen. Both surveyed a bridge across the stream, as a creeping barrage moved ever closer. Patton noted that the barrage was "very thin and not dangerous. I think each one [of us] wanted to leave, but each hated to say so, so we let it come over us."⁶⁸ Whether the bridge was mined is not known, but Patton walked safely across and led his tankers into the village. This would not be the last time that these two ambitious and heroic personalities would demonstrate their composure in combat, but as Patton's biographer Carlo d'Este noted, "one writer has observed: 'One properly placed German shell at this moment in World War I would have eliminated two major, inspiring, and controversial figures of World War II.'"⁶⁹

With Patton's tanks across the stream, MacArthur's brigade advanced through Essey on to Pannes, where they joined General Lenihan's 83rd Brigade, which had had a much easier time moving forward on the right of the 84th. By the end of the day, the Forty-second Division had advanced to roughly the same line that the First Division had reached. The attack on Sonnard Wood had cost the 3rd Battalion 200 casualties, but they had captured almost 300 prisoners and killed an undisclosed number of Germans.⁷⁰

*Lieutenant General H. Liggett*
Courtesy National Archives

To the right of the Forty-second, General Wright's Eighty-ninth Division went over the top on schedule, and he soon received reports that "everything was going very well." He noted that "There is no shelling by the Boche back of our lines—and I think he has withdrawn his guns."⁷¹ They kept going strong, as Wright stated, and he sent Colonel Conrad Babcock, late of the First Division and now in command of the 354th Infantry, to help work on the roads to speed up the division's advance. By 1700 hours they had pushed forward to roughly parallel the line of advance of the two divisions on their left. Casualties were about 500 to 600, with very few killed, and with about 3,000 prisoners on their hands. Wright stated that shrapnel had caused most of their casualties, and that "the infantry resistance seemed to melt away in front of our advance."⁷²

To the right of IV Corps, General Liggett's I Corps attacked the southeastern section of the salient and advanced rapidly. The hard-driving Second Division, under General Lejeune, surged forward over rough terrain, covering six miles in just over eight hours. They captured Thiacourt, the largest town in the salient, at 1100 hours, and seized the heights north of the town, giving the Americans control of the German supply route into the salient. The division took about 3,000 prisoners. They captured 92 artillery pieces lined up on railroad flatcars, an entire hospital train, an ammunition train, and 52 empty freight cars. The estimate of casualties in the Second Division was less than five percent, and most of them were wounded.⁷³

The Fifth Division, commanded by General McMahon, was to the right of the Second. Attacking into the fog and behind a curtain of shellfire and smoke, they swept through lightly held trenches, moving so fast that some of them ran into the rolling barrage, and were wounded. A couple of miles to the southeast, General Allen's Ninetieth Division encountered some of the toughest fighting in the salient but reached all of its objectives ahead of schedule, securing the extreme right of the southern face.⁷⁴ By the end of the first day of combat on the south face, IV Corps and I Corps had advanced beyond the objectives that had been planned for the second day.

Across on the west face, General Edwards's Twenty-sixth Division of General Cameron's V Corps attacked on schedule at 0800 hours, three hours later than the attack on the southern face (see map, p. 237). They rose from muddy trenches and made their way across no-man's land that was scarred by trenches in all directions, dotted with shattered trees, and with overlapping shell holes spread out before them. Belt after belt of barbed wire stretched out for miles. They were supported by French divisions on either side and had been assigned the deepest penetration in their sector. The assault troops stumbled forth across the pockmarked terrain, meeting little resistance until they encountered machine-gunners deeply dug in on a rise in the woods, protected by pillboxes and trenches. But the Yankee Division pressed forward, cleared the woods, and began sending groups of prisoners back to stockades in the rear. An observer noted that most of the prisoners "were serious-looking men of middle age who seemed to be glad to be out of the war." The majority of them wore clean uniforms, a sign that they had surrendered without resisting.[75] By the end of the day, some units were thrusting a long arm into the German lines, pressing forward toward the town of Vigneulles. It was located about 11 miles from the nose of the salient and the main road that the Germans would use to pull out of the salient ran through it.

By the afternoon of 12 September, First Army headquarters seemed confident that the St. Mihiel offensive would succeed. George Marshall turned to planning preliminary movements for the concentration of forces for the Meuse-Argonne operation.[76] When Pershing received the news that enemy soldiers and artillery were retreating along roads leading out of the salient, he ordered IV and V Corps to push forward without delay. He used the telephone to instruct General Cameron to send a regiment of the Twenty-sixth Division toward Vigneulles "with all possible speed."[77] Cameron sent the 1st Battalion of his 102nd Infantry, commanded by Marine Colonel Hiram I. Bearss, a veteran of the Philippines and Belleau Wood. Bearss ordered his men out of their shell holes, and on to Vigneulles. They left late that afternoon and captured 280 prisoners along the way. They arrived in the town at 0230 hours the next morning, woke up the surprised 10,000 inhabitants, and captured almost an entire German machine gun battalion that was preparing to evacuate the salient. For good measure, they also captured a German army band.[78]

General Dickman wrote that shortly after midnight on 12 September he succeeded in getting Pershing's order out to the 2nd Brigade of the First Division to advance to Vigneulles and the nearby town on Hattonville "to close all the roads to the north and east of these towns."[79] Summerall reinforced General Bamford's 2nd Brigade with all available machine guns, but by the time the frontline battalions had been readied, the brigade did not begin to move until 0315 hours the next morning, 45 minutes after Bearss's men had entered Vigneulles.[80] They had to march in the night through dense woods and found the roads leading northeast toward Vigneulles and Hattonville crowded with American artillery on the move.[81] Thus, they did not reach the latter town until 0620 hours and did not meet Bearss's men from the Twenty-sixth Division in Vigneulles until later that morning.[82] The two units had blocked the main road out of the salient, but of some 40,000 enemy soldiers at the tip, almost all managed to slip out before Bearss and Bamford had sprung their trap. Nevertheless, when Pershing received the news that the salient had been closed, he realized that his soldiers were "masters of the field."[83] As James Hallas points out, that day was also his 58th birthday, and "he could not have asked for a better present."[84]

In 1927, Dickman's book about his wartime service, *The Great Crusade*, was published. In it, he stated that the First Division was at least partly responsible for letting so many Germans escape on 12 September. Ignoring, or simply overlooking the communication problems and artillery traffic that clogged the roads and trails traveled by Bamford's men, Dickman wrote that

> If the 1st Division, even after receipt of the Corps order, had exercised for a short time the energy and skill in night marching and fighting which it exhibited later in the war, the Vigneulles-St. Benoit highway might have been reached from four to six hours sooner, resulting probably in a great increase of prisoners and captured material of war. However, in some of these things even our best divisions were still lacking in sufficient experience.[85]

If this sounds like a criticism of Summerall, that is, indeed, what it was. He and Dickman became embittered toward one another after Sedan, as shall be seen, and their mutual animosity lingered for the rest of their lives. In his comments on the Sedan incident, George Marshall recalled in 1957 that "the fight between Summerall and Dickman was very intense and went back to all sorts of jealousies." The "Dickman crowd," he continued, "were jealous of General Summerall's great reputation which he had made in the hard fighting."[86] In view of the combat record of the First Division, it seems rather extraordinary, if one is not aware of that relationship, that Dickman would state that the division, even if he had recognized it as one of the best, was "still lacking in sufficient experience." In his memoir, Summerall did not mention anything about the link-up with the battalion of the Twenty-sixth, but did describe the cavalry attack that Dickman had ordered. He wrote that "The day of the cavalry on the field of battle had ended. The fellow, Dickman, tried to discredit me for not having it charge. He knew nothing of conditions and he was totally ignorant of battle." He added punch to his seething resentment by noting that Dickman was "ignorant, foul-mouthed and brutal at the conference held with division commanders." Rather self-servingly, he stated that "It was a rule of the First Division never to criticize other troops. I always felt that I was fighting Germans and not Americans, and I never criticized other troops as other commanders did."[87] Obviously, after the war was over, he took off the gloves.

Another factor that limited Allied success, in spite of American efforts to conceal the preparations for the offensive from the enemy, was that by 10 September the Germans had determined the Americans would attack the salient with a major force.[88] German Supreme Headquarters and General Max von Gallwitz, commander of the army group that included Detachment C that held the salient, considered a preemptive attack. With the Americans rapidly increasing their buildup, General Ludendorff requested that von Gallwitz withdraw his forces to the Michael position, the defensive line of pillboxes and trenches that had been constructed along the base of the salient.[89] He began withdrawing some heavy artillery on 11 September, and when the American attack began on 12 September, Supreme Headquarters ordered that the lines be held to enable the withdrawal to continue. The swift Allied advance broke through many places along the hastily manned positions, forcing the Germans to evacuate as fast as possible to the Michael position.[90]

On 13 September, in order to improve his defensive position on the right flank of the breakthrough, Pershing ordered elements of the Eighty-second and Ninetieth Divisions to stage limited attacks on the extreme left of the German line.[91] These attacks would also help to conceal from von Gallwitz the concentration of men and guns to the Meuse-Argonne front, and deceive him about where the main American attack would occur. Indeed, the German commander believed that the increased American activity indicated that they might advance toward Metz, so he strengthened his line with four extra divisions. He despaired of mounting an offensive thrust to disrupt the American preparations and reported to Supreme Headquarters that "the only course left open to us is defense with counterattacks at suitable points."[92] For the next three days, American units attacked all along the German line in front of I Corps. They fought off German counterattacks, suffering 3,000 casualties,[93] but the salient had been seized, and First Army's position had been established and consolidated.

Colonel Mitchell's air service had been frustrated by foul weather during the first few days of the St. Mihiel offensive, but they took advantage of better weather conditions. They flew offensive patrols, attacked infantry and artillery positions, spotted for artillery, conducted high-level bombing runs and photographic reconnaissance.[94] Pershing commended their success, and their comprehensive missions undoubtedly added to von Gallwitz's expectation that the Americans would press their attack toward Metz.

Historian Ulrich Trumpener believes that von Gallwitz's divisions generally gave a good account of themselves in their defense of the St. Mihiel salient,[95] but by 16 September, Supreme Headquarters had determined that von Gallwitz's army had been defeated. Field Marshal von Hindenburg wrote his army group commander an angry and stinging criticism of his leadership. He stated that

> The defeat of Composite Army C on September 12 has rendered the situation of the Group of Armies critical. I have, insofar as the situation permits, adjusted the consumption of forces caused for the most part by faulty leadership and will also give further aid although it is very difficult for me to do so.... I can only hope that the Group of Armies employing the forces I have allotting to it will hold the position. The Group of Armies will bear the complete responsibility for this. I am not willing to admit that one American is worth 2 Germans. Whenever commander and troops have been determined to hold their positions and the artillery has been well organized, even weak German divisions have repulsed the mass attacks of American divisions and inflicted heavy losses on the enemy.[96]

In view of First Army's success and the Germans' rapid retreat, Pershing was sorely tempted to continue the advance toward Metz, but decided that it would become too involved and would risk delaying the Meuse-Argonne operation, "to which we were wholly committed."[97] Marshall wrote that he had no doubt that the First Army could have reached Metz by late afternoon on 13 September and could have captured the city by the next day. But, he and Grant stated vigorously that they were opposed to the idea, mainly because the American attack had lost its momentum and was out of range of its heavy artillery support; the Germans had a chance to reform scattered units and bring up reserves; and any advance would make impossible the concentration of men by the date set by Pershing for the Meuse-Argonne attack.[98] MacArthur wrote that he and his brigade adjutant made a nighttime reconnaissance of the area around Metz and found it "practically defenseless." He strongly recommended that his brigade lead an attack on the city, but Dickman, Liggett, and Pershing rejected any attack.[99] Liggett's reasons for opposing such an attack were particularly strong and sound. He maintained that the possibility of taking Metz existed only if the army was "a well-oiled, fully coordinated machine, which it was not as yet." He thought Foch had been wise to limit the attack to reducing the salient, thus protecting the American rear for the Meuse-Argonne attack. He contended that the German defenses in the salient had been strong and noted that they could have thrown in reserves to resist an attack on Metz, just as they had done, as shall be noted below, so easily and rapidly in the Meuse-Argonne. "This latter battle was the greater surprise of the two [to the Germans]," he wrote, "yet from the third day on they held us up until we paid in blood for every yard we gained." Even if the American army had "engaged to its uttermost" in an attack on Metz, he wrote, it probably would have spent the winter "mired in the mud of the Woevre, flanked to the east and the west."[100] In addition, a First Division intelligence report warned that the Germans had prepared a system of dams and dikes that they could exploit to inundate and turn the flat, marshy Woevre plain, as they had done in the Somme.[101]

Donald Smythe agreed that General Liggett's concerns about the army's expertise and efficiency were justified. American soldiers were still firing on their own planes; artillery barrages were not well coordinated with infantry attacks, as noted above; "Discipline was lax....Pilfering of prisoners was almost universal"; "animals were misued or abused"; and when telephone lines failed, commanders failed to use "a horse relay system" to restore communications, and remained out of touch; command headquarters were too far to the rear, and because they were not clearly marked, were at times difficult for messengers to locate. Smythe concluded that "Far from being impressed by the American effort, many felt that it revealed serious deficiencies which boded ill for the future." One of those was French Premier Georges Clemenceau, who got caught in a massive traffic jam on a visit to Pershing at Ligny on 15 September. Smythe notes that this monumental snarl "confirmed all his [Clemenceau's] fears about U.S. incapacity to handle large forces."[102]

Regardless of the German field marshal's negative assessment of American divisions, the French premier's fear of American mismanagement of big armies, and Donald Smythe's incisive criticisms, First Army had fulfilled its mission. Peshing's army had freed the Paris–Nancy railroad and reduced the salient; it had consolidated its defensive position; had threatened the fortress city of Metz, and misled von Gallwitz about the direction of its next major attack, while it began to prepare for the Meuse-Argonne operation. The army had captured nearly 16,000 prisoners and almost 443 guns and 752 machine guns. Its losses numbered about 10,000, including those lost in the consolidation of its position after 13 September.[103] In addition, Billy Mitchell's air service performed well and gained valuable experience for the Meuse-Argonne offensive. For Pershing, the victory "completely demonstrated the wisdom of building up a distinct American army." He believed that the result "must have tremendously heartened our people at home, as it gave them a tangible reason to believe that our contribution to the war would be the deciding factor." Most importantly, he thought that "The St. Mihiel victory probably did more than any single operation of the war to encourage our Allies....it brought assurance of the final defeat of a enemy whose armies had seemed well-nigh invincible." When he and Pétain visited the town of St. Mihiel on 13 September, the townspeople gave them an enthusiastic welcome in celebration of their deliverance from four years of German occupation. Pershing noted that "The French people of all classes were loud in their praise of Americans."[104]

While the Forty-second and Eighty-ninth Divisions of Dickman's IV Corps assisted I Corps in consolidating the defensive line along the base of the salient, the First Division, having completed its mission to meet the Twenty-sixth and slam shut the door that led out of the salient, moved to the reserve of IV Corps. They regrouped not far from Nonsard, in a wooded area that had been the site of a German rest camp. They found themselves in the midst of "artistic cottages and bungalows" that were filled with furniture and decorations the Germans had taken from surrounding villages. They had built clubhouses for officers and men and had equipped them with pianos, movie projectors and screens. The hastily retreating Germans had left behind several handsome horses in comfortable stables, as well as uniforms, various personal effects, and freshly cooked food.[105]

The First Division had earned their rest and the time to relax in the woods and enjoy the amenities the German army had left behind. They had advanced some nine miles in nineteen hours in the most important sector of the St. Mihiel salient. In a driving rain, they had attacked across marshy terrain and a flooded creek, through knee-deep mud and steeply banked trenches, and deep woods seemingly wrapped in barbed wire. Their losses were 3 officers and 90 men killed, 10 officers and 431 wounded, and 10 men captured and missing.[106]

Pershing visited division headquarters to express his satisfaction with the division's conduct of operations. Colonel Campbell King, chief of staff of the First Division, recorded that Pershing told them how much had been expected from the First Division, and that it had done its part "with great credit." In a tribute that revealed the deep emotional side of the commander in chief, he told Summerall and his headquarters staff, as King noted, that "he entertained a special feeling for the Division and its conduct on this, as well as on other occasions, fully justified this feeling." He left them with his regrets that his time was so limited that he could not stay longer and see more of the officers.[107] Surely, at this time, Summerall must have felt a strong emotional attachment to the man who had such great confidence in him, and whose personality and leadership had inspired Summerall, just as he had been inspired by the role models in his past. It is indeed unfortunate and sad that the antipathy he felt toward Pershing for his belated and critical reaction to the future episode of Sedan, should displace the strong, personal bond that undoubtedly had been forged between these two like-minded warriors on the battleground of France. Regrettably, the smile that crossed Summerall's face as he walked with Pershing along the Rupt de Mad would fade into a tight-lipped scorn that wiped out the memory of that happy day (see picture, p. 235).

After Pershing's visit to their headquarters, the men of the division spent their remaining few days in the sector behaving like tourists: walking in the woods, writing letters home, and visiting the heights of Montsec and Hattonchâtel, from which they could see the panorama of St. Mihiel battlefield stretching out before them.[108] As they gazed across the broken ground, splintered forests, and smoldering ruins of towns and villages, and returned to the comfortable surroundings of camp, their thoughts must have turned back many times to the war, and to the next mission their seemingly invincible commander would call upon them to fulfill. Once again, they would not have long to wait.

# Chapter Twelve

## *The Meuse-Argonne, "Racing" to Sedan, and Peace*

As First Army prepared for the St. Mihiel operation, British and French victories in Flanders and the area of Amiens forced Ludendorff's army back to the Hindenburg defensive line to protect its lateral communication. The German defeats had diminished German resources of men and matériel and undermined the army's morale. In despair, Ludendorff declared that "The war must be ended." Foch was eager to exploit the advantage the Allies held and keep the pressure on the German defenses. He was confident that a series of coordinated Allied attacks on the German line would break down the huge salient, known as the Laon bulge, which still remained after the German army had surged into Belgium and France. Foch also believed that success against the salient would prevent the enemy "from conducting any battle on a large scale, even a defensive one."[1]

On 3 September, the day after Foch had met with Pershing and Pétain to finalize the St. Mihiel operation and the American attack in the Meuse-Argonne, he sent the Allied commanders in chief more emphatic and sweeping instructions "to hurl the mass of their forces against the line from Cambrai—Saint-Quentin—Mézières, where they would reach the principal German lateral railway line. This meant the launching, west of the Meuse, of a new and powerful American attack."[2] The Allied armies would follow converging directions along the front. The British, supported on the left by French armies, would continue to attack eastward toward Cambrai and St. Quentin. The central units of the French armies would push the enemy across the Aisne and Ailette Rivers in the center of the line. The American offensive, "as powerful and violent as possible," would drive in the general direction of Mézières, "covered on the east by the Meuse, and supported on the left by an attack of the French Fourth Army." This offensive, he added, "will be prepared with the greatest rapidity in order that it may be launched, at the latest between the 20th and 25th of September."[3]

The Meuse-Argonne front that Marshal Foch assigned to First Army was located south of Verdun, extending about 18 miles east to west. As Pershing noted,

> it was ideal for defensive fighting. On the east, the heights of the Meuse commanded that river valley and on the west the rugged high hills of the Argonne Forest dominated the valley of the Aire River. In the center, the watershed between the Aire and the Meuse Rivers commanded both valleys, with the heights of Montfaucon, Cunel, Romagne, and of the Bois de Barricourt standing out as natural strong points. From these heights, observation points completely covered the entire area in front of the German lines.[4] (See map, p. 248)

The high points of Montfaucon, Cunel, Romagne, and Barricourt were along or near a massive ridge that ran up the center. It had a sharp summit, outcropping edges of rock and steeply sloping

*General Ferdinand Foch and General John J. Pershing at Val des Ecoliers, Chaumont, France*

Courtesy National Archives

sides and looked like the back of a razorback hog. It divided the area into two narrow defiles that forced attackers to fight their way through, while under artillery and machine gun fire from the brisling hogback in the center, from the Argonne Forest plateau to the west, and the Heights of the Meuse to the east. More hills, dense woods, and gulches covered with underbrush were scattered throughout the area.[5] General Liggett wrote that "the region was a natural fortress beside which the Virginia Wilderness in which Grant and Lee fought was a park."[6] To General Harbord, who had visited the area in June 1917 after the battle of Verdun, the area seemed as though "the Almighty had designed it as a barrier against the passage of an invader from either direction."[7]

The Germans had organized their defenses behind the Hindenburg line in the region into three main positions, or *stellungen*, named after Norse and Germanic legends—Giselher, Kriemhilde, and Freya—that Richard Wagner had incorporated into his great operatic cycle, *The Ring of the Nibelungen*. They were even more dense and challenging than any of Wagner's *Ring* operas. During the four years that the Germans had occupied the area, they had fortified the *stellungen* into a defensive labyrinth that protected their strategic lateral rail lines and secured the south face of the Laon bulge (see map, p. 248). General Harbord wrote that

> what nature had, perhaps without design, created in the way of defenses [thus qualifying his previous assessment of the Almighty's handiwork], military art had contributed every device known to modern war. Old, rusty, new, twisted, netted crossed and overlapping barbed wire was strung in endless miles with fortified strong points, dugouts, concrete machine-gun emplacements, skillfully selected natural machine-gun sites, and many lines of trenches, flanking and in parallel depth. It was probably the most comprehensive system of leisurely prepared field defenses known to history.[8]

General von Gallwitz's army group held the front from Verdun to the Argonne Forest with 13 divisions in line, with 11 divisions in reserve in the vicinity of Metz. First Army reported that the morale of these divisions was "below normal," and the quality of many was poor.[9] In addition, historian Paul Braim noted that their divisions were two-thirds below strength, although the German command structure was still effective, and the high command had emphasized the importance of a strong defense in Lorraine.[10]

In view of the rough and challenging terrain and formidable defenses, only five under-strength German divisions defended the area between the Meuse and the Argonne Forest. The wide "mouth" of the region opened to the north and made possible the rather rapid "funneling" of reinforcements. The east-west direction of the rail lines facilitated movement along the defensive lines. Perhaps these factors accounted for von Gallwitz's belief that an Allied attack was imminent against the Michel position in the St. Mihiel salient, rather than in the Meuse-Argonne area. He noted that a large part of the enemy artillery had moved forward in the salient, and that the "battle-tested" First and Second Divisions had been withdrawn so that the enemy could "grant his attack divisions a few days of rest…."[11] Also, Ludendorff reported on 22 September that "in view of the entry into the line of a new and only partly trained American division, an immediate attack [between the Meuse and Argonne] is improbable." He realized that a main French-American attack was coming but could not yet determine the probable direction.[12]

Meanwhile, Marshal Foch had set the time schedule for the great offensive that would strike the Laon salient "from the Meuse to the North Sea." On 26 September, the French and Americans would attack between the Suippe and the Meuse Rivers; on 27 September, the British First and Third Armies would attack in the general direction of Cambrai; on 28 September, the Flanders Group of Armies, commanded by King Albert I of Belgium, would attack between the sea and the Lys River; and on 29 September, the British Fourth Army, supported by the French First Army, would attack in the direction of Busigny, about 18 miles south of Cambrai.[13] Foch believed that these coordinated series of attacks would prevent tactical retreats and subsequent re-groupings of German forces to stop any one attack. The German army would be left reeling from one blow after the other, until the pounding forced it to give up the fight and collapse in defeat. He placed special importance on the French-American operation for the 26th. It required, he emphasized,

> that all its advantages be followed up without the slightest delay; that the rupture of the line of resistance be exploited uninterruptedly to as great a depth as possible. For this reason, halts in the development of the action must be avoided. This applies especially to the advance of the American Army between the Meuse and the French Fourth Army. As the strength of this Army relieves it from all risks, it must, *without further instructions*, and upon the initiative of its Commander, push its advance forward as far as possible.[14]

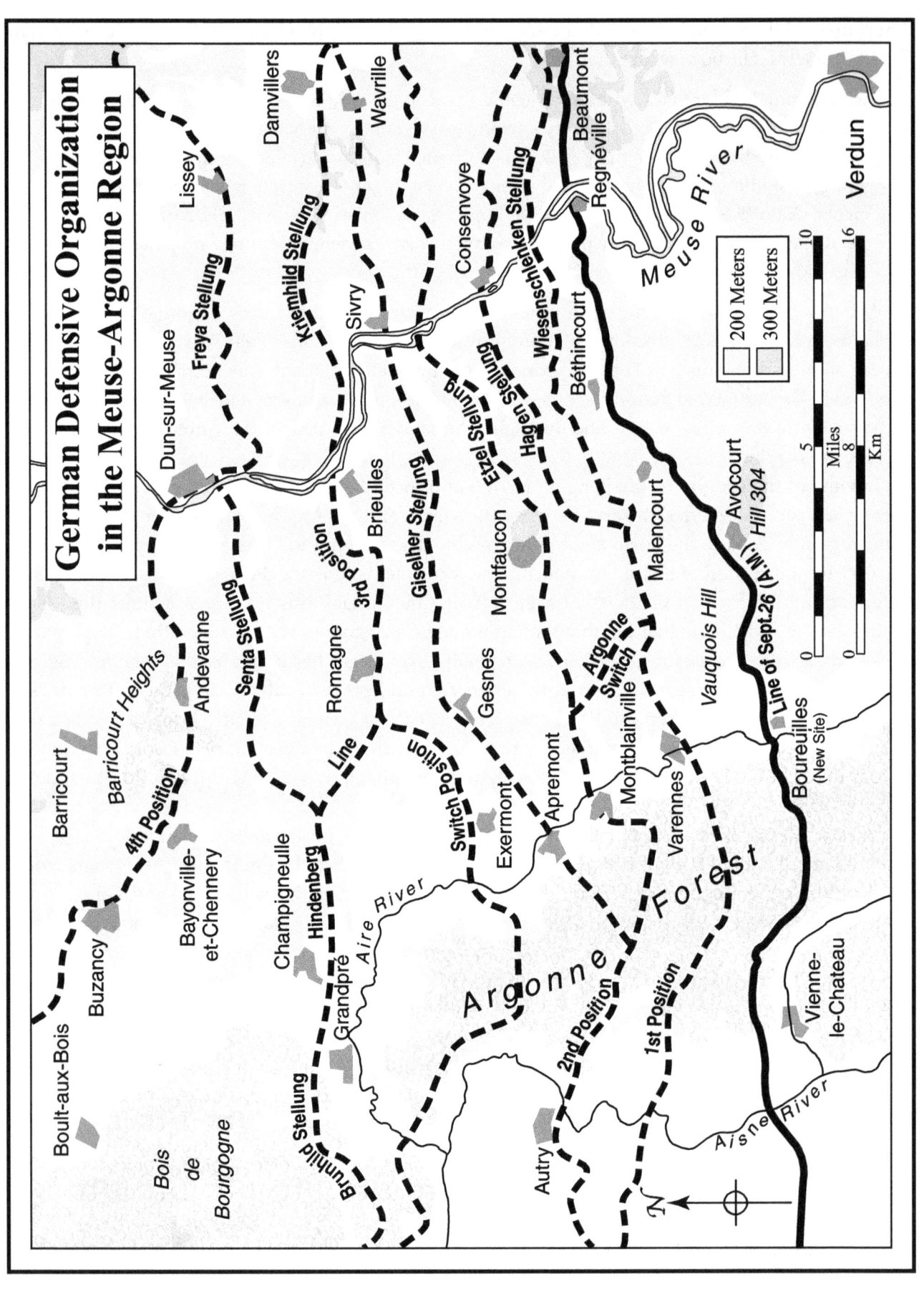

Meanwhile, George Marshall had taken charge of the movement of First Army from the St. Mihiel salient to the Meuse-Argonne, a distance of about 48 miles. It involved the transfer of three corps headquarters, 15 divisions, and various other army units, totaling about 600,000 men, 90,000 horses, almost 4,000 guns, and 900,000 tons of supplies and ammunition. Most of the men, guns, and matériel had to be withdrawn from the south face of the salient, moved westward, and then turned to the north, where they would replace some 200,000 French troops that would control the front until four days before the battle.[15] Marshall and his French counterpart managed to work out a plan that allowed the huge American force to move into the sector and the French to move out. Colonel Drum sent to the corps commanders an extract from Foch's chief of staff that emphasized the importance of surprise, and urged all commanders to take the '"strictest measure to avoid divulging their plans and operations."' They used only three farm roads, and, to achieve surprise, all movements were carried out at night. They also were encouraged to create the impression among their subordinates that the American concentration was intended to develop and exploit the '"Woevre operation."'[16] The rain pelted down, as usual, and huge traffic jams developed as men, animals, and matériel became mired in the muddy roads; solid columns had to be placed on the roads and mixed together different divisions and corps elements, thus adding to the confusion; faster moving elements crowded into slower moving ones; amid the chaos, trucks broke down and blocked stretches of the roads; and many French and American horses were so worn out that they could hardly be forced to move. Nevertheless, as Marshall noted, "the entire movement was carried out without a single element failing to reach its place on the date scheduled, which was, I understand, one day earlier than Marshall Foch considered possible."[17] For obvious reasons, Marshall became known as the "Wizard."

First Army's order of battle, from east to west, placed Bullard's III Corps on the right, with the Thirty-third Division, commanded by Major General George Bell, Jr., closest to the Meuse to cover the river and protect the army's flank; the Eightieth Division, commanded by Major General Adelbert Cronkhite, was in the center; and General Hines's Fourth Division was on the left. V Corps faced Montfaucon, and was commanded by General Cameron. It consisted of the Seventy-ninth Division, commanded by Major General Joseph E. Kuhn; the Thirty-seventh, commanded by Major General Charles S. Farnsworth; and the Ninety-first, under Major General John A. Johnston. General Liggett's I Corps was on the left of the army and included the Thirty-fifth Division, commanded by Major General Peter E. Taub; the Twenty-eighth Division, under Major General Charles H. Muir; and the Seventy-seventh Division, commanded by Major General Robert Alexander.[18] Colonel Patton's 1st Tank Brigade of 189 light tanks was assigned to support the Thirty-fifth and the Twenty-eighth Divisions. He had moved his brigade from St. Mihiel by train, thus avoiding the traffic snarls in the Meuse-Argonne sector. His tanks had been hampered in St. Mihiel when they ran low on fuel, so he and General S. D. Rockenbach had managed to stockpile 20,000 gallons of gasoline and oil to use after the first day.[19] Colonel Mitchell prepared his Air Service for the offensive by positioning over 800 aircraft, most of them American.

Just 10 days separated the conclusion of the St. Mihiel operation from the start of the Meuse-Argonne campaign; so, Pershing, as mentioned earlier, had to use untried and inexperienced divisions during the initial phases of the Meuse-Argonne attack. The battle-tested divisions, notably the First, Second, Twenty-sixth, and Forty-second, were not available. Of the nine divisions in the three corps, only four had had any front line duty, so, for most of these soldiers, this would be their first experience under fire. More than half were recent draftees, and some had never even fired a rifle.[20] The lone veteran division was the Thirty-third Division, which had fought with the British III Corps in the region of the Somme.

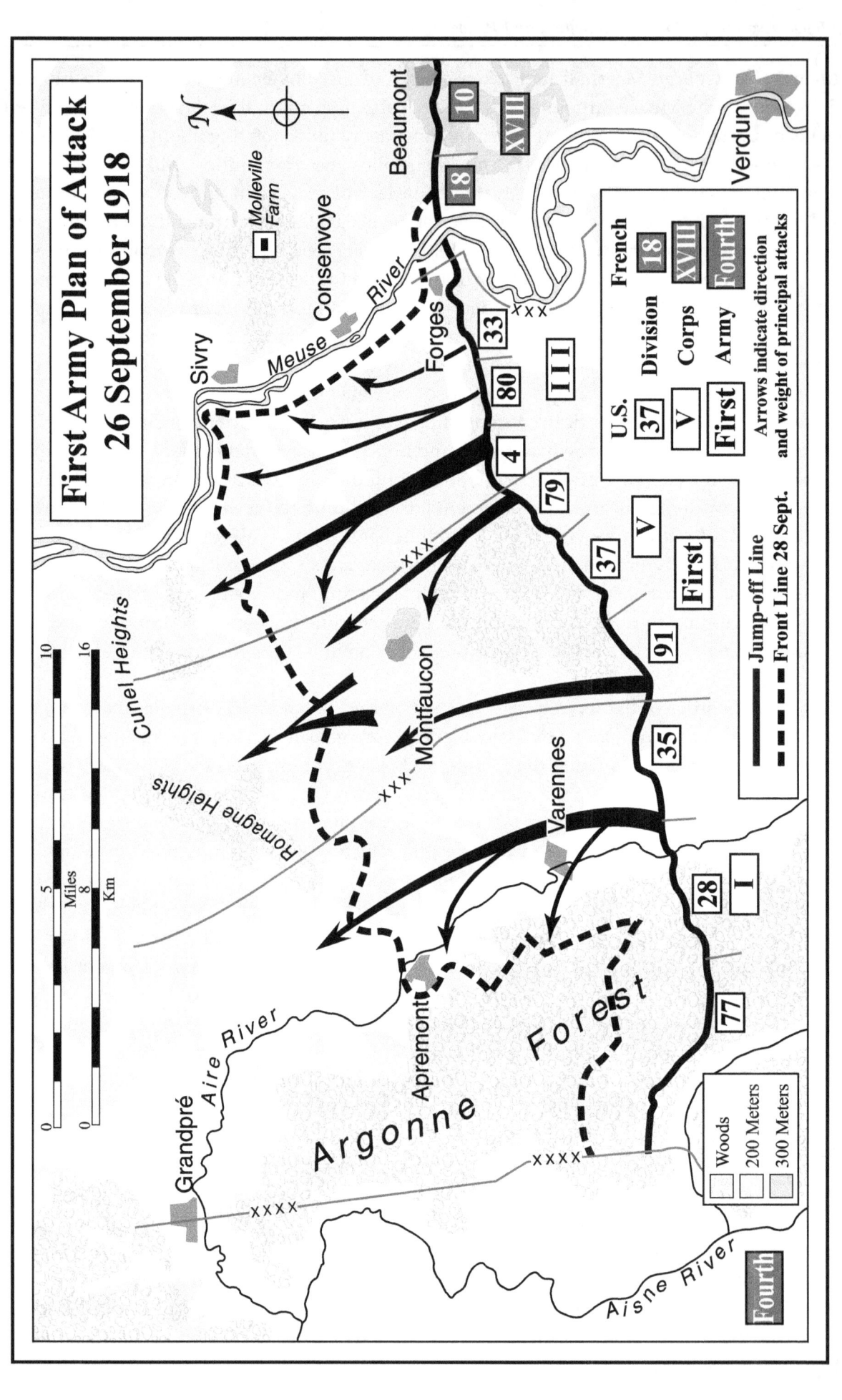

Pershing's plan for the Meuse-Argonne operation called for First Army to attack across the 20-mile front with its three corps abreast, "with all possible strength in the general direction of Mézières." He and General Pétain would coordinate the operations of the American army and the French Fourth Army (see map, p. 250).[21] General Liggett's I Corps would drive north along the Aire River and clear out the eastern portion of the Argonne Forest. Bullard's III Corps would advance in sector. General Cameron's V Corps had the toughest assignment: to advance up the hogback in the center and against Montfaucon, bypassing it on both flanks. Meanwhile I Corps and III Corps would advance up the Aire and Meuse valleys, respectively, driving two salients in the German lines, and assisting V Corps in seizing Montfaucon. These attacks would unhinge the *Giselher Stellung*, and enable Cameron's V Corps to attack and seize the heights of Romagne and Cunel, protected on both flanks by I and III Corps. Liggett's and Bullard's artillery would suppress German fire from the Argonne on the left and the Heights of the Meuse on the right, and the Americans would power through the *Kriemhilde Stellung*.[22] As the battle progressed, the Americans would link up with the French Fourth Army at Grandpré, on the left flank of I Corps.[23] Pershing realized that the "plan would require a rapid advance of ten miles through a densely fortified zone," but he counted on surprise and superior forces to overwhelm the defenders, before the German reinforcements arrived. GHQ estimated that nine additional German divisions could reinforce their defenses within three days, so Pershing calculated that the army's objectives had to be seized no later than by the end of the second day.[24] He later recalled General Pétain's opinion that the Americans "should not be able to get farther than Montfaucon before winter."[25]

On 25 September, Marshall spent most of the day checking with corps and division headquarters to make certain that last minute modifications in troop movements were clearly understood.[26] That afternoon Pershing visited them "to give a word of encouragement here and there to the leaders upon whom our success on the following day would depend. They were all alert and confident, and I returned feeling that all would go as planned."[27] As Donald Smythe stated, however, "No judgment was ever more wrong."[28]

At 0230 hours on 26 September, 2,275 guns, including massive 14-inch naval guns mounted on railroad flat cars, began firing a barrage on German front lines and rear areas from the Meuse to the Argonne. The artillery fire shifted to a rolling barrage at 0530 hours, and the infantry of three American corps climbed out of their trenches and moved forward about one hundred yards behind the exploding shells, across muddy, churned-up ground, in and out of shell holes, and into the heavy morning fog mixed with cordite smoke.[29] Supporting the assault, and firing their four 75-mm guns at the rate of 1,000 rounds per hour, was Battery D in the 129th Field Artillery Regiment of the Thirty-fifth Division in I Corps. Captain Harry S. Truman commanded the battery, and one month later wrote his wife Bess that '"My guns were so hot they would boil [the] wet gunnysacks we put on them to keep them cool."'[30] Major Brett's 344th Tank Battalion slowly ground forward with the Thirty-fifth. Colonel Patton moved up from his command post with six runners and a carrier pigeon. Using a compass to navigate through the fog, he advanced beyond his tanks, some of which had broken down, while others had become entangled in trench works some 125 yards behind him. He waited apprehensively as the fog began to lift, and German infantry and gunners spotted his tanks and the charging infantry of the Thirty-fifth Division.[31]

Elsewhere along the front of 20 miles, the attack of the First Army had, indeed, caught the Germans by surprise, and the doughboys quickly overran the initial German defenses. Fighting fiercely, German forces pulled back to their *Giselher Stellung*, and, as the fog began to lift and the sun broke through about 1000 hours, German machine guns began pouring flanking and frontal fire into American infantry as they burst into patches of open terrain. "Green" soldiers, like those in the three divisions that had never been in combat, lost liaison and cohesion, and rushed forward in bunches, as they had done at St. Mihiel, rather than singly, even milling about in the killing zone. Artillery support was poor since gunners found it difficult to determine the location of the attacking infantry.[32] As Marshall noted, "The first phase of the fighting was confusing in the extreme."[33]

In the center, V Corps's advance stalled in the approach ridges to Montfaucon. On the right, General Hines's Fourth Division of III Corps moved abreast of Montfaucon, but because V Corps had been pinned down on the approaches to the butte, his division had to wait four hours before it could move forward. This delay allowed the Germans to reorganize their defenses and reinforce Montfaucon and the village of Nantillois. Meanwhile, the Thirty-third Division of Bullard's corps came under heavy artillery fire from the heights east of the Meuse (see map, p. 250).[34]

On the left, I Corps slowly advanced, but intense machine gun fire from hidden positions in the Argonne Forest caused heavy casualties. On the right of Liggett's corps, the initial advance of the Thirty-fifth Division went well until the fog lifted. Then, German artillery and machine gun fire from the woods close to the village of Cheppy ripped into the division and thoroughly disrupted their attack. Bedlam prevailed, as soldiers scrambled to find their units; others panicked and fled toward the rear when they ran into Patton, who had taken refuge with his men behind a narrow-gauge railway cut. He ordered them to stay with him, and, as German fire increasingly endangered their position, he led them to cover on the reverse slope of a nearby hill. Looking back, Patton saw several tanks

*Lieutenant Colonel George S. Patton, Jr. near Langres, France*

Courtesy National Archives

stuck in trenches the Germans had abandoned. He ordered several men to start digging them out and moving them forward, but when nothing happened, he went himself, and ordered the crews to dig them out. When the tanks were freed, Patton led them and his infantry through the railway cut and over the hill. Machine gun fire swept through the attackers, and Patton was struck in the left upper thigh by a bullet that just missed his hip joint, sciatic nerve, and femoral artery. His orderly dragged him to a shell hole, where a medic bound his wound. As Patton lay in shock, a combined attack on the hill by his tanks and the 138th Regiment of the Thirty-fifth Division wiped out the German machine gun nests by early afternoon. Only then was Patton taken to an evacuation hospital. Within a few days he was transferred to a base hospital near Dijon, where he remained until late October, when he returned to his brigade.[35] Carlo d'Este said that Patton's wounding taught him that "even he was mortal." He also pointed out that the "joint action by Patton's tankers and 138th Regiment may well have been the first-ever example of tank-infantry cooperation in an offensive operation."[36]

On the second day of the attack, V Corps took Montfaucon in hard and bloody fighting, and all three corps came abreast. But casualties were mounting rapidly; rain had turned roads and trails into quagmires, and trucks and wagons bogged down, creating traffic jams that made the re-supply of units and the evacuation of wounded almost impossible. Many soldiers went without food for days. German reinforcements strengthened their formidable defenses, and American frontline units, rather than pressing forward the offensive, fought to improve their defensive positions, and had to repel strong German counterattacks. By 28 September, First Army had managed to shift all artillery forward, but only 53 of the original 140 tanks were still in action.[37] The great Meuse-Argonne offensive essentially had ground to a halt, in contrast to the British and French attacks in Flanders and in the center that drove the Germans back through the Hindenburg Line. The British victories were especially impressive since they had been won against the strongest concentration of German forces on the western front (see map, p. 250).[38]

The fierce German resistance that First Army encountered in the opening phase of the offensive belied the growing crisis in Germany and in the High Command. The massive Allied offensive against the Laon bulge, coupled with the disintegration in the Balkans of the Central Powers' Bulgarian ally, caused Ludendorff to collapse in a nervous fit on 26 September. He demanded that the government end the war, and a crown council agreed on 29 September to make an appeal to President Wilson.[39] On 3 October, Prince Maximilian of Baden, the new German chancellor, proposed an armistice and peace negotiations based on the president's Fourteen Points. The British and French were excluded from the negotiations and were not pleased, particularly since their demands were more stringent than those of the president. In response, Wilson toughened his demands to include a program of electoral reform in Germany, increased powers for the Reichstag, Germany's legislative body, and an armistice that would assure the military ascendancy of the Allies, as well as the evacuation of territory that German armies had occupied.[40] As Prince Max's government deliberated, the suffering of the German people increased. The burden of the war, and the effects of the British blockade of four years, produced hunger, deprivations, and poor diets that led to disease and the deaths of thousands. A powerful wave in favor of peace began to build throughout the nation.[41]

During the last week of September and into the first days of October, both sides knew that peace negotiations were under way, but this awareness in no way diminished the ferocity of the fighting. Ludendorff, having regained control of his nerves, ordered a stiff defense to prevent the kind of military collapse that would weaken Germany's negotiating position.[42] He argued that the German army could continue the fight. Foch, always pressing the attack, was concerned that commanders were too distant from the action, and '"did not seem to push it personally with the utmost energy, themselves supervising the execution of their orders."' He asked Pétain to order the various commanders in chief to ensure '"personal and active direction of the battle upon the field itself. *To encourage, inspire, and supervise, still remains a chief's principal task.*"' [his italics].[43]

Foch also was especially disappointed and frustrated by the stalled attack of First Army. He sent to Pershing a proposal by General Pétain to divide the command of Franco-American forces between Pershing and a French general.[44] Pershing objected strenuously and pointed out to Foch the many difficulties that would result from a change in organization.[45] In a pointed jab at Pershing and First Army, Foch replied that he would maintain the present organization of command, "under the condition that your attacks start without delay, and that, once begun, they be continued without any interruption such as those which have just arisen."[46] Donald Smythe noted that Pershing "hit the ceiling over this," but he also stated that Foch's response was "soft," and, that, at any rate, Pershing wanted to resume First Army's advance as soon as possible.[47]

In preparation for the renewed attack, Pershing moved his best divisions to the front lines to replace the battered and exhausted divisions that had, indeed, forced the Germans back to their defensive line of the *Kriemhilde Stellung*. The divisions on the flanks were left in place, but battle-tested, veteran divisions were moved into the army's center to lead the attack on the hogback and the heights beyond it. The four inexperienced divisions (Thirty-fifth, Ninety-first, Thirty-seventh, and Seventy-ninth) were replaced by the First, Thirty-second, and Third. Once they were in place, all three corps were ordered to advance independently rather than waiting for all to come abreast, as had occurred on the first day of the offensive.[48] Across the Meuse-Argonne front, there was no space for flanking attacks, so each division would have to press its attack straight forward against the powerful defenses that the Germans, working with the resources that nature had provided, had devised so creatively. Indeed, as Colonel George M. Russell, the historian of V Corps wrote, the German defense "was based on the terrain rather than upon organized positions."[49]

After the St. Mihiel operation, the First Division had been assigned to the reserve of III Corps, southwest of Verdun, and had begun to prepare for an attack on the right of III Corps against a "very strong Austrian division in front of Verdun."[50] Some of the officers and men who had been wounded at Soissons rejoined their old commands, and their morale and confidence were higher than ever. On 27 September, just as the division was about to begin its attack, Summerall received the order transferring the division to I Corps in the Meuse-Argonne, where it would relieve the Thirty-fifth Division, effective 30 September. The relief was to be completed by 0500 hours on 1 October.[51]

Summerall sent ahead Captain Gowenlock, his intelligence officer, to reconnoiter the Thirty-fifth's sector, and report to him that night. Gowenlock returned late that night and spoke of wooded ridges surrounded by deep ravines and defiles; of German shells exploding all around; of gory bodies in khaki and gray scattered everywhere; of the men of the Thirty-fifth lying in shell holes to avoid the machine gun bullets coming from bushes on the crest of a ridge across a ravine; of a captain with only 150 men left in his battalion; and of the cone-shaped Hill 240, and the steep ridge behind it known as Hill 272, that were separated by gullies and ravines and dotted with patches of forest and brush that made excellent cover for machine guns. Summerall replied that he would need more details, especially about machine gun and artillery positions, and Gowenlock said that he and his intelligence section would meet as soon as possible with their counterparts in the Thirty-fifth Division to gather additional information.[52] Early the next morning, Gowenlock and his two assistants left for Thirty-fifth's headquarters in the village of Cheppy, which was just beyond the place where Patton had been wounded. There, he would find men who confirmed every detail of his report to Summerall, as could many others who had survived the last few days in the Meuse-Argonne.

On 30 September, as the First Division completed preparations for yet another march to the front, Summerall assembled his men on a hillside and spoke to them about the campaign that lay before them. With Gowenlock's report fresh in his mind, he predicted that the battle on the hills and in the ravines of the Meuse-Argonne would be even more difficult and costly than the fight for Soissons. "'But you are men of the First Division,'" he said, and "'You will attack—you will keep echeloned in depth. You will take all your objectives, as the First Division has always done. You will advance—you will fight if necessary, until there are just two of you left—one echeloned behind the other.'"[53] Perhaps there were soldiers who were repelled, like Conrad Babcock had been, by what they considered Summerall's grim and depressing prediction of their fate. But, there were certainly many others, like Gowenlock, who grasped the nature of the war, understood the responsibility that rested upon the First Division, and trusted their commander to lead them to victory. Given their daunting mission to redeem the sacrifices of the Thirty-fifth Division, and to rekindle the fiery advance of First Army in the Meuse-Argonne, it seems appropriate that he would speak to them as urgently and realistically as possible.

That night, the division began the march of about six miles across the rear of First Army and toward the sector of the Thirty-fifth Division on the left of V Corps. The retreating Germans had mined the few roads leading northwest, and their artillery had blasted craters big enough to drop a house into, so the men had to pass through thick underbrush, up and down ravines, and through swampy depressions filled with mangled wheels, harnesses, and bloated horse carcasses. They felt their way forward, exchanging comments and gleaning information from the departing men of the Thirty-fifth, and began digging foxholes as they moved into a front line that had no clear definition.[54]

The men expected to attack at dawn on 1 October but soon got word that the attack had been delayed. Summerall had been ordered to wait until the Ninety-first Division on the right of First Division, and the Twenty-eighth Division on the left in I Corps had moved up to cover the flanks of the division as it advanced. As the sun rose over the hills to the north and east, German artillery from emplacements on reverse slopes and in the Argonne pounded the infantry with enfilading fire as the men crouched in their foxholes; enemy rifle and machine gun fire dropped anyone who exposed himself; gas shells exploded and drenched the ravines and hollows with mustard gas; and enemy airplanes swooped down and strafed the troops in their exposed positions. On orders from V Corps, Summerall sent out patrols at night; men were killed and captured, but prisoners were taken, and Gowenlock and his men grilled them incessantly. For three days the division endured the heavy German fire, losing an average of 500 men a day.[55] In his memoir, Summerall expressed resentment at the delay, without noting that it was necessary to allow the two divisions to move on either side of the First. He also disapproved of the order to send out night patrols, and noted that, as a result, the division sustained heavy casualties, and the soldiers that were captured "exposed us to the possibility of having the enemy learn our intentions." In addition, he stated that "we knew the enemy's disposition from the contact of our lines and patrols were needless."[56] Rather than wait on the arrival of flanking divisions and conduct patrols, what he wanted to do, it seems clear, was to attack, attack, attack. His wait was soon over.

By 4 October, First Army was ready to resume the offensive, and faced the defenses of the *Kriemhilde Stellung* that had been reinforced with fresh divisions. The mission of III Corps and V Corps, acting together, was to seize the heights of Cunel and Romagne; I Corps's mission was to support V Corps's attack on the Romagne Heights, and to neutralize artillery fire from the eastern flanks of the Argonne Forest. All three corps were ordered to maximize counterbattery fire, including the use of gas shells and smoke screens.[57] The First Division was to drive a deep wedge into the Aire Valley and seize the high ground dominated by Hills 240, 272, and 263, which loomed in the northeast over the ravine at Exermont and the village of Fléville (see map, p. 256).[58]

On 4 October, at 0530 hours, the infantry of First Army attacked behind a rolling barrage and immediately met intense resistance all across the front. The two brigades of the First Division surged

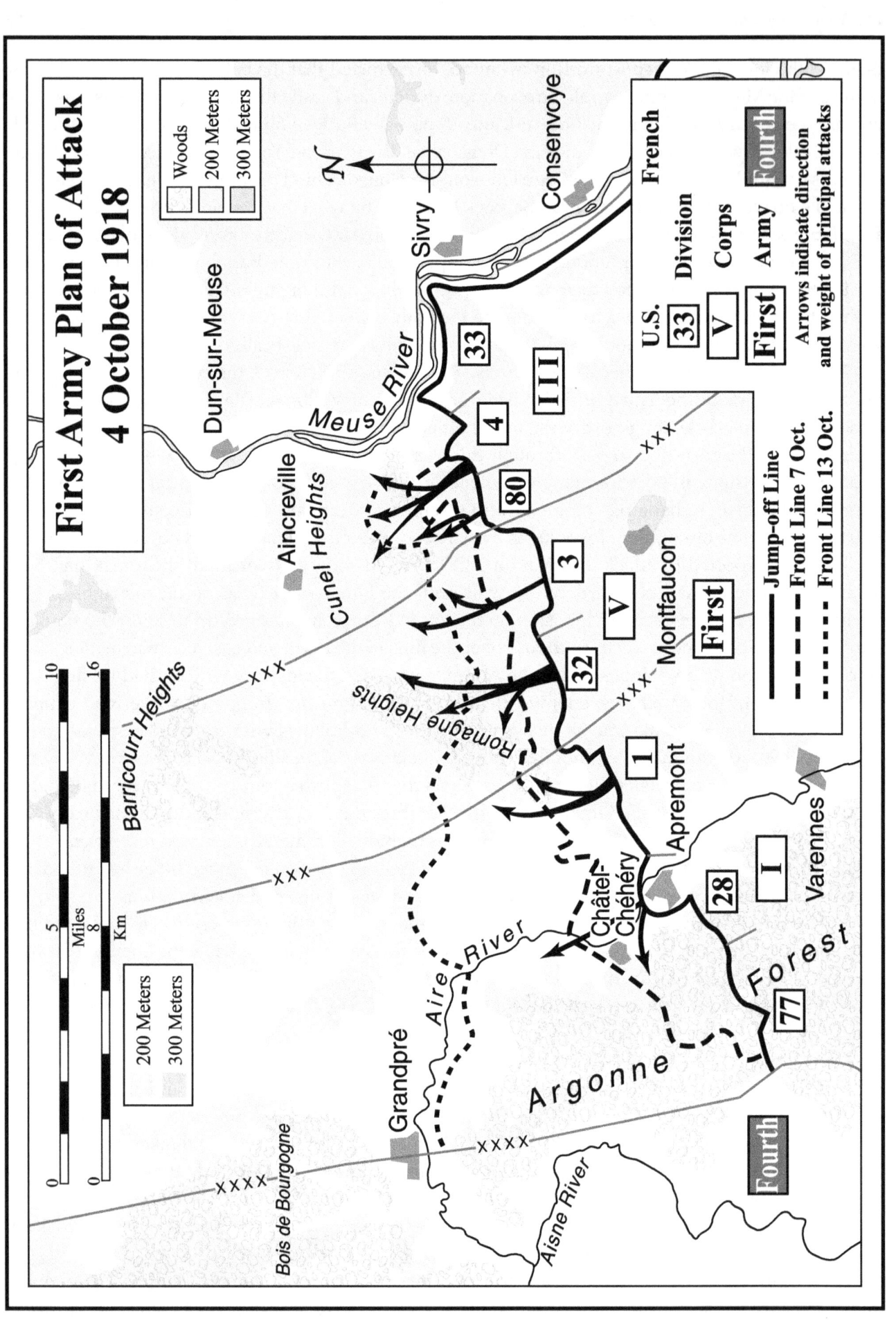

out of their foxholes to strike at the enemy who had for days relentlessly pinned them down and thinned their ranks. They charged into the forbidding landscape and defensive positions that Gowenlock had so accurately described, past the grisly remains of the dead of the Thirty-fifth Division, and into the enfiladed fire of machine guns and artillery. Two companies of 32 tanks from Patton's brigade led the advance, knocking out machine gun emplacements as the division's two infantry brigades moved into the woods before the Exermont ravine. By the time the 1st Brigade had fought through the woods and reached the ravine, only five tanks remained, and by the end of the day, only three were left. Eighty-four percent of their crews were casualties. The 1st Brigade had seized the ravine, but just beyond it, German artillery bombarded them from Hill 240 and fired gas shells into the artillery battery positions. On the right, the 2nd Brigade encountered "very heavy resistance" and was forced to halt about one mile short of the line held by the 1st Brigade. At dark, engineers came up to help dig trenches and build protection, as the division prepared for the next assault.[59] Meanwhile, Bullard's III Corps battled through German snipers and machine gun nests and fought toward the Cunel Heights, but neither the Eightieth nor the Fourth Division could make headway under the heavy fire from the Heights of the Meuse. Southwest of Cunel, Cameron's V Corps attacked over low ground and could make little headway, even with tanks leading the way.[60]

At 0615 hours on 5 October, all of First Division's artillery began firing in front of the 2nd Brigade as it prepared to move in line with the 1st Brigade. With both brigades abreast, they would then drive the attacking wedge to the village of Fléville, just west of Hill 272. Screened by smoke shells, the 2nd Brigade advanced behind a rolling barrage and fought through heavy fire from the right flank to link its front with the 1st Brigade. The slopes of Hill 272 "were a veritable machine gun hive," and the Ariétal Farm presented a fortified position at the base of the hill. Small groups of men filtered through the woods and slithered along depressions in the ground. They were able to outflank and capture the farm, but fire from the hill forced the advanced units to dig in. By the end of the day, the division had driven the wedge in the Aire Valley from Fléville to the Ariétal Farm, but the Germans repulsed all efforts to push out toward Hill 272.[61] As Summerall noted, "the fighting was desperate on both sides, and the losses were heavy."[62]

On 6 October, the division was ordered to assist the Thirty-second Division on its right and sent out a patrol to establish contact. As it moved through forest cover, the patrol leader noticed that the western slope of Hill 269 facing the Thirty-second was unoccupied. A detachment of engineers took it over and was driven off by a German attack, but regrouped, counterattacked and held the position. Attempts to infiltrate patrols from Ariétal Farm to Hill 272 were repulsed, and German fire from the hill had so severely depleted burial parties that there were not enough men left in them to bury the large number of dead that lay on the field. I Corps headquarters ordered the division to hold its position and not to attempt any further advance.[63]

As the First Division consolidated its position during the night of 6–7 October, General Liggett gave orders for a bold flank attack into the eastern ridges of the Argonne Forest. He realized that the advance of Summerall's division had made such an offensive possible, so he had moved the Eighty-second Division, commanded by General Duncan, from corps reserve into the First Division's zone and combined it with elements of the Twenty-eighth Division, under the command of General Muir. The advance of the two divisions would be supported by an attack of General Alexander's Seventy-seventh Division from the south. Liggett's operation could cut off the forest and force the Germans to retreat through the woods to the gap at Grandpré; it could clear the way for the French Fourth Army to advance into the forest from the west, and enable the Seventy-seventh Division to move forward and rescue a small force from the division that became known as the "Lost Battalion."[64]

Since 2 October, elements of three battalions of the Seventy-seventh Division had been cut off by strong enemy forces and encircled on a steep and rocky hillside deep in the Argonne. This group of 550 men had come under the command of Major Charles W. Wittlesley and were neither lost, nor were they a battalion. Major Whittlesley had organized them into a strong defensive square, and they were so close to the enemy positions that German artillery could not fire on them without endangering their own men. But, the Germans raked the American position with grenades and with fire from machine guns, mortars, and rifles. Their strength and supplies diminished rapidly, as the Germans beat back attacks to rescue them, and repeated attempts to aid them by air failed.[65]

On 7 October, I Corps artillery began a 15-hour preparatory bombardment of the eastern ridges of the forest, and the infantry attacked behind a rolling barrage. In the early morning hours of 8 October, reinforcements from the Seventy-seventh reached the "Lost Battalion," and the Germans began pulling back. Later that morning, Whittlesley and the remains of his command—194 men—marched out, having been without food or medical attention for 104 hours.[66] That same day, another dramatic episode occurred just to the northeast of Whittlesley's position. Corporal Alvin York, of the Eighty-second's 328th Regiment, using the sharp-shooting skills he had perfected in the mountains of eastern Tennesssee, picked off about 25 German machine gunners, and seized 35 machine guns. For good measure he brought in 132 enemy captives, including three officers. Among his many decorations, York was awarded the Congressional Medal of Honor and later received a stirring tribute from Summerall.[67]

Following the relief of Whittlesley and his men, the Seventy-seventh and Twenty-eighth Divisions forced the Germans to quit the Argonne "on the run," as Liggett described their retreat. By 10 October, the Seventy-seventh had reached the south bank of the Aire River and confronted Grandpré. Liggett's

*Sergeant Alvin C. York*

Courtesy National Archives

attack not only had rescued the "Lost Battalion," it also had freed the First Division from destructive flank fire from the forest and had put the Argonne permanently behind First Army.[68]

With its left flank secured by the success of the Eighty-second in the Argonne, the First Division was assigned to V Corps and joined the Thirty-second Division on the right in an attack on the dangerous hills and heavily defended forests that blocked their advance to the north. To strengthen the attack, a brigade from the Ninety-first Division was added to the First. At 0830 hours on 9 October, the artillery dropped a heavy barrage in front of the 2nd Brigade on the right, and it attacked toward the Bois de Romagne, just below Hill 272 to the southeast. The barrage then shifted to the front of the 1st Brigade on the left, and it advanced toward the dangerous Hill 272. Under the command of General William G. Haan, the Thirty-second Division advanced against Hill 287, yet another of the high, steep ridges, with wooden slopes that sheltered numerous machine gun nests. Known also as the Côte Dame Marie, it dominated the terrain and barred the path of the division toward the village of Romagne.[69] Haan decided to delay his attack until his patrols could scout the German positions on the côte.

As the furious fight unfolded, German units "viciously" attacked First Division engineers on the face of Hill 269, but the engineers held; German artillery shelled the entire line of attack, but division artillery responded with a dense barrage on Hill 272, and the 16th Regiment captured the peak, as Summerall noted, "in one of the hardest fought actions of the war."[70] Battalions from both brigades advanced and secured the line that extended from a point just north of the village of Sommerance on the left to the northern edge of the Bois de Romagne. For the next two days, the division sent out patrols that came under heavy fire. Their reports confirmed that a specially prepared assault would be necessary to break through the *Kriemhilde Stellung*. I Corps ordered that the division consolidate and hold its position.[71]

During this pause, "all available men" were organized into detachments to collect the bodies of the dead, and they buried their fallen comrades "with such brief religious ceremonies as were possible."[72] Losses had, indeed, been heavy, with over 1,500 men and almost 70 officers killed; more than 5,700 men and 128 officers had been wounded, and 92 men and officers were either missing or had been taken prisoner. Braim noted that the division's losses were the highest casualty figures of the campaign.[73] The First had captured almost 500 prisoners, but they could only estimate that the number of enemy killed "were very great, owing to his stubborn defense."[74] (See the tightly packed lines advance northward Oct. 1 to Oct. 31, map, p. 266)

While his men labored at their grim task, Summerall received orders at his headquarters that the Forty-second Division would relieve his exhausted and depleted division during the night of 11–12 October. Given his previous criticism of commanders requesting relief, it is highly unlikely that he would have asked that his division be relieved. He recorded in his memoir a conversation he overheard between his chief of staff, Lieutenant Colonel John N. Greely, and General Drum, Pershing's chief of staff at First Army headquarters, that seems to confirm this assumption. Colonel Greely, asserted Summerall, informed Drum that "The First Division never asks to be relieved. The high command knows the condition of the division as well as we do. When the high command wants to relieve it, we will go. Until then, we will continue the battle."[75]

At any rate, First Division retraced the bloody trail over which they had advanced two weeks before and assembled in the area around Cheppy, leaving behind about 100 men to finish the job of burying the dead. From Cheppy, they marched about 45 miles to the Vavincourt Area to the south. Replacements began to arrive immediately, while the veterans were deloused and reequipped for the next battle.[76]

Meanwhile, in the III Corps sector west of the Meuse, General Cronkhite's Eightieth Division pushed through woods and into the fields toward the Cunel Heights on 9 October, but German artillery and machine gun fire from the heights stopped their attack. General Hines's Fourth Division, on the right of the Eightieth, made progress through two heavy woods against a new German division. The fighting was stubborn, frequently hand-to-hand, and every foot of ground that the Americans gained was "bitterly contested." German resistance, like their attacks against the divisions in V Corps, was vicious.[77] The savage fighting left Hines and Conkhite reluctant to continue the assaults of their divisions. But Bullard and Pershing were losing patience with the stalled attacks and ordered the Fourth and Eightieth Divisions to resume their assaults. On 10 October, they managed to establish a firm foothold on Cunel–Brieulles road, and into the thick Bois de Forêt, just beyond the highway. The Germans showed no signs of collapsing, but III Corps had managed to pierce part of the *Kriemhilde Stellung* that confronted them.[78] First Army concluded, as had Summerall, that the period since 7 October had involved "some of the hardest infantry fighting on the western front."[79]

As Pershing himself noted, "The period of the battle from October 1st to the 11th involved the heaviest strain on the army and on me."[80] Casualties had reached 100,000, with influenza having claimed half of that number; the weather was cold and rainy, further depressing the fighting spirit of his men; the number of stragglers, known as "coffee boilers," or, more accurately, deserters, was rising alarmingly; roads remained muddy; many had been heavily damaged during the fighting, and the reinforcement of depleted divisions with men and matériel had become increasingly difficult.[81] Adding to the problem of re-supply was the fact that roads in the Meuse-Argonnne ran west to east, across the army's advance, rather than parallel to it. These logistical problems were exacerbated by the narrow front of 12 miles that extended west of the Meuse to the Argonne, where 200,000 American troops fought against pre-registered artillery and machine gun fire.[82]

Pershing, therefore, decided to broaden the American zone of attack to the high ground of the Argonne and east of the Meuse and to bring more American forces into the battle.[83] Marshal Foch once again had stated his concern that the Americans were not progressing as rapidly as the other Allies, and, rather pointedly informed Pershing that he "would like to see them advance."[84] Irritated by Foch's impatience, Pershing pointed out that the fight being waged by the Americans had drawn to their front a number of German divisions and had facilitated the advance of the other Allied armies. He informed Foch of his plans, and the French marshal agreed fully with them.[85]

When he mentioned Foch's remarks to Liggett at dinner a few days later, Liggett replied that the 40 German divisions that the Americans had drawn into their front explained why First Army was not moving faster, and, in part, why the British and French were advancing. He said that the Allies and the Germans knew the answer, and that the French marshal's comment left him "indignant."[86]

Effective 12 October, Pershing created a Second Army, commanded by Bullard, with responsibility for operations east of the Meuse River to the Moselle River. On 16 October, Pershing named Liggett to succeed him as commander of First Army. Already, on 10 October, he had told Liggett that he would appoint him as commander of First Army, and that Dickman would succeed him as I Corps commander.[87] Apparently at General Cameron's own request, but also because Cameron realized that Pershing was not pleased with his command of V Corps, he stepped down as V Corps commander, and returned to the Fourth Division, his old command.[88] In his place, Pershing appointed Summerall to command V Corps and Hines to take Bullard's position as commander of III Corps. As Liggett wrote, both of these two newly appointed corps commanders justified Pershing's confidence "brilliantly."[89] Pershing noted that his own status had become Commander of a Group of Armies.[90]

At GHQ, Liggett found that Pershing had ordered an attack on 14 October by First Army's three corps—I, III, and V— and asked, and was granted, permission to delay his taking command of the army until after the conclusion of that operation. During the next three days, he visited III and V Corps, as well as the French XVII Corps on the right of III Corps, "learning what I could while the battle was in progress," he wrote, "and in particular informing myself as to the temper of the troops and their commanders."[91]

Meantime, Summerall left for V Corps headquarters at midnight on 11–12 October. He was leaving as the First Division withdrew to its reserve position, so he did not have an opportunity to speak to his former command. Division headquarters published a farewell order, in which he expressed his pride and gratitude, and he telephoned General Drum to say that GHQ should give the division a citation in recognition of what they had accomplished. Drum asked Summerall to write the citation, which he did.[92] It was published as General Orders No. 201, on 19 November 1918, and stated the commander in chief's "extreme satisfaction with the conduct of the officers and men of the First Division in its advance west of the Meuse between October 4 and 11, 1918." The citation noted the success of the division against "eight hostile divisions, most of which were first-class troops and some of which were rested." It praised the division's "courage, fortitude and self-sacrificing devotion to duty" and noted the many enemy killed, and the large number of weapons it had captured. What was most remarkable about the citation was the paragraph that Pershing himself wrote. He said that "The Commander-in Chief has noted in this Division a special pride of service and a high state of morale, never broken by hardship or battle."[93] This was the only such commendation that Pershing ever awarded and indicated the high regard in which he held his favorite division. As he reflected on this special order, Summerall wrote in his memoir that "The effect on the division was all that I had anticipated and it is engraved on the hearts of the veterans while they live." Perhaps inadvertently, the anger and resentment toward Pershing that had gripped him for so long vanished in the moment in which he had recalled the citation, and the unique tribute that Pershing had offered to Summerall's own cherished command.

As he was driven to V Corps headquarters, Summerall noticed the miles of ambulances that were stalled on the muddy and congested roads and lamented the delays in reaching the field hospitals that would cost a great many lives. At 0200 hours on 12 October, he reached the small dugout that served as V Corps headquarters, and found General Cameron all alone, pacing back and forth. He had been one of Summerall's instructors in drawing at West Point. Summerall noted that he "had always liked him." Cameron had visited First Division's post of command during the recent advance, and Summerall appreciated the fact that he had never interfered with the division commanders. Summerall wrote that he later learned that Cameron had told Pershing that his corps could not accomplish all that the commander in chief expected of it, whereupon Pershing ordered him relieved. As Cameron left the dugout, he shook hands with Summerall, and said '"Goodbye, Jock, I hope you will do better than I have done."' Summerall recalled that Cameron entered his waiting car, and that he never saw him again. To Summerall, Cameron appeared to be "a crushed and broken-hearted man."[94]

The next morning, Summerall gathered his corps staff of about 80 officers to hear the report of Brigadier General Wilson B. Burtt, V Corps' chief of staff, who had just returned from a conference of First Army chiefs of staff. Burtt, a graduate of the West Point class of 1899, and an artilleryman, was a veteran of the Philippine Insurrection. He had been an observer on the western front in 1914 and 1915. Burtt delivered Pershing's order that V Corps would renew First Army's attack the following morning, 14 October.[95]

After breakfast, Summerall visited the posts of command of the Forty-second and Thirty-second Divisions, the two divisions that held the front of V Corps. The Forty-second, of course, was his old division, and he was familiar with its area, since the First Division had occupied it before being relieved by the Forty-second. He went on to visit and inspect the Thirty-second Division, which held the line on the right of the Forty-second, and had paused while its scouts checked out German positions on the Côte Dame Marie (see above). He renewed his acquaintance with its commander, General Haan, who had been a first classman at West Point when Summerall was a plebe, and had been a lieutenant when they both were in the 5th Artillery Regiment at the Presidio. He found that each brigade had a regiment of the other brigade in its sector. Not only that, but he found both brigade commanders at the headquarters of the first brigade he visited. While one might assume that some relaxation could be permitted after the division's tough fight in the recent attack of V Corps, Summerall believed that these conditions amounted to a "mixing of commands." He instructed the brigade commanders "to recover their own regiments and unite their brigades." Furthermore, he told them "to organize their lines in depth, with only a thin screen in the front line." Both adopted his suggestions "eagerly."[96] What General Haan thought about his corps commander's mixture of disciplinary advice with tactical instructions, after his division had distinguished itself by fighting up the face of the Côte Dame Marie earlier, is not known.

In its recent attack, First Army had advanced to the Hindenburg Line and had captured some important positions. Still, the German army was firmly entrenched to the west at Grandpré and across to the woods and hills of the *Kriemhilde Stellung* in the center, as well as in the sector extending eastward toward the Meuse River. For First Army to advance, these barriers had to be overcome. On 14 October, GHQ issued the order for the offensive to resume. I Corps would pin down the Germans on the left of V Corps by advancing toward Grandpré, while supporting V Corps on its right. The toughest task was assigned to V Corps: to seize the hills and woods in its front and drive the enemy from the Barricourt Heights that surmounted the *Kriemhilde Stellung*. III Corps would drive through the fortified defenses of Cunel and the forest beyond, then close with V Corps to seize the Barricourt Heights.[97]

The key to the heights was the group of hills known as the Côte de Châtillon. It loomed over the front of the Forty-second Division, and Summerall assigned its capture to the division's 84th Brigade, commanded by Brigadier General Douglas MacArthur.[98] The 83rd Brigade, commanded by Briga-

*Brigadier General Douglas MacArthur*
Courtesy National Archives

dier General Michael J. Lenihan, would attack on the left of the 84th, toward the village of St. Georges and the larger town of Landres-St. Georges. Historian James Cooke pointed out that it appeared that "combat power" was equally divided between the two brigades. But MacArthur's brigade would benefit from fighting under the cover of the woods, whereas Lenihan's brigade would be attacking in the open, and against wire, while under flanking machine gun fire from the Côte de Châtillon.[99]

Summerall and General Menoher, the division commander, approved MacArthur's plan to concentrate his men for the attack, rather than to spread them out along an attacking line.[100] They all understood the importance of the mission. In the evening prior to the attack, Summerall went directly to MacArthur's post of command. To MacArthur, Summerall seemed "tired and worn," so he "made" his corps commander drink "a cup of steaming black coffee, strong enough to blister the throat." With his voice "strained and harsh," and with somewhat singed vocal chords, Summerall said, "'Give me Châtillon, MacArthur, Give me Châtillon, or a list of five thousand casualties.'" Startled by Summerall's abruptness, MacArthur replied, "'All right, General, we'll take it, or my name will head the list.'"[101] Clearly, MacArthur understood that the man before him, who had forged the Forty-second Division's 67th artillery Brigade into a powerful fighting arm, and who had yet to be vanquished on the battlefield, meant what he said.

At 0830 hours on 14 October, V Corps attacked behind a heavy barrage from the 67th Artillery Brigade, the First Artillery Brigade of the First Division, nine batteries from I Corps artillery, nine batteries of 75-mm guns from a French artillery brigade, and three battalions of massive eight-inch guns from the 59th Coast Artillery.[102] MacArthur's 84th Brigade advanced through a misty rain, "slide-slipping forward from one bit of cover to another." Squads or platoons managed to envelop machine gun positions and "gained a toehold on some slope or deadly hillock." By nightfall they had taken Hill 288, and he decided to continue the assault. One battalion advanced from the west of the Côte de Châtillon, and another battalion attacked straight to the north. MacArthur wrote that they encountered "'a series of trenches with dug-outs and new wire with steel posts. It is strongly manned by both machine guns and infantry. One estimate puts the number of machine guns at 200.'" The battalions closed in from both sides. In the fight, companies were reduced to platoons and corporals took command.[103]

Meanwhile, on the right of MacArthur's brigade, General Haan had decided against a direct assault on the Côte Dame Marie and instead opted to seize the village of Romagne. His "reorganized" division, as Summerall termed the Thirty-second after he had straightened out the brigade commanders, fought "gallantly" and captured the village. They turned and attacked the Côte Dame Marie from its eastern flank and took the hill on 15 October. They moved up on the flank of MacArthur's brigade, as it fought to the heights of the Côte de Châtillon, and seized it the next day.[104] At the end, the battalion that had attacked the Côte de Châtillon from the right had only 300 men and 6 officers left, out of 1,450 men and 25 officers.[105]

To the left of MacArthur's brigade, Lenihan's 83rd Brigade attacked toward St. Georges, but it bogged down and could not advance. Tanks that had been promised to lead the attack failed to show up on time, and not surprisingly, many of them broke down once they did arrive. The Germans pounded the infantry with artillery and machine gun fire from the Côte de Châtillon and from the two towns. By 15 October, Summerall and Menoher had become impatient, and Summerall was irritated that there was a shortage of bangalore torpedoes that the infantry needed to blast through the German wire.[106] Historian Cooke stated that "Summerall had written off the 15th as far as the 83rd Brigade was concerned," and "That spelled serious problems for Lenihan as brigade commander."[107]

On the left of the 83rd Brigade, General Duncan's Eighty-second Division of Dickman's I Corps had advanced from Sommerance, and by 15 October, had reached the road that connected St. Georges with St. Juvin, just to the west of Sommerance. It had cooperated well with the 166th Regiment of Lenihan's brigade. Duncan went forward on 16 October and saw that his command was worn out, and that the Germans still held firm to the Landres-St. Georges line. Lenihan's brigade was even more exhausted and only 40 percent of the combat troops were left in the 165th Regiment.[108]

On the night of 15 October, Summerall called a meeting at General Menoher's command post. In his memoir, he makes it clear that weak and irresponsible leadership, and the failure of top commanders to establish their command posts close to the front, not the treacherous terrain and daunting resistance of the Germans, were responsible for the 83rd Brigade's failure to advance.[109] Those summoned to attend were Colonel Harry D. Mitchell, commander of the depleted 165th Regiment, Colonel Henry J. Reilly, son of the legendary captain of Reilly's Battery and commander of the division's artillery brigade, and Colonel Benson W. Hough, who commanded the 166th Regiment. Also present was Lieutenant Colonel Charles A. Dravo, the division's machine gun officer.[110] Summerall wrote that when he arrived, his "worst apprehensions were realized," for he found that "the division commander had never left his command post, which was far to the rear." He also noted that "the commander of the left brigade [General Lenihan of the 83rd] was confused and completely unstrung. He knew nothing of why the brigade had not advanced and had never left his command post. I saw that he was in no condition to remain in command and decided to relieve him."[111]

Summerall then moved to the command post of the 165th Regiment, the unit that had run into the German wire and had been pinned down by machine gun fire. He met Colonel Mitchell on his way to the meeting, and asked him why he had not attacked, and why he had never left his command post. Mitchell responded that "nearly all of his regiment had been killed or wounded and many bodies were caught in the enemy's wire." Summerall wrote that he asked Mitchell how he knew this, and he responded that some young staff officers had told him. "He was mentally defeated and in no condition to command," according to Summerall. "Of course," he continued, "the reports were not true and there had been few casualties."[112] This assertion is totally at odds with historian Cooke's statement that Mitchell's regiment had suffered heavy losses. In addition, in his history of the Forty-second Division, *Americans All*, Henry Reilly stated that "heavy flanking fire...was the main reason why the 83rd Brigade could not successfully break through the German position....It caused the heavy losses, particularly in the New York [165th] regiment." He added that the regiment, in spite of these losses, "held on to the position to which they had advanced and from which each of their unsuccessful attacks was made, leaving behind as evidence the bodies of their dead in the German wire."[113] Summerall finished with Mitchell by relieving him from command, "thus incurring the hostility of the regiment but he could not be trusted with men's lives," he concluded.[114] A more likely reason for the possibility of any such hostility would have been the regiment's reaction to what it considered Mitchell's unjustified removal.

Summerall also wrote that he found the other regimental commander, who was Colonel Hough of the 166th, far back from the front in his command post. This commander "had never gone to his lines, and did not know why the regiment had not attacked [sic]." To Summerall, Hough "seemed well poised and to realize that he had failed in his leadership. I explained what I expected of him and told him to move his command post well to the front and to visit his line at once. He assured me that he would do so."[115]

Summerall returned to division headquarters and told Menoher what he had seen. It was now Menoher's turn to receive the wrath of the corps commander. He told Menoher "to move his command post forward and to visit his commanders and lines at once and to report to me by telephone when he returned. I told him that if he did not do this, he knew what I would be compelled to do. He seemed responsive," he wrote, "but, although I had known him pleasantly for years, I realized that I had made an enemy of him. This I found later. I should have relieved him." Summerall concluded his stormy visit to division headquarters by telling Menoher to relieve Lenihan and replace him with "a colonel [Reilly] of an artillery regiment whom I had long known."[116] He failed to mention that Reilly commanded the division's artillery regiment. He also told Menoher to relieve "the colonel of the infantry regiment [Mitchell] and replace him by the division machine gun officer [Dravo]."[117] Menoher did as he was told, and relieved both officers.

General Lenihan did not go quietly. According to James Cooke's account, Lenihan demanded a hearing, and Colonel S. Field Dallam, V Corps Inspector General, was sent to investigate. Dallam, as Cooke states, believed that Lenihan had been "a victim of circumstances" and "had done all he could."[118] He recommended that Lenihan be restored to his command, but Summerall overruled his recommendation. General Liggett had decided earlier that he would recommend Lenihan to command the Twenty-sixth Division. When the report arrived on his desk, he overruled Menoher and Summerall and assigned Lenihan to command a brigade in the Seventy-seventh Division.[119] In his memoir, Summerall said nothing about Liggett's having overridden his relief of Lenihan. Rather, he concluded his own account of the incident by stating that "The brigade commander whom I relieved was a close friend and classmate of the army commander [Liggett] whose hostility I thereby incurred and who tried to hurt me later."[120]

If one considers in reverse order Summerall's account of his stormy session at Menoher's headquarters, an explanation of at least some of his actions is possible. Summerall's accusation that Liggett "tried to hurt me later," is another indication of his enmity toward another officer of high rank who like Pershing, criticized his ordering the First Division to march on Sedan later in the campaign. Liggett, as will be noted below, lost his temper over the incident and believed there was sufficient cause to take disciplinary action against Summerall, as well as against Brigadier General Frank Parker, Summerall's successor as First Division commander. Liggett decided to let the matter drop, but his reaction caused Summerall to place him and Lenihan, Liggett's "close friend," as well as Menoher, in the permanent company of his enemies. His linking of Liggett and Lenihan ruled out the possibility, even after lengthy reflection, that he might have acted precipitously in relieving Lenihan. As for Menoher, it was enough that he later lined up with the opposition to Summerall when he was the army's chief of staff.

The inspector general of V Corps, who recommended that the relief of Lenihan be overruled, apparently had nothing to do with the Sedan episode. Summerall could have stood his ground and recorded in his memoir that he was fully justified in relieving a commander who had faltered and failed on the battlefield, in spite of the inspector general's report. He also could have stated that, in his opinion, Pershing would have done the same thing, for that is exactly how the commander in chief had dealt with General Cameron, and, subsequently, with three division commanders.

Impatient with the slow progress of General Buck's Third Division in III Corps sector, Pershing visited Buck's headquarters on 15 October. He found the men "disorganized and apparently disheartened."[121] Three days later, he relieved Buck and replaced him with Brigadier General Preston Brown, the veteran chief of staff of the Second Division. That same day, he relieved General McMahon from command of the Fifth Division, replacing him with Major General Hanson Ely. McMahon's division had faltered while protecting the flank of General Haan's Thirty-second Division, and Pershing concluded that it was McMahon's fault. Pershing also removed General Edwards as commander of the Twenty-sixth Division. He had long since tired of Edwards's failure to enforce discipline in his division, his disregard of specific orders from GHQ, and his inflated ego.[122] Pershing replaced him with Brigadier Frank E. Bamford, who had been serving as interim commander of the First Division after Summerall had left to take over command of V Corps.

In the context of Summerall's mandate to MacArthur to take Châtillon, and considering what he could have said in his memoir about Lenihan's relief, and the actions that Pershing himself took against three division commanders, Summerall's removal of Colonel Mitchell is more understandable. What was wrong, and unfair to Mitchell, was Summerall's assertion that Mitchell had falsely reported that there had been few casualties in his regiment. Perhaps Mitchell was "mentally defeated and in no condition to command," but Father Francis Duffy wrote in defense of Mitchell that "No one who knows him could ever accuse Harry D. Mitchell of losing his nerve in battle. He liked a fight." At the same time, Duffy noted that Mitchell's modesty prevented him from strongly defending his action. He should have gauged Summerall's mood and responded "after the first ten minutes" with a plan for a new attack.[123] If Summerall had probed more deeply, he would have learned that the casualties in Mitchell's regiment were not few, but many. If there had been few casualties in Mitchell's regiment, it seems that Mitchell could have been trusted with men's lives, rather than the opposite.

The first two weeks of October had been tough on the Americans, and also on the British and French. General Haig had not succeeded in achieving a complete breakthrough of the Hindenburg Line, and a skillful and determined German defense had slowed down his attack. British and Belgian troops of King Albert's army group bogged down in the swampy ground east of Ypres, and Gourand's Fourth French Army on the left of Pershing's army was stalled. But, on 17 October, the British renewed their attack and

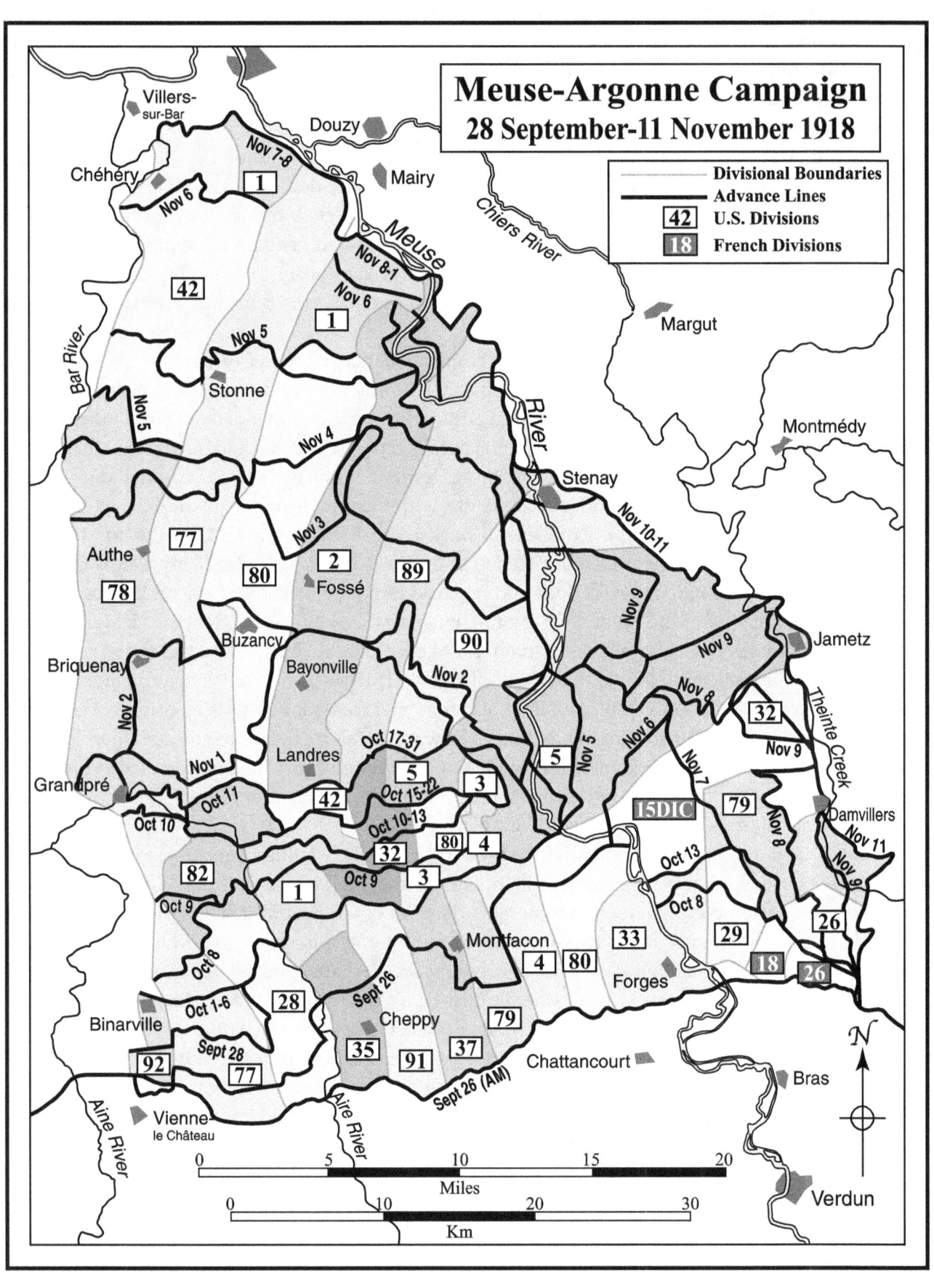

broke through the German line along the Selle River. Two days later, an Anglo-French drive crossed farther down, and King Albert's army group began moving again in Flanders.[124]

As difficult as the first 14 days of October had been for the Allies, for the Germans the entire month was even more wrenching and horrible. The German army had delayed the enemy advance, but that was about the best they could hope for. On 8 October, von Gallwitz's Fifth Army reported that there were so few army reserves available that it was impossible to relieve divisions that had been fighting for a long time.[125] A little over two weeks later, from north of the Meuse-Argonne, Crown Prince Rupprecht's headquarters reported to the High Command that their reserves soon would be "used up."[126]

On 20 October, Prince Maximilian's government completed negotiations with President Wilson and accepted the president's tough conditions for an armistice that he had set forth, as noted above, on 3 October. Later, when Wilson notified him that all correspondence would be submitted to the Allies, the stage was set for the negotiations that would lead to the end of the war with the signing of an armistice.[127] When the Kaiser supported his government's acceptance of Wilson's terms, Ludendorff resigned and fled to Sweden to write his memoirs. Paul von Hindenburg remained as commander in chief, and General Wilhelm Goerner replaced Ludendorff as quartermaster general and his first deputy. The October crises for the German Empire continued as soldiers in some divisions mutinied and refused to take their positions in the line. On 30 October, the Ottoman Empire signed an armistice with the Allies. Three days later, following the capture of Trieste by an Allied naval expedition, Austria-Hungary signed an armistice, and fighting ceased all along the Italian front.[128]

By the latter part of the crisis month of October, French Premier and War Minister Georges Clemenceau had decided that a serious problem existed in the American army. In a letter to Marshal Foch, dated 21 October, he made clear that General Pershing's failure to move his army forward in the Meuse-Argonne and allowing it to mark time had resulted in mounting casualties in the French army. Clemenceau believed that his positions as premier and war minister gave him authority over Foch, and he wrote him that

> You have watched at close range the development of General Pershing's exactions. Unfortunately, thanks to his invincible obstinacy, he has won out against you as well as against your immediate subordinates. To go over all of this again can only lead to useless regrets....
>
> Constitutionally, I am the head of the French Army....
>
> I would be a criminal if I allowed the French Army to wear itself out indefinitely in battle, without doing everything in my power to ensure that a Allied Army which has hurried to its aid was rendered capable of fulfilling the military rôle for which it is intended.[129]

What Clemenceau wanted, as the French marshal stated, was "nothing less than to effect a change in the chief command of the American Army." Foch wrote that he could not acquiesce in that "radical solution" and responded by stating his intention to maintaining his orders, that is, to continuing the existing command structure. He also pointed out that "this crisis is of the sort from which all improvised Armies suffer, and which always considerably impairs their effectiveness at the start." But he also stated that he planned to decrease the number of divisions under Pershing's command, "whenever operations being planned permit it. It is by manipulation of this sort that I expect to diminish the weaknesses of the High Command [of the American army], rather than by orders."[130] As Donald Smythe observed, Pershing would keep his command of the American army, "but would have fewer divisions to mess up with."[131] Foch closed his response by asserting "the magnitude of the effort made by the American Army....over particularly difficult country and in the face of serious resistance by the enemy."[132] With the subsequent advance of Pershing's army in the attack of 1 November and the impending collapse of the German army, Clemenceau let the matter drop, turning his attention to preparing for the armistice and the peace conference that would follow.[133]

While the German Empire struggled to survive, and Clemenceau and Foch sorted out their differences over Pershing's command of the American army, General Liggett had been busy reorganizing and retraining his command. He transferred the tired and worn Fourth Division to a training area and relieved the equally exhausted Thirty-second Division with General Wright's Eighty-ninth Division. He promoted George Marshall to colonel and appointed him to the position of chief of operations. At his headquarters he held daily meetings of the chiefs of artillery, Air Service, and engineers. Artillery support was developed to concentrate fire on the hills under attack by interdicting fire on rear slopes and rear approaches. Heavy counterbattery fire would target German artillery and infantry reserve positions. Liggett decided on the heavy use of gas, including mustard gas, the most lethal of all the poisonous chemicals used in the war. Patterned after the German army's Hutier tactics, special assault teams were trained to attack machine gun bunkers by fire and maneuver, crawling up to them to throw grenades or explosives into the bunkers. The attacking infantry would pass by these strong points, leaving them to be reduced by the assault teams.[134]

On 18 October, a few days before the Eighty-ninth Division relieved the Thirty-second, Summerall got word to General Wright that he wanted to talk to the officers of the Eighty-ninth to explain "their duties and the necessity for their leadership in combat." In his memoir, he noted that "My theme was that at all times every man must be under the eye of a leader in the appropriate grade and that men were only held up by fire when they wanted to be held up."[135] Historian Robert Ferrell noted that Wright's diary entry about Summerall's upcoming talk had an "acidulous tone," for the division commander did not feel that he needed a lecture.[136]

As a cold rain poured down, the officers assembled in a "great hollow square, one regiment's officers forming each side, the respective colonels alone in front, and the two brigade Commanders [Brigadier General Frank L. Winn of the 177th Brigade, and Brigadier General Thomas G. Hanson of the 178th Brigade] facing each other alone on opposite sides of the square."[137] Colonel Babcock, commanding the division's 354th Infantry Regiment, wrote that as he stood in the rain and mud,

> The Corps Commander drove up in his Cadillac limouzine [sic]. Feeling more than ever resentful over [Summerall's] treatment of me three months before [when Summerall transferred him out of the First Division], I could not help [but] compare his fine car, his warmly clad figure and dry uniform to the wet and mud coated uniforms of the hundreds of officers who had spent the past six days sleeping in the cold mud of the Argonne and eating under the almost continuous rains of October.[138]

Summerall noted the drenching rain, but, in contrast to Babcock's description, stated that "we thought little of it."[139] As he continued his embittered account of Summerall's visit, Babcock noted that after General Wright greeted him, Summerall stepped forward and, "in his best pontifical manner said, 'Good morning, gentlemen. I am glad to see you. I hope to see some of you again—not all of you, but some of you.'"[140] Babcock's assertion of this callous greeting may well be a contrived result of his bitterness, but it does not altogether conflict with the actual speech that Summerall delivered on that cold, rainy day to those who would lead their men in the next great attack of the Meuse-Argonne battle. Summerall stated proudly in his memoir that he took the account of his talk from the *History of the 89th Division*, so he obviously felt that he had made a strong and positive impression on the officers and men of the division. Quoting from that work, he wrote that

> ....The talk of General Summerall to the assembled officers was in tone grim, blunt and so[m]bre—the talk of a fighting man to fighting men. In substance, he spoke as follows: "When a division enters the line in attack, it is given an objective to take. That objective must be reached. There is no excuse for

failure. Either you take your objective or you do not take it. Casualties among officers will be heavy, as well as among men, although probably eighty percent of the wounded will come back. Officers must keep well to the front and when anything goes wrong, it is the duty of the next commander to go up and see what is the matter. The toll of casualties of the senior officers will, of necessity, be increased by this practice but the results are more than commensurate with the costs. Control is vital. Divisions have been frittered away by straggling or the pernicious practice of sending details to the rear. In this corps, it is the order that no riflemen are to be taken away from a company for any purpose. The best way to safeguard the wounded is to push ahead and defeat the enemy. Pitiful examples have recurred in the present offensive wherein units have allowed their strength to be weakened by details for carrying wounded and, in the face of a counterattack, have been driven back leaving their wounded to die. To halt plays the enemy's game, since he is fighting a defensive action with machine guns and artillery. To halt means losses. But if you push on the losses will not be much greater and you will have gained something. No officer should ever say that he is tired or allow his men to say it. No man is ever so tired that he cannot take another step forward.

Don't ask for relief. Those in higher command are constantly considering the matter of relief. It is expected that the full measure of the organization's strength will be demanded of it before it is pulled out. It must be so if we win. When you have reached the stage that the gains you are making do not justify the losses you are sustaining, you will be taken out. Don't worry about your flanks. Distribution in depth protects them. Troops must hold their ground. To fall back, allows the enemy to play his game on you causing losses and those losses, with the ones you have sustained in the advance, will be in vain. But even a squad or a platoon, if it holds its ground, will enable the whole line to advance. In the last few days, a patrol of twenty men, by fighting and holding its ground on a hill, enabled a whole division to advance. The best way to take machine guns is to go and take 'em. Press forward. The finest tribute that can be paid to a division is: 'It takes its objectives.'"

General Summerall concluded his talk with the characteristic remark that he would get down to see us as often as he could. That he would try to see us if things went well. If things did not go well, we would certainly see him soon.

Such appeals as those had a marked effect upon the conduct of the division in battle. It would be hard to conceive of a better fighting spirit than was shown by all ranks. The lesson of control was well learned; the total of straggling for the entire division was on a fraction of one percent.[141]

In his memoir, Babcock sharply criticized Summerall's talk as "the poorest exhibition of battle leadership possible to make. Instead of encouraging these fine young fellows, he was drawing a somber, terrifying picture of the days to come." He felt that Summerall should have praised the division for its previous service, and expressed his confidence that they would gain their objectives and be rewarded with "a well-earned rest." Had he done so, "They would have returned to their bivouacs heartened and confident of gaining their reward. As it was, the assembly broke up and even I felt a moment of depression....."[142] To show that his comments were not unique and attributable to his "dislike" of Summerall, Babcock quoted from the entry in a diary that was kept by one of the officers in his regiment. With stinging mockery, this officer wrote that

He [Summerall] talked for an hour while Colonel Lee of Division forced us to stand at attention in the rain and mud. The talk as to substance was good, but as to effect on morale, was disconcerting. Quite revealing as to what we might expect. Full of official platitudes—nice roll on the tongue—but coming from one in the safety of a corps command—well—"There is no such thing as being held up by machine gun fire—or shot up by your own artillery—or all shot to pieces. No Sir! tho I know of a case where only 4 men survived a company of 250 men, but even that company was not all shot to pieces." Wasn't it though? I am afraid the men have different ideas on that. Oh well, speeches must have lots of hot air in them.[143]

Babcock concluded his commentary on Summerall's arrival and talk in a hand-written notation that quoted from an article written by a Major Meade after the war. Meade wrote that the substance of Summerall's "little talk" was as follows:

> You officers are going into the hardest fight that the American Army has ever experienced. You have been thinking all along that you would be sent back into a rest camp. I want to tell you now that you will not be sent back to a rest camp until your regiment is so depleted of officers and men that it is absolutely useless as a fighting unit.

Meade ended his entry, as Babcock wrote, by stating that "The officers left this meeting with anything but the best feeling."[144]

Summerall's talk was a hard-hitting assessment of what he believed confronted the division when it attacked in the Meuse-Argonne. Understandably, he based his view on the combat that the army had just been through and had no reason to believe that the battle to come would be any easier. Summerall knew what Pershing expected of his commanders, and he himself had demonstrated repeatedly that he was in synch with his commander in chief's demand that officers take their objectives, and either die trying, or be relieved if they should fail. One can understand Babcock's lingering resentment, but while Summerall had removed him from command in the First Division, General Wright and others had praised his skill as a combat commander. On the other hand, he felt a commander of Summerall's rank should build morale and inspire their men for the battles ahead with praise and the promise of rewards; instead he had demanded that they attack and advance, regardless of the loss of life. Yet the historians of the Eighty-ninth Division thought that Summerall's talk had a positive effect on the division for the battle that lay ahead, and General Wright wrote that Summerall's talks "struck home and will bear fruit."[145] A few days later, after Summerall had to cancel a trip to the division to talk with men of the assaulting battalions, Wright wrote that "I was very sorry, as I had relied greatly on what he had to say to the men."[146] Historians Douglas Johnson and Rolfe Hillman believed that Summerall's address showed how he had matured as a combat commander, even though this development came only "after extensive command experience."[147] Summerall certainly made clear in his talk that he was determined to achieve victory in the fight ahead and was confident that his command would triumph. Perhaps this determination and conviction resulted from his maturation as a commander in the Great War, but these characteristics had been fixed in Summerall's character from the harsh and fragile conditions of his childhood, and through the years of iron at West Point. They were reaffirmed in his commands in the Far East and at home, before his rise to high command in the Great War. This affirmation also lay in Summerall's determination to preserve Captain Reilly's tradition that there were no excuses for failure.

The other division that Liggett replaced was the Thirty-second Division in Summerall's V Corps, and, as corps commander, he was much involved in process of their relief. He had no transportation to move them, and they were too exhausted from weeks of fighting to march very far. Anyway, he needed to keep them near enough to the line in case of an enemy attack, so he moved them out of the range of enemy artillery, although they were still in range of German bombers. They were deloused, given hot food and fresh uniforms.[148]

Summerall wrote that before the Thirty-second Division marched to the rear, General Haan came to his command post. As far as I know, there was no "Babcock" of the Thirty-second to write about Haan's visit, so we have only Summerall's rather self-serving description of it. When Haan arrived, he insisted that his division had to be taken at least 40 kilometers to the rear, where they could rest and be safe from any hostile fire. Then, according to Summerall, Haan "began to rave and use the most violent language. He said many other things with profanity and gross defiance," wrote Summerall, who replied "as calmly and in as low a voice as possible to offset his shouting." He told Haan that he could not talk to him "in that manner," whereupon the tired and overwrought commander's "whole manner changed and he looked crushed." Haan apologized, and after Summerall explained why the Thirty-second could not be moved as far as Haan wanted, he wrote that Haan "went away subdued and calm and to the end of his life he always showed me the greatest respect and friendship." Summerall believed that he had understood that Haan had experienced "a condition of neurosis from overstrain and by [my] being patient and calm, he was saved to recover and be a good commander and officer for several years."[149] One can be certain that subsequently Haan had nothing critical to say about Summerall and the future incident of Sedan. More importantly, and years later, the proud and octogenarian Summerall was confident that he always had been right in deciding which officers under his command in the AEF needed to be assured of their courage and ability, and which officers needed to be relieved. This confidence was another example of his conviction that his judgment, as one of the highest-ranking officers in the AEF, had been infallible.

After his conference with General Haan, Summerall wrote that he visited all of the batteries and companies of the division and praised their conduct in the line and their success. He explained why they could not be moved farther to the rear and assured them that they would be well fed, deloused, and that "everything possible would be done to prepare them to reenter the line as soon as they were needed." One could question just how they responded to this assurance, but to Summerall, "Their looks reassured me and I felt that the officers and men understood and would accept the situation in the proper spirit."[150]

Summerall's good feelings about the Thirty-second Division and his confidence that the Eighty-ninth was ready for battle were like Liggett's view of First Army, as the latter wrote that his army's morale was "as high again, I believe, as it had been in September, when the battle opened. Divisions had been filled up, supplies replenished, the artillery was in support positions, and the roads enormously bettered...."[151] Liggett, and certainly his V Corps commander, were confident that their men were ready to resume the Meuse-Argonne offensive.

General Liggett and General Henri Gourand, commander of the French Fourth Army on the left of Liggett's First Army, had agreed that the attack of the First and Second American Armies would begin on 1 November.[152] Gourand's army would advance toward Sedan from its bridgehead on the right bank of the Aisne River, drawing a large part of the German troops in the Argonne, and relieving pressure on the American First Army.[153] North of the French army, the British and Belgians would drive on Brussels. On their right, the French center and the British right would push in the Laon Bulge, as Gourand's Fourth Army and Liggett's First Army closed the gap from the south.[154] To the right of First Army, General Bullard's Second Army was deployed south of Verdun and well to the east of the Meuse, primarily for defense.[155]

The First Army was deployed in the heart of the Meuse-Argonne, from east to west, and would attack straight ahead in a power drive to uncover the line of the Meuse and the defenses of Sedan (see map, p. 266). General Ely's Fifth Division and General Allen's Ninetieth Division were in line east to west in General Hines's III Corps, with General Brown's Third Division in reserve. Summerall's V Corps was in the center, with General Wright's Eighty-ninth Division and General Lejeune's Second Division in line, and the First Division, commanded by Brigadier Frank Parker, and the Forty-second Division, under General Menoher, in reserve. I Corps, commanded by General Dickman, included the Eightieth Division, under General Cronkhite; the Seventy-seventh Division, under General Alexander; and General James H. McRae's Seventy-eighth Division in the offensive, with

General Duncan's Eighty-second Division in reserve. The recuperating Thirty-second Division was placed in First Army reserve.[156]

Summerall's V Corps would spearhead the attack and deliver the main blow along the front of First Army, the other corps in support. III Corps would advance past the Bois de Bourgogne (its artillery batteries neutralized by a massive gas attack) and capture the high ground east of Barricourt; I Corps would attack on the left flank of V Corps to seize Buzancy and Boult-aux-Bois, where they would link up with Gourand's Fourth Army.[157] As historian Braim points out, the AEF was now a far more professional fighting force than that which had begun the campaign in September.[158] Indeed, the divisions that composed the line on 1 November were solid, veteran units, and they were led by strong and vigorous commanders. They faced seven German divisions, all of which were tired, and far below their normal strength.[159] And, as noted earlier, their reserves were almost used up (see map, p. 275).

On 30 October, Summerall began a two-day "talking tour" of all the regiments in the Second, Eighty-ninth, and First Divisions, this time "Praising their accomplishments, and telling them that in the approaching battle we would end the war." But, remaining true to form, he told the other divisions that if any of their attacking troops faltered, he would "at once put the First Division in." He described General Parker as "the ablest combat leader in the war."[160] Summerall had recommended Parker to command the division, and Parker was in charge when the division "raced" to Sedan later. Summerall's praise of Parker might well have been enhanced by Parker's loyalty to his corps commander, as shall be seen, throughout the lingering controversy over the Sedan matter.

Summerall noted that he had talked to "nearly a hundred thousand men in the two days before the attack. My voice was very hoarse," he wrote, " but I was certain of success." When he reached his command post late on 31 October, he found Pershing and French General Paul Maistre, who commanded the French Group of Armies of the Center that included General Gourand's Fourth French Army. Pershing asked Summerall if he were sick, and he answered that his voice was hoarse from talking to the troops. When Pershing asked him what he thought about the prospects of the attack, Summmerall replied that he would "give him every foot of ground on schedule." Maistre said that the American losses had been very heavy, noted Summerall, who seems to have ended the discussion by telling Maistre that "if the French fought as hard as the Americans, their losses would be heavy also."[161]

For several days prior to the attack, huge 14-inch naval guns had been hurling 1,400 pound shells some 25 miles into rear areas of the German army. Two days before the attack, artillery shells exploded about 41.5 tons of gas on the Bois de Bourgogne, neutralizing the 11 German batteries in the sprawling forest.[162] Then, at 0330 hours on 1 November, the last great barrage of the war roared forth in a fire for destruction that Summerall said "used every weapon to its maximum power."[163] Gun barrels glowed in the darkness, as the artillery shelled enemy battery locations, reserve locations, crossroads, bridges, and areas where reserve units could be waiting.[164] The historian and novelist Fairfax Downey noted that "cannon enough to conquer hell" had been gathered, and that the guns pounded "like a million hammers."[165] Summerall had constructed the V Corps barrage plan that fired a sheet of shell, shrapnel, and bullets to a depth of 1,200 meters, or about the length of four football fields. It covered the advance of the entire corps along a front of over eight kilometers, or almost five miles. Hundreds of machine guns fired 600 shots a minute; 272 75-mm guns fired four rounds per minute; and 180 155-mm howitzers, 124 105-mm cannon, 24 eight-inch howitzers, and 8 six-inch mortars poured fire on enemy trenches, machine gun positions that had been located, and other known enemy positions.

At 0530 hours the barrage ceased for five minutes before the infantry attacked behind a rolling barrage that laid down a line of bursting shells 150 yards in front of their jump-off line; 200 yards beyond that line was a line of shrapnel bursts; and 150 yards beyond that was an intense machine gun barrage. As Summerall proudly and correctly noted, this massed fire became known as "'the Summerall Barrage.'" He also wrote, perhaps justifiably, that "It has probably never been equaled."[166]

The artillery fire overwhelmed the Germans and broke their defenses. As Summerall noted, "The effect was all we could want." Enemy machine gunners and gun crews abandoned their weapons without firing a shot; artillery teams of horses and drivers were killed before they could withdraw.[167] German infantrymen fled before their attackers, who stormed after them, and they by-passed enemy strong points, leaving them to be blasted by direct-fire weapons. Instead of climbing out of revetted trenches and attacking bunched together, as had so often happened in previous battles, the men of the attacking regiments dispersed widely as they advanced, using shell holes and other available cover. These tactics made it more difficult for German artillery and machine gun fire to score hits on the attacking infantry.[168]

In his introduction to General Wright's diary entry of 1 November, historian Robert Ferrell noted that Colonel Babcock "nicely displayed what experience taught." Babcock knew that German artillery would target his regiment where they would assemble for the attack, presumably from the edge of the Bois de Bantheville, south of their objective of the Barricourt Heights. Instead, Babcock placed his men out in the open, close to German machine gun nests, and when the enemy artillery began firing, their shells exploded on the fringe of the woods, while American guns fired on German machine gun nests to the north. Babcock's men were safe in the middle, waiting to attack.[169]

Ferrell's description of Babcock's action seems to confirm Johnson's and Hillman's assertion, noted in the previous chapter, that Babcock was an exceptional leader who could understand correctly, and react creatively, to the combat situations he faced, as they insist he had done at Soissons. They reinforced their conclusion by noting that General Wright's chief of staff reported to the AEF adjutant general on 15 November that "'I was forcibly impressed by the qualification of...Col. C. S. Babcock. [He is a] natural leader of men, forceful, physically and mentally apparently tireless, indifferent to danger, thoroughly versed in [his] profession.'"[170] In addition, General Wright wrote in his diary that Babcock had led his regiment "gallantly and successfully."[171] With Ferrell, Johnson and Hillman, and General Wright, as well as his chief of staff endorsing Babcock's innovative, successful, and courageous leadership, it seems obvious that Summerall acted precipitously and wrongly earlier in removing Babcock from his command in the First Division. It is, perhaps, ironic that Babcock, whom Summerall declared was "unsuited to be a combat regimental commander," will be remembered, not only for his courage and bravery, but also for his innovative tactical leadership of his regiment, one that helped Summerall's V Corps achieve victory in the Meuse-Argonne battle.

Late in the afternoon of 1 November, the Eighty-ninth's battalions had advanced about three miles beyond their jump-off line and had reached their objective: the Heights of Barricourt, the ridge that extended across the entire front of the division. From there they could look out across terrain that sloped all the way down to the Meuse River.[172] General Wright recorded in his diary that General Burtt, V Corps chief of staff, informed him that First Army had sent V Corps headquarters a message commending the officers and men of the division for their "good work" on 1 November, and that General Summerall had "heartedly concurred." Wright added that "It is a great source of satisfaction to me to feel that General Summerall is pleased."[173] Wright's feeling of satisfaction revealed an important aspect about Summerall's professorial, or as Babcock said, "pontifical" addresses. These talks were rather like lectures to "captive" audiences of cadets and stressed the necessity of personal sacrifices for the triumph of the cause that his men were fighting for. In these addresses, Summerall inspired men like Wright to please him. Wright's response indicates their belief that their success as commanders would be evaluated on the basis of their obedience to his will and commands. They also believed that if they faithfully followed him, they, and those whom they led, would reap their rewards in the triumph of Summerall's promise of victory.

On the left of the Eighty-ninth was General Lejeune's Second Division, and its cadre of veterans showed the value of their experience as well. As historian Mac Coffman wrote, they had learned that the Germans had always moved their machine guns close to the American line to avoid the barrage. Just before they attacked, Lejeune pulled back his troops 500 yards behind their front and started the rolling barrage there, wiping out the enemy gunners out in front in no-man's-land.[174]

To the right of V Corps, General Hines's III Corps advanced swiftly and seized the area west of Dun-sur-Meuse, protecting the flank of V Corps' advance. General Dickman's I Corps supported V Corps with supporting fire, and the Eightieth Division advanced along the left flank of V Corps. But the Seventy-seventh and Seventy-eighth Divisions of I Corps were unable to dislodge the Germans from the thick woods of the Bois des Loges and the village of Champigneulles.[175] Dickman wrote that "the situation in the I Corps was disappointing and there was gloom at our headquar-

*Major General John A. Lejeune*
Courtesy National Archives

ters."[176] Liggett visited Dickman's headquarters and thought they were depressed because they had missed the "Big Parade" the day before. Perhaps Dickman was also frustrated that Summerall's corps was leaving his corps in the dust. Summerall, sustaining his denunciation of Dickman, wrote in his account that to him, "the inaction of the 1st Corps was unpardonable, but it was glossed over by [Dickman's] friends at G. H. Q."[177] Liggett, at least, remained untroubled by I Corps' delay and assured Dickman that he would have the opportunity to catch up with the "procession" the next day.[178] That night the Germans pulled out of the Bois des Loges and Champigneulles. Historians Coffman and Smythe noted that they withdrew so fast that Dickman's corps, even with its infantry hastily loaded on trucks and in hot pursuit of the enemy, could not catch up with them.[179]

On 2 November, the advance continued (see map, p. 275). General Dickman's I Corps captured Buzancy. With General Lejeune's clearance and encouragement, the 9th Regiment of Lejeune's Second Division hit the German line on the southern edge in the Bois de Belval. They marched four miles in total darkness and pouring rain to seize the forest and captured enemy troops in their billets before the confused Germans had time to regroup and counterattack. They did not suffer a single casualty and missed capturing a German division commander and his staff by only five minutes.[180] General Wright's division took Nouart and fought hard toward Beauclair. On 3 November, they were told to stand by to be relieved by the First Division, but Wright asked that they remain in the line and continue their advance. He said that his troops "were in fine condition, were in touch with the situation, and would certainly make further progress the next day."[181] Never one to turn down the request of a fighting general to keep fighting, Summerall granted his request.[182]

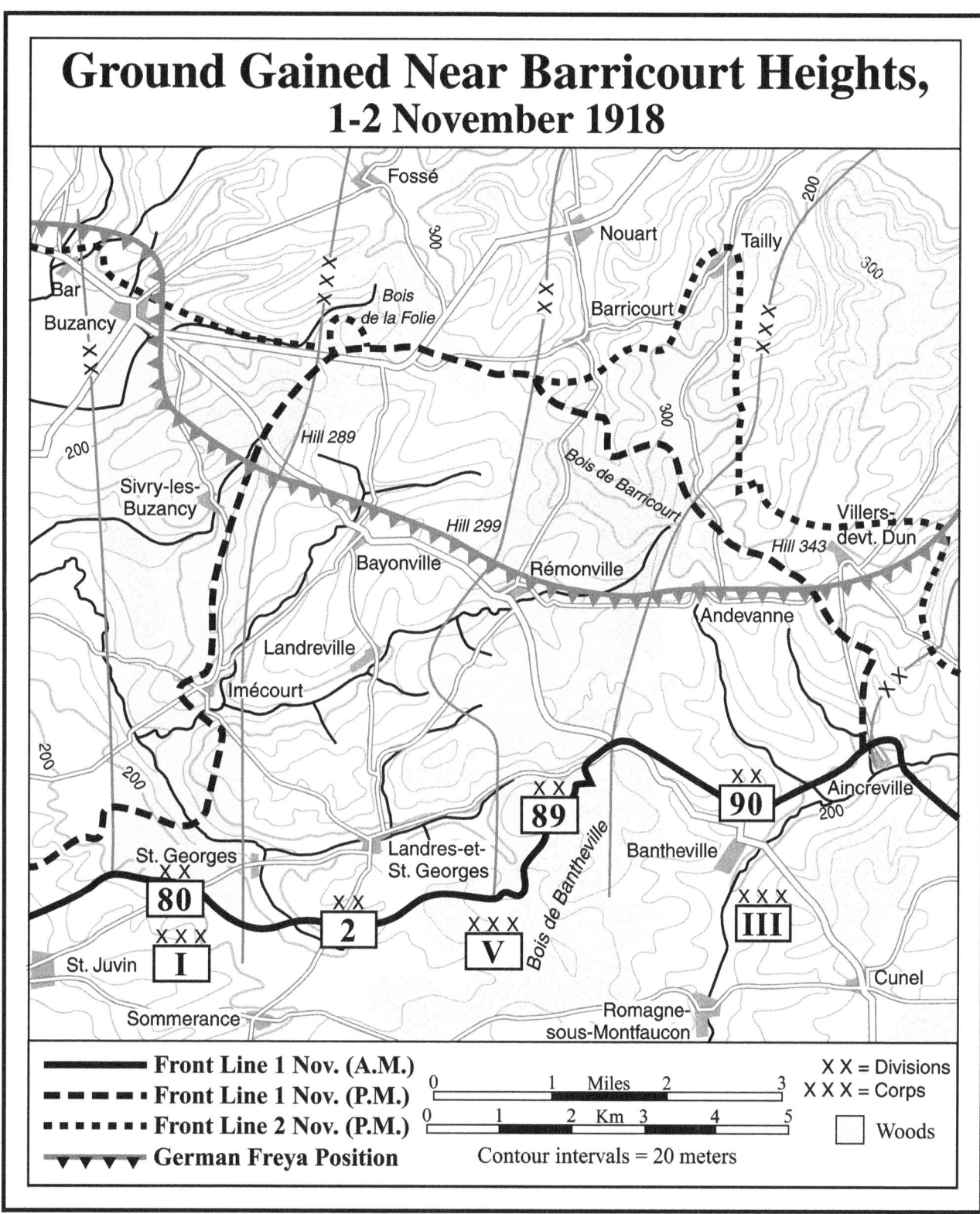

The Eighty-ninth resumed their advance on 4 November, but progress was slow and unsatisfactory, according to the division historian, Major C. J. Masseck. He also wrote that "The inactivity of our infantry was apparent." Historian James Hallas added that the subsequent attack of the infantry showed little vigor.[183] Summerall was not pleased, and neither was the division commander.[184] General Wright was especially dissatisfied with the commander of the 178th Brigade, Brigadier General Thomas G. Hanson, who always had "a reason for inactivity," noted historian Ferrell.[185] Wright called in Hanson and told him that "it was absolutely necessary for him to put more punch into his attack."[186] Wright finally managed to get Hanson and the rest of the division moving forward, and they reached their objective just beyond Beaufort on the south edge of the Bois de Dieulet.[187] Major Masseck wrote that "While the Division gained its objective, the attack was not driven with sufficient energy. Opportunity was undoubtedly lost to make large captures of men and material, and possibly hold an important river crossing.[188] That night, V Corps again directed that the division be relieved, but Wright requested that the division remain in the line, and Summerall, showing his patience, as well as his confidence in Wright's judgment, approved his request.[189]

Summerall assigned Wright the responsibility of seizing the north edge of the Bois de Dieulet so that the heavy artillery of the corps could move into the forest, from where it could reach the main line of German communications. By the end of the day, the division had captured its objective, and the artillery had been called forward to shell German positions and communications.[190] Wright also asked Summerall to authorize the advance of the division to the left and force a crossing of the Meuse River at Pouilly. Summerall approved it, but, as Wright wrote, "thought it ought to be done in real American style with plenty of artillery preparation."[191] For the next four days, Wright and his staff were busy planning the attack.[192]

As General Wright worked on the attack of the Eighty-ninth Division, Lejeune's Second Division continued to advance, reaching the Meuse on the left flank of Wright's division on 6 November.[193] In General Hines's III Corps, the Fifth Division, under General Ely, fought its way to the Meuse, and during the night of 4–5 November, established bridgeheads across the river south of Dun-sur-Meuse. Pershing wrote that they crossed the river "in a brilliant maneuver" and seized the heights of the Meuse. "Now for the first time since 1914," he stated, "the French positions around Verdun were completely free from the menace of these heights."[194]

By 5 November, First Army had advanced to the heights and onto the open ground in the valley of the Meuse. On 2 November, von Gallwitz noted the ground the Americans had gained and reported that

> there is nothing left to do than withdraw tonight into the so-called rearguard position....all of the front line commanders report that the Americans are attacking in mass formations in the general direction of Stenay, that the troops are fighting courageously but just cannot do anything. Therefore it has become imperative that the Army be withdrawn in rear of the Meuse and that said withdrawal be effected immediately.[195]

*Major General Hansen E. Ely*
Courtesy National Archives

Other German units west of the Meuse were equally desperate and reported that they could no longer hold their positions; that roads were "lacking and bottomless"; and that "no one knew where the enemy was or where our forces were."[196] During the night of 4–5 November, German forces began a phased, general withdrawal named *Kriegsmarsch* (march of war) that would enable them to disengage from the American attack, and reestablish defenses across the Meuse along the northeast bank of the river.[197] Elements from other divisions, and "whatever troops were still fit for combat," were sent in as reinforcements. "Everything available has been gotten together," reported von Gallwitz, "and the order given to drive the enemy back."[198] Indeed, as the Germans withdrew and narrowed their front against the American line of attack, their resistance stiffened, some units mounted counterattacks, and many died fighting in desperate hand to hand combat with the Americans.[199]

As the German army prepared for the *Kriegsmarsch*, turmoil erupted on the home front. On 3 November, sailors in the German High Seas Fleet seized control of the naval base at Kiel. During the next two days, revolutionaries took power in Hamburg, Bremen, Luebeck, and Munich, and soon after a democratic socialist republic was set up in Bavaria. The broken empire of Austria-Hungary had signed an armistice on 3 November, and on 8 November, negotiations for an armistice with Germany began in railroad passenger cars between Compiègne and Rethondes.[200] The Allied terms were severe and called for the evacuation of France, Belgium, Luxembourg, and Alsace-Lorraine within two weeks; the evacuation of bridgeheads over the Rhine at Cologne, Coblenz, and Mainz; and the surrender of weapons, airplanes, locomotives, box cars, and trucks.[201] The German delegation argued that the Allies had drawn up such severe terms in order to force them to refuse them and force Germany to proceed immediately with peace negotiations.[202] The tense negotiations continued, and the next day, after General Groener told him that the army would not march home under his leadership, Emperor William II abdicated and fled to Holland. Upheaval on the home front continued, as a new socialist government in Berlin proclaimed a republic.

Meanwhile, in the I Corps sector of First Army, General Cronkhite's Eightieth Division fought through fierce German resistance, advancing beyond Beaumont, where they were relieved on 5 November, by General Alexander's Seventy-seventh Division (see map, p. 282). By 6 November, Alexander's men had driven to the Meuse at Remilly-sur-Meuse, three miles south of Sedan. General McRae's Seventy-eighth Division captured Les Petites Armoises, northwest of Verrieres on 4 November, and was relieved by the Forty-second. General Menoher's division established its line north of Bulson, six miles south of Sedan.[203] On 5 November, the First Division marched all night through rain and over muddy roads and took over the sector of the Eightieth Division, just north of Beaumont on the left of V Corps. The First had been in corps reserve since 29 October, and when they arrived at 0400 hours on 6 November, they immediately attacked, "With an impatience born of days of waiting." By noon they had reached the Meuse and had captured Villemontry, on the west bank of the river, 10 miles south of Sedan.[204]

While revolutionary changes swept across Germany, and Allied and German representatives huddled in railroad cars at Compiègne, First Army pressed its attack toward and across the Meuse, and Pershing made a dramatic move of his own. As the French Fourth Army drove toward Sedan, the divisions in I and V Corps advanced past the French on the left of I Corps, until they were within a few miles of Sedan. Pershing noted in his diary that General Maistre had overstepped his authority by giving First Army the order to continue the attack. On 3 November, he met with Maistre to have a "very plain talk" about Maistre's order. "He was very nice about it," wrote Pershing, "and said it would not occur again."

Pershing also complained to Maistre about the French general's having drawn the boundary between his Fourth Corps and First Army to the right so that the Americans would strike the Meuse above Sedan. Maistre replied that he had done that because otherwise, the French would have no road to Sedan. With his French colleague backing up and on the defensive, Pershing then thrust home his statement that he wanted "my troops to take Sedan." Maistre managed to say "something about the line of communications." Pershing pressed his advantage and stated that "in case we arrived in front of Sedan first, we would oblique over in French territory and take it." As Pershing noted, Maistre said that "this would be alright, and repeated: 'Je ne demande pas m[i]eux.'"[205]

Pershing did not exclaim his delight in the outcome of his meeting with Maistre, but he must have considered it a high point of his command of the AEF. For too long he had listened to British and French criticism about the inefficiency of his staff and subordinate commands, as well as their complaints about the slow and often confused attacks by American units. As he noted in his diary, "we are not getting credit for all the work we are doing."[206] To erase that slight, and win for his forces the acclaim he believed they deserved, "It was the ambition of the First Army and mine that our troops should capture Sedan, which the French had lost in a decisive battle in 1870 [during the Franco-Prussian War]."[207] Where the French had lost, the Americans would win.

Sedan represented special historical importance and sentimental value for France. It was where Emperor Napoleon III and his army were surrounded and captured in a humiliating loss in 1870 to the army of King William I of Prussia, at the close of the Franco-Prussian War. The defeat destroyed the Second Empire of France and led to the creation of the German Empire in 1871. Sedan had been seized again by the Germans in their initial attack in 1914, and it is surprising that Maistre would concede its capture to the Americans, even under pressure from Pershing. As General Harbord wrote in his *The American Army in France*, Maistre "must have felt very much as the American Revolutionary Army would have felt if Rochambeau had asked to be permitted to elbow Washington out of the reviewing stand at Yorktown."[208]

On 5 November, Pershing spent the day on a visit to the front and called on General Dickman at I Corps headquarters. He told Dickman that he would like to see his corps "have the honor of taking Sedan, and he [Dickman] promised to do all in his power to have that honor." The next day he wrote that

> The French seem to be afraid we will beat them to Sedan and are constantly making efforts to get us to go more to the East. To-night our troops have arrived within 4 kilometers of Sedan and they say they are going to the town to-night. According to agreement with General Maestre [*sic*], if we arrive first we can take Sedan. I think we will do it.[209]

Pleased with Dickman's pledge, and excited about the prospect of First Army's capture of Sedan, an ebullient Pershing returned to his headquarters train at Souilly, the village where General Liggett's First Army headquarters was also located. At 1600 hours General Conner, AEF operations chief, came to the office of Liggett's chief of staff, Colonel Marshall, to discuss future plans. They reviewed the excellent progress of First Army. The Second, Eighty-ninth, and Ninetieth Divisions of V Corps had already reached the Meuse, and the Seventy-seventh and Forty-second Divisions of I Corps were steadily advancing on the left of V Corps (see map, p. 282).[210] After they had talked for about an hour, Conner suddenly told Marshall of General Pershing's desire that First Army capture Sedan. Marshall promptly called in a stenographer and dictated the following message from the commander in chief to the commanding generals of I and V Corps.

> General Pershing desires that the honor of entering Sedan should fall to the First American Army. He has every confidence that the troops of the First Corps, assisted on their right by the Fifth Corps will enable him to realize this desire. In transmitting the foregoing message, your attention is invited to the favorable opportunity now existing for pressing our advantage throughout the night.[211]

Conner wanted Marshall to send the message at once, but Marshall demurred, since Liggett and his chief of staff, General Drum, were away that afternoon. Marshall wrote that he "highly approved" of the opportunity to press the Germans hard throughout the night. He realized that Pershing's message meant a drastic change in operations and would involve the entry of First Army into the zone of the French Fourth Army, and without the French high command's having an opportunity to react or express an opinion. In this "predicament," he proposed to Conner a compromise that would delay sending the order until 1800 hours, and if neither Liggett nor Drum had returned by then, he would send it by telephone to the two corps commanders, Dickman in I Corps and Summerall in V Corps. Conner reacted without enthusiasm, but agreed, and left for his office. At 1750 hours, Marshall learned that Drum was back in his office and hurried over with a copy of the order.[212] Drum assumed that Pershing and Maistre had agreed on Sedan[213] and added a sentence that would make the order clearer. It read, "Boundaries will not be considered binding." With that addition at the end of the order, Drum approved the text, and signed it himself with the usual notation: "By command of Lieut. General Liggett." Marshall wrote that he had omitted the "amendment" through simple oversight, and he authenticated the message and telephoned it to the headquarters of Dickman and Summerall.[214]

The order of 5 November, and, especially the sentence that "Boundaries will not be considered binding," set off a hornet's nest of stinging recriminations and charges that would have unfortunate consequences for many years to come. To Marshall, the "amendment" seemed perfectly logical and necessary, since the First Corps would have to cross its left boundary into the zone of the French Fourth Army to comply with the order. General Drum felt the same way. In 1935, General Harbord, then chairman of the board of RCA, was about to finish the book that he would call *The American Army in France*, and asked Drum if he shed "any light on the order from your standpoint."[215] From his command in Hawaii, Drum explained that

> At the time General Pershing's instructions were received at Army Headquarters relative to Sedan, Sedan was not within the First Army zone of action. Consequently, some authority had to be given for the Army to go outside of its zone of action if General Pershing's desires for the capture of Sedan were to be carried out. The whole of the left wing of the Army had to move to the right of the Fourth French Army. When the left of the First American Army would move into French zone of action, the rest of the Army had to move accordingly to the northwest so that contact and covering operations could be carried out. Consequently, as the First Corps moved northwest on Sedan, the Fifth Corps should have conformed to that movement so as to support and protect the First Corps. If you read the order issued by First Army carefully, you will note two phrases "he has every confidence that the troops of the First Corps, <u>assisted on their right by the Fifth Corps,</u> will enable him to realize this desire." I have supplied the underscoring. How there be any misunderstanding of such language I do not know. At the end of the second paragraph of the order a statement is contained "boundaries will not be considered binding." Of course, if the First Corps was to move into the zone of action of the Fourth French Army, the army boundaries could not be considered binding. Then again, if the Fifth Corps was to assist the First Corps by operating on the right of the First Corps, the Fifth Corps' boundaries could not be considered as binding. Anyone with sound vision of a large battle command with an appreciation of the tactical handling of large commands will realize the full significance of the foregoing.[216]

Perhaps Liggett would have sent a different version, but Drum had neglected to show him the order that he had issued in Liggett's name. In addition, First Army headquarters failed to follow up

*Brigadier General Hugh A. Drum*

Courtesy National Archives

the order with instructions on how the two corps could coordinate their movements to the left toward Sedan.[217]

Summerall received the message from First Army at 1830 hours that evening. He wrote in his memoir that he "immediately" took copies to the three division commanders (Parker, Lejeune, and Wright, of the First, Second, and Eighty-ninth, respectively)[218] but, actually, he not leave his headquarters until the next morning and arrived at Parker's headquarters shortly after noon. He told Parker that Pershing desired that American troops be the first to reach Sedan. With the implication that Pershing wanted those troops to be the First Division, Summerall ordered Parker and the division "to proceed at once in the direction of Sedan, operating at night as well as by day."[219] Parker replied: "'I understand, Sir. I will now give my orders.'"[220]

While the First Division gathered itself to advance toward a new objective, Summerall moved on to General Lejeune's headquarters and told him to prepare the Second Division to march on Sedan; from there he went to see General Wright, at the headquarters of the Eighty-ninth, and also told him that General Pershing wanted to have American troops to be the first to reach Sedan.[221] He informed Wright that he was sending two divisions north, and the Eighty-ninth was to provide support by protecting the right flank of the advance. They were to push patrols across the Meuse and be prepared to follow the advance.[222] With the First Division leading the advance, Summerall planned for the entire V Corps to converge on Sedan.

While Summerall was bringing Pershing's message to his division commanders, Colonel Walter S. Grant, Marshall's colleague at First Army, arrived at Dickman's headquarters at 1850 hours with the same order to take Sedan, regardless of boundaries. Ten minutes later, General Drum showed up with the same message.²²³ Meanwhile, Menoher's Forty-second Division was pressing its attack toward the Meuse on the left of V Corps, and to right of the French Fourth Army. Alexander's Seventy-seventh Division was advancing toward the river on the right of the Forty-second, and to the left of Parker's First Division.

During the night of 6-7 November the Seventy-seventh paused and settled down, but not the Forty-second, which was far in advance of the French and closer to Sedan than any other Allied force. At 2230 hours, General MacArthur's 84th Brigade and Colonel Reilly's 83rd Brigade received the order from Menoher to drive with all possible speed toward Sedan without halting, and to take it that night, "even if the last man and officer drops in his tracks." (Shades of Summerall!) MacArthur's brigade was on the right of the division and had seized the heights of the Meuse on the west bank. With most of the enemy to his front across the river, he requested and received approval to wait until daylight to attack, so that his men could advance more securely over unfamiliar and rough terrain. That meant that Reilly's brigade, on the left of MacArthur's, would lead the division's attack on Sedan. Reilly immediately ordered his regimental commanders to start marching their battalions at 0200 hours and informed them that "Apparently the high command sets great value on the capture of Sedan immediately. Therefore it is up to us to make a final effort no matter what it costs us."²²⁴ Obviously, no one at I Corps headquarters had any intention of calling on V Corps for assistance, and, of course, neither MacArthur nor Reilly had any thoughts about doing so.

The First Division began their advance toward Sedan between 1900 and 2000 hours on the night of 6–7 November. They had just marched all night through rain and mud to take over the sector of the Eightieth Division and had captured Villemonty. They were worn out, and the weather was still overcast, cold, and rainy. As they set out, Parker noted that many of the men were "grumbling, swearing and criticizing higher authority," but "they were carried along by the real members of the First Division, just as a piece of rotten wood is carried by a strong tide."²²⁵ Apparently, he was not in the best of moods himself, and, quite likely, exhausted as well. Parker did not know what part of the area north of his division was occupied by American troops. So, in order to cover this territory as completely as possible, he decided to march the division in five columns, moving along roads roughly parallel to each other (see map, p. 282). The 16th Regiment advanced on the right flank along the road closest to the river, with the 18th Regiment on its left; the other columns were made up of the 28th Regiment to the left of the 18th, and the 26th Regiment advancing along the left flank. The 28th Regiment led the division, with Parker at its head. The three artillery regiments of the 1st Artillery Brigade were assigned to support the advancing columns and followed close behind them. The roads had been destroyed by German mines, and the men stumbled along on weary and sore feet, as the craving for sleep became "overpowering." Violent street fighting broke out in the towns, and machine gun and artillery fire hit the columns as they forced their way forward. As the *History of the First Division* stated, "The sufferings of that night march will remain one of the most memorable of the war's horrors."²²⁶

With his march under way, Parker sent a lieutenant to inform Colonel J. C. Montgomery, Dickman's chief of operations, that the corps commander had ordered him to march that night toward Sedan, and the First Division was advancing as directed. Parker's lieutenant reported at around 2000 hours to Montgomery, who noted that he had never heard of such a move. He immediately informed Brigadier General Malin Craig, I Corps chief of staff, and Craig said that he knew nothing about it either.²²⁷ Dickman wrote that the news that the First Division had crossed into the entire sector of the I Corps "was so extraordinary that it was felt, at first, that it could only be in obedience to direct orders from the highest authority...." He stated that his headquarters notified all concerned and did their best to help the First Division move forward their artillery, supplies, and ammunition. Dickman also wrote

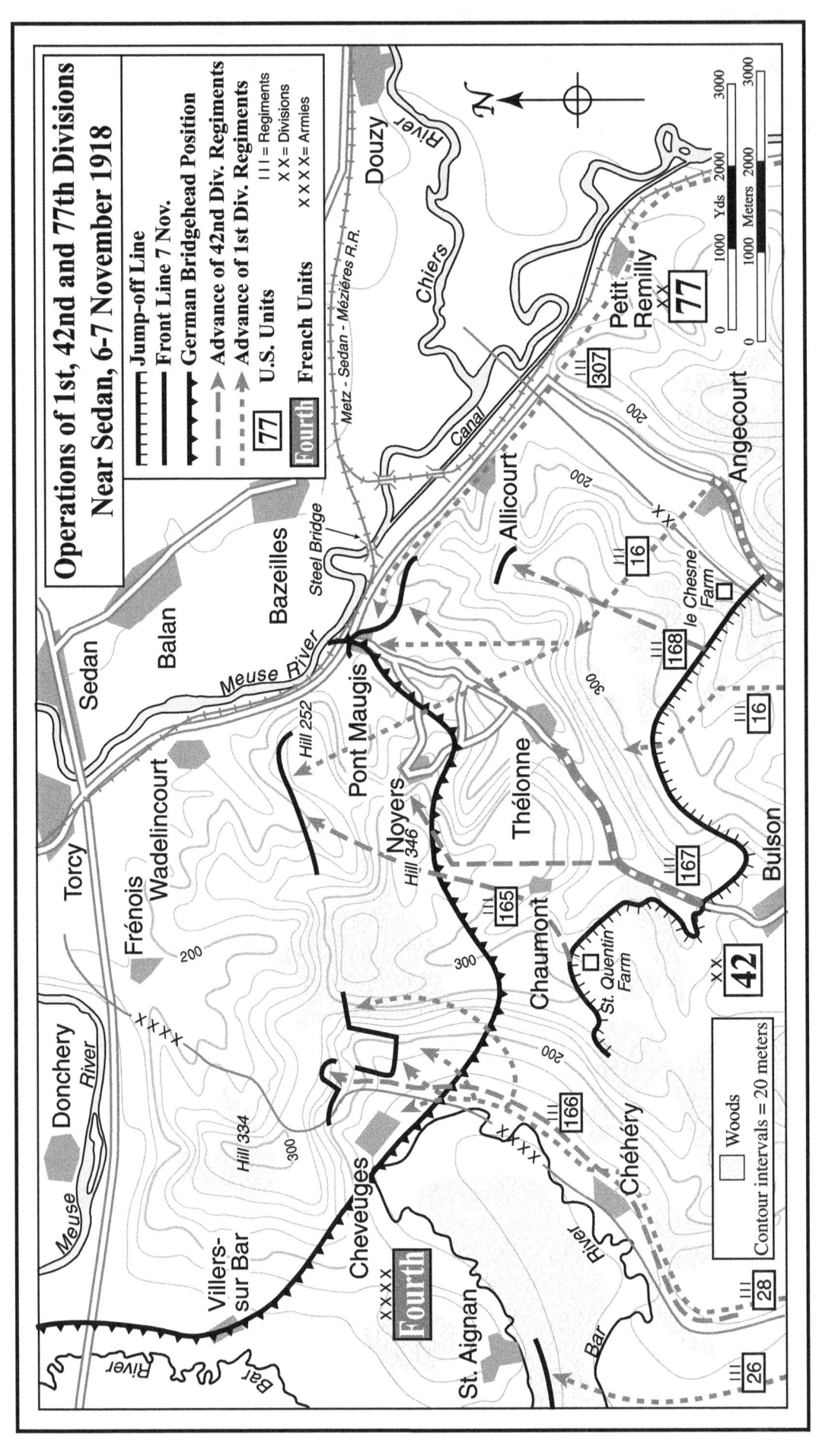

that he sent a wireless message to Summerall informing him that I Corps held the line south of Sedan to the extreme right of the corps sector.[228]

Meanwhile, in the morning hours of 7 November, the First Division fought through enemy machine gun and artillery fire along the roads and villages toward Sedan. As they advanced, the 16th, 18th, and 28th Regiments all encountered regiments of Reilly's and MacArthur's brigades of the Forty-second Division that were moving forward to reach and cross the Meuse and take Sedan (see map, p. 282). Some battalions of both divisions joined together to take German positions and moved closer to Sedan. In other units there was considerable confusion.[229] The commander of a machine gun battalion in MacArthur's brigade could not place his guns because American infantrymen suddenly appeared in front of his battalion. Traffic became snarled, phones lines went dead, and the confusion spread to General Alexander's Seventy-seventh Division, where he noted that detachments from the First Division had disrupted efforts to supply his men and had caused great confusion.[230]

The mix-ups and confusion continued. General MacArthur was awakened just before daybreak by an aide who told him that a brigade commander of the First Division was outside his room. "I was very much astonished to hear this," he wrote, "but went out and found it was Colonel [Hjalmar] Ericsson," who commanded the 1st Brigade of the division. MacArthur asked Ericsson what he was doing there. Ericsson showed MacArthur his orders and said that the 16th and 18th Regiments of his brigade were advancing on the river road along the Meuse.[231] The road ran across the front of MacArthur's brigade, perpendicular to its line of advance. MacArthur feared that in the darkness his men might mistake the Americans for Germans and start firing on them. He hurried forward to warn the different units, and to take charge of any problems that might result from the mixture of the two brigades. Fortunately, he ran into an advanced patrol from the First Division. He informed the lieutenant of the situation and told him to return to his battalion and explain the position of MacArthur's brigade and the danger that was involved.[232] As a relieved MacArthur stood smoking a cigarette, he noticed a soldier from the patrol looking at him "in a rather wishful way," so he offered the soldier a smoke. The doughboy thanked him, and as he lit it he said, "'I was thinking, if you had just a'bin a Boche general 'stead of an American one we would all of us got the D. S. C. [the Distinguished Service Cross].'" MacArthur laughed and gave him the whole pack. The soldier grinned and said, "'To tell the truth, sir, I would rather have the cigarettes than the medal.'" Later that afternoon, MacArthur learned that his "patrol friend" had been killed in the fighting before Sedan.[233]

A few hours later that morning, MacArthur was again surprised. As he stood wearing his garrison cap that drooped down over his ears, and non-regulation muffler (likely woven by his mother), holding a riding crop in his hand, another detachment from the 16th Regiment mistook him for a German spy, and arrested him. He explained who he was, and his "captors" went on their way.[234] For historian Donald Smythe, MacArthur's timely warning to the 16th Regiment averted "a debacle."[235]

Meanwhile, in the 83rd Brigade, as Colonel Reilly was busy dealing with complaints from the Fortieth French Division that his brigade was moving into their sector the lead battalion of the 28th Regiment suddenly appeared in the rear of his 166th Regiment. They said they had orders to take Sedan. Obviously concerned that the 28th would drive into the French sector and compound his problems with the French division, as well as disrupt his own command, Reillly ordered his men not to let the 28th pass them. The 28th then crowded up into the first line of the 166th, where both groups were held up by German fire (see map, p. 282). Next, a major from the Signal Corps of the First Division arrived at Chehery and said that was where he was going to establish the division command post. When he was told that he must be mistaken, he said no, and that the First Division was advancing in five columns, one behind him and the other four across the front of the division. General Parker then arrived, and told a lieutenant colonel of the 166th that he was going to the right of the division and advance on Sedan. Reilly received that report, and, not knowing what else to do, he ordered the 166th to advance as soon as they could.[236]

In the meantime, the liaison officer that Reilly had sent to the French division returned with the serious complaint from the division's chief of staff that the Americans were on the main road of the French sector, and were blocking the advance of his division. He requested "in the name of the General of the 40th French Division, that the American elements be removed farther east and away from this main road." Reilly immediately dispatched a motorcycle rider to Menoher with the message. Menoher then ordered Reilly to report "in person" to division headquarters. When he arrived, Menoher was reading the message to Dickman, whose voice was "loud and one of anger." Menoher called Reilly to the telephone. Dickman told him to find Parker and tell him that Dickman ordered him to withdraw the First Division immediately to the rear, and out of the sector of the Forty-second Division. "Do you understand that message?" thundered Dickman into Reilly's ear. Reilly said yes. Dickman again told him what he was to do and asked him to call Menoher to the phone. After Dickman repeated to Menoher the instructions he had given to Reilly, Menoher turned to Reilly, and told him that "There is nothing more except your prompt execution of them." Reilly left immediately along the road where he expected to find Parker.[237]

First Army had a real mess on its hands. At I Corps headquarters, Dickman's staff became more upset as liaison officers continued to relay French protests; one message stated that their artillery would have to fire in their own sector, and made clear that the presence of Americans in their front would not stop their firing.[238] While Reilly was out looking for Parker, Dickman got further word from Menoher that the situation between the First and Forty-second Divisions was intolerable. He recommended that First Army issue orders immediately to straighten out matters. Dickman ordered Menoher to take command of all the troops in the area and informed First Army headquarters about the situation.[239]

General Liggett wrote that he first learned that the First Division was not in the rear of V Corps, where it was supposed to be, when General Maistre called around noon on 7 November, to report that American troops were making it impossible for his Fortieth Division to move forward.[240] At first, Liggett insisted that the French must have misidentified those soldiers. When he was assured that the information was accurate, and that the troops were, indeed, from the First Division, he started for I Corps and V Corps headquarters as fast as he could travel. As he wrote,

> This was the only occasion in the war when I lost my temper completely. I had been holding this fine division back to be used when we crossed the Meuse, when we might have needed them very badly....the movement had thrown the First Corps front and the adjoining French front into such confusion that had the enemy chosen to counterattack in force at the moment a catastrophe might have resulted.[241]

When the now tempestuous Liggett arrived at I Corps headquarters, he found it "buzzing like a hornet's nest." Dickman and his staff swarmed around Liggett, with the inclination to hold him personally responsible for what they called an "'atrocity.'" Although MacArthur had taken his so-called capture as a joke, they were upset about that as well. Furious as he had been when he arrived, Liggett recovered his temper, and he calmed down and soothed Dickman and his staff. He then sent an order to V Corps to withdraw all of its troops from the zone of advance of I Corps and report when that had been accomplished.[242]

Indeed, while Liggett hurried to I Corps headquarters, Summerall was on the way to find Parker. When he arrived where the First Division headquarters had been the previous day, he was told that the division headquarters had been moved to Chehery. So off he went. He found Parker at Chehery at around 1400 hours. Parker told him that when the division reached Chehery, they had found elements of the Forty-second Division, and had advanced through them to high ground to the northeast. This was news to Summerall, who had not even been informed by Parker that he had moved his headquarters. Summerall ordered Parker to remove his troops from the entire area occupied by elements of I Corps. In case he encountered any serious resistance, Summerall told him that he should withdraw the division completely from the area, and hand over the front that it held to I Corps. After his meeting with Parker, Summerall stopped by the division's wireless station, where Liggett's order had just arrived, with the order to withdraw the First Division at once. Summerall then set out for corps headquarters. As Summerall returned to his headquarters, Colonel Reilly, who was still on the road searching for Parker, ran into Brigadier General Henry Butler, who commanded the 1st Artillery Brigade.[243] He told Butler that he had an order from General Dickman for General Parker and asked if he knew where Parker was. He answered that

> Oh, he's gone south. The whole division is moving out. He was in Chehery, but General Summerall drove in there "like a bat out of hell," with his usual recklessness under fire. Why he wasn't killed I don't know, because the Germans had direct observation and fire on the road as he dashed in. He ordered General Parker to immediately withdraw the division. Some of them are already out and the rest are withdrawing.[244]

A scenario had developed in Summerall's corps that was contrary to Captain Henry J. Reilly's directive to his officers at the Presidio and in China; namely, that there should never be anything to explain in his battery. It was an order that Summerall had often repeated to himself and to his own officers. But now it appeared that both he and Parker would have a lot to explain about what had happened in their commands.

While Summerall was racing to find Parker, Liggett left Dickman's headquarters and headed for V Corps headquarters at Nouart, about 15 miles to the southeast. On the way, the First Army commander's temper began to rise again. When he arrived, General Burtt, V Corps chief of staff, appeared, and found himself on the receiving end of a blast from his superior officer. Liggett was accompanied by his aide, Lieutenant Colonel Pierpont L. Stackpole, who recorded in his diary that Liggett told Burtt that the performance of the First Division was a "military atrocity," and that Parker "must have lost his head." He told Burtt to get them back at once, and Burtt said that he had already done that in response to telegrams from the army. Liggett asked him who had issued the order to the division in the first place, and who had developed such a plan. Burtt said that he supposed that General Summerall, General Parker, and he were responsible. Burtt pointed out the order came from First Army, but Liggett said he did not know about the order before it was sent, and, at any rate, it only called for V Corps to support I Corps on the right in taking Sedan, and "that no reasonable interpretation of the paragraph about limits would permit of the atrocity of marching one division across the front of another in pursuit of the enemy." He instructed Burtt to tell Summerall to send him a written statement at once, explaining who had given the order, and under whose authority it had been issued. Liggett and Stackpole returned to First Army headquarters in the evening. Summerall's statement arrived about midnight, but Stackpole called it "a lame affair, throwing the burden onto the memorandum."[245]

General Liggett returned to his headquarters that evening and sat down for a talk with Drum. Stackpole recorded Liggett's first calm and collected conclusions about what had happened in the First Army over the past 24 hours. He wrote that Liggett told Drum that the memorandum never should have been sent. Liggett thought it impossible that the First Division would move as it had, and that Parker's craziness and Summerall's ambition were behind it. Drum agreed, noted Stackpole, and mentioned the possibility of relief and court-martial for Parker and perhaps for Summerall as well.

But Stackpole also felt that Drum understood Liggett's point that the memorandum should not have been sent and realized "that he [Drum] himself had blundered."[246]

During that night of 8 November at First Army headquarters, General Pershing's involvement in the situation was also discussed. Stackpole noted that it appeared that Pershing had talked "excitedly" to Liggett about taking Sedan, and that Liggett was opposed to that idea, since he knew that the French would not stand for it. Stackpole also stated that on the night of 6 November, Pershing had gone to I Corps and told them to take Sedan, and had probably told V Corps to do the same thing. He noted that in a previous conversation Pershing had told Parker that the First Division could take any objective, and may have indicated to Summerall and Parker that the First Division "should join the race." Stackpole ended his account of the long night at headquarters by noting that Pershing's plans were in direct opposition to Liggett's of how the attack of First Army should be conducted. According to Stackpole, Drum should have known that, and it was another instance of his "ignorant meddling" that was involved in the entire situation.[247]

At any rate, before the night was over, General Liggett ordered an investigation. In his report to Liggett of 7 November, Summerall stated what would become his unyielding position; namely, that he was obeying orders that his corps would assist I Corps in taking Sedan, and that boundaries would not be considered binding. He also noted that he had directed Parker "to send an officer at once to the First Corps with a statement of the order he had received, and the direction of his march, so that there would be no misunderstanding as to firing upon areas in the front."[248] As noted above, Parker did send a lieutenant to I Corps, but the officer did not arrive until after the First Division's march was well under way, and its advance could hardly have been stopped.

In the last paragraph of his report to Liggett, Summerall stated that it was "a matter of profound regret" if the advance of the First Division "was not in compliance with the wishes of the Army Commander, and with the meaning of that order."[249] This was the only time that I have found, in all of his official reports, correspondence, and writing about the Sedan incident, that Summerall acknowledged that he might have misinterpreted what the order meant for him to do. He always insisted, as has been noted in this study, that his and Parker's actions had complied with the directive. But in his memoir, Summerall wrote that he could not give detailed orders to Parker, but that "the manifest thing was for the division to cross the Meuse wherever the river was reached that night. It did not occur to me that the division commander would do otherwise."[250] This assertion is disturbing and troubling, for Summerall certainly never stated this in any of his reports, statements, or correspondence. In addition, if he had assumed that the First Division would cross the Meuse, why had he ordered the Eighty-ninth to cross the river and support the First Division on its right flank, thus stringing out the attack on Sedan far to the east, and into the zone of the Second Army? Perhaps, indeed, his memory had become too clouded for him to recall all of his actual instructions to Parker. His assumption that Parker would do "the manifest thing" and cross the Meuse meant that Summerall, in the final analysis, had come to believe that Parker had misinterpreted Summerall's instructions, and that the confusion and controversy was Parker's fault.

In his report to General Summerall on 9 November, General Parker stated also that he had followed orders and went on to describe the arduous march of the division and the taking of their objectives. He noted that the First Division had encountered elements of the Seventy-seventh and Forty-second Division, as well as the Fortieth French Division. But Parker then stated that "nothing but the warmest and most cordial relations existed at all times between the First Division and these troops and there was not a single instance of any unpleasantness reported to me....nothing but the best feelings existed at all times and in all echelons."[251] Anyone familiar with what had happened on 6–7 November would have found it difficult to accept that self-serving assertion. But Summerall accepted it, and sent Parker's report to First Army headquarters the next day with his endorsement. At the same time, he stated that he accepted full responsibility for ordering the First Division to advance into the territory of I Corps, "in accordance with the instructions from the Army commander."[252]

In the meantime, General Pershing had showed up at Liggett's headquarters and, according to Stackpole, seemed "much amused at the rivalry between the 1st and 42nd, failing entirely to appreciate the serious consequences which might have resulted."[253] All units of the First Division had not yet left the area of the Forty-second; indeed, General Maistre reported that the 26th Infantry Regiment, commanded by Colonel Theodore Roosevelt, Jr., was still in the French sector, and seemed to be preparing to march down the Bar River valley and take Sedan from the western approaches. General Liggett's ire rose again. Once more, he made it clear to Drum that Pershing's directive was the cause of all the trouble, and that his memorandum should never have gone out.[254]

Liggett was also dissatisfied with Summerall's and Parker's report. He said that he really wanted Colonel Grant to investigate the matter, but would not take any action since he was convinced that "they [Summerall and Parker]will never do such a thing again, though if it had not occurred at the end of a successful operation, with no especially harmful consequences, he would have one or both courtmartialed."[255]

The next evening, General Parker showed up at Liggett's headquarters before dinner to explain his actions in person. Using what seemed to be his preferred descriptive terminology, Liggett told him that what had happened was a "military atrocity," and that he had told Burtt the same thing. He told Parker that he should have known that a division of 25,000 men could not be rushed out of its own sector into a narrow sector that was already crowded. Liggett acknowledged that in the final analysis, the memorandum "to go after Sedan was responsible," and that it never should have been sent out. He told Parker that "the whole episode showed the danger of too many masters and [the] duality of command." He sent Parker on his way with the advice "to take the thing to heart," and never do it again. Drum was there, and Stackpole noted again that much of what Liggett had said was directed at his chief of staff.[256]

The next day, 10 November, the persistent Parker was back again, this time to assure Liggett that the First Division had no intention of beating the Forty-second in a race to Sedan. Stackpole wrote that an exasperated Liggett told Parker to forget about it, but that he wanted him to be sure to tell Summerall that "it was a military atrocity and never do such a thing again." Before he left, Parker again "protested too much" about his honesty and good intentions. Afterwards, as Stackpole noted, Liggett said he did not believe Parker, and that Parker knew it. Drum said he was inclined to put Parker through "an argumentative inquisition," but Liggett rejected the idea and said that "the matter is closed."[257] Nevertheless, a few days later, a visit to Sedan and Chehery, where Parker had set up his headquarters in his advance on Sedan, seems to have reawakened Liggett's anger. As Stackpole wrote, Liggett said that both Parker and Summerall were responsible and repeated his conclusion that "if the operation had not been virtually concluded anyway both ought to have been tried by court martial; that he did not care to bring this about under the circumstances, though such proceedings were thoroughly appropriate."[258]

While Liggett managed, with some difficulty, to put the Sedan episode to rest, Dickman remained in high dudgeon. In a memorandum he submitted to Pershing's adjutant general on Christmas Eve, 1918, he asserted that the order of the corps commander [Summerall] to the First Division "was discourteous and fraught with the greatest danger to the troops of the 1st Corps and itself." He stated that Summerall had visited him at his headquarters and had told him that he had received orders from higher authority to march on Sedan. Dickman wrote that he had studied the orders that Summerall had received, and did not believe that First Army had ever contemplated the action that Summerall had taken, or had approved of it afterwards. He noted that on three different occasions Parker had tried to explain the matter to him, but that it could not be explained except on orders from Summerall, or because of "ignorance of the situation." In the last paragraph of his memorandum, he called for an investigation by a board of officers, and concluded that

> The whole performance was so clearly a serious violation of elementary military principles that I am unable to understand it except as a deliberate discourtesy to adjoining troops and the senior officer commanding them or as an example of loss of balance during moments of excitement and responsibility.[259]

The Allies had been victorious for over a month, and both Pershing and Liggett had decided to put aside the Sedan issue, so the investigation, which Dickman also said he would welcome, never took place. He went on to command the Third Army during the occupation of the Rhineland, but Stackpole noted that he continued to pester Liggett to head a board to consider "war lessons"; that is, the Sedan matter. Dickman persisted, as Stackpole wrote, in advancing "his hobby with some bitterness which is to show up Summerall and Parker in their wild move into his Corps in their rush at Sedan. General Liggett told him he thought it just as well to let that rest as it is."[260] Pershing also got tired of Dickman's fuming about Sedan and was irritated as well by his pompous behavior and tendency to take himself too seriously.[261] Stackpole wrote that Pershing told Liggett in late March 1919 that Dickman's command on the Rhine had not been successful and that he should be relieved. He noted that when Liggett pointed out that Dickman's relief would be a hard thing for him to accept and would ruin his chances for keeping his rank, Pershing was "not moved."[262] The next month, Pershing replaced him with Liggett. General Dickman died in 1927, the same year that *The Great Crusade* was published; Harbord noted that he "went to his grave embittered and unforgiving."[263]

During his post-war corps commands in France and Germany, General Summerall, unlike Dickman, seems to have kept his feelings about Sedan and Dickman under control. Nevertheless, as Stackpole observed, Liggett was troubled that Summerall was too concerned about his own reputation as V Corps commander as well as that of the First Division. Stackpole recorded that during a visit with Summerall's V Corps staff on 31 January 1919, Liggett gave a talk on the First Army offensive of November 1918 and said that "no one Corps, but the 1st Army as a unit accomplished the successful results from November 1st on, to which all corps and components contributed. His indirect allusion to the 1st Division-Sedan fiasco, in which Summerall participated, was not lost on Summerall."[264] After Summerall had assumed command of IV Corps of the occupation army in Germany, Liggett had lunch with him at Summerall's headquarters in Cochem Castle, high above the Moselle River. After the meal, as Liggett and Stackpole were returning to Third Army headquarters, Stackpole noted that Liggett mentioned that "as much as he liked Summerall he should never trust him in any affair where sentiment was involved; and that Frank Parker was a wild man anyway; Summerall's limit was a division and Parker's a regiment. All apropos of the Sedan incident."[265]

General Parker seems always to have seen himself as the man in the middle who was obeying orders from his superior officer, and whose career was damaged by Dickman's hostility toward him and toward General Summerall. He left in his personal papers the copy of a letter that he personally delivered to Dickman on 19 December 1919, explaining again that he was following orders, and that boundaries were not considered binding. He closed by apologizing to Dickman for having caused "inconvenience" to his comrades in the Forty-second and Seventy-seventh Divisions. Some years later he noted at the bottom of the letter that even though Dickman knew that "I had no choice in the Sedan matter but was acting under direct orders, personally given, General Dickman attacked me vigorously and succeeded for five years after the war in preventing my promotion to the permanent grade of brigadier general."[266] In the lingering aftermath of Sedan, he and Summerall cemented a close friendship and fused their explanations about the matter. When Summerall became the U.S. Army's chief of staff, he appointed Parker assistant chief of staff. For the rest of his life, Parker remained a devoted follower and staunch defender of his and Summerall's actions at Sedan, as well as a trustworthy trusted advisor to his former commander and mentor.

For more than a decade after the end of the war, Summerall exercised restraint regarding his inner thoughts and feelings about Sedan. As shall be noted, there were controversies and clashes with critics and rivals in his subsequent commands, as well as during his four-year term as the army's chief of staff. But his relations after the war with Pershing were fine and Pershing continued to rate him as one of his very best commanders. For Summerall, that era of good feelings changed forever with the publication in 1931 of General Pershing's two-volume memoir, *My Experiences in the World War*. In three paragraphs in volume two that dealt with the Sedan matter, he wrote first that

> On the afternoon of November 5th, the I Corps was directed to bend its energies to capture Sedan *'assisted on its right by the V Corps.'* [his italics]. A misconception in the V Corps of the exact intent of the orders resulted in the 1st Division erroneously going beyond the left boundary of the V Corps and marching directly across the sector of the I Corps during the late afternoon of the 6th and throughout the night....[267]

Pershing then described the confusion that resulted when the First Division mixed with the Forty-second and Seventy-seventh Divisions, and when elements of the three American divisions entered the zone of the Fourth French Army. He concluded by stating that

> Under normal conditions the action of the officer or officers responsible for this movement of the 1st Division directly across the zones of action of two other divisions could not have been overlooked, but the splendid record of that unit and the approach of the end of hostilities suggested leniency.[268]

Pershing's volumes appeared on 10 March 1931, just after Summerall officially had retired after more than 42 years of military service, the last four as army chief of staff. After his term as chief of staff ended in 1930, he and Laura moved to Eustis, Florida, and settled into a comfortable two-story house.

Pershing's version of the Sedan action caused Summerall to unleash an irate response in a letter that he wrote from his new home to the North American Newspaper Alliance on 1 April 1931, less than a month after Pershing's memoir was published. He wrote that Pershing's statements about V Corps and the First Division were "misleading and unjust," and that he had to respond "in the interests of truth, history, and fairness to the commander and troops concerned." Summerall said that the memorandum of 6 November 1918 had required the capture of Sedan by First Army, of which V Corps was a part. Thus the phrase "boundaries will not be considered binding" meant that V Corps, with the First Division in the lead, could advance, along with I Corps, toward Sedan. He insisted that if V Corps had not obeyed the order to advance and capture Sedan, "there would have been the usual ruthless relief and disgrace of the commanders concerned." He accused Pershing of deliberately defaming the First Division and noted that "these fighting men" stood united in disdaining "the faint praise with which General Pershing damns them throughout his story." Summerall concluded his epistle of three and a half typed pages by stating that

> Up to this moment I have been unswerving in my loyalty to Gen. Pershing. I must now taste the bitterness of misplaced trust and friendship. Towards others, I had resolved to carry out my motto of "Silence in life and pardon in death." But he has forced me to an issue of truth and I will fight him on that issue to the end.[269]

As shall be noted below, Pershing's account certainly was not the whole story, and, in several respects, was unfair to Summerall. Nevertheless, Summerall's friends succeeded in talking him out of sending the letter, even though, as mentioned earlier, he kept a copy for his files.

The anger and animosity that Summerall expressed in his repressed response to Pershing's words only intensified during the remaining years of his life, and, as has been noted frequently in this study, surfaced repeatedly in his memoir. Those feelings were rekindled and enflamed again in 1949, with the publication of *Eleven Generals: Studies in American Command*, by military historian Fletcher Pratt. In his chapter on Summerall, entitled "Sitting Bull II," Pratt lauded Summerall's bravery, and especially his mastery of artillery fire, but he ventured onto thin ice when he described the Sedan affair, writing that "the incident closed Summerall's fighting career with something of a shadow...."[270]

At age 82, having completed his 18th year as president of The Citadel, Summerall composed a lengthy response to Pratt's remarks. With no close friends to persuade him to file it away, he sent it to *The State* newspaper in Columbia, South Carolina, and it was published in the Sunday, 12 June 1949, edition. Summerall wrote his response in the third person and observed that "Mr. Pratt is supported by the misrepresentations...by high ranking officers who were motivated by enmity and jealously, and by newspaper men could not know the truth....It is regretted that his [Summerall's] accusers can not reply but they have recorded their charges and truth is independent of time and life and death."[271] He quoted the First Army memorandum of 6 November 1918, and, not surprisingly, stressed that the advance of V Corps was in response to direct orders that "boundaries would not be considered binding." He described in detail the success of V Corps; he based his account of the accomplishments of the First and Forty-second Division on *The History of the First Division* and Reilly's *Amercans All*, respectively. He praised Frank Parker's courage and leadership and noted that MacArthur said that he had not been arrested, but he had only been mistaken for a German.[272]

Summerall had ripped into Pershing in the letter that he did not send in 1931, but in the piece that he sent to *The State*, he seemed to qualify his criticism of the former commander in chief. He wrote that Pershing had made erroneous statements in his book, but he attributed these errors to the influence of Pershing's staff. Summerall insisted that they had been against him ever since they had attacked him in Paris in 1917 for advocating an increase in the amount of AEF artillery.

Summerall's harshest and most intense animosity was directed at his former nemesis, General Dickman, who had been dead for four years. Summerall resurrected him, and, in his article for *The State*, reinterred him without the slightest hint of regret. He wrote that Frank Parker had assured him that Dickman had been his "bitter personal enemy before the war." Summerall charged that Dickman's enmity merged with jealousy of his success at St. Mihiel, and escalated into Dickman's attempt to use his artillery, in some way, to discredit Summerall's plan to use his artillery in the V Corps's attack on 1 November. Summerall wrote that Liggett's statement in his book that Dickman's corps was not expected to make much progress on 2 November 1918 was false. According to Summerall, Liggett only said that because he and Dickman were close friends. Dickman had feared the success of V Corps, he asserted, and had done his best to hurt Summerall's standing. If that was not enough, Summerall said that Dickman was "wholly German in character and personality. Before the war he was known by his translations of German and his contacts with Germany." General Bullard had said that Summerall was "a fanatic in battle to defeat the Germans," so Summerall concluded that Dickman was bound inevitably to hate him. On the day of the armistice, he called on Dickman at his headquarters, apparently to bury the hatchet, but, as Summerall wrote, "General Dickman exclaimed angrily 'You played hell with my Corps.' This terminated the call [visit] and they never spoke to each other again."[273]

As they entered the last years of their lives, Summerall in his 83rd year, and Dickman in his final year, each revived and refreshed the bitter memories of the Sedan affair, and mounted an invigorated attack on the man and the men whom they held responsible. In addition to Harbord's assessment of the depth of Dickman's bitter animosity, as noted above, Dickman's unrestrained reaction led to his being removed from his command of Third Army, and his unbalanced version weakened his account of the Meuse-Argonne battle. Summerall's rebuke of any criticism of his actions at Sedan led him to believe during the last two decades of his life that he had been betrayed and victimized by men who had been jealous of his success, and had woven a conspiracy to blame him for errors of judgment and crucial mistakes for which he believed they were responsible. Like Dickman, the older he grew, the more embittered and unforgiving he became.

George Marshall was right when he stated many years later that "The fight between Summerall and Dickman was very intense and went back to all sorts of jealousies....They [Dickman and his staff] were jealous of General Summerall's great reputation which he had made in the hard fighting."[274] Indeed, Dickman was 10 years older than Summerall, and under the command of the younger major general, the First Division had become Pershing's favorite and was the only division to receive the commander in chief's special commendation. Donald Smythe wrote that the feelings between Summerall and Dickman were "partly responsible" for the Sedan incident. More decisive, he believed, was the close relationship that Drum and Marshall had with Pershing that led them to write the order that came from Pershing through Fox Conner, without checking first with Liggett, their immediate superior, or telling him afterwards about the order they had issued in his name.[275] Liggett repeatedly let Drum know that he had erred in sending the memorandum without Liggett's knowledge. He also made it clear to Drum that, had he seen the memorandum before Drum sent it, he would not have approved it. But Liggett, according to Stackpole, had told Pershing earlier that he was opposed to the idea, so it is doubtful that Pershing would have changed his mind even if Liggett reiterated his objections.

General Pershing told Dickman that he wanted his corps to take Sedan, and Stackpole came to believe that Pershing had told Parker and Summerall the same thing, although neither of them ever stated what Stackpole asserted. Drum and others, like Harbord, were right in pointing out that the order called for V Corps to assist I Corps in the attack. Summerall ordered his entire corps to advance on Sedan, and even though Dickman would certainly have rejected the assistance of the younger man whom he considered his rival, Summerall was wrong not to have initiated contact with him to offer and, possibly, plan for his corps to cooperate with Dickman's. For his part, General Parker's order that the First Division advance in five columns covering a front of over five miles with no knowledge or information about the location of I Corps units in his path might not have been crazy, but it certainly was impetuous and reckless. As noted, he informed Dickman of his advance, but only after the march of his exhausted division, with many disgruntled men, was well under way, and too late for Dickman to do much about it. In addition, Parker failed to inform Summerall of the location of his headquarters, thus increasing the amount of time it took for Summerall to locate him and stop his advance, adding to the duration of the conflict and confusion within First Army. Yet, even Summerall's and Parker's lack of caution and reflection, as they hastened to press the advance of their commands, was, in large part, the result of Pershing's demand that his commanders press their attacks behind the driving force of their leaders, and with maximum speed and vigor.

General Liggett was right again when he said to Stackpole, as already noted, that "the whole episode showed the danger of too many masters and [the] duality of command." Historian Mac Coffman added his insights into the matter by stating that "What happened on the road to Sedan was that personal feelings and relationships took precedence over professional training and common sense. Pershing wanted to beat the French; Summerall wanted his corps and the First Division in particular, to beat the rest of the American army [especially Dickman's I Corps]; Parker who had successfully commanded within the First, a regiment and brigade and now the division itself, wanted the honor for his division without regard for the rest of the army. In each case, the individual was not placing primary emphasis on the military requirements of the situation."[276]

In fact, the individual most responsible for the bizarre occurrences on the road to Sedan, and the officer who, as well, must be held, at least partially, accountable for the repercussions that followed was the commander in chief, General John J. Pershing. For reasons noted above, he was determined to snatch the prize of Sedan from the French, and he ignored the sage advice to the contrary from General Liggett. Pershing believed that the strength of his personality had forced General Maistre to concede the fortress-city to the superior power of the American First Army, and this conviction increased his confidence in the success of the operation. In his nighttime conversation with George Marshall, Fox Conner, Pershing's chief strategist, infused with Pershing's optimism, suddenly told Marshall that General Pershing wanted the Americans to take Sedan. Marshall reflected the same kind of optimistic outcome of his commander in chief as he wrote the order and later recorded that he "highly approved" of the action to press the Germans throughout the night. Pershing's desire was now operational, and with Drum's addition that boundaries would not be considered binding, First Army was authorized to sweep through and ahead of the French Fourth Army to win the prize. For the American army, the array of confusion, danger, disorder, recriminations, and animosities that followed was the unfortunate consequence.

While First Army was sorting out the "snafu" on the road to Sedan, Marshal Foch informed Pershing from the armistice negotiations at Compiègne that they had not determined when hostilities would cease. So, the American commander in chief proceeded with plans for a French and American offensive on 14 November.[277] In preparation, the First and Forty-second Divisions were granted a well-deserved rest in the rear. I Corps, minus the Seventy-seventh Division, was withdrawn and replaced by the French Fourth Army that advanced to the front of Mézières. The Seventy-seventh was attached to Summerall's V Corps.[278] Pershing then ordered General Bullard's Second Army, holding a defensive position since its formation in early October, to begin a general advance on 11 November, and Bullard ordered his divisions to make limited attacks on 10 November.[279] General Liggett ordered First Army to complete the capture of the heights east of the Meuse, and to "closely press the enemy all along its front and follow vigorously and promptly any hostile withdrawal." He directed V Corps to occupy the high ground east of the Meuse.[280]

At 1730 hour on 9 November, General Summerall convened a meeting at his headquarters of his two division commanders, General Wright of the Eighty-ninth, and General Lejeune of the Second, and their chiefs of staff, along with General Burtt, V Corps chief of staff, to plan the crossing of the Meuse and the advance northward. They discussed the operation in great detail and continued their discussion after dinner.[281] Summerall and his staff developed a plan for the Second and Eighty-ninth Divisions to force the river simultaneously between Pouilly and Mouzon, behind heavy artillery preparation. The main attack of the Second Division would be directed at Mouzon and would be made by the 6th Marine Regiment, reinforced by the 3rd Battalion of the 5th Marines. A secondary force would strike south of Mouzon at Letanne and clean up the area between the main attack and the Eighty-ninth, opening the way for Wright's division to advance from the south. This "Letanne force" would be made up of soldiers from both divisions, the 5th Marines, minus its 3rd Battalion, and a battalion from the Eighty-ninth Division.[282] The 178th Brigade of General Wright's division would cross at Pouilly and maintain liaison with the Second Division. His 177th Brigade would maintain combat liaison with the Ninetieth Division, cross the river at Stenay, and push northward, clearing the heights and gaining contact with the 178th (see map, p. 294).[283]

The Ninetieth Division was to the right of the Eighty-ninth and already had advanced units across the river. Lejeune proposed that the Ninetieth move north and clear the area, so that the Eighty-ninth could cross without opposition and force the enemy to withdraw opposite the Second Division. His Second Division would then cross the river and move to the north, paving the way for the Seventy-seventh Division, to the left of the Second, to cross and continue the corps' advance.[284] General Wright seemed to favor Lejeune's plan, for he was worried that the corps plan was too intricate, and required too much coordination and cooperation.[285]

The attack was scheduled to begin after the moon had set on the night of 10 November, and early that evening Summerall stopped by the headquarters of the Eighty-ninth. General Wright expressed his apprehension about the attack. He suggested that the entire movement be postponed, and that his division could be concentrated at Stenay and advance north, thus opening up the country for the Second Division. Summerall said that he thought Wright's plan was the best one, but that he had received from First Army the orders to cross (according to the corps plan that he had submitted the night before), and had to follow them. As he left, he said that "everything had been arranged and would go all right."[286]

At 2130 hours on 10 November, the corps artillery dropped a heavy barrage on the German batteries across the river, and the infantry got ready to cross the Meuse. General Lejeune's "Mouzon force" faced a thick cordon of German defenders along the river bank, which was made up of elements of three divisions, totaling about 1,000 men, backed up by strong artillery and aircraft. It was here that the Germans would make their stand against the Americans, for they were able to station only a few provisional regiments on the high ground east of the river. They were determined to fight stubbornly and desperately, for they felt, as did the Americans, that all would be lost if they could not deny the river crossing to the attack from the west. Under the cover of machine gun fire and artillery bursts from the divisional guns, the leathernecks began their advance toward the river at 1800 hours. Engineers labored to throw up bridges, but enemy artillery and machine gun fire wrecked every attempt, and at daylight the troops withdrew to covered positions. The Mouzon crossing had failed.[287]

At Letanne, the 5th Marines had better luck. Division artillery still could not silence German artillery and machine gun fire that demolished the bridges across the river, pinning down the American troops. Nevertheless, engineers and infantry managed to build a bridge, "a mere footway supported on floating logs,"[288] that, as Summerall wrote, was "carried on the shoulders of men and shoved across the river."[289] Between 1900 and 2030 hours, a marine battalion worked its way across the river. They were held up by fire from a German machine gun nest, but wiped it out, and reached the heights beyond Autreville just after daylight on 11 November (see map, p. 294).[290]

The combat liaison battalion from the Eighty-ninth, located on the extreme left of the marines, was not so fortunate. As they were preparing to cross the river, they were hit by a heavy concentration of German artillery fire and suffered 256 casualties before they could make their way to the other side.[291] Historian Robert Ferrell wrote that the dead included Major Mark Hanna, nephew of the Ohio political leader of the McKinley era, who had just been promoted. Ferrell noted that Colonel John Lee, the Eighty-ninth's chief of staff, said that a Marine lieutenant colonel, who was in command of Hanna's battalion, was responsible for the battalion's losses.[292]

Farther up river, the Eighty-ninth's operation went practically as planned. Wright's men had hidden boats in camouflaged positions and started moving them toward the river at 1800 hours. At 1930 hours the 177th Brigade began crossing east of Pouilly, as the division artillery shelled the river towns on the other side. While engineers were building a footbridge, enemy outposts discovered and fired on them, and temporarily halted their work. The engineers moved to a small creek leading to the river, constructed a catamaran, and slipped an infantry battalion across the river that suppressed the enemy fire. Other battalions followed and advanced to seize the heights above Pouilly. They moved down to the town and mopped it up, while capturing a large number of prisoners and equipment. To

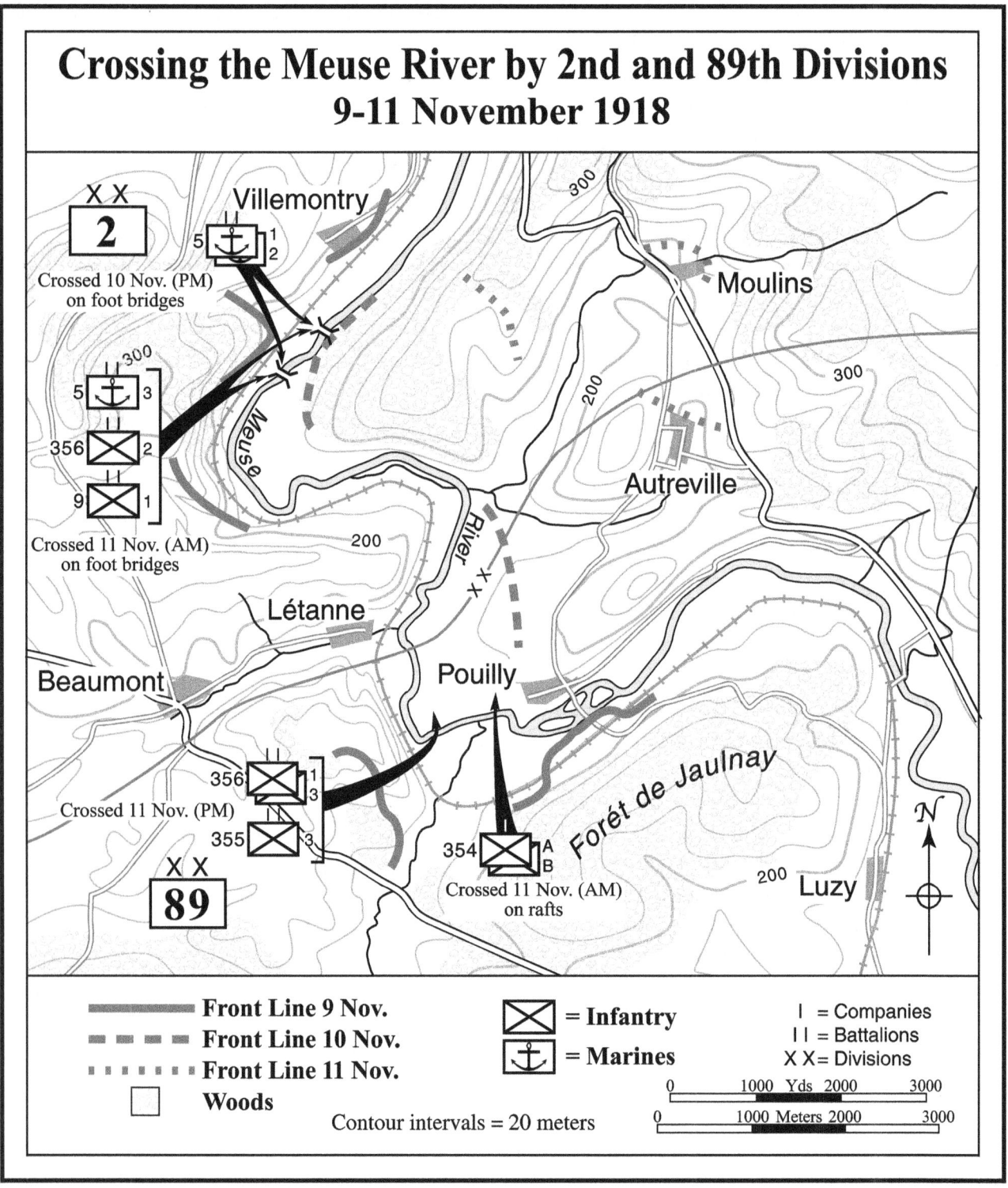

their south, the 177th Brigade crossed the river on a footbridge and followed elements of the Ninetieth Division.[293] At 0500 hours on 11 November, General Wright noted from his headquarters that the crossing and advance of his division had been very successful, and that they had taken their objectives with few losses in the face of opposition (see map, p. 294).[294]

Long after the war was over, and the euphoria of the Allied triumph and the luster of American victories had faded, the crossing of the Meuse was criticized for causing unnecessary American casualties. The critics, as Robert Ferrell pointed out, said that American soldiers "were driven like cattle to the slaughter, just as the war was ending."[295] Indeed, General Lejeune wrote that "The night of this last battle of the war was the most trying night I have ever experienced." He realized that an armistice was about to be signed and anguished over the loss of life that would occur, in what would be the last hours of the war. Yet, he noted, without criticism, General Pershing's reasons for pressing the attack, as well as Pershing's praise of the V Corps's gaining control of the Meuse River line. Lejeune also recalled that Marshal Foch had ordered the offensive to force the Germans to accept the armistice terms that they had argued were too harsh. He also said of Foch, that "No one desired more than he to conserve human life, but he felt certain that heroic measures, such as those he directed, would cost fewer lives by compelling the immediate submission of the enemy than would have been the case if the negotiations had dragged along for days and perhaps weeks."[296] In addition, German resistance along the river was expected to be "stubborn and even desperate," and necessitated a strong American attack to secure the Meuse in advance of the anticipated Allied offensive of 14 November. To drive home the point to the enemy that he had been defeated, General Bullard believed that the Allies "should press him to the last minute."[297]

As V Corps advanced across the Meuse, Summerall drove himself and his men hard and relentlessly, but after the Sedan episode, his planning seemed more careful and deliberate. He submitted the attack plan of V Corps to First Army only after extensive consultation with Wright and Lejeune. Wright believed that Summerall understood his concerns about the plan and even noted that Summerall agreed with his proposal to delay the attack. On the one hand, since First Army had already approved the plan that Summerall submitted, his comment to Wright could be considered gratuitous. On the other hand, it should more accurately be interpreted as an expression of confidence in Wright's leadership and in his ability to carry out the orders he had received. And, as Summerall assured him, everything did "go all right," although the liaison battalion with the Second Division took heavy casualties. Lejeune's "Mouzon force" was stopped, and hit hard at the river, but his "Letanne force" crossed the river and linked up with the Eighty-ninth Division to advance northward.

To reaffirm their total commitment to the battle at this critical juncture, units of two German divisions refused to yield. They mounted a desperate counterattack against the American position, and, in hand to hand fighting, the German major leading the attack was killed. The report of his division stated that "it was absolutely necessary to hold the enemy...if a catastrophe was to be avoided....[if not, the] division with all its artillery would have fallen an easy prey. The artillery...continued in action until the last moment. The enemy was unable to break this new line. At 11.00 o'clock the fierce fighting of November 11th ended. The hostile artillery, active until this last moment, ceased firing suddenly. The great success, which the enemy had undoubtedly promised himself for this last day, was denied him."[298] This was the nature of the enemy that the American army had to defeat on the last, violent front of the Great War. And it had taken another major offensive of First Army, spearheaded by Summerall's V Corps, to complete the final chapter of that mission.

At 2300 hours on the night of 10 November, the German delegation at Compeigne received authorization to accept the armistice terms. By 0505 hours on 11 November, the final details had been settled, and the signing completed at 0510 hours. Foch then declared the conference closed and notified the

Allied commanders by radio and telephone that "Hostilities will cease on the entire front on *November 11th* at 11 A. M. French time."[299]

Donald Smythe noted that Pershing was glad the war was over, and "he would dance a jig that night," but the commander in chief felt that the armistice was a mistake. The Allies, he insisted, could have captured and humiliated the German army. Instead, German soldiers could march back home, and claim that they had never been defeated. Indeed, on 11 November, General Karl von Einem, commander of the German Third Army, stated that they had been undefeated and had ended the war on enemy territory. Smythe wrote that 10 years later, Adolf Hitler was "propagating the same error."[300]

Marshal Foch's message arrived at First and Second Army at 0630 hours and at V Corps at 0830 hours. Wright's and Lejeune's divisions were still attacking, and Summerall recorded that he was "greatly amazed, and regarded it as only a delay gained by the Germans."[301] At 0610 hours, a division radio operator told General Lejeune that he had picked up the order from Marshal Foch, and Lejeune called General Burtt to see if it should be carried out. Reflecting Summerall's skepticism, Burtt cautioned that it could be a German hoax, and told Lejeune to wait for confirmation from V Corps. At 0845 hours, Burtt sent the confirmation and told Lejeune to hold the ground he would gain up to 1100 hours. For the next two hours, German artillery fire intensified, and Lejeune's artillery brigade "sent as good as it received."[302] Word of the signing of the armistice reached General Wright at 0845 hours, and he directed his command to keep fighting until 1100 hours.[303] At that hour, fighting ceased, and suddenly the western front lapsed into complete silence. As General Lejeune recalled, that silence "was the most impressive celebration of the Armistice that could possibly have taken place."[304]

Major Thomas Gowenlock, Summerall's trusted intelligence officer when he commanded the First Division, recalled his indelible thoughts when he heard the news of the armistice. He was in his dugout with two First Division colleagues at Romagne-sous-Montfaucon, located in the quiet center of what had been a bloody and bitterly contested battlefield of the Meuse-Argonne in mid-October. Gowenlock wrote that

> All over the world on November 11, 1918, people were celebrating, dancing in the streets, drinking champagne, hailing the Armistice that meant the end of the war. But at the front, there was no celebration. Many soldiers believed the Armistice only a temporary measure and that the war soon would go on. As night came, the quietness, unearthly in its penetration, began to eat into their souls. The men sat around log fires, the first they had ever had at the front. They were trying to reassure themselves that there were no enemy batteries spying on them from the next hill and no German bombing planes approaching to blast them out of existence. They talked in low tones. They were nervous. After the long months of intense strain, of keying themselves up to the daily mortal danger, of thinking always in terms of war and the enemy, the abrupt release from it all was physical and psychological agony. Some suffered a total nervous collapse. Some of a steadier temperament began to hope they would someday return to home and the embrace of loved ones. Some could think only of the crude little crosses that marked the graves of their comrades. Some fell into an exhausted sleep. All were bewildered by the sudden meaninglessness of their existence as soldiers—and through their teeming memories paraded that swiftly moving cavalcade of Cantigny, Soissons, St Mihiel, the Meuse-Argonne and Sedan.
>
> What was to come next? They did not know—and hardly cared. Their minds were numbed by the shock of peace. The past consumed their whole consciousness. The present did not exist—and the future was inconceivable.[305]

In later years, some of these stunned and weary soldiers might well reflect on the crucial impact they, and their compatriots, those who had fallen and those who had survived, had had on the course of the war. Their fighting, their suffering, and their deaths had restored to their Allied comrades the confidence that they would prevail, and had assured the defeat of the German Empire.

Still doubtful that the armistice would hold, Summerall set out on the afternoon of 11 November, to visit the troops. Realizing that attacking soldiers would need food and ammunition, he wrote that he had ordered a bridge to be built by the engineers of the Eighty-ninth Division. When he found that it had not been constructed, he asked the commanding officer of the engineer regiment why he had not obeyed the order. The officer replied that it would be against international law to build the bridge. Summerall noted that the officer was not in his right mind, and sent him to the rear. He ordered the engineers of the Second Division to build it, which they did. As he continued his tour of the front lines, he found the men in high spirits. He commended them for what they had achieved and told them that they must be ready to resume the attack. "That night," he noted, "fires were built and the men slept."[306] Summerall did not mention their reaction to the possibility of their returning to battle, but as they gazed into the warming flames and embers of the fires they had built, many must have shared the deep emotions of their fellow soldiers, as Gowenlock described them, at firesides all along the western front.

Summerall next visited the Second Division and recalled in his memoir that he learned later that the marine brigade in the division resented his order to cross the river, and blamed him for their losses, which, he wrote "they said were unnecessary." He noted correctly that he knew nothing about the impending armistice and was obeying orders from the high command. Still bristling from their criticism, he stated that General Lejeune had been responsible for selecting the marine brigade to cross the river, "without any reference to me. No doubt, he wanted to gain credit for the Marines." He added that marines "should never be employed with the Army or under army officers. They fight no better than the army and they complain, seek quick relief and try to gain publicity."[307]

As Robert Ferrell stated, and as noted above, Wright's chief of staff blamed a marine lieutenant colonel for the casualties in the Eighty-ninth's liaison battalion, but Summerall never mentioned that accusation, and apparently knew nothing about it. So, that remark is an unlikely source of his criticism of the marines' fighting skills, or their unwillingness to serve under army officers. Once again, it seemed that Summerall's resentment of criticism, as he understood it, had shaped his memory. Rather than stating that V Corps had planned the attack, and that General Lejeune was executing the order as he thought best, Summerall reacted to the marines' accusation and their losses by blaming Lejeune for trying to win fame for the marines. Apparently, Summerall did not read Lejeune's account of the Meuse crossing in the latter's *Reminiscences*, published in 1930. If he had read it, he certainly would have noted Lejeune's reservations about the V Corps' attack order. But, that did not mean that Lejeune blamed him for the marines' casualties. He would have read that Lejeune understood and accepted the reasons why the attack had to go forward. And that realization was why he anguished over the impending casualties. In fact, General Wright shared Lejeune's worries and told Summerall about his concerns. But Summerall did not recall or record any criticism from Wright or from the Eighty-ninth, so Lejeune and the marines received the full blast of Summerall's resentment. He struck back against what he considered an unfair charge with an accusation of his own that was just as unfair.

The armistice of 11 November provided for the withdrawal of German armies in districts on the left bank of the Rhine River, and the administration of these districts by local authorities under the control of Allied armies of occupation.[308] Summerall recalled in his memoir that visiting officers told him that "the thought existed in army that a third army would be formed and that I would command it," and that the V Corps would lead the advance of the army into Germany. He noted that V Corps headquarters was surprised, therefore, when they learned that their divisions were assigned to other corps, and that their headquarters had been ordered to Nogent-en-Bassigny, which was about 160 miles south of Verdun, and far from Germany.[309] Summerall did not mention that Pershing had appointed General Dickman to command Third Army, but that news must have been about as unpleasant as his surprise in not receiving that command. Yet, contrary to what might be expected, he never mentioned the "fall" of Dickman, when Pershing replaced him with Liggett as Third Army commander. He also heard that, in case General Pershing were disabled, Secretary Baker planned for Summerall to replace him. That Pershing remained commander in chief did not seem to trouble Summerall at all. But he did lash out at GHQ, where many of his "enemies" could be found. They were the "vipers," as he had come to call them, who had spoken contemptuously about "we of the troops...as only combat soldiers, belonging to an inferior quality." The sunshine of his success had brought out these "vipers," he said, and they had prevented his being moved up to command Third Army.[310]

Disappointed, and later embittered once again by what he considered as GHQ's prejudice against him, Summerall wrote that he left with his staff on 14 November for the new headquarters of V Corps. The Twenty-sixth, Twenty-ninth, and Second Divisions were under the command of V Corps, and they were all eager to go home. Summerall noted that his main problem was to keep up their morale while they waited to leave France. Training exercises helped little, but horse shows, inter-division athletic contests, and liberal leave policies were popular, and he felt that discipline, dress, bearing and "soldierly conduct" were excellent.[311]

Summerall was invited to a field day of Eighty-second Division that concluded with a review in his honor. General Duncan, an old friend and admirer, and commander of the division, told Summerall that he had just received the report of a board of officers about a Corporal York who had killed or wounded an entire German machine gun battalion. Duncan pointed out York, who was the division standard bearer, and was astride a horse right in the front of the division. Summerall called him forward and read a citation that carried across the snow-covered ground to the entire division. Summerall noted with pleasure that Alvin York was awarded the Medal of Honor, was promoted to sergeant, and became "one of the notable figures of the war."[312]

In early December, Summerall was admitted to the National Order of the Legion of Honor in a ceremony at Pershing's headquarters at Chaumont. Napoleon Bonaparte had established it as the premier order in France, and Summerall was one of a number of American general officers who received the honor in recognition of their outstanding military achievements in the war. He was awarded the rank of commander, which is the third highest degree of the order. This recognition entitles the recipient to wear the badge of the Legion suspended from a necklet, and it was Marshal Pétain himself who placed it around Summerall's neck.[313]

General Pershing hosted a lunch after the ceremony, and Summerall wrote that he was surprised to find himself seated on Pershing's right, since there were other general officers present who were senior to him. Pershing promptly asked Summerall to tell him about the advance of the First Division on Sedan. Summerall described the orders he had received and sketched on the tablecloth the roads that the division had followed. Pershing seemed entirely satisfied. Summerall wrote that it was at that point that he realized that Pershing had been "told lies about confusion in the 1st Corps."[314] That recollection, obviously, did not temper Summerall's later repudiation of Pershing's critical remarks in volume two of his *Experiences*.

After lunch, the guests adjourned to a large reception hall, where General Harbord asked Summerall to request Pershing to write a commendation for the Second Division. Summerall wrote that this request surprised him, since Harbord was very close to Pershing. Summerall asked Pershing's aide to request that Pershing see him and was subsequently taken to Pershing's bedroom, where Summerall found him sitting before a fire with his shoes off. Summerall wrote that he told Pershing about the superior record of the division and asked him to give the division a citation from GHQ. He noted that Pershing showed little interest, and that the citation was never made. He concluded that Harbord blamed him for not winning Pershing's approval of the citation, and for that reason decided later that "Harbord was one of my chief enemies."[315] He already had determined that Harbord was an integral part of GHQ's prejudice against him, and found yet another reason for placing his name on his list of "enemies."

Summerall recalled a more pleasant exchange with Marshal Pétain, when he asked Pétain how he had restored the morale of the French army after the disastrous offensive in the spring of 1917. He noted that Pétain seemed eager to respond, and answered that, rather than blaming the men, he praised them, told them they had done well, and allowed them to take leaves to go home. He established canteens where they could buy modest luxuries cheaply, and where they could meet and socialize together. He said that very few decorations had been handed out, so he had commanders recommend a large number of men to be decorated, and established a special medal to be awarded to regiments and divisions for courageous performance in combat. He observed correctly that "In a very little while, it was a different army and ready for combat."[316]

Christmas was approaching, and Summerall was notified that President Wilson would take Christmas dinner with a division of V Corps. The president had arrived on 14 December in Paris, where he had been greeted by a tumultuous reception by millions of cheering citizens. Summerall wrote that he was thrilled at the possibilities and thought that the president "would be gracious to the troops and say something to hearten and encourage the entire army." He suggested that Wilson dine with one hundred enlisted men from the Twenty-sixth Division who had received the Distinguished Service Cross. Instead, he was informed that Wilson wanted only officers at the dinner. Dinner was at 1200 hours and took place at near-by Fort Montigny-sur-Rois. Summerall was waiting to greet the president and recalled having spoken with Wilson several times at West Point before he became president and on several occasions after his inauguration. Instead of acknowledging Summerall, Wilson swept past him and remained at the dinner table for only very short time. He left without making any remarks to the officers. Summerall remembered being keenly disappointed that Wilson had ignored him and his officers. That reaction is certainly understandable, but perhaps Summerall could have considered the greater demands and enormous pressures the president faced at that point, and would have to face in the near as well as distant future. Instead he judged the president's indifference as a sign that he had become "a man drunk with power."[317]

As the winter lengthened, Summerall received in February 1919 his appointment to the permanent rank of brigadier general in the Regular Army. His new rank was one grade lower than the rank of major general that he held at the end of the war, and he noted the reduction without commenting on it.[318] Like other officers who remained in the Regular Army, he could not have been pleased about this reduction in rank. Yet, his tacit acceptance of it indicates that he understood that it was necessary for officers who held higher ranks in the war to revert to their prewar ranks, as the army decreased to its peacetime strength.

With its divisions having left for home, V Corps was demobilized, and IX Corps was established to supervise the training (to keep the soldiers busy) of eight divisions as they waited their turn to leave. One of these divisions was Captain Harry S. Truman's much-maligned Thirty-fifth. Summerall noted that the division was "filled with resentment" toward army inspectors who had submitted adverse reports after the division had been pulled out of action on 1 October, and relieved by the First Division. They also felt that they were the victims of Regular Army prejudice against all National Guard divisions.[319] Being stuck in the mud of yet another soggy winter did not lessen their resentment. Captain Truman took out his frustrations on all West Pointers, with Summerall excluded, perhaps believing that "most of them were "pompous, lazy, and overrated."³²⁰ Hoping to assuage their feelings, Summerall invited the division's staff, brigade, and regimental commanders to dinner at his headquarters and asked them to express their grievances, which they did far into the night. He assured them that their combat record was too good to be clouded by bitterness and revenge. He encouraged them to let the past rest and to emphasize the pride they felt in having been of such service to the command. He recalled that when he had finished, one of the officers told him that if they had had him as division commander, "there would have been no grievances."³²¹ Summerall should have written that the advice he had dispensed to that group of officers was advice that he himself should have taken and acted upon.

In early May, as spring finally dispelled the cold and rain of winter, Summerall left the command of IV Corps and was detailed to accompany members of the Committee on Military Affairs of the House of Representatives on a tour of the entire theater of operations of the American army, and across the Meuse bridgehead into army's zone of occupation. They called on the French General Charles Mangin, who lamented what he considered to be the losses in negotiations of all that the Allies had gained on the battlefield. Summerall intimated that he and the committee members agreed with Mangin's assessment. Summerall felt that he had made friends on the committee who proved to be helpful to his plans when he later served as army chief of staff.³²²

After his return from the "friendship tour" with the congressmen, Summerall took command of IV Corps, with headquarters at Cochem Castle. Three divisions, including the First Division, were assigned to the corps, while they waited to return home. As noted earlier, it was at Cochem Castle that

*Banquet table with President Wilson. Summerall is seated five places to the left of the president.*

Courtesy United Press International

Summerall hosted a dinner for General Liggett when he visited Summerall, just after Liggett had relieved Dickman as commander of III Army. Summerall and his staff spent a great deal of time accommodating visitors to the castle, many of whom spent the night. One evening, he escorted to dinner a lady whom he remembered as "quite superior in appearance." At the dinner table she told Summerall that she had come to find the body of her son, and said that she had found it. She showed him a picture of her son, who had been a young officer, and Summerall recognized him as an officer he knew who had been killed at Soissons. He told her that they had located a grave with his name on the cross, but later found that it was the grave of a German soldier. She said that she had found that grave, and was taken to where her son had left his brigade command post to go to the front line. She walked along a route that took her out of the First Division zone and into the French sector, where she found a helmet on a cross with his name written across it. The body was exhumed, and she told Summerall that it was the body of her son. She spoke of her pride in having raised such a boy, her only son, who had left Harvard College for the army, and had given his life for his country. Summerall told her how he admired her fortitude and wondered, as he wrote, "if all mothers could be so resigned."[323]

Meanwhile, in late April 1919, the Allies had completed the treaty of peace, and a German delegation, headed by the chancellor and foreign minister, arrived at Versailles to receive it. The Germans were stunned by the severity of the terms and submitted a counterproposal on 29 May. The Allies made only minor revisions, and the German delegation returned to Weimar on 18 June and urged the government to reject the treaty. When the cabinet decided to accept the document, the chancellor and foreign minister resigned, and the government of President Friedrich Ebert collapsed on 21 June. One day later, the German crews of the High Seas Fleet, interred at Scapa Flow, opened the sea cocks on their ships, and sank them. With renewed anger, the Allies demanded that Germany sign the treaty within 24 hours, and concentrated their forces, including the divisions of the AEF, to cross the Rhine and head east. Ninety minutes before the resumption of war, a hastily formed German government accepted the treaty, and two new representatives arrived at Versailles to sign the document.[324] The American divisions returned to their billets to wait further for their orders to go home.

While he waited at his headquarters, Summerall received the news that he had been selected as one of the American generals to witness the signing of the treaty in the Hall of Mirrors. It took place on 28 June 1919, exactly five years after the assassination of Archduke Francis Ferdinand of Austria-Hungary and his wife Sophie Chotek. As Summerall entered the hall, he passed by the long tables in the center and saw the treaty document opened to the signature page. When he went to his seat toward the front of the hall, he noticed the presence of President Woodrow Wilson, Premier Georges Clemenceau, British Prime Minister David Lloyd George, as well as the large number of Allied officers who filled the long hall. Many "distinguished looking ladies" stood along the walls before the gleaming mirrors. At 1550 hours, the German representatives entered with heads held high and stood before the document. Clemenceau told them, as Summerall recalled, "that they had been brought to [the] bar [of justice] for their crimes by the civilized world," and in the total silence that followed, the Germans signed the treaty. Immediately afterwards, a booming artillery salute shattered the quiet of the hall, and thundered to the world that the Great War was officially over. Wilson, Clemenceau, and Lloyd George stepped out on a terrace to greet the cheering crowds that had gathered in the sculptured gardens and around the sparkling fountains of the great château. For Summerall, "It was an impressive and historic occasion."[325]

When he returned to IV Corps headquarters, Summerall learned that the First Division would be the last one to leave occupied Germany. He wanted to tell them the news in person, so, in July he went to division headquarters at Montabaur, about 20 miles east of the bridgehead at Koblenz. He first spoke to the 2nd Brigade, and when he told them of the "honor" of being the first to arrive and the last to go, they were not particularly impressed by that distinction. He wrote that "the rest of the division accepted the news stoically," and soon they all seemed to be proud of the fact that they would be the last American soldiers to leave. While Summerall was at Montabaur, the division formed the Society of the First Division, AEF, and held a farewell dinner where they elected Summerall as the society's president. When the cheers subsided, he visited each table to say a few words before leaving to return to IV Corps headquarters.[326] The division did not have much longer to wait, and on 6 September, the last elements arrived in Hoboken.

The victories of the First Division and V Corps had established Summerall as a premier battlefield commander of the AEF. His hard-driving, relentless, and exhausting pursuit of the enemy had been costly, but the division's farewell tribute to his leadership confirmed their high regard for their favorite commander. Yet, Summerall's strong will, fortitude, and conviction that his tactical decisions were flawless, revealed a troubling authoritarian streak. His account of Colonel Mitchell's removal and report is marred by a tone of self-righteousness, and a refusal to acknowledge that generals, like all humans make mistakes, that do not necessarily bar them from being competent. His conviction of his own infallibility was to earn him many enemies in the future as it had in the past. As he reflected in his old age on the high commands that he had held, he rejected any criticism of his actions. To his dying day, he believed that those who disagreed with him such as Liggett, Babcock, and those who later served in the War Department, were doing so out of personal animosity. Perhaps the burdens of old age and loneliness, the conflicts and crises of the Great War and their lingering aftermath were to be compounded by an unhappy departure from The Citadel described later. Perhaps Summerall sought consolation in his belief that he had always been right, and that those who had opposed him had always been wrong and had been motivated by less than honorable motives.

# Chapter Thirteen

*Mission to Fiume and Homecoming*

After his farewell visit with the First Division, Summerall was busy tending to the demobilization of IV Corps and his transfer to Koblenz. Perhaps he hoped for a command that would take him home, but he wrote that he had been "warned" that he would be named to head a mission to Poland. Indeed, he was summoned to Paris in early July to meet with the peace commission, and reported to the Quai D' Orsay as directed, promptly at 0900 hours. Once again, he received no recognition from President Wilson, and it was Premier Clemenceau who told him why he had been summoned to Paris. Rather than being sent on a mission to Poland, Summerall was informed that he was to proceed at once to Fiume, as a member of an Interallied Commission of Inquiry. The other members were General H. E. Watts of Great Britain, General Mario Nicolis di Robilant of Italy, and General Stanislas Naulin of France. They were instructed "to adjust a conflict between the French and Italian troops at that place" and report to the peace commission in Paris.[1]

Fiume, now named Rijeka, was an Adriatic seaport on the eastern side of the Istrian peninsula, southeast of Trieste. Italians composed a larger majority of the population, but the inhabitants of the surrounding area were Slavic Croatians. It had been an important port for the nearly land-locked kingdom of the Dual Monarchy of the Austro-Hungarian Empire. When Hungarian authorities left the city in November 1918, Croatians from the suburb of Susak occupied the governor's office. Shortly afterwards, Italian warships sailed into the harbor, and Italian soldiers occupied Fiume proper and set up a National Council, consisting exclusively of Italian business leaders residing in the city. The council pledged allegiance to Italy and began working with Nationalists in the Italian parliament to annex the city. At the same time, the French hoped to use the city as a base from which they could more directly influence the new Kingdom of Serbs, Croats, and Slovenes (renamed Yugoslavia in 1930) and were supported by the Croatians. France sent a company of soldiers, with an American contingent, that entered Fiume on 17 November, backed up by French warships anchored in the harbor. During the next few months, tensions steadily increased between the French and their Croatian supporters on the one hand, and, on the other hand, Italian sympathizers who were stirring up trouble against the Americans as well.[2]

In the meantime, while conditions in Fiume became more tense, negotiations in Paris between President Wilson and the Italian delegation, headed by Premier Vittorio Orlando and Foreign Minister Sidney Sonnino, became increasingly difficult. Before the conference began, Wilson had approved the awarding of South Tyrol and its two million German-speaking inhabitants to Italy to assure them of his concern for their security against a future Austrian state. But these gains were not sufficient for Orlando and Sonnino, and they demanded more territory as just compensation for the enormous human and material resources that their country had sacrificed in the war. Throughout the negotiations, they had pressed Wilson hard to grant them Fiume. President Wilson considered the port an economic necessity for the emerging state of Yugoslavia and rejected the Italian demands as imperialistic. Thoroughly displeased with Wilson, Orlando and Sonnino bolted from the conference in late April, returning to Rome, where they received the enthusiastic endorsement of the parliament. They returned to Paris in May, as Italian patriots and heroes.[3]

On 29 April, Italy and Austria signed the treaty that gave the Brenner Pass to Italy, but this additional gain still was not enough to satisfy the Italians. Wilson, understandably, was even more resistant to their demands for Fiume. Nevertheless, Orlando signed the Versailles agreement and returned to Italy to face a parliament "Fiuming" over his failure to obtain the city. In June, the parliament angrily rejected his government, and joined the Italian population in hostility toward President Wilson. The new government of Premier Francesco Nitti and his foreign minister Tommaso Tittoni came to Paris and found Wilson even more uncompromising, and his stance on Fiume more intractable than ever.[4]

In early July, tension in Fiume escalated into violence. Several French sailors, joking with local girls, accidentally dislodged a patriotic ribbon one of the girls was wearing. Nearby, a group of citizens quickly decided that the girls were being attacked and beat up the sailors before they could return to their barracks.

Other incidents followed. In the early morning hours of a few days later, an Italian military patrol opened fire on three French sailors, killing one, and wounding another. The patrol arrested the third. By evening the city was in a nasty mood, when at sunset, one of the Italian warships opened fire on a barracks where French soldiers were staying, killing nine and wounding scores of others. The French command protested, and the matter was referred to the peace commission in Paris. It proceeded to create a commission of inquiry, headed by Summerall, to look into the matter.[5]

Summerall quickly assembled a small staff including his orderly Sergeant William M. Steamer. That afternoon they were joined by French General Naulin and his staff and boarded a train to Venice, where an Italian destroyer waited to take them to Fiume. On the journey and in Venice, Italian officers pressed Summerall to support Italy's claims to Fiume. Commander Bertolucci, a young Italian naval officer, told Summerall that his admiral had assigned him to be of service, and that he had arranged for a royal barge to take him to his hotel in Venice. At stops in Padua and other cities, Italian officers came on board to offer the compliments and services of local commanders. To all of these invitations and entreaties, Summerall wrote that he maintained his neutrality by accepting the Italians' hospitality only if the French general on the commission were included.

When the generals and their staffs arrived in Venice, a group of Italian officers escorted them to their hotel. As they crossed St. Mark's Square, Summerall recalled that their escort had to shield them from what he felt were the "very hostile" intentions of a large crowd. They arrived safely in Fiume, where Bertolucci arranged for a car to take Summerall and his party to their billets in an apartment house. On the way, when his car passed through thousands of "hostile" Italian soldiers and civilians, someone hurled a large stick through an open window, hitting Summerall in the chest. He wrote that he "pretended not to notice it," but observed that, once again, he had encountered a "very hostile crowd." The next day, Summerall and his staff had lunch on an American destroyer, the *Pittsburgh*, anchored in the harbor, and when the captain offered them accommodations on board, Summerall quickly accepted.[6]

In mid-July 1919, the commission began their investigation in the city hall of Fiume. Summerall was elected president, and French was adopted as the language, which Summerall noted he could use. In their early deliberations, they reviewed the historic importance of the city, its strategic and economic significance as a port, and the recent outbreaks of violence. For six weeks, during a very hot summer, they heard evidence in eight languages concerning the violence and casualties that had taken place, as well as the various claims to the city. As Summerall saw it, the French wanted the right to exploit the forest resources of the interior, and to use the port for shipping. He said that Yugoslavia claimed it as part of the territory granted them under the terms of the armistice. The Italians, he believed, asserted that it was theirs by right of occupancy and necessary for their security in the Adriatic.[7]

When the commission determined that they had heard all the evidence, they decided that each member would prepare a set of findings and recommendations. As Summerall stated, "the documents of the Englishman and the Frenchman were of little value" (he did not mention the Italian's), and his paper became the foundation for their recommendations. On 9 August, the commissioners completed their report. It reviewed the recent incidents of violence stating that disputes and contradictory claims by various self-appointed councils, rather than individuals, were responsible. Among its most significant recommendations was the election of a government under the control of an Interallied Military Commission that would guarantee the impartiality of the city, and the opening of a judicial inquiry into the deaths of the French and Italian soldiers.[8] The report said nothing about whether Fiume should belong to Italy or Yugoslavia.

On 10 August, the Allied generals boarded the *Pittsburgh* and sailed for Venice, where Summerall bought some gifts for Laura. They arrived the next day by train in Paris, where Summerall waited to be called to present his report to the peace commission. When he had heard nothing for several days, he went to the Quai D'Orsay and asked members of the American delegation if he was expected to present a report. He noted that they all said that they did not know, and so, wrote Summerall, "nothing was ever done about it." Looking back with petulance on this indifferent and uninformed reception, he added that "I never received any [additional] money for my expenses or those of my aides and orderly."[9]

Summerall's account of the response of the Americans on the peace commission differs significantly from historian J. N. Macdonald's statement in his study of the Fiume problem and its aftermath, entitled *A Political Escapade: The Story of Fiume and D'Annunzio*, published in 1921. Macdonald wrote that when the president (Summerall) of the Fiume commission returned to Paris, he handed to the council (peace commission) a full report, including findings and recommendations. He added that "These were accepted and approved of."[10] Perhaps Summerall believed that the commission was indifferent and ignorant because President Wilson, whom Summerall felt had deliberately snubbed him in the past, had influenced the committee to ignore his report. Summerall was right in stating that nothing came of his recommendations, but that was not the result of indifference, ignorance, or prejudice against him in Paris, but of developments that were transforming the situation in Fiume.

On 11 September, the Italian poet and adventurer Gabriele D'Annunzio seized Fiume with a force of Italian war veterans with the support of Benito Mussolini's Fascists. Fearful of becoming involved in a civil war, Allied forces withdrew from the city. The Italian government condemned D'Annunzio, but the Italian public was delighted. D'Annunzio declared himself *commandante* and proclaimed a constitution that would guarantee freedom of speech, secular education, universal suffrage, and religious freedom for all religions and "cults." It provided for a tricameral legislature and seven "rectors" elected by the legislature and serving one-year terms. He also proposed the League of Fiume, which would replace the League of Nations and would unify the people of the "third world," and protect them from the great powers.[11]

In Paris, the Allies decided to let Italy and Yugoslavia settle the question of Fiume by themselves, and in December 1920, the two governments signed the Treaty of Rapallo, establishing Fiume as a free state. D'Annunzio denounced the agreement and declared war on Italy. The Italian government responded by sending the warship *Andrea Doria* to the port, where it fired a shell into D'Annunzio's headquarters. He announced his abdication, in order, he said, to save the city from bloodshed and left peacefully.[12] His constitution was never revived and the League of Fiume proved just as ephemeral. The Italian government allowed him to return home, where he retired to a villa on Lake Garda and successfully sought fame as a poet, playwright, womanizer, and adventurer.

In January 1924, the Treaty of Rome assigned Fiume to Italy and the suburb of Susak to Yugoslavia, with joint administration of the port.[13] In his memoir, Summerall erroneously stated that his report recommended that the city and port of Fiume be given to Italy, and that Susak be awarded to Yugoslavia. So, once again, his memory had failed him. Perhaps, he had come to believe that his hard work in Fiume could not have been in vain. With that concept fixed in his mind, and neglecting to examine the copy of the commission's report that he had retained in his files, Summerall let his aged memory replace the futile endeavor at Fiume with the settlement of 1924. This agreement, not a settlement that resulted from Summerall's report of 9 August, resolved the difficult question of Fiume's post-war fate. The Italian government turned to face the country's troubled relations with its allies, as well as with its own people.

Summerall recalled with displeasure his reception by the Americans on the peace commission, but remembered with delight when Commander Bertolucci called on him to request his support in arranging for Bertolucci to come to Washington as an assistant naval attaché. The Italian also brought with him a request from Premier Orlando for Summerall to visit him at his hotel in Paris. Orlando thanked him for what the premier viewed as Summerall's fairness to Italy. It is understandable that Summerall noted the only words of appreciation that he remembered receiving for his work in Fiume. He returned Bertolucci's courtesies by asking Orlando to send him to Washington as assistant naval attaché, noting that Orlando said he would be glad to do so.[14]

Thus, Summerall's mission to Fiume ended without having had a real effect on the crises, or an impact on the final agreement. Nevertheless, his account of his patronage toward Bertolucci, and his description of his cordial reception by Orlando, reveal that skills he developed in dealing with public officials in his assignments across the United States may have helped to reduce the level of post-war tension between Orlando and Italian naval officers on the one hand, and the American authorities on the other hand.

While Summerall was engaged in Fiume, General Pershing and his aides, plus a large group of American generals, the AEF Band, and officers and men from the best American soldiers remaining in Europe, known as the Composite Regiment, had been enjoying the adulation of thousands as they marched in the London Victory Parade. That celebration was almost as glorious as the joyous reception they had received from the millions thronging Paris during the first great Victory Parade on 14 July, Bastille Day, 1919.[15]

Shortly after he had returned to Paris, Summerall received an invitation to accompany Pershing and a small entourage on a tour of Italy. He noted the invitation without excitement or enthusiasm, but stated that he enjoyed the luxurious accommodations the Italians provided at every stop along the route that took them through Turin, Genoa, and down to the capital. In Rome, they were introduced to King Victor Emmanuel III and treated to a lavish lunch at the Quirinal Palace. They were conducted on a tour of the Vatican and the historic sites of the city before traveling to Venice, the battlefields of the Assiago Plateau, and the Piave River area. Then it was on to Verona, where they attended the performance of an opera in the Roman amphitheater. They saw the gleaming, white cathedral in Milan, which Summerall described as "lace in marble." From Milan, they passed along the shores of Lake Garda, through the Brenner Pass into Tyrol, before crossing the Rhine and ending their journey back in Paris.[16]

On 1 September, Pershing, his staff, Summerall, and the remaining generals of the AEF, as well as the Composite Regiment, sailed from Brest aboard the world's largest ship, the *Leviathan*, and headed home. Commander Bartolucci's wish to be assigned as assistant naval attaché in Washington had been granted, and Summerall arranged for him to accompany the Americans. Pershing had been invited to address a joint session of Congress, and Summerall wrote that during the voyage Major Lloyd Briscom, a member of Pershing's staff, asked him what he thought Pershing should say in his speech. Summerall advised that modesty on Pershing's part was all-important, and that he should credit the soldiers, the Congress, and the support of the American people for the victory. Pershing spoke on 17 September, stressing the valor and devotion to duty of the country's soldiers, and was interrupted by applause over 25 times. Summerall was present, and must have been among those who applauded his commander in chief, although he said nothing in his memoir about the enthusiastic reception Pershing had received, or his reaction to the speech. He noted that Pershing did not use any specific words he had suggested, but he felt that his ideas had influenced Pershing's remarks.[17]

When the *Leviathan* eased toward its berth in New York Harbor on 8 September, the ship was welcomed by tugs, destroyer escorts, water jets, airplanes flying overhead, salute guns, whistles, horns, and cheering crowds on the piers.[18] As he disembarked, Summerall was handed orders assigning him to the command of the First Division at Camp Zachary Taylor, six miles south of Louisville, Kentucky, which had been the army's largest training camp. With these orders in hand, he stepped off the gangway and onto the dock, where he was met by his "precious wife and son." He remembered that moment as a time when "My cup of joy was full."[19]

On 10 September, New York City honored the victory of the AEF with a three-hour procession of the First Division and the Composite Regiment down Broadway from 110th Street to Washington Square. Pershing and his generals led the parade, as the crowd tossed roses and laurel in front of their path. Summerall called it a "characteristic New York reception." It was followed that night by a banquet. Summerall recalled that he sat with Brigadier General George Wingate, who had commanded the artillery brigade of the National Guard's Twenty-sixth Division. Wingate reminded him that many of his gunners had trained at Camp Tobyhanna and had spent the night of the armistice singing songs and telling stories about their experiences at the camp. Summerall remembered Wingate's account as a "tribute...to the influence of that training camp in 1913–1916 upon the war."[20]

On 17 September, the last great Victory Parade took place in Washington, with Pershing and his generals again leading the way. Summerall remembered the ovation they received as "overwhelming," noting that President Wilson and his cabinet reviewed the parade from in front of the White House. After Pershing's address to Congress, Summerall and his family returned to the Westmoreland Apartments, where Laura and Charles had lived since 1914, along with her elderly parents, Colonel and Mrs. Alfred Mordecai. Charles recently had received an appointment to West Point. He was taking a preparatory course at a school in Washington and would remain at the Westmoreland with his grandparents when his parents moved to Kentucky. On 30 September, the Summeralls left Union Station for Louisville, where Summerall looked forward to a reunion with the First Division.[21] It would be the continuation of a career that would see Summerall rise to the highest position in the American military, and to the command of another corps of cadets, whom he would help to become leaders in peace and war.

It was altogether fitting and proper that General Pershing held the place of honor at the head of the AEF on parade in Paris, London, New York, and Washington, and that he led his generals in their triumphal marches. He had demanded of general officers, and their subordinates, hard-driving and aggressive pursuit of the enemy, and foremost among the men of iron whose leadership embodied Pershing's ideal of command was Charles P. Summerall. Neither Pershing nor Summerall was an innovative or creative leader, but both men never wavered from their commitment to press their men forward with the utmost vigor. The courage to risk one's life in combat, and indifference to the pain and suffering of life on the march and in the trenches, were the standards that they believed measured the character of a soldier. When they concluded that their top subordinate commanders did not measure up to these standards, they did not hesitate to relieve them. Yet, criticism of Pershing's relief of officers like General Cameron, and Summerall's relief of Colonel Babcock and others, did not undermine the confidence of their officers and men in the leadership of both men, and their loyalty to each. Many of Summerall's colleagues shared George Marshall's assessment of Summerall that is quoted in the introduction of this study. In a confidential report that General Ely submitted in October 1918, he wrote that Summerall "is one of the best disciplinarians I have ever seen—severe, but absolutely just; understands human nature, adapting methods that fit the case. He is an indefatigable worker, giving personal attention of details to an extent unequalled by any officer who has come under my observation....[He is] Aggressive to the highest degree and will attack and advance when most commanders think it irresponsible." Ely concluded this glowing assessment by noting that Summerall "has held many responsible positions, always with marked success; his physical and moral courage, his example to his subordinates in personal and official conduct, his excellent judgment and intelligence, all unite to qualify him as a leader of marked distinction."[22]

Summerall's victorious leadership of Pershing's favorite division and his swift rise from brigade to corps commander indicates Pershing's high regard for his ability, and his stature in the AEF. He invited Summerall to witness the signing of the Versailles Treaty, and to accompany Pershing on his tour of Italy, and to sail with him on board the *Leviathan* on the homeward voyage. After the war, his admiration of Summerall remained just as high. In an efficiency report on general officers that Pershing wrote in 1922, when he was chief of staff, he rated Summerall as "an able, efficient, loyal officer, with an inspiring personality; a natural leader with exceptional ability. [He] Commanded in battle an artillery brigade, then the American 1st Division which had no equal in the World War, and finally a corps, and in all these positions he displayed superlative qualities of character and leadership."[23]

In the years before Pershing's comments about Sedan turned Summerall against his former commander in chief, there is clear evidence of his equally high regard for Pershing. In a letter he wrote to General Lejeune on 21 January 1919, when he was still commander of V Corps, he gave a totally different account of his meeting with Pershing after General Harbord had requested that he speak with the commander in chief about issuing a citation for the Second Division. Rather than Pershing's having ignored him, as an embittered Summerall had recalled in his memoir, he wrote that "It was my good fortune last Tuesday to sit at General Pershing's right at lunch....I then secured a personal interview with him and presented the matter as earnestly and as fully as possible. He was extremely kind, extremely sympathetic, and felt every desire to meet the citation if he could find it consistent with his policy."[24]

Summerall also showed at that time his high regard for the Second Division and his admiration for Lejeune, when he included in his letter of 21 January the citation that he had written for the signature of the commander in chief. In closing his letter, he wrote Lejeune that "Again assuring you of my highest regards, for you personally, and for the division as a whole, and of my abiding interest in you," and signed it "Faithfully yours."[25] In the citation he hoped Pershing would issue for the division, he wrote that "The Commander-in-Chief desires to make of record in the General Orders of the

American Expeditionary Forces, his extreme satisfaction with the conduct of the 2nd Division in the battles in which it has engaged, and his high commendation of the officers and soldiers of this division, their conspicuous courage, their fortitude and their lofty self-sacrifice in the performance of every duty that has been assigned to them." He praised their participation in battles at Chateau-Thierry, Soissons, St. Mihiel, in the offensive in Champagne, and in the Meuse-Argonne, as decisive in ending the war. He noted the division's exceptionally high morale and discipline, and stated that

> its officers and men have been filled with an unconquerable spirit, which has enabled them in every engagement to enforce their will upon the enemy. Its personnel is a tribute to American manhood, and its achievements will constitute a proud inheritance, not only of the American Army, but of the American people.[26]

In the glow of their shared victory in the war, his opinion of Lejeune and the marines contrasts sharply with his assessment in his memoir that they would fight no better than the army, complain, and "seek quick relief and try to gain publicity." But in January 1919, he had not "learned" of their resentment of his order to cross the Meuse, and it had not occurred to him to blame Lejeune for ordering the marine brigade to lead the crossing, as he asserted in his memoir. Unfortunately, and once again, his recollection of criticism had distorted his remembrance of his good intentions, as well as his encouraging and uplifting words to Lejeune, who would become commandant of the Marine Corps, and superintendent of Virginia Military Institute. It is also lamentable that Summerall and Pershing allowed their pride and vanity to shatter their mutual admiration and respect, and led Summerall to reject the legacy of the man whose leadership and fortitude in the war had been an example that Summerall faithfully had followed.

## Chapter Fourteen

*The Home Front and Hawaii*

Camp Zachary Taylor, the destination of the Summeralls as their train headed west for Louisville, had been the largest training camp in the army. It was built in the summer of 1917, and at one time housed 47,500 soldiers. More than 125,000 men from Kentucky, Illinois, and Indiana were trained there for service in the Great War. Many of these men, who had been fortunate to survive the war, including those of the First Division, were returning to the camp to be demobilized and discharged. The laws that had established the wartime army also entitled most of these soldiers to prompt discharges, and they left as soon as they could be separated. Altogether, 2,608,218 enlisted men and 128,436 officers of the wartime army were discharged by 30 June 1919; at one point, over 63,000 of these soldiers awaiting discharge were housed in tents at Camp Zachary Taylor.[1]

In the meantime, as the size of the army rapidly diminished, General Peyton C. March, Chief of the General Staff of the War Department, sent to Congress in January 1919 a plan for the reorganization of the army that would be the basis of the long-term military policy of the country. He proposed a permanent Regular Army of 500,000 men, or a force that was five times the size of the army authorized by the National Defense Act of 1916. It would be organized into five corps, each at half strength, and "expanded" in wartime with reserves. Universal military service of three months for all men between the ages of 19 and 21 would insure an adequate reserve force, organized and trained by the Regular Army. The nation's primary military reserve, the National Guard, was relegated to third place, behind the expandable Regular Army and the draftees in the Federal Reserves.[2]

With President Wilson's expending his energy and power to win public and Congressional support for the League of Nations, he showed no interest in March's proposal. In addition, the American people and the Congress were unwilling to spend the money to finance a large peacetime army, which involved a peacetime draft. Some people even thought that its very existence would facilitate the involvement of the country in another foreign war. Predictably, neither the president, Congress, nor the public supported March's bill.[3]

In October 1919, the Senate Military Affairs Committee, chaired by Republican James W. Wadsworth of New York, began hearings on a new military bill and invited General Pershing to testify. He had asked Hunter Liggett, John Hines, and Summerall to give him their views, although Summerall did not mention Pershing's request in his memoir. George Marshall was now Pershing's aide and summarized for his boss the testimony of various witnesses before the committee. Pershing supported a Regular Army of 300,000 officers and men at full strength, rather than an expandable force through reserve. Colonel John M. Palmer, Summerall's classmate at West Point, and veteran of the China Relief Expedition and World War I, proposed a much smaller Regular Army and a much larger federalized militia of citizen-soldiers that would be under their own officers but trained by the Regular Army. This citizen force would constitute the main wartime army, and would fight as companies, regiments, and divisions alongside the Regular Army rather than being absorbed into Regular Army units. Pershing agreed with Palmer's plan for the reserve, and both men supported universal peacetime military training for the citizen army.[4]

Colonel Palmer so impressed the Senate committee that Senator Wadsworth asked the War Department to release him to help the committee write the new military law. For the next nine months, Palmer worked with the committee and did much to craft the new bill that was signed into law on 4 June, as the National Defense Act of 1920. It provided for a Regular Army of 297,000 officers and men, close to the number that Pershing had recommended; a National Guard of 435,000 troops, and an Organized Reserve of unspecified numbers. These three components of the military would be known collectively as the Army of the United States (AUSA). All three would be filled by volunteers, not by universal, that is, compulsory military training.[5] The new law divided the country into nine army corps areas that replaced the old geographical military departments. To each corps area was assigned one Regular Army division, two National Guard divisions, and up to three Organized Reserve divisions. The components of each National Guard division would be determined by the states in each corps area, and the Regular Army division in each corps area would train the citizen formations.[6] The act also curtailed the autonomy of the old army bureaus by establishing a single promotion list that replaced the separate promotion lists for each branch. (Nevertheless, as Summerall would discover when he became army chief of staff, the heads of these old-line bureaus had retained enough power to thwart any attempt to reduce further their authority.) In addition, the law gave the four combat arms—infantry, cavalry, coast artillery, and field artillery—administrative headquarters in the War Department, with equal standing with the traditional bureaus. The law also created new arms and services—the Air Service, Chemical Warfare Service, and Finance Department—placing them on the same level as the bureaus. In addition to other duties, the combat arms headquarters was charged with the development of tactical doctrine for their arms, and was responsible to the General Staff; however, as military historian Larry H. Addington noted, this provision of the act "encouraged branch isolation." It also might have embolded the bureau chiefs in their determination to maintain their degree of autonomy. The General Staff was strengthened by assigning 93 officers to the office in Washington, including four assistant chiefs of staff. This number was far larger than the 19 that served under the National Defense Act of 1916, but considerably less than the 226 that the War Department had requested.[7]

The Act of 1920 established the army in which Summerall would continue to serve, and would head as chief of staff, until his retirement in 1931. It mandated constructive changes and laid impressive foundations, but, as Addington and Forrest Pogue observed, it had significant weaknesses. The latter wrote that its greatest weakness was the fact that the military organization it created depended upon a trained citizen army established through universal military training, which was not enacted. Pogue concluded that "the Army lost its position at the core of a citizen organization and reverted to a skeleton combat force which in case of war would again have to try to flesh itself out largely with another generation of raw recruits."[8]

Addington noted that Pershing and all of his successors as chief of staff, which would include Summerall, were "frustrated by public indifference and by congressional parsimony with military budgets." In 1921, Congress reduced the Regular Army to 150,000; the next year it mandated a further reduction to 137,000, discharging more than a thousand Regular officers; and in 1927, the year after Summerall was appointed chief of staff, an additional cut brought the number down to 118,750, with a corresponding reduction for activities and equipment. In addition, the training centers were eliminated, and National Guard units, dependent on federal funds, barely reached half of the strength authorized in 1920 and suffered as well from a lack training and equipment.[9] Even before Summerall became chief of staff, these were issues that would affect his commands in Hawaii, Texas, and New York. How he dealt with these problems in these commands would shape his policies as chief of staff.

In his memoir, Summerall mentioned nothing about the Act of 1920, as he wrote only about how he and Laura spent the year at Camp Taylor. They found a place to stay on post until they could rent a house, and were pleased that the people of Louisville received them with open arms. He noted that local women's organizations provided dances and recreation for the soldiers and helped to boost morale when many discharges were delayed because of the difficulty in finding replacements.[10] Indeed, the shortage of volunteer replacements occurred even though the pay of enlisted men was doubled during the war, and was attributed to the public's lack of interest in military service. Summerall sent a memorandum to the First Division refuting a series of articles in the Louisville newspapers charging that the army was so desperate for recruits that it was taking men whose conduct was such "that they would be sent to prison should they not enlist in the Army." He affirmed that "The First Division has not enlisted nor will it enlist anyone who would otherwise go to jail, all reports and or rumors to the contrary."[11]

Nevertheless, the army had difficulty in retaining officers, as well as enlisted personnel. The *New York Times* reported that officers' pay was so low that they were not able to meet the requirements of their positions, and could not afford to take care of their families. At Camp Dix in New Jersey, Summerall's next command, the paper stated that 1,500 officers returned to civilian life because they could not meet "modern expenses." With wartime ranks lowered in grades and salaries, colonels were reduced to lieutenants earning $200 per month, out of which they had to buy their food, uniforms, and meet other expenses before they could financially support their families. In addition, although living expenses after the war in many places had increased as much as 100 percent, the salary scale for officers had not been revised since 1908.[12]

During Summerall's tenure at Camp Taylor, discrepancies and irregularities in the office of the camp quartermaster indicated that at least some officers and men who remained were less than competent, and that policies and record keeping in the First Division were partly at fault. An audit of the accounts of the property officer revealed a shortage of some five thousand items valued at $4,000,000. The office of the inspector general of the War Department conducted an investigation and issued an initial report, stating that "in all large camps and demobilization centers there occurred a confusion of records which made any attempt at an accurate audit farcical." The report exonerated the property officer, concluding that the discrepancies resulted from inaccurate and incompetently kept records, a failed system of inventorying property, frequent turnover of property officers, and inexperienced and incompetent personnel in that office. It concluded that "In the instance of Camp Taylor, evidence in abundance exists to prove that conditions were even worse than in other camps." Without specifying specific policies or actions, the report stated that Summerall and the administration of the First Division had contributed to the "confusion of the property records," but did not specify what these policies or actions were.[13]

The inspector general's office conducted a reinvestigation and issued a final report in June 1922, after Summerall had left to command the Hawaiian Department. This report again cleared the property officer and concluded that "the shortage was a paper shortage and not a shortage in fact, and that much of the property unaccounted for was believed to be in the hands of the 1st Division at Camp Dix, and at stations throughout the 5th Corps Area to which property had been shipped without proper accounting being made."[14]

Summerall was given the opportunity to respond to the charges that, as commanding general of the First Division, he was responsible for the failure to keep accurate records. The report stated that Summerall had responded to the inspector general's charges against him and the division by asserting that the officer in charge of the investigation "was not qualified to make the investigation by reason of personal animus." But the report concluded that "The statements submitted by Major General Summerall fail to establish any animus on the part of the Inspector or even a basis of hostility." Summerall did not include any material about the case in his papers, but he did insist in his memoir that the inspector had "some grievance which I never knew." At the same time, the reinvestigation found that Summerall "could not be expected to know all the details and ramifications of property storage and accounting." It recommended that Summerall be informed that "the conclusion of the Inspector, to the effect that he individually was to some degree responsible for the conclusion in the property accounts, is not warranted...and no further action will be undertaken by the War Department."[15]

Thus, the War Department officially exonerated Summerall, but once again, he had attributed criticism of policies and actions to personal animosity toward him, even though the report found no basis for that accusation and was clear that he was not responsible for the "snafu" at Camp Taylor. And, since the "snafu" at Camp Taylor had occurred under his command, he again had violated Captain Reilly's dictum, which he had pledged to follow, that there should be nothing to explain away in his area of responsibility.

One reason that Summerall might not have been "minding the store" at Camp Taylor was the amount of time and energy he devoted to fulfilling what he described as his "pact with our [the First Division's] dead on the battlefields and erect some worthy memorial to them." He organized the First Division A. E. F. Memorial Association, and was elected president. They set a goal of $150,000 to finance the design and construction of the monument to be placed in the nation's capital, and members of the division contributed $5,000. To raise additional funds, Major Harcourt Harvey organized a circus extravaganza at Camp Taylor, complete with infantry, artillery, and cavalry exhibitions, with tanks, lions and elephants on parade, and plenty of clowns, balloons, and refreshments. It was a great success, wrote Summerall, especially after one of the lions attacked his keeper, and an exploding caisson caught the clothing of the gunners on fire and caused them to run with flames of fire shooting out behind them. No one was hurt, but the incidents generated a lot of publicity, with crowds coming "to see lions kill the keeper, and the cannoneers on fire." The circus moved on to Indianapolis where it performed for a week before capacity crowds, and then to Chicago, where it held performances at the lakeshore and drew overflow crowds there, as well. Even though there were no more lion attacks and blazing cannoneers, the Memorial Association cleared $100,000. Subsequent fundraisers in Chicago and Boston brought in additional contributions, including $1,500 from a gathering in Boston that included Dr. James Russell Lowell, president of Harvard University. Summerall wrote that while he was in Boston, a friend took him to meet Governor Calvin Coolidge, who, as might be expected, "said almost nothing," but later sent Summerall a copy of his book, *Have Faith in Massachusetts*.[16]

Within a year, the Memorial Association had collected more than the estimated cost of $150,000 for the monument. In September 1919, Summerall contacted Mr. Charles Moore, chairman of the Commission on Fine Arts, a federal agency that advises the government on matters of art and architecture, and suggested erecting a monument to the First Division in the capital. The commission met the next month to discuss Summerall's request and suggested that a memorial dedicated to the entire army would have more national significance. This idea was not acceptable to the division, since the funds for the monument came exclusively from First Division families and friends, and since soldiers in the division came from across the country, anyway. After lengthy deliberation, the commission finally agreed to support the division's proposal. They had concluded that the First Division memorial presented an opportunity to commemorate American soldiers and their victory in a contemporary and unique work of art, rather than erecting yet another equestrian statue, of which there were more than enough representations, mainly Civil War monuments, in the civic sculpture of the city.[17]

In the meantime, on 20 April 1920, Summerall was promoted to the rank of major general in the Regular Army. He received additional good news from Congressman Fred M. Blackman, of Alabama, that Charles, Jr., had been appointed to the U.S. Military Academy. He noted that he and Blackman had become friends when Summerall was with the Militia Bureau, and had been in Anniston to negotiate the purchase of an artillery range. Following his graduation from prep school, young Charles spent the summer at Camp Taylor. His proud parents went with him to Washington to put him on the train for the trip to West Point. His father recalled that "When we saw him go through the iron gate of the Union Station to the train, I realized that he was going into the world alone and that I could never do for him anything that I had not done. We were proud of him and his opportunity but our hearts were crushed at this definite separation. He amply rewarded us by his character, intellect and achievements." Not long afterwards, on a subsequent trip to the capital, Summerall learned that Commander Bartolucci, who had attached himself to Summerall on their way to Fiume, was gravely sick in the hospital. He found the Italian in agony with double mastoiditis, and his fiancée in tears at his bedside. A few days later, Bartolucci died. Summerall wrote that he often felt responsible, for if he had not secured Bartolucci's assignment in Washington, his Italian friend might never have contracted the fatal illness.[18]

When Summerall and Laura returned to Camp Taylor after seeing their son off to West Point, he learned that the War Department had decided to close down the installation to save money. The First Division was transferred to Camp Dix, outside Trenton, New Jersey, and the Summeralls arrived there in September 1920. He found the facilities at his new command post in poor condition. The *New York Times* reported that soldiers returning from overseas to Camp Dix were forced to live in unheated barracks, with many developing pneumonia. Summerall set the men to work repairing buildings, improving the barracks, and converting many of them into family quarters for the "hundreds of officers and men" who had married Kentucky girls.[19]

Summerall also encountered problems with authorities in the neighboring towns. In early October, the *Times* reported that a soldier from the First Division was playing with a machine gun that was a part of a display of army trophies at the Trenton Fair Grounds. Instead of blanks, the gun was loaded with live ammunition, and when the soldier pulled the trigger, the gun blew off the back of the head of a 39-year-old man. The soldier was arrested, and friction arose between the locals on the one hand, and the soldiers and authorities at the camp, on the other hand. Summerall declared many of the towns close to the camp off limits because, he said, of venereal disease. Tensions further mounted when the board of education in the town of Pemberton barred the children of officers and men from attending the local schools.[20]

The First Division seems to have assuaged the feelings of the locals, when it performed a massive sham battle in the evening of 10 November before about 10,000 of its own veterans and thousands of civilian visitors. The *Times* described the event as "the most spectacular of its kind ever staged in this country," and reported that General Pershing was present, along with other prominent army officers. When a single star shell signaled "zero hour" for the attack, tanks lumbered out from the woods, guns fired from their turrets, with doughboys charging behind and firing their rifles, as mines exploded ahead of them, and 155-mm guns blazed away to simulate counterbattery fire. The "titanic spectacle" took place in "a great natural amphitheater at the foot of Marne Hill, made as light as day tonight by batteries of searchlights and the dazzling brilliance of chemical contrivances."[21]

A few months later the better relations between the soldiers at Camp Dix and the local population suffered a setback when two men in army uniforms robbed a saloon in Trenton at gunpoint during the night of 5 May 1921. They took $60 from the till and fled in a taxi. A policeman stopped the car, but the soldiers and the driver beat him with their guns, badly chewed up one of his fingers, and fled toward the camp. The car sped on, crashing through a roadblock. The police gave chase, with the robbers and police emptying their guns, but both sides missed their targets in the dark, and the taxi disappeared into the night. The police notified the military police, who began a search of the camp, accompanied by the bruised policeman with a bandaged finger. They failed to find the suspects, and the *Times* reported that the robbers could have been civilians dressed in army uniforms.[22] Apparently the culprits never were captured, since a follow-up report did not appear in the *Times*, and Summerall provided no information on the incident in his memoir. Suffice it to say, that the fireworks around Camp Dix were not confined to the sham battle at "Marne Hill."

Writing the history of the First Division was the second major project that Summerall worked on while he was at Camp Dix. He arranged for the War Department to detail a number of officers and men to compile the records and maps of the division, but stated that he composed a draft of the history, and sent 100 mimeographed copies to officers and men who checked the facts. He wrote that he did not take credit as the author, "because I did not want to appear to be seeking distinction but I compiled it and wrote it entirely. I consider it an epic as a story," he continued, "and the English, imagery and sentiment are superior."[23] While one can question the epic status of the work, it is rich in the details of the training and fierce fights of the division; it vividly describes the suffering of the soldiers in their harsh winter encampments, as well as in their painful, exhausting marches, and shows how determined they were to maintain the fortitude and performance their hard-driving commanders demanded as an example to the entire AEF. General Pershing, still in Summerall's good graces, wrote a glowing foreword, and it is printed in his handwriting. He praised the division for establishing "the reputation of the American Soldier in Europe," and for maintaining "our ideals by the dignity and self-restraint of your bearing on German soil. The record of your achievements, and your sacrifices," he concluded, "will be a model for our armies in the future."[24] (Obviously I have used this *History* extensively, and, I hope, judiciously in this study.)

A Sergeant Glidden painted brilliant and colorful allegorical pictures and subdued watercolors for the book. His pastel allegories included a medallion on the frontispiece picturing a mounted and helmeted First Division crusader between two mounted, medieval knights dressed and armed for the crusades. The knights held banners high, which unfurled in the wind, while the First Division warrior gripped the staff of a blue flag embossed with a large, white "1." Hovering by his flag is an elongated figure of a maiden in gleaming white raiment raising a long, gold and silver sword high in her right hand. The title of the medallion is *The First Victorious Crusade*.

The plate facing the dedication on page xiii is entitled "The Gold Star" and commemorates the dead of the division. It displays the profile of the bust of a young doughboy, with a large, red "1" on the patch on his left shoulder, against the background of a red, stained glass window. To his right is a tall, blazing, golden torch, and to his left is a sword with the crucified Jesus suspended from the cross-handle. A banner, with "For Valor" written across it, is suspended below a cross that is placed behind the soldier's profile.

Opposite the page with the tribute to the division on page xxi is a richly colored plate with the figure of a modestly beautiful young woman striding forth in the center, encircled by a golden ring with the flags of all the Allied countries painted on it. Above the golden ring, to the left and right, are shields emblazoned with the emblems of the French Republic and Great Britain, respectively. A large shawl, with the shoulder patches of all the AEF wartime divisions embroidered on it, is draped over the woman's right arm, flowing into folds at her feet. On her head is a gold filigree crown, with a red "1" displayed on a laurel wreath attached to the crown above her forehead. She holds a palm fond in her right hand and cradles a sword in her left hand.

Sergeant Glidden's watercolors depict a winter scene at Seicheprey, with two soldiers huddled in a trench in a snow storm; a springtime scene at Cantigny, with the ruined village ablaze, and two groups of soldiers in foxholes on the edge of a green field with a swaying tree and a clump of red poppies nearby; a picture of summer at Soissons, with soldiers advancing through a field of golden wheat past fallen comrades, as planes fly overhead and clouds of smoke rise from artillery firing in the background; an autumn scene in the Argonne, with a line of soldiers, gleaming bayonets pointed skyward, striding forth beneath a large tree in full autumn colors, passing beyond a dead soldier in gray tangled in barbed wire that stretches around the tree; and the final scene, entitled *The Chosen Corps*, with two dark helmets tilted over the top of crosses placed on a hillside, with the pale, white figures of soldiers lined up diagonally across the back of the picture, stretching over a dark, green valley, almost to the horizon.[25] While Summerall's *History* may not be the epic he thought it to be, Glidden's allegorical pastels are among the most arresting examples of this genre. His watercolors are soft, gentle, and strangely touching illustrations of determined and courageous soldiers in combat.

When Summerall contacted The John C. Winston Company in Philadelphia about publishing the book, they agreed, but required a payment of $25,000 for printing 5,000 copies. Fortunately, the division had enough money from the liquidation of its canteen in Germany to finance the cost. After receiving permission from the division's judge advocate to use the surplus canteen funds for this purpose, Summerall ordered an edition of 5,000 copies. The *History* was bound in a handsome, thick cover, with the title printed in gold letters on the front at the top of a gold frame, with the Big Red One emblem encircled by gold, and Pershing's special commendation, likewise printed in gold letters, set in the gold frame at the bottom. The book was published in 1922, and Summerall anticipated robust sales. He was keenly disappointed, therefore, when it became clear that not only was the public not interested in buying the book, but that also the officers and men of the division bought few copies.[26] As noted above, with interest in the military in steep decline, both within and without the army, the lack of response to the *History* is not surprising.

While Summerall was disappointed by the reception of the *History*, he was pleased that his plans for the First Division monument were moving forward. In November 1920, the Commission on Fine Arts approved the site for the monument that Summerall had selected; namely in the park south of the State, War, and Navy Building, now the Eisenhower Executive Office Building. The next month, a joint resolution to erect the monument was introduced in Congress, and the House approved it in June 1921, followed by the Senate's approval in November.[27]

Summerall's idea and form for the monument seem to have been based on the Battle Monument at West Point. It commemorates the Regular Army soldiers of the United States who died in the Civil War, and is composed of a monolithic granite shaft surmounted by a winged female statue symbolizing victory, holding a trumpet and wreath. The names of the fallen soldiers are inscribed on the monument.[28]

During the summer of 1921, the Society of the First Division and the Fine Arts Commission selected Cass Gilbert as the architect, and Daniel Chester French as the sculptor for the monument. Gilbert was a prominent architect who had designed the Woolworth Building in New York, the tallest building in the country until 1930. He also had been one of the original members of the Commission, and was familiar with the capital city. Apparently, Gilbert suggested to Summerall that French be engaged as the sculptor. Like Gilbert, French had been an original member of the Commission, best known for his sculpture of the seated Abraham Lincoln in the Lincoln Memorial.[29]

The memorial association required that the names of all the war dead of the division be inscribed on the monument, and that the sculpture "typify the spirit of triumphant sacrifice and of service of the Division's dead."[30] Gilbert's design for the monument closely followed the form of the monument at West Point, and he proposed inscribing the honor roll of more than 5,500 on the granite base. The shaft would be a granite column 35 feet tall; the Victory sculpture would be gilded bronze, 15 feet tall, and would stand atop the column. The total height, from the ground to the top of the statue, would be 78 feet.[31]

During the winter of 1921–22, French designed the statue of Victory holding a flag in her right hand, with the left hand free and extended in a gesture of benediction. In April 1922, the Commission accepted the memorial as designed by Gilbert and French, and by April, the latter had finished a plaster model of the Victory. He sent a photograph of the sculpture to Summerall, at his command post in Hawaii, and received an unexpected response. Apparently, the figure not only violated Summerall's Victorian tastes, but also the concept of the memorial. He stated that it was "too voluptuous and not sufficiently spiritual. The abdomen is too prominent and the limbs suggest material rather than spiritual emotions....Let me repeat that our purpose is to preserve the spirit of triumph, of spiritual exaltation, of sacrifice, glorified by renunciation, of pride, and of reward."[32] For emphasis, Summerall had sent French a copy of the *History*. After reading the book, the sculptor conferred with Gilbert, and asked him to "convert" Summerall to support his design, by emphasizing that the statue would be observed from below and from a distance, and that its silhouette would make the greatest impression. Gilbert obliged his colleague, and Summerall responded by writing French that he had sent a cable to Gilbert approving the design. The general's letter enabled French to begin work on a full-size model of the statue, while Gilbert began the search for a granite monolith large enough to yield a column 35 feet tall.[33]

Meanwhile, Summerall was ordered to the command of the Hawaiian Department, and he and Laura left the rather contentious area of Camp Dix on 30 June 1921. After the cross-continental journey by rail, and a calm sea voyage from Los Angeles across over 2,500 miles of the Pacific, they arrived in the harbor of Honolulu on 5 August. They were promptly settled into the commanding general's quarters at Fort Shafter, located about 10 miles from Pearl Harbor, just minutes from downtown Honolulu. Fort Shafter had been constructed on former crown lands that had been ceded to the United States government after annexation. Their house faced the parade ground that was ringed by Royal Palms.[34]

Under the National Defense Act of 1920, an important part of the mission of the Regular Army was to garrison the nation's overseas possessions. The Pacific Army, divided into the Hawaiian and Philippine Departments, fulfilled that responsibility, but it was actually of far lesser importance than the navy in the defense of the Philippines and Hawaii. Early in the 20th century, when the United States feared that a resurgent Japan could threaten U.S. presence in the Philippines and its interests in China, the Joint Army and Navy Board, a consultative committee, had developed War Plan Orange, the basic study for a war with Japan. Taking advantage of the opportunity to gain Germany's Asian possessions and extend its imperial reach in the East, Japan declared war on the German Empire in 1914. The Japanese gained enclaves in China and Siberia, and seized Germany's central Pacific islands just north of the Equator. This island group of Micronesia—the Carolines, the Marianas, and the Marshalls—lay along the main routes to China and the Philippines. The U.S. feared that if the Japanese developed them as forward airfields and operating bases for their navy, they could threaten the American way stations of Guam, Midway, and Wake. After the war, Japanese forces withdrew from China and Russia, but remained in Micronesia, placing Japan in a strong position to return to China. They were now positioned to expand their power throughout southwest Asia at the expense of the rich but weakly defended colonies of the Dutch in the East Indies, the French in Indo-China, and the British in Malaya. In addition, Japanese control of the islands of Micronesia made it unlikely that the U.S. Navy could defend the Philippines, and stop Japan from exploiting either China's weakness or the vulnerability of the European colonial regimes. These concerns led the U.S. Navy to conclude that it needed a fleet "second to none" to curb British influence, but more importantly to deter Japan, the object of War Plan Orange.[35]

In response to these risks, Congressional budget cuts, and in hopes of forestalling a naval race among the leading naval powers, the administration of President Warren G. Harding called for an international meeting to limit naval armament. Known as the Washington Conference, it was held during the winter of 1921–22. Historian Robert Kaufman called it "the most ambitious pre-nuclear effort to limit arms in the history of the United States."[36] The conference produced the Washington Naval Treaty that set tonnage ratios for battleships and aircraft carriers of the United States, Great Britain, Japan, France, and Italy of 5, 5, 3, 1.75, and 1.75, respectively. The United States, Great Britain, and Japan also agreed not to construct permanent fortifications around their bases in the western Pacific.[37] On the one hand, this meant that the Japanese could not develop their Micronesian islands into naval bases. On the other hand, it also meant that the American army would have to maintain the status quo on fortifications in the Pacific, and could not establish a fortified naval base further west than Oahu or strengthen those in Manila Bay.[38]

For the army, as historian Brian Linn stated in his *Guardians of Empire: The U.S. Army in the Pacific, 1902–1940*, this latter provision was the most important part of the treaty. In the first decade after the war, the army affirmed that the primary mission of the Philippine Department was to hold Manila and Manila Bay, so that the U.S. fleet could launch an offensive to aid the defense of the Philippines if war broke out with Japan. The Washington Treaty, coupled with the decline of military budgets and manpower, made this mission more difficult, but the Joint Board still retained that mission until 1928, in spite of Congressional budget cuts that reduced the garrison of 13,251 by half. By then it was clear that the Philippine army was too weak to do more than secure the entrances to Manila Bay, and hold the area as long as possible.[39]

While the scope of the Philippine army diminished, Brian Linn quotes an Army War College committee's statement that "Hawaii remains at the forefront of our defense of the Pacific Coast and is vital to us." The mission of the army was to defend the naval base at Pearl Harbor against damage from aerial bombardment, or enemy sympathizers, and from attack by an enemy invasion force. Linn notes that this mission remained "virtually unchanged after 1919."[40]

Summerall's immediate predecessor as commander of the Hawaiian Department, Major General Charles G. Morton, outlined, in 1920, a defense plan for Oahu that was based upon this mission. It emphasized defense in depth and would use new 16-inch guns to deter the enemy's capital ships from approaching the harbors and southern shore, thus compelling the Japanese amphibious force to land soldiers on the northern and eastern coasts. Here the assault force would have to cross reefs and advance through beach cordons sighted in with artillery and machine gun fire. Moving rapidly on newly constructed roads, American forces would then counterattack and overwhelm the enemy on the shoreline. Morton requested a sizable increase of infantry, artillery, and cavalry, as well as funds for a major road construction project. Mainly because of repeated Congressional reductions in the War Department budget, criticism by the bureau chiefs in Washington, and decreases in the size of the army resulting from the National Defense Act of 1920, Morton's plan was never adopted.[41]

When Summerall arrived in Honolulu on 5 August, he was correct in stating in his memoir, therefore, that "There were no war plans." He said that before leaving for his new post, he had been told in Washington that Japan had considered an attack before the disarmament conference, so he believed

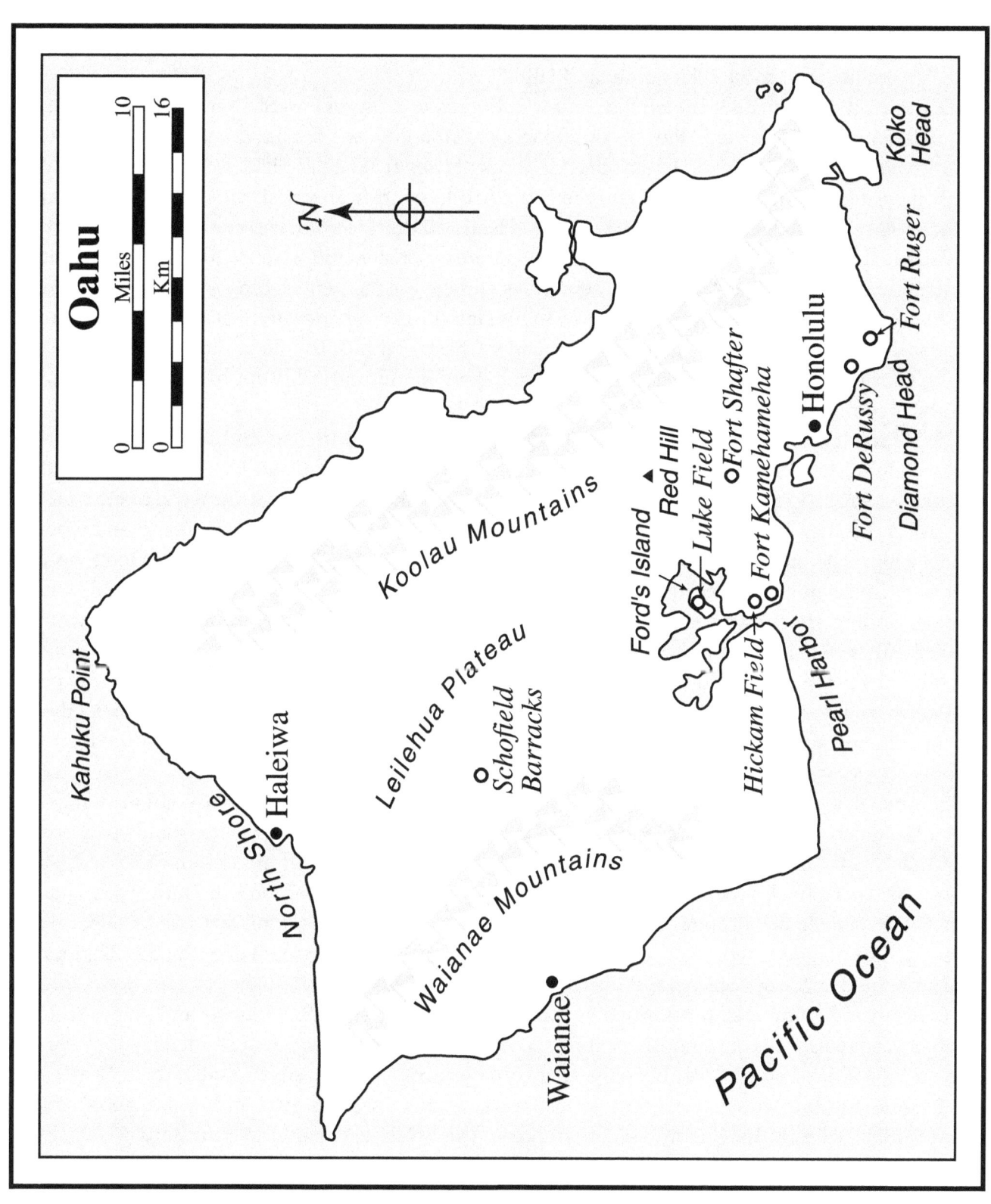

that "the situation was tense." Adding to the tension, in Summerall's view, was concern that the large Japanese minority, some 43 percent of Hawaii's population in 1921, had placed their loyalty to their homeland, and not to America. He noted that the General Staff had gathered a great deal of information on Japanese espionage that could be facilitated by the crews of Japanese merchant vessels sailing weekly from the west coast to Honolulu and Hilo.[42]

Summerall's command included the comfortable surroundings of Fort Shafter; the cantonment at Schofield Barracks that covered the open approaches to Honolulu and the naval base, and was located about five miles north of Pearl Harbor; the Air Service bases at Wheeler Field at Schofield and Luke Field on Ford Island in Pearl Harbor; and the Coast Artillery fortifications, situated at strategic points on the southern coast of Oahu, between Diamond Head and Pearl Harbor. He wrote that soon after his arrival, he ordered Major Leslie J. McNair, his operations officer, and Major Charles H. White, the assistant operations officer, "to seclude themselves and devote their entire time to the preparation of war plans." Unofficially, Summerall attached to his staff the commander of the Submarine Squadron Division 14 at Pearl Harbor, Lieutenant Commander Chester Nimitz, to collaborate with McNair and White. They finished the plan in August 1924, just in time for Summerall to approve it before his tour of duty as commanding general ended (see map, p. 319).[43]

The "Project for Defense of Oahu, Revision 1924," as the title made clear, and as Summerall stated in his memoir, was centered exclusively on stopping an invasion of Oahu by Orange, that is, the Japanese enemy, and the occupation of the island for use as an advanced base for naval operations in the eastern Pacific. The plan assumed that "Orange would hope for strategic surprise," and would open hostilities before a formal declaration of war. To achieve success, the enemy invasion force would have to establish at least two extensive beachheads on Oahu. Enemy air force bombardments would support landing attacks, and, should American ships be in action in Pearl Harbor, the enemy would attack them as well. Even if Orange should decide not to invade Oahu in the event of war, the mission of the enemy air force "would be the destruction of Pearl Harbor." The defenders also could expect the enemy to lay mines off Pearl Harbor and Honolulu, and launch submarine attacks into these harbors. Enemy sympathizers would try to destroy armaments, supplies, utilities, sabotage the two harbors, and prevent the utilization of the labor supply.[44]

Summerall's plan of defense depended upon a force on Oahu strong enough to compel Orange to expend so much time and effort, and impose on the enemy such a high cost, that he would be deterred from attacking the island. This deterrent force would be composed of an air force of some 304 planes and almost 7,000 personnel; a coast artillery corps of about 8,500; a mobile land force of 71,646; 648 military police; 1,453 personnel for chemical warfare service; and 11,591 civilian and military personnel for supply service, to include a medical depot of over 5,000, and a quartermaster depot of over 2,500. The grand total amounted to 100,698 officers and men, of which almost 7,000 were civilians.[45]

In his memoir, Summerall described how his plan would operate. Small boats and planes would conduct reconnaisance continuously within 100 miles of the shore, and would identify the enemy force at least a day before it would arrive at anchorage. Sixteen-inch guns mounted on railway cars and 240-mm mortars would shell enemy transports at anchor; machine guns and 75-mm guns would defend the beaches; if the enemy used poison gas, the defenders would use mustard gas against enemy ships.[46] In wartime, civilian labor would be used to lay contact mines and barbed wire, and to build field fortifications, improve physical defenses, and expand airfields. Defense in depth would be prepared in the rear of the beach defense line. From his headquarters at Schofield Barracks, as Brian Linn noted, Summerall would oversee air attacks, antiaircraft defense, and coastal artillery. Each sector would have a commander who could call for fire support, including shelling from the 16-inch guns. Roads were to be built and trails cut from Schofield Barracks to facilitate the rapid deployment of defensive forces down to the west coast. Cordons of soldiers would contain the Japanese population of Oahu, and prevent them from assembling.[47] To provide water for the garrison of over 100,000 men, a large reservoir was constructed above Schofield Barracks, and a refrigeration plan was built on the post to hold enough meat and perishables to last the men for six months. Summerall wrote that field exercises were frequently held "day and night," so that the troops became familiar with their missions and could be relied upon to reach their defensive positions quickly. He believed that he had "never seen better trained troops or higher morale than they developed." The coast artillery and the heavy mobile artillery conducted target practice, with half of their exercises held at night, and half during the day. Airplane spotters adjusted fire on long-range targets over the horizon.[48]

Predictably, Summerall insisted that "every command be made better by the appearance of the officers and men." Honor guards that welcomed visiting officers and dignitaries of high rank at Fort Shafter wore tailor-made uniforms that they purchased voluntarily; made sure that drivers kept their horses well-groomed and their horse-drawn vehicles spotless; even their names were stenciled on their harnesses and seats. "In a short time," he noted, "all was in excellent condition."[49]

In April 1925, a major test of Hawaii's defenses took place as Joint Army and Navy Exercise No. 3, involving some 50,000 soldiers, sailors, and marines. In his brief account of the exercise, Brian Linn noted that it resulted in a successful landing on the North Shore, "whereupon the umpires called if off, and declared the invaders victorious." Perhaps that is why Summerall did not mention the event in his memoirs, or include any information about it in his papers. At any rate, Linn wrote that, following Summerall's plan, the mobile forces performed well, the harbor defenders stuck to their guns, and the coast artillery at Pearl Harbor and Honolulu theoretically drove off the enemy battleships.[50]

Linn also wrote that the exercises "also revealed deep divisions between the services," especially between the army and navy. The army commander of the heavy coastal guns was "appalled" that the navy totally ignored the power of his guns that would have demolished four battleships as they steamed along pretending to bombard the shoreline. In addition, Linn stated that communications between the Hawaiian Department and the 14th Naval District "broke down completely." He quoted one observer's statement that Summerall and his naval counterpart "'could not cooperate in anything, not even calling on each other.'" Linn noted that during the exercise, the enemy air force had landed and secured a base on the island of Molokai. The army commander wanted to launch a combined attack on the base, but his naval counterpart refused to cooperate, because his planes were required to protect Pearl Harbor. The delay led to the destruction of the defender's air cover, resulting in the failure of the entire defense.[51]

Indeed, although Summerall stated that when he first arrived he "worked in the closest harmony" with the admiral who commanded the district, he wrote that the successor, Admiral John D. McDonald, "would have nothing to do with me."[52] Summerall did not explain what could have led to McDonald's attitude, but it might have been in reaction to Summerall's plan of defense, which he described as "against all Navy policy, and prevented the mission of the Navy to seek the enemy at sea and defeat him," and for the navy, this was "the best form of defense," but one with which he clearly did not agree.[53] It is possible that the failure of Admiral McDonald and General Summerall to communicate or cooperate was due to their holding so firmly and stubbornly to their own plans and intraservice viewpoints. If so, as far as Summerall was concerned, it would be consistent with his determination to press forward with his own plans and assert his own will, regardless of contrary advice or opposition. Regrettably, in the years ahead, as Brian Linn noted, the issue of interservice rivalry was not addressed, either in Honolulu or Washington. Each service continued to develop its own plans, while incorporating support from the other without insuring that it would be provided.[54]

Perhaps, with the rather enormous benefit of hindsight after the Japanese attack on Pearl Harbor on 7 December 1941, and with the past conflict with navy brass remaining in his memory, Summerall noted in his memoir that "It was inconceivable that any American ship would be in Pearl Harbor except two station destroyers and the twelve old model submarines which would at once attack the enemy ships. Any fleet in Pearl Harbor could be blocked by one of the Japanese merchant ships that passed near the channel every day or two." In addition, he wrote that "we did not want any part of the Navy in Hawaiian waters where it would be exposed to submarine attack without any warning."[55]

In the next few years, down almost to the end of Summerall's term as army chief of staff in 1930, the basic outline of his plan for the defense of Hawaii remained the framework for the defense of Hawaii. Ironically, but accurately, Summerall's 1924 Project for the Defense of Hawaii stated clearly that it was "based upon a fallacy regarding manpower," that is, a defense force of over 100,000.[56] Congressional cuts in the military budget steadily reduced the force, so that by the end of his term as army chief of staff in 1930, only about 14,000 soldiers and 18 airplanes remained in Hawaii. Nevertheless, Summerall's plan established not only the framework for Hawaii's defense, but it laid out a tactical means for accomplishing that goal, that, as Brian Linn noted, remained in place for over two decades. His plan, and the expansions of it by his immediate successors in Hawaii, as well as innovative and vigorous commanders in the Philippines, as Linn concludes in his excellent study of the Pacific Army, might well have kept the army from abandoning altogether the struggle to defend Hawaii, as well as the Philippines.[57]

In early November 1923, as Summerall and his staff continued to work on their plan for Hawaii's defense, Brigadier General Billy Mitchell, the assistant chief of the Air Service, arrived in Honolulu with his new bride, Elizabeth, on the first leg of an informal inspection tour of American installations in the Pacific. Mitchell's boss, Major General Mason Patrick, chief of the Air Service, had written ahead to Summerall that Mitchell would inspect the islands. The day before the Mitchells' ship docked in Honolulu Harbor, Summerall sent a radio message of greetings to the newlyweds, and on the evening of their arrival, the Summeralls hosted them in their home for dinner. Summerall had known Mitchell since the latter had entered the army, and, when Summerall led the First Division at St. Mihiel, Mitchell commanded a coalition force of more than 1,400 airmen in the largest single concentration of air power in the war. After the war, Mitchell was appointed assistant chief of the Air Service and became an assertive and outspoken advocate for the establishment of the Air Service as an independent branch of the armed forces.[58]

The day after his arrival, Mitchell began his inspection tour of the installations on Oahu, and found Summerall friendly and very much aware of the need to develop air power throughout the islands. Mitchell and his wife remained in Hawaii until the end of the year, and for the remainder of his stay, he kept a busy schedule: sitting in on critiques of recent maneuvers, instructing squadrons on how they should fly in formation, flying various types of airplanes at Wheeler and Luke Fields, visiting all the islands in the Hawaiian group, addressing groups of officers, playing polo, hiking in the mountains, fishing, shooting pheasants, wild pigs and sheep, and enjoying the social life of Honolulu. After they left Hawaii, Mitchell and his wife spent the next seven months visiting the Philippine Islands, India, China, Manchuria, Korea, and Japan. They returned to Washington in July 1924.[59]

On 1 December, Mitchell completed his inspection of the Air Service in Hawaii. He did not submit a final report, in which he predicted a Japanese air attack on Pearl Harbor, until he had returned to Washington from his Asian tour. Just before sailing from Honolulu for Manila, he sent a preliminary report to General Patrick, and left a copy of it with Summerall. In it, Mitchell criticized Summerall's defense plan for failing to develop any plans "for the employment of the Air Service in case of war," and for not handling the air force as an independent arm. He stated that the plan's system of defense

# The Home Front and Hawaii

was essentially "a garrison for the defense of a fortress," but "with the coming of air power, this system of defense...needs revision, the mission of the ground forces should remain the same....For the air force, however, the mission must be to prevent landing on any islands and to destroy any force either in the air, on the water, or under the water within the radius of their operation." In order to develop plans for these operations, arrange for defense against aircraft, train pilots and air crews, as well as manage logistical support, Mitchell recommended that the air force in Hawaii be placed under an air force commander and his staff, and handled as an independent arm.[60]

Just after Christmas, Summerall responded with a seven-page letter to Patrick, in which he challenged almost all of Mitchell's assertions and recommendation. He was especially critical of Mitchell's emphasis on the necessity of a unified Air Service command. He noted that the Department Air Officer "supervises the activities of all Air Service units, and makes appropriate recommendation to the Department Commander, with every assurance that they will receive favorable consideration. A separate air force operating virtually independent to the Department Commander would be an anomaly that would have little value in peace and war." Summerall also stated that Mitchell's assertion that no plans existed for the employment of the Air Service was wrong. He said that "Plans in the form of field orders have been in existence for several years," and that he "must deny, emphatically, the impression conveyed by General Mitchell that no plans are in existence."[61]

Mitchell had recommended that inter-island flying be inaugurated, but Summerall noted that it had been going on for over a year, even though progress had been slow. In a comment that subtly emphasized Mitchell's unfamiliarity with flying conditions in the islands, Summerall wrote that Mitchell wanted to fly from Oahu to Kauai, but the weather forced him to ship a plane by boat.[62] Looking back in his memoir on the confrontation with Mitchell that occurred before the latter's court-martial in 1925, Summerall added that when Mitchell tried to take off from Kauai, he flew his plane into a fence, because he had no intention of flying back to Oahu. That confirmed Summerall's opinion. He stated that Mitchell was a "showman" and always seemed "irresponsible, eccentric, and vain."[63]

Summerall concluded his letter to Patrick by stating, with patronizing emphasis, that his Department welcomed constructive criticism, and realized that "much benefit can be derived from the experience and knowledge of officers visiting it from the War Department and from other parts of the country." At the same time, he dismissed Mitchell's report for its "superficial impressions and academic discussions," which might "result in conclusions that are unfair to the command, whose officers and soldiers are laboring whole-heartedly to improve their efficiency and to fulfill their mission."[64]

In his response, General Patrick wrote that he "was inclined to regard General Mitchell's report as a theoretical treatise on the employment of Air Power in the Pacific, which, in all probability will undoubtedly be of extreme value some ten or fifteen years hence." Patrick assured Summerall that he had "every confidence in your knowledge and appreciation of the capabilities and limitations of the Air Force of your command," and closed by noting how much more valuable to the army were those Air Service officers who had had the opportunity "to be members of your highly esteemed command."[65]

With Billy Mitchell out of the way, at least for the time being, and with the defense plan for Hawaii well under development, Summerall resumed work he had begun to improve living conditions and services for the officers and men of his command. Barracks and a new mess hall were built for the men, and small vacation cottages were added to Kilauea Military Camp, near the Kilauea Volcano on the Big Island. There enlisted men and officers could spend a week enjoying complete relaxation, the high mountain scenery, the camp's post exchange, library, and restaurant, and with a cadre in charge of the facilities, and a medical officer in residence. Children at Schofield Barracks could not attend Hawaiian schools; so, Summerall provided buildings for classrooms, and the wives of officers who had experience served as teachers. Schofield Barracks was, actually, the second largest city on Oahu, and already had impressive entertainment facilities. In February 1920, 27 movies were shown to over 4,000 people; over 5,000 soldiers participated in various athletic events; and almost 4,000 students were enrolled in education classes.[66]

Summerall promoted boxing matches between army and navy personnel, and boasted that some of the army boxers became professionals after their discharge. He formed an entire company of football players and "they did nothing but train" to play the game. During Christmas time, after the football season was over in the U.S., the navy collected its best players and sent them to Pearl Harbor to play the army team. Summerall recalled that in the last minute of the game, the army scored a touchdown and won; when he crossed the field to congratulate the afore-mentioned Admiral McDonald on his team's performance, the navy commander, as one might well surmise, turned away and would not speak to him.[67]

Summerall's concern for the loyalty of the Japanese population in Hawaii led him to establish an innovative and successful ROTC program in Honolulu at McKinley High School, where most of the student body was Japanese. Strangely enough, Summerall did not mention the program in his memoir, or in his papers, but Brian Linn quoted Summerall's memorandum to the adjutant general that described the ROTC unit at McKinley as "'eminently successful and the Japanese students showed themselves to be capable of becoming very efficient military students. There is no better way of securing the loyalty of such people than to incorporate them in our military forces with the environment of obligation to duty that cannot fail to win their allegiance in most, if not all cases. Such a course would also tend to remove the resentment the Japanese citizens now feel at the discrimination that is made against them." Linn noted that the program was very popular and became "one of the most successful programs for tapping Japanese manpower." While the program resulted in far more officers than enlisted men in Hawaiian reserve organizations, it did produce a large and growing number of Japanese American ROTC graduates for the Pacific army.[68]

During their last summer in Hawaii, the Summeralls enjoyed the company of their son, Second Lieutenant Charles P. Summerall, Jr., who had been graduated from West Point in June 1924, and spent his graduation leave enjoying the social life of the city, playing water sports, and riding with his father. Summerall's friend Clark Williams, the Wall Street financier and former head of the Red Cross during the Great War, kept him up to date on the hearings of the Congressional committee that approved the plans for the First Division monument in May 1922.[69] On 28 April 1924, the 58-ton granite shaft was put in place on the pedestal, and on 2 May, the Victory statue was hoisted to the top of the column. It faced south, overlooking a long expanse of parkland toward the Mall. The dedication of the monument was scheduled for 4 October 1924.[70]

In the meantime, the Summeralls prepared for their return to the mainland and to his new post as commanding general of VIII Corps area at Fort Sam Houston, Texas. A few days before their departure, a lengthy article in the Sunday edition of the *Honolulu Advertiser*, on 10 August 1924, reviewed Summerall's tour of duty as commander of the Hawaiian Department. It featured an impressive picture that showed the bust of the general, with his smooth, firm countenance, and with his hair closely trimmed and carefully parted in the middle. His dark eyes gazed firmly to the left, over a crisp uniform blouse that was topped by a high, stiff collar, with the white rim of the liner showing just above the top of the collar.[71] It was a picture that showed the seriousness of the man, as well as the inner force that had driven him forward since the formative years of his youth in the sandy flatlands of Florida.

The *Advertiser* credited Summerall with developing "for the first time since the Island of Oahu has been garrisoned, a really comprehensive scheme....for its defense." It praised him for completing critical construction projects at Schofield Barracks; for the high degree of efficiency of the garrison, the Air

Service and the coast artillery; for the "noticeable improvement in service athletics in Hawaii" that culminated in the victory of the army's football team over the navy's; for maintaining high standards in the army school system, in spite of a cut-off of Congressional funding; for developing ROTC units in the public schools of Hawaii; and for providing the troops with a variety of recreational activities, including a large number of bathing beaches, and the development of the Kilauea Military Camp into a unique family recreational resort. The newspaper praised his successful efforts "to further and develop a hearty spirit of mutual helpfulness between the citizens of this Territory and the member of the Hawaiian Department. He has stressed the fact that the soldiers in Hawaii are 'citizens in uniform,' and that their interests are the interests of all other citizens." It noted the assistance of soldiers and army airmen in keeping up and developing forest reserves, and in supporting community welfare, health, and relief projects, as well as in supporting local businesses by the purchase of local supplies and materials. The article stated that under Summerall, the Hawaiian Department had "placed itself in the first rank of military efficiency, and stands today a competent and alert organization on the first line of the western defense of America." It concluded by wishing him a deeply appreciative "ALOHA."[72]

The *Advertiser* article certainly confirmed Summerall's own assessment of his work in Hawaii, and its particular praise of his cooperation with the civilian community is consistent with Summerall's previous success in building cordial relationships between his commands and their civilian neighbors. He weathered well the squall that Billy Mitchell stirred up, certainly to the satisfaction of Mitchell's boss, General Patrick, and left his island command stronger and more stable than it had been when he arrived. As Summerall and Laura returned to the mainland, he could look forward to a refreshing leave and the challenges of continental commands that lay ahead.

# Chapter Fifteen

## *Home to Stay and in Command: The VIII and II Corps Areas and Chief of Staff*

In August 1924, with Summerall nearing the end of his three-year tour of duty in Hawaii, he received orders to assume command of the VIII Corps Area at Fort Sam Houston, located outside San Antonio. He noted in his memoir that praise for his work in Hawaii came from many local organizations, including the laudatory article in the *Honolulu Advertiser*. On 12 August 1924, escorts brought the Summeralls to a pier at Pearl Harbor, where a group of their friends had gathered to place leis around their necks, and bid them bon voyage.[1] As he and Laura left Hawaii, Summerall could look back on his duty as the last milestone of his service beyond the secure borders of his country; he never again would serve, or even travel, outside the continental U.S.

The Summeralls sailed on an army transport and arrived a few days later in San Francisco to an enthusiastic welcome, which included members of the city council and prominent local citizens, as well as a "committee of ladies" that brought a bouquet of flowers for Laura. They were escorted to the Fairmont Hotel, where "a beautiful suite" had been reserved for them. During their brief stay, he made several talks to various civic organizations and noted in his memoir that he lamented to these audiences the reduction in the army's strength to a skeleton force of 118,000 men, and warned "of the heavy armament of Japan and the danger to the Pacific." This warning reflected the concerns that he had justifiably laid out in his plan for the defense of Hawaii. But a similar signal about the "heavy arming of the dictators"[2] in Europe was based on faulty hindsight that again failed to consider the fact that "the dictators" were not in power in 1924. Adolf Hitler was in prison in Germany; in the Soviet Union Lenin had died and Joseph Stalin was scheming to secure his power over the Communist Party and the sprawling expanse of the USSR; General Francisco Franco was leading Spanish forces in Morocco against the Rif rebellion; and Benito Mussolini had not yet established control over the Italian government and people.

After the Summeralls' festive reception in San Francisco, he and Laura enjoyed a few weeks on vacation in Santa Barbara, where they stayed with friends. He had received notice that the First Division Monument would be dedicated on 4 October and used the time in Santa Barbara to prepare the speech that he would give at the ceremony. Young Charles had joined his parents, and he and his mother preceded Summerall on the trip to Washington. Second Lieutenant Summerall had been ordered to report on 30 September to Fort Hoyle, Maryland, to join the 6th Artillery Regiment of the First Division, the latter the command which his father had prized above all others, and to which, of course, the Victory monument had been dedicated. His father followed a few days later, after tending to the final details of his assumption of command of the VIII Corps area.[3]

The dedication ceremony and the unveiling of the monument were scheduled for Saturday, 4 October 1924, the anniversary date of the First Division's entry into the Meuse-Argonne battle. From

Hawaii, Summerall had authorized General Frank Parker, who was first vice president of the First Division Society, to act for him in all matters pertaining to the memorial. Parker had worked closely with the First Division Memorial Association in planning for the dedication.[4] It began at 0945 hours, with a parade of the First Division, including many of its veterans, from Pennsylvania Avenue near the Capitol, moving westward to the monument. Summerall served as grand marshal, leading the parade, and Parker followed him. Next, came the massed bands of the division, and behind them marched a composite regiment of infantry from the 16th and 18th Regiments that were stationed near New York City. Thousands of spectators watched the procession, and more than 6,000 veterans and guests attended the ceremony. They were seated on the lawn on the south side of the monument, gazing up at the monument, with its base covered with white drapery and wrapped with a woven band supporting a laurel wreath. Flowers practically enveloped the dais that covered the terrace around the monument. General Parker presided, and the massed bands began the ceremonies by playing *America*. Colonel Adolphe H. Huguet, chairman of the memorial association's executive committee, gave the first speech, describing the monument and its history.[5] Parker then read a letter from General Pershing, in which he expressed deep regrets at being unable to attend, and wrote that "my heart is with you in these services, as the ties that bind me to that division are eternal."[6] Summerall spoke next, praising the "unconquerable spirit" of the division, and noted that "There was mutual confidence and comradeship in all ranks and elements, and it attained to the highest ideal of a fighting command." He praised Pershing as their "greatest leader" and quoted the commander in chief's famous praise of the division.[7] Predictably, Summerall omitted in his memoir this glowing reference to Pershing. He also did not mention Pershing's letter that expressed his regrets at not being able to attend, and his feelings of everlasting solidarity with the division.

President Coolidge arrived on the dais just after Summerall's speech, welcomed by a presidential salute fired by Lieutenant Summerall's Battery C of the 6th Artillery. Private First Class Daniel R. Edwards, who had received the Medal of Honor, released the drapery, and, as everyone stood and saluted, he exclaimed, "May we be worthy of them."[8] Battery C then fired a ceremonial cannon, and President Coolidge rose and delivered the dedication address. He used the occasion to appeal to the survivors to defend the Constitution at all times, and pledged himself to the treaties and covenants against war, and to the efforts to secure further disarmament. He traced the history of the division, reviewing its achievements at Cantigny, Soissons, St. Mihiel, and the Meuse-Argonne. He praised the Veterans Act of 1924, which had established the Veterans Bureau and provided over $40,000,000 for the building of 31 hospitals to care for the 25,000 to 30,000 disabled veterans of all wars. He noted that Germany and the Allies had recently adopted the Dawes Plan. He said that the American government was the "architect" of the plan that would help stabilize the German economy and currency, by rescheduling reparation payments and providing Germany with foreign loans. The president concluded that, as a result, "we shall have the satisfaction of knowing that we have done what we could to dispel the hatreds of war, restore the destruction it has wrought, and lay a firmer foundation for industrial prosperity and a more secure peace."[9] Not surprisingly, Coolidge said nothing about increasing the shrunken budget of the War Department. Apparently, and quite likely to the dismay of the generals who heard and read his words, he believed that economic strength through industrial development and prosperity among the nations of Europe and in this country would displace the risk of war.

Following the president's remarks, the benediction was given by the reverend Dr. Murray Bartlett, who had been the representative of the YMCA with the First Division in France. The massed bands of the division closed the day's ceremony with the playing of the national anthem. The dedication ceremonies concluded the following Sunday morning with a pilgrimage to the Tomb of the Unknown Soldier at Arlington National Cemetery.[10]

*General Summerall addressing reunion of First Division Veterans at First Division Monument*

Courtesy United Press International

The Summeralls left Washington that same afternoon, arriving in San Antonio at dawn on 6 October, after a long and tiring train ride. They were met at the station by Brigadier General Preston Brown, who had served as chief of staff under General Lejeune's command of the Second Division in the war and also as Summerall's chief of staff when he commanded IV Corps in Germany after the war. Brown commanded the Second Division, which was based at Fort Sam Houston, under the command of Summerall's VIII Corps Area. His new commander regarded Brown as "one of the most efficient officers in the army," and one his close friends. Brown escorted the Summeralls to their quarters at Fort Sam Houston, where they settled in, and soon afterwards hosted a reception for Brown's officers and their wives. It was the beginning of a very active and attractive social life on post and in San Antonio.[11]

Meanwhile, in Summerall's home state of Florida, the state legislature had approved a bill to finance the purchase of a small tract of land adjacent to the Dora Canal in the town of Tavares, the county seat of Lake County, and turn over the deed to the American Legion Post for a World War memorial park. The legionaries decided to name the park in honor of a son of an Astatula grocer and Lake County's most famous military commander, Major General Charles P. Summerall. The centerpiece of Summerall Park was a bronze statue of a doughboy on a marble pedestal, thrusting his rifle with fixed bayonet from the hip, and leaning forward as he advances in full stride up an inclined, rough-hewed block of granite. The unveiling of the statue and dedication ceremonies were scheduled for Armistice Day, 11 November 1924. Summerall was invited to deliver the dedication address as the guest of honor. As he stepped from his car to make his way to the rostrum to speak to "the largest crowd ever gathered in Lake County...his feet never touched the ground. He walked on a path of roses scattered by the school children of Lake County. It was a wonderful sight and showed the great popularity of the General in the section [of the state] where he had taught school before entering West Point." After his speech, Summerall reviewed a parade that was followed by a barbecue, a football and a basketball game, boat races, and a dance at the Lake County Country Club in nearby Eustis.[12] Eighty-two-year-old Chester Treadway was seven years old when the statue was dedicated and remembers that "I was somewhat awed by the general." Four years later, Summerall returned to Lake County for a short visit. He met the commander of the local American Legion post at the park and expressed his appreciation, noting that "I am profoundly grateful to Lake County for this tribute to me." Mrs. Sue Nunes never met Summerall, but she said that "From everything I've read about him, he's probably one of the greatest men from Lake County."[13]

Summerall returned to Fort Sam Houston and his command of the VIII Corps Area that included some 28 posts in the states of Texas, Colorado, Oklahoma, Arizona, New Mexico, and Wyoming. He anticipated a short stay of only three months at his new post since, as he noted in his memoir, "It was understood that I would succeed General Bullard in command of the 2nd Corps Area with headquarters at Governors Island, N. Y., when he retired in January 1925." Nevertheless, he made an inspection of all of the installations under his command and found the soldiers and conditions "in a high state of efficiency," with the exception of one post where he found a lack of heating stoves in the officer's quarters.[14]

The most significant and notable event during Summerall's brief but busy time in the VIII Corps Area centered around the final illness and death of Samuel Gompers, the organizer and long-serving president of the American Federation of Labor (AFL). Gompers had been born in London in 1850 and had immigrated with his parents at the age of 13. He began work as a cigar maker in New York City and joined a labor union, becoming its leader in 1875. He helped organize the AFL, becoming its president in 1896. He built the organization into a powerful force in support of an eight-hour working day, and greater involvement in political campaigns to secure the rights of labor to organize and engage in economic action.[15] Summerall believed that Gompers had been responsible for the railroad strike in 1894 that had involved the then Lieutenant Summerall in violence that broke out in California. As a result, Summerall noted that Gompers "had been deeply prejudiced against him."[16] The labor leader and his organization supported the election of Woodrow Wilson, and during Wilson's administration the AFL gained many of their objectives. During the war, Wilson named Gompers to the Council of National Defense, and he helped mobilize labor's support for the war. At the end of the war, the president appointed Gompers to the Commission on International Labor Legislation at the Versailles Peace Conference, where he helped to create the International Labor Organization.[17] Summerall gave Gompers great credit for his work during the war, and even "considered that he had somewhat redeemed himself."[18]

In early December, the elderly and ailing president of the AFL collapsed in Mexico City, where he and other officials of the organization had gone to attend a pan-American labor congress. Gompers was rushed by train to San Antonio and hospitalized, but died on the morning of 13 December.[19] Summerall sent General Brown to offer his condolences and any assistance and was surprised when Gompers' colleagues requested a military funeral. Brown pointed out that army regulations did not authorize a funeral for a civilian, but Summerall wrote that he would take full responsibility and instructed Brown to make the necessary arrangements. He wrote that he regarded the officials' request as "an opportunity for the Army to remove some of the hostility towards it by organized labor." A large military escort accompanied Gompers' body on a specially built catafalque to the train station, while soldiers from the Second Division lined both sides of the street, and division bands played funeral marches.[20] The *New York Times* reported that Texans filled the car carrying his body with flowers. Summerall traveled with the labor officials on the journey to Washington. He noted that an honor guard met their train at every station where soldiers were stationed nearby. At stops along the way, the lid of the casket was raised, and "Even after dark, large crowds were found at every station, bent on entering the train and obtaining a final look at the famous leader."[21]

On 16 December, a military honor guard met the train as it pulled into Union Station and escorted the casket to the Federation of Labor Building. It was placed in a flower-banked room, where Gompers' body lay in state until that night, when it was placed on board a train for New York. Early the next morning, the train arrived at Pennsylvania Station. The casket was placed on a military caisson draped with an American flag and drawn by six horses. A military honor guard, and an Honor Committee of over a hundred labor officials, escorted his body to the Elks Club, where it lay in state prior to the funeral there the next day. Mayor James J. Hylan ordered all municipal flags to be flown at half-mast during the funeral. Rabbi Stephen Wise officiated, and the eulogy was delivered by James Duncan, Gompers' successor as AFL president and his long-time friend. Senior AFL officials served as pallbearers; honorary pallbearers included Secretary of State Charles M. Hughes; former President William Howard Taft, Chief Justice of the U.S. Supreme Court; Governor Alfred E. Smith of New York; General Bullard, commander of the II Corps Area; Admiral Charles P. Plunkett, commandant, New York Navy Yard and the 3rd Naval District; Mayor Hylan; state and federal governmental officials, and labor leaders from across the country. After the service, the casket was escorted by a guard of honor to Pennsylvania Station and taken to Tarrytown, New York. After military salutes were fired and an army bugler sounded taps, Gompers was buried in Sleepy Hollow Cemetery. The *Times* viewed the funeral as an "acknowledgement of Mr. Gompers' friendship of men in all walks of life," and an event that "emphasized his pride in his American citizenship as the distinguishing mark of his life."[22] Summerall believed that the presence of the military, as well as the military rituals that were such a visible part of the funeral services, were of incalculable value to maintaining good relations between the army and organized labor. "During the rest of my service," he wrote, "labor officials were friendly to me and to the Army."²³

After returning to Fort Sam Houston, Summerall relinquished his command of the VIII Corps Area. He and Laura left for New York City on 11 January 1925, where he would take command of the II Corps Area, with headquarters at Fort Jay on Governor's Island in New York Harbor. With a golf course, well-manicured grounds, boating facilities, athletic playing fields, officers' quarters, office buildings, and barracks, Fort Jay was an attractive and comfortable post. The Summeralls settled into their spacious quarters in an old colonial mansion at Fort Jay that Laura outfitted with new furniture and carpets she purchased with money from an inheritance.²⁴

Summerall assumed command from General Bullard, one of his closest friends and admirers, and, of course, his long-ago mentor in the Philippines, as well as his predecessor as commander of the First Division in the war. After a number of ceremonial affairs, Bullard was honored at a large banquet at the Hotel Astor on 14 January. Members of the city's social elite, representatives of patriotic

*Bullard and Summerall, Governor's Island, 1925*
Courtesy United Press International

and veterans' groups, as well as army and National Guard officers, all joined in praise of Bullard and his achievements in more than 40 years of military service, and Summerall wrote that he "tried to pay suitable tribute to him." The *New York Times* printed a full-page article that described his long and successful service in the army, noting that "Since the war, few officers of the army have been better known in New York than General Bullard. His presence has been familiar at military gatherings in the city, and his humorous speeches have been widely appreciated."

On 16 January, as a band played *Auld Lang Syne*, Bullard left his quarters at Fort Jay, passed by a line of infantry with arms at "present," and stepped aboard a ferry that would take him to Manhattan, where he would live in retirement at the Hotel Wellington.²⁵ In 1925, Doubleday and Company published his memoirs, *Personalities and Reminiscences of the War*, and he became a vigorous advocate for rapid rearmament and modernization of military equipment as president of the National Security League. In one final tribute to his old friend (as noted previously), Summerall used his influence as army chief of staff to persuade Congress to restore Bullard and every other retired officer to their World War rank. Bullard died in September 1947, just over six months after his 86th birthday, and was buried in the post cemetery at West Point.²⁶

Summerall's new command included the First Division at Fort Dix and the coast artillery units of the Second Coast Artillery District. As provided by the National Defense Act of 1920, he was the patron of the National Guard organizations of New York, New Jersey, and Delaware, and was required to visit drills and summer camp for these units. Headquarters of the II Corps Area was also responsible for the citizen military training camp that was held every summer at Plattsburg, the college ROTC units in the area, and for supervising reserve officers who had received their commission after the war through the ROTC or citizen military training camps. In addition to these supervising duties, Summerall, like Bullard, also was charged with building public support for the military and encouraging the public's interest in military matters.[27] It was a task in which Bullard had had success, as the *Times* had reported, and one in which Summerall had excelled in the past. It gave him the opportunity to engage in civic and social activities, as well as in ceremonial occasions, in what he referred to in his memoirs as "the most important command in the Army."[28]

In one of his first trips from headquarters, he visited the governors of New York, New Jersey, and Delaware, and followed that journey with an inspection tour of all the posts in the three states. He wrote about being the dinner guest of the Chamber of Commerce in Albany, where he spoke with his "close friend," Governor Al Smith, who invited him after dinner to the executive mansion. He sat alone with Smith that night, except for the presence of the head of the state police, and waited with him until midnight, when the deadline passed for the governor to stop executions at Sing Sing Prison. In 1928, Smith won the nomination of the Democratic Party for president, and Summerall noted that the governor, known on the campaign trail as "The Happy Warrior," had told him that if elected, he would make Summerall secretary of war. Summerall wrote that he regarded Smith as "one of the ablest men I ever knew."[29]

The Summeralls maintained a "constant" social schedule, and, as he noted, generally went out to dinner or entertained at home. Summerall was made an honorary member of all the New York City clubs, and spoke at their meetings and at civic ceremonies. In his addresses to chamber of commerce meetings, Summerall wrote that he stressed the need to integrate interstate commerce into war plans, as well as the necessity of linking industrial development to national defense. He emphasized that if the country ever went to war again, everything and everyone, not just the soldiers, should be involved. When someone asked him if that included the people's money, Summerall answered that it did, and, at any rate, the money was less important than the lives of the men who fought. He became acquainted with the Rockefellers; with Judge Elbert H. Gary, president of the Iron and Steel Institute; with James Russell Lowell, president of Harvard University; and with Patrick E. Crowley, president of the New York Central Railroad. He was the featured speaker at a convention of the Grand Army of the Republic, where he met a small group of survivors of the Civil War, all of whom subsequently died during his stay at Fort Jay. He spoke at the dedication of a statue to General William T. Sherman in the Hall of Fame at New York University. The Summeralls became good friends with Edward Bowes, the Broadway conductor, composer, and arranger, who later achieved fame as the creator and host of the popular radio talent show *Major Bowes Original Amateur Hour*. They were also fond of his wife, the well-known and distinguished actress Margaret Illington, who, as Summerall noted, "brought us beautiful presents when she returned from abroad."[30]

As a good-will ambassador for the army, Summerall attended large public events like state fairs and visited towns close to the army posts in the II Corps Area, where he spoke to local organizations and was often entertained by local officials. A trip to inspect a fire that erupted at the naval ammunition depot at Lake Denmark, New Jersey, almost became the last journey of Summerall's life. Secretary of War Dwight F. Davis and his party came up from Washington and joined Summerall and his aides before they all rushed down to the scene. An army ammunition storage area, at the adjacent Picatinny Arsenal, containing rifle cartridges, grenades, depth charges, and torpedoes was within 1,000 feet of the navy depot. As Davis, Summerall, and their aides approached the fire, flames ignited the army munitions, and shells exploded intermittently, forcing the men to seek shelter where they could find it. They escaped harm, but the fire and explosions demolished officers' quarters and barracks, as well as a number of civilian houses across the road from the arsenal. A civilian employee was killed when a burning garage collapsed on him before he could escape, but there were no other casualties. Damages totaled over $3,000,000. After returning with Summerall to New York, Davis left for the capital, where he initiated an investigation into the causes of the fire, after making a preliminary announcement that a new policy of keeping arsenal buildings isolated and apart from other structures would be necessary.[31]

Meanwhile, from his safe headquarters at Fort Jay, Summerall continued his rapprochement with organized labor by offering the use of Fort Hamilton (where, as a young lieutenant, he first learned of the sinking of the battleship *Maine* in Havana Harbor), for Labor Day gatherings, and noted that he spoke at their meeting on Labor Day, 1925. Nevertheless, in spite of improved relations with the AFL, he asserted that many labor leaders remained "opposed to any military policy and regarded the Army as an enemy."[32] Indeed, the *Times* reported that there had been considerable criticism of military training camps at labor conventions, because the camps "tended to influence youth on a 'militaristic' trend."[33]

Secretary Davis acted to assuage these sentiments by inviting William Green, Samuel Gompers' successor as president of the AFL, and seven members of his executive council to Plattsburg to inspect the Civilian Military Training Camp. In mid-August 1926, Summerall escorted Green and his party, standing with them on the reviewing stand at the parade ground, as 1,600 student infantrymen passed in review in honor of the labor leaders. Much impressed with his reception, and the colorful parade his party had seen, Green responded with enthusiastic praise for the training camp and said that "there has been a wrong impression prevailing in some quarters as to the work, training, purposes and objectives of the military training camps. I think the American Federation of Labor through its organizations and officers can do much to acquaint the public mind with what General Summerall and his officers are doing toward the development of young men mentally, morally, and physically....We promise you we will go out and tell the people of what we have learned."[34] Summerall stated that "From that moment, the American Federation of Labor was a friend to the Army. We had no more opposition." He wrote that "Mr. Green never failed to send me a handsome Christmas card," and that the Summeralls included him in "at least one of our dinners afterwards in Washington."[35]

Under Green's leadership, the AFL won the right to bargain collectively and celebrated the passage of the Labor Standards Act of 1938, the first federal law that established the 40-hour week for all workers. When the Korean War broke out in 1950, President Truman appointed the labor leader to the National Committee on Mobilization.[36] It was, obviously, a politically sound choice. It was also a logical choice, due, in part, to Secretary Davis's and Summerall's success a generation earlier in winning Green's support for military training and preparedness. Undoubtedly, the cordial relationship with Green that Summerall would later cultivate during his term as army chief of staff helped to sustain the labor leader's backing for the military.

Toward the end of Summerall's first year as VIII Corps Area commander, in a far less cordial atmosphere than he would ever encounter in and around New York, his path and sword again crossed with those of Billy Mitchell. Since his return from his Asian tour and after submitting his report critical of Hawaii's air defenses, Mitchell had continued to promote air power in letters, articles, books, speeches and in numerous public addresses. In 1921 and 1923, Mitchell demonstrated air power's potential when his planes bombed two obsolete battleships that floated motionless and unarmed off the Virginia capes. Skeptics pointed out just how vulnerable were the vessels, but Mitchell's demonstration was still impressive. In 1923, a board headed by Major General William Lassiter, whom Pershing had considered before naming Summerall to command the 1st Artillery Brigade of the First Division, advised the War Department to proceed with caution in developing a separate air force. He urged that pilot strength, organization, and an expansible aviation industry needed to be developed in order to sustain an air force that could support ground forces and attack areas remote from those forces. Nevertheless, Mitchell widened his attacks on aviation policy and continued his criticism of aviation organization and equipment before Congressional committees, as well as in newspaper interviews and in numerous public addresses.[37]

On 2 September 1925, the USS *Shenandoah*, the navy's second rigid airship, broke apart and crashed in Ohio after encountering severe weather, killing 14 crewmen, as well as the captain. Reporters asked Mitchell for his reaction, and he stated that the accident was "the result of the incompetency, the criminal negligence, and the almost treasonable negligence of our national defense by the Navy and War Departments."[38] Four days later he called back the reporters and announced that he wanted every American to know "that we are going to better our National Defense, that we are on the warpath and that we are going to stay there until these conditions are remedied."[39] President Coolidge and the War Department had heard enough. The president attacked Mitchell in a speech in Omaha, and, after conducting an investigation, Secretary Davis announced the decision to court-martial Mitchell. He appointed Summerall as president of a court-martial board to try Mitchell on eight charges related to the Ninety-Six Articles of War, especially "conduct prejudicial to good order and military discipline" and "conduct of a nature to bring discredit upon the military service."[40]

The court-martial of Billy Mitchell began in Washington on 25 October 1925, in a room in an old, red brick building that was used as a warehouse to store old army desks, swivel chairs, and bookcases. In addition to Summerall, the court included five other major generals: Robert L. Howze, Douglas MacArthur, Fred W. Sladen, Benjamin Poore, and William S. Graves; as well as six brigadier generals: Albert L. Bowley, Edward K. King, Frank R. McCoy, Edwin B. Winans, George Le R. Irwin, and Ewing E. Booth. All six major generals had held division commands in the World War, and Graves had led the AEF contingent in Siberia during the Allied intervention in the Russian Civil War. The brigadier generals had been combat commanders during the war, and all held important commands in the peacetime army. The *New York Times* called the court the "most impressive ever assembled in the history of the United States Army."[41]

Mitchell's wife and the widow of the captain who had been killed in the *Shenandoah* accident, as well as 40 reporters, were among the audience of about 100 seated in the packed courtroom. The trial opened with the introduction of Mitchell's lead counsel, Congressman Frank Reid of Illinois, and his assistant, army Colonel Herbert H. White. Reid at once challenged Bowley's right to sit on the court because he had recently criticized Mitchell's advocacy of an independent air service, and was thus prejudiced and biased against his client. The jurors retired, and returned shortly to excuse Bowley.[42]

Congressman Reid then looked directly at Summerall and announced Mitchell's challenge to the general's right to be on the court and to serve as president. The *New York Times* stated that Reid mounted an attack on Summerall that "bristled with bitterness." Referring to a seven-page statement that Mitchell had prepared, Reid told the court that two years ago Mitchell had reported to the War Department that under Summerall's command of the Hawaiian Department, "the Air Force..., and the whole system of defense was inefficiently handled, badly organized, and that ignorance of its application was manifested by his staff. This handling and administration of these defenses would lead to certain defeat in case of war." He added that when Summerall responded to Mitchell's charges in a letter to General Patrick, the Chief of the Air Service, he "sidestepped them," and instead of taking remedial measures, he dismissed Mitchell's report for its "superficial impressions and academic discussions." Concluding his "attack on the fairness of General Summerall," Reid asserted that Mitchell believed that Summerall was "prejudiced in this case and should not be allowed to sit as a member of this courtmartial."[43]

The *Times* noted that Reid's attack had taken Summerall "apparently...completely by surprise," but, as he rose to his feet to respond, his "eyes blazed with indignation," and "his flushed face showed the deep resentment that he felt over the form which the challenge had taken." Summerall then declared that

> Until this moment, I did not know of the bitter personal hostility entertained for me by the accused. The extracts read from Colonel Mitchell's report on the Hawaiian Air Service of 1923 are probably correct. However, I had not thought that the report was made with hostile intent and I learn now for the first time that the report was personally hostile to me. I did not think there was hostility behind the report and therefore entertained no enmity toward Colonel Mitchell, although the report was untrue, unfair and ignorant.

In the same article, the *Times* reporter wrote that Summerall turned to his colleagues on the court and

> announced in a voice that carried to all parts of the room that under no circumstances would he continue to be a member of the court. The court, retiring for a moment, returned and formally announced that its President was excused. General Summerall was quoted as saying after he left the courtroom that had it been necessary in order to get off the court he would have appealed direct to the Secretary of War and the President.[44]

Historian Burke Davis wrote in *The Billy Mitchell Affair* that after Summerall had left the courtroom, he turned to a group of reporters who had followed him, and told them that "I have kept an open mind on Mitchell's case. I took him into my home as a friend when he came to Honolulu. I placed a private car at his disposal. I loaned him an airplane. Only ten minutes before court convened, I shook hands with him. Now it's all over. We're enemies Mitchell and I."[45] Back inside the courtroom, General Howze replaced Summerall as president, and Congressman Reid immediately challenged General Sladen, without citing a reason, as was Mitchell's privilege under military law. Sladen was also excused, but unlike Summerall, appeared not at all disconcerted. "In fact," as the *Times* reported, "he looked as if he welcomed the chance to get off the court."[46]

Mitchell's trial lasted over seven weeks. Three days before the verdict was reached, the *Times* reported that Summerall was called as a witness, and questioned by Congressman Reid whether he had stated to newspapermen that he and Mitchell were enemies. Summerall replied that he had no recollection of ever making such a statement, and that he was certain that he never did. Reid then asked: "Are you now friendly toward the accused?" Summerall replied: "I am indifferent toward the accused."[47] Outside the courtroom, in a parting gesture of conciliation and recognition of Mitchell's achievements, Summerall called him one of that "damned kind of soldier who's wonderful in war and terrible in peace."[48]

Summerall's recollection in his memoir of his confrontation with Mitchell at his court-martial was brief and tinged with bitterness that came from his flawed memory. Rather than recalling his balanced judgment of Mitchell as a soldier, he incorrectly stated that Mitchell had reported to the War Department that "I had no war plans [for the Hawaiian Department]." Perhaps he correctly wrote that "I had no recollection of his making a report." But having recalled many of the details of his own war plan, he should have made certain that he recorded accurately and fairly the only detailed and significant critique of those plans.[49] Indeed, Mitchell had reported that Summerall's plan lacked specific unit plans for the Air Service, but he had not stated that no war plan existed.

On 17 December 1925, the court-martial of Billy Mitchell ended with a verdict of guilty on all eight charges. He was suspended from rank, command, and duty, with the forfeiture of all pay and allowances for five years. President Coolidge approved the findings and sentence of the court-martial judges on 26 January 1926, and Mitchell resigned from the army on 1 February. Ten years later, at age 56, he died in New York City of complications from pneumonia and was buried in his home state of Wisconsin, in Milwaukee's Forest Home Cemetery. In 1946, Congress passed an act that awarded a special Medal of Honor to Mitchell. It was not the Congressional Medal of Honor, but a special award that Congress authorized.[50] The next year, the U.S. Air Force was created as a separate branch of the military, a goal that Mitchell had struggled to achieve. But, as Russell Weigley wrote, Mitchell's theories in the 1920s "were utterly disproportionate to the military aircraft available," and "World War II did not vindicate his prophecies about the decisiveness of air power in the next war."[51]

The last nine months of 1926 turned out to be much more enjoyable for Summerall than the preceding months of unpleasantness during the Mitchell court-martial. The management of the Metropolitan Opera had placed at his disposal a box and a number of seats, so he and Laura, as well as officers and their wives whom the Summeralls invited, continued their enjoyment of the Met's superb productions. In September, beaming in admiration for General Pershing, he walked up the gangway of the *Leviathan* to greet his former commander in chief, whom he still regarded as a mentor and great friend. General Pershing was the chairman of the American Battle Monuments Commission and had just returned home after three months in France. He had led the commission on battlefield tours and inspections of the cemeteries that contained about 30,000 American soldiers who had died in the World War. The commission determined the character of the monuments that would be erected in France, and published in 1927 *A Guide to the American Battle Fields in Europe* to commemorate the 10th anniversary of the U.S. entry into the war. Summerall escorted Pershing down the gangway to the pier, and, as the crowd gave "three ringing cheers," the former commander in chief "gave one of his rare smiles as he raised his derby hat and bowed in acknowledgment."[52] Summerall must have been smiling as well, as he and Pershing stepped into a waiting limousine that drove them to a reception at the Waldorf-Astoria Hotel, but predictably, he did not mention this happy occasion in his memoir.

In September, the Summeralls celebrated an even more joyous occasion: the marriage of their son Charles to Willis Julia Potter Reeder, daughter of Colonel and Mrs. Russell Potter Reeder. They were married at the post chapel at Fort Monroe, Virginia. The *New York Times* wrote that "The assembly was brilliant, with army and navy uniforms and the chapel was a bower of cut flowers, ferns, and growing plants." Summerall wrote that he and Laura were entertained by the post commander, Brigadier General Robert E. Callan, West Point class of 1896, an old friend and Coast Artillery officer, and his wife, and found the ceremony and reception at the officer's club to be "perfect."[53] With affection and graciousness, he noted that "It was a happy beginning of a happy life for [Charles and Julia] and for us in them. We did not lose our precious son, but we gained a darling daughter."[54]

On 7 September 1926, the *New York Times* reported that Summerall headed the list of major generals who were in line to succeed General Hines in the "blue-ribbon post" as army chief of staff.[55] Summerall was the senior major general of the line in the army, and, as noted previously, had worked smoothly with Secretary of War Davis in establishing a constructive relationship with AFL president Green. In addition, President Coolidge and Summerall not only had shared the rostrum at the dedication of the First Division monument, but, more importantly, held common feelings about Billy Mitchell and the outcome of his court-martial. Perhaps the president was impressed as well, not only with Summerall's strong leadership, but also his skillful handling of relations with the public and public officials.

Secretary Davis made the announcement on 21 September 1926 that Summerall would be the next chief of staff of the army, and on 2 October, the *Army and Navy Journal* published a digest of comments in the press under the headline "General Summerall's Appointment Wins Nation-Wide Approval."

The *Chicago Tribune* called him "the man for the place"; the Hearst papers wrote that "No man now in active service has seen more fighting than he, or has carried greater responsibilities"; the *New York Times* wrote that "No staff officer knows the army better than he,"' and noted that Summerall always had enjoyed "the good will of representative citizens"; the *Washington Star* stated that "there'll be general agreement that Summerall's selection is supremely excellent", and that "General Summerall has specialized in cementing the relations between the Army and the civilian population."[56] In his memoir, Summerall wrote that "my dear wife and I were deeply gratified" by the appointment, and that they were pleased by the complimentary newspaper editorials and letters they received from old friends.[57] Among those congratulatory letters was one from Major George Patton, who was stationed at the time at Schofield Barracks, Hawaii. In reply, Summerall wrote that "It has been one of my peculiar privileges to serve with you under varying circumstances and difficulties, and I have always felt the most sincere appreciation of your loyalty and admiration for your efficiency."[58]

When Summerall relinquished his command of the II Corps at Fort Jay on 20 November, his departure was much like General Bullard's almost two years earlier. With bayonets fixed and rifles at "present arms," the men of the 16th Infantry of the First Division formed a lane through which their departing commander walked to the ferry dock at Governor's Island. Summerall paused at the dock and thanked the men of his command for their loyal support and told them how fortunate he had been to command this "band of brothers." The band of the 16th Infantry played *Auld Lang Syne*, as Summerall stepped aboard the ferry that took him to Manhattan, and to a farewell dinner at the Waldorf-Astoria. It was a gala affair, with General Bullard presiding, and with speeches by Henry L. Stimson, Secretary of War under President William Howard Taft, and S. Stanwood Menken, Chairman of the Board of Directors of the National Security League. As noted earlier, Bullard served as president of the League, an organization that advocated conservative economic and political ideas, as well as compulsory military training in public schools. Sharing the dais was Summerall's and the army's friend, AFL President William Green, who also delivered a brief address. Green's speech was followed by remarks from actress Marie Dressler, the outspoken president of the Chorus Equity Association, a union that was the precursor of Actors Equity. In his address, Summerall predictably urged that the nation be prepared for war, not by "militarizing the country, but by citizenizing the military forces"; in other words, by making sure that the Regular Army had strong and well-trained citizen soldiers ready to join them to protect and defend the country.[59] It was a goal that would guide his work as chief of staff.

Summerall assumed his new duties on 21 November, and after he and Laura spent a few nights as guests in the new home of his former wartime aide A. B. Butler and his wife, they moved into the spacious quarters of the chief of staff, located near the crest of a hill at Fort Myer, Virginia. Under Summerall's direction, the War Department General Staff was responsible for recruiting, organizing, supplying, equipping, mobilizing, and training the army. He served at the pleasure of the president and the secretary of war, and acted as their agent. He also shared authority with the War Department bureau chiefs, who, as previously noted, dispensed most of the army's appropriations.

As historian and archivist Timothy K. Nenninger has noted, the army that Summerall led had been shaped by forces that he really could not control or change. The postwar "fetish" for economy in government, and the "dream" that wars had ended for all time, led to decreases in the size of the Regular Army to levels far below the goals of the National Defense Act of 1920, and to reduced appropriations for new weapons or major pieces of equipment, as well as for the maintenance and construction of barracks and quarters. The Congressional budget axe forced the National Guard to reduce its numbers to less than half of the 435,000-man force envisioned in 1920, and also prevented the reserves and the Regular Army from holding large scale maneuvers and field exercises. In 1924 and 1925,

*Secretary of War Dwight F. Davis (who also founded the Davis Cup international tennis competition) is in the center, flanked on his left by retiring army chief of staff Maj. Gen. John L. Hines, and on his right by Summerall, the army's new chief of staff*

Courtesy United Press International

scattered protests by students on college and university campuses across the country where ROTC were located disrupted training and instruction, and resulted in the abolition of the program at one state university. To Summerall, these developments were the result of "rampant" pacifism. He also found that the army's morale was low, and Nenninger concluded that "By the end of 1926 the Army had probably reached the nadir of its interwar existence....and readiness was virtually nonexistent." The Kellogg-Briand Pact that was signed in 1928 by 62 nations agreed not to use war as an instrument of national policy, seemed to embody American public opinion toward war and the military. All of these issues and developments led Summerall to focus his considerable energies on internal army issues and problems.[60]

As mentioned previously, Summerall had been concerned about the quality of life for enlisted men on his posts in Hawaii, Fort Sam Houston, and Fort Jay. He felt that their greatest needs had been for adequate housing and rations, followed by the lack of social and recreational facilities. On subsequent visits to other army posts he found families living in bachelors' quarters with no places to cook, and soldiers housed in flimsy, wartime barracks and remodeled warehouses with leaking roofs. Plumbing was out of repair, and water contamination was a frequent problem. The surgeon general reported that the daily ration allowance was not sufficient to provide soldiers with a properly varied diet. Clear evidence of the decline in morale that Summerall noted was an increase in the desertion rate to 7.39 percent of the total enlisted strength of the army in 1925, and the rising number of discharged men who did not reenlist.[61]

Summerall noted in his memoir that his most urgent duty was to familiarize himself with the army budget. He concluded that the budget was too small to take care of the appalling conditions that soldiers and their families had to endure, and he determined to "make an issue of the problem," as historian Nenninger noted, "in the War Department, with Congress, and with the public."[62] During an inspection tour of army posts on the West Coast, Summerall was invited to address a Chamber of Commerce luncheon on 11 October in San Diego. He listened as the mayor criticized the government for the "shameful way" the army housed the cavalry that protected the border with Mexico. Summerall agreed and said that such conditions existed throughout the country. He stated that the army was a mere skeleton, and living "like immigrants or like prisoners of war, instead of soldiers of the United States." He affirmed that the "housing situation in the army is a disgrace," and said that "until the Administration is aroused to the real need, nothing can be done and we shall continue to perish by fast degrees."[63] The next morning, Summerall received a telegram from Secretary Davis ordering him to return to Washington and report to the president. Assuming that his remarks had been reported to Coolidge, Summerall cancelled the rest of his inspection tour and left for the capital, expecting that he "would be relieved as Chief of Staff. I had no regret," he wrote, "and was willing to be sacrificed in such a cause."[64]

Summerall arrived amid speculation that the president not only would relieve him, but also Secretary Davis as well. He also found that "the papers were full of [reports about] the incident and vigorously defended me, demanding that conditions be improved."[65] Indeed, newspaper investigations, as well as studies undertaken by the House Committee on Military Affairs and various subcommittees, supported Summerall's assessment of housing conditions. In addition, Summerall ordered the G-4 Section (Supply) to prepare a report for Secretary Davis, and it outlined the facts about army housing. Also included in the report were examples of savings that Summerall had achieved on army posts, while managing to improve living conditions at the same time. In addition, in his San Diego speech Summerall had supported the president's policies aimed at greater economy and efficiency in government.[66] Nevertheless, he was worried when he entered the Oval Office and had prepared a statement for the president that assured Coolidge of his loyalty. Thus, he was pleased and reassured when the president "rose to meet me and shook hands cordially. Even his pet dog came and was very friendly." Reflecting, perhaps, on his respect for Summerall's judgment as well as the facts regarding army housing condition, the president then said, as Summerall recalled, "Well, General, the papers seemed to have exaggerated what you said in San Diego." They continued to talk for several minutes "in a friendly way," and the president said that he would support efforts to improve housing.[67] One week after Summerall's speech, the press reported that President Coolidge was satisfied that Summerall had been misquoted, and regarded the matter settled. Subsequently, Congress appropriated funds to build barracks for 28,652 soldiers, and new quarters for 1,443 non–commissioned officers and 1,534 officers. Summerall wrote that by the time his tour as chief of staff had ended, he had secured, with the president's approval, over 90 million dollars for army housing. As Timothy Nenninger stated, much of the success in obtaining the commitment and funds for new construction can be atttibuted to Summerall and his "forthright public statements."[68] Like General Pershing, President Coolidge valued the advice and opinions of strong men who held fast to their own positions and judgments.

Summerall also was concerned about another issue that weakened army morale: the daily ration allowance for the army, which was paid to units to defray the costs of food in mess halls. In the mid-1920s it was 30 cents, which was considerably less than the navy allowance of 50 cents, and, by mid-1925, inflation had increased the cost of food for the same ration to more than 36 cents. The daily caloric intake was sufficient, but the surgeon general noted that an allowance of more than one dollar was necessary to provide a properly varied diet.[69]

In January 1927, Summerall and Secretary Davis testified before the Military Affairs Committee. In his memoir, Summerall wrote that the men could not live on 30 cents a day. He recommended to the Military Affairs Committee the sum of four million dollars to raise the army ration to 50 cents. He and Secretary Davis pointed out that raising the allowance would reduce desertions, raise morale, and improve efficiency. The House of Representatives approved the increase, but fiscal conservatives in the Senate blocked passage because they considered the provision too costly.[70]

A concerned president invited Davis and Summerall to lunch at the White House, "where the greatest abundance of food was served." Afterwards, Coolidge turned to Summerall and asked, "General, what is this about increased appropriations for rations? You know you are breaking my budget, don't you?" Summerall explained the inclusion of the request in the House budget, and, as silence prevailed, the president's guests departed, with Summerall feeling once again that Coolidge would relieve him of his post. Instead, he and Davis managed to convince the president to issue an executive order fixing the allowance at 50 cents per man per day.[71] Once again, through his persuasive influence with the president and Congress, Summerall had achieved an important goal for the army.

Summerall seems also to have earned Coolidge's friendship, as well as his respect. He wrote that from time to time the president would send for him to talk in the Oval Office, and invited him for a weekend at Coolidge's summer home in Wisconsin. At the request of the House Committee on Military Affairs, Summerall's office undertook a study of the army's system of promotion and rank. One key recommendation called for the chief of staff to carry the rank of a four-star general, corresponding to the rank of full admiral for the Chief of Naval Operations. Summerall forwarded the report with this endorsement to the president, but recommended that the promotion to four-star rank would not apply to him as the incumbent chief of staff, but to his successors. Coolidge sent the report to Congress, and in an action that showed his esteem for Summerall, stated that he approved of the change only with the stipulation that the present army chief of staff be promoted to the four-star rank. Congress approved the measure, and Summerall receive his promotion on 23 February 1929. As he noted in his memoir, he was the only officer from the South ever to be promoted to the rank of full general to that time. This meant a great deal to Summerall, and he deeply appreciated the president's support. In his memoir he praised Coolidge as "the last real President who conformed to his duties under the Constitution. His high courage, clear understanding of national economy, and fidelity to duty were without a superior....He said the one necessity for national defense was being out of debt so that the resources of the nation would be available for war."[72]

Summerall did not have the kind of warm friendship that he had developed with President Coolidge with his successor, President Herbert Hoover, but he believed that he enjoyed a solid relationship with the new president, whom he served under from March 1929 to November 1930. When Secretary Davis left office, he was succeeded by James Good, and he and Summerall became close friends. But Good died late in 1929 and was succeeded by Patrick Hurley. Summerall believed that he had a good relationship with Hurley as well, and wrote that when he presented the army budget to Hoover and his cabinet, Hurley "complimented me heartily." But Timothy Nenninger pointed out that Summerall regarded Hurley "with some resentment," mainly because Hurley took his job more seriously than his predecessor, and had far more talent for the position.[73] Hurley later told Summerall to find an assistant secretary for planning industrial mobilization and for supervising the procurement of all army supplies. Summerall's first two choices could not take the position. His third choice was Frederick H. Payne, an industrialist from Massachusetts, who accepted the post. Summerall did not know Payne well and claimed that Payne came too much under the influence of the bureau chiefs. Nenninger points out that Summerall would not even speak with Payne and refused to work with him on planning for manpower mobilization. Finally, Hurley intervened and forced Summerall and his office to cooperate with Payne.

On another occasion, Summerall tried hard to prevent the appointment of a certain officer to succeed to the post of chief of ordnance, until Hurley, according to Surgeon General Merritt Ireland, told Summerall that he was going to make the appointment anyway.[74] Then, a few months before Summerall's term as chief of staff ended in November 1930, Nenninger notes that "much to Hurley's chagrin," Summerall wrote an article encouraging army officers to write newspaper pieces to inform the public about military matters. From Summerall's perspective, a view presumably not shared by Hurley, they could do this without criticizing either their military or civilian leaders. Based upon these issues with Hurley, Nenninger agrees with historian John R. M. Wilson that "Summerall came closer than any other interwar Chief of Staff to open opposition to a Secretary of War."[75]

Summerall's refusal to speak to Assistant Secretary Payne, who he believed was influenced by the bureau chiefs, indicates the deep rift that had developed between the chief of staff and

*Major General and Mrs. Summerall call at the White House to pay their New Year's respects to President Coolidge*

Courtesy United Press International

these officials. In addition, he believed that some of the officers on the General Staff as well as the bureau chiefs, many of whom had served on Pershing's staff in World War I, were prejudiced against him for having been "only a 'combat officer.'" For some time, he held weekly staff meetings in his office with the bureau and branch chiefs and the heads of the General Staff sections. But it seemed to him that these officers came reluctantly, and many felt that they did need to come at all, so he soon discontinued the meetings.[76] Therefore he tended to micromanage matters, taking his lunch in his office, and driving his staff just as hard as he had driven his officers and men in war.

Summerall could also come down hard on subordinates, as he had done in relieving combat commanders in the First Division during the war. On 21 March 1930, Lieutenant Colonel E. M. Shinkle, commander of the Aberdeen Proving Grounds in Maryland, met Summerall and Brigadier General Colden L'H. Ruggles, Assistant Chief of Ordnance, at the Aberdeen train station, and escorted them to the post to observe how 75-mm guns could be transported and fired from several new gun carriages. Shortly after the visit Shinkle submitted a report to the chief of ordnance. Prior to Summerall's arrival Shinkle noted that he was informed that the chief of staff "desires no salute or ceremony," and no orders to conduct honors or similar ceremonies were issued. As Summerall was conducted on his inspection, he, Ruggles, and Shinkle paused before one demonstration, and Shinkle began explaining a few things about the gun and carriage. Suddenly, Summerall interrupted him, and demanded to know the name of an officer standing about 20 feet away. Shinkle identified Major Shurtleff, who stepped forward and saluted. Summerall asked Shurtleff what he was doing there and told him that he should have reported immediately to the chief of staff. Shinkle quoted Summerall as telling Shurtleff that "I am accustomed to have officers report to me promptly when I inspect a post. You should have immediately reported to the Chief of Staff. I won't have you in my presence. Leave here immediately." Two other junior officers were standing by, and saluted smartly, whereupon they received from Summerall the same stinging reprimand for not reporting to the chief of staff, who also ordered them to leave immediately. He then turned to Shinkle and told him that he was "ashamed" of him and his officers, and that he had an undisciplined command. He ended the inspection by telling Shinkle that "I won't stay here any longer. I'm leaving immediately."[77]

In his report, Shinkle wrote that Summerall had discussed the incident with the press, and that the resulting publicity "has injured the reputation of Aberdeen Proving Ground as a government institution." He pointed out that Major Shurtleff was not directly connected with the demonstration, and that he and the other officers had not "omitted any outward show of disrespect." He noted also that he had complied with all of the instructions he had received from the chief of staff.[78]

The *New York Times* reported that "Army circles are wondering just what happened at the Aberdeen Proving Grounds....", and that "What ever it was, Colonel Shinkle had received a rebuke from General Summerall, who left in what was described as disgust." The *Times* article speculated that Summerall was displeased that "a young officer" had attempted to explain a weapon that Summerall was more familiar with than the officer himself.[79] Perhaps Summerall reacted to what he thought was an impertinent attempt by Shinkle to show that he knew more about guns than did the army's foremost artillerist as well as the army's chief of staff. In Summerall's view, perhaps, Shinkle's officers might well have been influenced by their commander against him, and they also had to be put in their place. At any rate, it is reasonable to concur with Timothy Nenninger's judgment that "Summerall had demonstrated publicly that he could be a martinet."

Summerall's authoritarian streak certainly did not lessen or eliminate the hostility that prevailed in the relations between Summerall and his bureau chiefs. He believed their exemption from control by the chief of staff by law was a mistake, and that their continued reappointment was the "greatest evil in the War Department," essentially because it "caused resentment in the Army and deprived good officers of any chance for promotion to Chief of Branch."[80] Both Secretary Davis and President Coolidge agreed that the chiefs and assistant chiefs should be limited to one four-year term in office, and some members of Congress favored the proposal.[81] But Summerall encountered strong resistance from several influential chiefs, who naturally wanted to keep their jobs and could summon political support. Also, his determination to impose his will, as well as his own hostility toward those who opposed him, alienated many officers.

One of Summerall's staunchest critics was Surgeon General Merritt Ireland. He wrote to his friend, and Summerall's predecessor as chief of staff, John L. Hines, that an army officer riding on a train with Summerall heard the chief of staff berating Ireland, George van Horn Moseley, the military assistant to the assistant secretary, and Quartermaster General B. Franklin Cheatham, as "three of the devils who had caused him a great deal of trouble." Ireland noted that Summerall had opposed his reappointment, and when the secretary of war approved it anyway, it made Summerall angry.[82] Hines lent a sympathetic ear to Ireland. Summerall wrote that when he succeeded Hines as army chief of staff, he "saw the pillars of the War Department crumbling,"[83] and Hines was offended. In addition, Summerall had sent Hines to the Philippines, even though Hines did not want to go, and had less than two years to serve before retirement.[84] Hines came to believe that he had turned the tables on Summerall, writing Ireland that "I have enjoyed my stay here in the Philippines very much. As a matter of fact, it has been the most pleasant form of punishment that I have ever undergone."[85] Quite probably, as Timothy Nenninger wrote, there were personal motives involved, but criticism of Summerall was also the result of how he conducted the daily business of his office. "Too often," stated Nenninger, "he made a decision and had the General Staff prepare a study to support the decision."[86]

Summerall certainly consulted with those whose counsel he valued, such as Frank Parker, his assistant chief of staff and successor as First Division commander, and fellow traveler on the "road to Sedan." But this circle was increasingly tight, and if others on the staff proposed different actions, as Conrad Babcock had during the battle of Soissons, they received Summerall's abrupt rejection. Summerall's style of command and control led Ireland to write Hines that after Douglas MacArthur succeeded Summerall, "everyone is laughing around here." He noted that people were no longer behaving as if they "expected to be hit with something, and every man is working on his job and happy."[87]

An even more tumultuous storm developed around Summerall's appointment in March 1929 of Colonel Stephen O. Fuqua to be chief of infantry, with the rank of major general. Fuqua had been promoted to colonel only a year earlier, and his new appointment and rank advanced him over 165 other army colonels who were eligible for the position. His career had been honorable, but not particularly brilliant or unusual. What was distinctive was his close association with Summerall. He had appointed Fuqua as chief of staff when he commanded the First Division; had named Fuqua as his assistant chief of staff in Hawaii; and had placed him in charge of the training section of the II Corps Area. When he received his appointment as chief of infantry, Fuqua was in command of the 16th Infantry at Fort Jay.

The *New York Times* reported that when Fuqua's nomination came before the Senate Committee on Military Affairs for confirmation, an "anonymous campaign" stressed that the close association between Summerall and Fuqua had been "the subject of comment for some years," and that "the decisive factor in the selection of Col. Fuqua was personal friendship." On the other hand, the *Times* reported that officials in the War Department pointed out that more than 130 colonels were senior to Fuqua when he was appointed.[88] In addition, the *Boston Transcript* pointed out that the chief of cavalry stood 27th on the list of 28 colonels when he was appointed, and that Quartermaster General Cheatham (one of Summerall's "devils"') was 11th out of 42 quartermaster colonels when he was made chief of that branch.[89] The secretary of war and the president approved Summerall's choice, and the Senate went on to confirm Fuqua. But Nenninger pointed out that the appointment continued to undermine Summerall's relations with senior officers in the army, and led to increased involvement of the civilian leadership in decisions that involved the promotion and appointment of senior army officers.[90]

Summerall omitted from his memoir any reference to the Fuqua furor. Considering the hostility he faced from several bureau chiefs, it is understandable that he wanted a chief who was not just friendly, but, more importantly, one who was loyal to him personally. Fuqua might not have been a brilliant officer, but Summerall knew from experience that he was competent, and, coupled with his loyalty, he was convinced that Fuqua was the logical choice. Predictably, Merritt Ireland stated of Summerall's appointment of Fuqua that he "will [n]ever get away with it."[91] But General Hines reacted differently, and wrote Fuqua that "It is very pleasing to your old friends to see your energy, efficiency and devotion to duty thus rewarded. Here's hoping for you every success in your new position."[92] Indeed, if Ireland, Moseley, Cheatham, and others had reacted to Fuqua's selection as Hines had done, a few years of collegiality could have replaced the strained relations among the most senior commanders of the army.

Summerall's troubles with the "cabal" of bureau chiefs did not divert his attention from aviation and mechanization, which were two major areas where his decisions, as Timothy Nenninger concluded, "had a profound and positive impact on how mechanization, in particular, developed in the U. S. Army."[93] In World War I, the tank corps operated independently of the other branches of the army, but the National Defense Act of 1920 placed all tanks in the infantry, and thus, the chief of infantry had control over the development of tank doctrine. According to historian David E. Johnson, this officer might have continued to dominate armor's development if Secretary of War Davis had not visited England early in 1927.[94]

During his visit, Davis observed a demonstration of the combined arms of the British Army's Experimental Mechanized Force on Salisbury Plain, the army's large training area some 50 miles south of London. Davis was impressed with the unit, and ordered Summerall to organize a similar unit for the U.S. Army. Summerall directed the Operations and Training Section (G-3) of the General Staff, under the direction of his close friend and colleague, Frank Parker, to study the creation of an experimental mechanized force. On 30 December 1927, he approved a plan that called for the organization of a unit that contained one infantry battalion, one field artillery battalion, two tank battalions, and an assortment of engineer, signal, medical, and maintenance units. These units assembled at Camp Meade in July, and over the next three months the Experimental Mechanized Force trained and conducted maneuvers to test and evaluate their equipment and tactics. The obsolete World War I equipment performed poorly, but the combined force demonstrated the potential to operate in an independent offensive capacity. In late September, in accordance with the limited purpose of the plan for the force, Summerall disbanded it, but by no means did he shelve plans for mechanization.

While planning for the Experimental Mechanized force was under way in the spring of 1928, Summerall also ordered Parker and the G-3 section of the General Staff to work on plans for a more permanent unit. This report was completed in March, and Summerall gave it his complete endorsement. It recommended a battalion of light, fast tanks as the core of a force that combined infantry, artillery, and support units. This unit would rely on surprise and speed, and spearhead an attack that would disrupt enemy reserves and rear installations, and serve as well as a counter-attack force. It would also serve as a laboratory for tactics and equipment. The report concluded with the recommendation that in fiscal 1930, the War Department should begin procuring new equipment, and establish a permanent mechanized unit.[95]

On 10 May, the War Department appointed a board of officers "to make recommendations for the development of a mechanical force within the Army and to study questions of defence [sic] against such forces."[96] The board recommended the formation of a permanent mechanized force, with its mission and organizational structure closely in parallel with those in Parker's report. On 31 May, Secretary Davis, with Summerall's support, pressed ahead with plans to establish the unit, although budgetary restraints slowed down their progress. The only dissenter among the bureau chiefs was Fuqua, of the infantry, whose opposition was essentially parochial, since the infantry no longer would exercise exclusive control over tanks, as it had since 1920.[97]

In his 1930 annual report, Summerall reaffirmed the army's commitment to the development of mechanization, and selected Colonel Daniel Van Voorhis to command the Mechanized Force. It became operational on 1 November 1930, just three weeks before Summerall's term as chief of staff ended, and began training at Fort Eustis, Virginia. Once again, as in the summer of 1928, obsolete and unreliable tanks and other equipment greatly limited operations. On 31 June 1931, the Mechanized Force came to an end, when new army chief Douglas MacArthur returned tanks to the infantry, while, at the same time requiring the cavalry to mechanize as well.[98]

The Mechanized Force, indeed, had a short existence, but as historian David E. Johnson wrote, "The establishment of a permanent mechanized force marked a milestone in the Army's tank development efforts."[99] And, as Timothy Nenninger stated, Summerall's "interest in mechanization was crucial to its development in the U.S. Army in the interwar years. When few senior officers were really interested in tanks and mechanization, Summerall's support helped overcome the innate conservatism and parochialism of the branch chiefs."[100] Summerall justifiably was pleased with the progress that had been made toward mechanization during his incumbency, writing in his memoir that when the Mechanized Force became operational, "This was the beginning of the armored force."[101]

Summerall had advanced army mechanization and noted in his final report as chief of staff the striking development of military aviation in the World War. He stated in his memoir that he "realized the potentials of aviation and the need for increasing and improving the Air Corps,"[102] but further development of the military strength of the air arm was limited by a number of factors. In the aftermath of the Mitchell court-martial, President Coolidge named New York banker Dwight Morrow to head a board to investigate air power doctrines and the creation of an independent air force. The Morrow Board recommended a modest increase in aviation, but did not endorse a separate air force. Its recommendation did influence Congress to give military aviation greater prestige by passing the Air Corps Act of 2 July 1926. The Act left army aviation under the control of the General Staff, but changed the name of the Air Service to the Air Corps, and provided for aviation representation in each General Staff division. It authorized an Assistant Secretary of War for Air, and a major general to serve as Chief of the Air Corps, assisted by three brigadier generals. The act also provided for a force of 1,650 officers, 15,000 enlisted men, and 1,800 modern airplanes, which were to be provided over a five-year period.[103]

Most significant for Summerall was the fact that even though the personnel strength of the Air Corps grew from 9,079 to 13,190 between July 1927 and July 1931, neither the Congress nor the Coolidge and Hoover Administrations were willing to fund an overall increase in army manpower. Thus, the entire growth in the manpower of the Air Corps came from transfers from other arms, and the funds for Air Corps operations, research and development, construction, housing, and other demands as well, came out of the army budget. Summerall supported the policy but stated his concerns that "The rest of the Army has, moreover, been required to reduce its troop strength to supply the commissioned and enlisted personnel of the Air Corps."[104] Although Summerall secured money for additional airplanes, he noted in his memoir that "the losses were about as great as the increase, so that progress was slow."[105] Thus, it is not surprising, and, indeed, quite logical, for Nenninger to describe Summerall as "an army traditionalist who did not want to see the established arms suffer to foster expansion of new technology."[106]

In July 1929, in his determination to reduce government spending, President Hoover ordered the General Staff to survey all military activities "with a view to making extensive reductions in the cost of the Army...without manifest injury to National Defense." Summerall informed the General Staff and the branch and bureau chiefs that he expected candid responses and appraisals of how they would cut costs within their own areas. He also requested recommendations from the army's senior commanders.[107]

Summerall made it clear that he wanted to convey to the president certain principles and conclusions that would define the relationship of the army to national defense. He believed that military preparedness must reflect international conditions, but that costs should be determined within the context of what the government needed to meet all needs. He also indicated that the Regular Army needed to be large enough to meet emergency defense requirements, and to train a larger force that would be raised in the event of a national emergency. He stated that the most important conclusion of the survey should state that the army budget needed to be stabilized, rather than raised or lowered. Stabilization would provide a balanced budget for the army within the context of the president's desire to reduce spending.[108]

Summerall's message to commanders and chiefs also included several questions about whether harbor and coast defenses were obsolete; whether horse cavalry was sufficiently valuable to maintain as a separate branch, and to what extent could motorization and aviation replace cavalry; whether the five-year Air Corps program should be curtailed or extended; and what was the relationship between the Air Corps and other branches; what were the costs of a conscript army in relation to the costs of the several civilian reserve components; could any of the civilian components be curtailed or abolished; and could the army be reduced to its strength in 1916, without endangering national security. His principles and questions indicated that the survey would be used to determine which programs could be reduced or eliminated.[109]

The replies Summerall received essentially ignored his directives, stressing the importance of a particular commander or chief's "domain." The War Plans Division (WPD) of the General Staff studied these responses and prepared a final report for President Hoover. It concluded that any significant reduction in the military budget would endanger national security, and called for the stabilization of the budget at the sum of $350 million. Hoover accepted Summerall's recommendation and made it an important goal of his administration.[110]

Throughout his tour as army chief, Summerall and Laura followed a busy social schedule, entertaining presidential cabinet members, diplomats, Congressmen, Senators and their wives, as well as army and navy officers and their wives. In his memoir, he praised Laura for her "grace, charm, and cordiality" that "captivated all who saw her." He wrote that he believed that "the Army was never as well represented or did its part as completely as when my dear wife presided over the residence and the social program of the Chief of Staff." He also noted that their entertaining "cost all of our pay and allowances and much of my dear wife's legacies from relatives."[111]

The Summeralls were especially pleased that their son Charles had been transferred to an artillery battery at Fort Myer. Because of the crowded housing conditions on post, similar to what Summerall had seen on army installations across the country, Lieutenant Summerall and his wife Julia lived in half of a single set of quarters. Julia was pregnant, and late at night in early September 1929, they all rushed to Walter Reed Hospital, where she gave birth to a baby boy. A few minutes later, undetected and to everyone's surprise, including the doctors, a baby girl arrived. The twins were named Charles

Pelot III and Julia Reeder, and soon became known to family and friends as Punch and Judy. An elderly woman who worked for Laura's family helped care for the children, and General Summerall stopped by every morning to see them on his way to the office. Soon they were christened in the Summerall's spacious house. Their grandfather wrote of them in his memoir that "They have been a great blessing in our lives and are all we could want them to be."[112]

On an evening late in the following November, President and Mrs. Hoover hosted the Summeralls at a small dinner. The next day, 30 November 1930, Summerall stepped down as army chief of staff, handing over his duties to Douglas MacArthur. On returning to Fort Myer, he received one final gun salute from the battery commanded by his son. He and Laura then left for Union Station and the trip to his native state of Florida, where they had purchased a house in the city of Eustis. They stayed for a few days in a boarding house until their new home was ready and were living comfortably there when Summerall's retirement became official on 31 March 1931.[113]

During his long interview with biographer Forrest Pogue, General George Marshall wrote that his admiration for Summerall was "very, very great," but that "as chief of staff, he was a failure because he didn't fit into that [role]...." Marshall believed that the mutual suspicions between Summerall and his critics, which lingered after the Sedan episode, limited his effectiveness as army chief.[114] Similarly, Timothy Nenninger concluded that Summerall was not a great chief of staff, and stated that Summerall's "personality, his immediate professional interests, and events during the time he served [as chief of staff], combined to limit his opportunities and ability to achieve greatness."[115] Yet, Summerall worked constructively, if, at times, awkwardly, with two presidents who were committed to significant economies in government. He skillfully managed the survey President Hoover

*General Summerall with his son, Lieutenant Charles P. Summerall, and twins, Julia and Charles*

Courtesy United Press International

ordered and supported the president on army budgets. But, in his final report as chief of staff, he expressed concern, as noted above, that increases in the Air Corps would come at the expense of other branches. He also warned that the figure of $350 million was not enough to support the army under the National Defense Act of 1920, and that "We cannot base our future defense upon the assumption that the armies of allies will assure us the time required for the preparation of our military effort."[116]

Summerall succeeded, as Nenninger also notes, in obtaining small increases for specific programs, like housing and the daily ration allowance. He prevented possible budget cuts and was instrumental in establishing the policy of stabilizing army budgets. Under his leadership of the army from 1924 to 1930, and even into the first three years of the Great Depression, War Department expenditures actually increased.[117] His support for military aviation was tempered by his concern that the Air Corps would siphon funds from the more traditional arms. Yet, his consistent support for mechanization helped to sustain development of the mechanized force. Indeed, in his important and incisive study of Summerall's term as army chief of staff, Timothy Nenninger correctly concludes that Summerall was "a conservative chief for a conservative era," and remained an "army traditionalist."[118] In his next and longest-lasting command as president of The Citadel, these conservative and traditionalist qualities would suit ideally the pressing needs and future development of the small military college in Charleston, South Carolina.

*Summerall, flanked by General Pershing in the funeral procession for General Tasker H. Bliss at Arlington National Cemetery, 12 November 1930, shortly before Summerall retired as army chief of staff (note the almost exact bearing and stride of Summerall and Pershing)*

Courtesy United Press International

# Chapter Sixteen

## *The Citadel*

In mid-March 1930, a few days after Summerall had reprimanded the clutch of officers at Aberdeen Proving Ground for "shameful" behavior, he received a letter from his close friend and assistant chief of staff Frank Parker. Concerned about the criticism in the press of Summerall's angry reaction at Aberdeen, Parker urged him to counteract the negative publicity by visiting conventions of the American Legion, and win their support for a campaign for political office after his retirement as chief of staff. They had discussed previously a possible schedule for these appearances, but Summerall wrote that after the Aberdeen incident, he felt that he was in an "exposed situation" and must avoid making the "slightest misstep." He feared that the press and the public would object to reimbursement by the government for mileage to these events, and that, in any event, the controller would deny payment. Although neither man defined the office Summerall should seek, Summerall noted in his response to Parker that his appearance at Legion conventions would suggest that he was advancing his "candidacy," and that would lead to protests to the secretary of war and to the president. It would also produce hostile articles in the press. Summerall concluded that he must refrain from any "active undertaking for the rest of the year, and decline all invitations, unless the Secretary wants me to represent him." He closed his letter to Parker by expressing his appreciation, and by urging him to "let someone else have the field. I simply want to get through without any further conflict and trust to fate for my future after next November."[1] Parker was not discouraged, and spelled out specifically what he previously only had implied: that Summerall should seek the presidency, and would be an unbeatable Democratic candidate. He wrote that "A soldier, Democrat, dry, well-known and popular will surely win in '32 and you are that man."[2]

After reading Parker's optimistic assessment of his prospects for the presidency, Summerall did an about-face. Shortly before he left Washington for his new home in Eustis, he assured Parker that "I shall not fail to do my part, if in your judgment circumstances should warrant." He stated that the real reason for his move to Florida was to place himself in a position of "readiness," since the state had "acquired importance and publicity," and "It would not be difficult to arouse enthusiasm there." He noted that the party machinery was in trouble, and that if he followed "a proper procedure" he would win their support.[3]

Summerall's hopes were encouraged when the mayor and city officials of Eustis welcomed him enthusiastically, and when Democratic Senator Duncan U. Fletcher of Florida hosted a reception in his honor. At the same time, he was worried about raising enough money to finance a campaign, and more importantly, whether his retirement pay and a small legacy left to his wife would be enough to provide for their living expenses.[4]

In the meantime, Colonel Oliver J. Bond, Citadel class of 1896, had decided to retire after 22 years as president, and inquired of Summerall whether he would be interested in succeeding him at the military college.[5] A few days later, the editor of *The Columbia Record* of South Carolina wrote Summerall that the president of the University of South Carolina would be delighted to have the general associated with the university in any capacity. He noted that the compensation would be "very modest," but the Summeralls could live in the recently renovated home of Woodrow Wilson, pending approval by the legislature.[6]

Summerall responded to Colonel Bond's inquiry that he might consider favorably an invitation to become president of The Citadel, and inquired about salary, campus housing, and the date for the beginning of the school year.[7] But before reaching a decision about whether to pursue a political course from Florida, or an educational course at the University of South Carolina or The Citadel, Summerall wrote General Parker for his advice. Parker responded that he had given "careful thought and analysis to your problem." He felt that after having served as army chief of staff, "To take the Citadel [position] would be a retrogression in your military life—a long retrogression—it will bury you in a far away town in the back water of this Nation's current of effort." He advised Summerall to avoid Charleston, where life is "lethargic," and where "one must grow up and live there to be able to enjoy it, or even understand it. Your past life precludes the possibility of your ever being happy in Charleston, and the Citadel is a military kindergarten, little calculated to stimulate your further efforts."[8] From a fellow South Carolinian (Parker was born in Georgetown), these were harsh words, but perhaps reflective of many others in the state who were not native Charlestonians or devotees of The Citadel and its proud alumni.

Parker also had a low regard for Florida. He wrote Summerall that is was "no place for you. At best it will always be a State where the principal elements are those either looking for a warm place in winter, or those trying to get something for nothing in speculation. The reports here are not enthusiastic concerning the present or future of Florida." But Parker was enthusiastic about Columbia. "It is the political center of the State," he wrote, "where the current of life, political and business runs strong. By all means, go there—your mother's family belong to that Section [of the state] and have long been identified with it. Many of your real friends are from South Carolina and from the neighborhood of Columbia."[9]

The day after Parker wrote his letter to Summerall, Colonel Bond mailed his response to the latter's inquiries about The Citadel presidency. The yearly salary would be $7,500; a house was provided on the "new campus" for the president, as well as quarters for all members of the faculty; and the school year would begin on 12 September. A few days later, Colonel John P. Thomas, chairman of the Board of Visitors, the policy-making body of the college, telegraphed Summerall that the board had unanimously elected him president, effective 12 September, and added that he hoped Summerall would accept. The general requested that he delay his decision until he could visit the college in early January 1931, and the Board agreed.[10]

On New Year's Day Summerall responded to Frank Parker's letter of advice and expressed reservations about taking a position in Columbia, South Carolina, where nothing could happen, he believed, without the "action of the Legislature." He noted the "isolation" of The Citadel, but concluded that "it offers a living which my retired pay will not give." He also made clear to Parker his continuing interest in a political career and was pleased that people in Florida were talking about his going to Congress or the Senate. Calculating the political effects of his accepting The Citadel's offer, Summerall decided that it would not weaken his "political prospects," but would instead more closely identify him with South Carolina, and, in any case, the position need not be permanent, "if something better comes up."[11] He noted in his memoir that Laura thought well of his becoming president of the military college, and on 11 January, he wrote Parker that he would leave the next day for Charleston "to decide about The Citadel. All want me, it is clear. I will be in a position in readiness. I can be available for any office if I am really wanted. I can go about and make speeches. They merely want my advertising value. I think I shall take it, but ask them to withhold publicity until June, so as to make the Florida demonstrations fall flat."[12]

The platform from which Summerall hoped to launch his political career was founded in 1822, as one of two arsenals, the other in Columbia, to support the militia against a possible slave uprising. During the nullification crisis in 1832, federal troops were withdrawn from the Charleston installation, known as the State Citadel, to nearby Fort Moultrie on Sullivan's Island. They were replaced by local militia. In 1842, the General Assembly combined the two arsenals into the South Carolina Military Academy in Charleston. Defense of society remained an important consideration, but South Carolina, like Virginia and other Southern states, believed that a military education would instill discipline, character, and patriotic devotion in its young men.[13]

After South Carolina seceded from the Union in December 1860, Citadel cadets helped to shore up the defenses around Charleston harbor. On 9 January 1861, with the American flag flying from its mast, the Northern merchant vessel *Star of the West* approached Fort Sumter to supply the Federal garrison commanded by Major Robert Anderson. Cadets assembled on Morris Island, fired cannon at the ship, and forced it to abort its mission. Citadel alumni would claim that these were the first shots fired in the Civil War.[14]

After the defeat of the Confederacy, Union soldiers occupied The Citadel in February 1865 and stayed until they were withdrawn in the spring of 1879. Led by former Confederate general Johnson Hagood, alumni and legislators urged the General Assembly to reopen the school. They pointed to Citadel alumni who were state leaders and argued that the institution could serve the state by combining an education with the virtues of military training and discipline. In addition, a useful, inexpensive education would unite the sons of all South Carolinians, whether rich or poor, into an egalitarian Corps of Cadets. Their arguments prevailed, and The Citadel reopened in downtown Charleston on Marion Square in October 1882.[15]

The cadet barracks soon were filled with "paying cadets," who were the sons of prosperous citizens, and with "beneficiary cadets," who came from poorer families in every county of the state, and were selected by competitive examinations to receive full scholarships. The number of cadets steadily increased. Even as World War I ended, and the influence and popularity of the military declined, the buildings on Marion Square could not accommodate the 350-man Corps of Cadets. In 1918, the city of Charleston transferred one hundred acres between Hampton Park and the Ashley River, just to the northwest of downtown, for the construction of a new campus. This "Greater Citadel" opened in 1922, with a towering barracks to house the cadets. The "Old Citadel" housed faculty members while new faculty quarters were under construction.[16]

By the end of the decade, enrollment had increased to over 700 cadets, and a second barracks was completed. Construction began on the Main College Building to house administrative offices, a library, classrooms, and laboratories. An important milestone had been achieved in 1924, when The Citadel met the higher education standards of the Southern Association of Colleges and was elected to membership in the organization, along with Furman University in Greenville.[17] Colonel Bond had led the college to academic respectability; he had guided the relocation and construction of a new campus; and he had presided over a substantial increase in the cadet corps, as well as a corresponding increase in college revenues.

After his lengthy service as president, Colonel Bond began looking forward to passing on his responsibilities to a successor, and a return to teaching as professor of mathematics. As the country and the state of South Carolina struggled to cope with the Great Depression, Bond became increasingly apprehensive about whether the state could continue to support the military college. The college budget for 1930 was reduced by 13 percent; funds for the completion of the Main College Building were disapproved; one of the most important private donors could no longer afford to honor his scholarship pledge; and, although the senior class was the largest in the school's history, losses in the other three classes had been considerable. In consequence, enrollment in the Corps of Cadets fell to fewer than 500.[18]

In the fall of 1930, Bond learned of the retirement of Summerall as army chief of staff. He concluded that because of the general's "recognized character, ability, and administrative talents," and with "preëminent distinction of promotion to the rank of general" he was the only man who could save the college from extinction, and preserve its future.[19] He would have been even more optimistic had he known that George Marshall regarded Summerall as "one of the greatest living exponents of the principle that much more can be done than ever seems possible, if there is a will to do it."[20] Bond received the unanimous approval of the Board of Visitors to offer the presidency to Summerall, but apparently, neither he nor the Board was aware of Summerall's political ambitions. Bond's colleagues on the Board shared his confidence and faith in Summerall, and even if they had known about the general's grander plans, the dire condition of the college's finances and the bleak prospects for its survival would have overcome any hesitancy to offer him the position.

After confiding in Frank Parker that he was thinking about accepting The Citadel's offer, Summerall arrived in Charleston on 12 January 1931. Colonel Bond and Colonel Thomas conducted him on a tour of the campus, which had begun to show the effects of meager funding and declining revenues. Summerall observed that the buildings were in "bad condition," and that none of the roads were paved. He found that the furniture in cadet rooms was obsolete, and they slept on iron-slatted beds with no springs. Only a few quarters had been provided for the faculty and staff, with the remainder residing at the Old Citadel in quarters that were in bad repair. The wooden washers in the laundry were worn out, and all the pressing was done by hand. The grass on the campus was cut only in the fall, and the man who cut it used it for hay. Since the Main College Building was not completed, the cadet store, canteen, post office, commandant's office, and several classrooms were located in the barracks.

Summerall wrote in his memoir that on this first visit to the campus, he asked Colonel Thomas whether his decisions "on matters of discipline would be final." The chairman "assured me that they would be. I would not have gone otherwise."[21] In his memoir, this was the first inquiry that he addressed to Thomas, and its prominence indicates that it was the most important issue that concerned Summerall and his relations with the Board. This matter of final authority in disciplinary cases had deeply troubled Colonel Bond, and would have a serious impact as well upon at least one of Summerall's successors.

After his inspection of the campus, Summerall went downtown to meet with Mayor Thomas P. Stoney at City Hall. Before informing his Citadel hosts of his decision, he returned to Eustis and conferred with Laura. On 15 January, he wrote W. W. Ball, editor of the *Charleston News and Courier*, and requested a one-month subscription to the paper, beginning with the 15 January edition.[22] The next day he wrote Frank Parker that he had decided to accept The Citadel presidency, effective 12 September.[23]

Summerall remained confident that The Citadel position would strengthen his chances for high political office. He confided to Parker that "S.C. [South Carolina] should take the lead in advancing me for a national place. The south is entitled to it. The time is most propitious. If we had the means and friends it could be done." He added that accepting The Citadel offer would be the "the safest thing for me to do and it will be a strategic position in readiness."²⁴ That same day Summerall wrote Colonel Thomas that he would accept the presidency of the college, and Thomas, rather than waiting until June, as Summerall had requested, officially announced the general's acceptance on the afternoon of 16 January. The announcement appeared in the 19 January edition of the *News and Courier*,²⁵ and, thanks to his subscription to the local paper, Summerall and Laura read all about it just a few days later.

In his enthusiastic reply to Summerall's acceptance, the Board chairman confirmed the general's salary and his residency on campus. Colonel Thomas also mentioned the possibility that the legislature would reduce college appropriations, but expressed confidence that Summerall's acceptance of The Citadel presidency "will be a very material aid in our securing the budget." For his part, Summerall expressed his belief that the college could not operate efficiently on a smaller budget. With concern for his own reputation and a pragmatic view forward, he cautioned that it would be an embarrassment to him if he attempted to lead a meritorious program without sufficient funds to accomplish it.²⁶

Author D. D. Nicholson described the effusive praise of Summerall's selection by state political and educational leaders, as well as local and regional newspapers. South Carolina State Senator John C. Long of Charleston said that Summerall's selection was "one of the biggest things that has happened, not only to The Citadel, but to Charleston in many a year." South Carolina Governor John G. Richards paid tribute to Summerall's splendid character and reputation as a soldier, and his great importance to education in the state. The president of the College of Charleston stated that Summerall's leadership of The Citadel would enhance the prestige of the military college, and the president of the Medical College of South Carolina in Charleston said that Summerall would guide the military college to even greater usefulness "in its special field of service." News of Summerall's acceptance had attracted interest from newspapers in many states. *The Raleigh News and Observer* in North

*The Citadel Campus, 1930*
Courtesy The Citadel Archives & Museum, Charleston, South Carolina

Carolina commended Charleston and the entire country for enabling Summerall to continue in useful service by training young men.[27] In an editorial in the *News and Courier*, W. W. Ball compared Summerall to General Robert E. Lee, who became the president of Washington University in Lexington, Virginia, after the Civil War. Ball wrote that Summerall, like Lee, had answered "the call of the South to lead the Southern youth" in an institution "supported by a commonwealth resolved that it shall grow and increase in good work, loved as few schools are or have been by a numerous and powerful body of alumni. In these two pictures the motive is the same."[28] Colonel Bond responded with a gracious letter, perhaps grateful letter to Ball, and thanked Ball for the reference to General Lee. Bond believed it "must deeply touch General Summerall."[29]

With tributes to his career, and with enthusiastic anticipation of his leadership of The Citadel resounding across the state and region, Summerall and Laura returned to Eustis to make preparations for their move to Charleston. In Eustis, Summerall studied The Citadel's catalogue and other college material that Bond had sent, and corresponded with Bond about scholarships and the appointment of an officer to the position of commandant of cadets. The commandant was responsible for enforcing discipline in the corps and reported directly to the president. Summerall's choice for this, one of the most important positions at the college, was Lieutenant Colonel John W. Lang, whom Summerall had appointed as chief of public relations during the last year of his term as army chief of staff. Lang had been graduated from West Point in 1907 and had served as military attaché at the embassy in Madrid during World War I. He also had been professor of military science and tactics at Lehigh University.[30] Summerall requested the War Department to assign Lang to The Citadel both as professor of military science and tactics and commandant, and on 28 March, General MacArthur, Summerall's successor as chief of staff, detailed Lieutenant Colonel Lang to The Citadel, where he was ordered to report for duty to the college president.[31]

On 10 March, Summerall came to Columbia to address the General Assembly. He told the legislators that he was honored to address them, and praised The Citadel for teaching young men to perform deeds and service "in the bravest, best sense of the terms." The Summeralls drove to The Citadel on 1 June for graduation week and were hosted by Colonel and Mrs. Bond. The next evening both men were honored at a banquet in the cadet mess hall hosted by the Association of Citadel Men, the official college alumni organization. During commencement exercises on 3 June, Summerall addressed the graduating class of 124 cadets. He praised the leadership of Bond and told the senior class that they must continue to fulfill their new duties and responsibilities as graduates as faithfully as they had fulfilled their duties as cadets.[32] He would later develop his call to faithful duty into a code of conduct to which he would hold every cadet accountable. As he soon would discover, this would not be a simple or an easy task.

After the general's triumphal reception at The Citadel, the Summeralls drove to Washington for a visit with their son and his family at Fort Myer. From there they headed south to spend the summer months in the historic village of Valle Crusis in the mountains of North Carolina. Summerall wrote Colonel Bond to inquire about the availability of scholarships, and Bond kept him informed about campus affairs. On 1 September, they moved into their spacious, two-story stucco quarters on The Citadel campus. When Laura suddenly became quite ill, her husband took her to Walter Reed Army Medical Center, where she remained until she was well enough to accompany her husband to Charleston to assume his duties as president of The Citadel on 12 September.[33]

Still vigorous and in robust health at the age of 64, Summerall embarked upon his new responsibilities with his customary energy and determination. In his memoir, he expressed dismay that cadet discipline was poor, and that cadets had been found drinking in the barracks. Doubtless, he considered discipline and abstinence essential requirements of those under his command, and The Citadel

Corps of Cadets would be no exception. He saw the need to assert a vision of what he expected of the cadets, and composed a creed to which all cadets should aspire. Entitled The Citadel Code, it remained the standard by which he expected every cadet to measure his own conduct. In each of the years since the end of Summerall's presidency in 1953, it has been printed in the cadet freshman handbook, entitled *The Guidon*. In the culture of the early 21st century, many cadets seem inclined to view parts of it as remote and irrelevant relics of an age that was bound by inflexible rules and prudish standards of youthful conduct. The code follows.

> To revere God, love my country, and be loyal to The Citadel. To be faithful, honest and sincere in every act and purpose and to know that honorable failure is better than success by unfairness or cheating.
>
> To perform every duty with fidelity and conscientiousness and to make duty my watchword.
>
> To obey all orders and regulations of The Citadel and of proper authority.
>
> To refrain from intoxicants, narcotics, licentiousness, profanity, vulgarity, disorder, and anything that might subject me to reproach or censure within or without the college.
>
> To be diligent in my academic studies and in my military training.
>
> To do nothing inconsistent with my status as a cadet.
>
> To take pride in my uniform and in the noble traditions of the college and never to do anything that would bring discredit to them.
>
> To be courteous and gentlemanly in my deportment, bearing, and speech, and to exhibit good manners on all occasions.
>
> To cultivate dignity, poise affability, and a quiet and firm demeanor.
>
> To make friends with refined, cultivated, and intellectual people.
>
> To improve my mind by reading and participation in intellectual and cultural activities.
>
> To keep my body healthy and strong by physical exercise and participation in many sports.
>
> To be generous and helpful to others and to endeavor to restrain them from wrongdoing.
>
> To face difficulties with courage and fortitude and not to complain or be discouraged.
>
> To be worthy of the sacrifices of my parents, the generosity of the state, and the efforts of all who teach and all who administer the college in order that I might receive an education and to recognize my obligation to them.
>
> To make the college better by reason of my being a cadet.
>
> To resolve to carry its standards into my future career and to place right above gain and a reputation for integrity above power.
>
> To remember always that that honor of being a Citadel cadet imposes upon me a corresponding obligation to live up to this code.
>
> The foregoing code is earnestly commended to all cadets as an interpretation of the ideals of The Citadel.

Summerall believed that it was his duty and that of all Citadel faculty, staff, and cadet officers to enforce the code, and he expected the Board to honor its commitment that his decisions on "matters of discipline would be final."

Colonel Lang moved quickly to abolish cadet social clubs in the barracks. These clubs were more like college fraternities and apparently distracted cadets' service and loyalty to the cadet companies into which the corps was organized. Lang also created the rank of cadet lieutenant colonel for the regimental commander. This high rank would signify not only a high level of authority, but also a corresponding high degree of responsibility for the cadet who held that position and rank. In keeping with The Citadel Code, Colonel Lang prepared *Customs and Courtesies*, a booklet that was given to all cadets to inform them about etiquette and conventions of social and military traditions. It was praised in newspaper editorials in Columbia and Charleston and distributed to the young men working in all of the camps of the Civilian Conservation Corps in South Carolina.[34] Summerall noted that under Lang discipline had begun to improve "at once," although he expressed some concern that progress was slow.[35] As will be considered below, the issue of discipline developed into a major crisis between Summerall and the Board as to which possessed final authority in "matters of discipline."

Meanwhile, during his first semester on campus, editorials began to appear in a number of Florida newspapers promoting Summerall's candidacy for governor of the state. The *Ocala Banner* was "strong for his candidacy," because Florida "needs as its chief executive the strongest man it can find." The *Sanford Herald* stated that "he could easily be elected and would make a great governor." The *Tampa Tribune* reported that Summerall's "boom had been launched," and the *Ft. Myers Press* noted that Summerall "would be an extraordinary human being if he passed up an opportunity to top off a distinguished military career by becoming governor of his home state."[36]

Thus, Summerall continued to hope for high political office when he returned to The Citadel to prepare to present the college budget to the state legislature. Indeed, the precarious condition of the college's finances might have encouraged him to consider other opportunities to serve his country. As the result of decreases in enrollment and budget reductions imposed by the General Assembly, the budget for fiscal year 1932 included a deficit of $19,000 that had accumulated during the last years of Colonel Bond's administration.[37] On 9 February 1932, Summerall presented the college budget to the South Carolina State Senate Finance Committee in Columbia. Senator Wylie Hamrick held Summerall accountable for the deficit and demanded to know by what authority he had taken such an action. Hamrick asked what good it did for the legislature to establish a definite appropriation, "if a department may spend more than is appropriated?"[38] Suddenly, Summerall rose from his seat and stated that as a general of the army and president of The Citadel he would not tolerate such disrespect, and said that he would resign immediately as president. He turned around abruptly, marched out of the committee room, and left for Charleston. The next morning, he submitted his resignation to the Board, effective immediately.[39]

As D. D. Nicholson wrote, "Not since the 1886 earthquake had anything shaken Charleston as did Summerall's resigning." The Board of Visitors called an emergency meeting and urged Summerall to stay; Charleston mayor Burnett R. Maybank headed a committee that called on Summerall in his office, and pleaded with him to withdraw his resignation; over the next few days, parents, alumni, and newspaper editors and citizens from across the state entered similar pleas. Most importantly, every member of the Corps of Cadets signed a petition appealing to Summerall to rescind his resignation, and presented it to him on 12 February.[40] Three days later, he told the Board that he would withdraw his resignation "because of the petition of the cadets." When the cadet commander announced Summerall's decision in the mess hall, the cadets celebrated with a rousing cheer.[41]

A few weeks later, Summerall wrote Frank Parker that he regretted the Columbia incident, but that "[Senator Hambrick's] hostility was bitter and the insult deliberate." He stated that he "could not risk letting them legislate me out of office by resolution or failing to appropriate my salary....I simply had to resign to protect myself from further indignity." His confidence that "Public sentiment was

*Summerall at his desk at The Citadel*

Courtesy The Citadel Archives & Museum, Charleston, South Carolina

aroused and vindicated me" was an important reason for his remaining at The Citadel. But when he stated "The loyalty of the cadets is like that of the First Division and the Charleston people gave me their whole support,"[42] he made clear which appeals had impressed him most deeply, and had influenced him most decisively to change his mind, and to resume his leadership of the college.

So, Summerall stayed, but so did the deficit. Nevertheless, the stand that he took before the senate committee added stature to his reputation in the state, and strengthened his position as the president of The Citadel. No legislator or legislative committee ever again challenged him about The Citadel's budget figures or his management of the college. Perhaps unknowingly, he had established the independence of The Citadel from the meddling and interference of politicians, and eliminated the possibility that state officials would attempt in the future to undermine or weaken the authority of the college's president.

The strong and enthusiastic support Summerall had received in the wake of the "incident in Columbia" seems also to have resolved the issue of his political future. He had written Parker on 2 January that he had decided not to run either for governor or Congress, because "there was no plan to raise money," and he could not afford to take a long leave from The Citadel or resign.[43] In the meantime, his supporters in Tampa had organized a campaign supporting Summerall for vice president on the Democratic ticket. On 11 January he wrote Parker that he believed he was well known nationally and could win the votes of "important groups such as the patriotic organizations and the women." He stated that he expected to receive support from Colonel Robert McCormick, who had served under Summerall in the First Division at Cantigny and was the publisher of the *Chicago Tribune*. But he also noted, less optimistically, that the vice presidential campaign "is the only thing that seems possible now and this is the last chance."[44]

On 15 February he wrote Parker that "the sentiment of the state was so overwhelming that I decided to remain." He stated again that he had given up the "idea of running for Governor or Congress." A week later he wrote to a friend in Tavares, Florida, that he was "deeply grateful for your faith in me," but that he had decided not to be a candidate for public office.[45] Although he did not address the question of his possible candidacy for vice president, never again in the letters or documents that survive did he mention that possibility. The enthusiastic reception of his decision to remain at the helm of The Citadel with the promise of a steady and adequate income had been decisive in his decision to forego politics, while making it possible for him to continue to serve his country by leading young men into manhood and maturity.

Summerall had solidified his position as Citadel president, but the college still confronted a financial crisis that threatened the survival of the Corps of Cadets, as well as the faculty and staff. As noted above, he had found the physical plant in a dilapidated and deteriorating condition, the Corps of Cadets declining toward 400, a worried insecure faculty, and a debt-ridden budget. He confronted these challenges with the same kind of resolute energy and aggressive action that had typified his commands in the World War. He was even more meticulous in his attention to detail that he had been in any of his peacetime commands, and he wielded his authority over subordinates as absolutely as he ever had in either war or peace.

Summerall began his campaign to save The Citadel by reducing his own salary by 45 percent and those of the faculty and staff by from 30 to 40 percent. He laid off many hourly wage earners, and cut the salaries of those who remained from 15 to 20 percent. He rationed the use of electricity and water; he had telephones, including his own, disconnected; and he ordered the use of lighter-weight paper to save money on catalog printing and mailing. He personally enforced every "decree" and made rounds to insure that lights and radiators were turned off in classrooms when they were not in use; if they were left on, he sent through the campus mail terse, hand-written notes written in pencil on strips of foolscap to those who were responsible. The General Assembly commended him for his economies, and Colonel McCormick praised him in a Sunday edition of the *Tribune* for setting an example for the whole country.[46]

Realizing that "the college would fail" if The Citadel did not succeed in attracting more students, Summerall began a campaign to increase enrollment by calling upon prominent and wealthy friends and admirers to denote money for scholarships. His good friend and Wall Street financier Clark Williams initially endowed five full scholarships, and later established fifteen more. Colonel McCormick donated a number of scholarships as well, and regularly featured articles on Summerall and The Citadel. Friends of the Summeralls in New York, Rhode Island and Washington, D.C., also endowed additional scholarships. By 1933, enrollment in the Corps of Cadets had increased to over 500, and three years later the total had reached almost 700.[47]

The successes of Summerall's first year, and the promise of better days ahead under his leadership, were threatened by a crisis that developed between the new president and the Board of Visitors over cadet discipline. A few weeks before commencement in June 1933, Colonel Lang informed Summerall that a cadet had scratched out the name of another cadet, and had written his name on some of the other cadet's clothes. Lang determined that the action was stealing, which was against college regulations, and recommended that the cadet be dismissed. Summerall concurred with Lang's decision and dismissed the cadet. But the cadet appealed to the Board, which then overruled Summerall's dismissal, and reinstated the cadet to give him a second chance. Lang promptly resigned, and Summerall was faced with a serious dilemma. Chairman Thomas had promised him that his would be the final authority in matters of cadet discipline, so he could resign because the Board had not honored the chairman's promise, and in doing so, had "so weakened my authority as to render my efforts useless."[48] If he remained, he would have to accept the reversal of the Board's decision, which Colonel Lang would not accept, as well as the prospect that the Board would reverse all of his future decisions involving cadet discipline.

In view of Summerall's recent reaction in Columbia to a challenge to his authority, as well as to the criticism of his actions and decisions during his military career (see his responses to the comments of Conrad Babcock, Dickman, Liggett, Mitchell, and Pershing), a stinging response or an abrupt resignation could certainly be predicted. Indeed, he wrote in his memoir that "Ordinarily, the failure of the Board to support me in carrying out its own regulations would have discredited me and so weakened my authority that as to render my efforts useless. I finally decided to take the position that I had done my duty and that the exercise of the superior authority of the Board could in no way reflect on me." He also stated that "although [in the future] the Board constantly reversed my action appeals to it [in] all cases of punishment, I felt no concern as to the consequences."[49]

Several factors and recent developments quite likely influenced Summerall's decision to accept the Board's breaking the promise that Colonel Thomas had made when it overturned the president's decision. He persuaded Lang to withdraw his resignation, and realized, perhaps, that when the Corps of Cadets, the faculty, public officials, as well as the Board of Visitors, appealed to him to withdraw his resignation after the confrontation in Columbia, he had gained the kind of support that would secure and sustain enough of his authority over the academic and military operations of the college to justify his remaining as president. Perhaps also he recalled that, on occasion, when Presidents Coolidge and Hoover had challenged his actions, he, nevertheless, had succeeded in remaining army chief of staff, and maintaining their support for his policies and programs. Perhaps in view of his wife's recent illness, he was reluctant to subject her to the emotional and physical demands that a move from their comfortable quarters on campus would impose. In addition, since he felt that his retirement pay was not enough to live on, and The Citadel presidency had been his only job offer with pay, he might well have decided that he could not afford to leave the college.

Nevertheless, when Summerall wrote that "I felt no concern as to the consequences" of the Board's reversal of his decision, he misjudged the impact and influence of his acceptance of their action. With enormous support from all the constituencies of the college, and from the public as well as from public and private officials, Summerall could have stood his ground, as he had done with Pershing in Paris, and with his commands on the battlegrounds of Asia and Europe, and demanded that Thomas and the Board honor the chairman's promise. At that point, it is highly unlikely and improbable that Thomas and his colleagues would have reversed his dismissal of the cadet. Thus triumphant, he would have made certain that his future actions and decisions, as well as those of his successors, to preserve the integrity of The Citadel Code and enforce the highest standards of cadet conduct would be respected and honored by the Board of Visitors, and, most importantly, by the Corps of Cadets.

Summerall's failure to take advantage of the opportunity to exert final authority in disciplinary matters would make his task of enforcing and strengthening The Citadel Code more difficult and frustrating for him. In view of his prestige and his crucial leadership of the college in desperate times, his resignation likely would have forced the Board to reverse its decision to overrule his decision. Even if he had left, the Board certainly would have been reluctant to overrule the disciplinary decisions of a successor, and thus precipitate another resignation or upheaval. Predictably, additional and even more serious disciplinary cases lay ahead, but with the chief operating officer of the college prevented from exercising ultimate authority in disciplinary decisions, the Board, and ultimately the Corps of Cadets, would remain in charge of these matters. In addition, the individual most responsible for instituting and preserving the integrity of The Citadel Code no longer would have the authority to insure that cadets would honor and sustain its principles. And, contrary to his assertion that he felt no concern about the consequences, within a decade he would face a challenge even more serious, and one which would make more difficult the president's authority to enforce discipline in the corps.

On 23 October 1935, President Franklin D. Roosevelt spoke on campus. His cheerful address could be seen as a harbinger of better days ahead. He recalled an earlier visit to the Old Citadel when he was assistant secretary of the navy, and said he was delighted to find that it had been "reproduced," and would be continued for "generations to come." The president told the crowd that he was "happy that The Citadel is under the command of my old friend, General Summerall," and was also happy to be welcomed by the governor and the mayor. His only unhappy reference was to the absence of "another old friend, your Senator James F. Byrnes."[50]

Roosevelt's remarks seemed to reflect the reemergence and resurgence of the college. Summerall's decision to remain as president; his tough financial restrictions; the generous support the college received from his friends and supporters; and an admiring and perhaps chastised state legislature, combined to pull The Citadel through the crises of the early thirties. By fiscal year 1936–1937, income had increased over the previous year by $119,000, state appropriations had increased by $7,000, and the number of cadets had grown to 888. Cadets slept on mattresses and box springs instead of matted straw pallets, and mowers cut the grass on the parade ground every week. Roads had been paved, and the library had been expanded and relocated to a large area in the Main College Building, which had been completed and renamed Bond Hall in September 1932.[51]

With loans and grants from the Works Project Administration of the federal government, and authorization from the legislature to issue bonds, The Citadel embarked on an even greater building program. By 1940, a new mess hall, chapel, and 24 faculty apartments had been constructed, Bond Hall had been doubled in size, a new barracks was started, and all barracks rooms and facilities had been refurbished and reequipped. Campus facilities were sufficient to accommodate a Corps of Cadets of 1,196, and The Citadel enrollment had increased to 1,196 cadets. Funding was solid and secure.[52]

When he assumed the presidency, Summerall was as concerned about the academic quality and standing of The Citadel as he was about the college's funding and physical plant. In his memoir, he commented that when he became president, "the college had no standing in the educational world," and that he had received from the University of Illinois a report that rated The Citadel as a third class college. To overcome that lowly distinction and elevate that ranking, he began a campaign that recalled his hard-driving attacks on the western front in the World War.

In Summerall's opinion, the fact that most of the faculty were Citadel graduates and only a few held advanced degrees was an important reason for its low ranking. He set aside funds to allow faculty who lacked advanced degrees to return to graduate school, pressuring them to take advantage of the opportunity. As a result, the percentage of faculty holding advanced and terminal degrees increased yearly.[53]

During the academic year 1935–1936, he contacted Princeton University to request recommendations for teachers who might be interested in coming to The Citadel. When Dr. A. D. G. Wiles was recommended, Summerall promptly hired him (there were no legally approved and collegial search processes then) and appointed him to head the English department. By 1940, the number of faculty members holding master's degrees had more than doubled, and the number holding doctoral degrees had increased by more than 50 percent.[54]

With the support and assistance of the faculty, he added a department of classics to teach Latin, Greek, and philosophy, as well as departments of electrical engineering and political science and government. He asked the State Department to prepare the curriculum for the department of political science and government, and sent a faculty member to Washington to prepare for the installation of the curriculum. He initiated a reform of the curriculum that eliminated a number of marginal courses and added more specialized courses in each departmental major. In 1935, The Citadel offered the Bachelor of Arts degree in English, Modern Languages and History, and Bachelor of Science degrees in Chemistry, Physics, Civil Engineering, Business Administration, and Pre-Medical. In 1939, the accrediting agency for collegiate civil engineering programs, the Engineers' Council for Professional Development, notified The Citadel that the college's program had been duly accredited.[55] Under Summerall's leadership, The Citadel had improved the professional qualifications of its faculty, established a strong and extensive academic program in the humanities, business administration, and pre-medicine, maintained its overall accreditation, and gained accreditation for its civil engineering program. Summerall's strong personality and his hard-driving will had sustained The Citadel, and had restored its vitality, viability, and respectability. But in other respects, Summerall's command and control of the college's planning and operations was not so fortuitous.

With his black cape flowing behind him as he made daily inspection tours of the campus, Summerall looked like "Batman" to the cadets and held the faculty and staff in awe. He hovered over the faculty and scrutinized their performance to make certain, as Captain Reilly had advised long ago, that there would be nothing to explain in his command. The memos he sent to faculty members who had neglected to turn off the lights and radiators when they left their classrooms left many of them fearful to check their mail slots. He would stand outside of classrooms to see if professors arrived punctually to their classes, and regularly visited classrooms. If a faculty member arrived late, or if Summerall concluded that the professor was poorly prepared or lacked proper elocution, he would send him a memo that called attention to his shortcomings, and demanded improvement. He would also send a copy to the professor's department head. He required each member of the faculty to submit a report at the beginning of the fall semester describing what each one had done during the summer to improve his teaching and expertise.[56]

On the one hand, Summerall's relentless scrutiny and driving of the faculty led them to improve their qualifications and performance, and doubtless convinced them to arrive on time for class, and turn off the lights and radiators when they left their classrooms. On the other hand, as Professor Wiles remembered, "Some of the faculty got so frightened that they could not do their best work."[57] Deans and department heads faithfully adopted Summerall's authoritarian style. Through their loyal obedience, they helped to solidify a strict hierarchy of authority, reinforcing Summerall's impact and helping to institutionalize and perpetuate an authoritarian system of college governance. Most faculty respected Summerall and were grateful for his having saved the institution and their livelihoods as Citadel professors, but many resented the imperialistic and paternalistic power he and his officials exercised over them. Fearing that their loyalty to The Citadel could be questioned, they chose not to speak out, or advocate a more collegial form of college governance. Rather, they confined their ideas for reform and restructuring to discreet discussions among themselves.[58]

After Summerall arrived at The Citadel he found that "hazing was practiced to an extreme degree. At one inspection Colonel Lang found that over 34 fourth classmen [freshmen] showed bruises from being beaten." Not only were the freshmen physically abused, but each senior cadet "detailed" a freshman to clean his room, care for his uniform and rifle, and perform various other services, that Summerall referred to as "menial."[59] In return for these services, the senior beneficiary "looked out" for the freshman, shepherding him through the physical and mental challenges of his freshman year.

After a few years of inspecting barracks and observing cadet conduct, Summerall realized the extent of the "detail" system. Undeterred by the Board's overruling of his decision to dismiss an offending cadet in 1933, he instructed Colonel Lang's successor as commandant, Lieutenant Colonel Jesse Gaston, to enact measures at the beginning of the 1937–1938 year to end the system.[60]

In the evening of 15–16 March 1938, after resentment had smoldered for months, the seniors in one of the two barracks staged what amounted to a riot. They set off firecrackers, threw trashcans down stairwells, and glass bottles and buckets of water onto the paved quadrangle in the center of the four-story structure. The uprising was brought under control a day later, and all 400 cadets in the barracks were placed on restriction. Summerall threatened to expel the entire senior class if the disturbance were repeated. He placed on probation all but three of the seniors in that barracks, commending those three as well as the cadets in the other barracks for their loyalty and sense of duty.[61] The "probationary" cadets stayed out of trouble the rest of the academic year and were graduated on time in June. Summerall, backed by the Board in this case, apparently had succeeded in his determination to eliminate the "detail" system.

Summerall's crackdown on the seniors' prized privilege of service by the freshmen did not keep them from continuing a springtime event that had become an annual tradition since Summerall became president. Beginning at 0715 hours on 4 March 1932, Summerall's 65th birthday, the entire corps marched to his quarters, and stood at attention while the band played a birthday tribute to the general. In response, he greeted them on the front steps in his dark blue, full-dress uniform, with shining brass buttons vertically aligned in parallel rows on the front of his blouse, his chest full of ribbons, and gleaming gold epaulets embroidered with four silver stars on each shoulder. Standing erect and as firmly as ever, he exclaimed, "Gentlemen, this is indeed a pleasant surprise."[62] Thus began the most memorable tradition of the Summerall years. In every year subsequent to 1932, the corps would assemble at his quarters early on the morning of his birthday, and Summerall would appear "per schedule" in his sartorial splendor to proclaim so all could hear, "Gentlemen, this is indeed a pleasant surprise." Succeeding classes of graduates, including his steadfast admirers in the class of 1954,[63] the last class to graduate under Summerall's leadership, would remember fondly these occasions. Their president seemed to enjoy them as much as he did. They remembered them as a time when the stern disciplinarian who was their president, revealed a softer, humorous nature that was more like their own youthful and cheerful exuberance. The birthday celebrations remained for them a reminder of their affection and esteem for their president, as well as their unique experience and education as Citadel cadets.[64]

During the war years of 1941–1945, the specter of the early 1930s rose again as enrollment in the Corps of Cadets declined precipitously, and the entire senior class was called to duty as officers.[65] Junior cadets assumed the seniors' positions as cadet officers, and, at times, the entire corps dwindled to fewer than 150. Fortunately for the continuation of the college and for the faculty and staff, whose jobs depended upon a viable student body, the War Department selected The Citadel as one of several hundred colleges and universities to participate in specialized military-collegiate training programs. Under the Army Specialized Training and Reassignment Program (STAR), selected soldiers were housed, classified and instructed for a period of from five to thirty days, and then designated for specific courses of study in the Army Specialized Training Program (ASTP). In these units, qualified trainees received special instruction in specified curricula for one or more 12-week terms. The Citadel was designated as a site for both programs, and soon the faculty and staff were busy training and educating thousands of young men. With Federal funds flowing in to support these programs, The Citadel was able to retain most of the faculty and staff, and keep the barracks full. By end of the war, more than 10,000 soldiers had been trained on campus by over 100 faculty members. For several

*Army Chief of Staff General George C. Marshall reviewing the
South Carolina Corps of Cadets with General Summerall*

Courtesy United Press International

months after the war, the navy leased several barracks to house sailors waiting for their discharges, and preparations were made to accommodate veteran students under the GI Bill.[66]

As the STAR and ASTP programs began to fill the barracks with soldiers headed to war, Colonel Clarence M. McMurray, professor of military science and tactics, and commandant of cadets, became convinced that hazing was still evident. He had been graduated from The Citadel in 1909 and had recently commanded an infantry regiment in Panama. He had reason to be concerned. Violations of cadet regulations by upperclassmen were frequent, especially those involving drinking and intoxication. The Board of Visitors regularly considered a number of appeals in their meetings on campus. In the year 1942 alone, they heard 42 appeals (amounting to about 10 percent of the entire Corps of Cadets), ranging from coming in after hours, placing "dummies" in beds to hide their absence, uniform violations, public drunkenness, and drinking in barracks.[67] It must have concerned McMurray that the Board either reduced or overruled his punishment orders for all but nine of the cases. In addition, he apparently believed repeated violations and hazing could compromise or interfered with the crucial task of preparing soldiers for war, or even compel the War Department to move its training programs to another institution. If that happened, The Citadel might well have to close down.

In mid-July 1943, a member of the junior class was expelled for hitting a freshman three times with a broom handle.[68] A few days later, the entire junior class (all of whom were pre-med students)—and led by Cadet Ronald Strong, the regimental commander—planned a protest against the bad food in the mess hall, and what some considered the commandant's policies that weakened their authority over the freshmen. Summerall was out of town, and with the Board of Visitors present at evening mess, McMurray entered to mess hall to sit with the Board. In his letter to General Summerall of 26 July 1943, McMurray stated that when he appeared, the cadets stopped eating and sat in silence.[69] Dr. R. L. Cockfield, later the superintendent of the Lake City South Carolina School Board, but then a member of that junior class, recalled that McMurray went into the kitchen to investigate, whereupon the cadets then resumed eating. When he returned they stopped eating again, and "silenced the commandant," as Dr. Cockfield stated.[70] When Cadet Strong sat silently, McMurray later wrote that he walked over to his table and asked him what was wrong. Strong answered nothing. McMurray then ordered the cadets to return to barracks, where he expressed his displeasure at what had occurred and relieved Strong as the regimental commander. Then he called all the junior officers together, and asked by seniority each of them in turn to take command. All refused. He then ordered other members of the junior class to serve as temporary cadet officers, pending the reorganization of the Corps of Cadets. McMurray placed Strong and the 16 other juniors who had refused to assume command under "room arrest" for refusing to obey orders.[71]

Colonel McMurray questioned at length the other members of the junior class about whether they had knowledge of a "conspiracy," to "silence" the commandant, or if they were aware of any intention by cadet officers to refuse command. He determined that they were not involved in any plan to silence the commandant or later to refuse command. Thus, McMurray limited his order of suspension to Strong and his 16 fellow officers. Strong was charged with "aiding and allowing a conspiracy, failure to take command...during a crisis....," and making false statements to the Board in his appeal. McMurray charged the others with disobeying a specific order, and also with making false statements to the Board. All 17 appealed to the Board to revoke their suspension.[72]

On 7 August, the Board of Visitors met to hear their appeals. Each cadet was allowed to make a statement and call witnesses in his own defense. They also were permitted to cross-examine other witnesses and statements of the commandant.[73] Colonel McMurray presented the evidence based upon his own statements and interviews with members of the junior class. Cadet Strong's father, an army major general, came from Washington to defend his son, and a marine major who had been graduated from The Citadel returned to represent his son and the remaining cadets. After hearing 14 hours of testimony, the Board concluded that the evidence presented by the commandant did not sustain the conspiracy change against Strong, nor did it indicate that he failed to act promptly. They also ruled that none of the other cadets had understood that the commandant intended one of them to take command upon Strong's relief. They further decided no cadet had intended disrespect for the commandant, and none had submitted false statements to the Board. In conclusion, they revoked the suspension of all 17 cadets and ruled that Strong be restored to his previous status. He later withdrew from The Citadel, but his classmates remained and completed their degrees.[74] The "mutiny" of 1943 was over, but its immediate and long-term impact was deep and decisive.

In General Order No. 3, dated 7 August 1943 (see above, endnote 72), Summerall excoriated the cadet officers who had "betrayed the trust and confidence placed in them and were disloyal to The Citadel." He noted that they had been deferred to continue their studies, and by their actions "have shown themselves unworthy of the preference given them over others not so favored. They have demonstrated that they are not officer material and are not fit to be officers of the armed forces. Their continuing presence constitutes a grave menace to the college and exposes it to disloyalty, antagonism, defiance of authority and outbreak. Their bad example to the lower classes is a lasting evil." Summerall closed his blistering rebuke by expressing renewed concern, which McMurray definitely shared with him, that evidence of this kind of behavior, added to "evil" of hazing, "before the disciplined soldiers present can only bring the college into disrepute," and endanger, he might well have added, its very existence.[75]

In a letter to Colonel Thomas, that he wrote on the same day that he issued General Order No. 3, Summerall affirmed equally strong concerns about his own authority, and the commandant's as well, to enforce discipline in the Corps of Cadets when the Board continued to overrule their decisions. Thomas had asked him "to state frankly what could be done to improve discipline at The Citadel." He wrote that "nothing can be done to improve discipline," since action by the college authorities [president and commandant] "is generally set aside upon appeal to the Board." He continued that "As long as the cadets believe that they can appeal to the Board of Visitors and have the punishment imposed by the authorities removed or have their offenses go unpunished when adjudged by the Board, there can be no permanent improvement and no military discipline."

Summerall then spelled out, for Colonel Thomas's edification, his own definition of, and his belief in, the great value of discipline. For his earlier admirers and critics of his command of subordinates on the march and in battle, or in times of peace, that definition would not have been a surprise. He wrote that "Discipline means making men do what they do not want to do and no way has ever been found to accomplish this but force; hence, the expression, 'enforce discipline.' It can not be maintained by appeasement, concessions, requests, condonation or acquittal. Talk about using tact and judgment is futile. The oppression exercised over fourth classmen [freshmen] is not discipline but the antithesis of discipline. This is shown by the indiscipline of those who were subjected to its so-called benefits as soon as they became the oppressors."

Summerall concluded by emphasizing the importance of his absolute authority in disciplinary matters in the military environment of The Citadel. That this authority should be upheld was even more crucial in wartime, when two separate and distinct groups of students existed side by side on campus. "In the military profession," he wrote, "guilt or innocence must be established by military men. No military organization could exist if officer and soldiers could appeal their cases to a civilian tribunal. The effect of the two systems is shown at The Citadel where soldiers of only a few months service are highly disciplined while cadets of two or three years at The Citadel are mutinous and insubordinate. Yet the soldiers must see that these cadets [are] being trained to become officers, perhaps over them. The Board has a right to follow any course it desires but the consequences are inevitable. It is only fair to recognize that when the college authorities have done their duty and have been sustained they are not responsible for the results."[76]

In spite of his condemnation of the Board's actions, Summerall elected to remain as president, largely for the same reasons he had asserted 10 years earlier, when the board initially overruled his decision to expel a cadet for disciplinary reasons. His decision to "soldier on" reaffirmed and essentially institutionalized the power of the Board to overrule the president's disciplinary authority over the Corps of Cadets. It would be extremely difficult or impossible for future Citadel presidents to eliminate the abuses of hazing or institute reforms of the traditions that governed freshman conduct or in the training of freshmen by upperclassmen. Thus, even as the college continued to remain a viable academic institution with a strong enrollment, the disturbing undercurrent of hazing and the potential for disruptive and debilitating upheaval would continue to loom over its existence.

Following the end of World War II, an influx of veteran students increased enrollment almost to full capacity, while the Corps of Cadets steadily was rebuilt to its prewar numbers. In 1946 there were 427 cadets and 245 veteran students on campus; in 1947 the numbers were 743 cadets and 1,095 veteran students; in 1948 the Corps of Cadets had reached the total of 1,046, with 1,225 veterans; by 1949 there were 1,141 cadets and 859 veterans; at the beginning of the decade of the 1950s, the number of veterans had begun to decline, but cadet enrollment gradually increased. Cadets and veterans attended classes together, but were housed in separate barracks and ate in separate mess halls. Married veterans lived off campus. By 1953, the Corps of Cadets had been organized into four battalions: infantry, artillery, engineers and ordnance, and air force and band. By 1953, cadet enrollment had reached 1,291, and the total number of veterans had fallen to 109. Faculty teaching loads were heavy, averaging 15.7 hours per week, with an average of 70.1 students per faculty member.[77]

Colonel McMurray retired in 1946, with high praise from Summerall for his service, and was succeeded over the next seven years by colonels T. I. Futch and J. H. Madison, whom Citadel author Nicholson credits with improvements in morale within the Corps of Cadets and among veteran students. In 1948, Colonel Futch and the cadet regimental commander received the Algernon Sidney Sullivan Award for distinguished service to the college.[78] With faculty and staff working hard to restore the strength and viability of the college, and with veterans and cadets coexisting peacefully and constructively, The Citadel was adapting well to the postwar conditions.

Summerall predictably kept a busy schedule in the community. He served as chairman of the local chapter of the Red Cross and the Salvation Army, and for a number of years was senior warden at the Episcopal Church of the Holy Communion, where he had been baptized and confirmed when he was a student in Dr. Porter's Holy Communion Church Institute. He was made Sovereign Grand Inspector General in South Carolina of the Masonic Order, and was elected to the organization's Supreme Council. He and Laura enjoyed the meetings of the Supreme Council in Washington, and they took many trips around the country to the annual reunions of the First Division Association.[79]

On campus, Summerall initiated another building program to accommodate a thriving enrollment. From his meticulous supervision of college spending during the war, the college had managed to accumulate $400,000 in savings from government funded tuition and rentals during the war. With an additional $600,000 in state appropriations, obtained without any legislator questioning of Summerall about The Citadel's budget, the college was able to add an academic building with 64 classrooms and office space for faculty, and an apartment building with 16 apartments for officers of the faculty and staff. In addition, the legislature authorized state loans that The Citadel would use in the future to build an apartment building for 24 families, an engineering building, a hospital ward for the college infirmary, a student activities building, and improvements to several existing college facilities.[80] Although many of these projects would not be completed until after Summerall had left the college presidency, he had laid the critical groundwork and secured the funding for the postwar resurgence, as well as the future growth and development of The Citadel.

As Summerall approached his 81st birthday and his 16th commencement at the college, he suffered the loss of his wife after almost 47 years of marriage. Laura Mordecai Summerall died on 23 April 1948, six years after she had suffered a severe stroke, which left her unable to participate in social and civic affairs at the side of her husband, or be at his side at social events and receptions on campus. Her condition also forced her to give up her own charitable activities such as teaching sewing to women at Red Cross centers, delivering food baskets to poor families, and working for the Army Relief Society, the organization that provided financial assistance to widows and orphans of deceased Regular Army soldiers.[81] Funeral services were held in The Citadel Chapel, and burial followed on 27 April, at Arlington National Cemetery. The shaded and spacious gravesite was on a gentle, sloping hillside facing eastward, overlooking the Potomac River and beyond to the Mall and the Capitol building.

After the saddened, octogenerian Citadel president returned to the college, he was engaged in a campaign against an enemy he considered as threatening as any he had faced on the battlefield; namely, Communism. Exercising his authoritarian control over the faculty, he told Colonel Wiles, the head of the English department and chairman of the library committee, that he would admit to the library

*Charles P. Summerall at home*

Courtesy Colonel Robert R. McCormick Research Center

books on Russia that were historical or geographical, but none that were either "ideological" or "speculative." He also told Wiles to review all books that the library purchased, and if he found "anything wrong with them, they should be thrown away." Wiles left a note in his papers that Summerall commonly referred to Russian Communism as "the devil loose in the world," and "wanted no books in the library that showed anything about communism in a favorable light."

On 25 July 1950, Summerall sent a memorandum to the registrar, the adjutant, heads of departments, and the librarian, noting that "A check of subversive books in the Library shows that six books ordered by department heads are barred by the Army. The publishers specialize in Communistic books. Heads of departments are responsible for the books ordered by them and they should protect the Library against inroads of Communistic literature." He followed this instruction with a memorandum to Wiles that listed the titles of "Propaganda leaflets or periodicals," such as *Soviet Russia Today* and *USSR* ("official publication of the Soviet Embassy"), and "Commercial Publications" such as *The New Republic*, *The Nation*, *Salute*, *The New Leader*, *Plain Talk*, and *The Daily Worker* ("Communist Newspaper").[82]

Colonel Wiles obediently informed the committee that "The President is concerned about the spread of communistic literature and about the discovery of some of it in the Citadel Library. He has therefore, asked the Library Committee...to examine all periodical and pamphlet literature in the Library and all books on political science, economics, and sociology, in order to weed out all that may be clearly communistic in their leanings." The library committee met and resolved that "all periodicals pamphlets, and books which present communism in a definitely favorable light be segregated and a list thereof presented to the President." Their report stated that "The following is a list of publications already stigmatized as communistic," and dutifully cited the publications Summerall had specified.[83]

Undoubtedly, Summerall and the faculty had reason enough to be concerned about the threat of the Soviet Union and Soviet Communism to national security. The Cold War had elevated tensions on both sides of what Winston Churchill had called the Iron Curtain, and the invasion by the Communist regime of North Korea of the Republic of South Korea in June 1950 confirmed fears that the power of communism threatened the free, democratic West. Yet, Wiles and his colleagues also were obligated to analyze and evaluate critically the ideas and assertions embodied in the "communistic" material, in order to involve their students in the most critical process of higher education, and, equally importantly, to preserve their own academic freedom.

Quite likely, if Wiles and others had taken such a determined stand, they would have received a blistering reprimand from Summerall, and would have placed at risk their employment at The Citadel. And they needed their jobs just as much as Summerall had needed his. In addition, they were reluctant to oppose the individual whom they admired and respected for his revitalization of The Citadel; for his rescue of the college from the Great Depression; and for his guidance of the institution safely through World War II and successfully into the postwar world. He had earned their respect for imposing upon himself greater sacrifices than those he expected from them. Also, they admired his ability to impress the public, and were grateful for his skill in winning the support of legislators while preventing their meddling in college policy and operations. Nevertheless, their silent submission to Summerall's power over them clearly reaffirmed the president's control and domination of academic matters. They unwittingly prepared the way for a successor to wield the same kind of intimidating authority over their own generation as well as the generations who would compose the future faculty.

In the spring of 1952, after more than 85 years of robust health and seemingly inexhaustible energy, Summerall suffered a serious prostate infection, and underwent surgery. After a lengthy hospital stay, he returned to campus, and dutifully went to his office every day. Apparently realizing that he could not continue indefinitely as president, he met with a committee of the Board of Visitors at his

*General Summerall with the Strom Thurmonds*

Courtesy The Citadel Archives & Museum, Charleston, South Carolina

home, and agreed with them that it was their duty to seek out someone to succeed him.[84] The committee then began contacting possible successors.

Meanwhile, the faculty realized that Summerall's iron grip on presidential authority might well be weakening. After the school year 1952–1953 had begun, Wiles and others noticed that, instead of walking, he had resorted to driving himself around the campus on his daily tours, and saw that he had trouble getting in and out of his car, as well as steering it. The wife of the college adjutant brought in his lunch every day, and she could see, as did others as well, that Summerall was losing weight, and looking increasingly frail.[85]

Besides seeing Summerall's physical decline, the Board also had seen his frailty, and had an additional reason to be concerned. In early June 1952, after consulting with Governor James F. Byrnes, the committee had contacted General Lucius D. Clay, who had retired from the army in 1949. He had served as Military Governor of the U.S. Occupation Zone in Germany, including managing the Berlin Airlift of 1948–49, and was serving on several corporate boards. Clay replied that he would not even consider the position of president of The Citadel until General Summerall had retired or resigned, or with his death the position became vacant.[86] On 3 September, the committee wrote Summerall that they had had difficulty getting a "distinguished man with military and administrative experience" to accept the position as long as Summerall was still in the office. "This is understandable," they wrote, because "out of their great respect for you...they do not wish to appear as seeking a post still occupied by you." The committee then delicately suggested that "if you have any intention of retiring, you might consider the propriety of notifying us of your intention to do so, effective, of course, at the end of six months, or at the end of the school term, just as you prefer. This would greatly assist us in securing your successor."[87]

Yet, Summerall, on his return to campus and with the start of a new academic year, chose not to go quietly. Despite the Board's cautious and sensitive approach to the question of his retirement and possible successor, he seemed offended by their handling of the matter. And also, perhaps, he had come to believe that the Board did not appreciate fully his rescue of The Citadel from oblivion, and his transformation of the college from an institution with "no standing in the educational world" into a viable institution of higher education. At any rate, rather than retiring as president, on 9 September he wrote Colonel James R. Westmoreland, chairman of the board, that he would resign effective on 30 June 1953.[88] That still was not good enough for General Clay, who refused emphatically the offer to accept the position.[89]

With Governor Byrnes then taking a more active role in the presidential search, he contacted General Mark W. Clark, who was ending his military career as commander in chief of the United Nations command in Korea. Clark cabled Byrnes that after completing his assignment in Korea, he would be interested in The Citadel position. After signing the armistice agreement that ended the Korean War in late July 1953, he went to Washington and talked with President Eisenhower about The Citadel presidency. Eisenhower complimented the college and its graduates, many of whom he had served with over the course of his military career. He also informed Clark that he had recently written a letter recommending for the position an old friend, General Willard S. Paul, but he told Clark that he thought Clark would be the better choice.[90]

Two weeks before his resignation was effective, Summerall was informed that General and Mrs. Clark, as well as Governor Byrnes would visit the campus. When they arrived at the Charleston airport, they were greeted by the mayor and other city officials, as well as several reporters, and escorted to The Citadel. The Corps of Cadets welcomed them with a parade and a review, and General Summerall received them in his spartan office, just off the mail hallway of Bond Hall. Its chief amenities were a bulky radiator behind his desk, a plain coat rack in one corner, and several hard-back chairs for guests.

*The Citadel campus with buildings constructed during Summerall's presidency*

Courtesy The Citadel Archives & Museum, Charleston, South Carolina

The meeting was rather awkward, and other than an exchange of pleasantries, little was said. Afterwards, Clark turned to Byrnes and said, "Is this the president's office? A little cubby hole like this?" When Mrs. Clark mentioned to Byrnes that she had seen Summerall's quarters on campus, he said, "Oh well, that house, we'll tear it down. We'll build you a house to your own specification." He turned to Clark and said, "And we'll get you a new dean." But Clark quickly replied, "Well, wait a minute. I'll get my own dean."[91] If any member of the faculty had overheard that response, he might well have realized that if General Clark became the president, his command of the faculty would be as authoritarian as Summerall's had been.

Before they left the campus, Byrnes pressed Clark to accept The Citadel presidency, but Clark said he needed time to think it over. He and his wife then left for Charlotte, North Carolina, where they stopped to visit an old friend. After discussing the matter with his wife, and perhaps also with his friend, Clark telephoned Byrnes, to tell him that he would accept The Citadel's offer. After New York City had showered the Clarks with a ticker-tape parade down Broadway, Clark retired from the army on 31 October 1953. Immediately he began preparations to take over as president of The Citadel.[92]

Meanwhile, General Summerall had long since departed the campus. As soon as Clark and his other guests had left his office, he began clearing his desk in preparation for an early departure. Two weeks later, in an interview in the *Charleston News and Courier*, he was quoted as saying that he had not made any specific plans for life in retirement, but he might write an autobiography for his family, but not for publication. He stated that he had no desire to travel, but "If I can go anywhere, do any good, that is what I want." In a parting jab at the Board of Visitors, he asserted that he was "proud of my age, but it means nothing. I am just as young as I ever was; I can do as much. What I ever was, I am. I've never lost my vital forces by indulgence, in liquor or tobacco." In two final statements that might well be taken as a summing up of Summerall's childhood, youth, and career as a serious-minded and conscientious servant of his country, he said that "I play no games. Work has been my hobby."[93]

Before Summerall took his leave of the campus, the Board of Visitors unanimously voted to name the cadet chapel as The General Charles Pelot Summerall Chapel, and honored him with a fine tribute to his character, fortitude, and to his long and distinguished service to The Citadel. The faculty honored him with a dinner in the mess hall and presented him with a television set. The next morning, on 30 June, he packed his own car, had lunch with a neighbor on campus, returned to his office for the last time, and turned over his keys to the college adjutant. He escorted Summerall to his car and said a tearful good-bye as the general drove away.[94]

When Summerall arrived in Aiken later that afternoon, he was welcomed by members of the Aiken Chamber of Commerce, Mayor Charles M. Jones and other city officials, and Strom Thurmond, former governor of South Carolina. A police escort led Summerall to his new home, known as White Hall, a spacious and handsome house located at the end of a drive lined with magnolia trees on a sprawling estate within the Aiken city limits.[95] In 1940, Colonel Robert R. McCormick, publisher of the *Chicago Tribune* and Citadel benefactor, had given the property to the college expressly for Summerall's residency in his retirement. As noted earlier, McCormick had served in the 5th Artillery Regiment as part of Summerall's 1st Artillery Brigade. He had even named his own estate west of Chicago in honor of the First Division's victory at Cantigny. Ironically, and perhaps of some slight irritation to its new resident, the street address of White Hall in Aiken was Whiskey Road. The Citadel had agreed to take care of all expenses for the care and upkeep of the house and grounds, and Summerall had to pay for only heat, light, water, telephone, and any personal services.[96] Despite his new address being on Whiskey Road, it had its compensations.

*The Citadel's Summerall Guards*
Courtesy The Citadel Archives & Museum, Charleston, South Carolina

At White Hall, Summerall lived by himself, assisted only by a housekeeper. His house was comfortably outfitted with his furniture from his quarters at The Citadel. Among the memorabilia, portraits, awards and decorations he had collected and received during the span of his long career, the flag of the First Division was prominent, as was a flag, emblazoned with an Imperial Dragon, that had flown from the walls that surrounded the Forbidden City in Peking. Occasionally he drove to Charleston to meet with the Masonic Lodge, to visit with friends, and had a pleasant dinner one evening with General and Mrs. Clark.[97] Summerall remained close to his son and family, but Charles Jr. had just returned to Boston (where he had lived as professor of Military Science and Tactics at Harvard University), after serving from 1952 to 1954 with the Military Assistance Advisory Group in the United Kingdom. Shortly thereafter he retired from the army with the rank of colonel after a distinguished 30-year career (he was awarded the Silver Star in World War II). So Charles Jr. was almost a thousand miles away as his father languished alone at White Hall.

Summerall's correspondence with Mrs. Maude J. Reynolds, the secretary of The Citadel's alumni association, who also handled Summerall's personal correspondence, reveals his growing despondency over his solitary existence. Although Summerall received visits from friends in Aiken, these letters also show his difficulty in coping with retirement after a lifetime of commitment to military and civilian service. On 8 July, one week after he arrived at White Hall, he wrote that "I am about settled, but no place could be home except The Citadel." A week later he wrote: "I am a like a ship adrift and hope some pilot will tell me what to do." In his third letter of that month, he thanked Mrs. Reynolds for her letter that he had just received, and the "nice" letters she had prepared for his signature. He added that "I hope you will set a date for your visit very soon. Of course, I am lonely. I can never have friends like those at The Citadel. Please give my warm regards to all." On 2 November, he expressed his hope that "I shall see you whenever possible. I wish that you would come and lunch with me some Sunday."[98]

During the next several months, Summerall's health, which had been improving, again weakened, and he went to the Johns Hopkins Hospital in Baltimore. After he returned to Aiken, he thanked Mrs. Reynolds for her letter of 24 June 1954, and informed her the next day that "They found nothing wrong with me at Johns Hopkins except too many white corpuscles." He asked her to bring his former secretary to see him, and, with a sad and nostalgic feeling, wrote that "My heart is always with The Citadel as I left it. I suppose I would hardly know it now." Two months later, he was admitted to Walter Reed Army Medical Center in Washington. To be near and to comfort their beloved father and father-in-law, Charles Jr. and his wife Julia rented their home in Massachusetts and leased a house in the capital. On 27 September he wrote a short letter, informing Mrs. Reynolds that he was "no better and I hate to think I am worse. I have not strength, and can eat very little." Some time later, he added an unsteady and faltering signature to a printed thank-you note for "sympathy and good wishes in my illness," and, just below his signature, stated that "I am too ill to write."[99] These few words to his devoted friend were, perhaps, the last that Summerall wrote. He died on 14 May 1955, three months after his 88th birthday, in the same room at Walter Reed where General Pershing had died on 15 July 1948, three months after his own 88th birthday.

On 17 May, Summerall's funeral was held in the chapel at Fort Myer. The flag-draped casket with his remains was carried on a caisson pulled by horses down the hill to the gravesite just below the grave of Captain Reilly, his long-ago superior and mentor. The honor guard of the Third Division fired a 17-gun artillery salute, followed by a volley of rifle fire. The bugler played taps, and General Summerall was laid to rest beside the grave of his dear wife. Space was reserved for their son Charles and his wife Julia. In bold capital letters SUMMERALL was inscribed across the front of the large granite gravestone, and the biblical verse from 2 Timothy, 4:7 was carved into back of the stone. It

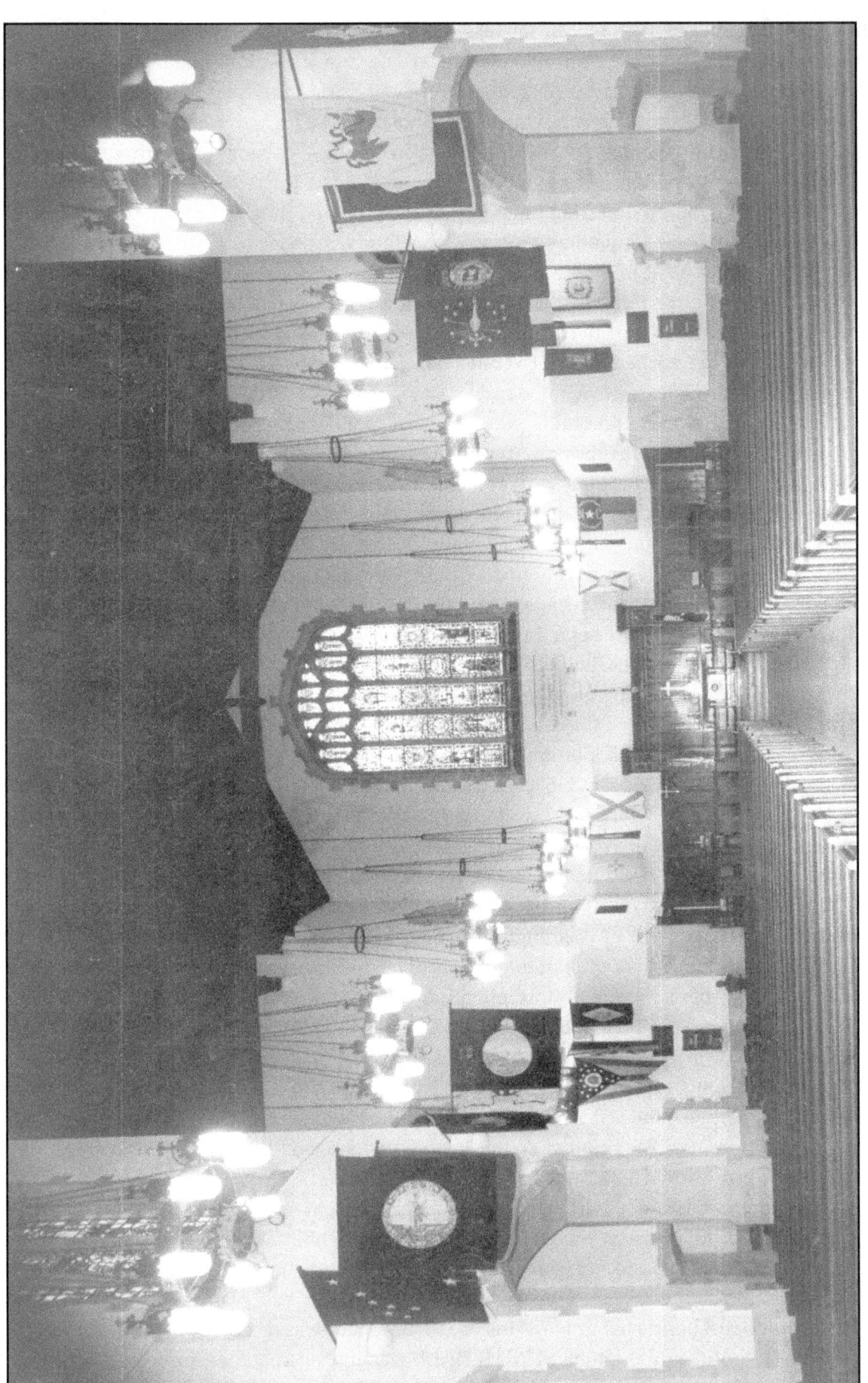

*Summerall Chapel, constructed 1936–37, bears the message "Remember Now Thy Creator in the Days of Thy Youth" at the front entrance to summarize the spiritual atmosphere of The Citadel*

Courtesy The Citadel Archives & Museum, Charleston, South Carolina

reads as follows. "I have fought a good fight, I have finished my course, I have kept the faith." This same verse is also inscribed into the tombstone of Captain Reilly, and it is a fitting tribute to Summerall's strength of mind and body. His strong personality and vigorous life inspired many of his followers, as he had been inspired by men like Captain Reilly, to dedicate their lives and energy to the mastery of the challenges they faced. Summerall, whatever the defeats and failures he had suffered, would be forever remembered for his triumphal deeds and indelible good works.

# Summerall Chronology

Born Blount's Ferry, FL ................................................................................................ 4 March 1867

Student, Holy Communion Church Institute, Charleston, SC .................................. 1882–1885

School teacher and principal, Astatula and Leesburg, FL ......................................... 1885–1888

Cadet, United States Military Academy, West Point, NY, First Captain, Class of 1892 .......... 1888–1892

Second Lieutenant, First Infantry, Benicia Barracks, CA ........................................... 1892–1893

Heavy Battery, Fifth Artillery, Coast Defenses of San Francisco, Presidio, CA ....... 1893–1896

Light Battery, Fifth Artillery, Fort Hamilton, New York Harbor, NY ....................... 1896–1898

Aide-de-Camp to General Graham, Department of the Gulf, Atlanta, GA,
   II Army Corps, Camp Alger, VA, and Camp Meade, PA ........................................ 1898

Aide-de-Camp to General Pennington, Department of the Gulf, Atlanta, GA ....... 1898–1899

First Lieutenant, Light Battery F, Fifth Artillery (Reilly's Battery),
   Participation in Philippine Insurrection ................................................................ 1899–1900

Participation in China Relief Expedition ................................................................... 1900–1901

Marriage to Laura Mordecai, Benicia Arsenal, CA ......................................................... 1901

Captain and Commanding Officer, 106th Company, Coast Artillery,
   Fort Walla Walla, WA; Commanding Officer, Fort Lawton, WA ........................ 1901–1902

Birth of Charles Pelot Summerall, Jr. ................................................................................. 1902

Post Commander, Camp Skagway, AK, and Fort Flagler, WA ................................. 1901–1903

Commanding Officer, Third Battery, Field Artillery, Camp George H. Thomas,
   Chickamauga Park, GA, and Fort Myer, VA ......................................................... 1903–1905

Senior Instructor, Artillery Tactics, U.S. Military Academy, West Point, NY .......... 1905–1911

Major and Commanding Officer, Second Battalion, Third Field Artillery,
   San Antonio, TX, Tobyhanna, PA, and Fort Myer, VA ......................................... 1911–1914

Assistant to Chief, Militia Bureau, War Department, in charge of the Field Artillery,
   National Guard, Washington, DC .......................................................................... 1914–1917

Member, Baker Mission, a military mission to study the organization, training and
   operations of the British and French armies in England and France ....................... 1917

Commanding General, 67th Field Artillery Brigade, Forty-second Division,
   Camp Mills, NY (left for France, October 1917) ........................................................ 1917

Commanding General, 1st Field Artillery Brigade, First Division, France ............. 1917–1918

| | |
|---|---|
| Commanding General, First Division, France | July–October 1918 |
| Commanding General, V Army Corps, France | October 1918–February 1919 |
| Commanding General, IX Army Corps, France | February–April 1919 |
| Commanding General, IV Army Corps, Germany | April–June 1919 |
| Member, Allied Mission of Generals, Inter-Allied Commission of Inquiry on Fiume, Italy | July–August 1919 |
| Attached to American Commission to negotiate Peace in Paris; invited to signing of the treaty at Versailles | July–August 1919 |
| Commanding General, First Division, Camp Zachary Taylor, KY, and Camp Dix, NJ | September 1919–June 1921 |
| Commanding General, Hawaiian Department, Honolulu, Territory of Hawaii | August 1921–August 1924 |
| Commanding General, VIII Corps Area, Fort Sam Houston, TX | October 1924–January 1925 |
| Commanding General, II Corps Area, Governors Island, NY | January 1925–November 1926 |
| Chief of Staff, U.S. Army | November 1926–November 1930 |
| At home in Eustis, FL, awaiting retirement | November 1930–March 1931 |
| President, The Citadel, Charleston, SC | September 1931–June 1953 |
| Died, Walter Reed Army Hospital, Washington, DC | 14 May 1955 |

Buried, Arlington National Cemetery

# Notes

## Introduction

1. Larry I. Bland, ed., *George C. Marshall Interviews and Reminiscences for Forrest C. Pogue* (George C. Marshall Research Foundation: Lexington, Virginia, 1991), p. 242. Hereinafter cited as Bland, *Marshall Interviews*.
2. Leonard J. Fullenkamp, "New Looks at the American Civil War," *Parameters*, US Army War College Quarterly, 28, no. 2 (Summer 1998): 150.

## Chapter One

1. Edward F. Keuchel, *A History of Columbia County, Florida* (Tallahassee, Florida: Sentry Press, 1981), Appendix 3, "Columbia County Original Land Purchases," p. 232. Hereinafter cited as Keuchel, *History*.
2. Charles Pelot Summerall, "The Way of Duty, Honor, Country: An Autobiography" (unpublished memoir, The Citadel Archives and Museum), p. 1. Late in life and mainly for his family, General Summerall dictated an intensely personal account of his life. It is rich in the details of his early life and in his account of his long military career, for which he had access to materials he had assembled. For those whom he considered friends and supporters, he had nothing but praise and appreciation. For many of those with whom he had had serious disagreements or conflicts over the course of his long career of military and civilian service he was equally critical. Hereinafter cited as Summerall memoir.
3. Lake City, Florida, Columbia County Court House, *Property Records, 1866–1869*.
4. Ibid.
5. Summerall memoir, pp. 1–2.
6. Ibid. Summerall quite likely was referring to the attempt of General Seymour to advance from Jacksonville into the interior to recruit blacks, and confiscate whatever food and supplies his men could find. In February 1864, his army was defeated by Confederate forces under General Joseph Finegan at the Battle of Olustee, some 13 miles east of Lake City. Seymour retreated to Jacksonville to prepare to make a stand against an attack that, however, never materialized. It was this Confederate victory at Olustee, coupled with the defeat of Union forces at Natural Bridge on the St. Marks River south of Tallahassee in March 1864 that saved the interior of Florida from invasion. Tallahassee was the only Confederate capital east of the Mississippi that Union forces failed to capture. However, this apparently was of little consolation to Governor John Milton, who committed suicide less than a month after the battle at Natural Bridge. See Charlton W. Tebeau, *A History of Florida* (Coral Gables, Florida: University of Miami Press, 1971), pp. 213–17. Hereinafter cited as Tebeau, *History*.
7. Florida. Board of State Institutions, *Soldiers of Florida in the Seminole Indian-Civil and Spanish-American Wars* (Live Oak, Florida: Democrat Print, 1903; repr., Macclenny, Florida: R. J. Perry, 1983), pp. 204, 226, 319.
8. "The War Between the States, 1861–1865, Glynn County Georgia, 26th Georgia Infantry Regiment, Brunswick Riflemen, 26th Georgia Infantry—A Brief History," http://petersnn.org/petersnn/csarifles.html, pp. 1–8.
9. Summerall memoir, pp. 1–2, 7–8.
10. Ibid., pp. 4–5.
11. Ibid., p. 3; "Thomas Postell Pelot, South Carolina Patriot," *The State Magazine*, 30 May 1954. Hereinafter cited as Pelot, *The State*; A. G. D. Wiles, untitled manuscript on the life of General Summerall, The Citadel Archives and Museum, Chap. 1, p. 4. Wiles received his Ph.D. degree from Princeton University, and came in 1936 to The Citadel as head of the Department of English, serving in that position until 1960. In that year he left The Citadel to become president of Newberry College in Clinton, South Carolina. He retired from that position in 1971. He became an admirer and confidant of Summerall and edited a copy of Summerall's memoir, which Wiles urged him to record. Wiles based his work largely on the memoir, on personal interviews with his subject, and on material found in the Summerall Papers at the Library of Congress. He also conducted research into military strategy and the tactics of the American Expeditionary Forces in World War I. Although of significance in this latter respect, Wiles's manuscript is limited by his effusive acclaim of Summerall's every action, whether in military or civilian life. Hereinafter referred to as Wiles manuscript.

12. *Official Records of the Union and Confederate Navies in the War of the Rebellion* (2 series, 31 vols., Washington: Government Printing Office, 1894–1927), Series I, 1:33. Hereinafter cited as *ORN*; all citations refer to Series 1. The *Lady Davis* originally was an iron tug and had been called the *James Gray*, but was renamed after Jefferson Davis's wife and saw service as a blockade runner. See Francis Boadman Crowinshield *Blockade Running During the Civil War and the Effect of Land and Water Transportation on the Confederacy* (Philadelphia: Porcupine Press, 1974), p. 96, and Philip van Doren Stern, *The Confederate Navy: A Pictorial History* (Garden City, New York: Doubleday and Company, 1962), p. 19.
13. Hunter to Pelot, May 31, 1864, *ORN*, 15:491.
14. Ibid.
15. Pelot to Hunter, June 1, 1864, *ORN*, 15:492; Price to Hunter, June 8, 1864, ibid., 15:501–502; Raimondo Luraghi, *A History of the Confederate Navy*, trans. Paolo E. Coletta (Annapolis, Maryland: Naval Institute Press, 1996), p. 308. Hereinafter cited as Luraghi, *History*.
16. Price to Hunter, June 8, 1864, *ORN*, 15:501–502; Luraghi, *History*, p. 308.
17. Hunter to Secretary of the Navy S. R. Mallory, June 4, 1864, *ORN*, 15:498. Other Confederate reports state that from four to six of their men were killed in the action. See *ORN*, 15:497–498.
18. Price to Hunter, June 8, 1864, *ORN*, 15:502. In his earlier report of June 4, 1864, to Secretary Mallory, Hunter states that the *Water Witch* carried a crew of 77 officers and men and lost 2 killed and 12 wounded. That would mean that 64 were taken as prisoners. Citing Hunter's message to Secretary Mallory of June 4, 1864 (see above, note 17), Raimondo Luraghi states that 77 of the Union crew were prisoners. He failed to note that the figure of 77 referred to the number of officers and crew, rather than to the number taken prisoners. See Luraghi, *History*, p. 309.
19. "a brave and gallant officer," Price to Hunter, June 8, 1864, *ORN*, 15:502; "a most gallant and accomplished officer," Captain C. R. Hansleiter, C.S. Army to Captain W. T. Taliaferro, Asst. Adj. Gen., Thunderbolt, June 4, 1864, *ORN*, 15:497; "most accomplished officers," W. H. Pierson, Acting Assistant Surgeon, U.S. Navy, to Mallory, September 10, 1864, *ORN*, 15:481 (Pierson was serving on the *Water Witch* and was captured in the attack); "whose conduct was beyond all praise," "Extract from an appendix to the report of the Secretary of the [Confederate] Navy, dated April 30, 1864," *ORN*, 15:506; Hunter to Captain S. S. Lee, Captain in Charge, June 9, 1864, *ORN*, 15:500. Lieutenant Pelot is buried in Laurel Grove Cemetery in Savannah, Georgia. On his gravestone is inscribed the tribute that he was "killed in defense of Savannah." See Pelot, *The State*.
20. Summerall memoir, p. 3.
21. Ibid., p. 2.
22. Keuchel, *History*, pp. 113–14; Tebeau, *History*, p. 217.
23. Summerall memoir, p. 7.
24. George Brown Tindall with David E. Shi, *America: A Narrative History*, 3rd ed., vol. 2 (New York: W. W. Norton and Company, 1992), p. 716. Hereinafter cited as Tindall and Shi, *America*.
25. Ibid., p. 717.
26. Quoted in ibid.
27. Jerrell H. Shofner, *Nor Is It Over Yet: Florida in the Era of Reconstruction, 1863–1877* (Gainesville, Florida: The University Presses of Florida, 1974), p. 220. Hereinafter cited as Shofner, *Reconstruction*.
28. Keuchel, *History*, p. 122.
29. Shofner, *Reconstruction*, p. 220.
30. Keuchel, *History*, p. 122.
31. Shofner, *Reconstruction*, p. 220.
32. Keuchel, *History*, p. 127; Tindall and Shi, *America*, p. 719.
33. Shofner, *Reconstruction*, p. 228; Keuchel, *History*, p. 122.
34. Keuchel, *History*, p. 128.
35. Ibid., p. 122.
36. Shofner, *Reconstruction*, p. 228; Keuchel, *History*, p. 130; Tebeau, *History*, p. 252.
37. Shofner, *Reconstruction*, p. 228; Keuchel, *History*, pp. 129–30.
38. Tindall and Shi, *America*, p. 721; Keuchel, *History*, pp. 130–35.
39. Tindall and Shi, *America*, p. 731; Keuchel, *History*, p. 135.
40. Summerall memoir, p. 7.
41. Wiles manuscript, Chap. 2, p. 2; Summerall memoir, p. 7.
42. Summerall memoir, p. 8.
43. Ibid., pp. 1, 7–8.
44. Ibid., p. 8.
45. Ibid.

46. Letter from General Summerall, written to the Lake County Historical Society when he was army chief of staff, quoted in William T. Kennedy, editor in chief, *History of Lake County, Florida: Narrative and Biographical* (Tavares, Florida: Lake County Historical Society, 1988), pp. 17–18. Hereinafter cited as Kennedy, *Lake County*.
47. Eustis Memorial Library, *Florida File*, Charles Pelot Summerall folder, Eustis, Florida. Hereinafter cited as Eustis Library, Summerall folder.
48. Eustis Memorial Library Archives, advertisement in the circular *Semi-Tropical: Lake Eustis, Orange [Lake] County Florida*, No. 14, October 14, 1882, Eustis, Florida.
49. Summerall memoir, p. 8.
50. Kennedy, *Lake County*, pp. 81–82.
51. Ibid., p. 82.
52. Summerall, memoir, p. 8.
53. Ibid., pp. 8–9.
54. A. Toomer Porter, *Led On! Step by Step: Scenes from Clerical, Military Educational, and Plantation Life in the South, 1828–1898* (New York: Arno Press, 1967), pp. 71–80, 91, 104. Hereinafter cited as Porter, *Led On!*
55. Ibid., pp. 121–35.
56. Ibid., pp. 210–18, 223–24.
57. Ibid., pp. 238–42, 307–29.
58. Ibid., pp. 313, 342–43, 358, 377.
59. Ibid., pp. 366–67.
60. Ibid., pp. 363–69.
61. Ibid., p. 380; Summerall memoir, p. 8.
62. Summerall memoir, p. 9.
63. Walter J. Fraser, Jr., *Charleston! Charleston!: The History of a Southern City* (Columbia, South Carolina: University of South Carolina Press, 1989), p. 304. Hereinafter cited as Fraser, *Charleston!*
64. Ibid., p. 307.
65. Summerall memoir, p. 8.
66. Wiles manuscript, Chap. 2, p. 6.
67. United States Military Academy, School History of Candidates, No. 1, 1880 to 1899, "Candidates for Admission, showing time of attendance at School, and time employed as teacher. Also the time employed in Private Study, during the Five Years previous to reporting to the Academy," United States Military Academy Archives, West Point, New York.
68. Summerall memoir, p. 8.
69. Ibid.
70. Ibid.
71. Fraser, *Charleston!*, pp. 323–24.
72. Summerall memoir, p. 9; Kennedy, *Lake County*, p. 69.
73. Summerall memoir, p. 9.
74. Ibid.
75. Eula Meeks, "Oldtimer Recalls Early Astatula," *Orlando Sentinel*, May 3, 1964. Hereinafter cited as Meeks, "Oldtimer."
76. "Centennial Edition," *Leesburg (Florida) Commercial*," May 20, 1987.
77. Ibid.; The Lake County Retired Teachers Association, *Through Schoolhouse Doors: A History of Lake County Schools* (n.p. 1982), pp. 130–31. Hereinafter cited as *Lake County Schools*.
78. Ibid., pp. 31–37.
79. Summerall memoir, p. 9.
80. *Lake County Schools*, p. 61.
81. Summerall memoir, p. 9.
82. *Lake County Schools*, p. 131. The authors of *Lake County Schools* credit Summerall with an impressive leap from small-town, public school principal to high military command when they state that "He was appointed principal of the public school in Leesburg in 1889 and served in this capacity until he became a general." Kennedy, *Lake County*, p. 35; Eustis Library, Summerall folder. Curiously enough, Summerall failed to mention in his memoir that he had served as principal of the Leesburg Public School.
83. Meeks, "Oldtimer."
84. Summerall memoir, p. 9.
85. Ibid., p. 10.
86. Ibid.; Wiles manuscript, Chap. 3, pp. 1–2.

87. Summerall memoir, p. 8.
88. Allan R. Millett, *The General: Robert L. Bullard and Officership in the United States Army, 1881–1925*, Contributions in Military History, Number 10 (Westport, Connecticut: Greenwood Press, 1975), p. 29. Hereinafter cited as Millett, *The General*.
89. Ibid.
90. Wiles manuscript, Chap. 3, p. 2.
91. Ibid.

## Chapter Two

1. Summerall memoir, p. 11.
2. Ibid.
3. *Descriptive Lists of Candidates, 1869 to 1892*, No. 2, United States Military Academy Archives, USMA Archives, USMA Library, West Point, New York.
4. Summerall memoir, pages 4–5, 12.
5. Summerall memoir, p. 11.
6. I. B. Holley, Jr., *General John M. Palmer, Citizen Soldiers, and the Army of a Democracy*, Contributions in Military History, Number 28 (Westport, Connecticut: Greenwood Press, 1982), p. 34. Hereinafter cited as Holley, *Palmer*.
7. Summerall memoir, p. 11.
8. Holley, *Palmer*, pp. 35–36.
9. *School History of Candidates, No. 1* (1880–1899), "Candidates for Admission, showing time of attendance at School, and time employed as Teacher. Also the time employed in Private Study, during the Five Years previous to reporting at the Academy," USMA Archives, USMA Library, West Point, New York.
10. *Post Orders No. 12, U.S. Military Academy*, USMA Archives, USMA Library, West Point, New York. Hereinafter cited as *Post Orders*; Holley, *Palmer*, p. 37.
11. Summerall memoir, p. 11.
12. Ibid.
13. Wiles manuscript, Chap. 3, p. 5.
14. Summerall memoir, p. 11.
15. Millett, *The General*, p. 34; Bracing required the plebe "to throw his shoulders back until the blades met, draw his chin in until it was depressed against his windpipe, draw his abdomen up and walk so that his toes touched the ground before his heels." See Thomas J. Fleming, *West Point: The Men and Times of the United States Military Academy* (New York: William Morrow and Company, 1969), p. 270. Hereinafter cited as Fleming, *West Point*.
16. Stephen E. Ambrose, *Duty, Honor, Country: A History of West Point* (Baltimore: The Johns Hopkins Press, 1966), p. 223. Hereinafter cited as Ambrose, *West Point*. Millett, *The General*, p. 35.
17. Holley, *Palmer*, pp. 36–38; Summerall memoir, p. 12.
18. *Delinquencies, No. 26*, USMA Archives, USMA Library, West Point. Hereinafter cited as *Delinquencies*.
19. Summerall memoir, p. 12.
20. *Delinquencies*.
21. Millett, *The General*, p. 35; Sidney Forman, *West Point: A History of the United States Military Academy* (New York: Columbia University Press, 1950), p. 170. Hereinafter cited as Forman, *West Point*.
22. Ambrose, *West Point*, pp. 223–25.
23. Millett, *The General*, p. 34.
24. Quoted in Carlo d'Este, *Patton: A Genius for War* (New York: HarperCollins, 1995), p. 72. Hereinafter cited as d'Este, *Patton*.
25. Ambrose, *West Point*, pp. 225–26; Fleming, *West Point*, pp. 270–71; Millett, *The General*, p. 35.
26. Summerall memoir, p. 11.
27. Millett, *The General*, p. 35.
28. Summerall memoir, p. 12.
29. Ibid.
30. Forman, *West Point*, p. 148.
31. Ibid.
32. Holley, *Palmer*, p. 38.
33. Summerall memoir, p.12. The young ladies were invited to West Point to attend dances, or hops, and other social events that were held during the summer for plebes and upperclassmen.
34. Millett, *The General*, p. 35.
35. Ibid.

36. Summerall memoir, p. 13.
37. Ibid., pp. 35–36.
38. *Regulations, U.S. Military Academy, 1883*, USMA Archives, USMA Library, West Point, New York. Hereinafter cited as *Regulations*; *Delinquencies*; Millett, *The General*, p. 36;
39. Millett, *The General*, p. 36.
40. Summerall memoir, p. 13; *Delinquencies*.
41. *School History of Candidates, No. 1, 1880 to 1899*, USMA Archives, USMA Library, West Point, NY. Hereinafter cited as *School History*.
42. *Delinquencies*.
43. Millett, *The General*, p. 37.
44. Summerall memoir, pp. 11, 13.
45. United States Military Academy, *1990 Register of Graduates and Former Cadets, 1802–1990, Dwight D. Eisenhower Centennial Edition* (West Point, New York: Association of Graduates, USMA, 1990), p. 285. Hereinafter cited as USMA, *Register*.
46. Summerall memoir, p. 13. Quite probably the verse in the Bible Summerall referred to is Deuteronomy 34:8, "And the children of Israel wept for Moses in the plains of Moab thirty days: so the days of weeping and mourning for Moses were ended."
47. Ibid., p. 14.
48. Millett, *The General*, p. 36.
49. Summerall memoir, p. 14.
50. Ibid.
51. *Post Orders*.
52. Summerall memoir, p. 16.
53. Heath Twichell, Jr., *Allen: The Biography of an Army Officer* (New Brunswick, New Jersey: Rutgers University Press, 1974), p. 20. Hereinafter cited as Twichell, *Allen*. Wiles manuscript, Chap. 3, pp. 7–8; Millett, *The General*, pp. 38–39.
54. Ambrose, *West Point*, pp. 90–91; Millett, *The General*, p. 38; Twichell, *Allen*, pp. 20–21.
55. Ambrose, *West Point*, p. 279.
56. Ibid., p. 197; Fleming, *West Point*, p. 232.
57. Ambrose, *West Point*, p. 202.
58. Millett, *The General*, pp. 37–38.
59. Frank Parker Papers, folder 1, 1854–1891, Southern Historical Collection, University of North Carolina–Chapel Hill, Chapel Hill, North Carolina. Hereinafter cited as Frank Parker Papers. Parker succeeded Summerall in command of the First Division of the AEF in World War I, and became one of his most loyal supporters as well as closest confidant in the post-war years.
60. Ibid., p. 38. See also Fleming, *West Point*, p. 234, and Twichell, *Allen*, pp. 21–22.
61. Millett, *The General*, p. 39; Twichell, *Allen*, p. 22.
62. Quotations are in Fleming, *West Point*, pp. 234–36.
63. Summerall memoir, p. 13.
64. Millett, *The General*, p. 41.
65. *CIRCUMSTANCES OF THE PARENTS OF CADETS, No. 2, 1880–1910*, USMA Archives, USMA Library, West Point, New York.
66. Summerall memoir, p. 11.
67. *Official Register of the Officers and Cadets of the U.S. Military Academy, West Point, N.Y. June 1989*, USMA Archives, USMA Library, West Point, New York. Hereinafter cited as *Official Register*.
68. Summerall memoir, p. 14.
69. *School History*; Summerall memoir, p. 14.
70. Ibid., p. 15.
71. *School History*.
72. Ibid., p. 16.
73. *School History*.
74. Summerall memoir, p. 14; USMA, *Register*, p. 314.
75. Ibid.
76. Ibid., pp. 14–15.
77. Ibid., p. 15.
78. Ibid.
79. USMA, *Register*, p. 313.

80. Summerall memoir, p. 15.
81. Ibid.
82. Holley, *Palmer*, p. 53.
83. Ambrose, *West Point*, pp. 303–04; Fleming, *West Point*, pp. 257–58.
84. Quoted in Holley, *Palmer*, p. 53.
85. Ibid., p. 54; Ambrose, *West Point*, p. 305; Fleming, *West Point*, p. 258.
86. Holley, *Palmer*, p. 54; Fleming, *West Point*, pp. 258–59; Ambrose, *West Point*, pp. 304–05.
87. Holley, *Palmer*, pp. 54–55; Ambrose, *West Point*, p. 305; Fleming, *West Point*, p. 259.
88. Holley, *Palmer*, p. 57; Ambrose, *West Point*, pp. 305–06; Summerall memoir, p. 15.
89. Summerall memoir, p. 16.
90. Holley, *Palmer*, p. 59.
91. Ibid., pp. 59–61.
92. Summerall memoir, pp. 16–17.
93. Ibid., p. 14.
94. Ibid., p. 15.
95. Ibid., p. 16.
96. Ibid., pp. 16–17.
97. USMA, *Register*, p. 313.
98. Summerall memoir, pp. 19, 21.
99. Charles P. Summerall to The Adjutant General, U.S. Army, July 11, 1892, Box 1401, 3672–3673, 1892, Document File, Appointment, Commission and Personal Branch, The Office of the Adjutant General, Record Group (RG) 94, National Archives and Records Administration, Washington, DC. Hereinafter cited as Summerall AGO File.
100. Ibid.
101. Summerall memoir, p. 17.
102. Ibid.
103. Fleming, *West Point*, pp. 207–63; Ambrose, *West Point*, pp. 191–218.
104. Fleming, *West Point*, p. 240; Ambrose, *West Point*, p. 206.
105. Quoted in Fleming, *West Point*, p. 240.

## Chapter Three

1. T. Harry Williams, *The History of American Wars from 1745 to 1918* (New York: Alfred A. Knopf, 1981), p. 303. Hereinafter cited as Williams, *American Wars*. Edward M. Coffman, *The Old Army: A Portrait of the American Army in Peacetime, 1784–1898* (New York and Oxford: Oxford University Press, 1986), p. 215. Hereinafter cited as Coffman, *Old Army*. Holley, *Palmer*, p. 64.
2. Millett, *The General*, p. 69.
3. Holley, *Palmer*, pp. 64–65; Williams, *American Wars*, p. 303; Coffman, *Old Army*, p. 230.
4. Coffman, *Old Army*, p. 283.
5. Ibid.
6. However, for those less inclined toward these edifying pursuits, this abundance of leisure often led to idleness and boredom, "which often required the stimulation of too much whiskey." Holley, *Palmer*, p. 65.
7. Coffman, *Old Army*, p. 284.
8. John F. Marszalem, "Sherman, William Tecumseh," in *The Oxford Companion to American Military History*, ed. in chief John Whiteclay Chambers II (Oxford and New York: Oxford University Press, 1999), p. 656. This volume hereinafter will be cited as *Oxford Companion*. Williams, *American Wars*, p. 308. As has been noted earlier, General Sherman had recommended to the secretary of war the transfer to Dr. Anthony T. Porter of the property and buildings of the Arsenal in Charleston, SC, for the purpose of expanding Dr. Porter's school for boys.
9. Williams, *American Wars*, p. 308; Coffman, *Old Army*, p. 270; Russell F. Weigley, *History of the United States Army, The Wars of the United States*, general ed. Louis Morton (New York: The Macmillan Company, 1967), pp. 273–74. Hereinafter cited as Weigley, *United States Army*. Timothy K. Nenninger, *The Leavenworth Schools and the Old Army: Education, Professionalism, and the Officer Corps of the United States Army, 1881–1918*, Contributions in Military History, Number 15 (Westport, Connecticut and London: Greenwood Press, 1978), p. 36. Hereinafter cited as Nenninger, *Leavenworth Schools*. Allan Millett and Peter Maslowski, *For the Common Defense: A Military History of the United States* (New York: The Free Press, 1984), p. 256. Hereinafter cited as Millett and Maslowski, *Common Defense*.
10. Williams, *American Wars*, p. 308.
11. Stephen E. Ambrose, *Upton and the Army* (Baton Rouge: Louisiana State University Press, 1964), p. 41. Hereinafter cited as Ambrose, *Upton*. Millett and Maslowski, *Common Defense*, p. 256.

12. Millett and Maslowski, *Common Defense*, pp. 256–57; Carol Reardon, "Upton, Emory," *Oxford Companion*, p. 745; Coffman, *Old Army*, p. 272.
13. Ambrose, *Upton*, pp. 96–110; Coffman, *Old Army*, pp. 272–73; Williams, *American Wars*, p. 309.
14. Ambrose, *Upton*, pp. 122–23; Millett and Maslowski, *Common Defense*, p. 257; Coffman, *Old Army*, p. 273; Williams, *American Wars*, p. 309; Weigley, *United States Army*, pp. 277–78.
15. Williams, *American Wars*, p. 309; Coffman, *Old Army*, p. 274; Millett and Maslowski, *Common Defense*, p. 258; Weigley, *United States Army*, p. 280.
16. "Revised Regulations for the Army of the United States, 1895," quoted in Weigley, *United States Army*, p. 285.
17. This discussion of the command structure is based on the following works: Williams, *American Wars*, pp. 304–05; Weigley, *United States Army*, pp. 288–89; Millett and Maslowski, *Common Defense*, pp. 263–64; and Millett, *The General*, pp. 49–50.
18. Summerall memoir, p. 18; Wiles manuscript, Chap. 40, pp. 1–2.
19. Summerall memoir, pp. 18–19.
20. Ibid.
21. Ibid., p. 18.
22. Ibid.
23. Rudyard Kipling, *American Notes* (London and New York: Standard Book Company, 1930), pp. 20–21.
24. Ibid., p. 19.
25. "Largest Hotel in the United States Now Going Up Here," http://www.sfmuseum.org/hist1/1873.html, June 2000; "San Francisco History: Population," http://www.sf50.com/sf/hgpop.html, June 2000.
26. For population figures see above, note 27, "San Francisco History: Population"; for historical data see "A Timeline of San Francisco History," http://www.zpub.com/sf/history/sfh2html, June 2000.
27. Walter J. Thompson, "Strolling on Sunday Afternoons," http://www.sf50.com/sf/hgsto13.html, June 2000.
28. Kipling, *American Notes*, p. 17.
29. "Early History: Camp Reynolds," http://www.angelisland.org, June 2000; Summerall memoir, p. 19.
30. Summerall memoir, p. 19.
31. Ibid.
32. Ibid.
33. Ibid.
34. Ibid., pp. 20–21.
35. Ibid., p. 19. Summerall's description of his days at Benicia Barracks recalls John Palmer's account noted above of the "abundant leisure" that was one of the "charms" of army life, but which also could lead to idleness, boredom, and the consumption of too much whiskey.
36. Ibid., p. 20.
37. Ibid., pp.19–20.
38. Kipling, *American Notes*, p. 53.
39. Summerall memoir, p. 20.
40. Kipling, *American Notes*, p. 53.
41. Summerall memoir, p. 20.
42. Ibid., p. 21.
43. James Parker, *The Old Army: Memories, 1872–1919* (Philadelphia: Dorrance and Company, 1929), p. 196. Hereinafter cited as Parker, *Memories*. Noel Garraux Harrison, *City of Canvas: Camp Russell A. Alger and The Spanish-American War* (Falls Church, Virginia: Falls Church Historical Commission and Fairfax County History Commission, 1988), p. 8. Hereinafter cited as Harrison, *City of Canvas*.
44. Summerall memoir, p. 21.
45. *Sacramento Bee*, July 16, 1894.
46. Summerall memoir, p. 21.
47. Ibid.
48. Ibid.
49. Summerall to The Adjutant General of the U.S. Army, January 24, 1893, Summerall AGO File.
50. Summerall memoir, p. 21.
51. Parker, *Memories*, pp. 196–97.
52. Summerall memoir, p. 21.
53. "1st Endorsement," Summerall to The Adjutant General of the U.S. Army, January 24, 1893, Summerall AGO File.
54. "3rd Endorsement," Ibid. The 2nd Endorsement was approved and recommended by the post commander, Lieut. Colonel James P. Casey, ibid.

55. "Presidio of San Francisco," http://www.nps.gov/prsf/prsfphot/cultureh.htm, http://www.nps.gov/prsf/prsfphot/spanyrs.htm, http://www.nps.gov/prsf/prsfphot/mexyrs.htm, http://www.nps.gov/prsf/prsfphot/ameryrs.htm, June 2000.
56. Colonel Herbert H. Hart, "Historic California Posts: Presidio of San Francisco," *The California Military Museum*, http://www.militarymuseum.org/Presidio.html, June 2000. These boards administered physical and professional examinations for all lieutenants and captains who were eligible for promotion. However, promotions were still granted on the basis of seniority, and some preference was still given to Civil War veterans; so these examinations were not competitive. Nevertheless, each officer who was up for promotion had to meet physical standards and demonstrate some professional competence. In addition, the secretary of war ordered in 1891 that all officers below the rank of colonel periodically submit a written report on their skills and measures they had taken to maintain and improve them. Their superiors also commented in an accompanying "efficiency report" on the officer's performance in a number of categories, including professional zeal, attention to duty, conduct and habits, condition and care of men, capacity for command, scientific attainments, prominent talents, peculiar fitness, and the performance of special duties. Although promotions were not speeded up, these measures succeeded in identifying those best qualified for special duties and served to maintain and raise standards. See Coffman, *Old Army*, p. 281, and "1894. Efficiency Report in Case of C. P. Summerall, March 1, 1894." Summerall AGO File. Hereinafter cited as "1894. Efficiency Report."
57. Monro MacCloskey, *Reilly's Battery: A Story of the Boxer Rebellion* (New York: Richard Rosen Press, 1969), p. 17. Hereinafter cited as MacCloskey, *Reilly's Battery*.
58. Summerall memoir, p. 22.
59. Weigley, *United States Army*, p. 284; Millett and Maslowski, *Common Defense*, p. 253; Joe C. Freeman, Stephan A. Haller, David M. Hansen, John A. Martin, Karen J. Weitze, *Seacoast Fortifications Preservation Manual Golden Gate National Recreational Area San Francisco, California* (San Francisco: National Park Service and KEA Environmental Golden Gate National Recreational Area, July 1999), http://www.nps.gov/goga/ftmanual/chapter2/chapter2.htm, June 2000. Hereinafter cited as Freeman, et al., *Seacoast Fortifications*.
60. Ibid.
61. Freeman et al., *Seacoast Fortifications*.
62. Summerall memoir, p. 22.
63. Ibid.
64. Freeman et al., *Seacoast Fortifications*.
65. Summerall memoir, p. 23.
66. Ibid., p. 22.
67. Ibid., p. 23.
68. Ibid., p. 19.
69. E. F. Land and James G. Maguire to the Honorable Secretary of War, July 19th 1893; H. W. Lawton, Lieut. Co., Inspector General, to General R. Williams, Adjutant General, U.S.A., Aug. 25, 1893; Summerall AGO File.
70. E. F. Land and James G. Maguire to Secretary of War, June 19th, 1893; H. W. Lawton, Lieut. Col., Inspector General, to General R. Williams, Adjutant General, U.S.A., August 25, 1893, Summerall AGO File.
71. Summerall memoir, p. 25.
72. The description of this incident is taken from an official account entitled "Proceedings of a Board of Survey re. shortage of funds in Post Exchange," contained in file labeled "'Controversies' and Attacks, 1894–1931," box 26, Charles P. Summerall MSS, Manuscripts Division, Library of Congress. Hereinafter cited as Summerall MSS. This account differs from Summerall's recollection in his memoirs, where he states that $300.00 in cash was missing when Drewes was found. He also said it was "necessary for me to refund this amount from personal funds, which I did by borrowing it from Mr. Winfield Jones." Summerall's version in his memoirs seems unnecessarily gratuitous, especially since he had deposited an official account in his papers. See Summerall memoir, p. 25.
73. Summerall memoir, p. 25.
74. See above, note 58.
75. The other terms were "Very Good," "Tolerable," "Indifferent," and "Bad."
76. "1894. Efficiency Report." Summerall AGO File.
77. Summerall memoir, p. 23.
78. Fairfax Downey, *Sound of the Guns* (New York: David McKay Company, 1955), pp. 180–81. Hereinafter cited as Downey, *Guns*; William Addleman Ganoe, *The History of the United States Army* (New York and London: D. Appleton-Century Company, 1942), p. 367. Hereinafter cited as Ganoe, *Army*.
79. Summerall memoir, p. 23. From 1911 to 1914, Summerall served as assistant to the chief of the militia bureau of the War Department, where he was in charge of the Field Artillery of the National Guard. In that capacity he traveled the nation securing sites for artillery training camps for the National Guard. So well located were many of these camps that they later were turned into army installations.
80. Ibid., pp. 23–24.

## Notes to Pages 42–47

81. Summerall to The Adjutant General, May 28th 1894, Summerall AGO File.
82. Summerall memoir, pp. 23–24.
83. Physical Examination, NY City, 13 June 1894, Summerall AGO File.
84. Summerall memoir, p. 24.
85. Tindall and Shi, *America*, pp. 709–11; Millett and Maslowski, *Common Defense*, pp. 242–43.
86. Millett and Maslowski, *Common Defense*, p. 243.
87. Ibid., pp. 244–45.
88. Tindall and Shi, *America*, pp. 720–21.
89. Millett and Maslowski, *Common Defense*, p. 247.
90. Coffman, *Old Army*, p. 246.
91. Millett and Maslowski, *Common Defense*, pp. 247–48; Tindall and Shi, *America*, pp. 793–94; for a more detailed account of the 1877 strike see Jerry M. Cooper, *The Army and Civil Disorder: Federal Military Intervention in Labor Disputes, 1877–1900*, Contributions in Military History, Number 19 (Westport, Connecticut: Greenwood Press, 1980), pp. 43–98. Hereinafter cited as Cooper, *Army and Civil Disorder*.
92. Cooper, *Army and Civil Disorder*, pp. 90–91.
93. Tindall and Shi, *America*, p. 803.
94. Ibid.; Cooper, *Army and Civil Disorder*, p. 114.
95. Cooper, *Army and Civil Disorder*, p. 114.
96. Tindall and Shi, *America*, pp. 803–04.
97. Cooper, *Army and Civil Disorder*, pp. 114, 118.
98. Paul H. Carlson, *"Pecos Bill": A Military Biography of William R. Shafter* (College Station, Texas: Texas A&M University Press, 1989), pp. 155–56. Hereinafter cited as Carlson, *"Pecos Bill"*.
99. Cooper, *Army and Civil Disorder*, p. 115.
100. Carlson, *"Pecos Bill"*, pp. 156–57.
101. Cooper, *Army and Civil Disorder*, pp. 118–19. Sacramento was also where the National Guard had been most sympathetic to the strikers, who brought ice water and sandwiches to Guardsmen, who in turn, handed over their arms and ammunition to the strikers. As a result, the Guardsmen retired to their camp outside the city and the strikers remained in control of the rail yard. See Captain J. J. O'Connell, First United States Infantry, "The Great Strike of 1894," *United Service* 15, no. 4 (April 1896): 309. O'Connell commanded "E" Company that had been assigned from the 1st Infantry Regiment to Colonel Graham's force of 540 men. Hereinafter cited as O'Connell, "Great Strike."
102. O'Connell reported that a dispatch warning of threats against Graham's command was handed to him by "Lieutenant Summerall, the efficient quartermaster of the colonel commanding." O'Connell, "Great Strike," p. 311.
103. Summerall memoir, p. 24. According to a description of the strike and the aftermath in Sacramento in the *Sacramento Bee* of 11 July 1894, the large river steamer *Alameda* was the only vessel used to transport Graham's command from Oakland to Sacramento, arriving in the capital city at 6 o'clock in the morning. *Sacramento Bee*, 11 July 1894.
104. Summerall memoir, p. 24.
105. *Sacramento Bee*, 11 July 1894; Cooper, *Army and Civil Disorder*, p. 120.
106. Cooper, *Army and Civil Disorder*, p. 120; *Sacramento Bee*, 12 July 1894; Summerall memoir, p. 24. According to the article of 12 July in the *Bee*, engineer Clark was one of Governor Leland Stanford's "old and faithful stand-bys," and had been designated by the former railroad magnate to serve as one of eight pallbearers at his funeral.
107. *Sacramento Bee*, 12 July 1894.
108. O'Connell, "Great Strike," p. 312.
109. *Sacramento Bee*, 11 July 1894; O'Connell, "Great Strike," p. 312; Cooper, *Army and Civil Disorder*, p. 120; Summerall memoir, p. 24.
110. O'Connell, "Great Strike," p. 312.
111. *Sacramento Bee*, 11 July 1894.
112. Ibid., 12 July 1894.
113. Ibid., 13 July 1894; Cooper, *Army and Civil Disorder*, pp. 120–21; O'Connell, "Great Strike," p. 312.
114. *Sacramento Bee*, 20 July 1894.
115. Summerall memoir, p. 24.
116. *Sacramento Bee*, 21 September 1894. In a review of Knox's performance, the *Woodland Mail* stated that, "Knox, from a Populistic [sic] as an artistic standpoint, would doubtless make a better sheriff than actor." Quoted in the *Bee*, 22 September 1894.
117. Ibid., 7 November 1894. Knox, still under indictment, finished last in a three-man field.
118. Ibid., 10 December 1894.
119. Ibid., 23 October, 26 October, 29 October, 9 November, 17 November 1894.

120. Summerall memoir, p. 24.
121. Summerall MSS, Box 4, folder 4. (See also below, p. 330).
122. "Efficiency Report In Case of Charles P. Summerall, 2nd Lieut 5th Arty...." June 30, 1895, Summerall AGO File.
123. Summerall memoir, p. 25.
124. Summerall Personnel File, 3672-ACP-1892, Appointment, Commission and Personnel Branch, Record Group 94, National Archives and Records Administration, Washington, DC.
125. Summerall memoir, p. 26.
126. Ibid., p. 25.
127. Ibid.
128. See above, Chap. 1, p. 5.
129. Summerall memoir, p. 25.
130. Ibid., p. 26.
131. For the Mordecai family see <http://www.lib.unc.edu/mss/inv/m/Mordecai_family.html>. Hereinafter cited as www.lib.unc. For Alfred Mordecai, Sr., see Fleming, *West Point*, p. 53; Boyd L. Dastrup, *The Field Artillery: History and Sourcebook* (Westport, Connecticut: Greenwood Press, 1994), p. 185; "Alfred Mordecai," *Who Was Who in North Carolina*, pp. 312–13; USMA, *Register*, p. 250. For John David Miley, see USMA, *Register*, p. 308.
132. Mordecai family genealogical chart, www.lib.unc.
133. Summerall memoir, p. 26.
134. Ibid.
135. Ibid.
136. Ibid.
137. Mordecai family genealogical chart, www. lib.unc.
138. Summerall memoir, p. 26.
139. Ibid.
140. http://www.dcmilitary.com/baseguides/mdw/hamilton.html, p. 1.
141. Summerall memoir, p. 26.
142. Article written by Ann Harding Gatley, no title or date of publication, in Summerall MSS, "Clippings, 1900–1925," Box 40.
143. Summerall memoir, p. 26.
144. Ibid., p. 27.
145. Ibid.
146. Tindall and Shi, *America*, p. 902.
147. Ibid.
148. Albert Beveridge, "The March of the Flag," in John L. Beatty and Oliver A. Johnson, eds., *Heritage of Western Civilization*, 8th ed., vol. 2 (Prentice Hall: Englewood Cliffs, New Jersey, 1995), 251.
149. Millett and Maslowski, *Common Defense*, pp. 259–61; Tindall and Shi, *America*, pp. 902–03.
150. http://www.cascobay.com/history/ussmaine/ussmaine.htm#specs.
151. Tindall and Shi, *America*, pp. 906–07; Hugh Thomas, "Remember the Maine?", *New York Review of Books*, April 23, 1998, p. 10. Hereinafter cited as Thomas, "Maine." Millett and Maslowski, *Common Defense*, pp. 267–68.
152. David F. Trask, "Spanish-American War (1898)," in *Oxford Companion*, p. 667. Hereinafter cited as Trask, "Spanish-American War". Thomas, "Maine," p. 10; Williams, *American Wars*, p. 319.
153. Thomas, "Maine", p. 10; Tindall and Shi, *America*, p. 908.
154. Thomas, "Maine", p. 10; David F. Trask, *The War with Spain in 1898, The Macmillan Wars of the United States*, general ed., Louis Morton (New York: Macmillan Publishing, 1981), pp. 24–25. Hereinafter cited as Trask, *War with Spain*.
155. Summerall memoir, p. 27.
156. E. F. McGlauchlin, 5th Artillery Adjutant, 1st Lieutenant, to Colonel John I. Rodgers, Commander 5th Artillery, Governor's Island, February 11, 1898, RECORDS OF U.S. REGULAR ARMY UNITS, Artillery Regiments: 1821–1901, 5th Regiment, Register of Letters Received, 1877–1884 and 1888–1901, Vol. 11, NM-93, Entry 247, Record Group 391, National Archives and Records Administration, Washington, DC.
157. Summerall memoir, p. 27.
158. Ibid.
159. Quoted in Thomas, "Maine", p. 10.
160. Quoted in Tindall and Shi, *America*, p. 909.
161. Thomas, "Maine", p. 10; Tindall and Shi, *America*, p. 910. The actual cause of the destruction of the *Maine* has remained uncertain and controversial. An inquiry by two Spanish naval officers concluded that an internal explosion sunk the ship. In his own account published in 1899, Captain Sigsbee speculated that an explosion from the outside

had destroyed his ship. A study commissioned by Admiral Hyman G. Rickover in the 1970's and conducted by naval researchers concluded that the *Maine* was destroyed by spontaneous combustion in a coal bunker that caused an explosion in an adjacent ammunition magazine. A more recent study by Peggy and Harold Samuels asserts that Spanish extremists opposed to Cuban independence planted a home-made mine that they exploded. In his article, Hugh Thomas supports the conclusions of the Rickover study, but apparently neglected to consider the work of the Samuels. See Rickover, Hyman G., *How the Battleship Maine Was Destroyed* (Washington: Navy History Division, Department of the Navy), 1976; Samuels, Peggy and Harold. *Remembering the Maine* (Washington: Smithsonian Institution Press), 1995; Sigsbee, Charles D. *The Maine: An Account of Her Destruction in Havana Harbor* (New York: Century), 1899.

162. Tindall and Shi, *America*, p. 895.
163. John M. Dobson, "McKinley, William (1843–1901)", *Oxford Companion*, p. 424. Hereafter cited as Dobson, "McKinley".
164. Quoted in Tindall and Shi, *America*, p. 910.
165. Dobson, "McKinley", p. 667.
166. Williams, *American Wars*, pp. 320–21; Tindall and Shi, *America*, pp. 910–11.
167. Harrison, *City of Canvas*, p. 8.
168. Summerall memoir, p. 28; Special Orders, Dept. of the Gulf, 1898, Entry 2020, Record Group 393. Pt. 1, Special Orders N. 15, Headquarters, Department of the Gulf, Atlanta, Georgia, April 13, 1898, National Archives and Records Administration, Washington, DC. Hereinafter cited as Special Orders, Entry 2020, Dept. of the Gulf.
169. Summerall memoir, p. 29.
170. Special Orders, Dept. of the Gulf, Special Orders, Entry 2020, NO. 18, April 18, 1898; ibid., Special Orders NO. 19. April 19, 1898.
171. Summerall memoir, p. 28.
172. Ibid., p. 29.
173. Special Orders, Dept. of the Gulf, Entry 2020, Special Orders NO. 84, May 17, 1898.
174. Williams, *American Wars*, pp. 322–24; Graham A. Cosmas, *An Army for Empire: The United States Army in the Spanish-American War* (Columbia, Missouri: University of Missouri Press, 1971), pp. 127–28. Hereinafter cited as Cosmas, *Army for Empire*.
175. Williams, *American Wars*, pp. 322–23; Millett and Maslowski, *Common Defense*, pp. 270–73; Trask, *War with Spain*, pp. 151–53, 155–58; Trask, "Spanish-American War"; *Oxford Companion*, p. 667.
176. Cosmas, *Army for Empire*, pp. 131–34; Millett and Maslowski, *Common Defense*, pp. 273, 275; Williams, *American Wars*, pp. 324–25.
177. Cosmas, *Army for Empire*, p. 132; Millett and Maslowski, *Common Defense*, p. 273.
178. Harrison, *City of Canvas*, p. 42.
179. Special Orders, Dept. of the Gulf, Entry 2020, Special Orders NO. 18, May 17, 1898; Harrison, *City of Canvas*, p. 3.
180. Harrison, *City of Canvas*, p. 3.
181. Ibid., pp. 1–3.
182. *The Democrat*, 29 June 1898, http://www.geneology.emcee.com/~baf/misc/sp_am_war/6.29.1898. Hartley's brother Charles also wrote letters to *The Democrat*. Their letters are recorded on the website address indicated above, and can be found by noting the date each letter was written, for example the letter written by Aaron Hartley is located on the website by the date 6.29.1898.
183. Cosmas, *Army for Empire*, pp. 127–28; Williams, *American Wars*, pp. 324–25; Trask, *War with Spain*, pp. 159–60.
184. Harrison, *City of Canvas*, pp. 53–54; Cosmas, *Army for Empire*, p. 249.
185. Ibid., pp. 55–56.
186. Aaron Hartley, 6.29.1898.
187. Harrison, *City of Canvas*, pp. 56–59; Cosmas, *Army for Empire*, p. 266.
188. Ibid., p. 59; Cosmas, *Army for Empire*, pp. 268–69.
189. Ibid., pp. 70–71; Cosmas, *Army for Empire*, p. 271.
190. Aaron Hartley, 8.07.1898.
191. Harrison, *City of Canvas*, p. 72.
192. Ibid., pp. 68–69; Summerall memoir, p. 29.
193. Summerall memoir, pp. 29–30.
194. Harrrison, *City of Canvas*, p. 69.
195. Ibid., p. 72; Cosmas, *Army for Empire*, pp. 272–73.
196. Charles Hartley, 8.03.1898.
197. Ibid., 9.07.1898.
198. Harrison, *City of Canvas*, p. 79.

199. Summerall memoir, p. 29.
200. Ibid., p. 32.
201. Graham to Adjutant General of the U.S. Army, July 9, 1898, Summerall AGO file.
202. Summerall to Hon. S. M. Sparkman, M.C., July 9, 1898, ibid.
203. S. M. Sparkman, M. C. Florida to Brig. Gen. H. C. Corbin, U.S.A., Adjutant General, War Department, July 9/98.
204. S. R. Mallory to Major [sic] Gen'l. H. C. Corbin, U.S.A, Adj'l. Gen'l. U.S.A., July 9th, 1898, ibid.
205. Pennington to Adjutant General, n.d., Special Orders, Entry 2020, Dept. of the Gulf. See also Special Orders, NOS. 9, 20, 26, 47, in ibid.
206. Summerall memoir, p. 32.
207. Pennington to Adjutant General, March 20, 1899, Special Orders, Dept. of the Gulf, 1898, Entry 2014.
208. Jones to Adjutant General Corbin, US Army, Washington, D.C., March 18, 1899, Summerall AGO file.

## Chapter Four

1. John A. Tilley, "Spanish-American War (1898)," in *Oxford Companion*, pp. 667–68. Hereinafter cited as Tilley, "Spanish-American War (1898)." Trask, *War with Spain*, p. 234.
2. Tilley, "Spanish-American War (1898)," p. 668.
3. Trask, *War with Spain*, pp. 234, 241–48.
4. Tilley, "Spanish-American War (1898)," p. 668.
5. MacCloskey, *Reilly's Battery*, pp. 24–25.
6. Ibid., pp. 25–26; Trask, *War with Spain*, p. 333.
7. Brian McAllister Linn, *The Philippine War, 1899–1902, Modern War Studies*, general ed. Theodore A Wilson (Lawrence, Kansas: University Press of Kansas, 2000), p. 15. Hereinafter cited as Linn, *Philippine War*. Brian McAllister Linn, *The U.S. Army and Counterinsurgency in the Philippine War, 1899–1902* (Chapel Hill and London: University of North Carolina Press, 1989), p. 3. Hereinafter cited as Linn, *U.S. Army and Counterinsurgency*.
8. Cosmas, *Army for Empire*, pp. 236–37.
9. Ronald H. Spector, "Dewey, George," in *Oxford Companion*, p. 216; Linn, *Philippine War*, p. 8; Williams, *American Wars*, p. 329.
10. Trask, *War with Spain*, pp. 74–75, 81; Cosmas, *Army for Empire*, p. 118.
11. Trask, *War with Spain*, pp. 97–102, quoted in Trask, ibid.
12. Ibid., pp. 102–05; Linn, *Philippine War*, p. 8; Cosmas, *Army for Empire*, pp. 118–19.
13. John Morgan Gates, *Schoolbooks and Krags: The United States Army in the Philippines, 1898–1902*, Contributions in Military History, Number 3 (Westport, Connecticut: Greenwood Press, 1973), pp. 12–13; Linn, *Philippine War*, p. 17; Trask, *War with Spain*, p. 393.
14. Linn, *Philippine War*, pp. 17–20; Trask, *War with Spain*, pp. 393–96.
15. Trask, *War with Spain*, pp. 398–402; Linn, *Philippine War*, p. 20.
16. Trask, *War with Spain*, pp. 402–05; Linn, *Philippine War*, pp. 21–23.
17. Trask, *War with Spain*, p. 382.
18. Williams, *American Wars*, pp. 340–41; Cosmas, *Army for Empire*, p. 121; Trask, *War with Spain*, p. 384; Linn, *Philippine War*, pp. 3–4.
19. Trask, *War with Spain*, pp. 385–86.
20. Linn, *Philippine War*, p. 21.
21. Ibid., p. 23; Trask, *War with Spain*, pp. 409–410.
22. Cosmas, *Army for Empire*, p. 240.
23. Trask, *War with Spain*, pp. 414–21; Cosmas, *Army for Empire*, pp. 240–42.
24. Linn, *Philippine War*, pp. 26–29.
25. Ibid., p. 63.
26. Ibid., pp. 35–36.
27. Ibid., p. 35; Millett, *The General*, p. 123.
28. Tindall and Shi, *America*, pp. 915–16; Trask, *War with Spain*, pp. 482–83.
29. Tindall and Shi, *America*, p. 916.
30. Quoted in Linn, *Philippine War*, p. 30.
31. Ibid., pp. 30–31.
32. Ibid., p. 34.
33. Williams, *American Wars*, p. 343.
34. Linn, *Philippine War*, pp. 34–37.

35. Ibid., pp. 42–64.
36. Ibid., pp. 89–90.
37. Millett and Maslowski, *Common Defense*, p. 290.
38. Linn, *Philippine War*, p. 93.
39. Linn, *U.S. Army and Counterinsurgency*, pp. 4–5; Linn, *Philippine War*, p. 91; Millett, *The General*, p. 122.
40. Linn, *Philippine War*, pp. 93–95.
41. Ibid., pp. 96–99.
42. Ibid., pp. 101–03.
43. MacCloskey, *Reilly's Battery*, p. 26; A. R. Ginsburgh, Captain, F. A. (DOL), "Rolling Along with Reilly," *The Field Artillery Journal*, Volume 23, No. 1 (January–February, 1933): 8. Hereinafter cited as Ginsburgh, "Rolling." Summerall memoir, p. 32.
44. Letters Received, March 31, 1899, Vol. 1, 1899, Department of the Gulf, A.G.O., Record Group 393, National Archives and Records Administration, Washington, D.C. See also copy of telegram from [John I.] Rodgers, Comdg. Colonel 5th Artillery, Headquarters, Fifth Artillery, Fort Hamilton, N. Y. H., March 30, 1899 to Lieut, Phillips, Fort Monroe, VA in Vol. 2, Artillery Regiment, 5th Artillery, RG 391.
45. Summerall memoir, p. 32.
46. Ibid.; MacCloskey, *Reilly's Battery*, p. 26.
47. Linn, *Philippine War*, pp. 13–14; "very sick" is from Summerall memoir, p. 32.
48. Ginsburgh, "Rolling," p. 8.
49. Summerall memoir, p. 32.
50. Ibid.
51. MacCloskey, *Reilly's Battery*, p. 26.
52. Linn, *Philippine War*, pp. 120–22.
53. Ibid., p. 120.
54. Ginsburgh, "Rolling," p. 9; MacCloskey, *Reilly's Battery*, p. 27; Summerall memoir, p. 33.
55. MacCloskey, *Reilly's Battery*, p. 30; Summerall memoir, p. 33.
56. Linn, *Philippine War*, p. 164; Parker, *Memories*, p. 240.
57. Millett, *The General*, p. 123.
58. MacCloskey, *Reilly's Battery*, p. 30.
59. Ibid., p. 31; Summerall memoir, p. 33.
60. Wiles manuscript, pp. 13–14.
61. Summerall memoir, p. 33.
62. Ibid.
63. Ibid., pp. 33–34. Parker's son, Courtlandt, commanded the 6th Artillery Regiment of the 1st Division, AEF, when Summerall led the division as commanding officer.
64. Summerall memoir, pp. 33–34; Parker, *Memories*, pp. 241–44.
65. Summerall memoir, p. 34.
66. MacCloskey, *Reilly's Battery*, p. 31.
67. Linn, *Philippine War*, p. 164; Millett, *The General*, p. 123; Parker, *Memories*, p. 240.
68. Parker, *Memories*, p. 241.
69. Summerall memoir, p. 34.
70. Millett, *The General*, pp. 24–29.
71. Ibid., p. 42.
72. Ibid., pp. 43–44.
73. Ibid., pp. 51–60.
74. Ibid., pp. 61–62, 74–80.
75. Ibid., pp. 82–83, 94–98.
76. Ibid., pp. 99–104.
77. Ibid., pp. 104–07.
78. Ibid., pp. 114–15.
79. Ibid., pp. 115, 118, 124.
80. Linn, *Philippine War*, pp. 162–63; Millett, *The General*, p. 124; Glenn Anthony May, *Battle for Batangas: A Philippine Province at War* (New Haven and London: Yale University Press, 1991), p. 95. Hereinafter cited as May, *Battle for Batangas*. See also TELEGRAMS, ETC., Pertaining to MAJOR GENERAL BATES' Expedition into the Southern Provinces of Luzon, January 1900, Entry 762, Box 2, Record Group 395, National Archives and Records Administration,

Washington, D.C. Hereinafter cited as RG 395/TELEGRAMS. I am grateful to Mr. Rolfe L. Hillman, III, for providing me with photocopies of these materials.

81. May, *Battle for Batangas*, pp. 95–96; Millett, *The General*, pp. 124–25.
82. May, *Battle for Batangas*, p. 107; Millett, *The General*, p. 125.
83. Summerall memoir, p. 34.
84. Ibid.
85. Ibid., p. 183.
86. Ibid.
87. Millett, *The General*, p. 462.
88. Summerall memoir, p. 183.
89. Ibid., p. 35.
90. Ibid.; Millett, *The General*, p. 125.
91. Summerall memoir, p. 35; Millett, *The General*, p. 125; Linn, *Philippine War*, p. 164.
92. Bullard to Adjutant General, U.S.A., Washington, D.C., March 7, 1900, Summerall AGO File. Summerall AGO File.
93. Summerall memoir, p. 35.
94. Millett, *The General*, p. 126; Linn, *Philippine War*, p. 164.
95. Parker to The Adjutant, 39th Infantry, U.S.V., March 11, 1900, Summerall AGO File.
96. First Endorsement, March 15, 1900, Bullard to Adjutant General, U.S.A., Washington, D.C. On 18 March, General Wheaton added his endorsement with recommendation, however, that Summerall be brevetted a captain. On 27 March, General Schwann approved Wheaton's recommendation. General Otis added his endorsement of Schwann's recommendation and forwarded the document to the Adjutant General of the Army on 30 March. Summerall AGO File.
97. Millett, *The General*, p. 126; Linn, *Philippine War*, pp. 164–65; May, *Battle for Batangas*, p. 107.
98. Linn, *Philippine War*, p. 165.
99. Summerall memoir, p. 35.
100. May, *Battle for Batangas*, pp. 101–06; Linn, *Philippine War*, pp. 165–66.
101. Millett, *The General*, p. 127; Linn, *Philippine War*, p. 166; May, *Battle for Batangas*, pp. 110–11. See also Gaines, Adjt. Gen'l, Lake Division to Col. Wagner, Bullard' [sic] Adj't. General, Jan. 11, 1900 in RG395/TELEGRAMS.
102. "Historical Sketch of the Foreign Service of the 10th Battery Field Artillery," Box 2, Summerall MSS; Summerall memoir, p. 35; May, *Battle for Batangas*, p. 108; Millett, *The General*, pp. 127–28; Linn, *Philippine War*, pp. 166–67. In his memoir, Summerall mistakenly cites 1 January 1900 as the date for the departure of Bullard's march to San Tomas.
103. Millett, *The General*, p. 128; May, *Battle for Batangas*, pp. 110–11; Linn, *Philippine War*, pp. 166–67.
104. "Clippings, 1900–1925," Box 40, Summerall MSS.
105. Ibid.
106. Meta Gardner to Hon. Elihu Root, Secretary of War, May 16th 1900, Summerall AGO File.
107. May, *Battle for Batangas*, pp. 112–14.
108. Barry, A. G. to Gen. Bates, Silang, (n.d.), RG395/TELEGRAMS; Millett, *The General*, p. 128; Summerall memoir, p. 36.
109. Summerall memoir, p. 36.
110. May, *Battle for Batangas*, p. 114; Summerall memoir, p. 36. See also Gaines, Adj't. to Col. Wagner, Gen. Bates, January 13, 1900, RG395/TELEGRAMS.
111. Linn, *Philippine War*, p. 167; May, *Battle for Batangas*, p. 117; Millett, *The General*, p. 129.
112. Summerall memoir, p. 36.
113. May, *Battle for Batangas*, p. 117; Millett, *The General*, p. 128.
114. Summerall memoir, p. 36.
115. Millett, *The General*, pp. 128–29; May, *Battle for Batangas*, pp. 118–20; Linn, *Philippine War*, p. 167.
116. Summerall memoir, p. 36.
117. May, *Battle for Batangas*, p. 120; Millett, *The General*, pp. 129–30.
118. Linn, *Philippine War*, p. 169; May, *Battle for Batangas*, p. 122.
119. Linn, *Philippine War*, p. 128; Dora Neill Raymond, *Captain Lee Hall of Texas* (Norman, Oklahoma: University of Oklahoma Press, 1940), pp. 305–06. Hereinafter cited as Raymond, *Captain Hall*.
120. Raymond, *Captain Hall*, pp. 245–58.
121. Ibid., pp. 265–318.
122. May, *Battle for Batangas*, pp. 122–23; Linn, *Philippine War*, p. 169. May and Linn differ on whether Schwann intended for all three columns to arrive together. May states that Schwann planned to have the center column, "which he was accompanying," to arrive first. Linn says that Schwann intended for the columns to arrive together. Both agree, however, that Muir's column did get there first.

123. May, *Battle for Batangas*, p. 123; Linn, *Philippine War*, p. 169.
124. Summerall memoir, p. 36.
125. Linn, *Philippine War*, p. 169; May, *Battle for Batangas*, p. 124.
126. Summerall memoir, p. 37.
127. Ibid.
128. Ibid.; Linn, *Philippine War*, p. 169; Raymond, *Captain Hall*, p. 323.
129. Summerall memoir, p. 37.
130. Linn, *Philippine War*, p. 169.
131. Summerall memoir, pp. 37–38.
132. Raymond, *Captain Hall*, pp. 324–40.
133. Summerall memoir, p. 38.
134. Linn, *Philippine War*, p. 169.
135. Brian M. Linn, "The Philippine War (1899–1902)," in *Oxford Companion*, p. 550. Hereinafter cited as Linn, "Philippine War."
136. Linn, "Philippine War," pp. 169–70, 185; May, *Battle for Batangas*, pp. 126–32.
137. Linn, "Philippine War," p. 550; May, *Battle for Batangas*, pp. 133–269; Linn, "Philippine War," pp. 185–328.
138. Summerall memoir, p. 38; MacCloskey, *Reilly's Battery*, p. 60.
139. Ibid.
140. Summerall memoir, p. 38.
141. Millett, *The General*, pp. 135–83, 189–300.
142. Rodgers to Colonel Ward, Asst. Adj. Gen., Washington, D.C., January 28, 1901, Artillery Regiment: 5th Artillery, RG 391.
143. "Proceedings of a board of officers convened at Manila, P.I., pursuant to the following orders: Special Orders, No 136. HEADQUARTERS DIVISION OF THE PHILIPPINES, Manila, P. I., May 25, 1901," Summerall AGO File.

## Chapter Five

1. Peter Fleming, *The Siege at Peking* (New York: Harper and Brothers, 1959), pp. 23–30, 43–45. Hereinafter cited as Fleming, *Siege*.
2. Diana Preston, *The Boxer Rebellion: The Dramatic Story of China's War on Foreigners That Shook the World in the Summer of 1900* (New York: Walker and Company, 2000); first published as *Besieged in Peking* (London: Constable and Company, 1999), pp. 25–27. Hereinafter cited as Preston, *Rebellion*; Fleming, *Siege*, pp. 36–38.
3. "Emergence of Modern China: II," http://www-chaos.umd.edu/history/modern 2.html, June 2002, p. 1.
4. See R. Ernest Dupuy and Trevor N. Dupuy, *The Encyclopedia of Military History From 3500 B.C. to the Present*, 2nd rev. ed. (New York: Harper and Row, 1986), pp. 864–66. Hereinafter cited as Dupuy and Dupuy, *Encyclopedia*.
5. Fleming, *Siege*, pp. 28–31.
6. Tindall and Shi, *America*, pp. 921–22.
7. "Emergence of Modern China: III," http://www-chaos.umd.edu/history/modern, 3 June 2002, p.1.
8. Herbert Hoover, *The Memoirs of Herbert Hoover—Years of Adventure, 1874–1920* (New York: The Macmillan Company, 1951), p. 47. Hereinafter cited as Hoover, *Memoirs*.
9. Ibid.
10. Chester C. Tan, *The Boxer Catastrophe*, Columbia Studies in the Social Sciences, Number 583, edited by the Faculty of Political Science of Columbia University (New York: Columbia University Press, 1955), pp. 36–52. Hereinafter cited as Tan, *Catastrophe*; Preston, *Rebellion*, pp. 22–23; Fleming, *Siege*, pp. 48–51.
11. Preston, *Rebellion*, p. 25; Fleming, *Siege*, p. 54.
12. Fleming, *Siege*, p. 51; Preston, *Rebellion*, p. 32.
13. Preston, *Rebellion*, pp. 36–37; Fleming, *Siege*, pp. 54–71.
14. Hoover, *Memoirs*, p. 48.
15. Fleming, *Siege*, p. 68; Preston, *Rebellion*, pp. 38–39, 58–59.
16. Anne Cipriano Venzon, ed., *General Smedley Darlington Butler: Letters of a Leatherneck, 1898–1931* (New York: Praeger, 1992), pp. 14–15. Hereinafter cited as Venzon, *Butler*; Richard O'Connor, *The Spirit Soldiers: A Historical Narrative of the Boxer Rebellion* (New York: G. P. Putnam's Sons, 1973), p. 107. Hereinafter cited as O'Connor, *Spirit Soldiers*.
17. Fleming, *Siege*, p. 72.
18. Ibid., p. 74; Preston, *Rebellion*, pp. 90–91, 107.
19. Fleming, *Siege*, pp. 77–79; Preston, *Rebellion*, pp. 93–97; O'Connor, *Spirit Soldiers*, pp. 105–06.
20. O'Connor, *Spirit Soldiers*, pp. 106–08.
21. Tan, *Catastrophe*, pp. 72–75; Fleming, *Siege*, p. 84.

22. Preston, *Rebellion*, pp. 97–98, 104; Fleming, *Siege*, pp. 87–90; Rt. Hon. the Earl Jellicoe, "The Boxer Rebellion," *Fifth Wellington Lecture* (Southampton, Great Britain: University of Southampton, 1993), p. 15. Hereinafter cited as Jellicoe, "Rebellion." Earl Jellicoe is the son of Admiral Sir John R. Jellicoe, who commanded the British Grand Fleet at the Battle of Jutland in 1916. The elder Jellicoe served as Seymour's chief of staff and was seriously wounded in the chest as the expedition retreated to Tientsin. Serving alongside Jellicoe under Seymour was the future Vice Admiral, Sir David Beatty, who led a battle-cruiser squadron of 52 ships at Jutland. Beatty also was wounded on the retreat, but not as severely as Jellicoe.
23. Preston, *Rebellion*, pp. 3–7, 138; Fleming, *Siege*, pp. 17–19.
24. Preston, *Rebellion*, p. 84.
25. Ibid., pp. 74–78; Fleming, *Siege*, pp. 92–94.
26. Fleming, *Siege*, p. 94; Preston, *Rebellion*, p. 78.
27. Preston, *Rebellion*, p. 79; Fleming, *Siege*, pp. 96–104.
28. Preston, *Rebellion*, pp. 81–83; Fleming, *Siege*, pp. 106–09; O'Connor, *Spirit Soldiers*, pp. 102–05.
29. Fleming, *Siege*, pp. 109–12; Preston, *Rebellion*, pp. 84–86; O'Connor, *Spirit Soldiers*, pp. 112–13.
30. Fleming, *Siege*, pp. 117–19; Preston, *Rebellion*, pp. 125–28, 130–32, 135; O'Connor, *Spirit Soldiers*, pp. 122–24.
31. O'Connor, *Spirit Soldiers*, pp. 136–41; Fleming, *Siege*, p. 156.
32. Fleming, *Siege*, pp. 121–22, 145–46, 151–52, 173; Preston, *Rebellion*, p. 138.
33. Preston, *Rebellion*, pp. 184–86.
34. Hoover, *Memoirs*, p. 49.
35. Brig.-Gen. A. S. Daggett, *America in the China Relief Expedition* (Kansas City: Hudson-Kimberly, 1903; repr., Nashville, Tennessee: The Battery Press, 1997), pp. 24–26. Hereinafter cited as Daggett, *Expedition*; Preston, *Rebellion*, p. 185.
36. Hoover, *Memoirs*, p. 52.
37. Preston, *Rebellion*, p. 184; O'Connor, *Spirit Soldiers*, pp. 149–50; Daggett, *Expedition*, pp. 28–29; Fleming, *Siege*, pp. 162–64.
38. Hoover, *Memoirs*, p. 53.
39. Preston, *Rebellion*, pp. 186–89; O'Connor, *Spirit Soldiers*, pp. 155–58; Daggett, *Expedition*, pp. 29–30; Fleming, *Siege*, pp. 163–65.
40. Preston, *Rebellion*, pp. 190–96; Fleming, *Siege*, pp. 168–71.
41. O'Connor, *Spirit Soldiers*, pp. 164–66, 169–74, 203–06; Fleming, *Siege*, p. 173; Preston, *Rebellion*, pp. 205–06.
42. Tan, *Catastrophe*, pp. 105–09; Preston, *Rebellion*, p. 206.
43. Preston, *Rebellion*, p. 208; Fleming, *Siege*, p. 179.
44. Preston, *Rebellion*, p. 211.
45. Daggett, *Expedition*, pp. 46–48, 55; Fleming, *Siege*, p. 181.
46. Lieutenant Burgess remained behind in Manila until his wound healed. He rejoined the battery in China on 6 August.
47. Summerall, memoir, p. 39; MacCloskey, *Reilly's Battery*, pp. 156–57.
48. MacCloskey, *Reilly's Battery*, pp. 157, 159; Summerall, memoir, p. 39.
49. Summerall, memoir, pp. 39–40; MacCloskey, *Reilly's Battery*, pp. 157–60.
50. MacCloskey, *Reilly's Battery*, p. 160; Summerall, memoir, p. 40; Venzon, *Butler*, p. 26, note 1.
51. Quoted in Lowell Thomas, *Old Gimlet Eye: The Adventures of Smedley D. Butler* (New York: Farrar & Rinehart, 1933), p. 67. Hereinafter cited as Thomas, *Butler*.
52. MacCloskey, *Reilly's Battery*, pp. 132, 133, 137; Fleming, *Siege*, 182–83; Preston, *Rebellion*, pp. 217–18.
53. O'Connor, *Spirit Soldiers*, pp. 220–22; Fleming, *Siege*, pp. 182–84; Preston, *Rebellion*, pp. 217–19; MacCloskey, *Reilly's Battery*, pp. 139–42; Daggett, *Expedition*, p. 58; Summerall memoir, p. 40.
54. Summerall memoir, p. 40; MacCloskey, *Reilly's Battery*, pp. 163–64.
55. Fleming, *Siege*, pp. 184–85; O'Connor, *Spirit Soldiers*, p. 223; Daggett, *Expedition*, pp. 63–64; Preston, *Rebellion*, pp. 220–21.
56. Fleming, *Siege*, p. 185; O'Connor, *Spirit Soldiers*, p. 223; Daggett, *Expedition*, p. 63.
57. O'Connor, *Spirit Soldiers*, p. 223; Fleming, *Siege*, p. 185.
58. Preston, *Rebellion*, pp. 220–24; Fleming, *Siege*, pp. 185–89; O'Connor, *Spirit Soldiers*, pp. 223–25.
59. Daggett, *Expedition*, pp. 73–74.
60. Quoted in Thomas, *Butler*, p. 69.
61. Daggett, *Expedition*, p. 72.
62. Summerall memoir, p. 40.
63. Daggett, *Expedition*, p. 73.
64. Summerall memoir, p. 40.
65. Fleming, *Siege*, p. 191.
66. Ibid., pp. 191–92; O'Connor, *Spirit Soldiers*, pp. 225–26; Preston, *Rebellion*, pp. 227–28.

67. Quoted in Thomas, *Butler*, p. 71.
68. Preston, *Rebellion*, pp. 228–29; Fleming, *Siege*, pp. 194, 199–200; O'Connor, *Spirit Soldiers*, p. 237; Daggett, *Expedition*, p. 75.
69. Fleming, *Siege*, p. 200; Thomas, *Butler*, p. 72.
70. Summerall memoir, p. 41.
71. Daggett, *Expedition*, pp. 76–77.
72. Fleming, *Siege*, p. 201.
73. Fleming, *Siege*, 201–03; Preston, *Rebellion*, 229.
74. Summerall memoir, p. 42.
75. Fleming, *Siege*, p. 203. In his memoir, Summerall also failed to acknowledge that the Japanese also had managed before him to breach one of the gates. However, his statement that "Nothing of the kind had ever been done before," technically was correct with respect to the Japanese, since they used high explosives to blast their way through the gate when their small caliber artillery guns, which the British derisively called "peashooters," proved totally ineffective against it.
76. Daggett, *Expedition*, pp. 80, 86; Summerall memoir, p. 41.
77. Quoted in Thomas, *Butler*, p. 73.
78. Quoted in Venzon, *Butler*, p. 28.
79. Thomas, *Butler*, p. 72.
80. Venzon, *Butler*, footnote 3, p. 28.
81. Ibid., pp. 81–84; O'Connor, *Spirit Soldiers*, 241–42; Preston, *Rebellion*, p. 242; MacCloskey, *Reilly's Battery*, p. 146. For his courageous climb to the top of the wall of the Tartar City, Corporal Titus was awarded the Congressional Medal of Honor, as well as a Purple Heart, for wounds he suffered later in the conflict. He received an appointment to the U.S. Military Academy, where President Theodore Roosevelt presented him with his medals. His son Calvin Pearl Titus, Jr., was admitted to West Point in 1936, but enlisted in the Army Air Corps before he was graduated with the class of 1940. During World War II, he served in North Africa and was awarded the Silver Star, two Air Medals, and a Purple Heart. 1970 Register of Graduates.
82. Fleming, *Siege*, pp. 205–06; Preston, *Rebellion*, p. 242; MacCloskey, *Reilly's Battery*, pp. 146–47.
83. Daggett, *Expedition*, p. 91.
84. Summerall memoir, p. 41.
85. Daggett, *Expedition*, p. 95; Summerall memoir, p. 41; MacCloskey, *Reilly's Battery*, p. 147.
86. Summerall memoir, p. 41.
87. Ibid., pp. 41–42.
88. Daggett, *Expedition*, p. 95.
89. Ibid., p. 96.
90. Summerall memoir, p. 43.
91. Daggett, *Expedition*, pp. 95–96; Summerall memoir, p. 42; O'Connor, *Spirit Soldiers*, p. 250.
92. Daggett, *Expedition*, p. 96.
93. See O'Connor, *Spirit Soldiers*, p. 250; Fleming, *Siege*, p. 218. Fleming regarded Chaffee's action as "an impulsive, self-centered, bull-in-a-china shop operation." Ibid.
94. Fleming, *Siege*, p. 217.
95. Summerall memoir, p. 42.
96. Ibid.; Daggett, *Expedition*, p. 96.
97. Daggett, *Expedition*, p. 97; Summerall memoir, p. 42.
98. MacCloskey, *Reilly's Battery*, pp. 170–71. In his account of this action, MacCloskey wove together his father's letters and diaries, as well as a history of Reilly's battery written by an anonymous historian. He provided no citations or notes to which one can attribute specific sources.
99. Summerall memoir, p. 42. Tough and hardened as he had become from the rigors of war in the Philippines and in China, it is doubtful that Summerall could have scratched with his thumbnail a cross in the metal covering the gate. Daggett, MacCloskey, and O'Connor stated that he marked the location of the cross beams with chalk (Daggett, *Expedition*, p. 97; MacCloskey, *Reilly's Battery*, p. 170; O'Connor, *Spirit Soldiers*, p. 250). Again, the memory of a proud, old man was faulty.
100. General Chaffee to Adjutant General, September 1, 1900, in Daggett, *Expedition*, p. 234. Lieutenant MacCloskey wrote that "Wounded mortally, he [Reilly] fell unconscious and died in Sergeant Follinsby's arms." Quoted in MacCloskey, *Reilly's Battery*, p. 173.
101. Summerall memoir, p. 43.
102. Daggett, *Expedition*, p. 99.
103. MacCloskey, *Reilly's Battery*, pp. 171–72; Summerall memoir, p. 42; Daggett, *Expedition*, p. 101.

104. See Preston, *Rebellion*, p. 253; O'Connor, *Spirit Soldiers*, pp. 250–51, and Daggett, *Expedition*, pp. 101–02. The "pop-gun" quotation is in Preston.
105. Daggett, *Expedition*, p. 101; Summerall memoir, p. 43.
106. Ibid., pp. 101–03; Summerall, p. 43.
107. Daggett, *Expedition*, p. 103.
108. Summerall memoir, p. 43.
109. Fleming, *Siege*, p. 219; Preston, *Rebellion*, p. 254; O'Connor, *Spirit Soldiers*, pp. 252–53; Daggett, *Expedition*, p. 103.
110. Daggett, *Expedition*, p. 104.
111. Fleming, *Siege*, pp. 219–20; O'Connor, *Spirit Soldiers*, p. 253; Preston, *Rebellion*, p. 254.
112. See Preston, *Rebellion*, pp. 262–74; O'Connor, *Spirit Soldiers*, pp. 253–60.
113. Summerall memoir, p. 43.
114. Quoted in Fleming, *Siege*, p. 220, and in O'Connor, *Spirit Soldiers*, p. 253. American casualties on the 14th and 15th were 7 killed and 29 wounded. See Daggett, *Expedition*, p. 104.
115. Summerall memoir, p. 46.
116. Wiles, manuscript, 6, 13.
117. Thomas, *Butler*, p. 76.
118. Preston, *Rebellion*, pp. 292–94; Fleming, *Siege*, pp. 244–46.
119. Summerall memoir, pp. 44–45. Summerall might well have been correct in asserting that the Americans left everything as they found it, but Diana Preston noted that English observers saw Russian soldiers with their trousers "simply bulging with loot," and German and French soldiers making off with jewels and vases of jade and gold. Preston, *Rebellion*, pp. 294–95. Peter Fleming noted also that "diplomats and senior officers openly stuffed their pockets [with treasures] as they went along." Fleming, *Siege*, p. 246. He did not, however, mention specifically whether any American diplomats or officers were involved.
120. Summerall memoir, p. 44.
121. Ibid., pp. 45–46.
122. Ibid., p. 45.
123. Ibid.
124. Holley, *Palmer*, p. 122.
125. Ibid., pp. 105, 108, 112, 123. Quotations are on p. 123.
126. Ibid., p. 124.
127. Summerall memoir, p. 45. Summerall's description of their meeting agrees with Palmer's, except that Summerall mistakenly wrote that Palmer was headed toward Peking rather than toward Tientsin. Ibid.
128. Holley, *Palmer*, p. 125; Chapter 10; Chapters 22–53.
129. Summerall memoir, pp. 45–46. The outstanding score of 95.71 he received on the examination certainly strengthened his chances for promotion. See above, Chapter 4: The Philippines, p. 93
130. See above, p. 104.
131. Preston, *Rebellion*, p. 306; Daggett, *Expedition*, pp. 141–42.
132. See ibid., pp. 306–07; Fleming, *Siege*, pp. 252–53; O'Connor, *Spirit Soldiers*, pp. 297–99. The British officer's remark is quoted in all three works.
133. Summerall memoir, p. 48.
134. Quite likely, Summerall mistakenly stated that Laura wrote in early 1900, rather than early in 1901, for it was in March 1901 when he was granted leave in Japan. Ibid., p. 47.
135. Ibid., p. 47.
136. Ibid.
137. Ibid.
138. Ibid., pp. 47–48.
139. Ibid., p. 48.
140. These various boards dealt with problems such as the amount of firewood allocated to the various kitchens, the amount of coal for each tent, and the price of horses to be sold to the American Legation. Record Group 395, 925–929, 960–962.
141. HEADQUARTERS, CHINA RELIEF EXPEDITION, Peking, China, February 28th 1901. General Orders NO. 11. Record Group 395, 425–479.
142. Summerall to The Adjutant General, China Relief Expedition, Fort Reilly, Peking, China, February 21st, 1901, Record Group 395/906, 609, 4/6 1901. Again, I am indebted to Rolf Hillman for providing me with copies of these records.
143. Summerall memoir, p. 49.

144. Ibid.
145. MacCloskey, *Reilly's Battery*, pp. 175–76.
146. Ganoe, *History*, pp. 411–12.
147. Summerall memoir, p. 50.
148. Tan, *Catastrophe*, p. 120 ; Fleming, *Siege*, p. 246; Preston, *Rebellion*, p. 345.
149. Tan, *Catastrophe*, p. 150–53.
150. Ibid., pp. 156, 216–23; Fleming, *Siege*, pp. 248–49.
151. Tan, *Catastrophe*, pp. 223–33; Fleming, *Siege*, pp. 249–50; O'Connor, *Spirit Soldiers*, pp. 324–25.
152. Tan, *Catastrophe*, pp. 233–36; Fleming, *Siege*, pp. 250–52; Preston, *Rebellion*, pp. 311–12.
153. Fleming, *Siege*, p. 250; Tan, *Catastrophe*, pp. 240–42.

## Chapter Six

1. Summerall memoir, p. 50.
2. Ibid.
3. Ibid.
4. Ibid.
5. Ibid.
6. Ibid.
7. Ibid., p. 51.
8. Ibid.
9. "Fort Walla Walla," Fort Walla Walla Museum, Fort Walla Walla, Washington. I am grateful to Ms. Laura Schulz, Collections Manager, Fort Walla Walla Museum, for providing me with this information.
10. Summerall memoir, p. 51.
11. *San Francisco Examiner*, 15 August 1901. Hereinafter cited as *Examiner*.
12. Summerall memoir, p. 51.
13. *Examiner*.
14. Summerall memoir, p. 51.
15. *Examiner*.
16. Summerall memoir, p. 51.
17. *Examiner*.
18. Summerall memoir, p. 52.
19. Ibid.
20. Ibid.
21. Ibid.
22. http://www.cityofseattle.net/neighborhoods/preservation/fortlawton.html, July 2003.
23. Summerall memoir, p. 52.
24. An extract from a report on an inspection of Fort Lawton in February 1902 made this clear. It read, "Captain C. P. Summerall, Artillery Corps, has been in command of the post [Fort Lawton] since August 22, 1901, and evinces special zeal and ability in his position, having not only organized two companies of coast artillery within the past two months with only the assistance of recently appointed lieutenants, but also put an unfinished post into good condition by the labor of his troops." Extract from the inspection report of Fort Lawton by Major H. E. Tutherly, 11th Cavalry, Acting, Inspector General, Department of the Columbia to General J. C. Breckinridge, Inspector General, War Department. The report was sent by Breckinridge to the secretary of war, and dated June 23, 1902; the extract is in Summerall's AGO file. Major Tutherly also inspected the "Camp at Skagway, Alaska," in July 1902, and also sent his report to Breckinridge, who sent it as well to the secretary of war. The extract is also in Summerall's AGO file and states that "The condition of the company which he has organized during the past eleven months, and administration and discipline here, bears evidence of his excellent abilities and exemplary character as an officer."
25. Summerall memoir, p. 53.
26. Howard Clifford, *The Skagway Story: A history of Alaska's most famous gold rush town and of some of the people who made that history*, ed. Byron Fish (Anchorage: Alaska Northwest Publishing Company, 1975), pp. 1–13. Hereinafter cited as Clifford, *Skagway*.
27. Ibid., p. 14–27, 46. Summerall remembered these violent times and wrote in his memoir that "Many desperate characters and outlaws had preyed upon the gold seekers and murder had become quite common. The story of 'Soapy' Smith illustrated the conditions." Pp. 56–57.
28. http://www.yukonalaska.com/akblkhist/early/24th.html. August 2003. Hereinafter cited as www.yukonalaska.

29. Clifford, *Skagway*, p. 28.
30. www.yukonalaska.
31. Clifford, *Skagway*, pp. 28–29.
32. Walter R. Hamilton, *The Yukon Story: A Sourdough's record of Goldrush Days and Yukon Progress from the earliest times to the present day* (Vancouver: Mitchell Press Limited, 1964), p. 229.
33. Philip C. Jessup, *Elihu Root*, vol. 1, *1845–1909* (New York: Dodd, Mead & Company, 1938), p. 391. Hereinafter cited as Jessup, *Root*.
34. Lewis L. Gould, *The Presidency of Theodore Roosevelt*, American Presidency Series, eds. Donald R McCoy, Clifford S. Griffin, Homer E. Socolofsky (Lawrence, Kansas: University Press of Kansas, 1991), p. 82. Hereinafter cited as Gould, *Roosevelt*.
35. Jessup, *Root*, pp. 391–92.
36. Ibid., p. 392; Gould, *Roosevelt*, p. 82.
37. Quoted in Gould, *Roosevelt*, p. 82. See also William N. Tilchin, *Theodore Roosevelt and the British Empire: A Study in Presidential Statecraft* (New York: St. Martin's Press: 1997), p. 38. Hereinafter cited as Tilchin, *Roosevelt*.
38. Gould, *Roosevelt*, p. 82; Tilchin, *Roosevelt*, pp. 36, 38.
39. Summerall memoir, p. 53.
40. Quoted in Jessup, *Root*, p. 392. It is very likely that Cortelyue was aware of Summerall's record in the Philippines and in China, and recognized his ability and potential. In addition, his attention could have been drawn to Summerall by learning from the army's Adjutant General, H. C. Corbin, of a request addressed to Corbin from the president of the University of Idaho, that Summerall be assigned to the university as commandant of their 40-man cadet corps. J [illegible]. Lean, President, University of Idaho, to Adjutant General H. C. Corbin, October 2, 1901, Summerall AGO file.
41. Summerall memoir, p. 53.
42. Ibid.
43. Ibid.
44. Hudson Struck, *The Alaskan Missions of the Episcopal Church: A brief sketch, historical and descriptive* (New York: Domestic and Foreign Missionary Society, 1920), Chapter IV: *The Invasion of the Gold Seekers*, http://www.justusanglican.org/resources/pc/usa/ak/stcuk/04.html.
45. Summerall memoir, p. 55. He noted that the hotel was run by a Mrs. Pullen [sic] who had packed her possessions, two young sons, and a daughter over the trail from Dyea to Skagway and took over the hotel.
46. Summerall memoir, p. 54; http://www.sheldonmuseum.org/hainesalaska.html.
47. Summerall memoir, p. 54.
48. Ibid., pp. 54–55.
49. Ibid., p. 55.
50. http://www.whitepassrailroad.com/history/index.html. Today, the railroad carries thousands of tourist passengers during the summer and fall, and has been designated as a Historic Civil Engineering Landmark, a distinction shared with the Panama Canal, the Eiffel Tower and the Statue of Liberty.
51. Summerall memoir, p. 55.
52. Clifford, *Skagway*, pp. 138–39; Summerall memoir, pp. 55–56.
53. Clifford, *Skagway*, p. 139.
54. Summerall memoir, p. 56.
55. Ibid., p. 57. Like Summerall, Wilds Richardson escaped the misery of Reconstruction in his home state of Texas by entering West Point, and was graduated in 1884. He returned as an instructor in 1892, where he certainly took note of the first captain of corps of cadets. He was, indeed, devoted to Alaska, where he served four tours of duty, spanning over 20 years. In 1905, he was appointed president of the Alaska Roads Commission, and directed the construction of the 380-mile road from Valdez northward to Fairbanks. It was later named the Richardson Trail. In the closing months of World War I, he commanded the 78th Infantry Brigade of the 39th Division. His Alaskan experience and combat record led General Pershing to place him in command of American soldiers that were part of the Allied invasion of northern Russia during the Russian Civil War, where he helped to resolve the confusion among the various allied armies fighting to defeat Bolshevik forces. After serving in that short-lived and unsuccessful intervention, Richardson returned home, and retired from the army in 1920. For the remaining nine years of his life, he worked diligently to see that the settlement of Alaska and its development would be managed in a gradual and rational manner that would conserve, rather than exploit, its resources. Brian Hart, "Richardson, Wilds Preston," *Handbook of Texas Online* (http://www.tshaonline.org/handbook/online/articles/fri12)
56. Summerall memoir, pp. 57–58.

## Chapter Seven

1. Summerall memoir, p. 58.
2. Ibid., p. 59.

3. http://www.u-s-history.com/pages/h1029.html.
4. http://www.u-s-historycom/pages/h1030.html.
5. Summerall memoir, p.59.
6. Ibid., pp. 59–60.
7. Ibid., p. 60.
8. Ibid.
9. Ibid., p. 61.
10. http://www.nps.gov/check/adhi/adhit.htm.
11. Summerall memoir, p. 61.
12. Ibid., p. 62.
13. Ibid., p. 61.
14. Ibid., p. 62.
15. Ibid., pp. 62–63.
16. Ibid., p. 63.
17. Ibid., pp. 63–64.
18. Ibid., p. 64.
19. Ibid.
20. Ibid., pp. 64–65. Since Summerall's battery frequently took part in important occasions or made special appearances, it is not surprising that he failed to remember an appearance at Gettysburg National Park. It is not clear what the occasion was, but Mr. Tom Nicholson, the chairman of the Gettysburg Park Commission, wrote the army chief of staff that "Every duty assigned to him [Summerall] and his officers was discharged with promptness and fidelity, and the greatest courtesy characterized all of his actions." Tom P. Nicholson to Lieut.-General Adna R. Chaffee, Chief of Staff, U.S. Army, June 1st, 1904, Summerall AGO file. As noted in Chapter V, Chaffee had been the commander of the army's China Relief Expedition, and was well aware of Summerall's record.
21. Ibid., p. 65.
22. Ibid.
23. Ibid., p. 67.
24. Ibid.
25. Ibid., pp. 67–68.
26. In the papers of General George S. Patton, Jr., I found a copy of a publication entitled "INFORMATION RELATIVE TO THE APPOINTMENT AND ADMISSION OF CADETS TO THE UNITED STATES MILITARY ACADEMY that lists the courses that cadets were required to take during this time. See the Papers of George S. Patton, Jr., Box 45, Personal 201File, 1903–1906. Hereinafter referred to as Patton Papers.
27. Ambrose, *Upton*, pp. 155–57; Nenninger, *Leavenworth Schools*, p. 54; William Addleman Ganoe, *The History of the United States Army* (New York and London: D. Appleton-Century Company, 1942), p. 418. Hereinafter cited as Ganoe, *Army*.
28. http://www.army.mil/cmh/documents/1901/Root-Ovr.htm.
29. http://www.army.mil/cmh/documents/1901/Root-Cmd.htm; Millett and Maslowski, *Common Defense*, pp. 310–11; Matthew Oyos, "Root, Elihu," *Oxford Companion*, p. 625.
30. http://www.army.mil/CMH-pg/documents/1901/Root-NG.htm; Millett and Maslowski, *Common Defense*, pp. 312–13.
31. Summerall memoir, p. 67.
32. Ibid., p. 68.
33. Patton Papers, Chronological File, Box 5. See also Martin Blumenson, *The Patton Papers, 1885–1940*, p. 156. Hereinafter referred to as Blumenson, *Patton Papers*.
34. Ibid.
35. Ibid., pp. 732, 804.
36. Quoted in Summerall memoir, p. 69.
37. Ibid., p. 67.
38. General Shipp to Summerall, October 30, 1905, Summerall MSS, Box 12. Shipp was not the first top college official who wanted Summerall to be commandant of cadets. As noted in the previous chapter, the president of the University of Idaho earlier had asked the adjutant general to assign Summerall to the university as commandant of the university's 40-man cadet corps.
39. General Mills to The Military Secretary, War Department, May 25, 1906, copy in Summerall MSS, Box 12.
40. EFFICIENCY REPORT IN CASE OF Charles P. Summerall, Captain, Artillery, U.S. Army, Reported by Brig. Gen. A. L. Mills, U.S. Army, Superintendent. Commanding Post of West Point, New York. Date, June 30, 1906, Summerall AGO file.

41. Shipp to Summerall, May 5, 1906, Summerall MSS, Box 12.
42. McCain to Shipp, June 15, 1906, ibid.
43. Summerall memoir, p. 67.
44. Summerall memoir, pp. 67, 69–70.
45. Ibid., pp. 69–70.
46. Ibid., p. 70.
47. Ibid., p. 68.
48. Col H. L. Scott to Adjutant General, June 30, 1910, Summerall AGO File.
49. General Barry to Summerall, April 3, 1911, Summerall MSS, Box 12.
50. General Davis to General Barry, April 19, 1911, ibid.
51. Summerall memoir, p. 72.
52. Ibid.
53. See note 43.
54. It is also worth noting that, under his careful and tight supervision, the battery did not lose a single man or horse during the long trek from Camp Thomas.

## Chapter Eight

1. Summerall memoir, p. 72.
2. Weigley, *United States Army*, p. 330.
3. Andrew J. Bacevich, "Leonard Wood," in *Oxford Companion*, pp. 809–10.
4. Weigley, *United States Army*, pp. 333–34.
5. Ibid.; Williams, *History*, pp. 335–36.
6. Summerall memoir, p. 72.
7. Ibid., pp. 72–73.
8. Weigley, *United States Army*, p. 334.
9. Summerall memoir, pp. 73–74.
10. Ibid., p. 73.
11. Summerall AGO file, Hq. Ft. Myer, Va., Jan. 7, 1913, To C.O., 3rd F. A., Ft. Sam Houston, Tex.
12. Summerall memoir, p. 74.
13. Another aspect of Secretary Root's reforms was the separation of the Artillery Branch into the Coast Artillery Corps and the Field Artillery, which Congress approved in 1907. For specialized field artillery training for officers, the army opened the School of Fire for Field Artillery at Fort Sill, Oklahoma in 1911. The Infantry and Cavalry School at Fort Leavenworth was named the School of the Line in 1910. See http://www.army.mil/cmh/documents/1901/Root-Schools.htm.
14. R. K. Evans, Brigadier General, General Staff, Chief, Division of Militia Affairs, MEMORANDUM FOR THE CHIEF OF STAFF, Subject: Purchase of approximately 12,000 acres of land for a Field Artillery range, in Garrett County, May 15, 1912, Western Maryland, Box no. 151, 28951–29397, Document file, 1908–1916, Record Group 168, Records of the National Guard Bureau, National Archives and Record Administration, Washington, DC. Hereinafter cited as Evans, RG 168 NG. W. J. Snow, Major, Field Artillery, MEMORANDUM: Arguments in favor of the establishment of a Field Artillery Range in the eastern part of the United States, May 31, 1912, in ibid. Hereinafter cited as Snow, RG 168 NG.
15. Summerall memoir, p. 75; Summerall, C. P., Major, F.A., DETAIL, to inspect site at Oakland, Md., for joint camp for Field Artillery, April 10 and April 25, 1912, Box 342, Index by individual, 1908–1916, Record Group 168, Records of the National Guard Bureau, National Archives and Records Administration, Washington, D.C. Hereinafter cited as Summerall, RG 168 NG.
16. Summerall memoir, p. 75.
17. Summerall to The Adjutant General, Eastern Division, Governor's Island, N.Y., Fort Myer, Virginia, April 10, 1912, in Box no. 151, 28951–29397, Document file, 1908–1916, Record Group 168, Records of the National Guard Bureau, National Archives and Record Administration, Washington, DC; Summerall to The Adjutant General, Eastern Division, Governor's Island, N.Y., Fort Myer, Virginia. Summerall RG 168, NG.
18. N.U. Bond, Superintendent, DuBois and Bond Brothers, Manufacturers and Dealers in Lumber, Oakland, Garrett County, Maryland, May 4, 1912, to Major Charles Pelot Summerall ? [apparently Summerall had not left his calling card] United States Army, Washington, D.C., in ibid.
19. Snow, RG 168 NG; E. J. [?] Greble, Colonel, General Staff, For the Field Artillery Committee, MEMORANDUM FOR THE CHIEF OF STAFF, May 15, 1912, in ibid; Evans, RG 168 NG.
20. Major General, Chief of Staff, [Wood's signature does not appear on the memorandum], MEMORANDUM FOR THE ADJUTANT GENERAL, May 14, 1912, in ibid.

Notes to Pages 155–162

21. Summerall, C. P., REPORT, Report on Field Artillery camp at Tobyhanna, Pa., August 12, 1912, in Summerall, RG 168 NG. Other than this report, I have located no official records that document the purchase of the land, or the comments of his superiors, like those that dealt with the acquisition of the property in Oakland.
22. http://www.dcnr.state.pa.us/stateparks/parks/Tobyhanna.aspx.
23. Summerall memoir, p. 75.
24. http://www.tobyhanna.army.mil/toby/facts/history/begin.html. Hereinafter cited as www.Tobyhanna. Summerall memoir, p. 75.
25. http://www.monroehistoricsociety.org/175thcolumns.html.
26. Ibid.
27. Ernest Hinds, Lieut. Colonel, 5th U.S. Field Artillery, to The Division Adjutant, First Red Division, Connecticutt [sic] Maneuver Division, August 22, 1916, in Summerall AGO file.
28. Fred A. Smith, Brigadier General, U.S. Army, Commanding the Red Army, to Lieut. Colonel Ernest Hinds, 5th Field Artillery, October 8, 1912, in ibid.
29. Summerall memoir, p. 75.
30. Ibid.
31. Leonard Wood, Major-General, Chief of Staff, to Major Charles P. Summerall, Commanding, 2d Battalion, 3d Field Artillery, 8 March 1903, in Summerall MSS, Correspondence and Memoranda, 1900–40, Box 2, 1900–19. Hereinafter cited as Summerall MSS, 2.
32. Summerall memoir, p. 74.
33. This regimen was required of all field officers as a test of their physical fitness. See Ganoe, *Army*, p. 434.
34. Summerall memoir, p. 78.
35. Ibid., p. 77.
36. Major Charles P. Summerall, 3rd Field Artillery, "The Camp of Instruction for Field Artillery at Tobyhanna, PA.", *The Field Artillery Journal*, Volume 4, No. 1 (January–March 1914): 21–22. Hereinafter cited as Summerall, "Tobyhanna".
37. Ibid., pp. 22–25.
38. Ibid., pp. 26–27.
39. Ibid., pp. 32–33.
40. Summerall memoir, p. 76.
41. Ibid.
42. Ibid.; Summerall, "Tobyhanna," pp. 32–34.
43. www.Tobyhanna.
44. Thomas H. Barry, Maj. Gen., Comdg., Eastern Dept., "Report on Camp of Instruction for Field Artillery," August 25, 1913, copy in Summerall MSS, 2.
45. Summerall memoir, p. 77.
46. Ibid.
47. Ibid., pp. 77–78.
48. Ibid., p. 78.
49. Ibid., p. 77.
50. Ibid.
51. Ibid., p. 78.
52. Leonard Wood, Major General, U.S. Army, Department Commander, September 4, 1914, to Major E. [sic] P. Summerall, Comdg. Field Artillery Camp of Instruction, Tobyhanna, Pa., copy in Summerall MSS, Box 2, Correspondence and Memoranda, 1900–1940.
53. Ibid.
54. Ibid.
55. Wiles manuscript, Chap. 9, pp. 13–14.
56. Summerall memoir, p. 79; www.lib.unc.
57. Wiles manuscript, Chap. 10, p. 1; Dupuy and Dupuy, *Encyclopedia*, pp. 933–39;
58. Dupuy and Dupuy, *Encyclopedia*, pp. 939, 942.
59. Matthew Heiser, "Lusitania," in Anne Cipriano Venzon, ed., Paul L. Miles, con. ed., *The United States in the First World War: An Encyclopedia, Military History of the United States* (Vol. 3), *Garland Reference Library of the Humanities* (Vol. 1205), (New York and London: Garland Publishing, Inc., 1995), pp. 357–58. This volume will be cited hereinafter as Venzon, *Encyclopedia*. See also David Trask, "Lusitania, Sinking Of The (1915)," in *Oxford Companion*, p. 404.
60. Summerall memoir, p. 80.
61. http://www.tobyhanna.army.mil/toby/facts/history/yale.html. Hereinafter cited as www. tobyhanna/yale. Revolutionary upheavals continued in Mexico, as civil war broke out between government troops of President Venustiano

Carranza, who had the backing of President Woodrow Wilson, and the forces of Villa, who often was called the "Robin Hood of Mexico." Angered by Wilson's support for Carranza, Villa's army attacked Columbus, New Mexico, in March 1916, and killed a number of civilians and soldiers. In response, Wilson ordered to Mexico the Punitive Expedition, consisting of 10,000 soldiers, commanded by Brigadier General John J. Pershing, "a very hard taskmaster," to destroy Villa's band. When fighting broke out between Mexican regulars and American soldiers, Wilson reinforced Pershing's force with Regular Army units and 112,000 National Guardsmen. Since neither the Mexican nor American governments wanted war, they managed to avoid a larger conflict. Pershing failed to capture Villa, but dispersed his army, and, with relations with Germany rapidly deteriorating toward war in early 1917, the president recalled the Expedition. Pershing had merged various cavalry, infantry, and artillery units, as well as new elements like field radio transmitters, machine guns, truck companies, and even a squadron of airplanes, into a fighting field command. In addition, he had given a position on his staff to an impatient and ambitious young lieutenant named George S. Patton, Jr. President Wilson was impressed with Pershing's adherence to the strict rules of engagement that the former had established, as well as Pershing's skillful training and administration of the entire Expedition. In addition to ending serious border incidents, Regular Army and National Guard soldiers gained valuable experience in the field, although this partial mobilization made clear the difficulties of full mobilization for a larger conflict. See http://www.army.mil/cmh/books/AMH/AMH-16.htm; Frank E. Vandiver, "Pershing, John Joseph (1860–1948)," in *Oxford Companion*, p. 547; Millett and Maslowski, *Common Defense*, p. 320.

62. Quoted in www.tobyhanna/yale.
63. Hugh L. Scott, Brigadier General, The Chief of Staff, to The Adjutant General, November 30, 1914, Box 42, Document File 1-1, 1908–1916, Record Group 168, Records of the National Guard Bureau, National Archives and Record Administration, Washington, D.C.; A. L. Mills, Brig. Gen.., General Staff, The Chief, Division of Militia Affairs, to The Chief of Staff, August 6, 1915, in ibid.; Summerall memoir, pp. 79–80. The camp in Alabama became Fort McClellan in World War II, and the one at Monterey was named Fort Fremont in World War I, and Fort Ord in World War II.
64. See above, endnote 61.
65. Summerall memoir, p. 81.
66. Ralph B. Levering, "Lodge, Henry Cabot (1850–1924)," in Venzon, *Encyclopedia*, pp. 349–50; James W. Pohl, "Garrison, Lindley Miller (1864–1932)," in ibid., p. 250; Jonathan M. Nielson, "Preparedness," in ibid., pp. 469–70. Hereinafter cited as Nielson, "Preparedness"; Millett and Maslowski, *Common Defense*, p. 323; Edward M. Coffman, *The War To End All Wars; The American Military Experience in World War I* (New York: Oxford University Press, 1968), p. 21. Hereinafter cited as Coffman, *War*.
67. Nielson, "Preparedness," p. 470; Millett and Maslowski, *Common Defense*, pp. 323–24; James W. Pohl, "Plattsburg Movement," in Venzon, *First World War*, p. 464. Hereinafter cited as Pohl, "Plattsburg."
68. Pohl, "Plattsburg," p. 464.
69. Kendrick A. Clements, "Wilson, Woodrow (1856–1924)," in Venzon, *Encyclopedia*, pp. 795–96; Millett and Maslowski, *Common Defense*, pp. 304–25; John Whiteclay Chambers II, "National Defense Acts (1916, 1920)," in *Oxford Companion*, pp. 464–65. Hereinafter cited as Chambers, "Acts."
70. Larry Addington, "National Defense Act of 1916," in Venzon, *Encyclopedia*, pp. 399–400; Millett and Maslowski, *Common Defense*, pp. 324–25; Chambers, "Acts," pp. 464–65; Weigley, *United States Army*, pp. 348–49; Ganoe, *Army*, pp. 457–58.
71. Summerall memoir, pp. 80–81.
72. http://en.wikipedia.org/w/index.php?title=aerial_bombing_of_cities&printable=yes.
73. Dupuy and Dupuy, *Encyclopedia*, pp. 959–60; Spencer C. Tucker, "Verdun, Battle of (1916)," in Spencer C. Tucker, ed., Laura Matysek and Justin D. Murphy, assoc. eds., *The European Powers in the First World War: An Encyclopedia* (New York & London: Garland Publishing Inc., 1996), pp. 714–18. This volume will be cited hereinafter as Tucker, *Encyclopedia*. See also http://en.wikipedia.org./wiki/Battle_of_Verdun.
74. Dupuy and Dupuy, *Encyclopedia*, pp. 961–62.
75. Ibid., p. 962.
76. Ibid., pp. 960–61; David T. Zabecki, "Somme, Battle of (1 July–19 November 1916)," in Tucker, *First World War*, pp. 648–51; http://en.wikipedia.org./wiki/Battle_of_the_Somme_(1916); http://www.firstworldwar.com/battles/somme.htm.
77. The Battle of Jutland was fought of the western coast of Denmark from 31 May to 1 June 1916, between the two great battle flotillas of Great Britain and Germany, led by their all-big-gun battleships. It ended essentially in a draw, but, for the Germans, that result persuaded them that they could not defeat the British Grand Fleet. See Eugene L. Rasor, "Jutland, Battle of," in. Tucker, *Encyclopedia*, pp. 390–93; http://www.firstworldwar.com/battle/sea.htm; Dupuy and Dupuy, *Encyclopedia*, pp. 964–67. Emperor William II had believed that Germany's High Seas Fleet would secure Germany's "place in the sun," which he believed Britain wanted to deny to his empire. He then implemented a massive program to build a navy so powerful that no other power, namely Great Britain, would place its navy at "risk" by engaging it in battle. The British became convinced that Germany's battle fleet was a threat to the security of their empire, and were determined to maintain their naval superiority at any cost. The "naval race" that ensued during the last two decades before 1914 increased the tension between them, and helped to propel them toward war.

78. Juergen Rohmer, "Submarine Warfare, Central Powers," in Tucker, *Encyclopedia*, pp. 670–71; Millett and Maslowski, *Common Defense*, p. 329; Dupuy and Dupuy, *Encyclopedia*, p. 968. Austrian historian Erich Zoellner states that Habsburg Emperor Charles VI and his foreign minister, Count Ottokar Czernin, believed that Berlin held "dangerous illusions" about the resources and strengths of the United States. However, in Vienna, as in Berlin, the emperor was under the dominant influence of "military circles," who supported this intensification of German naval warfare. See Erich Zoellner, *Geschichte Oesterreichs Von den Anfaengen bis zur Gegenwart*, 4. Auflage (Vienna: Verlag Fuer Gechichte und Politik, 1970), pp. 486–87.
79. Justin D. Murphy, "Zimmermann Telegram," in Venzon, *Encyclopedia*, pp. 815–16; Robert G. Waite, "Zimmerman Telegram," in Tucker, *Encyclopedia*, pp. 769–70.
80. Harvey A. DeWeerd, *President Wilson Fights His War: World War I and the American Intervention, The Wars of the United States*, general editor Louis Morton (New York: The Macmillan Company, 1968), pp. 21–22. Hereinafter cited as DeWeerd, *Wilson*. In a sense, Berlin responded to the entry of the U.S. on the side of Britain and France by arranging for the transportation of the Bolshevik revolutionary leader, Vladimir I. Lenin, from Switzerland to Russia. He arrived in the capital of Petrograd on 16 April (when the war broke out, the name of the capital city of St. Petersburg had been changed to Petrograd, because the name Peter I, the Great, had chosen when he founded the city in 1703, was considered too German-like in origin and pronunciation). Lenin soon gained control of the faltering Bolshevik Party and led the opposition to the faltering Provisional Government and its support of Russia's participation in the war. On 7 November, the Bolsheviks seized power in Petrograd, and three weeks later took control of Moscow. Lenin took Russia out of the war in December 1917, and signed a peace treaty with Germany at Brest-Litovsk in March 1918 that freed German soldiers to fight on the Western Front. In sharp contrast to the post-war vision of President Wilson, Lenin's view of a post-war world would eliminate capitalism, and make the world safe for communism. Their successors pursued these goals until the fall of the Bolshevik/Communist Empire of the Soviet Union in 1991 shattered the vision of its founder, and opened the former Soviet Empire to the ideas and ideals of Woodrow Wilson.
81. Ibid., pp. 202–03.
82. Ibid., p. 203; Smythe, *Pershing*, p. 5.
83. Smythe, *Pershing*, pp. 2–4.
84. John J. Pershing, *My Experiences in the World War* (New York: Frederick A. Stokes Company, 1931), Vol. 1, pp. 17–18. Hereinafter cited as Pershing, *War*.
85. Ibid., Vol. 2, p. 358.
86. Ibid., Vol. 1, p. 154.
87. John Whiteclay Chambers, "Selective Service," in Venzon, *Encyclopedia*, pp. 540–41; Coffman, *War*, pp. 74–75.
88. Pershing, *War*, Vol. 1, pp. 19–20; Smythe, *Pershing*, pp. 10–11.
89. Pershing, *War*, Vol. 1, p. 37.
90. After the March revolution in Russia, President Wilson named Elihu Root to head a mission to Russia to assure the Provisional Government of America's support, and to urge Russia to stay in the war. Army Chief of Staff Scott was a member of the delegation, known as the Root Mission, that arrived in Petrograd via Vladivostok and the Trans Siberian Railroad in June. They arranged for a loan of $74 million to the government, but they could do little to stop the disintegration of the Russian government and its army. They returned to Washington in August. See David Esposito, "Root Mission," in Venzon, *Encyclopedia*, pp. 506–07. Bliss was an exceptionally learned and eloquent officer who had been a former advisor to Secretary Root, and would later serve on the Allied Supreme War Council. He was also one of five American commissioners to the Versailles Peace Conference. See Bullitt Lowry, "Bliss, Tasker Howard (1853–1930)", in ibid., pp. 94–96.
91. Pershing, *War*, Vol. 1, pp. 37–40; Smythe, *Pershing*, pp. 11–12.
92. DeWeerd, *Wilson*, p. 205.
93. Summerall memoir, p. 82.
94. Smythe, *Pershing*, p. 42.
95. Summerall memoir, p. 82.
96. Ibid., p. 83.
97. Ibid.
98. Smythe, *Pershing*, p. 13.
99. A fine artillery officer, Lassiter rose to become chief of artillery for the Second Army when Pershing created it under Bullard's command in October 1918.
100. Summerall memoir, pp. 83–84.
101. Ibid., p. 84.
102. Ibid., p. 86.
103. Van Michael Leslie, "Messines, Battle of (7–14 June 1917)" in Tucker, *Encyclopedia*, pp. 478–79.
104. Summerall memoir, p. 85.
105. Ibid., pp. 85–86.

106. Smythe, *Pershing*, p. 36.
107. Ibid., p. 24.
108. Summerall memoir, p. 86; the quotation is from Summerall's report to the adjutant general, which is discussed below in the text, and cited below in note 118.
109. Summerall memoir, p. 86.
110. Historical Division, Department of the Army, *United States Army in the World War, 1917–1919*, 17 Vols. (Washington: Government Printing Office, 1948), Vol. 1, pp. 112–13. Hereinafter cited as *USA/WW*. See also Holley, *Palmer*, pp. 303–04.
111. Summerall memoir, p. 86.
112. Smythe, *Pershing*, p. 36.
113. Summerall memoir, p. 86.
114. Smythe, *Pershing*, pp. 36–37.
115. Address of Maj. Gen. J. G. Harbord, at the Army War College, April 29, 1933, *Personalities and Personal Relationships in the American Expeditionary Forces* (Washington: Government Printing Office, 1933), p. 6.
116. Quoted in Smythe, *Pershing*, p. 37.
117. *USA/WW*, Vol. 1, pp. 93–106; Smythe, *Pershing*, p. 37; Millett, *The General*, pp. 336–37.
118. Paul F. Braim, "United States Army: American Expeditionary Force (AEF)," in Venzon, *Encyclopedia*, p. 607. Hereinafter cited as Braim, "AEF"; Smythe, *Pershing*, pp. 37–38.
119. Summerall memoir, p. 87.
120. Report from the Artillery Section of Military Mission to England and France, to The Adjutant General of the Army, July 21, 1917, that Summerall entitled "Reply of the Military Mission to England and France to Criticisms made by the Operations Section, AEF, July, 1917," Summerall MSS, Box 26, "Controversies."
121. Summerall memoir, p. 87.

## Chapter Nine

1. James J. Cooke, *The Rainbow Division in the Great War, 1917–1919* (Westport, Connecticut: Praeger Publisher, 1994), p. 3. Hereinafter cited as Cooke, *Rainbow Division*; William Manchester, *American Caesar: Douglas MacArthur, 1880–1964* (Boston: Little, Brown and Company, 1978), p. 77. Hereinafter cited as Manchester, *American Caesar*.
2. Douglas MacArthur, *Reminiscences* (New York: McGraw-Hill Book Company, 1964), p. 44. Hereinafter cited as MacArthur, *Reminiscences*.
3. Manchester, *American Caesar*, p. 76.
4. MacArthur, *Reminiscences*, p. 44.
5. Ibid., pp. 45–46.
6. Pershing, *War*, 1, p. 25; MacArthur, *Reminiscences*, p. 51.
7. Summerall memoir, p. 88.
8. Cooke, *Rainbow Division*, p. 33.
9. Henry J. Reilly, *Americans All: The Rainbow at War: Official History of the 42nd Rainbow Division in the World War* (The F. J. Herr Printing Co.: Columbus, Ohio, 1936), p. 50. Hereinafter cited as Reilly, *Americans All*.
10. Summerall memoir, p. 88.
11. Cooke, *Rainbow Division*, p. 21.
12. Ibid., p. 15.
13. Summerall memoir, p. 88.
14. Ibid., pp. 88–89.
15. Summerall to Major Francis H. Schoeffel, Office Commander of the Port, Army Pier No. 1, Hoboken, N.J, in Record Group 120, World War I, Organizational Records, 42nd Division, Historical File 10.2-32.11, Entry 1240, Box 34. This collection will be cited hereinafter as RG 120, 42nd Division.
16. Summerall memoir, p. 89.
17. Ibid. In addition to his lively cartoons, Butler kept a diary of his service as Summerall's aide from 23 December 1917 through 12 October 1918.
18. Ibid.
19. David F. Trask, *The AEF and Coalition Warmaking, 1917–1918*, Modern War Studies, Theodore A. Wilson, General Editor (Lawrence, Kansas: University Press of Kansas, 1993), p. 42. Hereinafter cited as Trask, *AEF*.
20. Pershing, *War*, 1, pp. 80–85; Smythe, *Pershing*, pp. 27–28.
21. Memorandum from Summerall to Regimental Commanders, November 3, 1917, in RG 120, 42nd Division, Box 36.
22. Summerall memoir, p. 89.
23. Louis L. Collins, *History of the 151st Field Artillery, Rainbow Division* (Saint Paul, Minnesota: Minnesota War Records Commission, 1924), pp. 23–24. Hereinafter referred to as Collins, *History*.

24. USA/WW, 2, pp. 77–78; USA/WW, 3, pp. 667–68; Smythe, *Pershing*, pp. 61–62; Cooke, *Rainbow Division*, pp. 22–23;
25. MacArthur, *Reminiscences*, p. 53.
26. USA/WW, 3, pp. 669–70.
27. MacArthur, *Reminiscences*, p. 53; Cooke, *Rainbow Division*, p. 23.
28. Reilly, *Americans All*, pp. 97–99.
29. Ibid., p. 99.
30. Summerall memoir, p. 90.
31. Reilly, *Americans All*, p. 99.
32. Ibid.; Summerall memoir, p. 90.
33. Summerall to Regimental Commanders, November 3, 1917, in RG 120, 42nd Division, Box 36.
34. Summerall memoir, p. 90.
35. Cooke, *Rainbow Division*, p. 33.
36. Collins, *History*, p. 26.
37. Reilly, *Americans All*, p. 100.
38. Summerall memoir, p. 91.
39. Cooke, *Rainbow Division*, p. 33.
40. Summerall memoir, pp. 90–91.
41. Cooke, *Rainbow Division*, pp. 34–35, 39.
42. Summerall to Commanding General, 42nd Division, December 9, 1917, in RG 120, 42nd Division, Box 38.
43. Summerall MSS, box 2, folder 3.
44. Summerall memoir, p. 91.
45. General Orders No. 6, December 21, 1917, RG 120, 42nd Division, Box 36.
46. Summerall memoir, p. 91.
47. George C. Marshall, *Memoirs of My Services in the World War, 1917–1918* (Boston: Houghton Mifflin Company, 1976), p. 8. Hereinafter cited as Marshall, *Memoirs*.
48. Millett, *The General*, pp. 310–11.
49. Marshall, *Memoirs*, p. 3.
50. Ibid., pp. 7, 241–44.
51. Ibid., pp. 11–14.
52. Coffman, *War*, pp. 131–32.
53. The Society of the First Division, *History of the First Division during the World War, 1917–1919* (Philadelphia: The John C. Winston Company, 1922), p. 9. Hereinafter cited as *History of the First Division*.
54. Coffman, *War*, p. 132.
55. Ibid., p. 133.
56. *History of the First Division*, pp. 21–22.
57. Ibid., pp. 22–26.
58. Pershing, *War*, 1, p. 154.
59. Millett, *The General*, p. 320.
60. Ibid., p. 318.
61. Ibid., p. 321.
62. George C. Marshall, *George C. Marshall Interviews and Reminiscences for Forrest C. Pogue, Revised edition, with an introduction by Dr. Pogue*, Larry I. Bland, ed., Joellen K. Bland, asst. ed., Sharon Ritenour Stevens, photographs ed. (Lexington, Virginia: George C. Marshall Research Foundation, 1991), p. 197. Hereinafter cited as Marshall, *Interviews*.
63. Ibid., p. 198.
64. Ibid.
65. Robert Lee Bullard, *Personalities and Reminiscences of the War* (Garden City, New York: Doubleday, Page and Company, 1925), p. 95. Hereinafter cited as Bullard, *Personalities*.
66. Millett, *The General*, p. 322.
67. *History of the First Division*, pp. 27–35; Coffman, *War*, pp. 138–40.
68. Dupuy and Dupuy, *Encyclopedia*, pp. 972–73; Coffman, *War*, p. 154; Pershing, *War*, 1, pp. 203–04; Smythe, *Pershing*, p. 96.
69. Dupuy and Dupuy, *Encyclopedia*, pp. 971–72.
70. Pershing, *War*, 1, p. 216.
71. Headquarters American Expeditionary Forces, December 13, 1917, Confidential memorandum, From: Commander-in-Chief, and "Sent to certain General Officers," Subject: "Pessimism," copy in "Controversies and Attacks, 1894–1931," Summerall MSS, Box 26.

72. Marshall, *Interviews*, p. 211.
73. Ibid.
74. Millett, *The General*, p. 334.
75. Ibid., pp. 334–35; Gary Nichols, "Parker, Frank (1872–1947)," in Venzon, *Encyclopedia*, pp. 450–51.
76. Bullard, *Personalities*, pp. 112–13.
77. Summerall memoir, p. 91; *History of the First Division*, p. 40.
78. Summerall memoir, p. 91.
79. HEADQUARTERS FIELD ARTILLERY BRIGADE, FIRST DIVISION, AMERICAN EXPEDITIONARY FORCES, MEMORANDUM FOR ALL OFFICERS: December 30, 1917, First Field Artillery Brigade, Historical File, 4.21-10.2, Box 91, National Archives and Records Administration, Washington, DC. Hereinafter cited as First Field Artillery Brigade, Historical File. In his diary, Lieutenant Butler noted also the "ragged and greasy uniforms," and that many of the men were "unshaved & with long hair." *Butler's Diary*.
80. Ibid.
81. The Adjutant, F.A. Brigade, First Division, to Commanding Officer, 6th Field Artillery, ibid., Box 97.
82. Millett, *The General*, p. 341.
83. Bullard, *Personalities*, pp. 116–17.
84. MEMORANDUM No. 10, January 15, 1918, First Field Artillery Brigade, Historical File, Box 92.
85. Summerall memoir, pp. 91–92; Marshall, *Memoirs*, p. 53.
86. Summerall memoir, p. 92.
87. Marshall, *Memoirs*, p. 53.
88. Summerall memoir, p. 91.
89. *History of the First Division*, pp. 44–47; Summerall memoir, p. 92.
90. *History of the First Division*, pp. 42–44, 49–50; Millett, *The General*, pp. 341–42; Summerall memoir, pp. 92–93; Bullard, *Personalities*, pp. 131–33.
91. Millett, *The General*, p. 342; Bullard, *Personalities*, pp. 129–31.
92. Memorandum No. 21, January 23, 1918, First Field Artillery Brigade, Historical File, Box 97.
93. Summerall memoir, p. 93.
94. Ibid.
95. *Butler's Diary*.
96. Bullard, *Personalities*, p. 140; *History of the First Division*, p. 48.
97. Memorandum No. 33, February 1, 1918, First Field Artillery Brigade, Historical File, Box 92.
98. Coffman, *War*, p. 145.
99. Memorandum No. 47, February 19, 1918, First Field Artillery Brigade, Historical File, Box 92.
100. Summerall memoir, p. 93.
101. Coffman, *War*, pp. 147–48.
102. Summerall memoir, p. 94.
103. Quoted in Richard Norton Smith, *The Colonel: The Life and Legend of Robert R. McCormick, 1880–1955* (Boston: Houghton Mifflin Company, 1997), p. 191. Hereinafter cited as Smith, *The Colonel*.
104. Quoted in ibid., p. 199.
105. Ibid.
106. Millett, *The General*, pp. 344–45; *History of the First Division*, pp. 55–56.
107. *History of the First Division*, pp. 55–57.
108. Bullard, *Personalities*, pp. 154–55.
109. Millett, *The General*, p. 345; Summerall memoir, p. 93.
110. *History of the First Division*, pp. 54–55.
111. Summerall memoir, pp. 93–94.
112. Ibid., p. 94; Bullard, *Personalities*, pp. 150–51; Marshall, *Memoirs*, p. 72.
113. Summerall memoir, p. 94.
114. Bullard, *Personalities*, pp. 150–51; Marshall, *Memoirs*, pp. 71–72; Millett, *The General*, p. 345; *History of the First Division*, p. 58.
115. *History of the First Division*, pp. 58–61; Marshall, *Memoirs*, pp. 72–73; Millett, *The General*, p. 346.
116. *History of the First Division*, p. 63.
117. Ibid., pp. 63–64.

## Notes to Pages 195–201

118. David T. Zabecki, "Ludendorff Offensives, 1918," in Tucker, *First World War*, pp. 443–44. Hereinafter cited as Zabecki, "Ludendorff." Shipley Thomas, *The History of the A. E. F.* (New York: George H. Doran Company, 1920), p. 67. Hereinafter cited as Thomas, *AEF*; Trask, *AEF*, p. 48.
119. Pershing, *Experiences*, note 1, p. 365.
120. Ferdinand Foch, *The Memoirs of Marshal Foch*, translated by T. Bentley Mott (London: William Heinemann, Ltd), pp. 312–13. Hereinafter cited as Foch, *Memoirs*.
121. Ibid., p. 315.
122. Smythe, *Pershing*, p. 104; Pershing, *War*, 1, p. 379.
123. Trask, *AEF*, p. 54; Historical Section, Army War College, *Order of Battle of the Land Forces in the World War, American Expeditionary Forces, Divisions* (Washington: United States Government Printing Office, 1931), pp. 26–27, 118, 277. Hereinafter cited as *Order of Battle, Divisions*.
124. Historical Section, Army War College, *Order of Battle of the United States Land Forces in the World War, American Expeditionary Forces, General Headquarters, Armies, Army Corps, Services of Supply, and Separate Forces* (Washington: United States Government Printing Office, 1937), p. 197. Hereinafter cited as *Order of Battle, GHQ, Armies, Army Corps*. Paul F. Braim, "Liggett, Hunter (1857–1935)," in Venzon, *Encyclopedia*, p. 343. Hereinafter cited as Braim, "Liggett." James J. Cooke states that "Liggett's staff was solid and was ready for the fight. He had Colonel Malin Craig as his chief of staff, Lieutenant Colonel Stuart 'Tommy' Heintzelman as the G-3 [Operations], and the abrasive Colonel Billly Mitchell as his chief, air service." Cooke, *Generals*, p. 77. Summerall soon had a major disagreement with Craig, and, as shall be noted in the following chapters, came to resent Liggett's criticism over his role in the Sedan incident. Summerall also engaged in a bitter dispute with Mitchell over Summerall's plans for the defense of the Hawaiian Islands when Summerall commanded the Hawaiian Department from 1921 to 1924.
125. Pershing, *War*, p. 370.
126. Coffman, *War*, p. 155; Thomas, *AEF*, p. 68.
127. Bullard, *Personalities*, p. 175.
128. Millett, *The General*, p. 355.
129. Summerall memoir, p. 96.
130. Millett, *The General*, pp. 355–56; Cooke, *Generals*, p. 79.
131. Millett, *The General*, p. 356; Cooke, *Generals*, p. 79.
132. Bullard, *Personalities*, pp. 174–75.
133. Summerall memoir, p. 96. Actually, as Allan Millett points out, Pershing's investigators found the Twenty-sixth Division at fault for mishandling its liaison with the First Division. Millett, *The General*, p. 356.
134. Bullard, *Personalities*, pp. 177–79.
135. Ibid., p. 180.
136. Ibid.; Summerall, memoir, p. 96.
137. Marshall, *Memoirs*, p. 78.
138. Bullard, *Personalities*, pp. 180–81.
139. Zabecki, "Ludendorff," p. 444.
140. Ibid.; Dupuy and Dupuy, *Encyclopedia*, p. 979.
141. Quoted in Pershing, *War*, p. 396.
142. Smythe, *Pershing*, p. 106.
143. Pershing, *War*, 1, p. 392.
144. Quoted in ibid., pp. 393–95.
145. *History of the First Division*, p. 97.
146. Summerall memoir, p. 96.

### Chapter Ten

1. Allan R. Millett, "Cantigny, 28–31 May 1918," in Charles E. Heller and William A. Stofft, eds., *America's First Battles, 1776–1965* (Lawrence: University of Kansas Press, 1986), pp. 163–64. Hereinafter cited as Millett, "Cantigny"; Millett, *The General*, p. 358.
2. *History of the First Division*, pp. 69–72; John F. Votaw, "United States Army: First Division," in Venzon, *Encyclopedia*, p. 617. Hereinafter cited as Votaw, "First Division"; Millett, *The General*, p. 358; Millett, "Cantigny," p. 165.
3. Millett, "Cantigny," p. 165; Marshall, *Memoirs*, p. 82.
4. Summerall memoir, p. 97.
5. Ibid.; *History of the First Division*, pp. 76, 97.
6. USA/WW, 2, pp. 270–71.
7. Coffman, *War*, pp. 148–49; Smythe, *Pershing*, pp. 107–08.

8. Dupuy and Dupuy, *Encyclopedia*, p. 979.
9. Pershing, *War*, 2, p. 54; Coffman, *War*, p. 156.
10. Millett, "Cantigny," p. 168.
11. Ibid., pp. 168–70; Marshall, *Memoirs*, pp. 88–90; Summerall memoir, p. 98.
12. Thomas, *AEF*, p. 74; Marshall, *Memoirs*, p. 88.
13. Millett, "Cantigny,", pp. 170–71; Smythe, *Pershing*, p. 126; Marshall, *Memoirs*, pp. 90–91.
14. USA/WW, 4, p. 293.
15. Millett, "Cantigny," p. 171.
16. Ibid.; Summerall memoir, p. 98.
17. Marshall, *Memoirs*, p. 94.
18. Millett, "Cantigny," p. 171.
19. Marshall, *Memoirs*, p. 95.
20. Millett, "Cantigny," p. 172.
21. Marshall, *Memoirs*, p. 95; Millett, *The General*, p. 363.
22. USA/WW, 4, p. 341.
23. Bullard, *The General*, pp. 363–64.
24. Journal of Cantigny Operations, First Field Artillery Brigade, Historical File, Box 14. Hereinafter cited as Journal.
25. Marshall, *Memoirs*, p. 95.
26. Journal.
27. Millett, *The General*, p. 365.
28. Smythe, *Pershing*, p. 127, Journal.
29. Ibid., p. 128.
30. Quoted in ibid.; see also Marshall, *Memoirs*, p. 96.
31. Jeremiah M. Evarts, Captain, 18th Infantry, 1st Division, A.E.F., *Cantigny: A Corner of the War* (Privately Printed: n.d.) pp. 14–15.
32. Smythe, *Pershing*, p. 128.
33. Millett, *The General*, p. 366.
34. Marshall, *Memoirs*, pp. 98–99.
35. Millett, "Cantigny," p. 176; Millett, *The General*, p. 366.
36. Millett, "Cantigny," p. 179.
37. Ibid., p. 178.
38. Millett, *The General*, p. 367.
39. *History of the First Division*, p. 86.
40. Bullard, *Personalities*, p. 199.
41. *History of the First Division*, p. 350.
42. Marshall, *Memoirs*, p. 99.
43. Bullard, *Personalities*, p. 198.
44. *History of the First Division*, p. 347.
45. Ibid., p. 349.
46. Smythe, *Pershing*, pp. 128–29; Millett, *The General*, p. 367.
47. *Butler's Diary*.
48. Millett, "Cantigny," pp. 179–81.
49. Summerall memoir, p. 98.
50. Smyth, *Pershing*, pp. 144–45.
51. Millett, *The General*, pp. 368–69.
52. Summerall memoir, p. 99.
53. Bullard, *Personalities*, p. 206.
54. *Butler's Diary*.
55. *History of the First Division*, p. 92.
56. Marshall, *Memoirs*, p. 102.
57. Summerall memoir, p. 99.
58. Bullard, *Personalities*, pp. 206–07; Summerall memoir, p. 99. Summerall neglected to mention that General Vandenburg was present at this meeting, and Allan Millett wrote that it was Vandenburg, not Debeney, who expressed his pleasure at Bullard's assurance that the division would hold its position. See Millett, *The General*, p. 369.

59. Millett, *The General*, pp. 369–70; Marshall, *Memoirs*, pp. 107–08.
60. Marshall, *Memoirs*, p. 108; Summerall memoir, p. 99.
61. Marshall, *Memoirs*, p. 108.
62. Coffman, *War*, p. 224; Thomas, *AEF*, pp. 87–88.
63. Charles A. Endress, "United States Army: 3rd Division," in Venzon, *Encyclopedia*, p. 622. Hereinafter cited as Endress, "3rd Division."
64. Quoted in Thomas, *AEF*, p. 90.
65. American Battle Monuments Commission, *American Armies and Battlefields in Europe: A History, Guide, and Reference Book* (United States Government Printing Office: Washington, 1938), p. 47. Hereinafter cited as *American Armies*.
66. Coffman, *War*, p. 214; Smythe, *Pershing*, pp. 138–39.
67. Quoted in George B. Clark, "Belleau Wood, Battle of," in Venzon, *Encyclopedia*, p. 74. Hereinafter cited as Clark, "Belleau Wood."
68. Ibid., p. 77; Smythe, *Pershing*, p. 140.
69. Smythe, *Pershing*, p. 140.
70. Clark, "Belleau Wood," p. 77.
71. Coffman, *War*, p. 213; Smythe, *Pershing*, p. 133.
72. Coffman, *War*, p. 213.
73. Pershing, *War*, pp. 70–71.
74. Quoted in ibid., p. 71.
75. *Butler's Diary*.
76. Millett, *The General*, pp. 377–78.
77. Ibid., p. 370.
78. Quoted in Bullard, *Personalities*, p. 196.
79. Summerall memoir, p. 99
80. Major General Joseph Dorst Patch, *A Soldier's War: The First Infantry Division, AEF (1917–1918)*, (Corpus Christi, Texas: Mission Press, 1966), p. 104. Hereinafter cited as Patch, *War*.
81. Summerall memoir, p. 99.
82. Ibid., p. 100.
83. *History of the First Division*, p. 346.
84. Summerall memoir, p. 100.
85. Foch, *Memoirs*, p. 391.
86. Ibid.
87. Steven D. Fisher, "Mangin, Charles Marie Emmanuel (1866–1925)," in Tucker, *Encyclopedia*, p. 459.
88. Foch, *Memoirs*, p. 407.
89. Ibid; Coffman, *War*, p. 234.
90. Smythe, *Pershing*, p. 152; Millett, *The General*, pp. 380–81.
91. Millett, *The General*, p. 381.
92. Summerall memoir, p. 100.
93. *Butler's Diary*.
94. Summerall memoir, p. 100.
95. *Butler's Diary*.
96. Summerall memoir, p. 100; Bullard, *Personalities*, p. 211.
97. Smythe, *Pershing*, p. 152.
98. Ibid., pp. 152–53.
99. Dupuy and Dupuy, *Encyclopedia*, p. 980; Thomas, *AEF*, p. 121.
100. Douglas V. Johnson II and Rolfe L. Hillman, Jr., *Soissons, 1918* (College Station, Texas: Texas A&M University Press, 1999), p. 17. Dr. Johnson, a retired professor from the US Army War College, combined his expertise as a military historian with the extensive research into the history of the Battle of Soissons that the late Colonel Hillman had conducted, and completed the work that the latter had begun. Their book is based upon careful analysis of German and American sources, and a broad range of secondary materials. It clearly and forcefully presents a thorough and detailed analysis of unit actions, and especially of American military leadership during the battle. Hereinafter referred to as Johnson and Hillman, *Soissons*.
101. Millett, *The General*, p. 382.
102. James G. Harbord, *Leaves from a War Diary* (New York: Dodd, Mead &Company, 1931), p. 318. Hereinafter cited as Harbord, *Diary*.

103. *History of the First Division*, p. 104; Summerall memoir, p. 100; Johnson and Hillman, *Soissons*, pp. 40–42.
104. Johnson and Hillman, *Soissons*, pp. 44.
105. *Register of Graduates and Former Cadets of the United States Military Academy, Cullum Memorial Edition* (West Point Alumni Foundation, Inc.: West Point, New York, 1970), p. 295.
106. Johnson and Hillman, *Soissons*, pp. 51–53.
107. Harbord, *Diary*, p. 319.
108. Ibid., pp. 319–21.
109. Johnson and Hillman, *Soissons*, pp. 60, 62, 67, 73.
110. Ibid., p. 42.
111. *History of the First Division*, p. 107; James G. Harbord, *The American Army in France, 1917–1919* (Boston: Little, Brown, and Company, 1936), pp. 325–26. Hereinafter cited as Harbord, *Army*. Coffman, *War*, p. 236.
112. Harbord, *Diary*, p. 323; Johnson and Hillman, *Soissons*, p. 61.
113. Johnson and Hillman, *Soissons*, p. 42.
114. "WWR. 2nd Division, Vol. 5-Soissons, Doc 2, Item 18: War Diary, [Editorial Translation], GROUP OF ARMIES GERMAN CROWN PRINCE, July 18, 1918," in *USA/WW*, 5, p. 679. Hereinafter cited as "War Diary, July 18, 1918," *USA/WW*, 5.
115. *History of the First Division*, p. 113; Johnson and Hillman, *Soissons*, p. 46.
116. Johnson and Hillman, *Soissons*, pp. 46–47; *History of the First Division*, pp. 114–18; Coffman, *War*, pp. 239–40.
117. Johnson and Hillman, *Soissons*, pp. 47–51.
118. Ibid., pp. 51–56; Coffman, *War*, p. 240.
119. *History of the First Division*, pp. 121–22.
120. "War Diary, July 18, 1918," *USA/WW*, 5.
121. Harbord, *Army*, p. 328.
122. Johnson and Hillman, *Soissons*, pp. 63–84; Coffman, *War*, pp. 240–41; Harbord, *Diary*, pp. 321–27.
123. Harbord, *Army*, p. 333.
124. Harbord, *Diary*, p. 327.
125. Ibid.
126. Coffman, *War*, pp. 241–42; Johnson and Hillman, *Soissons*, pp. 103–04.
127. Johnson and Hillman, *Soissons*, p. 105; Coffman, *War*, p. 242.
128. Coffman, *War*, p. 242; Johnson and Hillman, *Soissons*, p. 107.
129. Johnson and Hillman, *Soissons*, p. 109.
130. Harbord, *Army*, p. 335.
131. Harbord, *Diary*, p. 328.
132. Johnson and Hillman, *Soissons*, pp. 112, 114.
133. Coffman, *War*, p. 242.
134. Smythe, *Pershing*, p. 157.
135. Johnson and Hillman, *Soissons*, p. 112.
136. As General Duffieux, of the French Armies of the North and Northeast, said of American losses, "That makes no difference. We are having great success around Soissons and to the south. Everything must get into the battle as soon as possible." *USA/WW*, 5, pp. 248–49.
137. Ibid., p. 92.
138. Ibid., pp. 93–94; Coffman, *War*, p. 243.; *History of the First Division*, p. 122.
139. *History of the First Division*, p. 122.
140. Johnson and Hillman, *Soissons*, p. 92.
141. Beaumont B. Buck, *Memories of Peace and War* (San Antonio, Texas: The Naylor Company, 1935), pp. 197–98. Hereinafter cited as Buck, *Memories*.
142. Johnson and Hillman, *Soissons*, pp. 93–94.
143. Ibid., p. 94.
144. Ibid., pp. 93–94.
145. Ibid., pp. 95–96.
146. Summerall memoir, p. 102.
147. Johnson and Hillman, *Soissons*, pp. 96–97.
148. Summerall memoir, p. 102.
149. Babcock to Summerall, 25 July 1918, Summerall MSS, container 2.

150. Conrad Stanton Babcock Papers, Hoover Institution of War, Revolution and Peace, Stanford, California, p. 529. Hereinafter cited as Babcock Papers. Babcock continued to press his case. On 4 August 1918, he reported to Summerall that his order to Huebner "to organize his battalion in depth, gave rise to the erroneous Division report that the 28th Infantry had withdrawn and was reorganizing behind the French. Nothing of this kind was ever thought of, and the 28th Infantry at no time withdrew or attempted to withdraw." In this same report, Babcock asserted that when Huebner's battalion attacked, "the barrage had long since left the troops," and that Huebner had reported that it was "impossible to keep up with the barrage from the very start." Memorandum from Babcock to Summerall, "Report on Operations south of Soissons, July 1918," Babcock Papers. As far as I can tell, Summerall did not respond to the memorandum.
151. Ibid.
152. *History of the First Division*, p. 126.
153. Coffman, *War*, p. 243; Buck, *Memories*, pp. 199–200.
154. Babcock Papers, p. 531; Johnson and Hillman, *Soissons*, p. 99.
155. Johnson and Hillman, *Soissons*, pp. 99–102.
156. *History of the First Division*, p. 128; *Butler's Diary*.
157. Johnson and Hillman, *Soissons*, p. 117.
158. *History of the First Division*, pp. 128–29.
159. Johnson and Hillman, *Soissons*, p. 119.
160. Buck, *Memories*, p. 198.
161. Johnson and Hillman, *Soissons*, pp. 117–18.
162. Babcock Papers, p. 534.
163. Johnson and Hillman, *Soissons*, pp. 118–19.
164. Babcock Papers, pp. 534–35.
165. Johnson and Hillman, *Soissons*, p. 120.
166. *Butler's Diary*.
167. Ibid.
168. Summerall memoir, p. 101.
169. Johnson and Hillman, *Soissons*, p. 120.
170. *History of the First Division*, pp. 131–32.
171. Ibid., p. 133; Johnson and Hillman, *Soissons*, p. 123.
172. Summerall memoir, pp. 101–02.
173. *Butler's Diary*.
174. Johnson and Hillman, *Soissons*, pp. 122–23.
175. Summerall memoir, p. 104.
176. Quoted in Smythe, *Pershing*, p. 157.
177. Summerall memoir, p. 102.
178. Buck, *Memories*, pp. 204–06.
179. Summerall memoir, p. 101.
180. Ibid.
181. See above, note 80.
182. Johnson and Hillman, *Soissons*, p. 124.
183. Patch, *War*, p. 39.
184. Quoted in Johnson and Hillman, *Soissons*, p. 124.
185. First Division Historical File, Historical Sketches, etc., Box 23, National Archives.
186. Patch, *War*, p. 39.
187. Summerall memoir, p. 102.
188. Patch, *War*, pp. 41–42.
189. Johnson and Hillman, *Soissons*, p. 126.
190. Thomas, *AEF*, p. 168; *History of the First Division*, pp. 135–36; Johnson and Hillman, *Soissons*, p. 135.
191. Summerall memoir, p. 104.
192. *Butler Diary*; *History of the First Division*, p. 137; *USA/WW*, 5, p. 307.
193. Johnson and Hillman, *Soissons*, p. 141; *History of the First Division*, p. 138.
194. *History of the First Division*, p. 128.
195. Summerall memoir, pp. 104–05.
196. Quoted in Dupuy and Dupuy, *Encyclopedia*, p. 982.

197. "HS Ger. File: 803-33.5: Fldr. V: Report Exhausted Divisions, [Editorial Translation], Operations Section, GROUP OF ARMIES GERMAN CROWN PRINCE, July 24, 1918," in *USA/WW*, 5, pp. 684–85.
198. Johnson and Hillman, *Soissons*, p. 141; for a summary of the tough fight to the Vesle, see Coffman, *War*, pp. 248–61.
199. *Butler's Diary*.
200. Thomas, *AEF*, p. 169; Coffman, *War*, p. 245; Johnson and Hillman, *Soissons*, p. 144; Summerall memoir, p. 105.
201. Pershing, *War*, 2, p. 161.
202. Quoted in *History of the First Division*, p. 142.
203. Summerall memoir, p. 105.
204. Johnson and Hillman, *Soissons*, p. 148.
205. Patch, *War*, p. 39.
206. Johnson and Hillman, *Soissons*, p. 155.
207. Ibid., p. 41.
208. Ibid., p. 155.
209. Coffman, *War*, p. 242.
210. Johnson and Hillman, *Soissons*, pp. 155–56.
211. Ibid., p. 146.
212. "Notes on use of machine guns in the operation of the 1st Division south of SOISSONS, and recommendations based thereon, August 5, 1918," *Command and Duties, A.E.F. France, September 1917–Nov. 1918*, container 14, Summerall MSS.
213. Ibid.
214. Memorandum, August 11, 1918, in ibid.
215. Ibid.
216. Pershing, *War*, 2, p. 188.

## *Chapter Eleven*

1. Foch, *Memoirs*, p. 424.
2. Ibid., p. 426.
3. Pershing, *War*, 2, p. 211.
4. Foch, *Memoirs*, p. 427.
5. Ibid., p. 431.
6. Ibid., pp. 427–28. Brey was adjacent to iron mines, and not far away were the coalmines of the Saar River basin. Both of these areas were critical to the production of German war material. In addition, the fortified city of Metz was a strategic rail center, and, as historian James H. Hallas noted, "a lynchpin in the German defensive line along the whole Western front." James H. Hallas, *Squandered Victory: The American First Army at St. Mihiel* (Westport, Connecticut: Praeger Publishers, 1995), p. 2. Hereinafter cited as Hallas, *St. Mihiel*.
7. Coffman, *War*, p. 263.
8. Ibid., p. 458.
9. Hallas, *St. Mihiel*, p. 2.
10. Pershing, *War*, 2, 262; *History of the First Division*, p. 154.
11. J. Michael Miller, "St. Mihiel Campaign," in Venzon, *Encyclopedia*, p. 522. Hereinafter cited as Miller, "St. Mihiel."
12. Pershing, *War*, 2, p. 263; Miller, "St. Mihiel," p. 522.
13. "American Expeditionary Forces, 1st Army Reports: Artillery-#621.01," Box 3374, National Archives and Records Administration; Smythe, *Pershing*, p. 179.
14. Pershing, *War*, 2, p. 263.
15. *Order of Battle, GHQ, Armies, Army Corps*, p. 89.
16. Pershing, *War*, 2, p. 226.
17. Coffman, *War*, p. 268.
18. Marshal, *Memoirs*, pp. 126, 129.
19. Ibid., pp. 127–28.
20. *History of the First Division*, pp. 143–44; Summerall memoir, p. 106.
21. *History of the First Division*, pp. 144–45, 147.
22. Memorandum, Headquarters, 1st Division, August 29, 1918, World War I Historical Records, 1st Division, RG 120, Historical file, 201 321.1-32.15, Box 29. Hereinafter cited as Memorandum, August 29, 1918.
23. *History of the First Division*, pp. 144–45.
24. Ibid., pp. 146–50.
25. *Order of Battle, Armies*, pp. 11, 13.

26. *History of the First Division*, p. 150.
27. Memorandum, August 29, 1918.
28. Ibid., p. 146.
29. Memorandum No. 107, Aug. 11, 1918, First Field Artillery Brigade, National Archives.
30. Summerall memoir, p. 106.
31. Ibid.
32. *Order of Battle, Armies*, p. 13.
33. *History of the First Division*, pp. 157–58.
34. Marshall, *Memoirs*, p. 127.
35. Ibid., p. 124; Pershing, *War*, 2, p. 263.
36. Dale E. Wilson, "Patton, George Smith, Jr. (1885–1945)," in Venzon, *Encyclopedia*, p. 452. Hereinafter cited as Wilson, "Patton."
37. Coffman, *War*, p. 268; Miller, "St. Mihiel," p. 524. In his memorandum of 24 July, General Foch stated that "Finally above all, surprise must be effected. Recent operations show that this a condition indispensable to success." Foch, *Memoirs*, p. 428. Pershing also wrote that "A tactical surprise was essential to success." Pershing, *War*, 2, p. 263. On 19 August, General Pétain expressed his concern to Pershing that American officers and soldiers had talked publicly about the "projects in the Woevre." He suggested that Pershing send American officers into other areas occupied by French troops, such as certain sectors of Lorraine, the Vosges, and Upper Alsace, to help divert the enemy's attention from the Woevre. *USA/WW*, 8, pp. 21–22. Pershing developed Pétain's suggestion into a plan to trick the Germans into believing that the American attack would come elsewhere. GHQ sent General Omar Bundy with a corps staff to Belfort, in Upper Alsace, close to the Swiss border, to plan an attack on Mulhouse. Artillery fire in the area increased, aircraft flew reconnaissance missions, and officers from 7 divisions were busy planning the operation. Only Pershing and a few officers at GHQ, like Brigadier General Fox Conner, assistant chief of staff, knew the entire enterprise was a deception. Conner informed Bundy that Colonel A. L. Conger had been directed to report to him, and was fully informed of the planned attack. Bundy and his officers believed they were preparing a major attack. He submitted a preliminary report to Pershing on 1 September, and stated that a more detailed report and plan of attack would follow in two days. See *USA/WW*, 8, p. 45. Pershing's scheme, which became known as the "Belfort ruse," not only deceived Bundy and his officers, but also, more importantly, the Germans. They sent three divisions into the area to strengthen their defenses. See *USA/WW*, 8, pp. 31–32, and Coffman, *War*, pp. 269–70.
38. Michael Grumelli, "Mitchell, William Lendrum (1879–1936)", in Venzon, *Encyclopedia*, pp. 389–90. Hereinafter cited as Grumelli, "Mitchell."
39. Smythe, *Pershing*, pp. 169–73.
40. Ibid., p. 174.
41. Foch, *Memoirs*, p. 462.
42. Ibid.
43. *USA/WW*, 8, pp. 38–40.
44. Ibid., pp. 43–44.
45. Smythe, *Pershing*, pp. 176–77.
46. Foch, *Memoirs*, pp. 464–65.
47. Smythe, *Pershing*, p. 177.
48. Marshall, *Memoirs*, p. 133.
49. Smythe, *Pershing*, p. 182.
50. James Controvich, "United States Army: 4th Division," in Venzon, *Encyclopedia*, p. 627. Hereinafter cited as Controvich "4th Division."
51. Smythe, *Pershing*, p. 182.
52. John J. Pershing and Hunter Liggett, *Report of the First Army, American Expeditionary Forces: Organization and Operations* (Fort Leavenworth, Kansas: The General Service Schools Press, 1923), p. 25. Hereinafter cited as Pershing and Liggett, *Report*.
53. Smythe, *Pershing*, p. 182.
54. Pershing and Liggett, *Report*, p. 24.
55. Pershing, *War*, pp. 286–87; Smythe, *Pershing*, p. 183.
56. Smythe, *Pershing*, p. 183.
57. Thomas R. Gowenlock, *Soldiers of Darkness* (Garden City, New York: Doubleday, Doran & Company, Inc., 1937), pp. 153–57. Hereinafter cited as Gowenlock, *Soldiers*.
58. Summerall memoir, p. 107. Patton assigned Major Sereno Brett's 344th Tank Battalion to the First Division's zone, and Captain Ranulf Compton's 345th Tank Battalion to the Forty-second Division's sector. Patton's boss, Brigadier General Samuel D. Rockenbach, head of the AEF Tanks Corps, had instructed Patton to maintain communications

with Rockenbach's headquarters. Instead Patton dashed around the battlefield on foot, initially keeping up with the lead elements of Compton's battalion, then with Brett's battalion. Occasionally he sent reports by messenger or carrier pigeon. Rockenbach was not pleased, but let Patton off with a reprimand. See Wilson, "Patton," p. 452. On Rockenbach's reaction, see d'Este, *Patton*, pp. 242–43.

59. Miller, "St. Mihiel," p. 524.
60. Joseph T. Dickman, *The Great Crusade: A Narrative of the World War* (New York: D. Appleton and Company, 1927), p. 152. Hereinafter cited as Dickman, *Crusade*.
61. Hallas, *St. Mihiel*, p. 103.
62. *History of the First Division*, p. 162.
63. Hallas, *St. Mihiel*, pp. 103–04; "Report on Operations Against St. Mihiel Salient, September 12–13, inclusive," First Division Historical File, National Archives. Hereinafter cited as First Division Report.
64. *History of the First Division*, pp. 162–64; Summerall memoir, p. 108. The first quotation is from *History of the First Division*; the second is from the Summerall memoir. See also First Division Report.
65. Hallas, *St. Mihiel*, pp. 157–58; *History of the First Division*, pp. 164–65;
66. Dickman, *Crusade*, p. 155.
67. Hallas, *St. Mihiel*, pp. 101–02.
68. Quoted in d'Este, *Patton*, p. 235.
69. Ibid.
70. Hallas, *St. Mihiel*, p. 102.
71. William M. Wright, *Meuse-Argonne Diary: A Division Commander in World War I*, ed. Robert H. Ferrell (Columbia and London: University of Missouri Press, 2004), p. 17. Hereinafter cited as Wright, *Meuse-Argonne*.
72. Ibid., pp. 17–19.
73. Miller, "St. Mihiel," p. 524; Hallas, *St. Mihiel*, p. 145.
74. Hallas, *St. Mihiel*, pp.117–22.
75. Ibid., pp. 128–32.
76. Marshall, *Memoirs*, p. 147.
77. Pershing, *War*, 2, p. 269.
78. Hallas, *St. Mihiel*, pp. 154, 157; Thomas, *AEF*, p. 226.
79. Dickman, *Crusade*, p. 155.
80. Hallas, *St. Mihiel*, pp. 177–78.
81. *History of the First Division*, p. 167; Hallas, *St. Mihiel*, p. 178; the First Division Report describes the night as so dark that the men had to march in a single file formation to maintain contact with each other.
82. *History of the First Division*, p. 167.
83. Pershing, *War*, 2, p. 270.
84. Hallas, *St. Mihiel*, p. 179.
85. Dickman, *Crusade*, pp. 156–57.
86. Bland, *Marshall Interviews*, p. 229.
87. Summerall memoir, pp. 107–08.
88. See German intelligence report of 9 September, in *USA/WW*, 8, p. 294.
89. Ludendorff's telegram to Gallwitz, ibid.; Hallas, *St. Mihiel*, pp. 77–78. See also the summary of operations by Lieutenant General Georg Fuchs, commander of the operations section of Composite Army Group C, in *USA/WW*, 8, p. 316.
90. Miller, "St. Mihiel," pp. 524–25.
91. Pershing *War*, 2, p. 270.
92. "Report of Operations to Supreme Headquarters, September 14, 1918," *USA/WW*, 8, p. 310; "Report of Operations to Supreme Headquarters, September 16, 1918," *USA/WW*, 8, p. 311.
93. Trask, *AEF*, pp. 111–12. James Hallas noted that those men who died in the effort to convince von Gallwitz that the Americans would attack Metz "would be largely forgotten." Hallas, *St. Mihiel*, p. 214.
94. Michael Carr, "United States Air Service," in Venzon, *Encyclopedia*, p. 606. Hereinafter cited as Carr, "Air Service."
95. Ulrich Trumpener, "Gallwitz, Max von (1852–1937)," in Tucker, *Encyclopedia*, p. 287. Hereinafter cited as Trumpener, "von Gallwitz."
96. "von Hindenburg to Group of Armies, von Gallwitz, September 17, 1918," in *USA/WW*, 8, p. 312.
97. Ibid., p. 270.
98. Marshall, *Memoirs*, p. 146.
99. MacArthur, *Reminiscences*, pp. 63–64.

100. Hunter Liggett, *A.E.F.: Ten Years Ago in France* (New York: Dodd, Mead and Company, 1928), pp. 159–61. Hereinafter cited as Liggett, *AEF*.
101. First Division Historical File, RG 120, 20.1, Box 21, National Archives. Hereinafter cited as First Division Historical File.
102. Smythe, *Pershing*, pp. 188–89.
103. Pershing, *War*, 2, 270.
104. Ibid., pp. 271, 272–73.
105. *History of the First Division*, pp. 167, 168–69.
106. Ibid., p. 168.
107. Memorandum No. 135, n.d., in First Division Historical File.
108. Ibid., p. 170.

## Chapter Twelve

1. Foch, *Memoirs*, pp. 476–77.
2. Ibid., pp. 468–69.
3. Ibid., p. 469.
4. Pershing, *War*, 2, p. 282.
5. To General Liggett, the shape and position of the forest was like Manhattan Island. See Liggett, *AEF*, p. 167.
6. Liggett, *AEF*, p. 167.
7. Harbord, *Army*, p. 432.
8. Harbord, *Army*, p. 433.
9. "First Army Field Orders, No. 20, September 20, 1918," *USA/WW*, 9, 82.
10. Paul F. Braim, *The Test of Battle: The American Expeditionary Forces in the Meuse-Argonne Campaign*, 2nd revised ed. (Shippensburg, Pennsylvania: White Mane Books, 1998), p. 85. Hereinafter cited as Braim, *Battle*, p. 85.
11. "Operations Report Operations Sect. No. 3801, Group of Armies Gallwitz to Supreme Headquarters in the Field, September 21, 1918," *USA/WW*, 9, p. 507.
12. "Situation Report, Operations Section No. 10,436, Supreme Headquarters in the Field, September 22, 1918," *USA/WW*, 9, p. 509. Considering the number of German divisions in the vicinity of Metz, Pershing thought that Ludendorff expected the Americans to renew the attack in St. Mihiel sector. See Pershing, *War*, 2, 290.
13. Foch, *Memoirs*, pp. 473–74.
14. Ibid., p. 475.
15. Braim, *Battle*, p. 79; Trask, *AEF*, p. 122.
16. Quoted in Drum's 191-31: Directive, "Plans for Operation West of the Meuse, September 16, 1918," *USA/WW*, 9, pp. 75–76.
17. "G-3 Report: Concentration of First Army, AEF, for Meuse-Argonne Operation, November 19, 1918," ibid, pp. 64–66.
18. Pershing *War*, 2, pp. 290–91.
19. d'Este, *Patton*, pp. 250–52.
20. Trask, *AEF*, p. 222; Paul F. Braim, "Meuse-Argonne Campaign," in Venzon, *Encyclopedia*, p. 382. Hereinafter cited as Braim, "Meuse-Argonne Campaign."
21. Pershing, *War*, 2, p. 291.
22. Smythe, *Pershing*, p. 194; Pershing, *War*, 2, pp. 292–93.
23. Braim, "Meuse-Argonne Campaign," p. 382.
24. Ibid.; Pershing, *War*, 2, 293.
25. Pershing, *War*, 2, p. 293.
26. Marshall, *Memoirs*, p. 160.
27. Pershing, *War*, 2, p. 294.
28. Smythe, *Pershing*, p. 195.
29. Ibid., pp. 195–97; Braim, "Meuse-Argonne Campaign," pp. 382–83; Trask, *AEF*, p. 125.
30. David McCullough, *Truman* (New York: Simon & Schuster, 1992), p. 129. Hereinafter cited as McCullough, *Truman*.
31. d'Este, *Patton*, pp. 254–55.
32. Braim, "Meuse-Argonne Campaign, " p. 383.
33. Marshall, *Memoirs*, p. 160.
34. Trask, *AEF*, p. 125; Braim, "Meuse-Argonne Campaign," p. 383.
35. d'Este, *Patton*, pp. 255–60, 262. For his leadership and heroism under fire, Patton was awarded the Distinguished Service Cross. Patton's participation in the war was over, but Historian Dale Wilson noted that his tank brigade "performed yeoman service in the following weeks." Wilson, "Patton," p. 453.

36. d'Este, *Patton*, pp. 260–61.
37. Braim, *Battle*, pp. 102–03; d'Este, *Patton*, p. 264.
38. Trask, *AEF*, p. 133.
39. Ibid., pp. 134–35.
40. Ibid., pp. 135–37.
41. DeWeerd, *Wilson*, p. 377.
42. Trask, *AEF*, p. 137.
43. Foch, *Memoirs*, pp. 480–81.
44. "Petain to Foch, September 30, 1918," *USA/WW*, 8, pp. 82.
45. "Pershing to Foch, October 2, 1918," ibid., 8, p. 83.
46. "Foch to Pershing, October 2, 1918," ibid., p. 85.
47. Smythe, *Pershing*, p. 204.
48. Ibid., pp. 203–05; Coffman, *War*, p. 321.
49. "History of the Fifth American Army Corps, prepared by Colonel George M. Russell," typescript in Summerall MSS., Box 16, Fifth Army Corps: History and Comments on Operations. Hereinafter cited as Summerall MSS, 16.
50. Summerall memoir, p. 109.
51. *History of the First Division*, pp. 175–76.
52. Gowenlock, *Soldiers*, pp. 189–200.
53. Quoted in ibid., pp. 205–06.
54. Ibid., pp. 205–06; Summerall memoir, p. 109.
55. Gowenlock, *Soldiers*, pp. 206–07; *History of the First Division*, pp. 182–83; Summerall memoir, p. 109. Gowenlock stated that the German planes were a part of Baron Von Richthofen's famous squadron.
56. Summerall memoir, p. 109.
57. Braim, *Battle*, p. 108; Trask, *AEF*, pp. 138–39.
58. *History of the First Division*, pp. 183–86.
59. Ibid., pp. 186–95; Summerall memoir, p. 109.
60. Millett, *The General*, p. 409; Braim, *Battle*, p. 111.
61. *History of the First Division*, pp. 195–200.
62. Summerall memoir, p. 110.
63. *History of the First Division*, pp. 202–03; Summerall memoir, p. 110.
64. Liggett, *AEF*, pp. 186–88; Braim, *Battle*, p. 116.
65. Michael J. Knapp, "'Lost' Battalion," in Venzon, *Encyclopedia*, pp. 353–54. Hereinafter cited as Knapp, 'Lost.'
66. Ibid., p. 354; Braim, *Battle*, p. 116.
67. In a review of the officers of the Eighty-second Division in February 1919, Summerall, commanding V Corps, addressed York, and commended his "courage, skill, and gallantry." He told him that his conduct reflected great credit on the American army and the American people, and that "Your deeds will be recorded in the history of this great war, and they will live as an inspiration, not only to your comrades, but to the generations that will come after us." Summerall MSS, "Report on General officers of Corps and Recommendations, etc.," Box 16.
68. Liggett, *AEF*, pp. 189–90.
69. *History of the First Division*, pp. 203–10; Summerall memoir, pp. 110–11; Richard Kehrberg, "United States Army: 32d Division," in Venzon, *Encyclopedia*, p. 645. Hereinafter cited as Kehrberg, "32d Division."
70. Summerall memoir, p. 110.
71. *History of the First Division*, pp. 208–11.
72. Ibid., p. 211.
73. Braim, *Battle*, p. 119.
74. *History of the First Division*, p. 213.
75. Summerall memoir, p. 111.
76. *History of the First Division*, p. 212.
77. "Report of First Army, October 12, 1918," *USA/WW*, 9, p. 254.
78. Millett, *The General*, pp. 410–11.
79. "Report of First Army, October 12, 1918," USA/WW, 9, p. 254.
80. Pershing, *War*, 2, p. 320.
81. Braim, *Battle*, p. 119; Trask, *AEF*, pp. 145–46. Pershing wrote that during the first five days of October, over 16,000 new cases were reported, and that the total number of influenza patients in hospitals totaled nearly 70,000. Pershing, *War*, 2, p. 327.

82. Trask, *AEF*, p. 141. Trask credits this observation to Braim.
83. Braim, "Meuse-Argonne," p. 385. Battle, p. 385.
84. "GHQ, AEF: Bound Volume H-1: Record, Notes on conversation between General Pershing and Marshal Foch at Bombon, October 13, 1918," *USA/WW*, 8, p. 92.
85. Ibid.
86. Liggett, *AEF*, p. 200.
87. Ibid., pp. 198–99.
88. Braim, *Battle*, p. 119.
89. Liggett, *AEF*, p. 200.
90. Pershing, *War*, 2, p. 336.
91. Liggett, *AEF*, p. 205.
92. Summerall memoir, p. 113.
93. *History of the First Division*, pp. 214–15.
94. Summerall memoir, p. 113.
95. Ibid., p. 114.
96. Ibid.
97. Pershing, *War*, 2, pp. 338–39.
98. Summerall memoir, p. 114.
99. Cooke, *Rainbow Division*, pp. 168–69.
100. MacArthur, *Reminiscences*, p. 66.
101. Ibid.
102. Cooke, *Rainbow Division*, p. 170.
103. MacArthur, *Reminiscences*, pp. 66–67.
104. Kehrberg, "32d Division," p. 645.
105. MacArthur, *Reminiscences*, p. 67.
106. Cooke, *Rainbow Division*, pp. 171–76.
107. Ibid., p. 176.
108. Ibid., pp. 177–78.
109. Summerall memoir, pp. 114–15.
110. Cooke, *Rainbow Division*, p. 178.
111. Summerall memoir, p. 114.
112. Ibid., p. 115.
113. Reilly, *Americans All*, p. 658.
114. Summerall memoir, p. 115.
115. Ibid.
116. Ibid.
117. Ibid.
118. Cooke, *Rainbow Division*, p. 178; Cooke, *Generals*, p. 71.
119. Cooke, *Rainbow Division*, p. 178.
120. Summerall memoir, p. 115.
121. Smythe, *Pershing*, p. 214.
122. Ibid., pp. 214–15.
123. Francis P. Duffy, *Father Duffy's Story: A Tale of Humor and Heroism, Of Life and Death With The Fighting Sixth-Ninth* (New York: George H. Doran Company, 1919), pp. 276–77.
124. Dupuy and Dupuy, *Encyclopedia*, pp. 984–85.
125. "HS German File: 811-33.5: Fldr. IV: War Diary [Extract], German Fifth Army, October 8, 1918," *USA/WW*, 9, p. 544.
126. "HS German File: 810-33.5: Fldr. V: Operations Report from Operations Section, Group of Armies, German Crown Prince, to Supreme Headquarters, Operations Section, October 25, 1918," ibid., p. 565.
127. Ibid., pp. 134–37.
128. Smythe, *Pershing*, p. 219; Dupuy and Dupuy, *Encyclopedia*, pp. 986, 988.
129. Foch, *Memoirs*, pp. 505.
130. Ibid., pp. 508–09.
131. Smythe, *Pershing*, 2, p. 217.
132. Foch, *Memoirs*, p. 509.

133. DeWeerd, *Wilson*, p. 354.
134. Coffman, *War*, p. 332.
135. Ibid., p. 115.
136. Wright, *Meuse-Argonne*, p. 105.
137. Quoted in Babcock Papers, p. 607-A.
138. Ibid., p. 605.
139. Summerall memoir, p. 115.
140. Babcock Papers, p. 605.
141. Summerall memoir, pp. 115–16.
142. Babcock Papers, pp. 605–06.
143. Ibid., p. 607-A.
144. Ibid.
145. Wright, *Meuse-Argonne*, p. 106.
146. Ibid., p. 126.
147. Johnson and Hillman, *Soissons*, p. 140.
148. Summerall memoir, p. 117.
149. Ibid.
150. Ibid.
151. Liggett, *AEF*, p. 217
152. Liggett, *AEF*, pp. 218–19.
153. Foch, *Memoirs*, p. 514.
154. Braim, *Battle*, p. 131.
155. Millett, *The General*, p. 423.
156. Braim, *Battle*, p. 131.
157. Trask, *AEF*, p. 159; Braim, *Battle*, p. 131.
158. Braim, "Meuse-Argonne," p. 385.
159. Smythe, *Pershing*, p. 224; Trask, *AEF*, p. 159.
160. Summerall memoir, p. 118.
161. Ibid., pp. 118–19.
162. Braim, *Battle*, p. 131; Coffman, *War*, p. 345.
163. Summerall memoir, p. 119.
164. Braim, *Battle*, pp. 131–32.
165. Fairfax Downey, *Sound of the Guns: The Story of American Artillery from the Ancient and Honorable Company to the Atom Cannon and Guided Missile* (New York: David McKay Company, Inc., 1955), p. 233.
166. Summerall memoir, p. 119.
167. Ibid.
168. Braim, *Battle*, p. 132; Robert Ferrell's introduction to General Wright's diary entry of 1 November, 1918, in Wright, *Meuse-Argonne*, p. 136.
169. Wright, *Meuse-Argonne*, p. 136.
170. Johnson and Hillman, *Soissons*, p. 139.
171. Wright, *Meuse-Argonne*, p. 140.
172. Ferrell's introduction as noted above in note 166, in ibid., pp. 136–37.
173. Wright, *Meuse-Argonne*, p. 140.
174. Coffman, *War*, p. 345; Smythe, *Pershing*, p. 225; Merrill L. Bartlett, *Lejeune: A Marine's Life, 1867–1942* (Columbia, South Carolina: University of South Carolina Press, 1991), p. 98. Hereinafter cited as Bartlett, *Lejeune*.
175. Braim, *Battle*, pp. 132–33.
176. Dickman, *Crusade*, p. 176.
177. Summerall memoir, pp. 119–20.
178. Liggett, *AEF*, p. 223.
179. Coffman, *War*, p. 346; Smythe, *Pershing*, p. 226.
180. Coffman, *War*, p. 347; Smythe, *Pershing*, p. 226; Pershing, *War*, p. 376; Bartlett, *Lejeune*, pp. 98–99.
181. C. J. Masseck, Major, 353rd Infantry, *Official Brief History 89th Division, U.S.A., 1917–1918–1919* (n.p, n.d.), p. 83. Hereinafter cited as Masseck, *89th Division*.
182. Ibid.

183. James Hallas, "United States Army: 89th Division", in Venzon, *Encyclopedia*, p. 682. Hereinafter cited as Hallas, "89th Division."
184. Wright, *Meuse-Argonne*, pp. 149–50.
185. Ferrell's introduction to diary entry of 5 November, 1918, in ibid., pp. 150–51.
186. Wright, *Meuse-Argonne*, p. 150.
187. Hallas, "89th Division," p. 682.
188. Masseck, *89th Division*, p. 34.
189. Wright, *Meuse-Argonne*, p. 150; Hallas, "89th Division," p. 682.
190. Hallas, "89th Division," p. 682.
191. Wright, *Meuse-Argonne*, p. 150.
192. Hallas, "89th Division," p. 683.
193. Braim, *Battle*, p. 135.
194. Pershing, *War*, p. 379.
195. "War Diary, Group of Armies Gallwitz, November 2, 1918," *USA/WW*, 9, p. 576.
196. "War Diary, German Third Army, November 3, 1918," ibid., p. 582.
197. "Order, Operations Section, Group of Armies German Crown Prince, November 4, 1918—p.m.," ibid., p. 584.
198. "War Diary, Group of Armies Gallwitz, November 5, 1918," ibid., p. 588.
199. Ibid.
200. Bernard A. Cook, "Germany, Revolutions of 1918," in Tucker, *Encyclopedia*, p. 303; Bullitt Lowry, "Armistices of 1918," in Venzon, *Encyclopedia*, pp. 49–50; DeWeerd, *Wilson*, p. 385.
201. DeWeerd, *Wilson*, pp. 385–86.
202. Foch, *Memoirs*, p. 553.
203. Braim, *Battle*, p. 135.
204. *History of the First Division*, pp 227–28.
205. Pershing Papers, Diaries, November 3, 1918, Container 7, Oct. 1918–Sept. 1919, Library of Congress, Washington, DC. Hereinafter cited as Pershing, Diaries.
206. Ibid.
207. Pershing, *War*, 2, p. 381.
208. Harbord, *Army*, p. 455.
209. Pershing Diaries, November 6, 1918.
210. Marshall, *Memoirs*, pp. 188–89.
211. Ibid., p. 189.
212. Ibid., p. 190.
213. Dickman, *Crusade*, p. 182; Coffman, *War*, p. 349.
214. Marshall, *Memoirs*, p. 190.
215. Harbord to Drum, July 26, 1935, The Hugh A. Drum Papers, Archives, U.S. Army Military History Institute, Carlisle Barracks, PA, Box 20. Hereinafter the collection will be cited as Drum Papers.
216. Drum to Harbord, August 8, 1935, ibid.
217. Donald Smythe, "A.E.F. Snafu at Sedan," *Prologue* (Fall 1973): p. 138. Hereinafter cited as Smythe, "Snafu."
218. Summerall memoir, p. 121.
219. Summerall to Liggett, 7 November 1918, World War I Organizational Records, 5th C, Historical File, 32.15, National Archives and Records Administration.
220. Summerall memoir, p. 121.
221. Ibid.
222. Wright, *Meuse-Argonne*, p. 154.
223. Smythe, "Snafu," p. 140.
224. Reilly, *Americans All*, pp. 795–96.
225. Parker memorandum to First Division, November 8, 1918, First Division Historical File, 32.15, Box 34.
226. *History of the First Division*, pp. 230–32.
227. On 21 December 1918, Colonel Montgomery stated this information in a memorandum for the chief of staff of Third Army, commanded by General Dickman, while he was serving as assistant chief of staff for the army's operations section. Copy in Drum Papers, Box 20.
228. Dickman, *Crusade*, p. 185.
229. Reilly, *Americans All*, pp. 798–99.
230. Smythe, "Snafu," p. 143.

231. Reilly, *Americans All*, p. 800.
232. MacArthur, *Reminiscences*, p. 69.
233. Ibid.
234. Smythe, "Snafu," p. 142.
235. Ibid.
236. Reilly, *Americans All*, p. 804.
237. Ibid., pp. 805–07.
238. Dickman, *Crusade*, p. 187; Harbord, *Army*, p. 459, note 27.
239. Ibid., pp. 187–88; Smythe, "Snafu" p. 144.
240. Dickman, *Crusade*, p. 187; Liggett, *AEF*, p. 229.
241. Liggett, *AEF*, p. 229.
242. Ibid., p. 230; Dickman, *Crusade*, p. 188.
243. Ibid., pp. 805–07.
244. Ibid., p. 807.
245. Pierpont L. Stackpole Diary, 1918–1919, Marshall Manuscripts Collection, George C. Marshall Foundation, Lexington, VA, Box 9, folder 1, p. 287–88. Hereinafter cited as Stackpole Diary.
246. Ibid.
247. Ibid.
248. Commanding General V Army Corps to Commanding General, First Army, 7 November 1918, World War I Organizational Records, 5th Corps, Historical File, 32.15, National Archives and Records Administration. Hereinafter cited as 5th Corps Historical File. A copy of this document is in the Parker Papers, #1516.
249. Ibid.
250. Summerall memoir, p. 121.
251. Commanding General, First Division, American E. F., to Commanding General, V Army Corps, 9 November 1918, Parker Papers, Box 2.
252. Headquarters, V Army Corps, A.E.F., to Commanding General, First Army, 10 November 1918, First Division, Historical File, 33.6-34.2, Box 487.
253. Stackpole Diary, p. 289.
254. Ibid.
255. Ibid.
256. Ibid., pp. 290–91.
257. Ibid., p. 291.
258. Ibid., p. 295.
259. Commanding General, 3rd Army, Am. E.F., to Adjutant General, G.H.Q., Am. E.F., Dec. 24, 1918, First Division, Historical Data, File 201–33.6, National Archives and Records Administration.
260. Stackpole Diary, p. 384.
261. Smythe, *Pershing*, 2, p. 245; Paul F. Braim, "Dickman, Joseph Theodore (1857–1927)," in Venzon, *Encyclopedia*, p. 203.
262. Stackpole Diary, pp. 356, 368.
263. Harbord, *Army*, pp. 459–60.
264. Stackpole Diary, pp. 336–37.
265. Ibid., pp. 396–97.
266. Parker Papers, Box 19, "Miscellaneous."
267. Pershing, *War*, 2, p. 381.
268. Ibid.
269. Summerall's letter to the North American Newspaper Alliance, April 1, 1931, Summerall MSS, Box 19.
270. Fletcher Pratt, *Eleven Generals: Studies in American Command* (New York: William Sloane Associates, 1949) p. 262. Pratt erroneously wrote that Summerall was born in Lake City, Florida, was the son of a long line of preachers, and intended to go into the ministry. Perhaps he thought that Dr. Porter's Holy Communion Church Institute was an Episcopal seminary. See pp. 245, 247.
271. "Summerall Criticizes Book on Generals; Cites Errors," *The State*, Sunday, June 12, 1949.
272. Ibid.
273. Ibid.
274. Pogue, *Marshall*, p. 188.
275. Smythe, "Snafu," p. 149.
276. Coffman, *War*, p. 353.

277. Smythe, *Pershing*, 2, pp. 230–31.
278. "Field Orders, No. 106, November 8, 1918," *USA/WW*, 9, p. 398.
279. Millett, *The General*, p. 424.
280. "Field Orders No. 105, November 8, 1918," *USA/WW*, 9, p. 395.
281. Wright, *Meuse-Argonne*, p. 160.
282. John A. Lejeune, *The Reminiscences of a Marine* (Philadelphia: Dorrance and Company, 1930), p. 399. Hereinafter cited as Lejeune, *Reminiscences*; Oliver Lyman Spaulding and John Womack Wright, *The Second Division American Expeditionary Force in France, 1917–1919*, Third in The Great War Series (repr., Nashville, Tennessee: The Battery Press, 1989), pp. 217–18. Hereinafter cited as Spalding and Womack, *Second Division*.
283. Wright, *Meuse-Argonne*, p. 163.
284. Lejeune, *Reminiscences*, p. 399.
285. Wright, *Meuse-Argonne*, p. 163.
286. Ibid.
287. Spaulding and Womack, *Second Division*, pp. 218–19.
288. Ibid., p. 219.
289. Summerall memoir, p. 122.
290. Spaulding and Womack, *Second Division*, p. 220.
291. Masseck, "89th Division," p. 39; Wright, *Meuse-Argonne*, p. 164.
292. Ferrell's comments in Wright, *Meuse-Argonne*, p. 164.
293. Masseck, "89th Division," pp. 38–39.
294. Wright, *Meuse-Argonne*, p. 165.
295. Ferrell's comments in Wright, *Meuse-Argonne*, p. 1546.
296. Lejeune, *Reminiscences*, pp. 400–01.
297. Bullard, *Personalities*, p. 312.
298. Spaulding and Womack, *Second Division*, pp. 221–22.
299. Foch, *Memoirs*, pp. 557, 569, 571.
300. Smythe, *Pershing*, p. 232.
301. Summerall memoir, p. 122.
302. Lejeune, *Reminiscences*, p. 402.
303. Wright, *Meuse-Argonne*, p. 165.
304. Lejeune, *Reminiscences*, pp. 402–03.
305. Gowenlock, *Soldiers*, pp. 265–66.
306. Summerall memoir, p. 122.
307. Ibid., p. 123.
308. Foch, *Memoirs*, p. 560.
309. Summerall memoir, p. 123.
310. Ibid.
311. Ibid.
312. Ibid.
313. Ibid., p. 124.
314. Ibid., p. 125.
315. Ibid.
316. Ibid., pp. 124–25.
317. Ibid., pp. 123–24.
318. Ibid., p. 125.
319. Ibid., p. 126.
320. McCullough, *Truman*, p. 137.
321. Summerall memoir, pp. 126–27.
322. Ibid., p. 127.
323. Ibid., pp. 127–28.
324. Edward L. Byrd, Jr., and Ingrid P. Westmoreland, "Versailles Treaty (28 June 1919)," in Venzon, *Encyclopedia*, pp. 719–22. In this excellent summary of the deliberations at Versailles, the authors present a balanced account of the Allied determination to impose severe terms on Germany, and the strong reaction of the German delegation to the terms that were worse than they had feared. On both sides, the bitterness of the negotiations replaced the hostility of the war.

325. Ibid., p. 722; Summerall memoir, p. 128.
326. Summerall memoir, p. 128.

## Chapter Thirteen

1. Ibid., p. 129; "Report of the Interallied Commission of Inquiry, Fiume, Italy," Summerall MSS, Box 17. Hereinafter cited as "Commission Report."
2. Douglas Wilson Johnson, "Fiume and the Adriatic Problem," in *What Really Happened at Paris: The Real Story of the Peace Conference, 1918–1919 By American Authors*, eds., Edward Mandell House and Charles Seymour (New York: C. Scribner's Sons, 1921), p. 120. Hereinafter cited as Johnson, "Fiume." John Woodhouse, *Gabriele D'Annunzio: Defiant Angel* (Oxford: Clarendon Press, 1998), p. 317. Hereinafter cited as Woodhouse, *D'Annunzio*. Michael A. Ledeen, *The First Duce: D'Annunzio at Fiume* (Baltimore: The Johns Hopkins University Press, 1977), pp. 29–32. Hereinafter cited as Ledeen, *First*.
3. René Albrecht-Carrié, *Italy at the Peace Conference*, The Paris Conference (New York: Columbia University Press for The Carnegie Endowment for International Peace, 1938; reprint, Hamden, Connecticut: Archon Books, 1966), pp. 114–52. Hereinafter cited as Albrecht-Carrié, *Italy*.
4. Ibid., pp. 194–200; Woodhouse, *D'Annunzio*, pp. 322–24.
5. "Report"; J. N. Macdonald, *A Political Escapade: The Story of Fiume and D'Annunzio* (London: John Murray, 1921), pp. 76–77. Hereinafter cited as Macdonald, *D'Annunzio*.
6. Summerall memoir, pp. 129–30.
7. Ibid., p. 130.
8. Ibid., p. 131.
9. Ibid.
10. Macdonald, *D'Annunzio*, p. 85.
11. Ledeen, *First*, pp. 164–77; Woodhouse, *D'Annunzio*, pp. 344, 377.
12. Albrecht-Carrié, *Italy*, p. 304. Historian Michael Ledeen wrote that D'Annunzio, with his appeal to the veterans of the Great War, his theatrical manner, and his triumphal march on Fiume, invented much of the street drama and tactics that Mussolini's Fascism and Hitler's Nazism would exploit. His constitution was not a totalitarian doctrine, but rather one that incorporated human rights, and was based upon direct democratic processes and frequent changes in leadership. It attracted those from right and left, young and old, fighters and pacifists, and the possessed and dispossessed. His ill-fated League of Fiume appealed to those who hoped to free the world from domination by rich and powerful men, and from the great powers these men had created. In a real sense, D'Annunzio's abortive movement was the beginning of what became known as "the third world movement." Ledeen, *First*, pp. x, 164–67.
13. Ibid.; Woodhouse, *D'Annunzio*, pp. 349–50.
14. Summerall memoir, p. 132.
15. Smythe, *Pershing*, pp. 256–57.
16. Summerall memoir, p. 132.
17. Ibid., pp. 133–34.
18. Smythe, *Pershing*, p. 259.
19. Summerall memoir, p. 133.
20. Ibid.
21. Ibid., 134.
22. *Office of the Adjutant General, Central Decimal Correspondence File, Bulky Packages, 201.6E.E. (10-12-18), Confidential Report on Efficiency of Officers who served in A.E.F.*, National Archives and Records Administration.
23. Pershing Papers, Misc. Records Relating to Officers, Officers Efficiency Reports, Summerall, Charles P., Maj. Gen.
24. Summerall to Lejeune, Headquarters Fifth Army Corps, 21st January 1919, Papers of John A. Lejeune, Containers 3-4, Manuscripts Division, Library of Congress, Washington, D.C.
25. Ibid.
26. Summerall to Adjutant General, American E.F., 21st January 1918, in ibid.

## Chapter Fourteen

1. Weigley, *United States Army*, p. 396; http://www.courier-journal.com/reweb/community/placetime/midcounty-camptaylor.html.
2. Weigley, *United States Army*, pp. 396–97; Larry Addington, "National Defense Act of 1920," in Venzon, *Encyclopedia*, pp. 400–401. Hereinafter cited as Addington, "Act of 1920."
3. Weigley, *United States Army*, pp. 395–97.
4. Ibid., pp. 397–99; Coffman, *Hilt*, p. 200; Smythe, *Pershing*, p. 266–67; Pogue, *Marshall*, pp. 207–09.
5. Weigley, *United States Army*, pp. 398–99; Smythe, *Pershing*, p. 267; Addington, "Act of 1920," p. 401.

6. Weigley, *United States Army*, pp. 399; Addington, "Act of 1920," p. 401.
7. Weigley, *United States Army*, p. 400; Addington, "Act of 1920," pp. 401–02.
8. Pogue, *Marshall*, p. 214.
9. Addington, "Act of 1920," p. 401; Weigley, *United States Army*, pp. 400–401.
10. Summerall memoir, p. 134.
11. First Division Historical File, 10.3, Box 8.
12. "See Low Army Pay Bringing a Crisis," *New York Times*, 7 September 1919.
13. "Investigation of Alleged Irregularities in Property Accounting at Camp Z. Taylor, Kentucky," Record Group 407 (The Adjutant General's Office), Central Decimal Files, Project Files, 1917–1925, Camp Taliferro, Calif. To Camp Zachary Taylor, Ky., Box No. 1249, folder 250.26, Camp Taylor to 333.9., pp. 1–6.
14. Ibid., p. 14.
15. Ibid., pp. 14–16.
16. Summerall memoir, pp. 134–35.
17. Ibid., p. 135; http://www.nps.gov/whho/historyculture/first-division-monument.htm, p. 3. Hereinafter cited as www.nps.gov/monument.
18. Summerall memoir, pp. 136–37.
19. "For Camp Dix Inquiry: General Scott Orders Investigation of the Conditions There," *New York Times*, 5 January 1919; Summerall memoir, p. 138.
20. "Held For Trenton Killing: Soldier is Arrested for Machine-Gun Tragedy at Fair," *New York Times*, 4 October 1920; "Camp Dix Still Bars Troops From Town, Civil and Military Authorities Fail to Settle Differences at Pemberton," *New York Times*, 22 January 1921; Summerall memoir, p. 138.
21. "Veterans Play at War at Camp Dix Reunion, Old First Division 'Goes Over the Top' in Gigantic Sham Battle," *New York Times*, 11 November 1920.
22. "Soldier-Robbers Fire on Policeman, Two, Believed to be From Camp Dix, Hold Up Saloon and Flee in Taxi," ibid., 6 May 1921.
23. Summerall memoir, p. 138.
24. *History of the First Division*, pp. xv–xvi.
25. For *Winter-Seicheprey*, see facing, p. 49; for *Spring-Cantigny*, see facing, p. 69; for *Summer-Soissons*, see facing, p. 99; for *Autumn-Argonne*, see facing, p. 177; and for *The Chosen Corps*, see facing, p. 269, in ibid.
26. Summerall memoir, p. 138.
27. www.nps.gov/monument, pp. 3–4.
28. Ibid., pp. 2–3.
29. Ibid., p. 4.
30. Summerall to French, June 1921, quoted in Michael Richman, *Daniel Chester French: An American Sculptor* (New York: The Metropolitan Museum of Art, for the National Trust for Historic Preservation, 1976), p. 187. Hereinafter cited as Richman, *French*.
31. www.nps.gov/monument, p. 4.
32. Quoted in Richman, *French*, pp. 189–90; Summerall wrote in his memoir that the figure of the Victory was "exquisite," but "too voluptuous." Summerall memoir, p. 136.
33. Ibid., p. 190.
34. http://www.usarpac.army.mil/history/shafter_printable.htm.
35. Allan R. Millett, *Semper Fidelis: The History of the United States Marine Corps*, The Macmillan Wars of the United States, gen. ed., Louis Morton (New York: The Free Press, 1980), p. 319. Hereinafter cited as Millett, *Semper Fidelis*.
36. Robert Gordon Kaufman, "Washington Naval Arms Limitation Treaty (1922)," in Chambers, *Oxford*, p. 788. Hereinafter cited as Kaufman, "Treaty."
37. Ibid.
38. Millett, *Semper Fidelis*, p. 320.
39. Brian McAllister Linn, *Guardians of Empire: The U.S. Army in the Pacific, 1902–1940* (Chapel Hill and London: The University of North Carolina Press, 1997), pp. 146, 185–87. Hereinafter cited as Linn, *Guardians*.
40. Ibid., p. 194.
41. Ibid., pp. 194–95.
42. Summerall memoir, p. 140.
43. Ibid.
44. Basic Defense Plans, Hawaiian Department, Red-Orange Situation, Defense Plans, 1920–26, Box No. 1, Record Group 395, U.S. Army overseas Operations and Commands, 1898–1942, Hdq, Hawaii Deprt. Hereinafter cited as Basic Defense Plans, RG 395.

45. Ibid.
46. Summerall memoir, p. 141.
47. Linn, *Guardians*, p. 196.
48. Summerall memoir, p. 142.
49. Ibid.
50. Linn, *Guardians*, pp. 198–99.
51. Ibid., p. 199.
52. As for Summerall's attitude toward the naval commander, he could have been miffed that the War Department had ruled that the naval commander in Hawaii, a rear admiral, would take precedence over the army commander, who held the rank, as Summerall did, of major general. See "Clash on Rank Unsettled, But Admiral Simpson Will Have Precedence on Denby Visit to Hawaii," *New York Times*, 17 June 1922.
53. Summerall memoir, pp. 141–42.
54. Linn, *Guardians*, p. 200.
55. Summerall memoir, p. 141.
56. Basic Defense Plans, RG 395.
57. Linn, *Guardians*, pp. 251–52.
58. Burke Davis, *The Billy Mitchell Affair* (New York: Random House, 1967), pp. 158–59. Hereinafter cited as Davis, *Mitchell*. Summerall memoir, p. 143.
59. Davis, *Mitchell*, pp. 160–61.
60. William Mitchell Papers, Subject File, 1918–1924: Pacific Problem: Strategical Aspect, Container 46, Manuscript Division, Library of Congress, Washington, DC. Hereinafter cited as Mitchell Papers.
61. Summerall to Patrick, 27 December 1923, Mitchell Papers, Correspondence, 1923–25, Container 10.
62. Ibid.
63. Summerall memoir, p. 143.
64. Summerall to Patrick, 27 December 1923, Mitchell Papers, Correspondence, 1923–25, Container 10.
65. Patrick to Summerall, 26 January, ibid.
66. Linn, *Guardians*, pp. 118–19; Summerall memoir, pp. 143–44.
67. Summerall memoir, p. 144.
68. Linn, *Guardians*, p. 155.
69. Summerall memoir, p. 145.
70. www.nps.gov/monument.
71. "Summerall Leaves Lasting Monument Here," *Honolulu Advertiser*, August 10, 1924, Summerall MSS, Clippings, 1900–1925, Container 40, folder Hawaii, San Francisco, 1922–25.
72. Ibid.

## *Chapter Fifteen*

1. Summerall memoir, p. 147.
2. Ibid.
3. Ibid.
4. Summerall to Parker, 25 January 1922, Parker Papers, #1516.
5. www.nps.gov/monument; "World Good Will Urged by Coolidge," *New York Times*, October 5, 1924. Hereinafter cited as "World Good Will."
6. "World Good Will."
7. "The Spirit of the First Division: Address by Major General Charles P. Summerall at the Unveiling of the First Division Monument, October 4, 1924", *The Field Artillery Journal*, 14 (November–December, 1924) : 516, 517.
8. www.nps.gov/monument.
9. "World Good Will."
10. Ibid.
11. Summerall memoir, p. 148.
12. Peter Emmett, Jr., *Lake County Florida: A Pictorial History* (Virginia Beach, Virginia: The Donning Company for the Lake County Historical Society, 1994), pp. 80–81.
13. Rick Reed, "Summerall Park Dedication: The General Returns to Lake for ceremony," *Leesburg (Florida) The Daily Commercial*, May 9, 2000, "Reminisce," sec. B, p. 14. After a change in ownership, the *Leesburg Commercial* was changed to *The Daily Commercial*.
14. Summerall memoir, p. 148.

Notes to Pages 330–339

15. http://www.aflcio.org/aboutus/history/history/gompers.cfm. Hereinafter cited as www.aflcio.
16. Summerall memoir, p. 148.
17. www.afl/cio.
18. Summerall memoir, p. 148.
19. "Followers Mourn as Gompers Passes," *New York Times*, December 16, 1924. Hereinafter cited as "Followers."
20. Summerall memoir, pp. 148–49.
21. Ibid., p. 149; "Followers."
22. "Plans for Gompers Funeral Ready," *New York Times*, December 16, 1924.
23. Summerall memoir, p. 149.
24. Millett, *The General*, p. 445; Summerall memoir, p. 150.
25. Summerall memoir, p. 150; Herbert B. Meyer, "The Last of the Army's Big Four Goes: Bullard Follows Liggett, Harbord and Pershing into Retirement—His Picturesque Successor," *New York Times*, January 11, 1925.
26. Millet, *The General*, pp. 460, 462, 470.
27. Ibid., pp. 447–48.
28. Summerall memoir, p. 150.
29. Ibid., p. 151.
30. Ibid., p. 152.
31. Ibid.; "Arsenal Employee Killed in Explosion: Civilian Burned to Death After Blast in Picatinny Storehouse," *New York Times*, May 29, 1925.
32. Summerall memoir, p. 152.
33. "Green Endorses Plattsburg Camp, Labor Chief Tells Trainees Visit Makes 'Very Deep Impression' Upon Himself and Council," *New York Times*, August 21, 1926. Hereinafter cited as "Green."
34. Ibid.
35. Summerall memoir, p. 152.
36. http://www..aflcio.org/aboutus/history/history/green.cfm.
37. Alfred F. Hurley, *Billy Mitchell: Crusader for Air Power* (Bloomington: Indiana University Press, 1975), pp. 90–101. Hereinafter cited as Hurley, *Mitchell*; Davis, *Mitchell*, pp. 192–208; Weigley, *United States Army*, pp. 412–13.
38. Quoted in Davis, *Mitchell*, p. 218, and Hurley, *Mitchell*, p. 101.
39. Quoted in Hurley, *Mitchell*, p. 101.
40. http://www.homeofheroes.com/wings/part1/6_survival.html. Hereinafter cited as www. homeofheroes; Davis, *Mitchell*, pp. 218, 234; Hurley, *Mitchell*, pp. 100–101.
41. "The Intense Drama of the Mitchell Trial," *New York Times*, November 15, 1925.
42. Davis, *Mitchell*, p. 240.
43. Mitchell Papers, Subject File (a), Court Martial 1925, Container 38, Manuscript Division, Library of Congress.
44. "Mitchell Protest Ousts Three Judges as Trial Begins," *New York Times*, October 29, 1925. Hereinafter cited as "Mitchell Protest."
45. Davis, *Mitchell*, p. 243.
46. "Mitchell Protest."
47. Quoted in "Summerall Denies Imperiling Fliers," *New York Times*, December 15, 1925.
48. www.homeofheroes.
49. Summerall memoir, p. 151.
50. www.homeofheroes.
51. Weigley, *United States Army*, p. 413.
52. "Pershing Returns; Cheers Greet Him," *New York Times*, September 7, 1926.
53. "Miss Reeder Bride of Lieut. Summerall," ibid., October 24, 1926.
54. Summerall memoir, p. 153.
55. "Summerall in Line for Chief of Staff," *New York Times*, September 7, 1926.
56. The digest is reprinted in the "Biographical Sketch of General Charles Pelot Summerall," Appendix C, First Division Museum, First Division Foundation and Museum, Cantigny.
57. Summerall memoir, p. 154.
58. Summerall to Patton, November 4, 1926, in Patton Papers, Box 12.
59. "To Honor Gen. Summerall. Troops Will Bid Farewell to Corps Commander Tomorrow," *New York Times*, November 18, 1926; "Double Farewell to Gen. Summerall," *New York Times*, November 20, 1926; Millett, *The General*, pp. 458–59.
60. Weigley, *United States Army*, pp. 400–401; Summerall memoir, p. 154; Timothy K. Nenninger, untitled article-length manuscript on Summerall's four years as army chief of staff, in the possession of the author, pp. 8–9. Dr. Nenninger

kindly gave me a copy of his manuscript, and it is the most complete and thorough analysis of Summerall's service in that office. Hereinafter cited as Nenninger manuscript.

61. Summerall memoir, pp. 155–56; Records of United States Army Commands, Second Corps Area, Adjutant General File, 1920–35, Record Group 394, entry 24, box 122, National Archives and Records Administration. Hereinafter cited as Records, Army Commands. Nenninger manuscript, p. 23.
62. Nenninger manuscript, p. 24.
63. Summerall memoir, p. 158; "Army Perishing Without Funds, Says Summerall," *New York Herald Tribune*, October 12, 1927, in Clippings, 1924–40, container 41, folder Army Housing, October 1927, in Summerall MSS. Hereinafter cited as Clippings, Summeral MSS.
64. Summerall memoir, p. 158.
65. Ibid.
66. See Clippings, Summerall MSS; Nenninger manuscript, p. 25.
67. Summerall memoir, p. 158; Nenninger manuscript, p. 26.
68. Clippings, Summerall MSS; Nenninger manuscript, p. 26.
69. Nenninger manuscript, pp. 26–27; Records, Army Commands.
70. Summerall memoir, p. 159; Nenninger manuscript, p. 27.
71. Ibid.
72. Summerall memoir, pp. 161–62.
73. Ibid., p. 166; Nenninger manuscript, pp. 11–12.
74. Nenninger manuscript, p. 12; Major General Merritt Ireland to Major General John L. Hines, July 8, 1930, John L. Hines Papers, General Correspondence, box 28, Library of Congress. Hereinafter cited as Hines MSS. Ireland and Hines strongly disagreed with Summerall's actions and decisions as army chief of staff.
75. John R. M. Wilson, "Herbert Hoover and the Armed Forces: A Study of Presidential Attitudes and Policy," Ph. D. Dissertation, Northwestern University, 1971, pp. 8, 200–202, I, and 49, cited in Nenninger manuscript, p. 12, endnote 26.
76. Summerall memoir, p. 154.
77. Lieutenant Colonel E. M. Shinkle, to Chief of Ordnance, March 25, 1930, copy in Pershing Papers, box 193, and Hines MSS, Personal File, box 34.
78. Ibid.
79. "Summerall Reproves Aberdeen Officers; General Walks Away During Ordnance Test," *New York Times*, March 25, 1930.
80. Summerall memoir, p. 154.
81. Nenninger manuscript, p. 15.
82. Ireland to Hines, December 12, 1930, Hines MSS, General Correspondence, box 28.
83. Ireland to Major General R. C. Davis, February 4, 1930, ibid.
84. Nenninger manuscript, p. 18.
85. Hines to Ireland, January 30, 1932, Hines MSS, Personal File, box 34.
86. Nenninger manuscript, p. 18.
87. Ireland to Hines, December 12, 1930, Hines MSS, General Correspondence, box 28.
88. "Hunt Slur Writer in Army Evaluation; War Chiefs Look Into Anonymous Attack on Gen. Fuqua, *New York Times*, 1929; Army Men Criticize Fuqua Promotion, ibid., April 2, 1929.
89. "Fuqua Jumped Over Heads of 160 Colonels," *Boston Transcript*, March 20, 1929.
90. Nenninger manuscript, p. 16.
91. Ireland to Hines, March 28, 1929, Hines MSS, General Correspondence, box 26.
92. Hines to Fuqua, April 3, 1929, ibid.
93. Nenninger manuscript, p. 19.
94. Ibid.; David E. Johnson, *Fast Tanks and Heavy Bombers: Innovation in the U.S. Army, 1917–1945*, Cornell Studies in Security Affairs (Ithaca and London: Cornell University Press, 1998), p. 96. Hereinafter referred to as Johnson, *Fast Tanks*.
95. Johnson, *Fast Tanks*, pp. 96–98; Nenninger manuscript, pp. 18–20.
96. Colonel Chas. S. Lincoln, to Adjutant General, October 1, 1928, Office of the Adjutant General, Central Files, 1926–39, General Files, Part I, box no. 2702, Record Group 407, National Archives and Records Administration.
97. Nenninger manuscript, p. 20; Johnson, *Fast Tanks*, p. 99.
98. Ibid.
99. Johnson, *Fast Tanks*, p. 99.
100. Nenninger manuscript, p. 21.
101. Summerall memoir, p. 163.

102. Ibid., p. 157.
103. Weigley, *United States Army*, p. 413; Millett and Maslowski, *Common Defense*, p. 371; Nenninger manuscript, p. 22.
104. Final Report of the Chief of Staff, *Annual Report of the War Department: Fiscal Year Ended June 30, 1930* (Washington: Government Printing Office, 1930), p. 45, copy in Summerall MSS. Hereinafter cited as Final Report.
105. Summerall memoir, p. 157.
106. Nenninger manuscript, p. 23.
107. Johnson, *Fast Tanks*, p. 110.
108. Ibid., pp. 110–11; Nenninger manuscript, pp. 28–29.
109. Johnson, *Fast Tanks*, p. 111.
110. Nenninger manuscript, pp. 30–31.
111. Summerall memoir, pp. 168–69.
112. Ibid., p. 169.
113. Ibid., pp. 169–70.
114. Bland, *Marshall Interviews*, p. 242.
115. Nenninger manuscript, p. 32.
116. Nenninger manuscript, p. 30; quotation from Final Report, p. 4.
117. Nenninger manuscript, p. 33.
118. Ibid.

## Chapter Sixteen

Although I have made additions to the text, this chapter on Summerall's presidency of The Citadel originally was published under the title of "General Charles P. Summerall and the Training, Command, and Education of the Citizen Soldier" in the book *Unknown Soldiers: The American Expeditionary Forces in Memory and Remembrance*, edited by Mark Snell, published by the Kent State University Press and copyrighted in 2008.

1. Summerall to Parker, March 24, 1930, Parker Papers, box 6.
2. Ibid., November 13, 1930, Summerall MSS, box 4.
3. Summerall to Parker, November 17, 1930, ibid., box 5.
4. Summerall memoir, p. 171.
5. D. D. Nicholson, Jr., *A History of The Citadel: The Years of Summerall and Clark* (Charleston, South Carolina: Association of Citadel Men, 1994), p. 2. Nicholson served as public relations officer and vice president for development under General Mark W. Clark, who succeeded Summerall in 1955. His book is based on his large collection of Citadel-related news items and alumni recollections, as well as research into Citadel records and cadet life. Hereinafter cited as Nicholson, *The Citadel*.
6. Fitz Hugh McMaster, editor, *The Columbia Record*, to Summerall, December 17, 1930, Summerall MSS, box 8.
7. O. J. Bond to Summerall, December 13, 1930, ibid.
8. Parker to Summerall, December 26, 1930, Parker Papers, box 6.
9. Ibid.
10. O. J. Bond to Summerall, December 13, 1930, Summerall MSS, box 8; Summerall memoir, p. 171; Nicholson, *The Citadel*, p. 11.
11. Summerall to Parker, January 1, 1931, Parker Papers, box 6.
12. Summerall memoir, p. 171.
13. Rod Andrew, Jr., *Long Gray Lines: The Southern Military School Tradition, 1839–1915* (Chapel Hill and London: The University of North Carolina Press, 2001), p. 11. Hereinafter cited as Andrew, *Long Gray Lines*. W. Gary Nichols, "Citadel, The," in *The South Carolina Encyclopedia*, ed. Walter Edgar, "A Project of the Humanities Council, SC" (Columbia: University of South Carolina Press, 2006), p. 176. Hereinafter cited as Nichols, "Citadel."
14. Andrew, *Long Gray Lines*, p. 25; Nichols, "Citadel," p. 176.
15. Andrew, *Long Gray Lines*, p. 39.
16. Nichols, "Citadel," p. 176.
17. O. J. Bond, *The Story of The Citadel* (Richmond, Virginia; Garrett and Massie, 1936; repr., Greenville, South Carolina: Southern Historical Press, 1989), pp. 206, 209–11. Hereinafter cited as Bond, *The Citadel*.
18. Nicholson, *The Citadel*, pp. 2–3.
19. Bond, *The Citadel*, p. 219.
20. Marshall, *Memoirs*, p. 78.
21. Summerall memoir, p. 172.
22. Summerall to W. W. Ball, January 15, 1931, W. W. Ball Papers, 1918–1946, Special Collections Library, Duke University, Durham, North Carolina. Hereinafter cited as Ball Papers.

23. Summerall to Parker, January 16, 1931, Parker Papers.
24. Ibid.
25. Nicholson, *The Citadel*, pp. 11–12.
26. Thomas to Summerall, December 19, 1931, and Summerall to Thomas, January 16, 1931, Minutes of the Board of Visitors, The Citadel Archives & Museum, Charleston, South Carolina.
27. Ibid., pp. 12–13.
28. "Per Schedule," The *Charleston News and Courier*, January 19, 1931.
29. Ball Papers.
30. Bond to Summerall, March 18, 1931, Summerall MSS, box 8; Wiles typescript, Chapter XXV, p. 15.
31. Copy of extract of Special Orders NO. 73, War Department, March 28, 1931, signed by General MacArthur, Summerall MSS, box 4.
32. Nicholson, *The Citadel*, pp. 16–18.
33. Summerall memoir, p. 171.
34. Nicholson, *The Citadel*, pp. 33–38.
35. Summerall memoir, p. 172.
36. "About Summerall and Governor's Race," title of excerpts from newspapers compiled by Florida Clipping Service, Tampa, in the *Tallahassee Democrat*, September 28, 1931, Summerall MSS, box 42.
37. Nicholson, *The Citadel*, p. 41.
38. "Summerall to Resign. General Resents Question on Deficit at The Citadel," *New York Times*, February 11, 1932.
39. Ibid.; Summerall memoir, pp. 172–73.
40. Summerall,MSS, box 10; Nicholson, *The Citadel*, pp. 41–42.
41. Summerall memoir, p. 173; "Summerall Retains Post. Withdraws Resignation as Head of South Carolina Citadel," *New York Times*, February 16, 1932; "Cadets Cheer As Summerall Says He Will Not Quit," *Charleston News and Courier*, February 16, 1932.
42. Summerall to Parker, March 7, 1932, Parker Papers, box 9.
43. Summerall to Parker, January 2, 1932, ibid.
44. Summerall to Parker, January 11, 1932, ibid.
45. Summerall to Parker, February 15, 1932 in ibid.; Summerall to H. C. Duncan, Tavares, Florida, February 23, 1932, Summerall MSS, box 9.
46. W. Gary Nichols, "The General As President: Charles P. Summerall and Mark W. Clark As Presidents of The Citadel," *South Carolina Historical Magazine* 95 no. 4 (October 1994): 319. Hereinafter cited as Nichols, "Summerall and Clark."
47. Ibid.; "Annual Report of The Citadel, 1932–33," in Minutes of The Board of Visitors, 1932–33, The Citadel Archives & Museum, Charleston, South Carolina. Hereinafter cited as "Annual Report."
48. Summerall memoir, p. 173.
49. Ibid.
50. "The President's Speech," *New York Times*, October 24, 1935.
51. Wiles typescript, Chapter XXV, pp. 19–21; Nicholson, *The Citadel*, pp. 93–94. Colonel Bond died at age 68, one year after the Board named the Main Administration Building in his honor. He had entered The Citadel in 1882, the year the institution reopened after the Civil War. After graduation he was appointed assistant professor of mathematics, and became president in 1908. When Summerall succeeded him, Bond returned to the faculty as professor of mathematics and dean of the college. At the time of his death, he had been connected with The Citadel as cadet, faculty member, president, and dean for a total of 49 years. See his obituary, "Col. Bond, Educator, 68, Dies—President for 23 Years of the Citadel Military College of Charleston, S. C.", *New York Times*, October 2, 1933.
52. "Annual Report, 1939–1940."
53. Summerall memoir, p. 175; Nicholson, *The Citadel*, p. 101.
54. Nicholson, *The Citadel*, p. 120.
55. Summerall memoir, p. 175; The Citadel Catalogue, 1935–1936; Nicholson, *The Citadel*, pp. 119–20.
56. Wiles typescript, Chapter XXV, p. 20; Nicholson, *The Citadel*, pp. 113–14.
57. Wiles typescript, Chapter XXV, p. 25.
58. Nichols, "Summerall and Clark," pp. 320–21.
59. Summerall memoir, p. 176.
60. Ibid.
61. Nicholson, *The Citadel*, pp. 130–34.
62. Ibid., pp. 23–24.
63. "Class of 1954: General Charles Pelot Summerall and 'His Last Boys' Assembled by Robert Soukup, Class of 1954."At the invitation of the author, Robert Soukup of Myrtle Beach, South Carolina, collected reminiscences of his class-

Notes to Pages 362–371

mates. Accompanied by his classmate Lewis Cauthen, he presented these recollections at the conclusion of a cadet seminar on the life of General Summerall at The Citadel in April 2005. Of the many fond and interesting reminiscences of these former cadets, the one most frequently mentioned and gleefully recalled is the birthday celebration.

64. Colonel John E. Burrows, U.S. Army Retired, Class of 1940, and former regimental commander, recalls that after the birthday "ceremony" in 1940, Summerall turned to reenter his quarters, and found the front door locked. While the cadets stood in formation waiting for him salute and dismiss them, he kept trying, without success, to open the door. Finally, Mrs. Summerall looked down from an upstairs window and noticed the problem. She came downstairs and opened the door, and her husband went quietly back inside, but not before saluting the cadets, and with a rare, slight smile across his face. Thanks to Jake Burrows for passing on one of his favorite stories.

65. Summerall memoir, p. 177.

66. "103 More Colleges Will Help to Train Army Specialists," *New York Times*, May 30, 1943; Nicholson, *The Citadel*, pp. 173–74, 210; Summerall memoir, pp. 177–78.

67. Board of Visitors Minutes, 1941 Sept. 20–1943 March 6, The Citadel Archives & Museum.

68. Board of Visitors Minutes, 1943 April 3–1945 Aug. 18, ibid.

69. McMurray to General Summerall, 26 July 1943, copy given to the author by Rear Admiral Arthur M. Wilcox, U.S. Navy, Retired. Admiral Wilcox is the son in law of Colonel McMurray, and had received from him this letter and carbon copies of the typewritten transcripts of the commandant's interviews with all of the cadets who had been suspended. I am grateful to Admiral Wilcox for placing all of this material in my hands. This material will be cited hereinafter as McMurray Records.

70. Interview by the author of Dr. Cockfield, 12 February 2007. Cadet Cockfield left The Citadel lacking only one course in physics to complete his graduation requirements, and enlisted in the Marine Corps. He participated in the Iwo Jima landings, and managed to survive that brutal campaign. He returned to The Citadel, and asked General Summerall if he had to take that physics course, which was not offered that term, in order to be graduated. Summerall told Cockfield that the time he spent on Iwo Jima was worth more than the physics course, and waived the requirement. Cockfield was graduated at the end of that term.

71. McMurray to Summerall, 26 July 1943, McMurray Records.

72. "General Orders No. 3, Headquarters of The Citadel, Office of the President, August 9, 1943," copy in McMurray Records. General Summerall distributed this general order to the commandant, each member of the board, and to the file of each member of the junior class, as well as specifically to the file of Cadet Strong. It summarized the charges against each cadet, and the findings of the Board of Visitors, as well as Summerall's reaction to the incident in the mess hall. Hereinafter cited as "General Order No. 3."

73. Nicholson, *The Citadel*, p. 217.

74. "General Order No. 3"; Nicholson, *The Citadel*, pp. 216–17.

75. "General Order No. 3."

76. Summerall to Thomas, August 9, 1943, McMurray Papers.

77. Annual Report of The Citadel,1946–1953, The Citadel Archives & Museum.

78. Nicholson, *The Citadel*, pp. 236, 245.

79. Summerall memoir, pp. 179–80; Wiles typescript, Chapter XXV, pp. 40–44.

80. Summerall memoir, pp. 174–75.

81. Wiles typescript, pp. 33–34. In his memoir, Summerall mentioned his wife's stroke, but said nothing about her death. As he had held private his deepest feelings of love of his wife, so he kept just as privately the great sadness and pain he surely felt in losing her.

82. Handwritten notes by Colonel Wiles, dated 5/18/50, and 6/22/53; lists of the publications specified by Summerall (n.d.); Wiles's instructions to the Library Committee (n.d.), ADG Wiles Papers, A1983.14, "Foreign Leaders-Summerall on, " The Citadel Archives & Museum.

83. Ibid.

84. Summerall to Colonel Westmoreland, 12 May 1952, Board of Visitors Minutes, 1948, Oct. 16–1953, July 11, The Citadel Archives and Museum.

85. Wiles typescript, Chapter XXV, p. 44.

86. Minutes of the Board of Visitors, June 13, 1952, The Citadel Archives and Museum.

87. Colonel Westmoreland to Summerall, September 3, 1952, Minutes of the Board of Visitors, 1948, Oct. 16–1953, July 11, The Citadel Archives and Museum.

88. Summerall to Colonel Westmoreland, June 30, 1953, ibid.

89. Minutes of the Board of Visitors, 1948, Oct. 16–1953, July 11, The Citadel Archives and Museum.

90. Forest S. Riggers, Jr., "Conversations Between General Mark W. Clark and Lieutenant Colonel Forest S. Riggers, Jr., "Senior Officers Debriefing Program, U.S. Army Military History Collection, Military History Institute, Carlisle Barracks, Pennsylvania, interview 4, pp. 52, 54.

91. Ibid., pp. 57–58.

92. Ibid., p. 58. General Clark served as Citadel president from 1955 to 1965. See Nichols, "Summerall and Clark," pp. 323–35.
93. Interview of Summerall by W. D. Workman, quoted in Wiles, typescript, Chapter XXV, pp. 47–48.
94. Wiles typescript, Chapter XXV, pp. 45–46.
95. "General Summerall Arrives Here To Begin Retirement," *Aiken Standard and Record*, July 1, 1953.
96. Minutes of the Board of Visitors, May 2, 1953, The Citadel Archives and Museum.
97. Wiles typescript, Chapter XXV, pp. 46–48.
98. Summerall to Mrs. Reynolds, Aiken, South Carolina, July 8, July 15, November 2, 1953. I am grateful to Mr. Edward J. Reynolds of Mount Pleasant, South Carolina, for sharing with the author Summerall's letters to his mother.
99. Summerall to Mrs. Reynolds, June 26, 1954. The thank-you note he signed is not dated.

# Bibliography

## Manuscript Collections

Hoover Institution of War, Revolution and Peace, Stanford, California
   Conrad Stanton Babcock Papers.

Manuscript Division, Library of Congress, Washington, D.C.
   John L. Hines Papers.
   John A. Lejeune Papers.
   William Mitchell Papers.
   George S. Patton, Jr. Papers.
   John J. Pershing Papers.
   Charles P. Summerall Papers.

Marshall Manuscript Collection, George C. Marshall Foundation, Lexington, Virginia
   Pierpont L. Stackpole Diary.

Southern Historical Collection, University of North Carolina–Chapel Hill, Chapel Hill, North Carolina
   Frank Parker Papers.

Special Collections Library, Duke University, Durham, North Carolina
   W. W. Ball Papers.

The Citadel Archives & Museum, Charleston, South Carolina
   Board of Visitors Minutes. 1941 Sept. 20–1943 March 6; 1943 April 3–1945 Aug. 18; 1948–Oct. 16–1953 July 11; 1952 June 13; 1953 May 2.
   Summerall, C. P. "Annual Report of The Citadel, 1932–1933."
   ———. "Annual Report of The Citadel, 1952–1953."
   Wiles, A. G. D. Untitled manuscript on the life of General Summerall.

United States Army Military History Institute, Carlisle Barracks, Pennsylvania
   Hugh A. Drum Papers.
   Senior Officers Debriefing Program. U.S. Army Military History Collection. Riggers, Forest S., Jr.
   "Conversations Between General Mark W. Clark and Lieutenant Colonel Forest S. Riggers, Jr.

United States Military Academy Library and Archives, West Point, New York
   Circumstances of the Parents of Cadets, No. 2, 1880–1910.
   Delinquencies, No. 256.
   Descriptive List of Candidates, 1869 to 1892, No. 2.
   Official Register of the Officers and Cadets of the U.S. Military Academy, West Point, New York.
   Post Orders No. 12, U.S. Military Academy.

Regulations, U.S. Military Academy.
School History of Candidates, No. 1, 1880 to 1899.

## Records in the National Archives and Records Administration

Record Group 94
- Office of the Adjutant General.
    - Summerall AGO file.
    - Appointment, Commission and Personnel Branch Document File.
    - *Central Decimal Correspondence File, Bulky Packages, 201.6E.E. (10-12-18), Confidential Report on Efficiency of Officers who served in the A.E.F.*

Record Group 120
- World War I Organizational Records.
    - American Expeditionary Forces.
        - First Division Historical File.
        - First Field Artillery Brigade Historical File.
        - 42nd Division Historical File.
        - 5th C[orps] Historical File.

Record Group 168
- Records of the National Guard Bureau.
    - Index by individual, 1908–1916.
    - Document file, 1908–1916.

Record Group 391
- Records of U.S. Regular Army Units.
    - Artillery Regiments: 1821–1905.
        - 5th Regiment, Register of Letters Received, 1877–1884, and 1888–1901, Vol. 2, Vol. 11.

Record Group 393
- Department of the Gulf.
    - Special Orders, No. 15, 18.
    - Letters Received, March 31, 1899, Vol. 1, 1899.

Record Group 395
- U.S. Army Overseas Operations and Commands, 1898–1902.
    - China Relief Expedition.
        - File 906.
        - File 425–479.
        - File 898.
- U.S. Army Overseas Operations and Commands, 1898–1942.
    - Hdq, Hawaii Deprt.

Record Group 407
- Office of Adjutant General.
    - Central Decimal Files, Project Files, 1917–1925, Camp Taliferro Calif.
    - Central Files, 1926–1939, General Files, Part 1.

## Primary Sources

Buck, B. Beaumont. *Memories of Peace and War.* San Antonio, Texas: The Naylor Company, 1935.

# Bibliography

Bullard, Robert Lee. *Personalities and Reminiscences of the War.* Garden City, New York: Doubleday, Page and Company, 1925.

Butler, Alban B. "Journal of Operations, December 23, 1917 through October 12, 1918." Cantigny/First Division Museum, Wheaton, Illinois.

"Class of 1954: General Charles Pelot Summerall and 'His Last Boys'— The Class of 1954: Memories— 50+ Years Later by my Classmates." Assembled by Robert Soukup, '54. Loose-leaf binder in the possession of the author.

Colonel Clarence C. McMurray Records. In the possession of Rear Admiral Arthur M. Wilcox, USN (Ret.).

Columbia County Court House, Lake City, Florida. *Property Records, 1866–1869.*

Daggett, A. S. *America in the China Relief Expedition.* Kansas City: Hudson Kimberly, 1903; reprint, Nashville, Tennessee: The Battery Press, 1997.

Dickman, Joseph T. *The Great Crusade: A Narrative of the World War.* New York: D. Appleton and Company, 1927.

Eustis Memorial Library Archives, Eustis, Florida. *Semi-Tropical: Lake Eustis, Orange* [Lake] *County, Florida*, No. 14, October 14, 1882.

Evarts, Jeremiah M. *Cantigny: A Corner of the War.* Privately printed.

Florida Board of State Institutions. *Soldiers of Florida in the Seminole Indian-Civil and Spanish-American Wars.* Live Oak, Florida: Democrat Print, 1903; reprint, Macclenny, Florida: R. J. Perry, 1983.

Harbord, James G. *Leaves from a War Diary.* New York: Dodd, Mead & Company, 1931.

Historical Division, Department of the Army. *United States Army in the World War, 1917–1919.* 17 vols. Washington: United States Government Printing Office, 1948.

Historical Section, Army War College. *Order of Battle of the United States Land Forces in the World War, American Expeditionary Forces, Divisions.* Washington: United States Government Printing Office, 1931.

———. *Order of Battle of the United States Land Forces in the World War, American Expeditionary Forces, General Headquarters, Armies, Army Corps, Services of Supply, and Separate Forces.* Washington: United States Government Printing Office, 1937.

Hoover, Herbert. *The Memoirs of Herbert Hoover—Years of Adventure, 1874-1920.* New York: The Macmillan Company, 1951.

Kipling, Rudyard. *American Notes.* London and New York: Standard Book Company, 1930.

Lejeune, John A. *The Reminiscences of a Marine.* Philadelphia: Dorrance and Company, 1930.

Letters of General Summerall to Mrs. Maude Reynolds, dated July 8, July 15, November 2, 1953; June 26, 1953. Copies in possession of the author.

Liggett, Hunter. *A.E.F.: Ten Years Ago in France.* New York: Dodd, Mead and Company, 1928.

Marshall, George C. *Marshall Interviews and Reminiscences for Forrest C. Pogue, Revised Edition, with an introduction by Dr. Pogue.* Larry I. Bland, Joellen K. Bland, asst. ed., Sharon Ritenour Stevens, photographs ed. Lexington, Virginia: George C. Marshall Research Foundation, 1991.

———. *Memoirs of My Services in the World War, 1917-1918.* Boston: Houghton Mifflin Company, 1976.

Masseck, C. J. *Official Brief History of the 89th Division, U.S.A., 1918–1919.* N.p., n.d.

*Official Records of the Union and Confederate Navies in the War of the Rebellion.* Series 1. Washington: United States Government Printing Office, 1894–1927.

Parker, James. *The Old Army: Memories, 1872–1919*. Philadelphia: Dorrance and Company, 1929.

Patch, Joseph Dorst. *A Soldier's War: The First Infantry Division, A.E.F. (1917–1918)*. Corpus Christi, Texas: Mission Press, 1966.

Pershing, John J. *My Experiences in the World War*. 2 vols. New York: Frederic A. Stokes Company, 1931.

——— and Hunter Liggett. *Report of the First Army, American Expeditionary Forces: Organization and Operations*. Fort Leavenworth, Kansas: The General Service Schools Press, 1923.

Wright, William M. *Meuse-Argonne Diary: A Division Commander in World War I*. Ed. Robert H. Ferrell. Columbia and London: University of Missouri Press, 2004.

## Books, Chapters in Books, and Speeches

Albrecht-Carrié, René. *Italy at the Peace Conference*. New York: Columbia University Press for The Carnegie Endowment for International Peace, 1938; reprint, Hamden, Connecticut: Archon Books, 1966.

Ambrose, Stephen E. *Duty, Honor, Country: A History of West Point*. Baltimore: The Johns Hopkins Press, 1966.

American Battle Monuments Commission. *American Armies and Battlefields in Europe: A History, Guide, and Reference Book*. United States Government Printing Office: Washington, 1938.

Andrew, Rod, Jr. *Long Gray Lines: The Southern Military School Tradition, 1839–1915*. Chapel Hill and London: The University of North Carolina Press, 2001.

Bartlett, Merrill L. *Lejeune: A Marine's Life, 1867–1942*. Columbia, South Carolina: University of South Carolina Press, 1991.

Beveridge, Albert. "The March of the Flag," in John L. Beatty and Oliver A. Johnson, eds. *Heritage of Western Civilization*, 8th ed., vol. 2. Prentice Hall: Englewood Cliffs, New Jersey, 1995.

Bond, O. J. *The Story of The Citadel*. Richmond, Virginia; Garrett and Massie, 1936; reprint, Greenville, South Carolina: Southern Historical Press, 1989.

Braim, Paul F. *The Test of Battle: The American Expeditionary Forces in the Meuse-Argonne Campaign*, 2nd revised ed. Shippensburg, Pennsylvania: White Mane Books, 1998.

Carlson, Paul H. *"Pecos Bill": A Military Biography of William R. Shafter*. College Station, Texas: Texas A&M University Press, 1989.

Clifford, Howard. *The Skagway Story: A history of Alaska's most famous gold rush town and of some of the people who made that history*. Ed. Byron Fish. Anchorage: Alaska Northwest Publishing Company, 1975.

Coffman, Edward M. *The Old Army: A Portrait of the American Army in Peacetime, 1784–1898*. New York and Oxford: Oxford University Press, 1986.

———. *The War To End All Wars: The American Military Experience in World War I*. New York: Oxford University Press, 1968.

Collins, Louis L. *History of the 151st Field Artillery, Rainbow Division*. Saint Paul, Minnesota: Minnesota War Records Commission, 1924.

Cooke, James J. *The Rainbow Division in the Great War, 1917–1919*. Westport, Connecticut: Praeger Publisher, 1994.

Cooper, Jerry M. *The Army and Civil Disorder: Federal Military Intervention in Labor Disputes, 1877–1900*. Contributions in Military History, Number 19. Westport, Connecticut: Greenwood Press, 1980.

Cosmas, Graham A. *An Army for Empire: The United States Army in the Spanish American War.* Columbia, Missouri: University of Missouri Press, 1971.

Crowinshield, Francis Boadman. *Blockade Running During the Civil War and the Effect of Land and Water Transportation on the Confederacy.* Philadelphia: Porcupine Press, 1974.

Daggett, A. S. *America in the China Relief Expedition.* Kansas City: Hudson Kimberly, 1903; reprint, Nashville, Tennessee: The Battery Press, 1997.

Dastrup, Boyd L. *The Field Artillery: History and Sourcebook.* Westport, Connecticut: Greenwood Press, 1994.

Davis, Burke. *The Billy Mitchell Affair.* New York: Random House, 1967.

d'Este, Carlo. *Patton: A Genius for War.* New York: HarperCollins, 1995.

DeWeerd, Harvey A. *President Wilson Fights His War: World War I and the America Intervention, The Wars of the United States*, gen. ed., Louis Morton. New York: The Macmillan Company, 1968.

Duffy, Francis P. *Father Duffy's Story: A Tale of Humor and Heroism, Of Life and Death With The Fighting Sixth-Ninth.* New York: George H. Doran Company, 1919.

*Downey, Fairfax. Sound of the Guns: The Story of American Artillery from the Ancient and Honorable Company to the Atom Cannon and Guided Missile.* New York: David McKay Company, Inc., 1955.

Fleming, Peter. *The Siege at Peking.* New York: Harper and Brothers, 1959.

Fleming, Thomas J., *West Point: The Men and Times of the United States Military Academy.* New York: William Morrow and Company, 1969.

Forman, Sidney. *West Point: A History of the United States Military Academy.* New York: Columbia University Press, 1950.

Fraser, Walter J., Jr. *Charleston! Charleston!: The History of a Southern City.* Columbia, South Carolina: University of South Carolina Press, 1989.

Ganoe, William Addleman. *The History of the United States Army.* New York and London: D. Appleton-Century Company, 1942.

Gates, John Morgan. *Schoolbooks and Krags: The United States Army in the Philippines, 1898–1902.* Contributions in Military History, Number 3. Westport, Connecticut: Greenwood Press, 1973.

Gould, Lewis L. *The Presidency of Theodore Roosevelt.* American Presidency Series, eds. Donald R McCoy, Clifford S. Griffin, Homer E. Socolofsky. Lawrence, Kansas: University Press of Kansas, 1991.

Gowenlock, Thomas R. *Soldiers of Darkness.* Doubleday, Doran & Company, Inc. Garden City, New York: 1937.

Hallas, James H. *Squandered Victory: The American First Army at St. Mihiel.* Westport, Connecticut: Praeger Publishers, 1995.

Hamilton, Walter R. *The Yukon Story: A Sourdough's record of Goldrush Days and Yukon Progress from the earliest times to the present day.* Vancouver: Mitchell Press Limited, 1964.

Harbord, James G. *The American Army in France, 1917–1919.* Boston: Little, Brown, and Company, 1936.

———. *Personalities and Personal Relationships in the American Expeditionary Forces.* Washington: United States Government Printing Office, 1933. Address of Maj. Gen. J. G. Harbord at the Army War College, April 29, 1933.

Harrison, Noel Garraux. *City of Canvas: Camp Russell A. Alger and The Spanish American War.* Falls Church, Virginia: Falls Church Historical Commission and Fairfax County History Commission, 1988.

Holley, I. B., Jr. *General John M. Palmer, Citizen Soldiers, and the Army of a Democracy*. Contributions in Military History, Number 28. Westport, Connecticut: Greenwood Press, 1982.

Hurley, Alfred F. *Billy Mitchell: Crusader for Air Power*. Bloomington: Indiana University Press, 1975.

Jellicoe, Rt. Hon. the Earl. "The Boxer Rebellion," *Fifth Wellington Lecture*. Southampton, Great Britain: University of Southampton, 1993.

Jessup, Philip C. *Elihu Root*, vol. 1, *1845–1909*. New York: Dodd, Mead & Company, 1938.

Johnson, David E. *Fast Tanks and Heavy Bombers: Innovation in the U.S. Army, 1917–1945*. Cornell Studies in Security Affairs, Ithaca and London: Cornell University Press, 1998.

Johnson, Douglas V., II and Rolfe L. Hillman, Jr. *Soissons, 1918*. College Station, Texas: Texas A&M University Press, 1999.

Johnson, Douglas Wilson. "Fiume and the Adriatic Problem," in *What Really Happened at Paris: The Real Story of the Peace Conference, 1918–1919 By American Authors*. Eds., Edward Mandell House and Charles Seymour. New York: C. Scribner's Sons, 1921.

Kennedy, William T., editor in chief, *History of Lake County, Florida: Narrative and Biographical*. Tavares, Florida: Lake County Historical Society, 1988.

Keuchel, *A History of Columbia County, Florida*. Tallahassee, Florida: Sentry Press, 1981.

Ledeen, Michael A. *The First Duce: D'Annunzio at Fiume*. Baltimore: The Johns Hopkins University Press, 1977.

Linn, Brian McAllister. *Guardians of Empire: The U.S. Army in the Pacific, 1902–1940*. Chapel Hill and London: The University of North Carolina Press, 1997.

———. *The Philippine War, 1899–1902*. Modern War Studies. gen. ed., Theodore A Wilson. Lawrence, Kansas: University Press of Kansas, 2000.

———. *The U.S. Army and Counterinsurgency in the Philippine War, 1899–1902*. Chapel Hill and London: University of North Carolina Press, 1989.

Luraghi, Raimondo. *A History of the Confederate Navy*. Trans. Paolo E. Coletta. Annapolis, Maryland: Naval Institute Press, 1996.

MacCloskey, Monro. *Reilly's Battery: A Story of the Boxer Rebellion*. New York: Richard Rosen Press, 1969.

Macdonald, J. N. *A Political Escapade: The Story of Fiume and D'Annunzio*. London: John Murray, 1921.

Manchester, William. *American Caesar: Douglas MacArthur, 1880–1964*. Boston: Little, Brown and Company, 1978.

May, Glenn Anthony. *Battle for Batangas: A Philippine Province at War*. New Haven and London: Yale University Press, 1991.

Millett, Allan R. "Cantigny, 28–31 May 1918," in Charles E. Heller and William A. Stofft, eds. *America's First Battles, 1776–1965*. Lawrence: University of Kansas Press, 1986.

———. *The General: Robert L. Bullard and Officership in the United States Army, 1881–1925*. Contributions in Military History, Number 10. Westport, Connecticut: Greenwood Press, 1975.

———. *Semper Fidelis: The History of the United States Marine Corps (The Macmillan Wars of the United States)* Gen. ed. Louis Morton. New York: The Free Press, 1980.

——— and Maslowski, Peter. *For the Common Defense: A Military History of the United States*. New York: The Free Press, 1984.

Nenninger, Timothy K. *The Leavenworth Schools and the Old Army: Education, Professionalism, and the Officer Corps of the United States Army, 1881–1918.* Contributions in Military History, Number 15. Westport, Connecticut and London: Greenwood Press, 1978.

Nicholson, D. D., Jr. *A History of The Citadel: The Years of Summerall and Clark.* Charleston, South Carolina: Association of Citadel Men, 1994.

O'Connor, Richard. *The Spirit Soldiers: A Historical Narrative of the Boxer Rebellion.* New York: G. P. Putnam's Sons, 1973.

Peter, Emmett, Jr. *Lake County Florida: A Pictorial History.* Virginia Beach, Virginia: The Donning Company for the Lake County Historical Society, 1994.

Porter, A. Toomer. *Led On! Step by Step: Scenes from Clerical, Military Educational, and Plantation Life in the South, 1828–1898.* New York: Arno Press, 1967.

Pratt, Fletcher. *Eleven Generals: Studies in American Command.* New York: William Sloane Associates, 1949.

Preston, Diana. *The Boxer Rebellion: The Dramatic Story of China's War on Foreigners That Shook the World in the Summer of 1900.* New York: Walker and Company, 2000; first published as *Besieged in Peking.* London: Constable and Company, 1999.

Raymond, Dora. *Captain Lee Hall of Texas.* Norman, Oklahoma: University of Oklahoma Press, 1940.

Reilly, Henry J. *Americans All: The Rainbow at War: Official History of the 42nd Rainbow Division in the World War.* Columbus, Ohio: The F. J. Herr Printing Co., 1936.

Richman, Michael. *Daniel Chester French: An American Sculptor.* New York: The Metropolitan Museum of Art, for the National Trust for Historic Preservation, 1976.

Rickover, Hyman G. *How the Battleship Maine Was Destroyed.* Washington: Navy History Division, Department of the Navy. 1976.

Samuels, Peggy and Harold Samuels. *Remembering the Maine.* Washington: Smithsonian Institution Press, 1995.

Shofner, Jerrell H. *Nor Is It Over Yet: Florida in the Era of Reconstruction, 1863–1877.* Gainesville, Florida: The University Presses of Florida, 1974.

Sigsbee, Charles D. *The Maine: An Account of Her Destruction in Havana Harbor.* New York: Century, 1899.

Smith, Richard Norton. *The Colonel: The Life and Legend of Robert R. McCormick, 1880–1955.* Boston: Houghton Mifflin Company, 1997.

Smythe, Donald. *Pershing: General of the Armies.* Bloomington: Indiana University Press, 1986.

Society of the First Division. *History of the First Division during the World War, 1917–1919.* Philadelphia: The John C. Winston Company, 1922.

Spaulding, Oliver Lyman and John Womack Wright. *The Second Division American Expeditionary Force in France, 1917–1919.* Third in The Great War Series, repr., Nashville, Tennessee: The Battery Press, 1989.

Stern, Philip van Doren. *The Confederate Navy: A Pictorial History.* Garden City, New York: Doubleday and Company, 1962.

Struck, Hudson. *The Alaskan Missions of the Episcopal Church: A brief sketch, historical and descriptive.* New York: Domestic and Foreign Missionary Society, 1920.

Tan, Chester C. *The Boxer Catastrophe.* Columbia Studies in the Social Sciences, Number 583, edited by the Faculty of Political Science of Columbia University. New York: Columbia University Press, 1955.

Tebeau, Charlton W. *A History of Florida*. Coral Gables, Florida: University of Miami Press, 1971.

Thomas, Lowell. *Old Gimlet Eye: The Adventures of Smedley D. Butler*. New York: Farrar & Rinehart, 1933.

Thomas, Shipley. *The History of the A.E.F.* New York: George H. Doran Company, 1920.

Tilchin, William N. *Theodore Roosevelt and the British Empire: A Study in Presidential Statecraft*. New York: St. Martin's Press: 1997.

Tindall, George Brown with David E. Shi. *America: A Narrative History*, 3rd ed., vol. 2. New York: W. W. Norton and Company, 1992.

Trask, David F. *The AEF and Coalition Warmaking, 1917–1918*. Modern War Studies, Theodore A. Wilson, gen. ed. Lawrence, Kansas: University Press of Kansas, 1993.

———. *The War with Spain in 1898*. The Macmillan Wars of the United States, gen. ed., Louis Morton. New York: Macmillan Publishing, 1981.

Twichell, Heath, Jr. *Allen: The Biography of an Army Officer*. New Brunswick, New Jersey: Rutgers University Press, 1974.

Venzon, Anne Cipriano. *General Smedley Darlington Butler: Letters of a Leatherneck, 1898–1931*. New York: Praeger, 1992.

Weigley, Russell F. *History of the United States Army, The Wars of the United States*. Gen. ed., Louis Morton. New York: The Macmillan Company, 1967.

Williams, T. Harry. *The History of American Wars from 1745 to 1918*. New York: Alfred A. Knopf, 1981.

Woodhouse, John. *Gabriele D'Annunzio: Defiant Angel*. Oxford: Clarendon Press, 1998.

Zoellner, Erich. *Geschichte Oesterreichs Von den Anfaengen bis zur Gegenwart*. 4. Auflage. Vienna: Verlag Fuer Geschichte und Politik, 1970.

## Articles

Fullenkamp, Leonard J., "New Looks at the American Civil War," *Parameters*, US Army War College Quarterly, 28, no. 2 (Summer 1998).

Ginsburg, A. R. Captain, F. A. (DOL), "Rolling Along with Reilly," *The Field Artillery Journal*, Volume 23, No. 1 (January–February, 1933).

Nichols, W. Gary. "The General As President: Charles P. Summerall and Mark W. Clark As Presidents of The Citadel," *South Carolina Historical Magazine* 95 no. 4 October 1994.

O'Connell, Captain J. J., First United States Infantry, "The Great Strike of 1894," *United Service* 15, no. 4 (April 1896).

Smythe, Donald. "A.E.F. Snafu at Sedan," *Prologue* (Fall 1973).

Summerall, Charles P. "The Camp of Instruction for Field Artillery at Tobyhanna, PA.", *The Field Artillery Journal*, Volume 4, No. 1 (January–March 1914).

———. "The Spirit of the First Division: Address by Major General Charles P. Summerall at the Unveiling of the Fist Division Monument, October 4, 1924", *The Field Artillery Journal*, 14 (November–December, 1924).

Thomas, Hugh. "Remember the Maine?", *New York Review of Books*, April 23, 1998.

## Internet Sources and Interviews

"A Timeline of San Francisco History," http://www.zpub.com/sf/history/sfh2html, June 2000.

Cockfield interview by the author of Dr. Cockfield, 12 February 2007.

"Early History: Camp Reynolds," http://www.angelisland.org, June 2000.

"Emergence of Modern China: II," http://www-chaos.umd.edu/history/modern 2.html, June 2002.

"Fort Lawton." http://www.cityofseattle.net/neighborhoods/preservation/fortlawton.html, July 2003.

Freeman, Joe C., Stephan A. Haller, David M. Hansen, John A. Martin, Karen J. Weitze, *Seacoast Fortifications Preservation Manual Golden Gate National Recreational Area San Francisco, California*. San Francisco: National Park Service and KEA Environmental Golden Gate National Recreational Area, July 1999, http://www.nps.gov/goga/ftmanual/chapter2/chapter2.htm, June 2000.

Gough, Terrence. "The Root Reforms and Command." U.S. Army Center of Military History. http://www.army.mil/cmh/documents/1901/Root-Cmd.htm.

*"Haines, Alaska."* http://www.sheldonmuseum.org/hainesalaska.html.

Hart, Colonel Herbert H. "Historic California Posts: Presidio of San Francisco," *The California Military Museum*. http://www.militarymuseum.org/Presidio.html, June 2000.

Hartley, Aaron. *The Democrat*, 29 June 1898. http://www.geneology.emcee.com/~baf/misc/sp_am_war/6.29.1898.

Jones, Vincent C. "Transition to Change, 1902–1917" in American Military History, Army Historical Series. http://www.army.mil/cmh/books/AMH/AMH-16.htm.

"Largest Hotel in the United States Now Going Up Here." http://www.sfmuseum.org/hist1/1873.html, June 2000.

McDuffy, Michael. "First World War.com." http://www.firstworldwar.com.

Monroe Historical Society. "When Monroe Became a Town." http://www.monroehistoricsociety.org/175thcolumns.html.

"Mordecai family." http://www.lib.unc.edu/mss/inv/m/Mordecai_family.html.

National Park Service. "Chicamauga." http://www.nps.gov/check/adhi/adhit.htm.

Pennsylvania Department of Conservation and Natural Resources. "Tobyhanna State Park." http://www.dcnr.state.pa.us/stateparks/parks/Tobyhanna.aspx.

Peters, N. "The War Between the States, 1861–1865, Glynn County Georgia, 26th Georgia Infantry Regiment, Brunswick Riflemen, 26th Georgia Infantry—A Brief History." http://petersnn.org/petersnn/csarifles.html.

"Presidio of San Francisco." http://www.nps.gov/prsf/prsfphot/cultureh.htm, http://www.nps.gov/prsf/prsfphot/spanyrs.htm, http://www.nps.gov/prsf/prsfphot/mexyrs.htm, http://www.nps.gov/prsf/prsfphot/ameryrs.htm, June 2000.

"San Francisco History: Population." http://www.sf50.com/sf/hgpop.html, June 2000.

Thompson, Walter J. "Strolling on Sunday Afternoons." http://www.sf50.com/sf/hgsto13.html, June 2000.

"Tobyhanna Facts." http://www.tobyhanna.army.mil/toby/facts/history/yale.html.

"White Pass Railroad." http://www.whitepassrailroad.com/history/index.html.

Wikipedia.org. "Aerial Bombing of Cities" http://en.wikipedia.org/w/index.php?title=aerial_bombing_of_cities&printable=yes.

Wikipedia.org. "Battle of the Somme" http://en.wikipedia.org./wiki/Battle_of_the_Somme_(1916).

"Richardson, Wilds Preston," Brian Hart, *Handbook of Texas Online*. http://www.tshaonline.org/handbook/online/articles/fri12.

Yarrison, James L. "The U.S. Army in the Root Reform Era, 1899–1917" U.S. Army Center of Military History. http://www.army.mil/cmh/documents/1901/Root-Ovr.htm.

"Yukon, Alaska." http://www.yukonalaska.com/akblkhist/early/24th.html. August 2003.

## Newspapers

*Aiken (South Carolina) Standard and Record*. July 1, 1953.

*Boston Transcript*. March 20, 1929.

*Charleston (South Carolina) News and Courier*. February 16, 1932.

*Leesburg (Florida) Commercial*. "Centennial Edition," May 20, 1987; Reed, Rick, "General Returns to Lake for ceremony," *Leesburg (Florida) The Daily Commercial*, special section entitled "Reminisce: Summerall Park Dedication."

*New York Times*. September 7, January 5, 1919; October 4, November 11, 1920; January 22, May 6, 1921; June 17, 1922; October 5, 1924, December 16, 1924; January 11, May 29, October 29, November 15, December 15, 1925; August 21, September 7, November 18, November 20, 1926; April 2, n.d., 1929; March 25, 1930; February 11, February 16, 1932; October 2, 1933; October 24, 1935; May 30, 1943.

*Orlando Sentinel*. May 3, 1964.

*Sacramento Bee*. July 11–13, 16, 20; September 21, 22; October 23, 26, 29; November 7, 9, 17; December 10, 1894.

*San Francisco Examiner*. August 15, 1901.

*The State (Columbia, South Carolina)*. June 12, 1949.

*The State Magazine*. May 30, 1954.

## Encyclopedias

Chambers, John Whiteclay, II, ed. in chief. *The Oxford Companion to American Military History*. Oxford and New York: Oxford University Press, 1999.

Dupuy, R. Ernest and Trevor N. Dupuy. *The Encyclopedia of Military History From 3500 B.C. to the Present*. 2nd rev. ed. New York: Harper and Row, 1986.

Edgar, Walter, ed. *The South Carolina Encyclopedia*. "A Project of the Humanities Council, SC." Columbia: University of South Carolina Press, 2006.

Tucker, Spencer C., ed., Laura Matysek and Justin Murphy, assoc. eds. *The European Powers in the First World War: An Encyclopedia*. Garland Reference Library of the Humanities. New York and London: Garland Publishing, Inc., 1996.

Venzon, Anne Cipriano, ed., Paul L. Miles, con. ed. *The United States in the First World War: An Encyclopedia*. Garland Reference Library of the Humanities. New York and London: Garland Publishing, Inc., 1995.

# Index

## A

Aberdeen Proving Grounds, Md., 342, 349
Addington, Larry H., x, 323
AEF, 463. *See also* American Expeditionary Forces
AEF (American Expeditionary Forces) in France
  Armies
    First Army, 80
      organization of, 209, 231, 273
      at St. Mihiel Salient, 229, 232–34, 240, 242–43
      in Meuse-Argonne, 245, 247, 249, 251, 253–55, 259–62, 271–73, 276
      during Sedan incident, 277–81, 284–93, 295
    Second Army, 260, 271, 286, 292, 296
    Third Army, 288, 291, 298
  Corps
    I Corps
      organization of, 195–96, 209
      at St. Mihiel Salient, 234, 239–41, 243
      in Meuse-Argonne, 249, 251–52, 254–55, 257–60, 262–63, 271–72, 274
      during Sedan incident, 277–79, 281, 283–87, 289, 291–92
    II Corps (only in U.S.A.), 330–32, 337, 343
    III Corps, 183
      at Soissons, 209–10, 225
      in Meuse-Argonne, 249, 251–52, 254–55, 257–60, 262, 265, 271–72, 274, 276
    IV Corps
      at St. Mihiel Salient, 232, 234–36, 238–40, 243
    V Corps
      Summerall and, xii, 93, 260–62, 264–65, 270–74, 276–80, 284–86, 288–92, 297–99, 302, 308
      at St. Mihiel Salient, 235, 240
      in Meuse-Argonne, 249, 251–55, 257, 259–65, 270–74, 276–77
      during Sedan incident; Pershing's role in, 277–78, 280–81, 284–86, 288–92, 295–96
      armistice, 296, 298–99
      limits and boundaries, 285, 289, 292
    VIII Corps (only in U.S.A.), 324, 326, 329, 331, 333
    IV Occupation Corps, 288, 300, 302, 303, 324
    IX Occupation Corps, 299
  Divisions
    First Division
      Summerall and, ix, xii, 36, 80, 93, 167, 183–85, 209, 285–88, 289–91, 298, 302
      Philippine Insurrection, 58, 59, 74, 76, 79, 80
      under Bullard, 187–88, 190, 192–95, 196–99, 201
      at Cantigny, 202, 204–8
      attack on Soissons, 209, 214–15, 217, 219, 224–26, 229
      at the St. Mihiel Salient, 230–32, 235–36, 238–43
      in Meuse-Argonne, 254–55, 257, 259, 261, 263, 265, 271–72, 274, 277
      during Sedan incident, 280–81, 283–87, 289, 300–302, 308
      celebrations of victory, 307, 310–11
      postwar problems and successes, 312–16, 322
      commemorations, 326–27, 331, 333, 336, 342–43, 357–58, 373
    Second Division, 196
      at Château-Thierry/Soissons, 207, 209–11, 215–17, 222
      at the St. Mihiel Salient, 239
      in Meuse-Argonne, 271, 274, 276
      during Sedan incident, 280, 292–93, 295, 297–98
      postwar events, 308, 329–30
    Third Division
      at Château-Thierry, 207, 209
      in Meuse-Argonne, 265, 271
    Fourth Division
      at the St. Mihiel Salient, 234–35
      in Meuse-Argonne, 249, 252, 257, 259–60, 268
    Fifth Division, 239, 265, 271, 276
    Twenty-sixth, 195–96, 209
      at the St. Mihiel Salient, 235–36, 249
    Twenty-eighth, 249, 255, 257, 298
    Twenty-ninth, 298
    Thirty-second, 180
      in Meuse-Argonne, 254, 257, 259, 261, 263, 265, 268, 270–72
    Thirty-third, 249, 252
    Thirty-fifth
      in Meuse-Argonne, 249, 251–55, 257
    Thirty-seventh, 249, 254
    Forty-second, 180
      Summerall and, 176, 190, 261
      at the St. Mihiel Salient, 195–96, 236, 238–39, 243, 249
      in Meuse-Argonne, 259, 261–62, 264, 277
      during Sedan incident, 279, 281, 284–88, 290, 292
    Seventy-seventh
      in Meuse-Argonne, 249, 257–58, 264, 271, 274, 277
      during Sedan incident, 278, 281, 283, 286, 288–89, 292

Seventy-eighth, 271, 274, 277
Seventy-ninth, 249
Eightieth
  in Meuse-Argonne, 249, 257, 259–60, 271, 274, 277, 281
Eighty-second
  at the St. Mihiel Salient, 235, 241
  in Meuse-Argonne, 259, 263, 272, 298
Eighty-ninth
  at the St. Mihiel Salient, 235, 238–39, 243
  in Meuse-Argonne, 268, 270–72, 274, 276, 278
  during Sedan incident, 280, 292–93, 295, 297
Ninety-first
  in Meuse-Argonne, 249, 254–55, 259
Brigades
  1st Artillery Brigade
    Summerall and, 50, 80, 183, 333, 372
    in combat, 202, 225, 285, 287
  67th Field Artillery Brigade, 176, 183
  1st Tank, 233, 249
Regiments
  Artillery
    4th Artillery, 33, 74
    5th Artillery, (Summerall's unit), 36, 37, 40, 41, 45, 50, 63, 84, 93, 123, 156, 192, 208, 261, 372
    129th Field Artillery, 251
  Infantry
    9th Infantry, 211, 215
    16th Infantry, 184, 187, 219
    18th Infantry, 187, 192–93, 202, 204, 214, 219
    23rd Infantry, 211, 215
    26th Infantry, 187, 202, 206, 210, 214, 221–24, 287
    28th Infantry, 202, 204, 210, 212, 220
    354th Infantry, 239, 268
Agricultural Grounds, Manila, 125, 127, 135
Aguinaldo y Famy, Emilio, 67–69, 70–72, 77, 80, 87, 92
Aiken, S.C., xii, 12, 384, 385, 442, 452
Air Corps Act of 1926, 345
Aire River, 257, 263, 270
Aisne River, 178, 283
Alaskan duty, 145, 149, 410, 449
Albert I, King of Belgium, 259
Alexander, Robert, 261, 283
Alger, Russell A., 68, 70, 71, 91, 97, 159. *See also* Camp Alger
Allenby, Edmund, 165
Alsace-Lorraine, 277
Ambrose, Stephen E., 19
*American, The* (Manila news paper), 84
*American Army in France, The*, 216, 278–79
American Battle Monuments Commission, 336
American Expeditionary Forces (AEF), 12, 45, 179, 180, 242, 321
American Expeditionary Forces V Corps, 12, 105, 246, 247, 252, 261, 263–69, 271–75, 276–77, 282–86, 288–93, 296–98, 300, 301, 303, 308–11, 314, 320. *See also* AEF in France
American Federation of Labor (AFL), 47, 59, 341, 345
American Legion Post, Tavares, Fla., 329
American Railway Union (ARU), 42, 44, 45–46, 47

*Americans All: The Rainbow at War*, 192
Amiens, France, 194–96, 199, 208, 229, 245
Anderson, George S., 85, 86, 87
Anderson, Robert, 351
Anderson, Thomas M., 68
*Andrea Doria*, 306
Angel Island, San Francisco, 34, 37, 44
Anniston, Ala., 78, 162, 314
Ansauville sector, France, 189–92, 194, 196–97, 201, 223, 229, 232, 235
Apopka City, Fla., 9
Appalachian Mountains, 142
Argonne Forest, 179, 245–47, 251–52, 254–55, 257. *See also* Meuse-Argonne
Ariétal Farm, France, 257
Arlington National Cemetery, xii, 123, 144, 327, 366
*Armies of Asia and Europe, The*, 30
*Army and Navy Journal*, 336
Army-Navy game, origins of, 23–25
Army of Liberation (Philippines), 69, 71, 72, 77, 79
Army Specialized Training and Reassignment Program (STAR), 362
Army Specialized Training Program (ASPT), 362
Army Staff College, 183
Army War College, 147, 168, 318
*Army-Navy Journal*, 85
Arnold, Harold H., 148
Artillery Corps, 93
Ashley River, 351
Asiatic Squadron, 55, 66
Assiago Plateau, 306
Astatula, Fla., 6, 9, 10, 22, 26, 27, 32, 329
*Astor*, 8, 22
Astor, Viscountess, 171
Astor, Waldorf, Lord, 171
Atlanta, Ga., 33, 48, 54–56, 61, 62, 64, 78
Austro-Hungarian Empire. *See* Dual Monarchy
Austro-Hungarian forces (World War I), 165, 186, 230, 231
Austro-Hungarians (Boxer Rebellion), 96, 99, 106, 107
Automatic rifles, 184, 231
Autreville, France, 293

**B**

Babcock, Conrad S., 210, 217–19, 220, 226, 239, 255, 268–70, 273, 302, 308, 343, 359, 411n150
Babson, Rose Douglas, 78
Baker, Chauncey B., 169, 174
Baker, Newton C., 163, 166–67, 169, 171–72, 174–76, 184, 298
Baker Mission, 171, 172, 174, 377
Balfour, Arthur, 166
Balkans, 70, 158, 253
Ball, W. W., 352, 354
*Baltic* (steamer), 169, 170
Baltimore and Ohio Railroad, 141
Baltimore, Md., 155, 157, 373
Bamford, Frank E., 204, 211, 219, 240, 265
Bangalore torpedo tubes, 193, 232
Bar River, 287
Barnhardt, George, 23

*Index*

Barricourt (Heights), 244, 246, 262, 272, 273
Barry, Thomas H., 34, 151, 158–59
Bartlett, Murray, 327
Batangas Bay, 87
Batangas City, 87, 90
Batangas Province (Philippines), 71, 72, 76, 80, 84, 85, 90, 91
Bates, John C., 79, 84, 85, 90
Batson, Matthew, 87
Batteries
   Battery K, 5th Artillery, 37, 38, 39
   Battery L, 5th Artillery, 45, 46
   Battery Marcus Miller, 38, 39
   Light Battery F, 5th Artillery, 63, 72, 84
   10th Battery Field Artillery (new organization of Reilly's Battery), 123
Battle Monument, West Point, 316
Battle of Caporetto, 186, 190, 194
Battle of Jutland, 165, 402n77
Battle of Messines, 171, 173, 175, 197
Battle of Mézières, 233, 234, 245, 251, 292
"Battle of Newton," 155
Battle of the Marne, 161
Battle of Vimy, 173, 175
Bavaria, 277
Bay of Biscay, 179
Bay of Chihli, China, 95, 96, 103, 105, 122
Bearss, Hiram I., 240
Beatty, David, 394n22
Beaufort, S.C., 2
Beaumont, France, 191, 192, 277
Beauvais, France, 195, 196, 208, 210
BEF, 233. *See also* British Expeditionary Forces
"Belfort ruse," 413n37
Belgium, 160, 245, 247, 277
Bell, George, Jr., 249
Bell, J. Franklin, 183
Belleau Wood, 207, 209, 240
Bengal Cavalry, 106, 107
Bengal Lancers, 106
Benicia Arsenal, Calif., 121, 128
Benicia Barracks, 34, 36, 37, 45
Berdoulat, Pierre E., 209, 216
Berlin, 166, 222, 277
Berlin Airlift, 370
Bertolucci (commander), 304, 306
Berzy-le-Sec, France, 217, 219–22, 224
Besancon, France, 184
Beveridge, Albert J., 51–52
Big Red One, 236, 316. *See also* First Division
*Billy Mitchell Affair, The*, 335
Biñan, Philippines, 80, 83
Black soldiers (3rd Alabama), 78–79
Blackman, Fred M., 314
Bliss, Tasker H., 169, 170, 175, 186, 195, 403n90
Blount's Ferry, Fla., 1, 3
Blue Devils, 184, 185. *See also* Chasseurs Alpine
Blue Team (mock battle for New York), 155

Board of Visitors, The Citadel, 350, 356, 358, 359, 363–65, 368, 371, 372
Bois de Belval, 274
Bois de Bourgogne, 282
Bois de Dieulet, 276
Bois de la Brigade de Marine, 207
Bolshevik Party, Russia, 186
Bond, Oliver J., The Citadel, 350–52, 354, 360, 370, 428n51
Bond Hall, 360, 370
Booth, Ewing H., 334
*Boston Transcript*, 343
Bouconville, France, 189
Boult-aux-Bois, 272
Bowes, Edward, 332
Bowley, Albert L., 334
Boxer Protocol, 124
Boxer Rebellion, China, 113, 124
Boxers, xi, 38, 96, 98, 99, 101–4, 106, 108, 117, 120, 124, 125
Braim, Paul, 247, 259, 272
Breckinridge, John C., 40
Bremen, Germany, 277
Brenner Pass, 304, 307
Brest-Litovsk Armistice, 186
Brett, Sereno, 413n58
Briscom, Lloyd, 307
British Army's Experimental Mechanized Force, 344
British Expeditionary Forces, 160
British Isles, 161
British Legation (Boxer Rebellion), 99, 101, 102, 104, 112
Brooklyn Navy Yard, 53
Brooks, Sidney, 96
Brown, Preston, 211, 216, 217, 269, 329, 330
Brunswick Rifles, 2
Brusilov, Alexi A., 165
Brussels, 271
Buchanan, James, 140
Buck, Beaumont B., 187, 201
Buckner, Simon Bolivar, 148
Bullard, Robert Lee, 15, 18, 19
  in the Philippines, 77–78, 79, 80, 82–87, 91–93
    during World War I, 153, 167, 183, 185, 187–89, 191–93, 202, 205, 206, 208–10, 222, 260
    aftermath, 290, 295, 329, 330–32, 337
Bulson, France, 277
Bundy, Omar, 183, 209, 413n37
Burgess, Louis R., 72, 75, 92, 93, 122, 130
Burnham, William P., 235
Burrows, John E., 429n64
Burtt, Wilson B., 261, 285, 287, 292, 296
Butler, Alban B., 209, 220–21, 225–26, 337, 404n17, 406n79
Butler, Henry, 285
Butler, Smedley D., 106
Buzancy, France, 217, 223, 224, 272, 274
Byrnes, James F., 360, 370, 371

**C**

Cadorna, Luigi, 165
Calamba, Philippines, 75–77, 79, 80, 82–85, 87, 91, 92

Callan, Robert E., 336
Caloocan, Philippines, 71
Calvin, Alfred H., 122–23
Cambrai, France, 194, 233, 245, 247
Cameron, George H., 234, 235, 240, 249, 260–61, 265, 308
Camp Alger, Va., 56–60, 85, 142
Camp Dewey, Philippines, 92, 93
Camp Dix, N.J., 312–15
Camp George H. Thomas, 141. *See also* Camp Thomas
Camp Meade, Pa., 59, 60–61, 344
Camp Mills, N.Y., 176–78
Camp Otis, Philippines, 74–75
Camp Reilly, China, 120, 122, 123
Camp Reynolds, Calif., 34
Camp Shipp, Ala., 78
Camp Thomas, Ga., 142, 151
Camp Tobyhanna, Pa., 307
Camp Wikoff, N.Y., 64
Camp Zachary Taylor, Ky., 307, 310
Campbell, Charles, 56
Campbell, Emma, 56
Cantigny, France, battle of, 199, 201, 202, 204–6, 210–12, 226, 296
  after the War, 316, 327, 358, 372
*Captain Lee Hall of Texas*, 91
Carnegie Foundation, 158
Carranza, Venustiano, 401–2n61
Cavite Province, Philippines, 66–68, 71, 72, 75–77, 79, 83–85, 91–92
Central Pacific Railroad, 44, 45
Cervera y Topete, Pascual, 63
Chaffee, Adna, 104, 106, 109, 110, 113–17, 119, 120–21, 123, 125
Chambers, John Whiteclay II, 168
Charles VI, Habsburg emperor, 403n78
Charleston, S.C., xi, xii, 35, 39, 54, 370, 371, 373
  Holy Communion Church Institute at (school established by the Rev. A. Toomer Porter), 5, 7–8, 11, 22, 35, 39
  The Citadel at, 348, 350, 351
Charleston Female Academy, 8
*Charleston News and Courier*, ix, 357, 371
Chasseurs Alpine Infantry, 184. *See also* Blue Devils
Château de Tartigny/Château Tartigny, 206, 208
Château de Vincennes, 172
Château-Thierry, France, 205–9, 210, 215–16, 224, 230, 233, 309
Chauchat automatic rifles, 184
Chaudon, France, 211, 214, 217
Chaumont, France, 179, 184–86, 195, 207, 209, 298
Cheatham, Benjamin Franklin, 84, 85
Chehery, France, 283–85, 287
Chemical Warfare Service, 187, 311
Chemin des Dames, France, 166, 195, 202, 205, 206
Cheyenne, Wyo., 42, 44
Chiang, Li Hung, 117, 123, 124
Chicago, 40, 44, 120, 141, 313
*Chicago Tribune*, 126, 177, 192, 337, 358, 372
Chickamauga Military Park, 56, 141, 142, 144
Chief of Branch, 343

Chien Men, Peking, 99, 101, 102, 112–15, 117, 118, 123
Chih Hua Men, 109, 110
Chihli, Gulf of, 105, 121
Chihli Province, China, 95, 96, 103
China (Boxer Rebellion), 106, 108, 110, 117, 119, 120–25
  Relief and World War I, 310, 317, 318, 322
  return from, 127, 128, 140, 151, 226, 285
Chotek, Sophie, 301
Citadel, The (Military College of South Carolina), xi, xii, 8–9, 353, 354, 356, 357
Citadel Code, The, 355, 356, 359–60
Civil War
  as part of Summerall family background, xi, 1–2, 7–8, 11
  at The Citadel, 351, 354
  battlefields and memorials of, 141, 143, 144, 314, 316, 332
  legacy for the Army, 29–30, 43
  veterans of, 15, 18–19, 37–38, 54, 60, 67, 71, 78, 108
Clark, George B., 207
Clark, Grenville, 163
Clark, Helen, 129
Clark, Mark W., 370, 371
Clark, Miriam, 129
Clark, Samuel C., 45, 47
Clark, Walt, ix
Clay, Lucius D., 370
Clemenceau, Georges, 185, 193, 195, 243, 267, 268, 301, 303
Cleveland, Grover, 11, 44
Cleveland, Ohio, 163, 175
Clifford, Howard, 132, 133
Coastal defenses, 38, 39. *See also* harbor defenses
Coblenz, Germany, 277
Cochem Castle, France, 288, 300
Cockfield, R. L., ix, 364, 429n70
Coe, Frank, 183
Coetquidan, France, 180–82, 185, 196
Coffman, Edward M. ("Mac"), ix, 29, 184, 227, 274, 291
College of Charleston, S.C., 8, 353
Collins, James L., 183
Collins, Louis, 180, 181
Cologne, Germany, 277
Columbia, S.C., 7, 240, 350, 354
Columbia County, Fla., 1, 3, 4–5, 91
Columbia Female Seminary, S.C., 6
*Columbia Record*, 350
Columbia River, 140
Columbian Exposition, Chicago, 40
Columbian Guard, 40
Commission on Fine Arts, 313, 316
Committee on Military Affairs, 300, 339, 340, 343
Communistic books (Citadel Library), 368
Compiègne, France, 210, 277, 292
Composite Regiment, 306, 307
Compromise of 1877, 4
Compton, Ranulf, 413–14n58
Conant, Sherman, 11
Confederate Savannah Squadron, 2
Confederate States Army (CSA), 1
Conger, Edwin V., 117

Congressional Medal of Honor, 258, 336
Connecticut Maneuver Campaign, 156
Conner, Fox, 231
Cooke, James J., 177, 181, 182, 262, 263, 264
Coolidge, Calvin, 313, 334, 336, 339–41, 343, 345, 359
Cooper, Jerry M., 44
Corbin, H. C., 60–62, 398n40
Corps of Cadets, The Citadel, 351, 352, 355, 356, 358–60, 363–66, 370
Corps of Cadets, VMI, 143
Corps of Cadets, West Point, 13, 18, 23, 24, 148, 226
Corregidor Island, Philippines, 66, 74, 128
Cortelyou, George B., 133, 134, 137
Cosmas, Graham, 68
Côte Dame Marie, France, 259, 261–62, 263
Côte de Châtillon, France, 262–63
Council of National Defense, 164, 330
Craig, Malin, 196, 281, 407n124
Crise River, 219, 223
*Cristobal Colon*, 63
Crittenden farm, 58, 59
Crowder, Enoch H., 168
Crowell, Benedict, 175
Crowley, Patrick F., 332
Cuba, 51–56, 59, 67–69
  veterans of, 72, 78, 131, 133, 144, 147, 152, 168, 211
Cunel, 245, 251, 255, 257, 259, 260, 262
*Customs and Courtesies* (The Citadel), 356
Czernin, Ottokar, 403n78

**D**

Daggett, A. S., 104, 107–10, 112–17, 395n99
Dallam, S. Field, 264
Dammartin-en-Goele, France, 226
Danford, Robert M., 162
D'Annunzio, Gabriele, 305, 306, 422n12
Dardanelles Campaign, 172
Daugherty, Charles, 10, 11
Davis, Burke, 335
Davis, Dwight F., 332–34, 336, 339–41, 343–45
Davis, George B., 151
Dawes Plan, 327
Dawson, Alaska, 132, 137
Debeney, Marie Eugene, 191–92, 199, 206, 408n58
Debs, Eugene V., 44, 47
Defense Act of 1920, 311, 312, 323, 329, 330, 343, 344, 348
Denis, George, 44
Department of California, 42, 44
Department of the East, 53
Department of the Gulf, 54, 61, 64
Department of the Interior, 87
Depression, The, ix, xii, 348, 352, 368
D'Este, Carlo, 239, 253
Devers, Jacob L., 148
Dewey, George, 55–56, 66–69, 71
Dick Act (Militia Act), 147
Dickman, Joseph T., 207, 234, 235, 238, 240–42, 260, 271, 274, 278–79, 281
  feud with Summerall, 284, 287–88, 290–91, 298, 301, 359

Distinguished Service Cross (D.S.C.), 208, 212, 283, 299
Division of Militia Affairs, 147, 155
Dodge Commission, 60, 61
Dommiers Plateau, France, 209, 211, 212, 215
Doubs River, 184
Doullens, France, 195
Dravo, Charles A., 263, 264
Dressler, Marie, 337
Drewes, Charles H., 40, 41
Drum, Hugh, 168, 231, 249, 259, 261, 279, 280, 285–87, 291
Dual Monarchy (Austro-Hungarian Empire), 165, 166, 303
Duffy, Francis P., 265
Duncan, George B., 187, 191, 257, 263, 298
Duncan, James, 330
Dunn Loring, Va., 56, 58
Dun-sur-Meuse, France, 274

**E**

East Asiatic Corps, 120
Eastern Front (World War I), 194
Ebert, Friedrich, 301
École Superieure de Guerre, 187
Edwards, Clarence, 186, 196, 201, 235, 265
Edwards, Daniel R., 327
Eichelberger, Robert L., 148
El Caney, Cuba, 63, 64
El Paso, Texas, 167
*Eleven Generals: Studies in American Command*, 290
Ely, Hanson, 187, 201, 204, 210, 222, 265, 276, 308
Endicott, William C., 38
Episcopal Church of the Holy Communion, 366
Ericsson, Hjalmar, 283
Eustis, Fla., 6, 8–9, 39, 48–49, 54, 85, 289
  as first retirement home, 329, 347, 349, 352, 354
*Eustis Lake Region* newspaper, 4, 12, 85, 86
Evans, R. K., 155
Evarts, Jeremiah M., 204
Exermont, France, 255, 257
Experimental Mechanized Force, 344

**F**

Falls Church, Va., 55, 56
Farnsworth, Charles S., 249
Feland, Logan, 211
Ferdinand, Francis (Austrian Archduke), 301
Ferrell, Robert, 268, 273, 276, 293, 295, 297
Filipino, 66, 68, 70–72, 77, 82, 84, 90–91, 93
First Division AEF Memorial Association, 327
First Division Monument, 316, 324, 336
First Moroccan Division (part of First French Army), 189, 210–11, 214–15, 217, 219, 223, 226
First World War, 33. *See also* Great War
Fists of Righteous Harmony (Boxer Rebellion), 95, 96
Fiume (Rijeka), Italy, 303–6, 314
Fleming, Peter, 98, 107–9
Fleming, Thomas, 27
Fletcher, Duncan U., 349
Fléville, France, 255, 257
*Flintshire* (transport), 104, 105, 127

Florida, effects of Reconstruction on, 3–4
*Florida Times-Union, The*, 11
Foch, Ferdinand, 195–96, 207, 208, 224, 230–31, 233–34, 242, 245, 247, 249, 254, 260, 267, 292, 295–96, 413n37
Forbidden City, Peking, 99, 104, 116–18, 125, 373
Fort Cook, Neb., 79
Fort Flagler, Wash., 137–39, 141
Fort Hamilton, N.Y., 50, 51, 53, 64, 72, 93
Fort Jay, N.Y., 331–33, 337, 339, 343
Fort Lawton, Wash., 130, 131
Fort Leavenworth, Kans., 30, 31, 183
Fort Monroe, Va., 61, 336
Fort Myer, Va., 59, 141–42, 144–46, 152–53, 155–59, 337, 346–47, 354, 373
Fort Point, Calif., 37, 38
Fort Sam Houston, Texas, 54, 324, 326, 329, 331, 339
Fort Shafter, Hawaii, 317, 320, 321
Fort Sill, Okla., 154
Fort Sumter, S.C., 2
Fort Walla Walla, Wash., 129, 130
Fort Winfield Scott, Calif., 39, 50
Fourth Army (British), 225, 247
Fourth Army (French), 172, 234, 245, 251, 257, 271–72, 277, 279, 281, 292
French, Daniel Chester, 316–17
French Foreign Legion (part of First Moroccan Division), 210–11, 225
*Ft. Myers Press*, 356
Fullenkamp, Leonard J., xi
Funston, Frederick, 92
Fuqua, Stephen O., 343–45
Futch, T. I., 366

## G

Gallieni, Joseph S., 160
Gardener, Cornelius, 87
Garrison, Lindley M., 162
Gary, Elbert H., 332
Gaselee, Alfred, 104, 106, 107
Gaston, Jesse, 362
Gatley, George, 51
Gatling gun, 82
General Assembly of South Carolina, 351, 354, 356, 358
General Order No. 3, The Citadel, 364–65
General Organization Project (GOP), 173
*Georgia* (floating battery), 2–3
German Empire, 30, 31, 52, 165–66, 180, 204, 267–68, 297, 317
German High Seas Fleet, 277, 301
Gilbert, Cass, 316–17
Girard, Alfred C., 57
*Giselher Stellung* (German position), 251
Glendale, Fla., 6
Glidden (Sergeant), 315
Goerner, Wilhelm, 267
Golden Gate, San Francisco, 37, 38, 39, 50, 68, 74, 128
Gomez, Maximo, 52
Gompers, Samuel, 47, 329, 330
Gondrecourt Training Area, France, 184–86, 188, 190, 232

Good, James, 341
Gould, Lewis L., 133
Gourand, Henri, 172, 182, 271
Governors Island, N.Y., 53, 170, 331, 357
Gowenlock, Thomas R., 236, 254, 255, 296–97
Graham, William Montrose, 36, 37, 38, 40, 41, 42, 45, 46, 47–48, 54, 55, 56
  during Spanish-American War, 57, 58, 59, 60, 61, 62
Grandpré, France, 251, 257–58, 262
Grant, F. D., 76
Grant, Ulysses S., 30, 246
Grant, Walter, 231, 234, 242, 280, 287
Graves, William S., 334
*Great Crusade, The*, 238, 240, 288
Great Lakes, 38
Great Railroad Strike of 1877, 43
Great War (1914–1918), xii, 30, 36, 51, 80, 120–21, 148, 161, 175, 270–71, 301, 302, 310, 324. *See also* First World War
Greely, John N., 259
Green, William, 333, 337
Greene, Francis V., 68
Greenwood, S.C., 2, 3
Grenades, 168, 184, 186, 232, 258, 268, 332
Guadalupe Heights, 75
Guadalupe River, 75
Guam, 69
Guantanamo Bay, Cuba, 63
*Guide to the American Battle Fields in Europe, A*, 336
*Guidon, The*, 355

## H

Haan, William G., 259, 261, 263, 270, 271
Hagood, Johnson, 351
Haig, Sir Douglas, 197, 229, 233, 265
Haines Mission, Alaska, 135–37
Hall, Lee, 87, 90–91, 93
Hallas, James H., 230, 240, 276
Hamilton, Alexander, 50
Hampton Park, Charleston, S.C., 351
Hamrick, Wylie, 356
Hanlin College and Library, Peking, 99, 102
Hanna, Mark, 293
Hanson, Thomas G., 268, 276
Harbor defenses, 38–39. *See also* coastal defenses
Harbord, James G., 168, 172–73, 180, 196, 209–11, 215–17, 227, 246, 278–79, 288, 291, 298–99, 308
Harding, Ann, 51
Harding, Warren G., 318
Hartley, Aaron Ward, 56, 58
Harvey, Harcourt, 313
Havana, Cuba, 53
Havana Harbor, 53
*Have Faith in Massachusetts*, 313
Hawkins, Hamilton S., 16
Hayes, Rutherford B., 4, 44
Hearst, William Randolph, 53
Hearst papers, 51
Heintzelman, Stuart "Tommy," 407n124

## Index

Hillman, Rolfe, Jr., 210, 216–22, 225–27, 273, 409n100
Hinds, Ernest, 156
Hines, John L., 168, 186, 187, 191, 211, 235, 260
   dissension with Summerall, 336, 343, 344
*History of the 89th Division*, 268
*History of the First Division*, 184, 193, 198, 219, 232, 236, 281, 290
*History of the Rainbow Division in the Great War*, 177
Hoboken, N.J., 178, 184, 302
Holland, 277
Holy Communion (church) Institute (school), Charleston, S.C., 6, 7, 8. *See also* Charleston, S.C.
Hong Kong, 55, 64, 66, 67, 95
Honolulu, Hawaii, 64, 74, 335
   Summerall in command of Hawaiian Department, 317, 320–22, 324
*Honolulu Advertiser*, 324–25, 326
Honshu, Japan, 95
Hoover, Herbert, 95, 96, 102, 103
   as president, 341, 345–47, 359
Hoover Institution, ix
Hotchkiss machine gun, 76, 82, 83, 92, 184
Hotel Crillon, Paris, 174
Hough, Benson W., 263–64
House Committee on Military Affairs, 339–40
Hovey, Henry W., 133
Howze, Robert L., 149, 150, 334, 335
Hoyle, Eli D., 142, 144
Hudson Bay Company, 140
Hudson River, 12, 15
Huebner, Clarence, 232, 234, 238–39, 411n150
Hughes, Charles M., 330
Huguet, Adolphe H., 327
Hundred Days' Reform (China), 95
Hunter, William W., 2–3
Hurley, Patrick, 341
Hylan, James J., 330

### I

Illington, Margaret, 332
Imperial City, Peking, 38, 99, 113–18
Indian Frontier, 29
*Infantry Tactics*, 30
*Influence of Sea Power Upon History, 1660–1783*, 52
Inter-allied Commission of Inquiry on Fiume, Italy, 303
Ireland, Merritt, 341, 343, 344
Irish Sea, 161
Irwin, George Le R., 334
Isonzo River, 165

### J

Jackson, Thomas J. "Stonewall," 50
Jacksonville, Fla., 10, 11, 12, 22, 27, 54, 85
Jáudenes y Alvarez, Don Fermin, 68, 69
Jellicoe, Earl, 394n22
Jellicoe, John R., 394n22
Jervey, James, 24
Joffre, Joseph J. C., 160–61, 164, 166
Johns Hopkins Hospital, 373
Johnson, David E., 344–45
Johnson, Douglas, 210, 216–22, 225–27, 273, 409n100
Johnson, Elisha G., 4
Johnston, John A., 249
Johnston, Joseph F., 78
Joint Army and Naval Exercise No. 3, 321
Joint Army and Navy Board, 317–18
Jones, Brooks, 35, 40, 48
Jones, C. H., 11, 85
Jones, Charles M., 372
Jones, Winfield S., 35, 40, 48, 54, 61–62, 129, 130, 141

### K

Kapitunan (Philippines), 66, 67
Kaufman, Robert, 318
Kellogg, Donald W., 17, 20
Kellogg-Briand Pact, 339
Kelly, D. O., 129
Kerensky, Alexander, 186
Key West, Fla., 54
Keyes, Roger, 107
Kilauea Military Camp, 323, 325
King, Campbell, 183, 187, 217, 243
King, Edward K., 334
Kipling, Rudyard, 33, 34, 35–36
Kline, Jacob, 76, 77, 80
Klondike Gold Rush, 132, 134, 137
Klondike River, 131–33
Knox, Harry A., 45–46, 47
Korea, 95, 105, 322, 365, 370
Korean War, 333, 370
*Kriegsmarsch*, 277
*Kriemhilde Stellung*, 251, 254–55, 259–60, 262
Ku Klux Klan, 4, 5, 43
Kuang Hsu, 95
Kuhn, Joseph E., 249
Kwangchow, China, 95

### L

Labor Standards Act of 1938, 333
*Lady Davis* (Confederate tug), 2
Laguna, Philippines, 71
*Laguna de Bay* (gunboat), 71
Laguna de Bay, 71, 72
Lake Apopka, Fla., 6
Lake Bennett, Alaska, 136
Lake City, Fla., 1, 3, 4
Lake County, Fla., 6, 9, 10
Lake Eustis, Fla., 6
Land, E. F., 40
Lang, John W., 354, 356, 358, 359, 361
Langhorne, George, 84
Lassiter, William, 170, 187, 196, 333
Lawton, Henry W., 40, 63, 72, 74, 75, 79, 131
Lawton-Gordon-Evans Brigade, 2
League of Fiume, 305, 306
Le Valdahon, France, 184, 192
Lee, Fitzhugh, 53
Lee, Robert E., 50, 53, 354
*Leelanaw* (transport), 74–75

Leesburg, Fla., 9, 10, 11, 32
*Leesburg Commercial*, 10
Lejeune, John A., 235, 239, 280, 295–97, 308, 309
Lenihan, Michael J., 262–65
Lenin, Vladimir, 326, 403n80
Leon bulge, xii, 564
*Leviathan*, 307, 336
Lexington, Va., xi, 143, 354
Li Peng-hing, 104
Liggett, Hunter, 80, 196, 242, 246, 258, 260, 407n124
  involved in controversy, 264–65, 268, 270–71, 274, 279, 284–88, 290–92, 301, 302, 310
Lilly, William, 182
Lime Point Military Reservation, 39
Linievitch, N. P., 109, 113
Linn, Brian, 68, 69, 70, 92, 318–19, 321–22, 324
Liscum, Emerson H., 102, 103
Live Oak, Fla., 5, 6
Liverpool, England, 161, 169–71, 174
Lloyd George, David, 195, 201, 301
Lodge, Henry Cabot, 51, 52
Long, John C., 353
Long, John D., 53, 66, 68
Long Island, N.Y., 148, 150, 176
Longwy-Briey region, France, 179
Lorraine, France, 179, 184, 195–96, 229, 247, 277
"Lost Battalion," 257–59
Louisville, Ky., 307, 310, 312
Lowell, James Russell, 313, 332
Ludendorff, Erich, 165, 194–95, 197, 201, 209–10, 225, 241, 245, 247, 253, 267
Luebeck, Germany, 277
*Lusitania*, 161, 162
Luxembourg, 277
Luzon, Philippines, 70, 71, 72, 79, 80
Lynn Canal, Alaska, 131, 132, 135
Lys River, 247

## M

Macabebe Scouts (Philippines), 80, 87, 90, 91
MacArthur, Arthur, 68, 104
MacArthur, Douglas, 176–77, 180, 238, 242, 262–63, 265, 283, 290, 334, 343, 345, 347
MacArthur, Mary Pinckney, 178
MacDonald, Claude, 101
Macdonald, J. N., 305
Machenau, G., 122
MacInturff, Margaret, 129–31, 134–36, 139
Mackenzie, Ronald Slidell, 18
Madison, J. H., 336
Madrid, Spain, 53, 67, 354
Maguire, James G., 40
Mahan, Albert Thayer, 52
Main College Building, The Citadel, 351–52, 360
Maistre, Paul, 272, 277–78, 284, 292
*Major Bowes Original Amateur Hour*, 332
Mallory, Stephen M., 60
Malolos, Philippines, 71, 72
Malone, Paul B., 211, 233
Malvar, Miguel, 76
Manassas, Va., 58
Manchuria, 95, 322
Mangin, Charles, 209–10, 219, 226, 300
Manifest Destiny, 52
Manila, 54, 55, 64, 66, 67, 68, 69, 70, 71, 72, 74, 75, 76, 77, 80
Manila Bay, 55, 66, 72, 74, 79
Mann, William A., 176, 180
March, Peyton C., 310
Mare Island, Calif., 44, 45
Marines, 45, 46, 74
"Marne Hill," 314–15
Marne River, 161, 202, 205, 206
Marshall, George C., xi
  during World War I, 183–85, 187, 197, 202, 205, 231–32, 234, 241, 249, 252, 278–79, 291–92
  postwar career, 310, 347, 352
*Mary Powell* (paddle wheeler), 12
Masseck, C. J., 276
Maybank, Burnett R., 356
McAlexander, Ulysses G., 187, 210
McAndrew, James W., 185, 231
McCain, Henry P., 149, 150
McCloskey, Manus, 64, 74–75, 105, 395n99
McCormick, Robert R., 192–93, 358, 372
McCoy, Frank R., 334
McCrea, Tully, 93
McDonald, John D., 321, 324
McKays, Henry, 150, 152
McKinley, William, 53, 54, 66, 67–68, 70
McKinley High School, 324
McKinstry, Charles H., 183, 187
McMahon, John, 235, 239, 265
McMaster, George H., 22
McMurray, Clarence, 363–66
McNair, Leslie J., 184, 320
McRae, James H., 271
Meade, George G., 59
Meade, George S., 36
Meeks, Eula, 381n75
Menken, S. Starwood, 337
Menoher, George T., 180, 182, 235, 262–65, 271, 281, 284
Merritt, Wesley, 67, 68, 69, 341
Messines Ridge, France, 171, 173, 175, 197
Metz, France, 179, 241–43, 247
Meuse-Argonne operations, 93, 183, 230, 233–34, 236, 240–43, 245, 247, 249, 251, 253, 255, 258–60, 267–68, 270, 271, 273. *See also* Argonne Forest
  World War I remembered, 296, 309, 316, 326, 327
Meuse River, 234, 260, 262, 273, 276, 295
Mexican War, 50
Mézières, France, 233, 234, 251, 292
Micheler, Joseph, 197
Michie, Dennis Mahan, 23, 24
Michie, Peter Smith, 27–28
Miles, Nelson A., 56, 59, 63
*(The) Military Policy of the United States*, 31

*Index*

Miley, John David, 49, 50, 51, 63
Miley, Sara Mordecai, 49, 50
Military Reconstruction Act of March 1867, 43
Militia Bureau, National Guard, 47
Millett, Allan R., 11, 20, 78, 79, 205
Mills, A. L., 148–50
Mills, Ogden, 172
Mississippi River, 42, 145, 154
Missy-aux-Bois, France, 211, 214, 217
Missy Ravine, 212, 214, 217, 219
Mitchell, Billy, 141, 233, 249, 322–23, 325, 359, 407n124
  court-martial of, 333–36, 345
Mitchell, Harry D., 263–65
Mobile, Ala., 78–79
Montauk Point, 64
Montdidier, France, 197, 199, 205, 206
Monterey, Calif., 34
Montfaucon, France, 245, 249, 251–53, 296
Montojo, Patricio, 55, 66
Moore, Charles, 133, 313
Moore, William "Billy," 132
Mordecai, Alfred, Jr., xi, 49, 128, 129, 307
Mordecai, Alfred, Sr., 49
Mordecai, Laura, xi. *See also* Summerall, Laura Mordecai
  background of, 49–50
  correspondence with Summerall, 50, 51, 55, 60–61, 62, 64, 74
  trip to Japan, 121, 122, 127, 226
  wedding of, 129–30
Mordecai, Sally Maynadier, 49
Moret, Segismundo, 52
Moros, 92
Morrow, Dwight, 345
Morton, Charles G., 318
Moseley, George Van Horn, 20, 343, 344
Moselle River, 229–30, 260, 288
Mott, T. Bentley, 20
Muir, Charles H., 87, 90, 249, 257, 392n122
*My Experiences in the World War*, 289

**N**

Nagasaki, Japan, 105, 121, 122, 127, 226
Nancy, France, 179, 184–85, 230–31, 233, 243
National Committee on Mobilization, 333
National Defense Act of 1916, 164, 166, 176, 310–11
National Guard, xii, 30, 42
  in strikes, 43, 44, 47
    post-war experiences, 310–11, 331, 337
    Spanish-American War, 55, 57
    training of, 147–48, 154, 157–58, 160, 162
    World War I, 176–77, 182, 299
National Relief Commission, 57
National Security League, 331, 337
Naulin, Stanislas, 303, 304
Naval War College, Newport, R.I., 52
Nenninger, Timothy K., ix, 337, 339–41, 343–48, 425–26n60
Neville, Wendell C., 211
Newcomb, Warren, 64
"New Imperialism," 51–52

*Newport* (troop transport), 74
New York Board of Engineers, 38
New York City, 12, 23, 26, 42, 50, 52, 54, 149, 155, 164, 170, 177–78, 182–83, 307, 327, 329, 332, 371
*New York Journal*, 53
*New York Times*, 160, 312, 314, 330–31, 334, 336, 342–43
*New York World*, 53
Nicholson, D. D., 353, 356, 366, 427n5
Nicholson, Tom, 399n20
Nimitz, Chester, 320
Nitti, Francesco, 304
North Atlantic Squadron, 63
Nunes, Sue, 329

**O**

O'Connell, Capt., 45
Officer Reserve Corps (ORC), 164
Ogden, Utah, 72, 74
Olney, Richard, 44
*Olympia* (troop transport), 79
Open Door Note, 95
Ordnance Department, 42, 60
*Ordnance Manual*, 49
Orlando, Vittorio, 303, 304, 306
Otis, Elwell S., 69, 70, 71, 72, 74, 79, 80

**P**

Page, Walter Hines, 166, 171
*Pak Ling* (troop transport), 127, 128
Palace Hotel, San Francisco, 32, 33, 35
Palmer, John McCauley, 14, 16, 22, 23
  in Army, 29, 30, 120, 168, 310, 311
Panic of 1873, 5, 43
Panic of 1893, 44
Paris, 69, 70, 160, 168, 172, 177–79, 183–85, 194–95, 199, 202, 207–9, 214, 217, 224, 227, 229–30, 233, 243, 290, 303–7, 359
  Treaty of Paris, 70
Parker, Frank, 20, 187, 191, 211, 265, 271–72, 280–81, 284–89, 291, 327, 344, 349–50, 352, 356–58
Parker, James, 77, 78, 93
Parker, John Henry, 82, 83
Pasig River, 70, 71, 72, 75
Patch, Alexander H., 148
Patch, Joseph, 222–24
Patterson, Joseph M., 192
Patrick, Mason, 322–23, 325, 334
Patton, George S., Jr., 148, 226, 233, 236, 238–39, 251–54, 337, 401–2n61, 415n35
Payne, Frederick H., 341
Peace of Paris, 59
Pei Ho River, 98–99, 102, 105–8, 119, 130
Peking, China, xi, 38, 107–10, 117, 119, 120, 122–25, 129, 136, 177, 373
Pelot, Charles Moore (maternal grandfather), 2
Pelot, Margaret Ford (maternal grandmother), 2
Pelot, Susan (aunt; mother's sister), 9
Pelot, Thomas Postell (maternal uncle), 2–3, 11
Pendry, A. S., 6

Pennington, A. C. M., 61, 62
*Pennsylvania* (troop transport), 79
Perry, Matthew, 94
Pershing, John J., 80
  early career of, 167
  in command of the AEF in France, 167–69, 401–2n61
  mission to London and the Baker Mission, 169–70, 173–76
  use of National Guard, 180–83
  relationship with Summerall, 185–87
  training and personnel issues, 185, 192, 194, 205
  effort for an American Army, 195–98, 201, 205
  questions of command in combat, 207–9, 217, 221, 231, 233, 235–36, 240–44
  final campaigns in France, 245, 249, 251, 254, 260–61, 265, 270, 272, 276–80, 286–90, 415n12, 416n81
  postwar controversies, 290–92, 296, 298, 306–11, 314–15, 327, 333, 336, 340, 359, 373
*Personalities and Reminiscences of the War*, 331
Pétain, Henri Philippe, 164, 196, 208, 226, 234, 245, 253–54, 299
Philippine Insurrection, xi, 66, 68–72, 74, 75–77, 78–80
Philippine Islands, 54, 59, 64, 66
  Philippines, 38, 59, 66, 67, 68, 69, 70, 71, 72, 74, 75, 78, 79, 80
Piave River, 186, 306
Picatinny Arsenal, 332
Plattsburg Movement, 163–64, 332–33
Plebe Barracks, 14, 15, 16, 17, 19
Ploisy Ravine, France, 217, 219–20
Plumer, Herbert, 171
Plunkett, Charles P., 330
Pogue, Forrest, 311, 347
Pohl, James W., 163
*Political Escapade: The Story of Fiume and D'Annunzio, A*, 305
Poore, Benjamin, 334
Port Arthur, 95
Porter, Rev. Anthony Toomer, 5–6
  founder and principal, 7–8, 9
  Holy Communion Church Institute, 20, 22, 35, 39, 55, 384n8
Potter Reeder, Russell, 336
Post Exchange Officer, 40, 41
Pratt, E. Spencer, 67
Pratt, Fletcher, 290, 420n270
Presidio of San Francisco, 35, 37, 129, 130, 133, 167, 261, 285
  description of, 37, 41, 42, 47–48, 51, 62, 63, 74, 76, 77
Price, Joseph, 3
Prince, Leonard Morton, 14, 23, 24, 25
"Project for the Defense of Oahu, Revision 1924," 320–22
Providence, Fla., 1, 3, 4, 43, 49
Puerto Rico, 54, 55, 63, 69, 78
Pulitzer, Joseph, 53
Pullman Strike, 44
Punitive Expedition to Mexico (1916), 22, 166, 401–2n61

## Q

Quai D'Orsay, 303, 305
Quakers, 159
Quekemeyer, John G., 169, 170
Quincy, Fla., 3

## R

Race to Sedan, 170, 226; Chapter Twelve. *See also* Sedan incident
Rainbow Division, 188–90, 192
*Raleigh News and Observer, The*, 353
Rawlinson, Henry S., 145
Raymond, Dora Neill, 91
Reconstruction, 3, 4, 5, 6
Reconstruction Acts of 1867, 3–4
Reed, Edward B., 162
Regular Army. *See* U.S. Army
Regulators, 5
Reid, Frank (Alaska), 132–33
Reid, Frank (Illinois congressman), 334–35
Reilly, Henry J., 37–38, 41, 42, 62, 63–64, 72, 75, 76, 92
  in China, 104, 105, 112–15, 117–18
  later references to, 123, 125, 127, 129, 160, 173, 373, 375
Reilly, Henry J. (son), 176–77, 180–81, 263–64, 281, 283–84, 361
Remember the Maine, 53, 56
Reminiscences, 297
*Resolute* (cruiser), 64
Reynolds, Edward, 430n98
Reynolds, Maude, ix, 373, 430n98
Richards, John G., 353
Richardson, Wilds P., 136, 137, 398n55
Rickover, Hyman G., 388–89n161
Ridgway, Thomas, 119, 123
*Ring of the Nibelungen, The*, 246
Rio Grande River, 80, 87
Roberts, Captain, 46
Roberts, Frederick Sleigh, 171
Robilant, Mario Nicolis di, 303
Rockenbach, Samuel, 413–14n58
Rock Island Arsenal, Ill., 145
Rodgers, John J., 93
Romagne, France, 245, 255, 259, 263, 296
Rome, 184, 304, 306
Roosevelt, Franklin D., 360
Roosevelt, Theodore, 51, 52, 63, 92, 134, 137, 152, 162–63, 176
Roosevelt, Theodore, Jr., 202, 217, 219, 287
Root, Elihu, 79, 85, 133–34, 137, 146–47, 152, 400n13
"Root Mission," 403n90
Rosario Strait, 140
"Rough Riders," 63, 152
Ruger, Thomas H., 44
Ruggles, Colden L'H., 342
Rupt de Mad, France, 191, 230, 236, 238, 244
Russell, George M., 254
Russia, 51, 131, 159, 317
  during Boxer Rebellion, 94–95, 103, 113
  in World War I, 165, 194
  Summerall's distrust of, 362, 368
Russian Civil War, 334

## S

Saar coalfields, 179
Sacramento, Calif., 45, 46, 48

*Index*

*Sacramento Bee*, 36, 46, 47
Sagasta, Praxades, 52, 53, 54
Saint-Quentin, France, 245. *See also* St. Quentin
*Sampson* (gunboat), 3
Sampson, William, 63
San Antonio, Texas, 54, 91, 152–53, 326, 329, 330
San Cristobal River, 82
San Francisco, xi, 26
  defenses of, 38, 39
  first assignment, 32, 33, 35, 40
  social life in, 35–36
  strike, 42, 44, 50, 62
  mentions of, 72, 78, 92, 120, 127, 130, 326
*San Francisco Examiner*, 129, 130
San Jose, Philippines, 90
San Juan, P. R., 63
San Juan Heights, 63, 64
*Sanford Herald*, 356
Santa Cruz, 72
Santiago de Cuba, 54, 63
Santo Tomas, Philippines, 84, 87
*Savannah* (ironclad), 3
Savannah, Ga., 3, 54
Schofield, John M., 44
Schofield Barracks, Hawaii, 320–21, 323–24, 337
School of Application for Infantry and Cavalry, 31
Schwann, Theodore, 79–80, 87, 90, 392n122
Scott, Hugh L., 151
Seattle, Wash., 130–31, 134, 137, 139
Second Army Corps (Spanish-American War), 55–59, 60–63
Second Reconstruction Act, 43
Secretary of War, 38
Sedan and Sedan incident, Chapter Twelve. Also 175, 194, 196, 198, 233, 241, 244, 265
  rivalry with French, 271–72, 277–81, 283–92, 295–96, 298
  criticism of and resentment by Summerall, 173, 291, 343, 347
Seicheprey, 189, 192, 201, 316
Selective Draft Act (1917), 168
Senate Military Affairs Committee, 30–31
Seymour, Edward, 98
Seymour, Truman, 1
Seymour Expedition, 99
Shafter, William R., 37, 44, 62, 63
*Sheridan* (steamship), 121–22
Sherman, William Tecumseh, 7, 30, 31–32, 384n8
Shinkle, E. M., 342
Shipp, Scott, 143, 148–49
Shurtleff (major), 342
Sibert, William L., 183, 185–87
Signal Corps, 152, 283
Sigsbee, Charles D., 388–89n161
Simpson, William Hood, 148
Skagway, Alaska, 131–37
*Skagway Daily Alaskan*, 133
Skerrett, Lt., 45, 46
"skins," 17–18, 19
Sladen, Fred W., 74, 334, 335

Smith, Alfred E., 330, 332
Smith, Fred A., 156, 187, 193
Smith, Hamilton A., 211, 222–23, 226
Smith, Jefferson, 132–33
Smythe, Donald, 167, 172–73, 204, 207, 234, 242–43, 251, 254, 267, 283, 296
Snow, William J., 155
Society of the First Division, 302, 316
Soissons, France, 202, 207, 209–10, 212, 214–17, 219, 223–28, 233, 235, 254–55, 273, 296, 301
  postwar reflections, 309, 316, 327, 343
Somme River, 165, 194
Sonnino, Sidney, 303, 304
Soukop, Robert, 428–29n63
South Carolina, 2–3
Southern Pacific Railway, 48
Southern Railway, 56
Spaatz, Carl, 148
Spain, 51, 52, 53, 54, 55, 63, 64, 66, 67, 69, 78
Spanish-American War, 37, 51, 52, 53, 54, 55, 63–64, 66
Sparkman, S. M., 60
*Spirit Soldiers*, 107
Springfield, Mass., 50, 51
Springfield, Mass., Arsenal, 49, 51
St. Mihiel Salient, France, 179, 189, 196, 229–34, 236, 240–41, 243, 245, 249, 252, 254, 290, 322, 327
St. Nazaire, 179–81, 184
St. Quentin, 194, 233, 245
Stackpole, Pierpont L., 285–88, 291
*Star of the West*, 351
Staunton Military Academy, Va., 142, 144
Steamer, William H., 192
*Stellungen, Giselher, Kriemhilde, Freya* (German defenses), 246
Sternberg, George M., 57
Stimson, Henry L., 152, 162, 337
Stoney, Thomas P., 352
Straits of San Juan de Fuca, 138, 139
*Strassenbau* (German offensive), 209–10
Strong, Ronald, 363, 364
Sullivan's Island, 54, 351
Summerall Family
  Summerall, Bryant. *See* Summerall, Elbanan
  Summerall, Charles Pelot
    (childhood), xi, xii, 1–3, 5, 6
    schooling of, 6, 8–9; attitude toward discipline, 8–9
    teaching career of, 9–10
    application to West Point, 10–11
  Summerall, West Point years, 12–28
    processing of candidates/tests, 12–13
    system of hazing, 14–15, 17
    attitude toward criticism, 16–17
    disciplinary actions, 17–18; honors and promotions, 18
    schedule and academics, 19–20; code of conduct, 21, 22
    promotion to First Captain, 23–25, 26
    career choices, 26–27
    finances of, 32, 34
  Summerall, first assignment, 32–37
    transfer to artillery, 37

home leave, 48–49
  transfers to N.Y., 50–54; to Texas, 94
  during Spanish-American War, 55–60; promotion to First Lieutenant, 61
  combat in Philippines, 72, 74, 75–80
China and the Boxer Rebellion, 94–126
home and marriage, 127–38
  marriage, 129–30
  first home, 131
  Alaska, 131–38
  birth of Charles, Jr., 134
career moves and West Point, 139–51
coming of the Great War, 152–75
Over There with the Artillery, 176–98. *See also* AEF (American Expeditionary Forces) in France
  promotion to brigadier general, 176
  training and discipline for combat, 184–91
  under fire; problem of gas attacks, 192–98
Price of victory, 199–218
Summerall as artillery general
  Cantigny, 199–204
  Château-Thierry, 205–8
  promotion to major general, and command of First Division, 209
Summerall as infantry general
  Soissons, 209–28
St. Mihiel Salient, 229–244
  role of the American Army, 229–35
  St. Mihiel offensive, 236–44
The Meuse-Argonne, "Racing to Sedan" and Peace, 245–302
  Meuse-Argonne, 245–68, 271–77
  Summerall's attitude toward his men and combat, 268–70
  peace negotiations and unrest in Germany, 277, 295–96
  race to Sedan, 278–88
  criticism of Summerall's actions, 288–92, 302
  armistice, and reversion to rank of brigadier general, 296–99
  Summerall, praise of Sgt. York, 298, 416n67
Mission to Fiume and homecoming, 303–9
  Summerall as member of Interallied Commission of Inquiry, 303–5
  return to the United States and victory parades, 307–8
Home Front, 310–25
  changes in the Army and National Guard, 310–12
  president of the AEF First Division Memorial Association, 313–14, 316–17
  *History of the First Division*, 314–16
  in command of the Hawaiian Department, 317–18, 320–25
  Naval vs. Army rank, 424n52
in command and Chief of Staff, 326–48
  in command of the VIII Corps area at Fort Sam Houston, 326–27, 329–32
  reunion with Laura and social life, 329–31, 332, 336, 346
  in command of II Corps area, 331–36
  as Army Chief of Staff, 336
    difficulties with economic cutbacks, 336–37, 338–40
    promotion to four-star general, 340–41

friction between chief of staff and bureau chiefs, 341–44
    aviation and mechanization, 344–48
  President of The Citadel, 349–76
    political and educational ambitions, 349–54, 356–58
    presidency of The Citadel, 354–71
    Laura's illness and death, 354, 366
    financial and disciplinary problems, 358–60, 362–65
    academic reforms, 360–61, 362–66
    General Order No. 3, The Citadel, 364–65, 429n72
    Masonic Order, 366
    death and funeral of, 373
Summerall, Charles P., personal
  character of, 25–26, 27–28, 36; teetotaler, 35
  evaluations of, 41, 47–48, 61–62, 226–27, 271, 289–91, 295, 307–9, 312–13
  infantry/artillery attitude, 76–77
  promotions, 61 (1st Lt.); 130 (captain); 151 (major); 308 (brigadier general); 209 (major general); 314 (major general Regular Army); 340 (four-star general); 386n56
Summerall, Charles Jr. (son), 144–46, 150–53, 156–57
  appointment to West Point, 314
  posted to 6th Artillery, First Division, 326
  marriage and family, 336, 346–47
  retirement from Army and academic career, 373
Summerall, Elbanan Bryant (father), 1–5
  economic difficulties of, 4–6, 8
  death of, 48–49
Summerall, Hetty (grandmother), 1
Summerall, Julia (daughter-in-law), 336, 346, 373
  birth of Charles III and Julia Reeder (twins), 346–47
Summerall, Laura Mordecai, 130–31, 134, 136–37, 139, 144–46, 152, 156–57, 162, 167, 169, 171, 178, 182. *See also* Mordecai, Laura
  Army social life, 329–31, 332, 336, 346
  retirement and The Citadel, 289, 305, 307, 312, 314, 317, 325–26, 331, 336, 346–47, 350, 352–54
  death of, 366
Summerall, Meta Margaret Ann (sister), 1, 3, 6, 11, 39
Summerall, Margaret Cornelia Pelot (mother), 1, 2, 5, 6
  teaching career of, 3, 5, 6, 49
  death of, 54–55
Summerall, William Bryant (brother), 1, 3, 5
  at school and on staff, 5–6, 8, 9
  career in medicine, 39–40, 48
  in Atlanta, 54
Summerall, William (grandfather), 1
Summerall, Willis Julia Potter Reeder, 336. *See* Summerall, Julia
Summerall Park, 329
Supreme War Council (Allied), 186, 195, 207
Susak, 303, 306
Swift, Eben, 30

### T

Taft, William Howard, 152–53, 330, 357
Taiping Rebellion, 94
Taku, town of, 96, 98, 104, 121
Taku Bar, 103, 105
Taku forts, 98, 101, 105, 124

Tampa, Fla., 63
*Tampa Tribune*, 356
Tanks (Mechanized Force), 344–45
Tartar City, Peking, 99, 101, 110, 112
Taub, Peter E., 249
Taylor, William, 84
Temple of Agriculture, 99, 117
Temple of Heaven, 99
Tennessee River, 142
Thayer, Sylvanus, 19
Third Reich, 180
Thomas, John P., 2
Thoroughfare Gap, 58
Thurmond, Strom, 372
Tientsin, China, 96, 98–99, 101–8, 119–23, 130
Tiernan, Major, 74
Tittoni, Tommaso, 304
Titus, Calvin Pearl, 110, 113, 395n81
Titus, Calvin Pearl, Jr., 395n81
Tobyhanna, Pa., 155, 157–60, 162, 164, 177, 182, 307
Toral, Jose, 63
Trask, David, 68
Treadway, Chester, 329
Treat, Charles G., 154
Treaty of Paris, 70
Treaty of Rapallo, 305–6
Treaty of Rome, 306
Treaty of Simonoseki, 95
Treaty of Washington, 138, 318
Trías, Mariano, 71, 72
Triple Alliance, 159, 165–66
Triple Entente, 159
Truman, Harry S., 251, 299, 333
Trumpener, Ulrich, 242
Tsu Hsi, Dowager Empress of China, 95–96, 98, 104, 117, 123–24
Tsungli Yamen (Chinese Foreign Office), 96, 101
Tulane University, New Orleans, 39–40, 48
Tung Chih Men, 109
Tung Pien Men, 109–10, 112
Turin, 306
Turner, Frederick Jackson, 51
Tutherly, H. E., 397n24
Tuxedo Park, N.Y., 26, 27, 32, 34, 36, 51, 62
Tybee Island, Ga., 54
Typhoid fever, 58, 59
Tyrol, Italy, 303, 307

## U

Umatilla, Fla., 6, 8
Union Pacific, 44, 45
*United States Army in the World War*, 173
United States Arsenal, Charleston, S.C. (home of Holy Communion Church Institute), 7–8
United States Military Academy (USMA), West Point, xi, 10, 12–14, 19, 49, 314. *See also* West Point
United States Naval Academy (USNA), 2, 11, 23, 24
Upton, Emory, 30, 31–32
Upton, LaRoy, 211

U.S. Air Force, 323, 334
  establishment of, 336
U. S. Army
  size and function, 29–30, 70–71, 133, 142, 154–55, 158, 160, 163–64, 174, 310–11, 316–17, 337, 346, 366
  in war, 54, 55–56, 60, 63, 69, 176–77, 183, 299
U.S. Army Air Corps, 345–46, 348
U.S. Navy, 2, 318, 321–22
USS *A. B. Thompson*, 2
USS *Maine*, 52–53
USS *Monocacy*, 98
USS *Newark*, 98
USS *Olympia*, 66, 68
USS *Pittsburgh*, 304, 305
USS *President Lincoln*, 178
USS *Shenandoah*, 334

## V

Vallejo, Calif., 35
Vandenburg, Charles A., 205, 206, 408n58
Van Voorhis, Daniel, 345
Vassilievski, N. A., 109–10
Vatican, Rome, 306
Vauxcastille, France, 215
Verdun-sur-Meuse, France, 164–66, 230, 245–47, 254, 276, 298
Versailles/Versailles Treaty, 207, 301, 304, 308, 330, 421n324
Veterans Act of 1924, 327
Victor Emmanuel III, 306
Villa, Francisco "Pancho", 162, 166, 401–2n61
Virginia Military Institute (VMI), xi, 142–43, 149, 183, 309
*Vizcaya*, 53
Von Below, Otto, 186
Von Falkenhayn, Erich, 164
Von Gallwitz, Max, 241, 243, 276–77
Von Hindenburg, Paul, 165, 242, 267
Von Hutier, Oskar, 186, 199
Von Kettler, Clemons, 99, 101
Von Waldersee, Alfred, 104, 120–21

## W

Wadsworth, James W., 310–11
Wagner, Arthur L., 30
Walter Reed Army Medical Center (WRAMC), xii, 346, 354, 373
War Department, Washington, D.C., xii, 11
  reforms, 30, 31–32, 47, 56, 57, 58–59, 78–79
  communications with, 120, 133, 136, 141, 147–50, 155, 162–63, 167, 169, 173–74, 180, 185, 205, 302, 327, 333–35, 337, 342–45, 348, 354, 362–63
  Summerall and, 176, 183, 310–15, 318, 321
War Plan Orange, 317–18
War Plans Division of the General Staff (WPD), 346
Warren, Helen Frances, 167
Washington, D.C., 60, 141
Washington Conference, 318
Washington Naval Treaty, 318
*Washington Star*, 337
*Water Witch* (Union gun boat), 3
West Battery, 38, 39

Westmoreland, James R., 370
West Point, xi, xii. *See also* United States Military Academy
    Summerall as cadet, 10–11, 12–28, 78
    Summerall as instructor of artillery tactics, 146, 148–51
Weyler, Valeriano, 52
Wheaton, Lloyd, 71, 72, 79
Wheeler, Joseph, 63
Wheeler Field, Pearl Harbor, Hawaii, 320, 322
White, Charles H., 320
White, Herbert H., 334
White Hall, 372–73
White Pass and Yukon Railroad, 132, 133, 136
Whitney, Henry, 25
Wilcox, Arthur M., ix, 429n69
Wiles, A. D. G., 11, 118, 160, 360–61, 366, 368, 370
Williams, Clark, 232, 324, 358
Williams, R., 40
Williams, T. Harry, 68, 70
Wilson, John R. M., 341
Wilson, Woodrow, 47, 156, 161–63, 166, 168–69, 176, 253, 403n80
Winans, Edwin B., 334
Wingate, George, 307
Winn, Frank L., 268
Wise, Stephen, 330

Wittlesley, Charles W., 258
Wood, Leonard, 152, 155–56, 159, 163
Woodburn Manor, 56, 57–58. *See also* Camp Alger
Woodland, Yolo County, Calif., 47
Worden, Salter D., 47
Works Project Administration, 360
World's Fair, Chicago, 40
Wright, William M., 33

## Y

Yale University, 162, 177
Yellow fever, 64
Yellow River, 96
York, Alvin C., 114, 258, 298, 416n67
Young, Samuel B. M., 87
Ypres, Belgium, 171, 265
Yugoslavia, 303–6
Yukon Field Force, 132
Yukon Route, 133, 136–37
Yukon Territory, 131–32, 136

## Z

Zapote Bridge, 75, 80
Zapote River, 75
Zeppelin Airships, 164
Zimmermann Telegram, 166

## *The Author*

W. GARY NICHOLS is Emeritus Professor, School of Humanities and Social Science, Department of History, The Citadel, the Military College of South Carolina, in Charleston, where he served as a member of the faculty from 1965 to 2007. He received his B.A., M.A., and Ph.D. degrees from the University of Alabama and was a Rotary International Fellow at the University of Vienna, Austria. He was selected as a Citadel Development Foundation Faculty Fellow and has served as Director of The Citadel-University of Charleston Master of Arts in History Program. Dr. Nichols lectures frequently on the life and career of General Charles P. Summerall as well as the AEF in World War I.

— *COVER ILLUSTRATION* —
*GENERAL CHARLES P. SUMMERALL*
The Citadel Archives

White Mane Publishing Co., Inc.

*To Request a Catalog Please Write to:*
**WHITE MANE PUBLISHING COMPANY, INC.**
P.O. Box 708 • Shippensburg, PA 17257
e-mail: marketing@whitemane.com
*Our Catalog is also available online*
www.whitemane.com
Cover Design by Angela Guyer

www.ingramcontent.com/pod-product-compliance
Lightning Source LLC
Chambersburg PA
CBHW081755300426
44116CB00014B/2121